André Malraux

ANDRÉ MALRAUX

A

Biography

Curtis Cate

FROMM INTERNATIONAL PUBLISHING CORPORATION

NEW YORK

First Edition 1997

LIBRARY OF CONGRESS CATALOGING-IN-PUBLICATION DATA

Cate, Curtis, 1924-
André Malraux : a biography / Curtis Cate.
p.   cm.
Includes bibliographical references and index.
ISBN 0-88064-171-1 (hc)
French–20th century–biography. 2. Novelists,
French–20th century–Biography.   3.   Art historians–France-
-Biography. 4. Statesmen–France–Biography.   I. Title.
PQ2625.A716Z64313   1997
843'.912–dc20   96-27987
CIP

Manufactured in the United States of America
10 9 8 7 6 5 4 3 2 1

To
Elena

Contents

Preface

With the sole exception of Charles de Gaulle, no Frenchman in this century has inspired as much hagiographic adulation or been more the 'victim' of his legendary myth than André Malraux. That I should make this claim about a man who was a writer is in itself an extraordinary tribute; and if I have used the word 'victim' ironically, it is because Malraux was to a large extent the sculptor of his own heroic image, making little or no attempt to correct the apocryphal embellishments encouraged by his tumultuous career. For a long time I was myself taken in by several of his legendary 'feats'. Indeed, in April 1962, when the *New York Times Magazine* asked me to write a profile of Malraux, on the eve of his first visit to Washington as France's Minister for Cultural Affairs, I blithely listed two such exploits: that Malraux had distinguished himself in 1936 by personally heaving out bombs from an overflying aeroplane on to trenches occupied by Franco's Nationalists, and that later, in 1940, he had managed to escape from a German prisoner-of-war camp and make it across the demarcation-line into the 'unoccupied' zone of southern France disguised as a carpenter and carrying two planks on his shoulder.

The actual circumstances of André Malraux's successful flight to freedom in November 1940 (fully described for the first time in the twenty-ninth chapter of this book) strike me as being both more interesting and more plausible, and one more example of how, as so often happens, the lived reality is more fascinating than the hackneyed fiction. This is the reward that recompenses the painstaking biographer. It is even, I venture to add, the *raison d'être* of biography.

Twenty years ago, when Jean Lacouture undertook to set the record straight in several key respects, Malraux himself was still alive and his wife Clara had published only half of her autobiographical reminiscences. Three years later and shortly before Malraux's death in November 1976, Suzanne Chantal came out with a book devoted to her friend, Josette Clotis, who had been André's mistress for eleven years and the mother of his two sons. Since it raised the curtain on a little-known aspect of Malraux's life, this book was an immediate best-seller. Two years later Malraux's nephew Alain added his own, equally revealing story, as the son of André's second wife, Madeleine. And this is not to mention a number of other books, some written by friends and contemporaries, which illuminated areas of Malraux's life that had been hurriedly skimmed over, bypassed, or neglected in Jean Lacouture's biography.

That an American should have undertaken to complete the biographical task Lacouture left unfinished in 1973 is not a little surprising. I suspect that it was the awesome range of Malraux's multiple activities which discouraged others in France from tackling a full-scale biographical narrative. Be that as it may, it is a curious fact that, whereas the number of articles and essays that have been written about Malraux and his books runs into the thousands, the number of biographies he has inspired can be counted on the fingers of one hand.

Biographical research is apt to be a voyage of discovery. This at any rate has been my experience – first with Antoine de Saint-Exupéry (the only great French writer-adventurer of the twentieth century who can stand comparison with Malraux), then with George Sand, and now with the author of *La Condition humaine* (Man's Fate). There were in particular two popular stereotypes, particularly cherished by left-wing intellectuals, which I wanted to elucidate: the first was Malraux's 'betrayal' of the revolutionary ideals of his youth when, after the Second World War, he joined General de Gaulle in an anti-communist crusade; the second was the 'betrayal' of his literary vocation when, during the same period, he turned his back on novel-writing and became a politician.

Fallen idols often arouse this kind of *dépit amoureux* (amorous resentment) in the hearts of dismayed enthusiasts. But quite aside from the element of left-wing animus – so evident, for example, in the hostility towards Malraux exhibited after 1945 by Jean-Paul Sartre and even more by Simone de Beauvoir – these biased interpretations were and still are due to our casual habit of pigeon-holing outstanding individuals as being essentially this or that: in Malraux's case a writer, and, more specifically, a novelist.

Now, obviously, certain human beings are *born* writers, just as others are *born* painters or musicians. It is almost as though their life course, their personal destiny, was charted in advance, being essentially unilinear and unidimensional. One cannot imagine Marcel Proust doing something other than writing, just as one cannot imagine James Joyce making impassioned speeches and drafting political manifestos.

But there also exist human beings whose genius is so many- sided and whose curiosity is so all-embracing that they overflow the narrow banks of a single speciality. Such a man was Prosper Mérimée, an unusually versatile novelist (author of *Carmen*) who was also an archaeologist, a historian, a linguist, a folklore scholar, a dramatist, a senator and an official protector of public monuments. Another, on an even higher plane, was Goethe, who was not only poet, playwright, novelist, and autobiographer, but an amateur philosopher, a scientific researcher fascinated by light and problems of refraction, a biologist who anticipated Darwin's theories concerning the origin of species, a privy councillor and administrative official. It is to this species of polymathic, or even better, polyactive, human beings that André Malraux belongs.

Lest anyone think this is an exaggeration, let me briefly review this extraordinary man's multiple activities. The first thing to be noted is that André Malraux did not begin his life as a writer, even of short stories. He began his life as a *chineur* – a bibliophilic 'scout' and purveyor of rare books who had achieved such a precocious virtuosity in this field by the time he was seventeen that he could turn his back on secondary school studies and strike out on his own. Within one year he was helping to found a literary monthly as well as writing articles of literary criticism. Before another year was over he was the literary and artistic director of a rare-book publishing company. All of these activities, admittedly, had to do with the written word or the drawn (engraved, lithographed, or wood-cut) image; but basically they were four distinct occupations – more than enough to tax the energies of a young man of nineteen.

This was rapidly followed by an adventurous prenuptial honeymoon (described in the fourth chapter of this book), culminating in a happy marriage to an affluent young woman (Clara Goldschmidt), who was able to launch her husband on a new career as a globe-trotting connoisseur of art. In this connection it is well to recall the remark Malraux once made of himself (in 1945, to his young admirer, Roger Stéphane): '*Je suis entré en art, comme on entre en religion*' – or, roughly translated, 'I took to art as one takes to religion and monastic life.'

Being a globe-trotting *aficionado* of art cannot, strictly speaking, be regarded as a profession. But I don't think that Malraux's speculative ventures in buying and selling shares on the Paris Bourse can be eliminated from the list of his diverse activities. For what these stock-market operations revealed was an extraordinary readiness to take risks, a taste for the 'dangerous living' Nietzsche had made so fashionable. Nor, certainly, can one eliminate from Malraux's polymorphous achievements his swiftly acquired expertise in Brahmanic and Buddhist art and archaeology, which made it possible for him to stage a statue-lifting raid on a neglected Cambodian temple. Stock-market speculator . . . archaeologist . . . temple-robber – adding these three to the previous four, we get seven different activities indulged in by a young man who, when finally arrested in the Cambodian capital of Phnom Penh in December 1923, was only twenty-two years old.

But this was only a beginning. No sooner was he exonerated by a Court of Appeals of the charges of 'piracy' and 'vandalism' than he returned to the Far East as the co-editor, co-publisher, and leading editorialist of a daily newspaper dedicated to attacking a scandalously corrupt regime in southern Indochina. This was the eighth phase, or, to use a favourite Malraux word, the eighth 'metamorphosis' in this astonishing career.

When, one year later, the crestfallen editor returned to Paris like a beaten dog, he was under contract to write a novel about his temple-pilfering adventure. Instead, he surprised his publisher (Bernard Grasset) by writing *La Tentation de l'Occident* (The Temptation of the West): a book of meditations about the enduring (or disappearing) differences between East and West during a period of convulsive change in which he poetically expressed the existentialist anguish of France's post-war generation, ten years before Jean-Paul Sartre. The book's philosophical subtleties so overawed one reviewer that he roundly declared that 'Montesquieu's Persians look like simpletons compared to Mr André Malraux's Chinese.' Malraux the novelist had not yet burst on to the stage, but Malraux the prose-poet and philosopher was already visible and present. Intentionally or unintentionally, it was his ninth metamorphosis.

It is, as I suggest in this book, a mistake to assume that in the life of someone who has been brilliantly successful everything was preordained and that genius was bound to triumph. Had Malraux in the spring of 1926 (when he was still only twenty-four years old) been quintessentially a novelist, he would immediately have put his nose to the grindstone and churned out the kind of adventurous novel his publisher was so eagerly awaiting. Instead, what does the real (as opposed to the stereotypical) Malraux do? He returns to his first love, rare-book publishing, and, discreetly and on the side, to a kind of second but particularly lucrative love: pornographic publishing. Since it would be stretching matters a bit to chalk this up as another of André Malraux's signal 'achievements', I will make no further mention of it here and simply direct the interested reader's attention to the thirteenth chapter of this book.

Finally in 1928 Malraux made his mark as a novelist. Paradoxically entitled *Les Conquérants* (The Conquerors), this novel was in reality the chronicle of a defeat, the story of a 'strangled revolution' (as Trotsky later called it), of a revolution done to death in Canton – a Chinese city which, despite the promotional brouhaha, Malraux *had not yet visited*. Like three of the four novels that were to follow, this was a *roman engagé*, or what I prefer to call a *roman de combat*: a novel in which the author – this 'poet of violent defeat', as his friend Nicola Chiaromonte later put it – took up the cudgels once again, as he had previously done as a journalist in Indochina, on behalf of the humiliated and oppressed.

If what I am suggesting – that Malraux was not quintessentially a novelist – sounds heretical, let me quote what he himself had to say on the subject, in a letter written to his friend, Eddy Du Perron, in 1929:

> For critics (I am speaking of those who are not born idiots) the honest-to-god truth is that they like novels and that we do not like them. The longer I live, the more I realize our deep-seated indifference to what these fine fellows call 'the art of the novel' . . . There are people who have

something to express, and who never accomplish masterpieces (Montaigne, Pascal, Goya, the sculptors of Chartres) because one cannot dominate a passion that attacks the world; and there are those who 'produce objects'. But the critic, basically, is a man who likes 'objects' and not the expression of human beings.

Although this may have been written in a moment of pique, it was not a spur-of-the-moment outburst. Four years later, in a letter addressed to Edmund Wilson, Malraux candidly admitted that 'the role played by objectivity in my books is not of primary importance, and *Les Conquérants* is an "expressionist" novel like, with all due allowances, *Wuthering Heights* and *The Brothers Karamazov*'. Malraux's meaning in his letter to Eddy Du Perron would, I think, have been clearer if he had used the word 'intensity' rather than 'expression' as a contrast to run-of-the-mill novels. If *Wuthering Heights* and *The Brothers Karamazov* were singled out as magnificent prototypes of 'expressionist' novel-writing, it was clearly, for Malraux, because Emily Brontë and Dostoevsky had personally and intensely experienced the human temptations, the torments, and the passions they had undertaken to describe. Or, to put it more simply, in blunt terms Ernest Hemingway would have had no trouble understanding: a novelist, before putting pen to paper, must first of all have lived.

Living, however, is one thing; thinking, or more exactly asking what is the purpose of life and thus of action, is another. In Malraux's novels doing and thinking, the purposeful action and the philosophical doubt are inseparable, and it is precisely this metaphysical dimension which make them so different from Hemingway's earthier creations. To quote once again the anti-fascist Italian intellectual, Nicola Chiaromonte:

History, the event, the occasion, transcend all truth. The humiliation of the intellect, in fact, makes Malraux gamble on the deed even as the weakness of the human condition made Pascal gamble on God. 'To tie oneself to a great action of some kind, not to let go of it, to be haunted and intoxicated by it' [*Les Conquérants*, 1928] is the only issue. A man of any magnanimity cannot do less. And it is Malraux's contention [Chiaromonte wrote this in 1948] that in our time a 'great action' can only mean one thing: a *battle*, and a reason for it.

As can be seen, not for one moment did it occur to Chiaromonte – who knew what he was talking about, since he had served as a volunteer machine-gunner with Malraux's bomber squadron in 1936 – that the author of *Les Conquérants*, of *La Voie royale*, and of *La Condition humaine* could have chosen a life of adventure simply to provide himself with exciting material for future novels.

The proof of this was clearly given when, after Hitler's accession to the Chancellorship of Germany and the Reichstag fire of 1933, Malraux plunged impetuously into a new career – as an anti-fascist platform speaker. Most of the speeches delivered over the next three years (1933–5) were extemporaneous performances, nourished by Malraux's phenomenal memory and quick-wittedness. They were not, in most cases, carefully prepared orations, memorized in advance – as Winston Churchill and Charles de Gaulle used to do with theirs – but impassioned improvizations charged with such fire and eloquence that they exercized an extraordinary, almost incantatory spell on Malraux's audiences. No one, I think, has better described the public impact of such speeches than the French playwright, Henri-René Lenormand, who attended the International Writers Congress of June 1935, which Malraux had helped to organize and where he found himself competing with literary and political stars of the first magnitude, such as André Gide, E. M. Forster, Aldous Huxley, Robert Musil, Count Carlo Sforza, and the anti-fascist firebrand, Gaetano Salvemini.

> The rapidity of his [Malraux's] associations and of his delivery, his indifference as to whether or not he was being understood, his scorn of all concessions, of any adjustments to mediocrity, to the foreseeable sloth of his listeners, made each of his interventions seem like a magical operation. With his long body erect behind the table of the *praesidium*, his head slightly bent toward the microphone, he spoke in a low, hurried voice ... The crowd received the message in deep silence, then erupted into ardent applause ... After him, the loftiest intellects of the century, a Gide, a Huxley, seemed like professors embarrassed by their trains of thought and the difficulties of diction.

It is also worth noting that Malraux's intense speech-making was essentially a surrogate, a *faute de mieux* substitute for an impatient man of action who sought to work off his anti-nazi frustrations in a national context of somnambulistic lethargy by dashing off yet another *roman de combat* – *Le Temps du Mépris* (Days of Wrath) – this time describing the tribulations of a German Communist inside a Nazi prison. It turned out to be Malraux's weakest novel, precisely because it violated the rule implicitly laid down in his letter to Eddy Du Perron and sought to describe a reality the author had not personally experienced and about which he knew little.

Parodying Jean-Paul Sartre's nutshell definition of Existentialism – 'Existence precedes Essence' – one could say that the unspoken axiom underlying all of Malraux's novels was: 'Action precedes fiction'. He proved it again in June 1936, when the Spanish Republic was shaken to its foundations by a military insurrection, when he promptly abandoned his speech-making and everything else in order to help recruit pilots for a fighter-and-bomber squadron, which he then proceeded to direct, from various airbases in Spain, even though he had *never* piloted an aeroplane.

After being twice wounded – the second time in a crash which might have cost him his life – what does Lieutenant-Colonel André Malraux do ... now that his squadron has been reduced by losses to a couple of Potez bombers and half-a-dozen surviving fighter planes? He undertakes a tour of the United States, not to promote one of his novels, but to deliver fund-raising speeches on behalf of the Spanish Republic and to raise money for a volunteer ambulance corps. Then, after writing one more *roman de combat* – defiantly titled *L'Espoir* (Man's Hope) to honour the desperate courage of his Republican comrades-in-arms – he transforms himself overnight (though lacking previous experience) into a film-director and produces a remarkable *film de combat* (*Sierra de Teruel*), now generally regarded, in its sadly truncated and unpolished state, as being a minor masterpiece of cinematography. The *teniente coronel* of 1936 thus became the *cinéaste* of 1938. It was his thirteenth metamorphosis. But it was by no means the last.

Desperately unhappy because he could not gain admission to the French Air Force, when the Second World War broke out in September 1939 the former lieutenant-colonel volunteered for service as a simple private in a 'mechanized cavalry' unit, was captured by *Wehrmacht* troops during the débâcle of 1940, then managed to escape with the help of his half-brother Roland. Three-and-a-half years later, the erstwhile anti-militaristic draft-dodger of 1923 pulled off a flabbergasting feat of self-promotion by assuming the rank of colonel and the *nom de guerre* of 'Berger', getting himself officially recognized thereafter as the commander of a 'brigade' of Resistance fighters. If a novelist dared to invent such an implausible plot, it would almost certainly result in highly suspect fiction.

Once the Second World War was over, it only remained for Malraux to discard his distinctive beret, duffel coat, boots, and breeches and don the polished shoes and double-breasted suit of a cabinet minister in General de Gaulle's first post-war government. 'Colonel Berger' was thus transformed into 'Monsieur le Ministre' – his fifteenth and final metamorphosis.

In the 1965–6 edition of *Who's Who in France*, which I have carefully preserved because it indicates among other things that he attended the Lycée Condorcet and graduated from the Ecole des Langues Orientales (two glorious fibs!), one finds, after MALRAUX, André: 'Homme de Lettres. Ministre d'Etat.' So be it. But what follows, almost filling an entire column of small-type print, makes it clear that these two attributes need to be expanded to embrace all of this extraordinary individual's manifold activities and achievements.

Writers, and particularly famous writers, often tend to be exhibitionists, if only because they are selfconsciously posing for posterity. André Gide expressed this *péché mignon* ('darling sin') of the writer's craft by keeping a kind of 'public' diary. Vladimir Nabokov exhibited it by strewing his novels with minefields of arcane literary references, subtle word plots and puzzles. George Sand did so by pouring out her arch-romantic soul in hundreds, indeed in thousands of letters of more or less 'unpremeditated art' (Henry James' description), many of which she correctly assumed would be carefully preserved for future generations.

But what of André Malraux? A consummate exhibitionist? No doubt. A man capable of writing a Cubistic masterpiece of 'antibiographical' reminiscences (*Antimémoires*) cannot be exonerated of the charge. And yet . . . and yet . . . if we examine André Malraux's more private writings, what do we find? He never kept a diary, and most of his letters are disappointingly terse and to the point. No long-winded regrets, complaints, or apologias. No dramatic flourishes. No trace of epistolatory coquetry. Nothing but incisive and sometimes elliptic formulations, often drafted in the telegraphic style that characterizes the sharp, staccato beginning of *Les Conquérants* and later of *L'Espoir*. In short, they are not the kind of letters a professional *homme de lettres* is apt to write. They are the letters of a tense, time-rationed intellectual, for whom action, service in a noble cause, and an anguished search for human significance in a godless cosmos were far more important than fiction.

1

From Montmartre to Bondy

Rare today are the strollers who, having reached the summit of Montmartre, are tempted to wander down the less sun-blessed northern slope, even though it was here, in a rustic tavern on the corner of Rue Saint-Vincent and Rue des Saules, that a bearded guitarist sporting a scarlet pirate's cap used to entertain the bohemian clients of his Lapin Agile. Fewer still are those who stop at no. 12, Rue Cortot, to visit the Museum of Old Montmartre, which an enterprising architect installed in a small seventeenth-century town house once inhabited by a member of Molière's theatre troupe. Those familiar with the history of Impressionism may recall that it was here Renoir stored his *Moulin de la Galette* and painted *La Balançoire* and *Un Jardin à Montmartre*. But almost nobody wanders as far as the Rue Damrémont, named after one of Napoleon's soldiers, for whose heroic death, while besieging the Algerian citadel of Constantine in 1837, Berlioz composed his famous *Requiem*. Yet it was at no. 53, in one of the typically bourgeois houses lining this nondescript street, that Georges André Malraux was born on November 3, 1901.

Of André Malraux's early years we know precious little. He resented the conditions of his upbringing and preferred to draw a curtain over this period of his life. 'Almost all of the writers I know like their childhood,' he explained more than once to friends and interviewers, before recording his own aversion in *Antimémoires*: 'I detest mine.' In this respect he was the very opposite of Marcel Proust and Osbert Sitwell, or, going further back, of Jean-Jacques Rousseau, Chateaubriand, and George Sand.

No less typically, André Malraux seems to have been less fascinated by his father, a sedentary Parisian stockbroker, than he was by his truculent grandfather, Alphonse Malraux, a short, strong-willed individual whose pointed grey-white beard made him look a bit like Napoleon III. Brought up in the lee of the windswept grasses and sand-dunes of Dunkirk, this irascible skipper had followed the seafaring tradition of his forebears – with the single exception of a Calais innkeeper, virtually all Malraux males for generations back had been fishermen, boat-riggers, or corsairs – making a name for himself as a master cooper, wine-importer, and fishing-fleet owner.

But, like the ill-fated emperor he vaguely resembled, he too had finally been overtaken by misfortune, as a result of a fierce Atlantic storm off the coasts of Newfoundland in which most of his cod- and herring-fishing vessels had foundered.

One story André Malraux liked to tell about this cantankerous 'old Viking' graphically illustrates his independent-mindedness. Shocked by the Catholic Church's indulgent attitude towards well-to-do 'sinners' who, in exchange for their generous contributions, were excused from the meatless rigours of the Lenten fast, Alphonse Malraux berated the local priest for the practice and then decided to go to Rome to lodge a personal protest with the Pope. In Rome he was kept waiting for more than a week, then finally received at the Vatican in a routine audience along with twenty others. But when the Holy Father appeared, Alphonse Malraux barely had time to kneel down and kiss the papal slipper as the Pontiff moved unconcernedly on. Outraged by this cavalier treatment, the frustrated protester tramped back to his hotel, packed his bag in a huff and took the first train back to Dunkirk. Thenceforth regarding himself as a faithful follower of Christ, if not of his vicars, he attended Mass every Sunday *outside* the local church, kneeling down for a few minutes in the weed- and thistle-infested angle formed by nave and transept, from where, through a stained-glass window, he could hear the ritual tinkling of the silver bell before and after the elevation of the host.

One thing at any rate is certain and unobscured by the rolling mists of later embellishments. Although unhappily married to the masterful Alphonse, his grudging wife Mathilde bore him five children: two girls and three boys – Maurice, Julien, and Fernand – all three of whom became businessmen. Fernand was André Malraux's father.

We know only slightly more about Fernand Malraux than we do about Alphonse. His father's misfortunes at sea seem to have stunted any inclination the young man may have felt for a life spent behind the tiller, and not long after the completion of his studies, which may have included a year or two in engineering, he left Dunkirk for Paris. Here he acquired considerable experience in investment banking and stock-market transactions. He seems to have been reasonably affluent, for a photo dating from 1910 shows him at the wheel of an open four-seat roadster, which in those days was a luxury.

Fernand Malraux's fondness for the stock market was more than matched by a latent desire to be 'creative' – this was the Jules Verne and Thomas Edison heyday of individual invention – one that caused him to devote many leisure hours to the concoction of 'fantastic' devices: an 'unbreakable' light-bulb, a skid-proof and unpuncturable tyre, an anti-splash tap nozzle – which he reckoned would make him a fortune if only he could find an interested manufacturer.

More significant for the impact they were to have on his son André were Fernand Malraux's good looks and debonair ways. For this jovial *bon vivant*, with his brown hair parted down the middle, a straight nose, bushy moustache and fleshy chin, had two blue eyes which would light up and twinkle merrily in the presence of the 'second sex'. A natural charmer, he possessed, as his future daughter-in-law once put it, 'the easy-going way of speech of the man who is fond of women and whom women like'.

One of those who succumbed to this confident masculine charm was a young brunette whose Italianate pupils seemed to float against the white of her eyes above delicately rounded lower lids – a distinctive feature André Malraux was to inherit. They met, it seems, during summer holidays spent at the seaside resort of Malo-les-Bains, near Dunkirk – a significant biographical detail since it indicates that the social status of her father, Jean-François Lamy, who had emigrated from a village in the Jura mountains and set himself up as a baker in the suburban town of Saint-Maur-des-Fossés, south-east of Paris, was by no means a lowly one. He was indeed a prosperous baker, to judge from a photograph that has survived and shows a solemn bourgeois entrepreneur sporting a moustache almost as bristling as Nietzsche's.

That photograph must have been taken in the 1880s, for in October 1891 in his forty-third year, Jean-François Lamy died. Sometime thereafter his widow Adrienne (born in Paris, though of distant Italian ancestry) sold the bakery at Saint-Maur-des-Fossés and moved with her two daughters, Berthe Félicie and Marie Valentine, to Bondy, on the eastern periphery of Paris. One thing certain, for it figures in the official registry: on March 24, 1900 Fernand Malraux and the dark-eyed Berthe Lamy were married in the *mairie* (town hall) of Paris's 18th *arrondissement*.

Almost certainly it was Berthe Lamy's good looks and lustrous eyes which first attracted Fernand Malraux's roving gaze. Surviving photographs make her look less pretty than her younger sister, Marie, and do not do justice to her beauty. As for other aspects of her personality, we know next to nothing. The only written descriptions of Berthe date from much later (1924), but they are worth quoting since they do at least afford us an inkling of her qualities. The first, that of the publisher René-Louis Doyon, portrays her as a 'distinguished, simple, and sweet lady' and a 'worthy mother'. The second, from her daughter-in-law Clara, is more detailed, portraying her as 'tall, slim, pretty, youthful in aspect and behaviour, with the voice of a young girl' – one who, though discreet, was unaffected and warm-hearted.

Nineteen months after her marriage to Fernand, Berthe Malraux gave birth to a son – born by a fortuitous coincidence on November 3, 1901, her own twenty-fourth birthday. The baby was christened Georges, his father's second name, followed by André, which his parents and he invariably used thereafter. One year later, on Christmas Day of 1902, she gave birth to a second boy, named Raymond Fernand, who would have provided André with fraternal company and competition had he not died three months later. The young André was thus brought up as an only child. Although he was too young at the time to comprehend what had happened, this may have been one of the first 'humiliations' he later complained of, as having marked his unhappy youth.

The few photos that exist of the young André Malraux suggest an unsmiling disposition, a questioning vivacity, and above all a stubborn determination revealed by the pursing of his lips. Almost certainly he was a headstrong and not easily managed infant, and the fact that he was a hypersensitive as well as an only child – with no brother or sister to distract his attention – soon made him sense that the relations between his parents were growing increasingly strained. During one particularly violent dispute, the four-year-old boy is even reported to have shouted, 'Stop! Stop! Or else I'll call the gamekeeper!'

The root cause was Fernand Malraux's fickle temperament: that of a polygamic *hommes à femmes* who found feminine temptation just too delicious to resist, and whose extramarital adventures relieved the boredom of domestic life. Berthe Malraux, however, refused to submit to this humiliating treatment. She was also too straightforward a person to resort to revenge by cuckolding her husband. And so, by mutual consent, in 1905 husband and wife agreed to part. For Fernand Malraux, who had no taste for solitude, this involved a welcome liberation and freedom to resume his predatory celibacy. But for his wife, Berthe, the rupture was a blistering defeat, forcing her to abandon the apartment on the lively Rue Damrémont and to seek refuge under her mother's more humble roof in the town of Bondy.

This move from his father's comfortable apartment in Montmartre to the cramped quarters of his grandmother's small house on the Rue de la Gare in Bondy came as a traumatic shock to the highly sensitive, impressionable young boy. Located almost a kilometre from the railway station which had given the street its name, no. 16 was a small two-storey house, wedged in between other nondescript abodes, almost all of them garnished with shutters, and a few with dormer windows thrusting out from the sloping tiled roofs. Most of the ground floor served as a grocery, with a door opening inwards from the pavement. From the cobbled street a garage entrance led, under two upper floors, to an inner courtyard behind. To the left, a door opened into a kind of back-shop storeroom, which was partly transformed into a combination playroom and study for the young André.

The psychological turmoil generated by the sudden, wrenching move from Montmartre to Bondy could, according to classic Freudian interpretation, have turned the young André into a kind of 'mama's boy'. But interestingly, this did not happen. With the passage of the months his father, whom he now saw infrequently, grew in stature into an almost mythical figure, heroically embellished as adults tend to be in the imagination of the young, and inseparably associated in his mind with the metropolitan glamour of Paris and everything that the little town of Bondy was so obviously not. The transfiguration was facilitated by a debonaire absence that contrasted so markedly with the constricting omnipresence of a straitlaced matriarchy.

Of the three women who presided over André's youth – his mother, Aunt Marie, and Grandmother Adrienne – it was the strong-willed grandmother who ruled the roost. Years later Adrienne Lamy so impressed her granddaughter-in-law Clara Malraux that she described her as being as 'tall and straight-backed as a Franz Hals regent . . . A grand lady, she ruled over her universe with energy. Endowed with a well-nourished mind, and lucid to the very end, she spent most of her time reading.' Although she had less leisure time in 1905, it was Grandmother Adrienne who more than anybody else encouraged the young André to develop a precocious passion for literature. His mother presumably seconded this wholesome development, but her own contribution to domestic discipline was not always inspired. The adult André later complained of her constant insistence that he was ugly because his ears stuck out. If this was meant to warn him not to rely on good looks to get ahead in the world, it certainly succeeded. But it left a psychological scar which was never fully healed.

His literary education, in any case, was greatly facilitated by the proximity of what was then called the Bibliothèque Populaire Libre de Bondy – a lending library, open on Tuesdays and Fridays, which a stoutly republican refugee from Alsace had established in the 1870s 'for the instruction and improvement of all'. By 1900 the library had found a fairly permanent home on Bondy's most prominent thoroughfare, the Rue Saint-Denis, so named because it ran through the town in a westerly direction, pointed, across several miles of intervening land, towards the suburb and chapel of Saint-Denis.

Barely 150 metres separated the Lamy sisters' grocery shop from the lending library, so that it was within easy walking distance for the young André, who had only to turn left when he reached the Place du Marché, next to the recently rebuilt church (half destroyed during the Franco-Prussian War), and continue on in a westerly direction. Although the rules officially prohibited the loaning out of books to minors, the kind-hearted 'Père Jésu' (his family name was indeed Jésu, without a terminal *s*), who presided over this institution of intellectual improvement, was willing to relax the regulations for Adrienne Lamy's alert, bright-eyed grandson.

A great deal of nonsense has been written about the town of Bondy, partly inspired by André Malraux, who never ceased to disparage it as a kind of suburban 'hole'. Located too close to Paris to have developed a distinctive personality of its own, Bondy had once boasted a pillared château, where Emperor Alexander I of Russia had set up his headquarters in March 1814, shortly before Napoleon's first abdication. By the time the young André Malraux appeared on the scene, there was virtually nothing left of the magnificent forest which had extended to the east and south-east as far as the Marne. Once renowned as a hide-out for highwaymen and robbers, who would lie in wait for coaches plying back and forth between Paris, Meaux, and Reims, the forest of Bondy had gradually been sold off to make room for plots of cultivated land and suburban housing. Nevertheless, surrounded as it was by wheatfields, orchards, and market gardens, Bondy, which had a population of 5,000 in 1905, was not an unpleasant place to live, offering ample space for refreshing walks and bicycling excursions.

Paradoxical as it may sound, Bondy in the first years of this century was in some respects closer to Paris than it is today. Traffic jams on motorways and incoming roads were unknown, and anyone could travel to the Gare de l'Est (twenty-five minutes by train) or ride all the way to the Paris Opéra in an electric tram. Concerts and plays in the capital were advertised on local hoardings, as well as in the weekly *L'Echo du Raincy*, and a special post-midnight local known as the *train de théâtre* was regularly laid on by the Chemins de Fer de l'Est to carry theatre- or opera-goers home to Bondy and other nearby towns.

On the same Rue Saint-Denis – some distance beyond the lending library, a bistro, a hardware store, and the modest town hall – was a handsome three-storey house with shuttered windows known as the Institution Dugand. This was the private school where the not quite five-year-old André Malraux was enrolled in October 1906. The mere fact that Adrienne Lamy and her daughter Berthe should have insisted on sending André to a private rather than to a state school, with the full approval and financial support of Papa Fernand, attests to the family's determination to give the boy a better-than-average education. This is further corroborated by the spontaneous reaction of someone who had been one of André's neighbours: when asked by Jean Astruc, a local historian, if he could pick out the young Malraux on a photograph showing a number of Bondy youths milling around in the street in knee-length knickerbockers and straw hats, he immediately replied in the negative. 'I would be greatly surprised if his family let him loose on the streets like that. He was closely supervised. He was a *petit monsieur*' – which is to say, a cut above the average, a young man brought up to realize that he was somebody.

In the autumn of 1907 André and sixteen other students were joined by a short, brown-haired boy with round black eyes named Louis Chevasson, destined to become one of Malraux's life-long friends. Years later, when Jean Lacouture asked him if André's childhood had been an unhappy one, Chevasson protested:

But no, no! Being pampered by three women didn't affect him in the least. His mother was a delightful person, and he saw his father almost every week in Paris, and often in the company of his mother. It has been suggested that his facial twitches were due to harsh treatment at school. This is absurd. André was always plagued by facial twitches. As for the poverty in which he is supposed to have lived, it's simply an invention. The grocery store on the Rue de la Gare was a flourishing concern and our friend never lacked anything.

Several of Malraux's biographers have emphasized his first literary enthusiasms – beginning, understandably, with Alexandre Dumas' *Three
Musketeers*. Robert Payne even devoted a full page to Dumas' little-known
novel, *Georges* – the story of a half-French, half-native adventurer from
Mauritius who, after many martial and amorous exploits in various countries, returns home and foments an uprising against the British governor of
the island.

Such childish enthusiasms are normal. What is more significant for the
light it sheds on his later passion for art was the enthusiasm young André
developed for drawing, watercolours, and even oil painting. We know this
thanks to the recollections of Henry Robert, a slightly older student attending the *école communale* who had joined a boy scout troop formed by the
primary school's headmaster. The idea of being drilled and taking orders
from a 'corporal' – Henry's official rank – probably did not much appeal to
the eleven-year-old André, but the prospect of being able to get away for a
day or two from the grocery store in the Rue de la Gare, and of camping
out in tents, building camp-fires, and roaming the countryside proved
irresistible; and so, after badgering his mother and grandmother, he was
granted permission to become a boy scout and was fitted out, like the others,
with a khaki shirt and tie, knee-length shorts, boots and leggings, a tin
water-canteen attached to a diagonal shoulder-strap, and the distinctive
bushman's hat.

Meanwhile, Fernand Malraux had given his son a bicycle – a garish orange
machine equipped with wooden wheel-rims and solid, puncture-proof tyres.
This velocipedic marvel aroused the envy of André's fellow scout and
'corporal', Henry, whose father was not rich enough to offer him such an
expensive toy. Every Thursday afternoon, when all schoolchildren had a
half-day's holiday, and almost every Sunday, the young Robert would come
over to no. 16, Rue de la Gare to see his friend. While André exercised his
talents with the brush – painting figures and designs on glossy paper,
stretched canvas, and even on china plates – his friend Henry would take
the orange velocipede out for a 'spin' around the countryside and to the
nearby woods of Villemonble.

Often, during these artistic sessions, André would burst into song – and
not just any popular folk-tune but operatic airs from Massenet's *Manon* or
Werther. Exactly where he had picked them up is not clear. But since
gramophones were not yet being mass-produced, he had probably heard
them at piano recitals sponsored by the local musical society or during a
matinée treat offered to him by his mother at the Châtelet Theatre or the
Opéra-Comique in Paris. In any case, these joyous bursts of song pay tribute
to a gift that was to work wonders: a prodigiously retentive memory.

According to Louis Chevasson, André enjoyed his first experience of the
theatre during the summer of 1912 when his mother, grandmother, and aunt
took the not yet eleven-year-old boy to see a stage-adaptation of Victor
Hugo's *Les Misérables*, performed under a tent erected on the Place du

Marché. The spring and summer of this year were also marked by two notable occurrences. During a summer-holiday trip to Dunkirk André gashed his knee and it became so infected that it was feared for a moment that the leg might have to be amputated. The other occurrence, of which André knew nothing at the time, was the birth in May of a half-brother named Roland – the fruit of an affair Fernand Malraux had started with Marie-Louise Godard, daughter of an engineer who had helped to develop the railway network in French Indochina.

One year later, in May 1913, André was awarded a school certificate, officially terminating the first stage of his elementary education. His two best subjects were history and drawing, in which he was first in his class, followed by spelling, where he was second, whereas he ranked eighth in French and English. His lacklustre performance in these last two subjects was one of the reasons why his mother decided that André needed special tutoring to enable him to move on to a school better equipped for secondary education than the Institution Dugand, with its tiny staff of two teachers. He was accordingly entrusted to the care of a schoolmistress, Paulette Thouvenin, the daughter of a local gamekeeper. In a group photo taken of her 'charges' – four girls and four boys – André Malraux appears neatly dressed in tie, stiff collar, curved three-button jacket with an elegant watch-chain looped between the top button-hole and upper-breast pocket, and the usual knee-length breeches, woollen stockings and laced boots. Years later, when interviewed by Robert Payne, Paulette Thouvenin had not forgotten the 'pouting, taciturn lad, with his fine bearing, always well dressed, and who kept himself a bit aloof from the other students . . . He read a great deal, remembered everything he read, and could quote his sources when a subject came up for discussion.'

The purpose of this extra-curricular schooling was to prepare the teenaged André for admission to a *lycée* in Paris. But before this could happen the town of Bondy, like the rest of France, was turned upside-down by the dramatic events of July 1914, culminating in the British and French declarations of war against Germany on August 4th. Fernand Malraux was called up for service in the Army, where his enthusiasm for mechanical devices eventually won him admission to the fledgling tank corps. The boy scouts lost their scoutmaster, and the erstwhile 'corporal' and section chief, Henry Robert, was put to work by his patriotic father in a nearby munitions factory, where boys and adults worked night and day on twelve-hour shifts turning out shells for the front.

For several critical days in early September Bondy seemed about to relive the dramatic experiences of 1870, when it had been briefly occupied by the Prussians. The town was flooded by panic-stricken refugees, flocking in from Reims and Meaux, while the ministers of Premier René Viviani's government left Paris for Bordeaux. On September 3rd General Maunoury, commanding the French Sixth Army, set up his headquarters in the town hall of Le Raincy, a couple of miles to the south-east, and three nights later

500 taxi-cabs, requisitioned by General Gallieni, the military governor of Paris, transported some 4,000 French infantrymen out along the dusty highway bordering the Ourcq canal to join the counter-offensive against General von Kluck's exposed right wing – the first phase of what came to be called the Battle of the Marne.

That the four years of grim warfare which ensued made an indelible impression on the young André, there can be no doubt. Had he been old enough to see action at the front, he might well have become a nihilist – like Louis-Ferdinand Céline or the early surrealists of the Dada school, André Breton, Louis Aragon, and Philippe Soupault. Fortunately he was spared the grim experience of life in the trenches. Instead, he lived such experiences indirectly – from what he heard from adults or read and saw in gruesomely illustrated weeklies – but with such imaginative intensity that more than half a century later he was able to describe, in macabre and hallucinating detail, a gas attack on the Eastern front in 1915 as though he had personally witnessed it. Never, during those grim years, was death long absent from his thoughts. It partly explains his fascination with devils and demonic forces, and his metaphysical obsession with the age-old themes of doom, destiny, destruction, which mark so many of his works.

The early months of the war also coincided, in his case, with the kind of slow, spiritual moulting which overtakes young persons, and particularly the religiously-inclined, as they advance into adolescence. There is good reason to believe that he treated the Bible very seriously and was a passionate 'believer' right up until his first communion. The most striking written proof of this is to be found in a fragment of his later novel, *Les Conquérants* (probably written in 1927), which he finally discarded, among other reasons because it was too obviously autobiographical.

A child of an extreme, and completely nervous sensibility, he had, like all those who live in a world of dreams, an abhorrence of the sensibility of the heart. For him, Catholicism represented the appeal of a world superior to the one he lived in . . . When, two years after his first communion (from which he had expected a transformation, but which had brought him nothing), he found himself in a world – of studies, friendships, scholarship – which paid no heed to religion; when he began, not to doubt but to feel that the religious sentiment imbuing him was turning into something particular, rather than being something as necessary and general as life itself, the notion of sin, which alone had remained potent within him, began to change; it seemed to him that those sins to which he remained chained were perhaps not weaknesses, but rather victories. Obscurely but violently, with the puerility of early adolescence, his detachment from the faith assumed the appearance of a battle against Christ.

The war, which disrupted so many French families, undermining the constraints that had traditionally restricted the activities of 'well behaved' young boys and girls, contributed less to free André Malraux from the matriarchal rule of the Lamy trio at no. 16, Rue de la Gare than the change of school he was finally granted in 1915. From the understaffed Institution Dugand at Bondy he now moved to an Ecole Primaire Supérieure located on the Rue de Turbigo, near the central market place of Les Halles. Despite its rather pompous title, this was an institution of secondary education which, towards the end of the war, was renamed more simply the Lycée Turgot, in honour of the eighteenth-century political theorist whose economic reforms, had they been implemented, might have saved the *Ancien Régime* from the revolutionary convulsions of 1789.

What, for André, had previously been a weekly trip to the capital to see his father now became a daily routine, as he took the train to the Gare de l'Est or travelled in by tram, returning home in the evening unaccompanied by his mother. At the Rue de Turbigo school André Malraux soon won himself the curious nickname 'l'Espagnol' ('the Spaniard') – a tribute to the sombre intensity of his gaze and a seriousness of purpose which left little room for childish guffaws and facile laughter. He seems to have been a better-than-average student. During his first year (1915–16) he was again top of his class in history and drawing, second in spelling, third in both French literature and English, fourth in geography and mathematics, fifth in handwriting, and sixth in chemistry and natural sciences. Because of the shortage of teachers, many of whom had been conscripted, neither Greek nor Latin figured on the curriculum. In overall standing he was the third best student in his class.

During his second year (1916–17) he developed such a keen interest in clay modelling that he came first in this discipline. The following academic year (1917–18) he moved up to first place in handwriting, as in clay modelling, and to second place in French literature. He was placed third in diction and drawing and fifth in a course of 'civic instruction', and sank to eighth place in the natural sciences. The most significant changes were the decline in his artistic skill with the pencil (from first to third place) and his ascension in French literature, where, according to one of his Turbigo schoolmates, Marcel Brandin, he was second only to the *lycée*'s star pupil, the son of a Jewish cloth-maker named Perlman. It was probably his failure to maintain his lead in drawing which prompted the frustrated artist, during these crucial adolescent years, to seek pre-eminence in another field. Adolescence in boys is an age of wild day-dreaming in which, depending on their interests and aptitudes, they imagine themselves one day becoming a great poet or painter, a new Tolstoy or Balzac, a second Nelson or Bonaparte, or even, like Dostoevsky's adolescent, a penny-pinching Rothschild. André Malraux was no exception. Years later, when he was already well into his sixties, he told an interviewer: 'Long before I was sixteen I wanted to become a great writer. But my friends and I were persuaded that a great writer, like a great painter, had to be *maudit*' – ie 'damned' in the eyes of a scandalized society. 'He had to be half-starved in the traditions of Symbolism and

Baudelaire . . . In my hopes the feeling of revolt was far stronger than the aspiration to notoriety.'

This last sentence should be taken with a grain of salt. Save for certain psycho-masochistic individuals, no adolescent, no matter how morbid his romantic longing may be, wants to die poetically of hunger without some prospect of posthumous revenge over the stodgy dolts who failed to appreciate his iconoclastic genius during his tragic lifetime. However, the statement sheds a revealing light on the young Malraux's deliberate determination to make a name for himself as a 'scandalous' innovator in the field of letters.

It would be difficult to find a more succinct statement of his personal feelings about this period of his schooling than those expressed with such candid bitterness some thirty years before by Maurice Barrès, whose influence on André Malraux's first literary works was enormous. In *Sous l'oeil des Barbares* (Under the Eyes of the Barbarians – the barbarians being all those who surrounded him) Barrès summed up his own and what he felt to be the 'normal' sentiments of a sensitive *lycée* student in 1880 as 'the experience of disgust that the pedantry of the teachers arouses in a discriminating soul, the vulgarity of the schoolmates, the obscenity of the distractions'; all of which he strives to overcome by taking refuge in a dreamworld of 'ideal nobility'.

If the Rue de Turbigo school symbolized everything that was most staid and static, conventional and humdrum in contemporary society, the truly exciting finds in the field of culture were to be found outside the classroom, and above all among the bookstalls lining the stone *quais* of the Seine. The occasional Sunday concerts of the Colonne orchestra, which he and his friend, Louis Chevasson, attended, like the Comédie Française productions of Racine's *Andromaque*, Molière's *Le Médecin malgré lui*, and Corneille's *Le Cid*, which they saw during these wartime months, were rare 'treats', if only because of the cost involved. Even the silently flickering 'cinematograph', for which André Malraux developed a veritable passion from 1916 on, cost a certain amount for admission at a time when cinemas were still a rarity. Yet a keen nose and a sharp eye for rare book editions, picked up from unsuspecting quayside vendors and then sold to Left Bank booksellers at a higher price, could provide the adolescent prowlers with valuable pocket money. In this 'sport', thanks to a passionate interest in poetry, a natural affinity with what was unconventional and 'avant-garde', an ability to size up the literary worth of an author on the basis of a few quickly read pages, a sharp memory for titles, dates, authors' and publishers' names, and other points of detail, André Malraux soon displayed a precocious expertise. Indeed, as his familiarity with 'off-beat' or 'forbidden' works grew, so did his dissatisfaction with his pedantic teachers.

Meanwhile the bloody, man-devouring war – 'The War for Right and Civilization', as it was sententiously called by France's rear-line super-patriots – was gradually drawing to a close amid the weekly jibes of Maurice Maréchal's *Canard enchaîné* ('The Chained Duck'). The United States had at last entered the fray, in distant Petrograd the hypnotic 'priest', Rasputin, had been murdered, Tsar Nicholas II and Kerensky overthrown, and a new Bolshevik regime forcibly installed by Red Guards and revolutionary seamen. The Second German Reich was tottering towards collapse, after throwing its last manpower reserves into the second Battle of the Marne – which once again had German troops approaching uncomfortably close to Bondy and the north-eastern approaches to Paris.

Just what was going on in the sixteen-year-old André's mind during those momentous summer and autumn months of 1918 it is impossible to say. It is doubtful, however, if Malraux suffered any deep-seated feeling of regret at being too young to see action at the front, if only because the four years of trench warfare France had undergone were totally lacking in the swirling colour, movement, and panache of Napoleon's campaigns, which the young Alfred de Musset had felt so cruelly cheated to have missed.

In late September André Malraux decided to launch his own offensive, aimed at improving his educational lot by moving from the Rue de Turbigo establishment to the more prestigious Lycée Condorcet, situated further west, not far from the Gare Saint-Lazare and the Paris Opéra. The great Symbolist poet, Stéphane Mallarmé, had once taught there, as had a celebrated author of history manuals named Jalliffier, to say nothing of an expert *maître d'armes*, Adolphe Ruzé, who initiated young Parisians in the dashing art of fencing. Unfortunately, unlike those of his hero, Marshal Foch, the young applicant's bold offensive failed. His scholastic credentials did not impress the administrators of the Lycée Condorcet.

André Malraux's response to this rebuff, one of the cruellest yet suffered in seventeen not altogether happy years, was one of a petulant adolescent. Since he could not gain admission to the school of his choice, then to hell with scholastic education and the coveted baccalaureate! No matter what, he wasn't going to return to the classroom drudgery of the Lycée Turgot. Rimbaud, after all, had run away from home and school three times when he was only fourteen, but this had not kept him from becoming one of the most original of modern poets.

2

A Most Resourceful Rebel

Just how André Malraux's parents reacted to their son's decision to terminate his education is one of the mysteries obscuring the early years of his life. At Bondy his mother, Grandmother Adrienne, and his Aunt Marie must have received the news with dismay. The altercations it sparked may well have troubled the celebration of André's birthday on November 3, even though he was offered an 'educational' evening – Leconte de Lisle's *Orestie* at the Châtelet Theatre in Paris. By this time all three members of the trio realized that he was a headstrong youth; but since it was virtually impossible to force a seventeen-year-old to persist in his studies if he was adamantly opposed to them, they decided that the only thing to do was to let the stubborn André be taught by bitter experience that the peddling of supposedly rare editions of volumes picked up from the bookstalls along the Seine was a sure recipe for pauperdom. After which, they supposed, having returned to his senses, the wayward boy would be welcomed back, forgiven, and, duly chastened by the harsh realities of life, would meekly go back to his school bench.

Fernand Malraux had other, more urgent, problems to deal with. His first task was to get himself demobilized as fast as possible, then join his mistress, Marie-Louise Godard, and their six-year-old son Roland, and re-establish himself in the brokerage business. If his firstborn, André, was bent on making a fool of himself, he could do little to stop him, though by cutting off further allowances he could make his displeasure felt and get his son to perceive the error of his ways.

The rebellious adolescent's 'flight from scholastic drudgery' was almost certainly abetted by the euphoria which swept over the country eight days after his seventeenth birthday. On November 3rd the Paris Opéra, which had interrupted performances in June because of the long-range bombardments of the occasionally lethal 'Big Bertha', was reopened – a sure sign that the Allies now had the Germans on the run. Then, on November 10th, came the dramatic news that Kaiser Wilhelm had fled from Berlin, where German revolutionaries, inspired by what Lenin and his Bolsheviks had achieved the previous year, had invaded the Reichstag.

The frenzied crowds did not appear in Paris until the next morning – a typically cold, damp, dreary morning, wanly lit by a misty autumn sun. The glad tidings that an armistice had at last been signed were greeted by salvos of artillery fire, the wild ringing of church bells, cries of tearful rapture in the suddenly thronged streets, and the spontaneous formation of processions of jubilant Parisians, who began marching towards the Place de la Concorde, singing the 'Marseillaise', 'Madelon', and 'It's a Long Way to Tipperary'.

President Woodrow Wilson's arrival in the capital, ten days before Christmas, ignited another spasm of popular jubilation. But after the tumult and the shouting had died down, the prevailing feeling was more guilt-ridden than euphoric, so formidable to the survivors seemed the tasks of having to rebuild a shattered country which had lost 1,350,000 dead – 17 percent of those conscripted – and which now had to care for 660,000 invalids, 10 percent of whom were crippled for life. Not to mention the task of rebuilding a fragmented continent that had witnessed the collapse of three dynasties, where new frontiers had to be drawn for many of the thirty-two countries represented at the Conference of Versailles, and which seemed acutely threatened (particularly in Germany and Hungary) by the Bolshevik virus.

None of these staggering problems were of immediate concern to the young André Malraux. That the precarious new life he had chosen was full of risks, that it was an almost reckless gamble, he was fully aware, but this only made the challenge more exciting. He may not yet have discovered Nietzsche, but he was already convinced, like Stendhal's Julien Sorel, that getting ahead in the world is essentially a question of will-power and driving ambition. Now that he had chosen to live dangerously there could be no turning back. 'Between eighteen and twenty years of age,' as he explained a dozen years later to the Franco-American writer, Julien Green, 'life is like a market where one buys shares – not with money but with acts. Most men buy nothing.'

What neither of his parents realized was the precocious understanding their son André had already acquired of the rare-book trade and of its intricate connections with the world of pictorial art. At this time a rare limited-edition book was almost invariably a book that included illustrations – supplied, not by a photographer but by an artist skilled in the execution of drypoints, etchings, lithographs, or woodcuts.

Although many authors and artists had been called up or had volunteered for service in 1914 or later, Paris throughout the war had remained a cosmopolitan centre of the literary, graphic, and musical arts. This was due to the presence in the capital of talented foreigners – like Picasso, Juan Gris, Chaim Soutine, Marc Chagall, Amedeo Modigliani, Constantin Brancusi – who were not eligible for military service. Certain famous hostesses and patronesses of the arts – the Princesse de Polignac, the Baronne d'Oettingen, the Petersburg-born Misia Sert – maintained literary salons, and one of them, a Chilean *grande dame* with the gritty Basque name of Eugenia Errazuris, even kept Blaise Cendrars from starving, at a time when the

Swiss-born poet-author was learning to write with his left hand, having lost most of his right arm at the front in September 1915. Probably no single event during those grim wartime months more dramatically illustrated this astonishing resilience and what might be called the *union sacrée* of the arts than the May 17, 1917 première of *Parade*: a sophisticated variety show ('the first Cubist ballet', Apollinaire called it), which was staged by Diaghilev with a script written by the effervescent Jean Cocteau, music composed by Debussy's friend and rival, Erik Satie, stage sets designed by Picasso, and choreography worked out by Leonid Massine.

It is certainly no accident that one of the first people André Malraux chose to call on was the Greek-born painter and engraver, Demetrios Galanis. Like his Lithuanian colleague, Louis Marcoussis, Galanis had begun his career as a cartoonist for French and German satirical magazines before making his mark as an engraver and book illustrator. Galanis' studio-apartment was located on the Rue Cortot, a picturesque cobbled street located not far from the summit of the Butte, on the northern slope of Montmartre. The house, overlooking a small, tree-filled garden and a charming seventeenth-century mansion, had been inhabited by the painter Raoul Dufy, the poet Pierre Reverdy, and by a turbulent artistic trio composed of the painter Suzanne Valadon, her painter-husband André Utter, and her bibulous painter-son, Maurice Utrillo. All this André Malraux discovered later, for in January 1919, when he first rang the doorbell of no. 12, Rue Cortot, he was greeted by Galanis' wife, whose husband had not yet been discharged from military service. She was so impressed by the young stranger's familiarity with her husband's work that she noted his address. A few weeks later the seventeen-year-old admirer was finally able to meet the thirty-five-year-old engraver, establishing a fruitful friendship which was to last for years.

Malraux's progress in enlarging his circle of acquaintances in this literary-artistic milieu was prodigiously rapid. Paris was then a far more closely-knit intellectual and artistic community than is the case today. Famous painters and poets could easily be found in the particular bistros and cafés they frequented. The only passport needed to 'crash' such circles was a quick wit, original ideas, and a keen understanding of literary and artistic matters, such as André Malraux had been able to acquire through his book-peddling activities.

The soundest tribute ever paid to his capacities as a *chineur* (a rare-book hound) is that of the first bookseller and publisher with whom, for eighteen months, he was closely associated: René-Louis Doyon. A long-faced, bespectacled 'mandarin' (as he liked to call himself), he was an ardent bookworm who had decided to become a publisher. Being anything but rich, Doyon had started out more modestly by establishing a small bookshop and lending library in a dark passageway called the Passage de la Madeleine. This covered walk connected the Place de la Madeleine to the Rue Boissy d'Anglas – a convenient north–south street, running parallel to the Rue

Royale, which debouched into the Place de la Concorde between the Hôtel Crillon and a terraced men's club called L'Epatant (Tip-Top), which today is the site of the US Embassy. It rapidly dawned on Doyon, as he pored over his account-books in the tiny mezzanine office above the shop, that the sophisticated works of turn-of-the-century authors and poets lining the shelves of his tiny lending library could not possibly appeal to a local clientèle made up of waitresses,.dressmakers, *midinettes*, and secretaries, and that if he was going to survive he would have to make a speciality of selling off-beat books capable of attracting wealthy bibliophiles, who would not mind dropping in to a dingy book-crammed den provided it could offer them rare items missing from their library collections. But to be able to satisfy such exacting connoisseurs he needed a reliable supplier.

One day, during this same year of 1919, fate or destiny – the word that was to loom so large in Malraux's later works – presented Doyon with a godsend: an admirably efficient, punctual *chineur*. The providential visitor was a tall, brown-haired young man, who struck him as 'distinguished, and simply but most correctly dressed'. Every morning, having scoured the bookstalls of the *quais* or visited second-hand dealers, the spruce André Malraux would turn up punctually with his harvest at 11 o'clock. 'He fixed the prices, asked for his due, and then left. Little by little our relations became less strict; we began talking, exchanging ideas. He had very definite literary opinions and was often quite sarcastic in his judgements.'

Doyon's valuable testimony sheds light on another Malraux talent – as an incisive purveyor of literary gossip. 'Despite his cold appearance and a certain reserve in his behaviour, Malraux was not lacking in malice or even in cruel barbs, which contrasted with his air of being aloof and superior to the world he had to deal with every day.'

Thus ably seconded, Doyon could bring out his own books under the La Connaissance imprint. They included a limited edition of Stendhal's letters to his sister Pauline (each copy including one original letter, the rest being printed); a French version of Stendhal's *Chroniques italiennes*, translated by a *dame de lettres* and would-be poet exotically named Sanda Mahali, who for years had kept a fretful Jules Laforgue on tenterhooks in a typically Victorian fever of unconsummated passion; and – most important of all in terms of success – a limited edition (500 copies) of Mérimée's supposedly anonymous biography of H. B. (Henry Beyle, which is to say Stendhal), which sold out in a couple of days.

Far less successful was the first book Malraux recommended to Doyon. This was *La Passion de Jésus-Christ*, a French translation of the recorded visions of the famous Bavarian mystic, Anna Katharina Emmerich (the 'Nun of Dülmen'), as described by the Romantic poet, Clemens Brentano, in *Das bittere Leiden unseres Herrn Jesu Christi*. The original nineteenth-century edition had gone through twenty-five reprints in forty-four years, but the tastes of the French reading public had since changed, for Doyon found few takers.

Malraux's second proposal – a reprint of Görres' *La Mystique divine, naturelle et diabolique* – was equally curious and revealing of his youthful fascination with the irrational, the oneiric and demonic, which was soon to find expression in his earliest writings. A brilliant radical journalist who, in 1814, had helped to found the liberal *Rheinische Merkur*, Joseph von Görres (1776–1848) had later become a violently anti-Prussian Catholic, and he had spent the last years of his life compiling an anthology of Christian mysticism (*Die christliche Mystik*) in which magic, necromancy, witchcraft and sorcery, demonic possession and exorcism figure prominently. Doyon, whose literary tastes were less baroque, was understandably reluctant to republish this neo-Gothic pilgrimage through the wild dreamlands of the irrational.

He was more receptive to his young colleague's third suggestion: that they bring out several volumes of so far 'unpublished' notes, prose poems, aphorisms, and other literary fragments written by the tragically short-lived Symbolist poet, Jules Laforgue (1860–87). It is a tribute to the seventeen-year-old Malraux's literary acumen that he should have developed such a keen interest in the work of this wistful poet – 'the Heinrich Heine of France', as he has been called – whose laments about a godless universe, flavoured by sprinklings of disarming humour, were later the delight, and even at times the inspiration, of poets and authors as varied as Guillaume Apollinaire, Léon-Paul Fargue, T. S. Eliot, Ezra Pound, André Gide, Henry Miller, and Jacques Prévert. However, the unscholarly manner in which these fragments were presented – without source references and as so far 'unpublished' writings – later aroused the critical wrath of a rival editor (G. Jean-Aubry), who pointed out that these texts had already been published in various magazines.

With Malraux's active encouragement Doyon decided to expand his publishing activities by bringing out a literary monthly predictably named – a lively imagination was not one of Doyon's virtues – *La Connaissance*. The pompous tone of the lead article could not mask the lacklustre contents of the first issue, published in January 1920. Tucked in among other miscellaneous items – covering everything from the 'Epidermis of Women' to the 'Evolution of Management in Industry' – was a short Malraux contribution entitled 'Les Origines de la Poésie cubiste' ('The Origins of Cubist Poetry').

It is difficult not to agree with Doyon's later assessment in terming it '*sommaire*' – a cursory treatment of the subject. The very brevity of the article – five-and-a-half small-format pages, roughly 1,350 words – devoted to four distinctly different poets (Apollinaire, Max Jacob, Pierre Reverdy, and Blaise Cendrars), virtually excluded any possibility of analytical profundity. No attempt was made to explain the reasons for the catch-all appellation given to this so-called 'Cubist poetry'.

Indeed, the opening paragraph was nothing less than a cruel pastiche, ironically parodying the preciously convoluted, *fin-de-siècle* style affected by the poetic masters of a 'school' whose death throes the brash young critic did not hesitate to mock:

When Symbolism, having become a senile literary movement, splashed around in the precursory water-rippling of its definitive dissolution, young men who had little desire to publish flabby (though potentially prize-winning) poems, furbelows of stunning glozes, set out in search of an artist capable of producing a work from which a new aesthetic could be extirpated without plagiarism.

The reaction to Malraux's article was not long in coming. In the February 20th issue of *Comoedia*, a daily specializing in a coverage of the arts, a critic with the double-barrelled name of Valmy-Baysse took the whippersnapper to task for his impertinent denigration of a 'senile' Symbolism. To which the whippersnapper riposted with a letter explaining that he had 'in no sense attacked Symbolism' and that he felt 'a loyal admiration' for 'this movement, one of the most beautiful and assuredly the most artistic of French literary movements'.

It did not take the fledgling bibliophile and critic long to size up Doyon as a worthy but not particularly inspired bookseller. In the meantime, thanks to friends he had made in the literary-artistic world, Malraux had established contact with a far more enterprising editor, Florent Fels, and a bolder publisher, Simon Kra.

A turbulent Left Bank youngster, Florent Fels had developed a passion for modern painting thanks to his grandmother's lover, Théodore Duret, the trailblazing critic who had done so much to promote the cause of Impressionist artists like Renoir, Monet, Sisley, Pissarro and Seurat. After two years in the trenches, Fels had ended up in 1918 serving as an interpreter for a US Army Intelligence unit based in Paris. Duly fitted out with a brand-new US army uniform, the ex-*poilu* had staged a spectacular return from the front, appearing like a Santa Claus at Juan Gris' shabby Bateau-Lavoir studio in Montmartre with a sackful of 'goodies' – everything from US Army canned goods and chocolates to Old Gold and Camel cigarettes – which were joyfully distributed to Maurice Utrillo, Suzanne Valadon, André Utter, Demetrios Galanis, and the droll poet-painter, Max Jacob. Right up until the moment of his discharge in 1919, Florent Fels happily continued raiding US Army canteen stores to keep his bohemian painter friends properly supplied with foodstuffs and cigarettes. Not having been born with any notable talent for painting or composing poems, he finally decided that he could best help them by using his discharge pay to finance the launching of a new literary-artistic review dynamically called *Action*.

The first person whose talents he enlisted was Max Jacob. A plump baldheaded man with soft watery blue-green spaniel-like eyes, a fleshy nose almost as red as Mr Punch's, big ears, and the chubby hands of a peasant, Max (as he was known to everyone) had left the Rue Ravignan, which he had helped make famous with his friend, Pablo Picasso. He moved around the corner to the Rue Gabrielle, where he established residence in a kind of inner-court cavern that had a strange décor faintly reminiscent of a sooth-sayer's den – with zodiacal and other inscriptions on the walls – illuminated by a single oil-lamp and surrounded by a welter of books, scribbled poems, drawings, goauches, watercolours, cigarette ends, mugs and brushes. Here, dressed in a pair of velvet corduroy trousers held up by a piece of string, and a kind of Robin Hood hunting jacket, he regularly received his friends. This standard accoutrement was crowned, when he went out, by an incongruous bowler hat, or replaced for evening outings by his only other 'suit' – a frock-coat, complete with striped trousers, a moiré-silk waistcoat, monocle, and collapsible top hat. Literary and artistic pilgrims were welcome to visit this 'monument' of mystico-bohemian-Breton eccentricity – he had been converted to Catholicism in 1915, after experiencing a second vision of Christ – and, if they showed any spark of originality, they might be invited to share a *boeuf à la ficelle* or a *sauté* of lamb with this gifted entertainer at the restaurant-grocery located on the other side of the street. For it was in this modest bistro, as Fels later recalled, that 'the élite of the painters and writers of the future would take their places, around a circular table and beneath a suspended lamp-carrier, which served as an autodrome for flies'.

André Malraux's pilgrimage to Max Jacob's exotic habitat probably took place in November 1919, shortly before the appearance of his first piece of literary criticism. The initial impression made on Max by the young dandy, who turned up with kid gloves, a tasselled cane, and a pearl-headed tie pin, may not have been too favourable. However, the intense, dark-eyed youth, whose good looks were marred only by a nervous twitch, soon made it clear that he was an erudite connoisseur of French literature and art.

The second person whom Florent Fels recruited for his new review was another literary 'star', André Salmon – like Picasso and Max Jacob a former pillar of the artistico-bohemian world of the Montmartre Butte. A lean, lanky pipe-smoker with long, gaunt, and faintly equine features, Salmon had spent some of his early years in St Petersburg as the son of a French consular official who was an amateur watercolourist of some talent. In 1903 his gift for humorous versification had attracted the attention of Paul Fort, the celebrated 'prince of poets' whose Tuesday evening get-togethers at the Closerie des Lilas (near the southern end of the Luxembourg Gardens) had made this terrace-flanked restaurant one of the poles of Montparnasse's intellectual life. Almost exactly the same age as Apollinaire (born in 1880), with whom he immediately got on well, Salmon so shared his enthusiasm for modern painting that he was willing to leave the Left Bank in order to share the impoverished existence of Pablo Picasso, Juan Gris, Van Dongen, and Ricardo Casals in the ramshackle wooden beehive of a house known as the Bateau-Lavoir (literally, the 'Boat-Wash House'), on the corner of the Rue Ravignan, where painters, sculptors, poets, actors and seamstresses had to go downstairs to fill their jugs, cans, and cauldrons with water from the one and only pump.

Shortly after his marriage – an act of recklessness for one so poor, but duly hailed by a moving Apollinaire poem – a friend persuaded Salmon that journalism was not necessarily bondage. To his astonishment he was hired by Léon Bailby, the enlightened boss of the daily *L'Intransigeant*. One day the newspaper's art critic fell ill, and Salmon was asked to 'cover' the Salon des Indépendants. This was the chance of a lifetime. Salmon's article heaped praise on the works of Matisse, Rouault, Braque, Delaunay, Friesz, Vlaminck, and Van Dongen, and scorn on the paintings of the highly prized 'academic' artists. The article created such a sensation that Bailby decided to let Salmon sound off again on behalf of his Montmartre friends and others; a little later, when Salmon joined the staff of another daily, he persuaded Bailby to choose Apollinaire to succeed him. From then on Picasso, the Cubists, and the *Fauves* had two journalistic champions to uphold them.

The first number of *Action*, published in February 1920 with a pompous streamer proclaiming it (and successive numbers) to be 'individualist notebooks of philosophy and art', was a hodge-podge of critical articles and pieces of fiction. The most startling contribution was the work of André Malraux's friend, the poet Georges Gabory. It took the form of an 'Eloge de Landru' – an apologia on behalf of one of the most accomplished serial murderers France had ever known: a twentieth-century Bluebeard who had lured no fewer than ten lady-friends to his cottage west of Paris, where they had been killed, chopped up, and reduced to ashes in the kitchen stove. This short, tongue-in-cheek essay, denigrating the cult of human rights and equality and upholding not merely the right but the duty of 'superior men – artists, emperors, madmen, and lovers' to give free rein to their individual volition, was almost certainly a subtle exercise in *reductio ad absurdum*, intended to mock Maurice Barrès' egocentric *culte du Moi*, Nietzsche's rash deification of the Superman, and Gabriele d'Annunzio's jingoistic 'voluntarism', forcefully expressed the previous September by his flamboyant invasion of Fiume.

From the start Fels had wanted to provide his artist friends with a monthly in which their avant-garde works would be made better known through visual means. This objective was attained with the second (March 1920) number of *Action*, which was adorned with black-and-white photographic reproductions of paintings by Braque, Derain, Galanis, Juan Gris, André Gromaire, Marcoussis, Pablo Picasso, Dunoyer de Segonzac, and Fels' close friend, Maurice de Vlaminck.

André Malraux made his début as a contributor in the monthly's third (April 1920) issue. His subject was 'Les Chants de Maldoror' – a long prose-poem composed during the late 1860s by an aspiring bard named Isidore Ducasse, who had adopted the pen-name of Comte de Lautréamont.

If the adjective 'flippant' aptly describes the so-called 'origins' of Cubist poetry, 'glib' is the word for the young critic's treatment of the 'Genesis' of the 'Chants de Maldoror'. At the time little research had been done on this mysterious French prose-poet, about whom almost nothing is known beyond the fact that he was born in Montevideo, the capital of Uruguay, in 1846, and that he died during the Prussian siege of Paris in November 1870. One can therefore forgive certain elementary errors of fact in the article, such as Malraux's belief that Isidore Ducasse had left Montevideo at the age of twenty out of hatred for his family, had come to Paris and had taken up residence in a small hotel, where he spent his days playing the piano and his nights scribbling and consuming such quantities of coffee that he maintained himself in a permanent fever of intoxication. More surprising, given his taste for *maudit* poets and their 'scandalous' works, was the ferocity of Malraux's attack on Ducasse-Lautréamont, who was accused of having plagiarized 'romantic English clichés' popularized by Matthew Gregory Lewis (author of *Ambrosio, The Monk, The Castle Spectre*, etc) and Edgar Allan Poe; of having borrowed shamelessly from Milton's *Paradise Lost*, Byron's *Manfred*, and Mickiewicz's *Konrad Wallenrod*; of having indulged in the 'infantile sadism' and satanism which were the fashion with many French intellectuals of Théophile Gautier's generation. The question that naturally arises is why, being so unimpressed by the childish sadism of 'Les Chants de Maldoror', André Malraux should should have been so eager to debunk it. The answer is to be found in the literary-artistic context of this year 1920, the first months of which were dominated by the explosive irruption on to the Paris scene of a group of obstreperous nihilists known as the Dadaists.

Written by a would-be 'poet' who died when he was only twenty-four, the six 'Cantos' of 'Maldoror' (the neo-Gothic name Ducasse-Lautréamont chose for the Spirit of Malevolence in the world) are with little doubt the most sustained exercise in nihilistic blasphemy to be found in all of French literature. They reflected the despair which overcame many post-Romantic Europeans at the realization, so forcefully proclaimed by Schopenhauer (the first Western philosopher to have made a serious study of biology), that the zoological world of animals, and thus of human beings, is one of heartless and never-ending cruelty, making a mockery of the notion of divine benevolence.

By 1919 the 'Chants de Maldoror' had become such a rarity in Paris bookshops that André Breton had to spend days in the manuscript department of the Bibliothèque Nationale laboriously copying out Ducasse-Lautréamont's deceptively named 'Poésies' (the ironic 'postscript' he added to his earlier work in a bogus repudiation of his Cantos). For the twenty-three-year-old André Breton, as for his closest associates in the Dada movement – the twenty-two-year-old Louis Aragon, the twenty-three-year-old Philippe Soupault, the twenty-four-year-old Théodore Fraenkel and Paul Eluard – Lautréamont, that satanic idol-smasher and God-mocking blasphemer, was nothing less than a prophet and the trailblazing precursor of their own nihilistic, convention-defying sentiments. Four, five, or six years older than André Malraux, all of these determined rebels had served at one moment or another in the French Army, most of them with medical units, and had emerged from the war utterly disgusted by the futile bloodshed they had witnessed. Aesthetes all of them to the tips of their artistic fingers, these rebellious sons of the bourgeoisie were at this time politically uncommitted and not directly motivated by any Marxist enthusiasm for the revolutionary upheavals in Russia. But they were possessed by the same furious desire to destroy the conventions of 'respectable' society and to build, on their ruins, a new world – a *Nouveau Monde* – the title they had originally chosen for their literary monthly. In the battle to impose this utopian 'new world' on the ruins of the old, Lautréamont's 'Chants de Maldoror' loomed large as a kind of intellectual battering-ram to be used against the fortresses of cultural conservatism.

One writer who had learned to his cost just what Dadaism consisted of was André Salmon, who had been invited to sponsor a 'spectacle' organized by Breton's Dadaist group in a supposedly 'central' Paris cinema, far removed from the *littérateurs* of the Left Bank and the art galleries of the Opéra-Madeleine area. The several hundred spectators who filled the cinema on this January 23, 1920 were most of them shopkeepers. They soon began leaving the theatre, annoyed by Salmon's introductory speech, discussing abstract questions of poetry which were way above their heads. There was, however, considerable commotion when two new Picabia 'works of art' were 'unveiled' – one a blackboard drawing which the master then proceeded to erase, thus emphasizing its exemplary 'instantaneity', the other a 'masterpiece' featuring the five salacious letters – LHOOQ – which, when pronounced out loud, became 'elle a chaud au cul' ('she has a hot arse'). But what brought tempers to a boil, since it made it clear that this 'cultural matinée' was a carefully planned exercise in provocation, was the electrifying appearance on the stage of the diminutive, dark-haired, dark-skinned Romanian mischief-maker, Tristan Tzara, who, instead of reciting some of his avant-garde poems, proceeded to read the text of a speech that had recently been delivered in the Chamber of Deputies by the notoriously reactionary Léon Daudet. Feeling that their good faith had been abused, Salmon and Juan Gris began berating the 'actors' of this Dada comedy and were promptly joined by many members of the audience, including Florent Fels, whose voice could be heard above the uproar, shouting: '*A Zurich!*' ('Back to Zurich!', where Tzara had staged the first Dada 'manifestations' at the Cabaret Voltaire as early as 1916), and even: '*Au poteau!*' ('To the firing-post!' – ie to be shot).

This first Dada explosion was soon followed by a second uproar at the Salon des Indépendants art show at the Grand Palais, during which a series of provocative manifestos were solemnly read out loud. It was in the midst of this cultural brouhaha, given lavish coverage in the Paris press, that André Malraux wrote his article denigrating Lautréamont's 'Maldoror' as being little more than an adolescent exercise in provocation. Given Florent Fels' strong anti-Dadaist feelings, nothing in the spring of 1920 could have been calculated to give him greater pleasure than a sharp attack on their idol. Nor was it an accident if, in the same April 1920 issue of *Action*, Malraux's critical assault on 'Les Chants de Maldoror' should have been placed next to an article by the veteran Cubist painter, Albert Gleizes. In this article Dadaism was condemned as one more symptom of the spiritual decomposition of capitalist society, promoted by the irresponsible sons of wealthy bourgeois families and encouraged by cultural snobs, ever on the look-out for 'modern tendencies', avant-garde thrills, and the latest 'great event of the season'.

3

Author, Publisher and Troubadour

André Malraux's next contribution to *Action* was published in the fourth issue, which did not come out until July 1920 – proof that the new literary-artistic review was already having trouble surviving as a monthly. To earn his living, Florent Fels had been obliged to take a night-time job as proof reader and then page-editor for a financial newsheet. Malraux, for his part, kept the wolf from the door by continuing his fairly-lucrative activities as a rare-book *chineur* and by supervising the preparation of limited editions of rare books brought out under the imprint of Les Editions du Sagittaire, a new publishing company launched by Simon Kra during the spring of this eventful 1920.

The son of a bookseller who had once served as librarian for a Rothschild millionaire, the massive, corpulent Simon Kra in his younger years had been a globe-trotting music-hall entertainer. In 1910 he had even performed his celebrated 'diabolo' act on the stage of London's Palladium Theatre together with a baggy-trousered medical student named Charles Chaplin and an equally obscure juggler called Blaise Cendrars. After marrying a rich heiress, Simon Kra decided to surpass his father by publishing as well as peddling books. Lacking personal experience, however, he welcomed the collaboration of the young enterprising expert, André Malraux.

Malraux boldly proposed that they bring out a series of superbly illustrated books which, unlike most rare editions (limited to 100 carefully numbered copies), could have print runs of up to 1,000 copies. Though a gamble, this proposal was based on the elementary calculation that a larger print run would allow for a lower sale price, and also in the belief that it would be no harder to persuade 600, 700, or 800 well-to-do bibliophiles to invest in handsomely illustrated editions of works so far unpublished in book form than it would be to persuade 100 connoisseurs. Undermined by inflation and catastrophic budget deficits, the value of the franc, which throughout the first fourteen years of the century had remained rock-solid at five francs to the gold dollar, had gone into a tail-spin after the conclusion of hostilities, dropping to an abysmal 16 francs 25 centimes by April of 1920. The cost of living over the same sixteen months had increased fourfold, giving rise to massive speculation. Many French men and women now began to invest in rare books, as they did in gold, antiques, and paintings, as an insurance against rising prices. Malraux's gamble thus paid off. Within three weeks of the first notice in the profession's trade paper, *Journal de la librairie*, announcing the forthcoming publication by the Editions du Sagittaire of a series of rare books the first two titles on the list had been bought in advance by eager 'takers'. The first – Remy de Gourmont's *Livret de l'Imagier*, with seven woodcuts by an up-and-coming young artist named Jean-Gabriel Daragnès – was one of the many books Malraux had come across during his explorations of Symbolist and post-Symbolist literature. The second, Charles Baudelaire's little-known *Causeries* ('Chats'), was a reprint of newspaper articles Baudelaire had written in 1846 and 1847 with two other colleagues; it was illustrated by fourteen woodcuts based on water-colours painted by Baudelaire's much-admired contemporary, Constantin Guys (1802–98), which were printed in red ink, the better to suggest the delicacy of the originals. Indeed, the demand for this particular rare book was so great that more than 200 Holland paper copies had to be added at the last moment to those originally subscribed to, raising the total print order to 750 copies. Equally successful were the three titles that followed.

The year 1920 began with the first Dada provocations and was marked in February by the sensational première of *Le Boeuf sur le Toit* ('The Ox on the Roof') – 'an American farce concocted by a Parisian who had never been in America' (as its librettist, Jean Cocteau, put it) with jazzy avant-garde music by Darius Milhaud and dance numbers worked out by the choreographer, Leonid Massine. It was also a momentous year for the eighteen-year-old André Malraux. So prosperous did the young publisher, bibliophile, and literary critic become that he could soon take the risk of promoting the publication of volumes of poetry (usually the least saleable of literary works) by Max Jacob, Pierre Reverdy, Georges Gabory, and a young prodigy sponsored by Cocteau named Raymond Radiguet. He was even able to live it up, treating friends to expensive lunches or to evenings in the sultry cabarets of Montmartre.

For a while the most favoured of these friends seems to have been Georges Gabory. Largely self-educated – a quality certain to appeal to André – this young poetry-lover had been brought up in relatively poor surroundings in the uninspiring suburb of Clichy-la-Garenne, north-east of Paris. In the morning, again like André, he had to commute to Paris by train or bus.

The two friends usually spent several hours together every day, except for Sunday. As Gabory later recalled: 'Most often I would meet him [André] in the early afternoon at Kra's place on the Rue Blanche' – the street that runs up the steep foothill of Montmartre from the garment-sellers' district of the Rue Lafayette to the erotic flesh-pots of Pigalle. The corpulent Kra

would discuss, shout, raise his arms to heaven – [explaining that] the printer was demanding to be paid, the clients were dragging their feet, etc. It was a piece of theatre comedy, a music-hall number crowned by bursts of laughter. Malraux and I would emerge and cross half of Paris on foot, in any kind of weather and always without an umbrella.

During these long 'aesthetic' walks the two *aficionados*, both of them gifted with superior memories, would vie with each other in reciting verses written by Baudelaire or by any other poet who sprang to mind. On the picturesquely named Rue Croulebarbe ('Crumblebeard Street') or in the Gobelins district of south-eastern Paris Malraux would inspect the work of Ducros, Lefèvre, and Colas, three printers he regularly dealt with. When it was cold, he and Gabory would warm themselves with hot chocolate and soft brioches at a tea-room gaily named 'Frolic's'. From there they would move on and across the Seine to the Forum bar, behind the Madeleine, where they would sip newly-discovered cocktails: Manhattans, dry Martinis, an occasional Alaska, or the even more exotic Bijou, recently imported from America. Sometimes, with the same casual generosity, André would treat his friend to a lunch at Larue, Marguery, or the equally fashionable Noël Peters, located in a covered passageway behind the Opéra. 'Everywhere Malraux paid,' George Gabory wistfully recalled years later. 'I was poor, he was already rich, at any rate he always had money, and money which he spent . . .'

As the literary and artistic director of the Sagittaire publishing company, André was soon sufficiently prosperous to be able to rent a small bachelor's flat in the 17th *arrondissement*, not far from the Arc de Triomphe. To Bondy, already receding into the distance of an unregretted past, he now returned infrequently. Having won his financial independence by his own unaided ingenuity, he was more than ready to celebrate his 'emancipation' by sampling the tempting night-life offered by Montmartre at the Moulin Rouge and the equally famous Bal Tabarin, where André picked up a 'piece of fluff' who, in Gabory's words, 'displayed the childish grace of a monkey'.

Although blasphemy held no particular appeal for the young Malraux, he was already fascinated by the farcical, the monstrous, the grotesque. This became evident with his first fictional experiment, an initial fragment of which appeared in the fifth (October 1920) issue of *Action*. It was a three-part fantasy, describing the vicissitudes of the Seven Deadly Sins. The title he gave to this bizarre 'cautionary tale' was *Lunes en papier* ('Paper Moons'). The opening scene – featuring a laughing moon whose high-pitched chimes drop out, like teeth, slowly descending to earth like spent fireworks and blossoming on the surface of a lake into paper flowers containing two-eyed moonlets – was clearly inspired by Jules Laforgue's *L'Imitation de Notre-Dame la Lune*, as well as by Cyrano de Bergerac (for the detail of the falling teeth). But the kaleidoscopic bedlam that followed – with balloons assaulting a fairy-tale palace and trussing up its puppet-show inhabitants (Punches, Judys, gendarmes, gamekeepers, garrulous concierges, rustic gentlemen with red umbrellas, etc) only to be intoxicated on fine old brandy and tied up in their turn by a subtle, calculating cat – probably startled rather than enchanted Max Jacob, to whom this long prose poem was dedicated.

Given the precocious erudition of its author, *Lunes en papier* was a veritable anthology of themes, ideas, and images derived from a wide variety of sources. Indeed, it is such a plum cake of oddities that years later the Belgian scholar, André Vandegans, needed close to fifty pages to analyse its various elements.

The most interesting aspect of *Lunes en papier*, viewed in the context of Malraux's later works of fiction, is the prominence accorded to the subjects of war and death. The seven sins who are the main protagonists are not only deadly but mortal – in French, *les sept péchés mortels* conveniently expressing both meanings. In fact, two of them – Envy and Avarice – die and have to be replaced. Malraux may not have attached any particular significance to this burlesque detail, reserving his philosophical irony for a subsequent passage, where the five remaining sins (Anger, Gluttony, Laziness, Lust, and Pride) question the two replacements (one absurdly named Hifili, the other a former musician) as to the nature of God and what should be done about Him. Hifili says that he had once met God long ago, adding, 'This old man is very friendly' – a clear allusion to the naive Christian belief in *le bon Dieu* (the good Lord). Whereupon the musician chimes in: 'Friendly, yes, but a bit vulgar' – an ironic dig at those who, for aristocratic reasons, feel, like Goethe, that 'religion is made for others'. To this Pride replies that God is not vulgar. 'As he has grown older, he has grown completely unaware of what is going on. He has already changed his name and costume many times without attaching any importance to it; but this time Satan, who is no fool, has arranged to take his place, and neither God nor anybody else has noticed it. Since Satan has replaced him, we could replace Satan. What do you think?'

'Our power would be almost nil,' objects Anger. 'Death, Satan's best friend, is destroying us.'

'I have thought about it,' Pride replies. 'It is extremely simple to pay no heed to it; it is enough to kill Death.'

The idea that Satan has replaced God on earth, or to put it slightly differently, that life on earth is basically satanic, is not a new one. It is at least as old as the Zoroastrians, with their notion of the evil god, Angra Mainu (the 'lord of this world' of St John) forever warring with the good god of the 'other world', Ahura Mazda, the god of light. Even the idea that death itself is mortal was not basically original; in the sense of being overcome by faith and piety, it figured in many medieval mystery plays. But where Malraux can be said to have added a new, twentieth-century twist was by pitting the apprehensive sins – afraid that they too are threatened and may die (ie, in today's world the omnipresent sense of sin is largely a spent force) – against death, here represented as the ennui-stricken Queen of the *Royaume-Farfelu* (the 'Crazy Kingdom').

In the third and concluding section, Pride, in doctor's disguise, gains access to the Queen (Death), portrayed as a shivering skeleton dressed (against the cold) in a tuxedo – another 'borrowing' from Jules Laforgue, who liked to make drawings of dandified skeletons dressed in top hats and carrying canes. Lacking the courage to commit suicide, which would have been the easiest way to get rid of her Baudelairean ennui, Her Royal Majesty, Death, willingly consents to soak her bones (made of aluminium replacements) in what turns out to be an acid-filled bath. And thus, after a final soliloquy, Death dies, with a cigarette planted in her mouth, not only resigned but mockingly defiant. For the final triumph of the sins, in eliminating their hated enemy, turns out to be hollow. Although their own survival is now assured, they no longer know where to begin in exploiting their triumph, and burying their faces in their hands, they weep.

One can read several meanings into this strange conclusion: that life has lost its savour because the notions of divinity, and its opposite, damnation, have withered; or, probably closer to Malraux's intention, the idea that death is what gives life its inherent density, bringing people face-to-face with eternal truths. Whatever the interpretation, this tragic finale was the first indication that a more serious Malraux was beginning to emerge from behind the painted masks of Symbolism, post-Symbolism, and Cubism, which he, as a connoisseur of the plastic and literary arts, had so light-heartedly assumed.

It only remained to find a publisher, and, if possible, an artist to illustrate this weird tale. Both problems were solved thanks to the influential patronage of Max Jacob. Some time during the summer or early autumn of 1920 he introduced the eighteen-year-old André Malraux to the avant-garde art dealer, Daniel-Henry Kahnweiler, who, to make his clients better known to wealthy bibliophiles with numerous connections in the upper bourgeoisie, had gone into rare-book publishing as early as 1911.

Exactly what Kahnweiler thought of *Lunes en papier* we do not know. René-Louis Doyon, to whom Malraux read a few fragments, was impressed by his emotional earnestness as well as by 'the completely cerebral quality of his lyricism'. As a dealer who had been one of the first to appreciate the non-literal 'cerebrality' of Cubist painting, Kahnweiler was not one to be put off by a highly fanciful piece of fiction. The manuscript was accepted, and Kahnweiler's protégé, Fernand Léger, was hired to illustrate this limited edition (100 copies) with a number of solid, black-mass woodcuts – for him a new and unfamiliar medium.

Even before the publication of *Lunes en papier* in April 1921, Malraux had begun work on a second fantasy, written in the form of a diary kept by a puppet fireman: that is to say, by one of those traditional 'blockhead' figures, lined up inside the gaily coloured booths of country fairs, which clients are invited to knock down by heaving wooden balls at their usually leering, jeering, red-cheeked faces.

This 'farcical tale' was every bit as macabre as *Lunes en papier*, and more gratuitously cruel. Three of its four tableaux consist of scenes of combat, during which an impressive number of corpses are piled up. Only in one – the second, graced by the appearance of an 'old splenetic devil' (once again symbolizing the decadence of religious beliefs) – is there the slightest trace of humour.

It had been Malraux's intention to have this second fantasy published by Simon Kra as part of a new series of Sagittaire books he had announced in several trade-publication advertisements during the spring of 1921. However, his decision to launch this new limited-edition series with a collection of poems by Georges Gabory – *Coeurs à prendre* (Hearts to be Taken) – was hardly judicious in terms of profit-making. Almost unknown as a poet, Gabory could not be expected to arouse the interest of the bibliophiles who had subscribed to the first series of limited-edition books, featuring such celebrities as Charles Baudelaire, Jules Laforgue, and Remy de Gourmont. Simon Kra now informed his 'literary and artistic director' that he was discontinuing the series. Malraux thus found himself without a publisher for his second work of fiction.

Simon Kra proved more responsive to another proposal made to him by his enterprising associate: that they undertake to bring out clandestine editions of erotic works. These could be made more enticing by the inclusion of salacious illustrations, and then peddled under the counter at fancy prices. Two Marquis de Sade fragments were chosen. The first, *Les Amis du crime* (extracted from *La Nouvelle Justine*) was illustrated by Paul-Albert Moras; the second, *Le Bordel de Venise* (from *L'Histoire de Juliette*), reserved for 'amateurs' of gymnastic fornication, was 'embellished' by watercolour prints of multiple orgies penned and painted by an artist called Couperyn – a pseudonym used by Malraux's friend, the Belgian lithographer and painter, Georges Drains.

André Malraux may well have had a hand in the preparation of other pornographic works brought out under bogus imprints. In tracking down such works he was encouraged by a young contemporary, destined to become a leading twentieth-century connoisseur of French erotica: Pascal Pia.

Even more of a self-made youth than Malraux, Pierre Durand – to give him his real name – had lost his father, killed at the front, in 1915. In 1916 he had left his mother, whom he disliked, and began to work in various menial capacities for shipping and insurance companies, and later with money-changers. He had also worked as a barman and been involved for a while in the clandestine importation of cocaine. In 1918 he had found more interesting employment with an eccentric stockbroker and part-time author, Frédéric Lachèvre, who had asked him to undertake some basic research on the origins of atheism. It was probably from Lachèvre, a great admirer of the libertine authors and poets of the sixteenth and seventeenth centuries (Théophile de Viau, Claude d'Esternod, Cyrano de Bergerac, etc), that Pascal Pia (as he soon renamed himself) acquired his own taste for erotic literature – one that rivalled his passion for the poetry of Baudelaire and Apollinaire. It was probably while rummaging through Left Bank bookshops in search of little-known 'obscene' works that Pascal Pia first ran into another keen-nosed book-hound named André Malraux.

It was difficult not to like this tall, affable, brown-haired youth, who was witty, ironic, and gifted with a memory as prodigious as Malraux's own. There was hardly a poem that André could begin reciting without his friend Pascal being able to continue it with only minor errors or omissions. Equally impressive, and a source of great amusement, was his repertory of ribald verse. To amuse themselves, if not those they were supposed to entertain, the two 'troubadours' would stroll through the streets and enter carriage-way forecourts, singing bawdy songs – less in the faint hope of earning a few *sous* with which to pay for supper than as an act of wilful defiance, calculated to outrage staid members of the bourgeoisie. It was in the same tongue-in-cheek spirit that André encouraged his friend Pascal to haunt René-Louis Doyon's little bookshop in the sombre Galerie de la Madeleine, for the mischievous pleasure of seeing how this somewhat prim publisher would react to Pascal Pia's latest speleological *trouvaille* in the subterranean depths of 'forbidden' literature.

4

Clara

Florent Fels may not have been a brilliant magazine editor, but he had at least one salient virtue: tolerance. Like many others who had seen action at the front, he had never felt much sympathy for the super-patriotic bombast and 'Down with the *Boches*!' hysteria indulged in by armchair editors. The most strident Germanophobe in the field of the arts during the 1914–18 war had been Camille Saint-Saëns. In 1915 the octogenarian composer had launched a violent newspaper campaign with a series of articles which had driven Wagner operas from the Paris stage 'for the duration'; notwithstanding the polemical counter-attacks of Jean Marnold, music critic for the liberal monthly, *Mercure de France*, who had likened such narrow-minded fulminations to the 'prose of an epileptic sub-veterinary'. When, in November 1920 the director of the Concerts Colonne had decided to defy the super-patriots by staging scenes from Wagner's *Meistersinger* – still banned along with other Wagner works from the repertory of the Paris Opéra – Fels had made a point of attending the première at the Châtelet Theatre along with his friends Max Jacob, Francis Poulenc, Darius Milhaud, and Jean Cocteau.

It was in the same tolerant spirit that Fels opened the pages of *Action* to articles devoted to artistic and literary developments beyond the Rhine. The first of these articles appeared in the monthly's second number. It was devoted to German Expressionism and was written by an authority on the subject: Ivan Goll, a cosmopolitan Alsatian poet who had helped to launch the Expressionist movement in pre-war Berlin.

Although neither Ivan Goll nor his wife Claire ever became really close friends with André Malraux, they inadvertently transformed his life by opening a door past which he might have walked quite unsuspectingly, had he never met them. Opportunities of this kind can easily be missed. For if the opening of a particular door may owe much to chance, what one chooses to do thereafter is a matter of volition.

A convivial *bon vivant*, Florent Fels liked to give literary dinners to which contributors to *Action* were invited. It was at one of these dinners, organized in a restaurant located on one of the handsomely colonnaded walks of the

Palais Royal, that André Malraux – whose attitude toward the 'fair sex' had so far oscillated between frivolous sensuality and intellectual condescension – met a remarkable young woman who soon transformed his sedentary existence into something far more mobile and exciting.

Of medium height – she was 5 feet 6 inches tall – with light brown hair, blue-grey eyes, and a frequent flutter of the eyelashes suggesting both timidity and nervous tension, Clara Goldschmidt was the bilingual offspring of German-Jewish parents who had established residence in France. Her mother's well-to-do family came from the Prussian-Saxon city of Magdeburg, on the Elbe, in central Germany, while her hard-working father, Otto Goldschmidt, had built up his family's leather-tanning business, based in Paris, into an international enterprise. His premature death in 1912 had not affected the conditions of affluence in which she had been brought up – with a cook, a maid, an Austrian governess, and private tutoring in English. By the time the war broke out two years later – a wrenching war for the cruelly separated members of the Goldschmidt and Heynemann clans – the sixteen-year-old Clara was already fluent in three languages (French, German, and English); to these, after the war was over, she added Italian, easily acquired during a four-month stay in Florence. From early childhood she had developed a passion for literature. She dreamed of becoming a new poetic prodigy, a female Heinrich Heine. For this pampered day-dreamer who thrilled to the verses of Baudelaire, Gérard de Nerval, Alfred de Musset, Victor Hugo, and Jules Laforgue, a university education led inexorably to the teaching profession, from which she shrank in abhorrence. She longed for something more poetic and exciting, a life that would bring her into contact with writers, poets, artists.

Chance here played a major role. With the help of a former neighbour who had once lived near the Goldschmidt villa in Auteuil, she met the actor, Pierre Bertin, who agreed to give her lessons in poetic declamation. Impressed by her memory, literary enthusiasms, and fluency in four languages, Bertin introduced her to his childhood friend, Florent Fels. And thus it came about that, at the age of twenty-three, Clara Goldschmidt joined the *Action* 'family' as a translator – like Ivan and Claire Goll, whom she immediately befriended.

André Malraux never dwelled on the circumstances of his first meeting with Clara Goldschmidt at the *Action* dinner party given by Florent Fels. Fortunately we have her own fairly detailed account written up some forty years later in the first volume of her memoirs. Seated between a nondescript translator from Luxembourg and André Salmon's wife, she became aware of the presence, further down the table, of a garrulous young man who was apparently telling his neighbour, Jane Mortier, stories funny enough to make her ample form shake with laughter. He was 'a very tall and slender adolescent with eyes that were too big, and the pupils of which did not fill the immense curved globe; a white line stretched below the iris, of a watery green hue.'

At the end of the meal Jane Mortier, the plump, piano-playing wife of a well-to-do amateur painter who had been helping Florent Fels foot the printers' bills, left her seat and came up to Clara. Bending down, she suggested in a whisper that they go somewhere to dance. A few minutes later Clara found herself in the street with four others: Jane Mortier, Ivan Goll, the Luxembourg translator, and the slender young man with the large, penetrating eyes. Descending several stone steps, they pushed their way into a nightclub, festooned with tricolour garlands, called Le Caveau Révolution-naire (The Revolutionary Den). Not until the very end of the evening was Clara Goldschmidt invited to dance by the young stranger – a tango, which he danced rather awkwardly.

They met again the following Sunday in Ivan and Claire Goll's two-room apartment, located only five minutes away on foot from the Goldschmidt family's villa in Auteuil. Clara enjoyed these Sunday afternoon get-toge-thers, in an apartment adorned with canvases by Alexei Yavlinsky and Robert Delaunay, and with a bust by Alexander Archipenko boldly placed on the mantelpiece. Here the animated conversations were conducted in German as well as French by writers and artists as varied as the Cubist painter Albert Gleizes, the poet Céline Arnauld, the essayist Paul Dermée, the painter Marc Chagall and his wife Bella. Clara Goldschmidt now had time to study André Malraux's features:

a long, slightly drooping mouth, a chin whose triangle seemed slight compared to the height of the forehead, with pretty teeth and admirable hands. We installed ourselves in the rectangle of a window alcove and chatted away quietly in the midst of the hubbub caused by the others . . . His voice, with its faintly Parisian accent, rattled off curiously dense sentences, which it took a bit of effort to understand, enough to delight me; I sensed immediately that I was an initiate, a member of the same sect as my companion. So did he . . . He spoke to me of the poets of the High Middle Ages, of French satirists I knew nothing about. I spoke to him about Hölderlin and Novalis, we talked of Nietzsche, of Dostoevsky, of Tolstoy, whose *War and Peace* he had not yet read, and of El Greco.

She talked to him about Italy, of the Tuscan painters she had grown to love during her previous year's stay in Florence, casually adding, 'I'm going back to Italy in August.'

'I will accompany you,' he said without a moment's hesitation.

The swift answer thrilled her. Yes, why not? What a wonderful idea! This was the sort of adventure for which she had secretly been pining for years.

At the age of twenty-three Clara Goldschmidt was a highly frustrated virgin. She had long resented the greater latitude accorded to young men, expected to indulge in premarital 'experiences' while still in their teens. Why should young women not be granted the same freedom? The idea of being prematurely married without first tasting the forbidden fruit of premarital love appalled her, conjuring up a vision of imprisonment à deux.

When her older brother André, three years her senior, had returned from military service, he had been appalled by the 'scandalous' nonchalance with which she had cut her hair short, thrown away her corsets, was using lipstick, wearing knee-length skirts and entering cafés unescorted. His high-handed determination to act as her 'tutor' (their father being dead) had struck her as particularly hypocritical, since he himself was soon having affairs, often returning home at dawn. She was no less shocked by his cynical advice: 'First get married, then you can make a fool of yourself under another name.'

Returning from Ivan and Claire Goll's party that fateful Sunday afternoon, Clara Goldschmidt was in a radiant mood. 'How nice it is to be intelligent,' she remarked to her mother, 'for then one appeals to intelligent men.'

The intelligent young man she was thinking of was so intrigued by the superior knowledge and taste of this unusually well-read and cosmopolitan young woman that he took the trouble to telephone her at 10 o'clock the next morning. 'I love your voice,' were André Malraux's first words. Stretched out on the bed in her mother's room, Clara Goldschmidt felt like purring.

It was easier now – away from the Golls' crowded living room – to catch and savour each carefully chosen word in his rapid flow of speech. And so the minutes flew by, as recklessly unheeded by the languidly reclining Clara as by the invisible André. Her impatient mother kept coming into the room, obviously annoyed by this interminable conversation.

The next day André Malraux turned up at the Goldschmidts' three-storey villa, located, along with nine other houses, in a private enclosure known as l'Avenue des Chalets. He must have been impressed by the luxury of the garden and the presence of a maid to open the front door – so different from the cramped family life he had known at Bondy. Clara Goldschmidt clearly belonged to the upper bourgeoisie, on a level of affluence even higher than that enjoyed by Fernard Malraux.

Upstairs in her bedroom, they said not a word about her August trip to Italy, but talked about the things each wanted to show the other. From then on they saw each other every day. He took her to visit the Gustave Moreau Museum and showed her albums of drawings by James Ensor and Toulouse-Lautrec. She took him on excursions through the labyrinthine Trocadéro – that rococo masterpiece of Victorian bad taste, with its green-glassed rotunda and neo-Turkish minarets – where they studied the grimacing idols, plumed serpents, and foreign folklore of the ethnographic museum. She taught him how to row on the artificial lake of the Bois de Boulogne, he took her to horse races at Auteuil and Longchamp, where she developed a fondness for betting as keen as his own. Wherever they went, they talked and talked; of Nietzsche (by whom André was already obsessed), of Symbolists and post-Symbolists, of the 'eternal feminine' dear (among others) to Goethe and Jules Laforgue. He had a surprisingly off-hand way of separating their contemporaries into two distinct categories: those who were 'amusing' and those who were 'not amusing' – the worst offenders in this respect were André Breton and his fellow Dadaists, who took themselves far too seriously. One day, in what was clearly meant to be the *ne plus ultra* in his hierarchy of commendations, he said: 'I know only one person who is as intelligent as you – Max Jacob.'

Although Max had chosen this moment to retire to a Benedictine monastery on the Loire, the Montmartre Butte, of which he had long been the uncrowned bohemian king, was still associated in Clara's imagination with the naughty gaiety of can-can dancers kicking up their dark-stockinged legs in a flurry of lifted skirts – all those alluring cabarets and 'dens of iniquity' which, as a properly brought-up young lady, she had been unable to visit except through the drawings of Toulouse-Lautrec. André seemed surprised one day when, in answer to his question – 'Have you ever been to a *bal musette*?' (a plebeian 'ball' where partners from the humbler strata of society waltz, tango, and fox-trot to the accompaniment of accordions) – she answered, 'No.' This was a lacuna in her education which her young companion – she was after all four years older than he – felt it to be his masculine duty to fill.

The day chosen was a Sunday – a Sunday which began with a 'not amusing' literary get-together which several *Action* editors had chosen to stage, south of Paris, in a forest clearing surrounded by wooden huts. To honour the occasion Clara had put on a white worsted-and-silk dress, covered for the train trip out and back by an elegant grey velvet cape with a deep-blue satin lining. Over her dust-coloured hair she had placed a black sun-bonnet crowned with dark muslin, around her neck was a pearl necklace and she wore a diamond bracelet and a diamond ring.

This is not the kind of attire normally worn when going to a *bal musette* to 'see how the other half live'. But on this particular Sunday neither André nor Clara gave the matter a thought. They were probably both a bit flushed by the wine they had drunk at Noël Peters' celebrated restaurant when, some time after midnight, they turned up at a dance-hall located on a dark Left Bank street. The couple – 'too young and too luxurious', as Clara later recalled the scene – attracted a great deal of sniggering attention. But when the first stranger came up and invited her to dance, André whispered to her not to refuse. She laughed light-heartedly as she was shoved and bumped around over the floorboards by her clumsy partner amid the unfamiliar odour of perspiring bodies, cheap perfumes, and Pernod.

It all seemed a bit unreal, as unreal as what followed when, finally, André and she got up to leave. Outside in the dimly lit street several men from the *bal musette* barged rudely past them and then, a little further on, suddenly stopped, turned, and began to advance menacingly towards them. With his left hand André pushed Clara behind him, leaving his bent arm slightly outstretched to protect her, while with his right hand he dug into his pocket. A pistol shot was fired by one of the shadowy figures ahead, whereupon

André riposted with a revolver shot of his own. A moment later the dark figures vanished.

On the Montmartre Butte, during the early years of the century, painters, tavern-keepers, and poets were often armed against possible attacks by lawless thugs, and Picasso, who never went out without his Browning automatic, would occasionally pull it out and fire a couple of shots in the night air in moments of wild Andalucian-Catalan exuberance. André Malraux may well have been influenced by this example.

Gripping André's left hand, Clara suddenly felt blood trickling into her palm. The bullet fired by their molesters had passed between two knuckles. On the nearby Avenue des Gobelins they stopped by a sidewalk pump to wash away the blood. Clara said that they must disinfect the wound to keep it from getting worse and that she had what was needed at home.

In the taxi they clung to each other, bound by a new feeling of shared danger. At the Avenue des Chalets villa, Clara quietly opened the garden gate, and they tiptoed across the gravel to the front door, hoping that their crunching steps would not wake her mother. All in vain. For after they had crept up the carpeted stairs to Clara's bedroom, her mother suddenly emerged in a nightgown from her own bedroom and demanded to know what on earth 'your companion is doing here in the middle of the night?'

'He dropped me off, and he's come to pick up a book,' replied Clara airily, hastily hiding the bottle of peroxide disinfectant she was about to open.

A day or two later, seated on the same cushion-covered couch in the blue wallpapered bedroom, Clara and André exchanged their first hesitant, and then increasingly ardent, kisses. Leaving the villa, they took a taxi to what had once been one of Guillaume Apollinaire's favourite haunts – the O'Steen bar, located within earshot of the train whistles of the Gare Saint-Lazare. That night, or it may have been slightly later – it was at any rate a July 14th – she accompanied André to his rented room, and while outside the dark sky was rocked and brilliantly festooned by exploding necklaces of fireworks, they celebrated the national holiday and the storming of the Bastille by giving free rein to their passion.

Before parting, they agreed to meet the next day at the Hôtel Ritz, on the Place Vendôme. But when Clara turned up at the appointed time, there was no sign of André. Gradually yielding to panicky apprehensions and to a bitter suspicion that she had been 'had' by an artful seducer, she got up from her armchair, climbed into a taxi, and went home. She had barely reached the landing opposite her bedroom when the telephone began to ring. An anxious André was calling to find out what was wrong. He too had gone to the Ritz, had looked around, but had been unable to find her.

Half an hour later he joined her at the Goldschmidt villa. But such was Clara's rapturous relief at again beholding her 'lover' that it was only after he had left that she fully grasped what had happened. While she was waiting fretfully in the tapestried salon of the Ritz, André had gone to see his father for permission to marry her. The earnest plea had been rebuffed – one more crazy whim on the part of a headstrong adolescent who had run away from school, who had no fixed employment, who was still only nineteen years and eight months old. And who, as though that weren't enough, was now proposing to marry a Jewess!

The thwarted minor, however, was in no mood to abandon his plan to accompany Clara on her August trip to Italy. The next time he saw his father, he begged permission to be allowed to make a trip to Florence. The contemplation of all those masterpieces by Giotto, Botticelli, Donatello, Verocchio, Michelangelo, and others – none of them well represented in the Louvre – would be of great educational as well as psychological value and would help to overcome his youthful infatuation for Mlle Goldschmidt. Relieved to hear his son express such reasonable sentiments, Fernand Malraux gave him written authorization to obtain a passport, not realizing that Mlle Goldschmidt was also bound for Florence, still less that they would be travelling in the same *wagon-lit*.

Mme Goldschmidt was also kept in the dark during the planning of this premarital honeymoon. When the day of departure came, André remained discreetly out of sight, while Clara said goodbye to her mother. Only after the train had pulled out of the station did André reappear. In the restaurant car they laughed at the generous gullibility of Papa Fernand, so easily persuaded of the purely 'cultural' purpose of this clandestine elopement.

But early the next morning, after another night of shared rapture, Clara was rudely awoken by an insistent rapping on her compartment door. The *wagon-lit* steward asked her to accompany him to his cubicle, where he informed her that a gentleman in the compartment next to hers had asked to see the register and had exclaimed, on seeing her name, 'What a pity! A young girl from such a fine family.' After giving the steward a tip, Clara was allowed to examine the register in her turn. She recognized the name of her overly-inquisitive neighbour: a friend of her older brother.

When André appeared, casually dressed, like a pantomime clown, in striped silk pyjamas, he asked what had happened. Bad luck, she explained, had given her a nosy neighbour who was certain to inform her older brother that she had not been travelling on this train alone. There would be a terrible scene, her mother would have a fit, her brothers would throw her out of the house, and her Goldschmidt uncle – the one who since her father's death controlled the family's purse strings – would cut her off without a further penny.

André refused to be disconcerted: 'Would our getting married help to straighten things out?'

'Of course.'

'Now my father won't be able to oppose it any longer,' he reassured her.

'We will divorce in six months,' she suggested, afraid that he might think that this contretemps was forcing his hand.

'I'm going to have it out with that fellow next door,' announced the prospective husband in a resolute tone.

'What a numbskull, with that sickly curiosity of his!' he declared, after returning from his excoriatory mission. 'I told him that as a simple matter of fact we were engaged to be married, and were here with the authorization of our parents. But first, I proposed a small duel.'

She took him in her arms and was still laughing when there was a discreet tap on the door. It was the brown-uniformed steward once again. He handed Clara a visiting card, on which was a scribbled message. Monsieur Z (the importunate neighbour) 'presents his respectful homage to Mlle Goldschmidt and assures her that the incident will not get beyond the limits of this railway carriage'.

Doubting the sincerity of this pledge, Clara and André, after registering at their modest Florentine hotel, went to the city's central post office and sent off a telegram to Mme Goldschmidt announcing their engagement.

Gradually Clara's feeling of remorse at not having responded more affirmatively to André's offer to marry her – she still looked upon marriage as a form of bondage – was submerged by the visual pleasures offered them by the museums they visited. Although she spoke Italian, which he did not, and knew exactly which frescoed chapels, cool *cortiles*, and rusticated *palazzi* contained her favourite paintings and statuary, her intense young companion kept surprising her by the extraordinary extent of his knowledge, by occasional caustic comments, and above all by totally unexpected associations and comparisons with other, seemingly dissimilar works of art.

The misty mornings, the scorching afternoons, the cooler evenings, the feverish nights passed as in a dream, interrupted only by occasional lovers' quarrels brought on by Clara's contradictory desires and misgivings about their common future, and his aggrieved susceptibility. They climbed the hill to Fiesole, they stretched out near the cemetery of San Miniato al Monte and watched the evening sun gild Florence's umbred walls and roofs.

One evening, as they were strolling along the embankment overlooking the sadly shrunken Arno, the twinkle of lanterns on the other bank gave André an idea. 'Why don't we leave Florence and go on to Venice?' Clara thought it a wonderful suggestion, particularly since she had just received a peremptory telegram from her mother: 'Return immediately without your companion.' Since they had both decided to live dangerously, this was no time to stop.

The month of August is not the best season of the year for visiting the foetid canals of Venice. Though they decided to live it up in style by occupying a room at the Hotel Danieli, as George Sand and Alfred de Musset had done before them, Clara at first was strangely unmoved by the watery magic of the city of the Doges, and even by the polychrome view, beyond their Gothic windows, of the golden dome of San Giorgio floating like a mirage above the raft-like island of the Salute. The realization that she still had so much to learn, and consequently to experience, revived her distrust of marriage as a form of crippling bondage, leading her to insist again that they spell out their future relationship from the start.

'Whether married or not, we can't limit ourselves to each other. Naturally, in six months' time we'll divorce.'

To which a frowning André replied: 'Is it really necessary to fix all this in advance?'

These theoretical considerations soon seemed academic. Before they knew it, they had run out of money and hardly had enough left to settle the hotel bill and pay the extra train fares. The misnamed Orient Express, which had been lumbering its way north and westward through a number of now sovereign Balkan countries, was twelve hours late, and, unable to afford another meal, Clara and André spent their last hours on the sun-baked Lido, slowly sucking out the juice from a few remaining grapes.

By the time they reached the Swiss border, hunger was gnawing at their empty stomachs. Clara still had a few Swiss francs in her purse – enough to buy five sandwiches from a platform vendor.

The return of the prodigal couple was less stormy than Clara had feared. Her Aunt Jeanne, a member of the Goldschmidt clan, had insisted on accompanying her sister-in-law – Clara's mother – to the station to offer moral support.

'Is it really worth while?' she inquired – by which presumably she meant the prospective marriage, not the illicit honeymoon.

'Are you happy?' was the more charitable question asked by Clara's widowed mother.

What she said to André Malraux, looking leaner than ever in his famished condition, we unfortunately do not know, for Clara did not bother to record it. He may even have arranged to keep out of sight, once again.

At the Goldschmidt villa, Clara's older brother, who was also called André, was characteristically caustic. 'You have dishonoured us. I am leaving for America,' he announced, while trying to squeeze an overly large foot into a tight shoe.

'First put on your shoes,' was Clara's sensible suggestion.

The next day the twenty-seven-year-old André Goldschmidt met the nineteen-year-old André Malraux at Fouquet's, the fashionable restaurant on the Champs-Elysées. To Clara's relief, neither challenged the other to a duel, and by the end of the meal they were on the best of terms. Outwardly, at any rate. 'It's true she's quite intelligent,' Goldschmidt conceded about his sister during the discussion. 'The trouble is she's completely crazy.'

Probably nothing could have sounded more enticing to the intense young suitor. When he went to see his father, André was more determined than ever to get married. His father, realizing that he had been outwitted by his eldest son – for by this time he was the father of two others, brought into the world by Marie-Louise Godard – graciously yielded to the inevitable.

A day or two later he paid a ceremonial call on Mme Goldschmidt. 'I didn't want my son to get married so young but since our children have placed before us a *fait accompli*, we have no choice.'

'He could have spared himself this sentence,' was Mme Goldschmidt's aggrieved comment after he had left.

Fernand Malraux's opinion of Clara was less reproachful. 'She is charming,' he told his son André, 'and for a Jewess very simply dressed.'

Clara had already suggested that she and André be allowed to occupy the third floor of the Goldschmidt villa, which could be made into a separate apartment. The suggestion was welcomed by her mother and her brother, since this would enable them to keep an eye on this 'crazy couple'. Clara, however, was not satisfied. Obtaining a rent-free place to live was not enough; she wanted the financial means to sustain a truly independent and exciting life. But she encountered resistance when she went to see the uncle who was now handling the family's financial affairs.

'Your uncle is a beggar and you are just a poor girl,' the canny businessman protested. When he saw that she meant business, he proposed giving her an annual allowance – another way of keeping her on a tight rein. But she was having none of it. She wanted her share of her father's fortune, and she wanted it now.

A week before the wedding date Clara went to the town hall of the 16th *arrondissement* and handed the administrative secretary 300 francs, saying that she wanted no mention of their respective dates of birth during the ceremony.

'I see,' nodded the official. 'The future wife is a bit old.'

'It's me,' answered Clara.

'Oh,' said the official sadly, 'so the husband is too old?'

'No,' she replied, 'he's too young.'

The forthcoming marriage, as she knew better than anyone, was merely a formality. Ever since their return from Italy, she had been crossing the Seine every day to join André at his Left Bank hotel, and they had been spending their evenings together. Persistent lack of sleep had begun to crease her face and caused her to lose weight.

There was no let-up in the breathless tension, right up until the last moment. On the morning scheduled for the ceremony (October 21st) she was trying on her wedding hat (specially made for her by her older brother's latest mistress) when André turned up at the villa, looking utterly distraught. 'I can't cram all my things into my bags,' he explained.

'I'm coming with you,' said Clara. 'I'll take an empty suitcase and we'll stuff all the left-overs into it.'

Her mother shook her head in disbelief. 'You'll be late,' she predicted. The ceremony was due to begin in three-quarters of an hour.

Reaching the hotel, André asked Clara to take care of the bill, while he dashed upstairs and finished packing.

'Madame,' said Clara to the cashier, 'please hurry, I'm due to be married in twenty minutes.'

'Ah,' said the woman, finally raising her eyes as André appeared, weighed down by his luggage. 'Aren't you the little one that's been going every morning to see this boy? Regularizing the situation, eh?'

At the town hall Clara's black velvet two-piece with grey trim, designed and tailored for her by the famous *couturier* Paul Poiret, looked suitably smart, next to the slender youth she was about to marry. Even more striking was Fernand Malraux, looking more debonair than ever with his dashing cavalryman's moustache and well-cut clothes.

'You will be happy, you are young,' the urbane mayor assured the bridal pair.

However, not everyone present was fully satisfied.

'Odd,' remarked one of Clara's aunts, after the ceremony was over. 'They didn't read out the birth dates.'

Even more critical was the censorious Aunt Jeanne. 'You should have chosen the father,' she whispered to Clara when they were alone for a moment. 'He's much better looking than the son.'

5

New Horizons

André's and Clara's second honeymoon lacked the illicit piquancy of the first. Their destination, this time, was central Europe. From Strasbourg, where they stopped to admire the gabled façades of the houses and the Gothic statuary on the cathedral, they moved on to their next destination, Prague.

With its hill-crowning Hradčany castle and its towered bridge lined with baroque statues of gesticulating saints, Prague is one of the most beautiful of European cities. But it is by no means the most lively. So, after several days André and Clara decided to move on to Vienna. The moment was ill-chosen, for Vienna was no longer the carefree city of Strauss waltzes. Long queues of impoverished citizens, including officers of the former Imperial and Royal Army, were lined up outside soup kitchens. Particularly shocking was the contrast between such pathetic scenes of misery and the life of luxury enjoyed by foreigners and profiteers, out to make the most of the collapse of the Austrian schilling. But when Clara suggested that this and other European countries needed a cleansing revolution – like the one that Rosa Luxemburg and Karl Liebknecht had tried but failed to impose in Germany – André accused her of being 'one of those who want to kill everybody for the benefit of a few'.

André Malraux, at the age of twenty, knew no more about sociology and economics than did his wife, Clara. There was, however, one field in which he fancied himself to be something of an expert, thanks to 'inside' information and advice obtained from his father: that of speculative finance. Already in 1920 he had begun buying and selling shares on the Paris Bourse. The risks involved were sufficient justification, adding zest to a life which otherwise might have been too static and conventional for a young man who was determined to live dangerously. These are the kind of sentiments that naturally appeal to novices when luck is with them, and in the late autumn of 1921 André Malraux was more than ever persuaded that 'fortune smiles on the brave'. Clara too was quite ready to believe it, and after their return to Paris she willingly accepted André's proposal that he act as her 'investment banker'.

In December they made a second trip abroad – this time to visit Clara's maternal grandfather and her uncles in Magdeburg. From Magdeburg they moved on to Berlin, now flooded with White Russian refugees, whose tumultuous ways added to the turbulence caused by inflation and the almost daily decline in the value of the mark. The uncertainties of the future had encouraged a most un-Prussian spirit of moral laxity and 'let's live for the moment!' fever – blatantly evident in the night-clubs and cabarets they visited, frequented (in Clara's words) by 'touching Gretchens and young blond pederasts'. The same irreverent mood was manifest in the field of contemporary art, notably in the starkly realistic canvases of the violently anti-militaristic Expressionist painter, Otto Dix. In the bookstores Clara snapped up a number of Expressionist works by the playwright Georg Kaiser and the poet Franz Werfel as well as several books by Sigmund Freud. But the most exciting discovery during this trip was Robert Wiene's *The Cabinet of Dr Caligari*, which she and André saw in a Berlin cinema. So impressed were they by this masterpiece of silent cinematography that they decided after their return to Paris to go into the business of importing German Expressionist films for French audiences.

Other trips abroad soon followed. They also made a second trip to Berlin. It was probably on this occasion that Clara picked up the second volume of Oswald Spengler's *Untergang des Abendlandes* ('Decline of the West') – an epoch-making work which was now enjoying an enormous vogue as a historico-philosophical manifestation of the melancholy *Zeitgeist* of post-war Germany. Thanks to Clara – for it was years before it was translated into French – Spengler's dogmatic opus was destined, some time later, to cast its crepuscular shadow over André Malraux's first serious book, *La Tentation de l'Occident*.

In Paris the newlyweds installed themselves on the upper floor of the Goldschmidt villa, where the living room walls were covered by woodcuts by Derain, a portrait by Galanis, a Picasso collage, and a painting of a bare-breasted woman by Kisling. Often they joined the family in the downstairs dining room. Thanks to his gift of the gab, André was able to disguise the fact that his position in the world of letters was anything but solid. He was no longer the literary and artistic director of Simon Kra's Editions du Sagittaire, and though he was exploring the possibilities of bringing out other illustrated works of rare erotica with the connivance of Pascal Pia, this was not an activity he could air over the lunch or dinner table.

Meanwhile *Action* was in serious trouble. Its founder, Florent Fels, had lost his job with the financial sheet that had been employing him, and to keep body and soul together he had teamed up with several enterprising journalists to launch a new weekly, *Les Nouvelles Littéraires*, designed to appeal to a far wider public. *Action*'s mainstays had more or less retired from the field. The task of editing *Action* was largely entrusted to the obscure poet, Georges Gabory, 'aided' by his equally unprestigious and often absent friend, André Malraux. Indeed, it was something of a miracle that Fels and Gabory were able to bring out three successive issues of *Action* in October, November, and December 1921. But this super-human effort was followed by two months of silence, and finally in March 1922, slightly more than two years after the appearance of the first number, Florent Fels' literary-artistic review quietly gave up the ghost.

This twelfth and final issue of *Action* also included André Malraux's sixth and most significant contribution. Entitled 'Aspects d'André Gide', this relatively short but pithy article was the young critic's first serious attempt to deal with a major writer in more than a couple of glib paragraphs.

The previous autumn Gide had brought out a 500-page anthology containing what he felt to be most quintessential in his published works. This had moved Henri Massis, a fervent follower of the anti-republican firebrand, Charles Maurras, to write a scathing article in the fortnightly *Revue Universelle* (an arch-conservative, ultra-Catholic publication), in which Gide (a notorious pederast) was accused of being 'demonic' and a devious corrupter of French youth. To this Malraux replied that the suffering sinners in Gide's books were in their own way seekers of the divine, hungering after God. Though clearly no saint, Gide was in essence preaching a form of love, and though no philosopher, he had become a 'director of conscience' for many young persons 'who like to be directed'.

This little essay was exceedingly deft. Malraux praised Gide for the 'subtlety which makes him the most heeded critic of our time' and described him as 'the greatest living French writer' – two lavish compliments which could not but find favour in the eyes of a consummate narcissist like Gide.

Malraux was too acutely aware of the fragility of his present situation not to realize how vitally important it was for him to find new outlets for his literary talents now that *Action* was about to collapse. Gide was one of those who, in 1909, had helped the author-banker, Jean Schlumberger (a Protestant like himself), and the actor, Jacques Copeau, to found the *Nouvelle Revue Française*, which, after a period of wartime interruption, had regained its position as France's most prestigious literary monthly. To be published in the *NRF*, as it was universally referred to, was considered a consecration for any budding author.

One day a grateful André said to his wife Clara: 'But for you I would have remained a library rat.' That there was a lot of truth in this admission is incontestable. Without her money, never could he have made so many culturally enriching trips to foreign countries, archaeological sites, churches, chapels, and museums. But there is no reason to believe that he would not have succeeded in the end, thanks to his formidable erudition, impressive volubility, and the solid friendships he was beginning to make in the world of arts and letters.

Far and away the most important of these friends was Marcel Arland, who was two years older than André. Born and brought up near Langres –

Diderot's birthplace – in a south-eastern region of France bordering on Champagne, Burgundy and Lorraine, Arland, who was of partly peasant, partly rural-bourgeois stock, had come to Paris shortly after the Armistice of 1918 to complete his studies. At this time young university students eligible for the draft were permitted to serve half-time – their mornings being reserved for parade-ground drill and other military chores, while the rest of the day was devoted to academic studies. The twenty-year-old *élève-aspirant* soon discovered that he was as indifferent to the pontifications of Sorbonne professors as to the discipline of military life. He ceased to attend lectures and even disappeared from his barracks for weeks at a time. Instead, he devoted most of his hours to browsing through bookshops and helping to edit an officially sanctioned undergraduate review. The extra-curricular experience he thus acquired proved invaluable, enabling him to approach well-known authors, such as Marcel Proust, Paul Claudel, François Mauriac, Jean Giraudoux and Paul Morand.

It was probably in the spring of 1921, during a visit made to Demetrios Galanis' apartment-studio on the Rue Cortot, that André Malraux first met Marcel Arland. No one at first sight could have seemed less inspiring than this serious young man with his shock of brown hair, his robust chin, and eyes somewhat distorted behind thick lenses – the kind of nondescript face befitting a bank clerk, accountant, or notary. But it did not take Malraux long to realize that the appearance was deceptive and this nonconforming part-time officer-cadet shared his own enthusiasm for Dostoevsky, Nietzsche, Maurice Barrès and André Gide. Soon they were as inseparable as André had once been with Georges Gabory, arranging to meet every day at the Forum bar behind the Madeleine, where their conversations often began with the ritual formula: 'Well, what have you been reading?'

Clara, for her part, was struck by the contrast between Arland's round-faced, almost babyish features and the earnestness of a 'man of the East' – an earnestness which, in literary matters, attained the 'fervour of a militant monk'. At times, in his denunciations of established values and conventions, Marcel Arland seemed more of a rebel than André, even harbouring a sympathy for the iconoclastic pronunciamentos of the Dadaists.

Arland was soon a frequent visitor to the Malrauxs' apartment in the Goldschmidt villa, the decoration of which struck him as curiously 'bold and funereal' – probably due to the odd conjunction of avant-garde pictures and old-fashioned dark wood furniture. Here their discussions were as long as they were intense and heated. How was one to steer one's life in an increasingly confused, absurd and godless world? Where is one to draw the line between corrosive negation and slavish adherence to established values? Is sheer novelty enough to justify artistic experimentation? To what extent is man the victim of historical fatality, to what extent can he be the master of his destiny? And so on.

Clara usually kept out of these debates. Flattering though it was to be regarded by André as the most intelligent woman he had ever met, she was by now familiar enough with his secret as well as overt ways of thought to realize that his attitude to intellectual women was distinctly condescending. In moments of intense debate with Marcel Arland, an excessive intrusion on her part was bound to break the spell. For if Pascal Pia, with his gift for poetic plagiarism, appealed to the lighter, playful side of Malraux's personality, Marcel Arland appealed to a deeper strain of intelligence, where the issues involved were no laughing matter.

It would probably be difficult to find a better description of the intellectual climate of this post-war period, dominated as it was by the sudden opening of vast new horizons in the realms of science, history, and religion, than the one Clara herself provided decades later, in the second volume of her memoirs:

> Accordingly, since the world was emerging without justification from an imbecilic war, we wanted discovery to replace faith – knowing full well that every discovery could be only incomplete . . . Shaken to the core by the collapse of the Catholic universe, we no longer aspired to a single totality . . .
>
> Yes, our generation wanted to know everything, and it was given the means to know a great deal . . . We were acquiring new senses, on canvases we were painting what human eyes had never seen before, we were subjecting our verses to syntaxes intimately linked to our beings. And since we were taking our first steps in the world, like children, we were given toys – the automobile, the aeroplane, the cinema.
>
> Nevertheless, though dazzled by novelty, we were desperate. Never had we more needed God than after this war in which no Walhalla was there to welcome the heroes. The world order of our parents had led to the worst massacres mankind had ever known. We wanted to have nothing to do with them – they who did not know how to appreciate a book, nor a film, nor a new painting, nor a new poem. *Ex officio*, they were guilty on all counts . . . If I continued to love my mother, it was because she had become my daughter.
>
> In this general wasteland of values, each of us acquired a new importance. Fulfilling ourselves according to our own devices became the only mission we were willing to assume . . . For us the only ones who mattered were heroes, artists, saints.

It was in a similar state of mind, at once anxious, hopeful, and defiant, that André Malraux, armed with the recommendation of his friend, Marcel Arland, went to call on the Catholic novelist, François Mauriac. Mauriac was sufficiently impressed by the visitor – 'that bristling little bird of prey, with the magnificent eye' – to be able, fifteen years later, to recall their meeting and the fundamental problems they discussed. Though not a 'believer', Malraux was careful to treat religion with respect. 'Already at the age of eighteen, when he spoke of Christ, this refractory individual knew whom he was talking about,' Mauriac later wrote. 'Nothing in him recalls that ghastly species of old Masonic radicals who drool over the fate of the sweet vagabond of Judea; Malraux is acquainted with Christ: this sweet vagabond is his tough adversary.'

Less receptive, at any rate initially, was another luminary in the world of letters: Jacques Rivière, the serious-minded editor of the *NRF*. We have Clara's word for it that Rivière failed to appreciate Malraux's 'somewhat aggressive brilliance', refusing several of his literary offspring on the grounds that when he had 'several weighty works' to boast of, he would 'regret having given the public what was no more than inconsequential fantasy'.

However, now that he had gained admission to the *NRF*'s small manuscript-crammed offices at 3, Rue de Grenelle, André, encouraged by his friend Marcel, was in no mood to give up. Since Rivière was not interested in fantastic fiction, he suggested that he let him try his hand at book reviews – a genre in which he had by now acquired a certain experience. This time Jacques Rivière was genuinely impressed. The July 1922 issue of the *NRF* included a review of Arthur Gobineau's masterly novella, *L'Abbaye de Typhaine*, and the following (August) issue a favourable review of a booklet of aphorisms which André's one-time idol, Max Jacob, had brought out under the title, *Art poétique*. They were the first two of some sixty articles of literary criticism which Malraux was to write for the *NRF* over the next four decades.

6

A Shot in the Dark

And thus the weeks went by, in carefree rounds of self-education, intermittent work (for André) and nocturnal outings. In the mornings André would disappear on some mysterious mission, to conspire with Pascal Pia, consult with Georges Gabory, or argue with Jacques Rivière. Almost every afternoon he would arrange to meet Marcel Arland at the Forum bar, where he would snap up the evening paper and scrutinize the latest stock-market quotations.

Before André and Clara realized it, eight months had passed since the first honeymoon trip to Italy. Clara reminded André of their premarital pact: after six months of marriage, they would agree to divorce. André, however, was in no hurry to be separated from this exceptionally intelligent, affluent, and co-operative wife: 'Couldn't we put the money a divorce is bound to cost us to better use – for example, by going to Tunisia?'

So off they went to Tunisia, where they viewed the sad vestiges of ancient Carthage, sipped Turkish coffee in the raucous souks, and travelled in a dirty railway carriage to the old walled city of Kairouan.

Another such trip took them to Cologne. They may have met the museum's archaeological director, Alfred Salmony, through Ivan and Claire Goll, since, like the Golls, he was a fervent Expressionist. In Paris, in any case, Salmony visited Clara and André in their upstairs apartment in the Goldschmidt villa, bringing with him a briefcase full of photographs of art works. These he spread out over the large black-lacquered tray, mounted on a wooden base, on which André used to prepare the illustrated 'dummies' for books he wanted to have published. The art of photography was still young, hence the intense surprise experienced by both André and Clara; for what was novel here was the range of photographs displayed, far exceeding the limits of the Mediterranean world and including art works from India and China. As Clara later recalled this moment of breath-taking revelation: 'It was the first time I had found myself in the presence of a Thai sculpture. Then came the combination of a Han head and a Romanesque head.'

It would be simplistic to claim that it was at this precise moment that the idea of an 'imaginary museum' or of a 'museum without walls' – which he did so much to popularize later – first dawned on Malraux. The 'graphic revolution' brought about by the development of photographic reproduction was bound sooner or later to extend the average citizen's awareness of other worlds and cultures. But what kind of 'higher' appreciation is acquired thanks to the deliberate juxtaposition of a Chinese Han-dynasty head and a Romanesque head? André Malraux thought he had found the answer to this question by declaring, in the introductory preface he had written for the catalogue of an exhibition of Demetrios Galanis' works (in the spring of 1922):

> We can only feel through comparison. Whoever is familiar with *Andromaque* or *Phèdre* will have a clearer feel of what French genius is by reading *A Midsummer Night's Dream* than by reading all the other tragedies of Racine. The genius of the Greeks will be better understood by pitting a Greek statue against an Egyptian statue than through a familiarity with one hundred Greek statues.

In the late spring of 1923 the part-time critic and globe-trotting connoisseur of ancient and modern art was suddenly confronted with a most disagreeable prospect: that of having to complete a two-year period of compulsory military duty.

During the recent war he had shared the patriotic fervour of his schoolmates. He had even felt a filial pride because his father had served in the tank corps. But this admiration was focused on individual courage under fire and did not in any way embrace the *métier* of arms as such.

Malraux's feelings on the subject were essentially of an aesthetic order. During the previous summer he and Clara had been invited to spend several days in the country house, charmingly named Bois-Dormant (Sleeping Wood), near Orléans, to which Fernand Malraux had retired after marrying Marie-Louise Godard (now the mother of two handsome sons: Roland, now ten years old, and Claude, who was now almost two-and-a-half). One evening, after they had gone up to their bedroom, André shocked Clara by expressing admiration for the way in which young French officers, just graduated from the military academy of Saint-Cyr, had, in August 1914, charged into battle in scarlet trousers, blue cloaks, and cadet shakos topped with a panache of white feathers – a full dress-uniform which had made them ideal targets for German machine-gunners. What an admirable, what a magnificent *beau geste*! Clara, who had known at least one Saint-Cyrien who had lost his life in such a crazy charge, could find nothing admirable in this kind of reckless behaviour.

André kept insisting that, yes, 'the gesture was beautiful, that's enough in itself!'

Clara lost her temper: 'When you defend this kind of gesture, you yourself are as stupid as a Saint-Cyrien!'

'And you, when you say such things, are as cowardly as a Jewess!'

Stung to the quick, she had got up, dressed, and left the house. A breathless André soon caught up with her, and they finally made their peace – for, if there was one accusation that could not be levelled at her husband, it was that of being anti-semitic.

However, wartime panache was one thing; quite another was the mind-numbing drudgery of military drill and barrack chores, dished out and directed by humourless parade ground sergeants and choleric officers. As Clara later noted, 'Going to the theatre was not one of our strong points, and the only plays we took in with relish were, in their caricatural way, frankly anti-militaristic: *Le Train de 8h.47*, or *Les Gaîtés de l'Escadron*'.

Several years before, André had been exonerated from military service after a summary medical examination had revealed that in his youth he had been subject to bouts of rheumatic fever. But since then the confident euphoria of the immediate post-war period had evaporated, and confronted with a drastically reduced birth rate and the need to maintain the 'finest army in the world', the government in Paris had decided to crack down on the *réformés* (the 'exemptees') and to induct all those who (in Clara's words) were not 'hunch-backed, club-footed, or peg-legged'.

Come what might, André and Clara were determined not to allow such a 'calamity' to interrupt their married life. When at last the dreaded summons arrived indicating that he would have to proceed to Strasbourg, Clara consulted her younger brother Georges, who had completed his compulsory military service in Alsace. Georges agreed to help them, saying that in Strasbourg he had befriended a doctor who could probably find ways of having André declared unfit for military duty.

Without saying a word to Mama Goldschmidt, the three anti-military conspirators boarded the train and headed east. In Strasbourg, where they found lodgings in a cheap *pension*, Georges went to see his doctor friend, while André, looking like a tough young hoodlum with a bristling crew cut, slunk off in the direction of the induction centre. Here, through a typical mix-up in military administration, the 6-foot-tall recruit was formally enrolled in the hussars, where the maximum prescribed height had long been fixed at 5 feet 5 inches. The farcically uniformed hussar deliberately compounded the misassignment by absorbing massive quantities of caffeine tablets, which aggravated his facial twitches and lent a frightening plausibility to his claim to be a victim of heart palpitations and other cardiac anomalies. At night, without bothering to open his bed, he would sneak out of the barracks and return to the *pension*, where a worried Clara piled blankets over his shivering and sweating form.

This semi-comic ordeal was maintained through three tense weeks, before being terminated by an enlightened member of the medical corps, who had been 'briefed' by Georges Goldschmidt's doctor friend. 'Yes,' agreed the military physician after subjecting the bizarrely-dressed hussar to a perfunctory examination, 'a fellow like you can be better employed than in messing around here.' And without further ado, he signed the precious papers exonerating the tensely twitching *littérateur* from further military service.

Elated by this triumphant dénouement, André threw caution to the winds. They must immediately celebrate this hard-won victory over the forces of military obtuseness. 'After all we've been through, we need a change of air and scenery,' André insisted, refusing to be upset by the news from Paris, where the latest stock-market quotations had stopped rising. This was just one of those periodic troughs or 'valleys' through which share prices occasionally slump before resuming their normal ascent. Clara could relax, there was nothing to worry about. Now that they had reached the Rhine, why ruin the chance of seeing more of this fabled river that had given rise to so many myths and legends? Yes, why not? Accordingly, they boarded a river-steamer, making their way downstream as far as Koblenz and beyond, in a leisurely Siegfriedian journey. Not once during this idyllic voyage did either of them open a newspaper.

A rude shock awaited them when they finally returned to Paris. The recent 'sag' in the Paris Bourse had turned into a slump, and for certain shares, into a crash. This was the case with a large number of 'fabulous' shares in a Mexican silver-mining concern which André had decided to buy after attending several board meetings with the leading stockholders, all members of the same 'sympathetic' family. Overnight these shares had lost nine-tenths of their value and had been reduced almost to worthless paper.

It was several weeks before André realized the full extent of the catastrophe. Quite simply, they were ruined. For two years he and Clara had floated on a cloud, in the serene conviction that the bonanza could last forever. The return to earth was a jolting experience.

André, however, was not one to spend his time wringing his hands in despair, and, happily for him, Clara was not the kind of wife who indulged in bitter recriminations. They were companions in the sombre hour of disaster as they had been companions in the radiant days of good fortune. Once again it was her duty to help her husband – which she did by persuading her mother to let them recover some shares in a Mulhouse bank.

This additional windfall, added to their privileged situation as members of the Goldschmidt household, kept them going for several months. But the question inevitably arose: what was André going to do next? He could not hope to live on the meagre income derived from the sale of two or three articles per annum to the *NRF*. André was no longer associated in any way with Simon Kra's company, while Pascal Pia, called up for military service, had been forced to suspend his activities in pornographic publishing. In a similar plight Guillaume Apollinaire had not hesitated to take a humble clerk's job in a bank on the Rue Laffitte – a 'solution' which in the early years of the century had enabled him to offer 'princely' meals to his half-starved friends Picasso, Max Jacob, and André Salmon at Vincent's Italian restaurant, or Frédé's Lapin Agile, which they gratefully accepted while secretly deploring this un-bohemian compromise with reality. André Malraux felt much the same way. For when Clara questioned him as to his future intentions, he calmly replied: 'You really don't think I am going to work?' The idea was promptly discarded as deplorably bourgeois.

Meanwhile, André was turning over new projects in his restless brain. He had long been fascinated by ancient civilizations. Pascal Pia, who had spent many hours with him at the Bibliothèque Nationale, had been much struck by his young friend's passionate interest in the accounts of journeys made to distant Mongolia and Cathay by medieval travellers such as Marco Polo, Plano Carpini and his fellow Franciscan, Guillaume Rubruquis. Equally remarkable, for a once rebellious schoolboy, was Malraux's familiarity with Hindu mythology, and in particular with the *Ramayana* and the *Mahabharata* epics, roughly speaking the *Iliad* and the *Odyssey* of Indian folklore.

By the early 1920s once-legendary places such as Isphahan, Herat, Samarkand, Kashgar, Shangtu, and Lhasa were no longer as remote and inaccessible as they had once been. The penetration of the darkest jungles of Africa, the cutting of the Suez Canal, the steady development of safer steamships had given rise to an enthralling new kind of descriptive-novelistic literature, the pioneers of which were Joseph Conrad, Pierre Loti and Henry Rider Haggard. In 1896 a French adaptation of Allan Quatermain's adventurous search for King Solomon's legendary mines had proved such a success that the publisher, Hetzel, had brought out two further versions of this Rider Haggard novel in 1898 and 1900. Twelve years later, Pierre Loti's *Le Pèlerin d'Angkor* went through forty-two editions in one year. André Malraux could easily fancy himself treading in these authors' enterprising footsteps. The only trouble was that he lacked the professional qualifications which had made possible their exciting excursions into distant hinterlands. Conrad had been a seafaring mariner and river-boat captain; Loti had been an officer in the French Navy; Rider Haggard had served as a jurist and lawcourt judge with the British authorities in southern Africa.

One day André startled Clara by asking her if she was familiar with the itinerary followed by medieval pilgrims travelling from Flanders to Santiago de Compostela, in Spanish Galicia. She was frankly puzzled by the question.

'Never mind,' he said. 'That Pilgrims' Way was dotted with cathedrals, most of which have come down to us relatively intact. But in addition to these mighty sanctuaries there must have existed small chapels, many of which have disappeared.'

'Ah,' Clara admitted. 'I have never given much thought to the matter.'

'Well,' André went on, 'from Siam to Cambodia, all along the "Royal Way" leading from the Dangrek mountains to Angkor, there were great temples which have been located and written up in the Inventory, but there must surely have been others, small ones that are still unknown today.'

'Yes,' agreed Clara, wondering what on earth he was driving at.

'Well,' said André, as though it was the most natural thing in the world to propose, 'we go to some little temple in Cambodia, we remove several statues, and we sell them in the United States – which will enable us to live comfortably for two or three years.'

Surprised though she was, Clara would have been even more startled if her unconventional husband had suddenly informed her that he was going into the import-export business.

The mere fact that he could allude so casually to the official Inventory that the French had made of Khmer temples in Cambodia makes it clear that Malraux had already done quite a bit of preparatory work on the subject. In 1898 the Governor-General of Indochina, Paul Doumer, had decided to follow the example set by the British in India and Burma by establishing a local school for the systematic study of Far Eastern cultures. In reality this Ecole Française d'Extrême-Orient was less a 'school' than a tiny staff of philological specialists, headed by a Sanskrit scholar named Louis Finot, who among other things were entrusted with the task of inventorying, protecting, and deciphering the archaeological treasures of Indochina. The most remarkable of these treasures – in quantity, physical size, and wealth of decoration – were located in Cambodia, where scores of stone temples, markedly different from the wooden pagodas of Siam and China, had been discovered by French naval officers from the early 1860s on. Built of reddish sandstone and dark maroon laterite, they bore proud witness to the existence of a once-mighty kingdom which had flourished for some 600 years – from the early ninth to the early fifteenth century and which at its apogee had extended into Cochin China to the east, and to the north and north-west, far into neighbouring Siam.

The task of inventorying these many sanctuaries and temples was entrusted to an experienced topographer, Captain Edmond Lunet de Lajonquière. In 1901 he had spent six months on horseback exploring the tropical vegetation and water-logged periphery of Cambodia's 'Great Lake' (the Tonlé Sap), and in particular its north-western rim, where the now jungle-engulfed Khmer sanctuaries and temples were in places so densely concentrated that it was almost impossible to pin-point them all on a medium-size archaeological map without having the names merge into an illegible red-ink cluster. In 1902, when he completed the first volume of his Inventory, the number of visited sanctuaries and temples already reached 290, but two to three times as many temples still remained to be charted, photographed, and described. Indeed, it was not until 1911 that the enterprising cavalryman, now promoted to the rank of major, could complete his work of jungle reconnaissance, with a more definitive archaeological map and a third volume of his *Inventaire descriptif des monuments du Cambodge*, in which 910 Khmer temples, sanctuaries, bridges, sacred water-basins and reservoirs were described, in some cases with carefully drawn ground plans.

As a trained topographer, Lunet was careful to point out that most of these sanctuaries were built along five great axes radiating out from the capital city of Angkor Thom. And of these main axes, extending like the military highroads of ancient Rome in almost straight lines across the periodically flooded central plain of Cambodia, the most important, to judge by the number of extant temples and ruined bridges, was the one running in a roughly north-by-north-west direction from Angkor Thom all the way to the sandstone cliffs of the Dangrek mountains, marking the border between Cambodia and Siam, and on to the major Khmer temple at Phimai, in southern Thailand. To Lunet's tidy military mind, this north-west axis clearly reflected the Khmer kings' determination to extend the frontiers of their 'empire' well into the territory of their long-standing foes, the Thais. But what it suggested to the more romantically inclined André Malraux was something rather different: a 'pilgrims' way', or even a 'Royal Way', trodden by adoring subjects anxious to behold their god-king sovereign in his imposing capital of Angkor Thom.

While the prospect of discovering a new temple hidden in the jungle naturally appealed to Malraux's sense of adventure, it was but one aspect of a complex scheme which was anything but altruistically inspired. It was common knowledge that 'adventurers' of one kind or another had been going into the Cambodian hinterland, and that the Khmer sculptures they had managed to tear from the jungle's insidious grip were now highly prized by American museums. Since the colonial bureaucrats on the spot seemed to be making so little personal effort to locate and preserve old Khmer temples, which the dense vegetation was slowly devouring, he saw no reason why a 'treasure-saving' expedition, mounted and financed by himself, could be regarded as a form of 'piracy'. Once a Khmer temple had been thoroughly reconnoitred and inventoried, it naturally became untouchable; but he was persuaded that there were others that had so far been overlooked and abandoned to their fate.

This hunch was reinforced by a long ninety-page article which he came upon in the 1919 annual *Bulletin* published by the Ecole Française d'Extrème-Orient. Its author, Henri Parmentier, argued that during the reign of King Indravarman I (AD 877–889) a transitional form of Khmer art had developed, between the earliest unadorned brick temples of the seventh and eighth centuries and the monumental stone temples of Angkor dating from the thirteenth century. A particularly striking sandstone specimen of this intermediate phase – the temple of Içvarapura – had been accidentally discovered in 1914 by a French lieutenant named Marec – employed by the Colonial Geological Service – a dozen miles north-east of Angkor at a place known to the local inhabitants as Banteay Srei ('Citadel of Women'). An architect had been assigned the task of prospecting the ruins, but, like Marec, had been recalled to France after the outbreak of the 1914 war, and it was not until 1916 that Parmentier himself had been able to complete an initial survey. The photographs illustrating the article showed that several towers of the small Banteay Srei temple were still standing, despite the subterranean thrust of tree roots, which had toppled part of the structure. The curved lintels, like the cornices and niched pilasters of the surviving doorways, were adorned with exquisite carvings. A fine fragment, in which the Hindu god Shiva was shown seated cross-legged with his goddess-wife Uma reposing on one thigh, had been removed to the Museum of Phnom

Penh, but nowhere could Malraux find an indication that this recently discovered ruin had been added to Lunet de Lajonquière's official Inventory.

That such a 'jewel' of early Khmer architecture should have remained undiscovered for so long was enough to galvanize Malraux's explorational energies. A few weeks of voracious reading had made him an expert on Khmer art, and for the rest he could rely on an exceptionally nimble brain and a glib tongue. No one could accuse him of not having done his homework. Joseph Hackin, the Luxembourg-born director of the Guimet Museum, which housed (and still houses) a permanent exhibition of Far Eastern art objects, was sufficiently impressed by the young enthusiast's broad range of artistic knowledge not to challenge Malraux's bogus credentials as a former student of the Ecole des Langues Orientales. He was even more impressed by his neatly dressed visitor's readiness to organize and finance an 'archaeological' expedition aimed at uncovering new Khmer temples. The canny Luxembourger saw no reason to discourage such self-sacrificing philanthropy and agreed to give Malraux several letters of recommendation, which the self-taught archaeologist was instructed to present to Louis Finot, director of the Ecole Française d'Extrême-Orient in Hanoi.

Armed with these precious credentials, Malraux had little trouble obtaining an *ordre de mission* from officials at the Ministry of Colonies, only too happy to encourage enterprising archaeologists provided it did not cost the French state a centime of expense. Two troublesome strings, however, were attached to this official authorization granting Malraux the right to employ requisitioned bullocks for his jungle explorations. First, the young explorer could not lay personal claim to any objects he might uncover during his search. Second, he had to compile a complete report on his findings and make a personal donation of from 100,000 to 200,000 francs to the all-too-impecunious Ecole Française d'Extrême-Orient. Malraux had to accept both of these irksome conditions, though he had no intention of abiding by either.

To set out on such an expedition just with Clara would have been an act of madness. André also needed a male companion. The ideal candidate was the ingenious Pascal Pia, but he was away in Algeria completing his term of compulsory military service. For lack of anyone better André decided to enlist the services of his old Bondy schoolmate, Louis Chevasson – to the dismay of Clara, who had always considered him an uninspiring nonentity.

Clara had several seamstresses prepare a suitable explorer's uniform, consisting of a lightweight hunter's jacket with a buckled belt and large pockets, a pair of jodhpurs, covered below the knees by leggings, and an Australian bushman's hat pierced with holes for ventilation. André acquired his own tropical gear. They also bought quinine pills, hypodermic needles, various anti-snake vaccines, a battery-operated flash-bulb camera, and half a dozen hacksaws needed for dislodging the stones they intended to 'save' from the voracious Cambodian jungle.

There remained one other problem: what to do with those valuable pieces of Khmer sculpture once they had prised them free and had smuggled them out of Indochina. For a solution to this problem André and Clara appealed to Daniel-Henry Kahnweiler. Ancient Hindu or Buddhist sculpture was not Kahnweiler's speciality, and he may well have raised a critical eyebrow while listening to Malraux's audacious project. But he agreed to consult friends in Berlin, to get a rough estimate of what a bas-relief sculpture could fetch if sold to a museum or at a public auction. The answer, to judge by a semi-autobiographical passage in Malraux's later novel, *La Voie royale*, was a minimum of 30,000 francs for a small figure, and as much as 200,000 francs (or about $13,000) for a handsome sculpture of an *Apsara* (dancing goddess).

Kahnweiler must have made some passing mention to his friend Max Jacob of this extraordinary venture; for in a letter sent on October 12, 1923 from his Benedictine monastery, the self-exiled bohemian author, who prided himself on his powers of clairvoyance, predicted that the young Malraux would 'find his chosen path in the Orient. He will become an Orientalist and will end up at the Collège de France, like Claudel. He is made for professorial chairs.'

Far more sceptical about the outcome of this 'archaeological' expedition were the members of Clara's family. Particularly pathetic was her mother, who had lost her adored husband and who feared she was now about to lose her only daughter. Clara too was stricken by a sense of foreboding.

The evening of their departure, in the taxi that was taking them to the station, she broke down and cried, much to André's surprise. As she later described this painful moment,

He kept speaking to me of a future that would be finer than the past, and which nonetheless would suit him. He felt neither the risk, nor the suffering, nor above all the death of myself, which was threatened by the morrow. I was crying because I knew that on our return I would no longer have a mother and I would no longer have brothers, I would no longer have a home, no longer have money.

Those lines, written forty years after the event, forcefully expressed the bitterness of lived experiences. Even in this exaggerated form, they graphically illustrate the difference in mood between André Malraux's confident faith in a shining future and his wife's private apprehensions, which she did her best to smother.

7

Fortune Favours the Bold

It was Friday, October 13th when their train pulled into the station at Marseilles. This might have seemed an evil omen, had either of them been in a mood to give up. But once on board the *Angkor* – for such was the liner's name – Clara's fears were forgotten. With casual temerity they had decided to travel first class, leaving Louis Chevasson, who was to follow in another steamship, the dubious pleasure of 'roughing it' in second class. It was almost as though they expected miraculous riches to start raining down on them once they reached their first destination: Siam. Here there were plenty of Buddhist temples as well as dealers in ancient statuary from whom it should be possible to buy fine pieces of sculpture for sale to some American museum.

In terms of human company the three-week voyage was a definite disappointment. They had nothing in common with the smug colonial officials and well-fed majors and colonels who were travelling with them in first class. But fortunately there were interesting stops along the way to distract them from the monotony of shipboard 'entertainment'. At the mountain-girt port of Djibouti they had themselves rowed to shore after sundown and spent a torrid evening in the Somali quarter watching some dark-skinned Bacchantes shed their clothes and go into frenzied oscillations – a scene of contagious sensuality which later helped inspire the curious brothel scene in the early pages of *La Voie royale*.

An accidental fire in the *Angkor*'s coal bunkers delayed their departure from Djibouti. Cloudless blue skies and brilliant sunshine continued to accompany them all the way to the Bab-el-Mandeb ('Gate of Death') straits, at the southern end of the Red Sea, and for some distance out in to the Indian Ocean. But as they approached Ceylon the sky clouded over, the sea turned from deep blue to a dirty green, and they were swallowed up in the damp mists and persistent drizzle of the monsoon. At Colombo, heedless of the rain, dark loin-clothed rickshaw drivers were waiting to pull them through the city's wet streets and they realized they had entered a different world, one marked by dripping heat and tropical vegetation.

At Singapore they disembarked, only to discover that they had just missed the steamer for Bangkok. The alternative scheme André had worked out, aimed at exploring the Siamese end of the 'Royal Way' from Angkor to Phimai, had to be abandoned. An implacable Asiatic fate seemed to be pushing them relentlessly towards the accomplishment of their predatory assault on the Cambodian jungle. They did not have enough money to wait for the next sailing for Bangkok – particularly since they had rashly chosen to put up at the Raffles Hotel, where they spent a night in a 'luxurious absence of comfort' (Clara's description) in beds veiled by mosquito nets and fanned overhead by punkahs, which were moved by strings attached to the toes of invisible Chinese 'boys'.

Their next stop was Saigon – 'a charming provincial town' it seemed to Clara, with its carefully planned parallel streets and avenues, lined with lush, green-lawned gardens filled with brilliant red and orange flamboyants. Their final destination was Hanoi, administrative capital of the five component parts of French Indochina (Tonking, Annam, Cochin China, Laos, and Cambodia) and the seat of the Ecole Française d'Extrême-Orient. Here, amid the strident clamour of street vendors, soup merchants, black-turbaned house-boys and rickshaw coolies, they had the impression of having entered China.

Heavy raindrops were still falling from enormous leaves, their pitter-patter mingling with the raucous croaks of hidden frogs, when Malraux turned up at the garden-surrounded headquarters of the Ecole Française d'Extrême-Orient. In the absence of Louis Finot, he was received by the interim director, Leonard Aurousseau, a Chinese scholar who proceeded to play a subtle cat-and-mouse game with this mysterious young interloper from Paris.

From Hanoi André Malraux returned with Clara to Saigon, where they were joined by Louis Chevasson. Here they met Henri Parmentier, the now white-bearded architect-turned-archaeologist whose description of the Banteay Srei temple had so impressed Malraux in Paris. Together they boarded the steamboat that was to take them up one of the branches of the Mekong delta to the Cambodian capital of Phnom Penh.

Parmentier was more outgoing than the wary Aurousseau, being visibly impressed by Malraux's familiarity with the different styles in the evolution of Siamese-Buddhist and Khmer art. Flattered to discover that this young amateur had read some of his contributions to the publications of the Ecole Française d'Extrême-Orient, Parmentier let an amused Clara know how much he admired the 'disinterestedness' displayed by her wealthy husband, who could have chosen to dissipate his fortune on less worthy undertakings.

As they chugged their way north past riverbanks of banana trees and mangroves, he treated his fellow passengers to a friendly lecture on the geographical idiosyncracies of Cambodia's Tonlé Sap, explaining how during the late spring and early summer the floodwaters of the Mekong caused the Great Lake's water-level to rise by several metres, inundating miles of adjacent forest, swamps and rice paddies.

In Phnom Penh André, Clara, and Louis Chevasson added a few indispensable items to their camping gear. But their most valuable acquisition turned out to be a local 'boy', who was brought to them by Parmentier's own man-servant. He was a versatile young Cambodian with the concise name of Xa, who said he knew how to cook, bake bread, sew and iron clothes. His familiarity with the local language and his countrymen's ways proved invaluable from the very start; for it was Xa who, without asking questions, led them straight to a market where they bought a number of long Chinese trunks made of redolent camphor-wood.

Twenty-two years before, when Pierre Loti had travelled over the same pewter-coloured waters of the Tonlé Sap, marvelling at the endless miles of drunken forest marking the impenetrable lakeside, his river-steamer had been met in the leafy bay of the Siemreap estuary by quaintly roofed sampans. In one of these he had been rowed for several hours through an aquatic underbrush of tree trunks, reeds, and clinging vines that teemed with lizards, grasshoppers, toads, tiny river-snakes, moths and dragon-flies by the hundreds. Two decades of progress had eliminated the sampans; instead they travelled in a modern cutter, through whose windows André, Clara, and Louis Chevasson watched the cloying vegetation brush past the panes. 'Branches caked with mud coagulated by the heat, vertical filaments of slime, rings of dried foam marked the topmost level of the flood,' as Malraux later graphically described this first exposure to the Cambodian jungle. 'In each opening, beyond the leaves, he tried to glimpse the towers of Angkor Wat above the skyline of trees bent and twisted by the lake winds; in vain, the leaves, reddened in the twilight, closed in on this paludal universe.' A universe filled with 'slimy shellfish bubbling inside their shells, filthy crickets . . . Before him rose the forest, the enemy, like a clenched fist.'

Finally the branches parted. Beyond the small wooden dockside a Ford roadster was waiting to pick them up. It had been dispatched by Henri Marchal, the *conservateur* who had been labouring for ten years to free the broad moats, the flagstoned causeways and the triumphal arches of the Angkor Thom complex (a perfect square, 3 kilometres long by 3 kilometres wide) from the encroaching vegetation. At the *conservateur*'s house they were offered an aperitif and assured by Marchal that they could obtain all the bullocks, carts, and native drivers they wished. The Cinzano, though chilled, went straight to Clara's head; when, a little later, they were driven past rice fields and clumps of forest to the monumental ruins of Angkor Wat and then to the bristling pile of the Bayon, with its fifty pineapple-shaped towers and 200 god-king faces, she saw all the cryptically smiling lips and the cobra-headed *nagas* in an unnerving double focus.

Several days were needed to assemble four carts, eight bullocks, and eight drivers needed for this jungle exploration. Malraux had ample time to get to know the local 'delegate' of the French residency in Phnom Penh, an unfriendly administrative busybody named Crémazy who did not dare to thwart a 'mission' sponsored by the Ministry of Colonies in Paris.

Malraux's original intention was to strike out in a north-western direction in the hope of unearthing an undiscovered temple along or close to the axis of the 'Royal Way' that had once linked Angkor to Phimai in Siam. But such a hit-or-miss method of exploration could well involve weeks of fruitless effort and leave them utterly penniless. The air of casual affluence André and Clara had had to assume for weeks in order to sustain the illusion that they were well-heeled 'philanthropists' had by now severely strained their financial resources. And so, at a last-minute council of war, André reluctantly proposed that the 'Royal Way' scheme be abandoned, and that instead they head north-east towards the still unclassified sanctuary of Banteay Srei. There at least they were certain to find what they were looking for.

Early the next morning André, Clara, and Louis Chevasson set out on horses so small that André's feet dragged along the soggy ground. They were preceded by a bare-shouldered guide named Svay, who had been 'lent' to them by the local French delegate, Crémazy, while the four carts, each carrying two loin-clothed drivers and pulled by a pair of grey bullocks, lumbered along behind. The rutted track took them through a monotonously flat landscape of tall trees and patchy underbrush which was crossed by shallow streams they had no trouble fording. Their first night in the jungle was spent in a native *sala*, a Cambodian guest-house built on wooden stilts and reached by ladder-like steps, where they shared the single bedroom, divided by an improvised canvas partition, with a Chinese porcelain salesman who protected himself from mosquitos by wreathing himself in opium smoke.

This tranquil night must have calmed Malraux's nervous anxieties about the trek into the jungle. But the heartening illusion was of short duration. For as they continued their slow advance into the jungle, the tree trunks seemed to close in on them, the sinuous vines became more intertwined, the roots wriggled across the pathway more treacherously, the dark green air became more stifling, the red earth more viscous. Mosquitos attacked them from the front, from the sides, and, after they had passed through each angry swarm, from the rear.

At the village of Rohal, where they stopped for the second night, André and his companions received a shock. None of the villagers had ever heard of a Khmer temple located nearby at Banteay Srei. André could almost hear the mocking laughter of the monkeys, and indeed of all the jungle's teeming, creeping, crawling, clawing, stinging wildlife, at this new victory of the alien, hostile, ferociously non-human world they were rashly undertaking to disturb. Finally, after persistent questioning, Xa found an emaciated village elder who seemed to recall having once seen a pile of stones half hidden among trees and ferns not too far away. Promised a good reward, he agreed to guide them to it.

The next morning the bullocks and carts were left behind with several drivers. The others, armed with machetes and led by the old-timer, began to hack and scythe a new pathway through the dank vegetation, scattering ants and beetles, which raced up the slimy tree trunks, destroying enormous spiders' webs and disturbing all sorts of bugs and nameless beasts whose heads peered forth from under carapaces next to surfaces of moss. The tall, whitish termite heaps, on which the termites themselves were never to be seen, raised their summits of abandoned planets in the prevailing gloom, as though they had been born in a corruption of the air, in a stench of toadstools, in the presence of tiny leeches, stuck beneath the leaves like fly-eggs . . .

The unity of the forest now imposed itself . . . [making it difficult] to separate beings from forms, moving life from oozing life; an unknown power tied the fungus-growths to the trees, generating a bubbling of all sorts of provisional things on a ground resembling marshy foam, in fuming woods dating from the very beginnings of the world. What human action still had a meaning? What act of will-power still retained its force? Everything here grew soft and spongy, trying to accommodate itself to this world, at once repellent and beckoning, like the glance of half-wits, and which attacked the nerves with the same abject power as those spiders suspended between branches, from which at first he had so much trouble turning away his eyes.

For Malraux, whose sleep was often perturbed by monstrous dreams of geometric traps being woven by gigantic spiders, this daunting incursion into the dank forest's arachnoid depths must have been a nightmarish experience, as the passage from *La Voie royale* cited above so vividly suggests. Progress was so slow that André, Clara, and Louis Chevasson soon dismounted, feeling a bit ridiculous and uneasy, as they led their small mounts forward by the reins. Though they were armed with carbines and revolvers, all three felt helpless and at the mercy of inscrutable Buddhist peasants who cared little for the Brahmanic temples that once had been the glory of their country.

Then, after several hours of hacking, the aged guide raised his machete. Up ahead, through the intervening vines and leafy underbrush, they could see a stone gateway, and beyond it a little forecourt flanked by two partly crumbled, partly moss-covered walls of a lovely rose hue. To Clara, as to André, this 'Trianon of the Forest' loomed up before them like an incarnation of 'grace and dignity, more beautiful than all the temples we had so far seen . . .'.

The little temple had once had three towers that had gradually been toppled by the imperious thrust of tree roots, leaving stumps nine to ten feet high, surrounded by mounds of fallen stones half-covered by bushes and lianas. A cursory inspection showed that parts of the remaining walls carried exquisite carvings, which had not been chipped or smashed.

Back at Rohal, André was relieved to discover that their cart-drivers, like the aged guide, were not in the least curious to know what he, Clara, and Louis Chevasson proposed to do with the ruined temple. Only two Cambodians accompanied them on the second trip to the sanctuary – the faithful Xa and the local guide, Svay, whose mission, as they later discovered, was to report on everything he saw and heard. When they reached the little temple, whose stones in the afternoon light had taken on a darker, more russet and even purple hue, André politely asked the two Cambodians to leave them alone and to come back in a couple of hours. Neither made any fuss.

The grating of the saws seemed to bring the jungle suddenly to life, setting off a flight of heavy-winged birds. Each time the sawing stopped they caught the sound of stealthy footsteps. It was unnerving to realize that they were not alone in this tensely listening forest and that their every move was being watched. But by and by, after more intervals of breathless silence, the soft footsteps gave way to the sudden rustling of leaves as the monkeys above and around them resumed their acrobatic leaps from branch to branch.

Infinitely more troublesome was the fragility of their hacksaws, the metal teeth of which kept snapping. The ancient Khmers had used no mortar in piling precisely chiselled stone on stone. Malraux and Chevasson soon realized that they were exerting themselves for nothing. What was required were crowbars to lever each stone from its seat. Fortunately the hacksaws with the broken teeth and several wedges proved strong enough to move the sculpted blocks.

Each 'rescue' operation required a great deal of sweat, giving Malraux and Chevasson an acute physical impression of what it must have cost the ancient Khmers to erect so many massive monuments of stone in this suffocating jungle heat. By the end of the third day seven corner stones, several of them representing the figures of two exquisite *devatas* (protective goddesses), had been pried loose and were ready to be eased into their camphor-wood 'coffins'. This final step required the assistance of the Cambodian ox-drivers, divesting the expedition of the last shreds of an already tattered secrecy.

The convoy's homeward march, thanks to the added weight bearing down on the four carts' creaking axles, took even longer than the outbound expedition. It was also less fraught with suspense, as they emerged from the forest's suffocating depths into woodlands of a brighter green where once again they could glimpse the sun. But the final nine-hour stretch proved too much for Clara. Dizzied from her little horse's waddling movements, she finally lost her balance and fell exhausted from her mount.

By this time they were within sight of the craggy towers of Angkor. Up till now Malraux had not stopped to consider what sort of explanation the explorers should offer to local French officials surprised by the premature return of these young 'archaeologists' from an excursion that had barely lasted one week. Clara's momentary malaise provided André with a conveni-ent explanation: his wife had succumbed to a sudden attack of dysentery, and this had forced them to interrupt their explorations. At the guest-house there was a flurry of solicitude, and over her protests a young Annamite doctor was summoned to give her an intestine-disinfecting injection.

It is not easy to fathom exactly what was going on in André Malraux's mind at this moment. It required a great deal of naïveté to suppose that one could smuggle out seven large crates full of Khmer statuary without arousing the suspicions of the local French authorities, and Malraux, for all his youth, was anything but naive. Fifteen or twenty years before, a bored young bank clerk named Géry Pierret had one day quietly 'lifted' two small Phoenician statues from the Louvre and had turned them over to his friend, Guillaume Apollinaire, arguing that his action did not constitute a 'theft' since the Museum's curators would not have left them exposed in an open display case if they had been objects of priceless value. There was, however, a staggering difference in degree between the easy 'lifting' from a museum of two inconspicuous statuettes and the cumbersome removal from a Khmer temple of seven heavy stones, so weighty that a truck had to be requisitioned to transport them from the Angkor rest-house to the Siemreap wharf. Here the camphor-wood 'coffins' were loaded on to the river cutter and later lowered into the hold of the Great Lake steamer that was to take the three adventurers back to the Cambodian capital of Phnom Penh. Did Malraux seriously believe that he could get away with such an act of larceny? If not, he was careful to conceal his misgivings from Clara. The means might be murky, but the end was of crystalline simplicity. Fortune, once again, was bound to favour the bold.

8

The Temple-Plunderers of Angkor

Since the die was now cast, there was no point in needlessly fretting about what might happen next. There was something almost Asiatic in Malraux's fatalistic resignation. On board he, Clara, and Louis Chevasson slept fitfully beneath the protective mosquito nets of their cabin bunks as the Tonlé Sap steamer ploughed its way across the opaque waters of the Great Lake, bound for Phnom Penh and Saigon.

In the meantime Crémazy had been tipped off by the director of the Angkor guest-house and a warning message had been telegraphed to the French authorities in Phnom Penh. At Kompong-Chnang, some sixty miles north of the Cambodian capital, a French archaeologist boarded the steamer and was shown the seven 'Chinese coffins', earmarked for shipment to the firm of Berthot & Charrière, in Saigon.

It was still dark in the early morning of this December 24, 1924 when the thump of the diesel engines gradually subsided into silence. It was soon broken by several imperious knocks on André's and Clara's cabin door. Outside, three plainclothes officials were waiting to accompany them into the dark, suffocating hold. The seven crates were picked out by the beams of several torches.

'They are yours?'

'Yes, registered in our names,' answered Malraux, brazenly adding: 'But at the moment of our departure from Siemreap they were empty.'

'All right, open them,' ordered the plainclothesmen.

One by one the lids were lifted with a curiously singsong plaint. Inside, as though embalmed in strongly scented camphor, were the seven fragments of Khmer sculpture. The inspectors then informed the 'owners' that they could not continue their journey to Saigon as they were subject to arrest. The seven crates were impounded. The three temple-robbers were ordered to return to their cabins. Malraux's reaction was strangely calm. His rapid diction seemed only slightly more nervous than usual as he assured Clara that this setback would delay the fulfilment of their plans by a day or two, no more.

A native policeman escorted them to Phnom Penh's finest hostelry, the Manolis, managed by an enterprising Greek. They were given a large bedroom, containing a huge mosquito-netted double bed. The ground-floor dining room, cooled by electric ceiling fans, seemed luxurious compared to the Angkor guest-house, with its slow-moving punkah. And to prove that they could treat adversity with the contempt it deserves, they appeared for the New Year's Eve dinner impeccably attired – André in a white dinner jacket, Clara in a *haute couture* grey and gold dress.

During the first week they almost had to pinch themselves to realize that they were under house-arrest, so lax was the surveillance, so unobstructed the pleasant evening drives in a horsedrawn *calèche*. Xa continued to serve them with the same stubborn fidelity, glad to be able to explain to them in what ways Cambodians differed from Annamites, and to emphasize the inferior status of his mistress, who was forced to walk a good yard behind him in the street and forbidden to venture above his shoulder level when in bed.

A nerve-wracking tedium, as implacable as the midday heat, soon supplanted these initial surprises. They were separated by an invisible wall from Phnom Penh's colonial society, being pointedly shunned, on the dance-floor and elsewhere, as pariahs. 'Never come to the colonies as a university lecturer,' Malraux warned his friend Marcel Arland at the end of his second week in the Cambodian capital. 'I write this with the utmost seriousness – never. The cities of the colonies smack neither of Africa nor of Asia, but of the most abject provincialism.' New restrictions ended their pleasant evening drives and made this atmosphere doubly stifling. Clara in her turn was indicted by an embarrassed young magistrate as one of the 'temple-sackers' (*pilleurs de temple*) whose predatory assault on the ruins of Banteay Srei had obliged Henri Parmentier to interrupt his Angkor Thom inspection in order to make a second, damage-estimating visit to the desecrated sanctuary.

So debilitating was the heat during these dry months that they preferred to remain indoors for much of the day, stretched out naked on the sweat-drenched sheet behind shuttered windows. Although they sought to combat the insidious boredom by reciting poems, both might have been driven mad by enforced inactivity had they not discovered the existence of a well-stocked municipal library.

But as the days dissolved into weeks, and the weeks into months, the accumulating strains became increasingly difficult to bear. The establishment of an official 'case' against them necessitated an investigation of their suspect activities in France – information which, once gathered, had to travel back to Saigon by slow boat. Soon the money needed to pay the Hotel Manolis' steadily lengthening bill had run out. A telegraphic SOS had elicited a welcome cheque from André's indulgent father, providing them with enough to pay for three weeks of room and board – less than half the time they had already spent in Mr Manolis' hotel. Meanwhile the examining magistrates in Paris had uncovered some highly embarrassing facts about M. Georges André Malraux. Not only were his archaeological credentials nil, but in addition to his dubious status as a would-be *homme de lettres*, he was a social parasite who had lived as a boarder in his mother-in-law's house, and – even more damning proof of premeditated crime – he was a calculating art thief who had sought to contact interested dealers in Asiatic statuary.

Clara had long hoped to be able to keep the truth about their arrest from reaching the Goldschmidt household, where she feared the reaction would be violent. It was. It took the form of a peremptory letter from her mother, ordering her to divorce her disreputable husband immediately.

Louis Chevasson had generously offered to assume the entire blame for the piratical assault on Banteay Srei, in order to exonerate André. But it did not take the examining magistrates in Phnom Penh long to realize that André Malraux was the real brain behind this 'archaeological' foray. The local authorities had no intention of releasing such a dangerous temple-robber now that he had been caught red-handed.

Finally it occurred to Clara that she, being a woman, was the one most likely to be freed if some subterfuge could be found to speed up the legal process. Why not simulate an attempted suicide, to draw attention to their desperate plight?

The faithful Xa was dispatched to the nearest pharmacy to buy two tubes of Gardenal tranquillizers. Clara and André decided that a tube and a half should suffice to induce a plausibly comatose state without pushing her over the brink. In the evening André descended to the dining room alone, explaining to the waiter that his wife was suffering from a headache. Ten minutes later, he went upstairs and found Clara stretched out in a still conscious but unusually grey state. 'You've taken too many!' he exclaimed, and in a panic that was anything but feigned, he rushed out into the corridor and began shouting for a doctor, for a first aid team, for an ambulance.

A doctor, several medical assistants, and two stretcher-bearers were quickly recruited to transport Clara's inert form to the hospital. The small procession was accompanied by a highly perturbed André and a tearful Xa, who kept repeating to a vaguely conscious Clara, 'You are nasty, you are nasty! Why did you make me buy this evil medicine?'

In the hospital Clara was assigned a huge bedroom overlooking a closed courtyard. It contained a mosquito-netted bed big enough for two; but André had to return to the Hotel Manolis for his meals. Clara's ruse had failed. No change of heart was displayed by the local magistrates. The 'temple-robbers' had simply exchanged one prison for another.

To keep from going mad Clara tried her hand at translating, while André kept her regularly supplied with philosophical and sociological works borrowed from the local library. He also brought back illustrated books for Xa, who turned up every afternoon around 5 o'clock to visit Clara. Although it was weeks, and soon months, since he had been paid a cent for his services, he continued to regard M. and Mme Malraux as his real masters, even after finding employment with others. His gradual realization that they were truly poor made a deep impression. He could see no reason why they should be blamed for 'crimes' so many others had committed with impunity.

One day he asked Clara why she and Monsieur had not explained at the outset exactly what they were looking for. 'I would have found you some heads, without anybody knowing anything about it.' Clara looked at him with admiring disbelief.

A week or so later Xa brought her two extraordinary presents: the head of an *apsara* (dancing goddess) not unlike the two they had removed from Banteay Srei, and a two-foot-high *hari-hara* (a Hindu deity, half-Vishnu, half-Shiva), which, André assured her, was a very rare piece. Both were tucked away in her trunk, and later brought triumphantly back to France.

Soon six months had passed – three of them at the Hotel Manolis, three of them at the hospital – with no sign of immediate relief. An uncomfortably hot, dry spring was followed, wih the onset of the monsoon, by a hot and clammy summer. Every now and then André received a letter from France – sometimes from his father, at others from his mother – but for Clara there was not a word of commiseration. Having disgraced the Goldschmidt family by her marriage to an unscrupulous adventurer, she had forfeited her right to further pity; she had ceased to exist. Her pariah-like status in Phnom Penh was duplicated by ostracism at home.

And so, with each passing week, their plight grew grimmer, their mounting debts more crippling. Again it was Clara who came up with a 'solution'. Her threat to end her days at a single stroke by simulating suicide had failed, so why not try a threat of slow death by starvation?

The first days of this hunger strike failed to impress her hospital guardians, beginning with the chief nurse, Mme Elisabeth. But neither her maternal embraces, nor the entreaties of the other nurses could shake Clara's determination to waste away. She lost weight, growing so feeble that André had to keep her from collapsing as they took their daily walk around the inner courtyard. This did not keep him from carrying on a pensive monologue about the ways in which 'the oriental will face up to the need to become an individual', or a critical self-examination, intended to reassure her about their common future – 'You must not despair, one day I'll end up being Gabriele d'Annunzio!'

As the needle on the scales relentlessly kept dropping – from 40 kilograms to 39, from 39 to 38 – the doctor became increasingly alarmed. The examining magistrate too suffered a change of heart. Twice he came to Clara's hospital bedside to assure her that, according to the terms of the law, 'a wife is duty-bound to follow her husband in all places'. Since the evidence indicated that she was in no sense the initiator of the temple-robbing venture, she had merely performed her uxorial duties in accompanying her husband to Cambodia. In a word, she was '*free! free!*' – as Mme Elisabeth kept repeating to her.

The hunger strike thus victoriously concluded, Clara had André draft a telegram addressed to her mother, announcing her official exoneration from the judicial charges brought against her. This time there was a swift and favourable response. Clara received a cheque to cover hospital expenses and a prepaid steamship ticket.

The examining magistrate had by now completed the legal preliminaries. André and Louis Chevasson were due to be tried just two weeks after Clara's departure. 'Everything is fine,' André sought to reassure her. 'They don't have a single serious element to condemn us. You'll see. I'll be embarking in my turn before your arrival in France.'

Given Clara's weak condition, the hospital management arranged to have her transported by ambulance to Saigon, where she was to embark on a homeward-bound liner. The final parting was strangely silent, charged with an intensity words seemed powerless to express. André, as she later recalled, stood near the stretcher, then leant over her. 'He said nothing, I said nothing. But when the vehicle took off, I saw him standing there in the middle of the road, in his white summer suit, a pith-helmet on his head and a semi-stiff collar around his neck, his arms hanging limply down, apart from the others, an orphan.'

Two weeks later André Malraux and Louis Chevasson were brought to trial before a local Phnom Penh court for the 'removal of bas-relief fragments purloined from the temple of Banteay Srei, in the Angkor group'. This unusual case – unusual because the temple-robbers had been caught and were being tried, whereas scores of French colonial officials had quietly acquired pieces of Khmer sculpture for the embellishment of their living rooms – had attracted considerable attention in the Saigon press, and the hot courtroom was well-filled with curious spectators when the two-day trial opened on June 24, 1924.

The charges against Louis Chevasson were speedily dealt with. The public prosecutor could find no elements in his past to suggest that he had ever harboured subversive views and might constitute a threat to the established order. Radically different was the checkered past and peppery personality of Georges André Malraux, an impetuous young man who had not bothered to complete his normal *lycée* studies, had preferred to consort with bohemian painters and writers of dangerously anarchistic views – one of them, a poet named Georges Gabory, had even praised the multiple murderer, Landru – and who, rather than seek honest employment, had married the wealthy daughter of German–Jewish immigrants and had gambled away her fortune on the Paris Bourse.

The young Malraux's courtroom behaviour did little to belie this unflattering portrayal, for less than ever was he now prepared to curb his sharp tongue when interrogated by the prosecutor and presiding judge. 'He is a tall, lean boy, with a beardless face brightened by two eyes of an extreme vivacity,' wrote the correspondent of Saigon's leading French newspaper, the highly prejudiced *L'Impartial*, who was forced to admit that Malraux 'defended his positions with a surprising energy, refuting all the points of the judicial inquiry'.

Stubbornly convinced that he had committed no crime in seeking to rescue a few sculptured fragments from an abandoned temple, Malraux was further embittered to discover that the prosecution had been granted access to confidential information supplied by the Ministry of Colonies in Paris, some of it in coded messages, which neither he nor his lawyer were allowed to see. Of the witnesses summoned to testify against the temple-sackers, the most virulent was the French Resident's local representative, Crémazy, who blackened the record as much as possible while playing up his own personal merits as a vigilant protector of Cambodian 'treasures'. Far less biased was the testimony of Henri Parmentier, understandably irked to discover that the friendly encouragement he had offered to the young explorers had been so ill requited.

The surprising range of Georges André Malraux's erudition even proved an embarrassment to the lawyers of the defence, who had trouble pleading the youthful 'innocence' of their clients. A weightier argument was that used by Malraux's lawyer, Percevaux, who pointed out that the little temple at Banteay Srei had not been officially 'classified', so that it could not seriously be claimed that a 'crime' had been committed.

The presiding judge paid no attention to such subtle considerations. As far as he was concerned, the basic facts were simple. Two adventurers from metropolitan France, masquerading as 'explorers', had abused the trust of professional archaeologists and administrative officials in order to perpetrate an act of 'vulgar theft'. They must therefore be punished for discrediting France's tutelary role as an enlightened colonial power. Four days later, on July 21, he handed down his sentence: three years of prison for André Malraux, eighteen months for Louis Chevasson, found guilty of 'fruitful vandalism'.

The two convicted 'vandals' immediately appealed the harsh sentence to a higher court located in Saigon. In late July Malraux and Chevasson were officially transferred from their 'house-arrest' at the Hotel Manolis in Phnom Penh to another hotel-prison (the Continental) in the capital of Cochin China. Here the prevailing atmosphere was only slightly less provincial, but the hostility of the local French press even more blatantly evident. That the two temple-robbers should have dared to challenge the first judicial verdict and to hire the services of two eminent members of the Saigon bar was, for the editor of *L'Impartial*, another act of impudent defiance, meriting an exemplary chastisement.

In the meantime, Clara Malraux was gradually recovering her strength, if not her peace of mind, on the liner that was taking her back to France. A telegram from André, which she received in the middle of the Indian Ocean, assured her that: 'Everything went well. See you soon.' But the absence of a simpler statement – 'have won trial' – made her suspect that her penniless husband would not be embarking soon on another ship bound for France.

She herself had already been subjected to a humiliating affront at her dining room table when two women had complained to the head waiter about her unwanted presence. She had hoped to retain an unobtrusive anonymity during the three-week voyage, but this was denied her by these two fellow passengers, daughters of a lawcourt clerk in Phnom Penh.

This disagreeable experience would have shattered what was left of her self-confidence had she not befriended a director of French teaching missions in China, a man who had fled Europe after the horrors of the Great War (which had cost him his right, violin-playing hand) and who had taken the trouble to master Mandarin Chinese. Full of scorn for the pettiness of French colonial officialdom, he was delighted to outsnub the snobs who had ostracized Clara by inviting her to join him at *his* dining room table. The affable stranger soon became an inseparable companion, providing her with a psychological crutch on which she was happy to lean.

One day, as Clara was explaining André's predicament, her new Chinese-speaking friend nodded towards a wiry man with a dark suntanned face who had been pacing up and down the deck.

'You don't know that fellow? You should. It's Monin, the lawyer.'

She had never met him, but Paul Monin was a familiar name. A left-wing radical, perhaps even a Bolshevik, he had 'sold out' to Annamese patriots, whose cause he was ever ready to defend. He was an incorrigible troublemaker who had denounced various cases of financial skulduggery; he had organized at least one strike in Saigon, had even challenged La Chevrotière, editor of the misnamed *L'Impartial*, to a duel. In a word, he was a thorn in the flank of the colonial authorities in Saigon and their most detested *bête noire*.

Shortly after the liner had left Djibouti, Clara Malraux boldly seated herself in an armchair Monin habitually occupied near the bar, and when the swarthy, blue-eyed lawyer came up to protest at this 'usurpation', introduced herself. Monin soon made it clear that he knew a great deal about the 'temple-robbers' case. Unwittingly, he explained, the young explorers had fallen foul of a venal colonial administration which rigged elections, stifled the press, crushed the native peasantry through a pitiless system of taxation and shamelessly enriched itself through bribes, monopolistic business deals and sordid speculation in Indochinese property, while hypocritically claiming to be promoting 'justice', progress, and 'Western civilization'.

When they docked at Marseilles, Monin gave Clara his card and urged her to get in touch with him in Paris. It was comforting to realize that on board ship she had made a second and potentially far more useful friend. But it did nothing to alleviate her immediate predicament. For she was by now almost penniless. At Port Said she had dispatched a telegram to her father-in-law, Fernand Malraux, asking him to meet her in Marseilles, but there was no sign of him on the wharf.

'You seem upset,' said her Chinese-speaking companion, who by this time had become her lover – a shipboard romance which had restored her shattered self-confidence in her feminine ability to charm.

'Very much so,' she admitted. The steward had just handed her Fernand Malraux's answering cable: 'Telegram arrived too late. Call me at Orléans. Affectionately. Father.' In her handbag she had just 200 francs left, too little to pay for the train fare back to Paris. Mortified, she blurted out the bitter truth. A few minutes later her companion returned from his cabin and handed her a book she had previously lent him. Discretely tucked inside was an envelope containing enough money to cover her immediate needs.

Aware that she could expect no pity from her family, Clara, on reaching Paris, headed straight for the Place de Clichy, at the western extremity of Montmartre's red-light district, where a former chambermaid of the Goldschmidts now ran a hotel. The welcome, as the 'prodigal daughter' had anticipated, was wonderfully warm, but followed by lively protests: 'My, what an uproar you've stirred up!'

'Oh, it's nothing,' Clara replied, trying to sound light-hearted.

'Nothing?' exclaimed the good Jeanne. 'Why, the papers are full of his condemnation.'

Now for the first time Clara was brought face to face with the ugly truth. Far from getting himself acquitted, André had been sentenced to three years in prison. The news had got back to Paris, where it had inspired far from flattering comments in certain newspapers. For *Le Journal*, André Malraux was no more than a 'burlesque adventurer'. Even more sarcastic was the ultra-conservative *Le Matin*, in a long, front-page article headlined, 'THE MAN WITH THE ROSE CONDEMNED TO THREE YEARS IN JAIL'. The reporter painted a ferocious portrait of a 'curious kind of crook' who had started out as a dilettantish dandy, parading around with a rose in his buttonhole and trying to pass himself off as a genuine *homme de lettres*:

> Georges Malraux had sought in vain to focus attention on himself, first of all by publishing a novel, *Lunes en papier*, which went unnoticed. Every now and then his person attracted the momentary notice of the Paris public, when Georges Malraux turned up at the theatre for a dress rehearsal most bizarrely hatted and draped in a black-velvet cape lined with white satin . . .

To Clara's horror, worse was yet to come:

> The *Man with the Rose* could not conceivably have lived in just any house of bourgeois appearance. In fact, Georges Malraux resided at no. 10 Avenue des Chalets, in Paris, in a cottage rented by his mother-in-law at a price of 10,000 francs.
>
> The in-laws still inhabit the house on the Avenue des Chalets, but for some time now they have completely lost interest in the fate of somebody whose name literature has been unable to render famous. Nevertheless,

the *Man with the Rose*'s habitat is not devoid of interest. A delirious cubism confers on his installation an undoubted originality . . .

Clara could well imagine the indignation with which her poor mother and brothers had greeted this embarrassing notoriety. But they had only themselves to blame for having provided the examining magistrates with such damning information.

The next day Clara decided to confront her outraged family. Outwardly, nothing seemed to have changed at the Goldschmidt villa – neither the red and blue carpeted stairs leading up to the second floor, nor the large living room with the English-style furniture and the famous portrait of Whistler's mother hung between the two windows. But for Clara, now a rejected stranger, this was no longer home.

The reception was stormy. Her two brothers remained standing, as did she, pelting her furiously with peremptory accusations and injunctions – 'An immediate divorce! . . . You must divorce immediately! . . . You aren't going to remain married to that good-for-nothing, to that common-law criminal!'

'No! . . . Never! . . . Of course, I'm going to stay with him! Now, more so than ever!' she no less heatedly retorted.

'You must leave this boy. You must leave him. . . . This boy has always lied,' her mother, whose hair had suddenly turned white, kept tearfully repeating.

'He never even obtained his baccalaureate,' chimed in Clara's younger brother, the same one who had accompanied them to Strasbourg and masterminded André's exemption from military service. Now he too was ready to believe the worst of this abominable brother-in-law, and also of his father. For Fernand Malraux too was a bluffer. He had never been a bank director (as André had airily claimed during the Phnom Penh trial), merely an employee in some obscure establishment. He had hoodwinked them at the time of Clara's engagement by turning up in a hired car!

The atmosphere became so electrically charged that one of her brothers came up and slapped Clara in the face as she tried to pick up three letters that were waiting for her on a desk. There was a brief remonstrance from their weeping mother; this gave Clara a chance to slip them into her handbag.

After more acrimonious exchanges a doctor turned up to examine their mother, who had long suffered from stomach ulcers. Clara now had a chance to open the letters. The first, from Florent Fels, expressed his heartfelt sympathy. The second, from André Breton, was more surprising; if she needed help in any way, she could count on his support – this from a former Dadaist, turned Surrealist, for whom André had never felt much affinity. The third letter, from a former suitor, urged his 'little princess' to repair their past errors by getting a divorce and marrying him.

The brothers returned, saying that the doctor would like to have a word with Clara. Her mother, the doctor explained, had suffered severely from the nervous strains of the past few weeks and she was going to retire for a few days to an agreeable rest-home near Paris. It would greatly help if Clara could remain with her. Made to feel guilty for this psychological distress, Clara agreed to accompany her mother to the rest-home – only to discover, when they had reached this 'idyllic' retreat, that it was she her brothers were proposing to intern. Several tense hours followed, during which three doctors tried to persuade her that the harrowing experiences of the past few months had deranged her mentally and that she was in urgent need of a rest. Suddenly panicking, she ran out of the building, but was stopped at the gate by one of her brothers: 'You've been too much talked about! This has got to stop!' Led back to her panel of medical tormentors, Clara realized that she had behaved like a frightened schoolgirl. Since she was in complete control of her mental faculties, they had no right to confine her without her consent. A consent she stubbornly refused to give them despite two hours of tedious 'persuasion'. Finally the three doctors gave up – to the disgust of Clara's two brothers, who were, however, kind enough to drive their unrepentant sister back to Jeanne's hotel in the family car.

Haunted by visions of an emaciated André, condemned to spend thirty months in a Saigon prison where he might go mad, succumb to some tropical disease or be surreptitiously poisoned, Clara passed a sleepless night. Now that they knew her whereabouts, her furious brothers might return at any moment and drag her away for further 'interrogation' and some kind of forcible internment. There was not a minute to be lost.

At 6 am she got up and crept out of the hotel without saying goodbye to the hospitable Jeanne. The 3 francs 25 centimes left in her purse just sufficed to pay the taxi-fare as far as the Rue Fontaine, where André Breton lived. She had trouble waking the disgruntled concierge, who finally yielded to Clara's desperate determination – 'It's a case of life or death!' – and let her climb, or rather race, up the four flights of stairs.

'I'm Clara Malraux,' she exclaimed breathlessly to the small woman in a brown dressing gown who finally answered her insistent ringing by opening the door. A moment later, feeling faint and dizzy, she collapsed and let herself be stretched out on a sofa.

When she came to, she was comforted by the reassuring sight of André Breton's woolly head and the welcoming smile of his dark-haired wife, Suzanne.

Later, over cups of morning coffee, the first concrete steps were taken and plans discussed for the future. A telegram was dispatched to Fernand Malraux at Orléans, another to Marcel Arland, who was spending his summer vacation near his home town of Langres. Clara also telephoned Paul Monin, the lawyer, to indicate her new address. In the early afternoon Fernand Malraux turned up, visibly upset to have learned the news of his son's trial and condemnation for theft from the newspapers.

'Swear to me that he's innocent!' he insisted to Clara, who was ready to swear anything to regain the goodwill of this benevolent father-in-law. Little persuasion was needed, for at that moment Paul Monin appeared. In a few devastating sentences he painted a black picture of the administrative set-up in southern Indochina, a vast web of favouritism and corruption designed to enrich the governor of Cochin China, a handful of sycophantic 'natives' and powerful French business and commercial groups, at the expense of a cruelly taxed Annamite peasantry. There was nothing at all surprising about the severity of the sentences meted out to André Malraux and Louis Chevasson. The local 'overlords' were a law unto themselves, and there was nothing they detested more than prying interlopers from metropolitan France.

Seated around the dining room table, they debated what should be done. Monin could not offer much immediate help, since he was not returning to Indochina for some weeks – by which time the Appelate Court in Saigon would have handed down its verdict. But André Malraux and Louis Chevasson had fortunately chosen two of the most highly respected members of the Saigon bar to defend them. The important thing was to supply them with the ammunition needed to demolish the image that had been maliciously fabricated in Phnom Penh and Saigon of an unscrupulous adventurer (Malraux) who had been reduced to 'temple-pillaging' by his failures in literature and journalism.

Breton volunteered to write an article on behalf of Malraux. But a single article written by an iconoclastic nonconformist would have not the slightest impact on the judges in Saigon. Something of heavier calibre was needed: for example, an 'open letter' of protest signed by some of France's most celebrated writers – men like André Gide, François Mauriac, Jacques Rivière. Clara was given a pencil and a few minutes later she had prepared a preliminary draft. The text was then reworked, Monin insisting that it avoid all criticism of the overly harsh sentence handed down in Phnom Penh and that it invoke the finest traditions of French justice in defending the country's 'intellectual heritage'. That evening, when Marcel Arland arrived, a carefully worded 'open letter' was ready for distribution to potential signatories.

Meanwhile, Malraux's first mentor in rare-book publishing, René-Louis Doyon, had taken up the cudgels for his former associate – in a laudatory article published in the August 9th number of L'Eclair, a conservative Paris daily which had previously printed a critical dispatch under the arresting title: 'The poet André Malraux was plundering the temples of Angkor'. In his apologia Doyon regretted the 'particularly aggressive, gratuitously ironic, and even nasty' tone employed by the Paris press against his former associate. This highly cerebral young writer, who had a 'rabid taste for aesthetics', had been overly inspired by the examples of Rimbaud and Lord Seymour (a French Beau Brummel), but his audacity was not that of an ordinary thief and did not deserve to be so severely condemned in court and cruelly stigmatized in the press.

Clara hurried over to the little bookshop in the dark Galerie de la Madeleine to express her heartfelt thanks. 'I had never previously met

Doyon,' she later recalled, and 'in a mixture of gratitude and exaltation I flung my arms around his neck'.

Though vitally important, the articles and petitions now being prepared were clearly not enough. Something had to be done, to enable a penniless André to pay the Hotel Manolis bill, as well as the new debts he was accumulating at the Continental in Saigon. Generous as ever, 'Papa' Fernand had given Clara money to cover her immediate expenses in Paris, but far more was needed for André. Breton and Doyon, both outraged by the way she had been treated, made several trips to the Goldschmidt villa. A pearl necklace, a diamond ring she had inherited from her grandmother, the woodcuts by Derain, the Picasso collage, the Kisling painting, the African fetish, were all sold, along with a few rare books, to pay for André's debts.

On August 12th Fernand Malraux wrote a long letter to his son in which he expressed admiration for all his daughter-in-law had been able to accomplish in just four days.

Clara is a good little wife . . . Now feeling confident and secure, she bustles about like a watchful bee and acts with a perspicacity which surprises me and fills me with admiration. No initiative is too much for her, and she amazes me by the sureness of her deductions when, with perfect common sense and an unquestionable sense of what is appropriate, she arranges with friends to draw up the main points for articles which others then write almost under her dictation . . . You did well to send her back to France.

Almost everywhere the reactions were prompt and sympathetic. Typical was François Mauriac's response to Marcel Arland's appeal. 'I am not one of those who believe that genius gives one every right . . . But this marvellous boy, André Malraux, whom you had me meet, his adventure seems to me so "literary", so Rimbaudian, that I shudder to think the price it will cost him. . . . He must be saved.'

On August 16th André Breton's article was published in the weekly *Nouvelles littéraires*. It began with a fine flourish, inspired by a translated verse from Hölderlin's *Hyperion*, which Breton had found among Clara Malraux's papers at the Goldschmidt villa and which he had mistakenly attributed to André: 'Farewell, prudence. "Everywhere one looks," says André Malraux, "there lies a buried joy." ' The article continued in the same exalted vein, praising the young Malraux's 'fiery and somewhat heroic temperament' and even 'the abduction carried out on the persons of two or three stone dancing-girls, from an unknown temple in the vicinity of Angkor. Who really cares about the conservation in their native land of these works of art?' But for this 'crime' the author of *Lunes en papier* was being made to pay an intolerably high price, particularly since his published works were products of 'today's most secret intellectual activity', and were 'remarkable experiments in a laboratory to which the general public is not admitted'.

'A modern writer's lyricism and his comprehension of Cubist painting,' Breton concluded, 'cannot be invoked by the many as a proof of immorality.'

From his monastic retreat at Saint-Benoît-sur-Loire Max Jacob offered his wholehearted support. But it was at the annual literary conference held at Pontigny, in Burgundy, that Marcel Arland accomplished wonders, obtaining a dozen signatures for the 'open letter' of protest Clara Malraux had prepared three weeks before with the help of Paul Monin and André Breton. Published in the September 6th issue of *Les Nouvelles Littéraires*, it is worth quoting in full, for the impact it had in Paris and in distant Saigon:

> The undersigned, upset by the condemnation that has struck André Malraux, have confidence in the consideration that [French] Justice habitually displays toward those who contribute to augment the intellectual patrimony of our country. They undertake to guarantee the intelligence and real literary worth of this person, whose youth and already completed work hold out very high hopes [for the future]. They would greatly deplore a loss resulting from the application of a sanction that would prevent André Malraux from accomplishing what all have had a right to expect of him.

There followed, in a more or less descending order of influence and prestige, the names of Edmond Jaloux, André Gide, François Mauriac, Pierre Mac Orlan, Jean Paulhan, André Maurois, Jacques Rivière, Max Jacob, François Le Gris, Maurice Martin du Gard, Gaston Gallimard, Raymond Gallimard, Philippe Soupault, Florent Fels, Louis Aragon, Pierre de Lanux, Guy de Pourtalès, Pascal Pia, André Harlaire, André Desson – to which were added, modestly appended at the end, the signatures of two of the three prime movers of this unusual petition: André Breton and Marcel Arland.

This and other published texts and lists of signatories were cabled by Clara to Saigon. They reached André at a moment when his prospects seemed distinctly bleak. In early September the ferociously hostile *L'Impartial* reprinted the sarcastic *Le Matin* article about 'The Man with the Rose'. A wrathful Malraux stormed into the newspaper's offices and demanded to see the editor-in-chief and publisher, Henry de Lachevrotière. To pacify the incensed youth, Lachevrotière offered him an interview with one of his correspondents – a proposal Malraux imprudently accepted.

The result, published in the September 16th issue of *L'Impartial*, did nothing to enhance his already tarred image. The young 'explorer' rashly belittled the value of the temple stones he had removed from the sanctuary of Banteay Srei, dismissing them as 'a few truncated bas-reliefs' forming 'a mass of stone' not more than four feet high – an affirmation which could only make the reader wonder why he should have been so intent to lay hands on such a heap of rubble. Malraux also inflated his father's position in the world of finance by claiming that he was a 'legendary figure of the Paris

Bourse' and also the director of 'one of the largest international petroleum companies' (significantly unnamed) — two gratuitous fibs which were bound to reinforce the fallacious impression that he had always been a pampered *fils à papa*.

On October 8th, André Malraux and Louis Chevasson appeared before the higher court in Saigon. The underlying issue was not simply the immediate fate of the two temple-robbers but the tangled question of just who was the rightful owner of the ruined sanctuary of Banteay Srei. The public prosecutor argued that Malraux and his accomplice, Chevasson, had deliberately abused the confidence of the Ministry of Colonies in Paris in order to obtain an official authorization to undertake an act of premeditated theft on a temple which, along with Angkor, the French had retrieved from Siam in 1907 and reintegrated into the kingdom of Cambodia. The Banteay Srei ruins could not therefore be regarded as an ownerless site. Georges André Malraux was not only a liar who had concealed his real intentions, he was a thief who had tried to make off with treasures belonging to the King of Cambodia. He therefore deserved the three-year prison sentence meted out in Phnom Penh.

Malraux's defender, Maître Joseph Béziat, a burly, strong-featured lawyer endowed with a stentorian voice, refused to be intimidated by these well-argued accusations. It was true, he conceded, that the region of Angkor had been detached from Siam and added to Cambodia by a treaty signed in 1907, and that it had subsequently been turned over to the Cambodian Crown by a decision of the Governor-General of Indochina. But this transfer, confirmed by a French presidential decree issued eight years later (in itself an anomaly) in 1915, had never been officially approved by the French parliament in Paris. If the question of the 'property rights' to Angkor and other ruins was complex and unclear, this was not the case with their official 'protection'. The Angkor Thom complex had been officially added to the Inventory years before, but though the Banteay Srei sanctuary had been visited by Henri Parmentier as early as 1916, the competent French authorities had not bothered to have the remaining 'débris' classified as a 'monument' worthy of being preserved and restored. Those ruins were thus *res derelictae* (like a shipwrecked vessel), to which any enterprising explorer was free to help himself. It was sheer hypocrisy to single out André Malraux for exemplary punishment. 'How many others,' the lawyer boomed, 'have taken from Angkor artistic riches of far greater importance. . . . If my client is punished for the peccadillo thus committed, then in the past admirals, senior residents, and other mandarins of equal importance should have been prosecuted and condemned for depradations they committed to the detriment of the same monuments.' He concluded by painting a completely different picture of André Malraux, a young author whose literary talents had been recognized by many prominent writers and critics — as could be judged by the elogious articles and petitions on his behalf (including the 'open letter'), which he proceeded to read to the court.

Chevasson's defender, Louis Gallois-Montbrun, was no less mordant in attacking the sanctimonious hypocrisy of office bureaucrats who had developed a belated passion for 'protecting' ruins they knew next to nothing about. 'Khmer art! Khmer art!' he cried sarcastically. It was a veritable 'fit of archaeologitis' that had seized on people who had never for one moment dreamed of venturing into the jungle.

On October 28th, some ten months after their arrest, the Saigon court virtually absolved the two 'felons' of the grave charges brought against them. André Malraux was condemned to a suspended prison sentence of one year, Louis Chevasson to one of eight months. This time André's laconic telegram to Clara was more explicit: 'One year suspended sentence'. Three days later he and Chevasson boarded the *Chantilly* for the homeward trip to France.

9

Convicted, but Not Cowed

Clara was waiting on the wharf when the *Chantilly* docked at Marseilles three weeks later. But the shared joy of this homecoming was spoiled when André suddenly asked her, in a peevish tone: 'But what have you been up to with my mother?'

Once again it was a shock for Clara to realize how hypersensitive her husband was to everything concerning his mother's family. Totally absorbed by his tribulations in Indochina, Malraux had not bothered to imagine the troubles his wife had encountered after her return to Paris.

As they walked towards the customs shed, Clara explained that she had written a letter to his mother to reassure her about André. His mother had asked to see her, they had met and had taken a liking to each other, bound as they were by a common sense of adversity and the need to find a new home. For the little suburban house and grocery store at Bondy had finally been sold. Being herself homeless, Clara had accepted Grandmother Adrienne's generous hospitality and had moved into their small apartment on the Avenue Edgar Quinet, near the Montparnasse railway station.

In mid-September, when Paul Monin was about to return to Saigon, she had urged him to look up André. 'You'll see, he's extraordinary. Everything acquires a meaning when he speaks. I'm sure you'll hit it off with him.'

Her intuition had not betrayed her. Not only had Paul Monin and André Malraux hit it off, they had begun seeing each other every day. The indignities to which 'native' Vietnamese were constantly subjected by local French settlers and a corrupt administration had made Malraux increasingly angry. He was still determined to regain possession of the sculptured stones he had rescued from the jungle depths of Banteay Srei, by taking the Saigon verdict to a higher court of appeal. But for the moment his intellectual energies were concentrated on another, nobler, more ambitious mission.

So sure by now was André of Clara's steadfast loyalty that he did not even ask for her preliminary consent. He simply announced his decision. 'You and I will be leaving again for Saigon in a month or six weeks' time . . . Well, once we have the necessary funds. The Annamites need a free newspaper. Monin and I are going to run it.'

In Paris André and Clara moved into an apartment conveniently located right above the one that was now occupied by his mother, Grandmother Adrienne, and his Aunt Marie. The fare might be frugal and the maid-service non-existent, but the atmosphere at Grandmother Adrienne's lunch and dinner table was less strained and stilted than had been the case in the Goldschmidts' elegantly furnished dining room.

André in any case had no intention of remaining cooped up at home when there was so much to be done and so many people to be seen. René-Louis Doyon was one of the first Malraux went to thank for his support. Far less agreeable was the visit made to André Breton and his wife Simone. 'Why did you go to those people who are my enemies?' had been André's spontaneous reaction to the news that Clara had accepted their hospitality. She herself had trouble appreciating the deep-rooted hostility André felt for Breton and the Surrealist movement. But Malraux was too independent-minded and instinctively hostile to Breton's stubborn belief in the creative potential of the unconscious and the merits of 'automatic writing' to make any genuine rapprochement possible.

Within a day or two of André's return to Paris, his relations with Clara were subjected to a major crisis. From Saigon he had brought back a small bag of Indian hemp which, when chewed, enveloped one in a cloud of idyllic music, while the words uttered conjured up a sequence of brightly coloured pictures. It was absolutely harmless, he assured a sceptical Clara, leaving behind no bitter aftertaste or perilous addiction. When she agreed to try some, one evening before dinner, the chewed weed generated such a painful impression of unreality that she was forced to leave the table and go upstairs to their bedroom. Here, instead of delicious music and wondrously coloured images, she experienced a hallucinatory loss of identity. Staggering to her feet, she made for the window and tried to wrench it open with the intention of flinging herself out into the street; fortunately André appeared to see how things were going. Obviously, they were not going according to plan. He tried to soothe her by reciting poems, but this 'therapy' had not the slightest effect. She kept trying to reach the window, beyond which could be heard the shrill train whistles and puffs of steam from Montparnasse station.

At the height of this grim psychedelic struggle Clara murmured, 'Did I already tell you that I went to bed with Charles G?' – and here she added the name of the compassionate Chinese-speaking companion she had befriended during her voyage back to France. Not long before, Fernand Malraux, who was more subtle and intuitive than was suggested by the carefree twinkle in his bright blue eyes, had offered her this friendly warning: 'You must never tell your husband all the truth. My son is like the others. Don't idealize him too much.' It was sound advice, but now it was too late. The truth, defying her volition, had leapt from her lips.

The effect was electric. Before making another dark descent into the depths of distress, she briefly glimpsed 'a young man seated at the foot of the bed, and who was crying'.

Later, after a tense, all-night vigil, a deeply hurt André could not still his reproaches. 'Why did you do that?' he asked, or more probably repeated for the fifteenth time. To which he added, after a moment of tense silence: 'If you hadn't saved my life, I would leave you.'

The psychic wounds inflicted by this chance confession were never fully healed. A few days later, when they went to spend a weekend in Fernand Malraux's house at Orléans, the complaints and recriminations were as bitter as ever. They attempted a candid 'explanation' while alone together in the garden. But once again André could not restrain himself. 'Why did you do that?' This by now pointless question was followed by a gratuitous expostulation: 'And with that numbskull!'

'He's not a numbskull!' Clara heatedly replied. The sullen silence that followed left the issue half-buried. Later that evening in their bedroom it again reared its head.

'Just think what that fellow must now be imagining!' observed André bitterly. 'He has a right to despise you.'

'He doesn't despise me!' insisted Clara sharply.

'I know what a man thinks of a woman he has had' was the report. It was an absurd rejoinder, one worthy of an immature Julien Sorel, not of a man of the world.

'I am not an object whose value depends solely on the personality of its buyer,' was Clara's proud answer.

Fortunately for both of them there were enough practical problems to keep their minds occupied by other matters. 'I'm not prepared to put up with failure,' André kept repeating to his father, as he outlined his and Paul Monin's plans for founding a newspaper whose mission it would be to expose everything that was rotten, misguided and corrupt in the French colonial administration of southern Indochina. Fernand Malraux's scepticism ('Just one more of André's crazy schemes!') was soon transmuted into grudging admiration. This new undertaking was a good bit worthier than trying to pry stones away from an abandoned temple.

'When you reach Singapore,' he told André and Clara, 'you will find 50,000 francs waiting for you in the bank. It's up to you to get there. I must also make it plain that you should not expect any further sum from me.'

This generous pledge of support had a galvanizing effect on André, who spent a hectic week trying to obtain exclusive reproduction rights for Indochina for articles published in French satirical and other weeklies. On January 12, 1925, two days before they were to leave for Marseilles, a surprise telegram was brought to the Avenue Edgar Quinet apartment asking M. André Malraux to get in touch with the publisher, Bernard Grasset, as soon as possible. André was so busy that he felt like ignoring the dispatch. But his mother and grandmother insisted that he respond to this startling invitation, and at 2 o'clock the next day Malraux was ushered into Bernard Grasset's office.

A dynamic publisher who cared little for esoteric literature, Grasset had recently launched a successful series of adventure novels set in more or less exotic places. The author of *Lunes en papier* and 'The Origins of Cubist Poetry' did not interest him. But André Malraux, the bold 'temple-robber of Angkor', whose literary talents so many French writers, beginning with François Mauriac (a Grasset author) had publicly praised, was quite a different proposition; this ambitious young man with a stomach for adventure would bear watching.

In vain the young man protested that he had no completed manuscript to offer. Grasset waved aside these modest scruples. He was certain that M. Malraux was a person of genuine literary talent. Before André knew what was happening, he was invited to sign a contract form pledging him to deliver three books to the publisher. In return, Bernard Grasset was willing to make an advance of 3,000 francs – offered to him on the spot in the form of three 1,000-franc banknotes (roughly equivalent to three $200 bills). 'Now,' said Grasset, giving the astonished 'temple-robber' a paternal pat on the back, 'don't take too much time, if you can, giving me your little book. Just think of the marvellous publicity so many writers recently gave you.'

André's and Clara's second voyage to the Orient differed radically from the first. Obliged to count every penny, they bought third-class tickets. They were separated, each having to share a kind of cabin-dormitory with five others: Army non-coms and petty officials in the case of André, their equally boring wives in the case of Clara. The stench of vomit was sickening, the shouts and wailing of disobedient children was deafening, but most disagreeable of all was the scorn for this third-class 'chattel' shown by dining room waiters and other members of the crew.

In Singapore they avoided the celebrated Raffles and chose a humbler hotel. The 50,000 francs Fernand Malraux had promised were waiting for them at the bank, but with the Indochinese currency now pegged at more than 10 francs to the piaster, André decided to take no chances. As they had decided to make a detour via Bangkok, it was in a second-class railway carriage with hard wooden seats that they made the long, hot, sticky overland trip up the Malay peninsula to Kuala Lumpur and beyond, surrounded by talkative Chinamen who devoured fruit and cakes, spat out seeds, laughed, rolled dice and gambled with tireless gusto.

Bangkok, with its punted sampans and floating market, its gilded pagodas and its orange-robed Buddhist monks, struck them as being the happiest and most untroubled Oriental city they had yet seen. But their first-class steamship voyage from Bangkok turned out to be a luxury they would have done better to forgo. No one on the Saigon dockside could possibly have been impressed by the ageing tub which had rolled and pitched its way across a stormy Gulf of Siam and had come close to foundering when a jarring wave had half ripped away the rudder.

Paul Monin was waiting for them on the wharf, his lean body, next to the Annamite beside him, making him look taller than he really was, while his suntanned face, beneath the white pith-helmet, seemed singularly dark for a European. He drove the new arrivals to Saigon's fanciest hotel, the Continental, already familiar to André, who had spent three months there with Louis Chevasson prior to their second trial. He and Clara were given a spacious corner bedroom looking out beyond a balcony on to Saigon's most important thoroughfare, the Rue Catinat. Directly opposite was the French-run theatre, behind them was a redolent opium factory – officially tolerated by the local authorities because it was supposed to supply a soporific antidote to the dangerous effervescence of Annamite hotheads – and some distance away, flanked by luxuriant flame-trees, was Monin's house.

It was in Monin's house that André and Clara now spent most of the daytime hours. Monin's waiting-room was transformed into an editorial reference room, where tables and even chairs began to disappear under mountains of newspapers. His living room was similarly sacrificed to the needs of the moment, as the stiff, black-lacquered chairs, with their Chinese scrollwork, were displaced to make room for new tables needed both for typewriters and as space for the composition of articles and preparation of layout sheets and dummies.

Intelligent journalism, particularly of the hard-hitting kind they envisaged, requires the prior constitution of detailed files on specific topics and individuals. No one knew this better than Monin, who had already twice sought to supplement his legal activities on behalf of the downtrodden and oppressed by launching a newspaper. The second – the *Saigon Républicain* – had survived an arbitrary crackdown by the authorities simply because one of its Radical Socialist French editors was an indolent opium addict, while the other was a spineless printer who was being bribed by henchmen working for Maurice Cognacq, the Lieutenant-Governor of Cochin China, to soften the paper's attacks on local iniquities and administrative abuses.

To avoid a repetition of his previous journalistic setbacks, Monin had to put together an effective editorial team and extend the new paper's readership beyond the limits of Saigon's European community, barely 7,000 strong. He began by recruiting two volunteers from among his Vietnamese admirers. The first, named Vinh, was a soft-spoken young man from Saigon who had been forced to marry a girl his widowed mother had adopted, and whose longing for personal as well as national emancipation was in almost schizophrenic conflict with loyalty to ancestral tradition. Much tougher in looks as well as behaviour was the squat, sturdy, dark-featured Hin, a student from the central highlands of Annam who had turned his back on the privileged life he could have enjoyed with his influential uncle at the imperial court of Hué, preferring to join other anti-colonial 'patriots' in Saigon.

Of even greater value was an older journalist named Eugène Dejean de la Batie. The son of a senior French diplomat, he had proudly chosen to espouse the cause of his Annamite mother and had helped one of the founders of a moderate Constitutionalist Party to launch an independent 'opposition' newspaper called *L'Echo annamite*. As a *métis* (of mixed blood), he automatically enjoyed French citizenship – a privilege (including voting rights) denied to all but a handful of Annamites– and could thus assume an irksome responsibility as publisher of *L'Indochine*.

Although Governor Cognacq and his subordinates were not allowed to subsidize individual newspapers, they had devised an ingenious way of getting around this official prohibition by 'encouraging' Vietnamese administrative officials in the countryside to subscribe to newspapers favourable to the colonial status quo. In this way Saigon's leading French daily, *L'Impartial*, which brazenly proclaimed itself to be an 'organ for the defence of French interests in Indochina', was assured of 1,800 subscriptions. The next most important newspaper in terms of circulation, *L'Opinion* (owned by the arch-conservative Banque d'Indochine and run by a retired army colonel), could count on a solid 'fund' of 1,200 subscriptions, while three other newssheets of smaller dimensions (four pages each) were each assured of 600 subscriptions.

Given the existing set-up, Monin knew that there was little hope of winning many readers away from the ranks of this 'captive audience'. The majority of his readers would have to be found from among the thousands of French-speaking Vietnamese who lacked a daily newspaper willing to take up the cudgels on their behalf.

Of crucial importance for fund-raising purposes, because it was a genuine 'bastion' of finance and commercial activity, was the teeming suburb of Cholon – the picturesque 'Chinatown' situated a half-hour ride by tram or taxi from the centre of Saigon. Here, in a bustling labyrinth of restaurants and gambling halls, grocery stalls and opium-dens, where (as Clara Malraux later noted) the 'smell of soy sauce was mingled with that of the jasmine blossoms worn above the ear by little prostitutes in shorts', were a number of wealthy merchants. Refugees from the decadent 'Middle Kingdom' of the last Manchu emperors, they had recently acquired a new sense of national pride thanks to the revolutionary upheavals brought about by Sun Yat-sen and his disciples of the Kuomintang in the South Chinese Republic of Canton.

In the pulsing streets of Cholon Chinese youths could often be seen brandishing posters bearing inflammatory inscriptions: 'Confucius said . . . Lao-Tse said . . . Our ancestors said . . . So it must be false.' Older members of the community – wealthy merchants such as Dong Thuan or Dang Dai – may not have subscribed to such sacrilegious sentiments and slogans, but like the rest they were firmly committed to policies of change – in China and elsewhere.

In mid-May Monin, who was now acting as their legal adviser, was invited to a banquet in Cholon by Dong Thuan, Dang Dai, and other members of the local Kuomintang chapter. For André, as for Clara, it was a memorable experience. In a rich Chinese décor of red, green, and gold screens and partitions, the three European guests were graciously asked to take their places at a large banquet table. Clara found herself alone among this strange company of seated menfolk, some of whom, as the evening progressed, casually doffed the white shirts covering their hairless chests and bellies on which not a trace of perspiration was to be seen.

The banquet was the occasion for an official presentation to Paul Monin of a sizeable sum of money – voluntary donations contributed by Kuomintang supporters from all over Indochina. Finally toasts were proposed with tiny glasses filled with various kinds of translucent firewater. Whereupon, in a sudden deafening din of firecrackers exploding in the street below, they were informed by their laughing hosts that all three of them had been admitted to the Kuomintang. More Cantonese delicacies had to be consumed before Monin could deliver a speech of thanks, in which he praised the Russian and German governments for having recently renounced their extraterritorial privileges in China. After this, André Malraux stood up and in a rapid burst of speech assured those present: 'Together we are going to make a newspaper. Together we are going to fight. It would be false to think that our aims are totally the same. What draws us together, what unites us, are the enemies we have in common.'

With the money thus collected by their Chinese friends, Monin and Malraux were able to cable the advance payments due to Hachette's Messageries and to the Fayard publishing company for the right to reproduce articles, humorous squibs, and short stories from *Candide*, the satirical *Canard enchaîné*, and other Paris weeklies. Monin, however, was still not satisfied. He wanted to have their future daily, *L'Indochine*, appear in *quoc-ngu* (Annamite words written in a Latin script) as well as in a French edition – something that could project its influence into the most backward provinces of Cochin China, Annam, and even Tonking. Accordingly Malraux was dispatched to Hanoi, where Maurice Monguillot, the acting Governor-General, declined to receive the former 'temple-robber'. A secretarial assistant informed the young editor-to-be that there was no need for one more *quoc-ngu* newspaper in a country whose censors were already overworked.

Clara, who was simultaneously dispatched by boat to Singapore, was more successful in her mission. Though she too was closely shadowed by local police agents, she was able to meet the publishers of two English-language papers, who welcomed the idea of a fruitful exchange of copies and the appearance in French of translated news items culled from their pages. They had nothing to fear, Clara reassured them. *L'Indochine* was going to be a 'really serious' newspaper – unlike others she did not care to name.

10

Fishing in Troubled Waters

Monin and Malraux had decided to launch their new daily in mid-June. The moment seemed propitious. In early May Governor Maurice Cognacq had suffered a serious setback when a local shipper and freight handler named Rouelle had been elected mayor of Saigon as a result of municipal elections ordered by the Ministry of Colonies in Paris. This had put an end to three years of arbitrary rule exercised by a municipal commission dominated by two Cognacq cronies. With *L'Indochine* spearheading the offensive, there was a good chance that reports of Governor Cognacq's misdeeds would at last get back to Paris and be taken seriously by leaders of Edouard Herriot's left-wing coalition.

As the critical launching date approached, the tempo of activity grew increasingly feverish. Monin, Malraux, and Clara spent more and more time at the printer's workshop, which was run by a half-French, half-Annamite named Louis Vinh. It was a primitive establishment in which the type-setting, as Clara vividly recalled years later, had to be done manually.

> Yellow fingers grasp the lead type, fit them into place next to each other, then push them into frames, which are carried into the room next door where the press, with a broad fan-like movement, forces the sheets of paper down on them. In the first room the heat is hardly bearable, in the second the air whips our sweat-drenched bodies. As long as the paper lasted, we suffered colds and sore throats . . . we could hardly touch the paper, even lightly, without marking it with the moisture from our hands. The cage-like den in which the type setting was done was lit by a ceiling skylight, and there was no fan to refresh us.

The first trial number of *L'Indochine*, advertised on its front page as being a 'Daily Newspaper for a Franco-Annamite Rapprochement', was published on Wednesday, June 17, 1925. It created a sensation. Though limited to six pages – two less than the front-running *L'Impartial* – it was far more impressive than the four-page newssheets that had been allowed to subsist by the local administration to sustain the illusion that the press in

Cochin China was free. It was printed on better paper, and an entire page – the last – was reserved for a well laid-out spread of photographic illustrations. The inside pages contained a lively 'review of the local press', a so far 'unpublished' translation of a short story by Leo Tolstoy, and an intelligent review of recent books by two popular novelists, written by a noted Paris critic. Thanks to Malraux's diligent spadework in Paris, *L'Indochine*, in terms of literary quality, had at a single bound outstripped all its Saigon rivals.

The most sensational item in this trial number was a front-page interview which Paul Painlevé had granted to the newspaper's Paris correspondent. At the time the interview was given, almost two months before, Painlevé, a famous mathematician and former cabinet minister, held the post of speaker of France's lower house, the Chamber of Deputies. But in the interim, thanks to a cabinet reshuffle, he had replaced Edouard Herriot, the Radical Socialist mayor of Lyons, as prime minister. It was thus the head of the current French government, no less, who had deigned to offer the fledgling newspaper some wise words of encouragement.

L'Indochine's Paris correspondent had focused his first questions on the thorny issue of Annamite culture and French educational opportunities. While many primary schools had been set up (often run by Catholic or other missionary groups) for the colony's 20 million Vietnamese, the French authorities had seen fit to establish exactly six *lycées* capable of dispensing an advanced level of secondary education, and of these six no fewer than three were reserved exclusively for young European boys and girls. Nor was this all. Although 100,000 Vietnamese 'volunteers' had been conscripted and shipped to France to work in factories or to fight in the trenches during the 1914–18 war, the colonial authorities had shown themselves reluctant to grant the Annamite visas to continue their studies in metropolitan France. Experience had shown that it was in Paris, once the home of hotheads like Gracchus Babeuf and Karl Marx's contemporary, Joseph Proudhon, that young Annamite were infected by the revolutionary 'virus' – not in Saigon, where subversive books could be seized, where the Annamite press was censored and French-language newspapers bullied, intimidated, and, if necessary, suppressed.

Paul Painlevé was probably only dimly aware of the crippling discriminations imposed on the Annamites, in effect captives deprived of basic rights in their own country. But as a former professor and a member of an avowedly left-wing coalition, he naturally favoured improved educational facilities for them, no less than for French boys and girls. 'Common instruction, common education,' he roundly declared, 'are the best and most complete means of assimilation between diverse races. There is no entente, no accord without an interpenetration of minds . . . Access to our teaching system at all levels must be accessible to the Annamites.' This first, unambiguous affirmation was immediately followed by a second: 'The French and native press must be free to express itself.'

In a central 'box' published on the first page of *l'Indochine*, Malraux and Monin outlined their 'programme' in several trenchant sentences: '*L'Indochine* is a free newspaper open to all and without any links to banks or commercial groups. As a matter of principle it will respect the temperament of its contributors . . . The polemicists will write with acerbity, the moderates with moderation.'

Any doubts as to which of these two categories André Malraux belonged were dispelled with the publication the next day (Thursday, June 18th) of the second number of *L'Indochine*. The main item on the front page, filling two left-hand columns, was a 'first letter' addressed by a certain Jacques Tournebroche (Jim Turnspit) to his 'good master' and former mentor, Jérôme Coignard – the name Anatole France had given to the learned as well as epicurean abbé of his entertaining novel, *La Rotisserie de la Reine Pédauque*. In this 'letter', Jacques Tournebroche, a kind of much-travelled Candide figure, described a visit he had made to an exotic land ruled by a Governor named Je Menotte ('I Handcuff'). To Saigon readers it was instantly clear that this Governor was none other than Maurice Cognacq, and that what the not so naive author-traveller Tournebroche Malraux was lampooning was the system of authoritarian rule Cognacq had imposed on the native subjects of Cochin China with the help of two dreaded associates – a sadistic colonial official named Darles, and André Arnoux, head of the omnipresent Sûreté (security police).

Towards the end Malraux discarded Jacques Tournebroche's gently chiding tone and gave full vent to his indignation: 'And if you think that the Annamites we have educated have the right only to keep quiet, what wasp was it that stung you into shouting it from the rooftops?' This was a pointed reference to Governor I Handcuff's shameless justification of 'native stupidity'. One day, during an argument with the Annamite editor of a dissident weekly, Cognacq had cut him short with these blunt words: 'If you want to manufacture intellectuals, go to Moscow. You would do well to realize that the seeds you want to sow in this country will never sprout . . . that everywhere you will find Dr Cognacq waiting for you.'

This subtle exercise in *lèse*-governership was a mere beginning. No less caustic was another item in which one of the French administration's 'captive' newspapers, the bi-weekly *Progrès annamite*, was witheringly dismissed in a few sharp sentences: 'The very great discretion of this honourable newssheet does not keep it from having five readers.' The first of them being Dr Cognacq, the obedient organ's chief 'paying pig', and the fourth Dr Lê-quang-Trinh, 'nicknamed the Doctor of Love by his aristocratic clientèle' for the good reason (not specifically mentioned) that he was an accredited inspector of local prostitutes and brothels.

The noisy intrusion of such an uninhibited newcomer into the stagnant backwaters of Saigon journalism was bound to arouse a storm. But it broke faster than Monin and Malraux had anticipated. On June 17th, the conservative *Courrier Saïgonnais* published a brief note acknowledging receipt of an advance copy of *L'Indochine*'s first trial number and wishing the newcomer 'long life and prosperity'. This snippet had been surreptitiously inserted into a corner of the front page by a Vietnamese member of the paper's staff, in the absence of the liberal editor-in-chief, Camille Devilar. Devilar had been recently bought out by a local magnate, Jean de La Pommeraye, president of the Saigon Chamber of Commerce, director of the subsidized Société des Grands Hôtels, and general manager of the Société des Distilleries de l'Indochine, which had established a monopoly on the local manufacture of various kinds of firewater. When the friendly 'welcome' extended to *L'Indochine* was brought to his horrified attention, the new owner exploded. The next morning the *Courrier Saïgonnais* published an indignant retraction. The newspaper wanted its readers to know that it had not changed its editorial policy, that it condemned M. Monin's 'deplorable anti-French enterprise', and that it rejected 'even a semblance of distant solidarity with fishers in troubled waters and fomentors of disorder'.

Amused by this embarrassed disclaimer, Monin and Malraux decided to take offence at this charge of being 'anti-French'. Two seconds were dispatched to the offices of the *Courrier Saïgonnais*. To combat the debilitating torpor induced by the humid heat, Monin and Malraux had taken up fencing, parrying and lunging at each other for a half-hour every day on the terrace rooftop of the lawyer's house. Monin had already crossed swords with his arch-enemy, Henry Chavigny de Lachevrotière, editor-in-chief of *L'Impartial*, and he must have known that the obese, myopic La Pommeraye would not dare to answer a challenge to a duel with rapiers. But a craven refusal would make first-class 'copy'. Which is exactly what happened. The seconds made three visits to his newspaper but were unable to meet the invisible M. de La Pommeraye. The *Courrier Saïgonnais*' 'increasingly anonymous management' was accordingly ridiculed in the next day's issue of *L'Indochine*.

By Saturday, June 20th, when the fourth number of *L'Indochine* appeared, the brash newcomer needed no further publicity. The paper this time featured a front-page 'Letter to M. de La Pommeraye', in which caricatural insult – a profile drawing emphasizing the magnate's bald pate, pince-nez, toothbrush moustache, tiny hump nose, and thick neck – was added to verbal injury. He was hailed as a 'philanthropist' whose education, alas, had been sadly neglected, since he had never learned the difference between a piaster and a franc (at this time one Indochinese piaster was worth about ten francs); the surest proof of this crass ignorance being a crooked deal in which he had arranged to buy cinema film in France at a price of 30 francs a metre and to sell it to the colonial administration in Saigon for 30 piasters a metre – a mere ten times what it had cost him!

This fourth number of *L'Indochine*, with a price tag of 10 centimes, was the first to be publicly sold, rather than distributed free of charge. After several hours of uncertainty, publishers, editors, and printers realized that they had passed the crucial test. There was no dearth of buyers.

These first exhilarating weeks of daily journalism were probably among the most intensely happy André Malraux had yet known. Already in Paris he had tended to judge people according to a criterion of pomposity, and nothing had annoyed him more about the Dadaist revolt against sacrosanct conventions than the sententious seriousness of purpose of André Breton and his followers. But in Saigon the grim seriousness of purpose exhibited by the well-entrenched nabobs of the established colonial order did not even have the saving grace of literary or artistic merit. Crass philistines to a man, the Maurice Cognacqs and Ernest Outreys, the La Pommerayes and Henry Chavignys were pompous nobodies whose absurd claims to 'superiority' over 'backward natives' could flourish only in a closed, semi-chloroformed, carefully policed society. As Maurice Monribot, editor-in-chief of the arch-conservative *L'Opinion*, had one day explained to a local editor, the Vietnamese did not have 'the right to insult France' (a euphemism for freedom of expression) because their ancestors had not fought and died on the barricades, like the freedom-loving Paris revolutionaries of 1830 – a gem of colonial 'thinking' which *L'Indochine* was happy to expose in its June 25th issue.

Years later, in reminiscing about these 'heroic' days in Saigon, a friend whom Clara Malraux had not seen in years recalled how uninhibited and saucy her husband André had seemed to him at this time. 'A guy brimful of humour, who didn't take himself seriously and still less the others – the gang of scoundrels who were plundering the country. My own father among them . . .'

On June 22nd, *L'Indochine* launched another attack, by exposing a property scandal engineered with the connivance of the former Municipal Commission, which was going to cost the city of Saigon enormous sums of money. Increasingly alarmed, Maurice Cognacq invited Malraux to call on him at his gubernatorial offices.

Malraux's reaction to this attempted intimidation was characteristically cheeky. In a second letter addressed to 'Mr I Handcuff', he thanked the Governor for the personal interest he had taken in him and for the 'grace' of operating methods that were 'full of grandeur'. Unfortunately, Mr I Handcuff had read too many adventure stories about galley-slave whippers and prison guards and this had affected his manners. 'You are great, but your hands are still a bit dirty.' Being great, however, he would never dream of 'having a newspaper boycotted that displeases you. That would be the gesture of a valet, and absolutely unworthy of a Governor.' And so on.

The next day (Friday, June 26th) Paul Monin opened up with the heavy artillery. In a two-column, front-page editorial entitled, 'Disorder, Illegality, Anarchy', he pointed his guns on 'the most evil functionary Cochin China has ever had' – a man (unnamed, but it was clearly Governor Cognacq) who with the help of a 'black gang' and of four servile institutions – the Chambers of Commerce and of Agriculture and the Municipal and Colonial Councils – had fastened his dictatorial grip on the province. There was, for example, the scandalous case of Bernard Labaste, 'a tiny bearded and voracious rat' who had clung to his position as president of the Chamber of Agriculture for seventeen months beyond the legal term, and who had managed to appropriate 130,000 of the 175,000 piasters that had been intended for distribution to French and native farmers in 1923. The editorial ended with this two-fisted question: 'How much longer will the Republic tolerate such a scandal, which suffices to demoralize the country?'

For Maurice Cognacq the warning was unmistakable. As an active member of the Radical Socialist Party, Paul Monin had influential friends in Paris who could make life very difficult for the Governor if fully informed of what was going on behind the scenes in 'his' bailiwick of Cochin China. Monin, and his impertinent 'joker', Malraux, had to be silenced.

Governor Cognacq's counter-offensive came not a moment too soon. For on July 6th Louis Gallois-Montbrun, the doyen of the Saigon bar who had so eloquently defended Louis Chevasson, accorded *L'Indochine* a frank interview, in which France's 'civilizing mission' in Indochina was scathingly exposed for what it had in fact become. At first few pioneers from metropolitan France could be persuaded to take any interest in the colony. But once the capital investments began to flow in, they were followed by unscrupulous 'sharks'. 'They have become more and more numerous, with ever longer teeth.'

On the very day these words were published, one of the most flagrantly successful of these 'sharks' opened up with a broadside against *L'Indochine*. In a long front-page article headlined, 'Denial by Mr Paul Painlevé', the readers of *L'Impartial* were informed that the French Prime Minister had known nothing of the 'activities of Monin and Malraux' and that he had 'never authorized them to use his name' for their journalistic purposes.

To Monin and Malraux it was glaringly apparent that Henry Chavigny de Lachevrotière was again indulging in mendacious mischief. The first number of *L'Indochine*, featuring the Painlevé interview, had appeared on Wednesday, June 17th. It was now Monday, July 6th. Since surface ship mail required at least three weeks to travel from Saigon to Marseilles, *L'Impartial*'s Paris correspondent could not possibly have shown the French Prime Minister a copy of this first issue. What he had shown a disconcerted Painlevé could only have been a garbled version of the interview, cabled to him by Chavigny.

The next day, July 7th, the editors of *L'Indochine* replied with a blunt front-page rebuttal, printed across all six columns:

After threatening our native readers with imprisonment, after resorting to the most shameless blackmail against our contributors by threatening reprisals against their families, after having tried by the most vile and cowardly means to prevent us from appearing, our good friends of the Government of Cochin China have just mounted a little campaign of defamation which, we must admit, surpasses in meanness everything they have so far achieved . . .

Unlike *L'Impartial*, we will not seek to employ dishonestly twisted telegrams. We will submit the text of his interview to Mr. Painlevé. AND WE BOLDLY ASSERT THAT WE WILL PUBLISH IN THIS VERY PLACE HIS APPROVAL AND RECOGNITION OF THIS TEXT.

The same front page of the July 7th number featured a short sharp blast, aimed at Chavigny de Lachevrotière, who had managed to sit out the 1914–18 war in Saigon. Signed by Paul Monin, it bore the challenging title: 'Traitors?'

'Yes,' it began, 'I have asked all the good Frenchmen, those who served in the war, not those who displayed their cowardice, which is to say desertion, like the filthy guttersnipe of *L'Impartial*, to ascertain on which side were the traitors.'

The verbal cannonade by this time had reached a new pitch of intensity, also enveloping Malraux in clouds of smoke and shrapnel. The Tuesday, July 7th issue of *L'Impartial* carried a front-page editorial, sarcastically entitled: 'Will Indochina become the prey of audacious adventurers?' The most brazen of these adventurers was, of course, Malraux, described as having 'one day disembarked here along with several accomplices who came here solely to steal part of the artistic treasures bequeathed to us by the ancient Khmer civilization, in order to resell them for fancy sums of cash to international antique dealers'.

In terms of vulgar mud-slinging this was about par for the course. Infinitely wittier was Malraux's answering 'First letter', addressed, in the next day's issue of *L'Indochine*, to 'MONSIEUR HENRY D'EN-AVANT-POUR-L'ARRIÉRE – Mr Henry of Forward-March-to-the-Rear. To Anglo-Saxon readers this ironic appellation recalls William Gilbert's famous lines about the Duke of Plaza Toro, who preferred to lead his regiment from behind because he found it less exciting. The French connotation dated from the recent war, when the satirical *Canard enchaîné* had hardly let a week go by without mocking the rear-line super-patriots who had tirelessly egged on the mud-splattered *poilus* of the trenches to new heights of heroism, while simultaneously clamouring for dire punishment to be meted out to all the *embusqués* (literally, 'those hiding in ambush') who had managed to dodge the draft. With mordant sarcasm Malraux undertook to list some of Lachevrotière's egregious virtues as a 'stern moralist and healthy journalist'. His article was peppered with barbed references to Lachevrotière's 'immaculate past', to his exploits as a police informer, to his modest beginnings as a semi-literate reporter employed by the newspaper, *L'Opinion*, before effecting a spectacular metamorphosis as the affluent editor-in-chief of the influential *L'Impartial*.

In the final paragraph the 'audacious adventurer and unsavoury journalist' (as Malraux described himself) flung down the gauntlet by resorting to calculated insult. 'I want to tell you that I regard you as a grotesque fellow and a coward. Any jury of honour will admit that one can fight [a duel] with a man whose conviction has been quashed. But there is not one that will admit that one can fight with somebody who has offered proof of cowardice in wartime.'

Malraux wanted everyone in Saigon to know that he was afraid of nothing and of nobody. It amused him to play the part of a 'fisher in troubled waters', a furious 'anti-patriot', a 'disturber of the peace', and even of a seemingly hot-headed d'Artagnan. For when Dr Lê-quang-Trinh joined the baying bloodhounds of the pro-administration press by righteously asserting that his *Progrès annamite* numbered no 'convicted common criminal, no thief of the bas-reliefs of Angkor' among the members of its staff, Malraux marched over to his editorial office and treated the local inspector of prostitutes and brothels to a serious tongue-lashing.

Articles ridiculing Chavigny were now featured almost daily in *L'Indochine*. With his customary heavy-handedness Chavigny had let it be known that he had no intention, as a gentleman, of crossing swords with an uncouth ruffian who was also a burglar. This was a *faux-pas* his light-footed adversary was quick to exploit. He, André Malraux, was quite happy to be regarded as a mere commoner, adding: 'I make no distinction between a black, a gentleman, a yellow-skin, a commoner,' etc.

It would be a mistake to conclude that the almost boyish glee Malraux derived from this polemical mud-slinging was simply a manifestation of impish insolence. For underlying the sarcasm was a deep sense of outrage over the crimes that were daily being committed, combined with a feeling of compassion for the sufferings of the downtrodden peasants of the provinces of Cochin China.

An opportunity for expressing this compassion now presented itself with the revelation of a new scandal. In early May Governor Cognacq had undertaken an inspection tour of the western and south-western provinces of Cochin China, including the fertile rice-growing regions of Baclieu and Camau. Some of the most productive rice paddies were temporary grants or 'concessions' that had been offered years before to Vietnamese peasants, encouraged to carve new plots of cultivable land from the tiger-infested jungle on the understanding that they would eventually be allowed to buy the ground they had laboured hard to adapt and develop. The Governor and the equally venal members of his entourage had immediately glimpsed the opportunity of pulling off a lucrative deal by ordering some of these concessions to be put up for sale at a public auction, but under conditions that would make it impossible for poor peasants to acquire a solid right to the lands they had been working.

On July 11th *L'Indochine* opened fire on this new conspiracy with a bluntly worded front-page article, in which Monin pointed out that the tables had been deliberately tilted to favour the richest landowners of Cochin China or a speculative consortium, able to buy up thousands of hectares at the ridiculously undervalued price of 10 piasters per hectare, which could later be resold for ten or twenty times the purchase price. The predictable outcome was going to be the callous eviction of hundreds of hard-working Annamite peasants and their families who would be reduced overnight to a state of abject poverty.

Monin's announced intention of bringing the Baclieu–Camau land-grab scheme to the attention of the interim Governor-General, Maurice Monguillot, soon due to visit Saigon, brought tempers in the Cognacq–Chavigny camp to a new boil. Rumours, filtering out from the Governor's offices, indicated that Monin and Malraux were going to be assaulted by hired 'thugs' during one of their evening strolls through the streets of Saigon.

The two editors responded to this new threat by boldly proclaiming their determination to continue these unconventional evening strolls, 'alone and without arms. If we are struck' – by lead-filled canes, as rumour had it – 'the public will judge for itself. But,' the defiant text confidently predicted, 'since the aggressors have already been paid, there is every reason to believe that they will do nothing.'

One week later, after the publication of more protesting letters from about-to-be-despoiled peasants, which no other Saigon newspaper had dared to publish, Malraux personally joined the fray. What was novel about this third 'letter to Mr Henry Chavigny of Forward-March-to-the-Rear', now accorded a new title as Professeur de Délicatesse, were not the now familiar barbs aimed at Chavigny's 'aristocratic' pretensions and 'nobility' of character; it was the tone of compassion – worthy of a Dickens, a Victor Hugo, an Emile Zola – used by Malraux to describe the peasants who were about to be dispossessed:

They were poor. Bit by bit, they turned the bush into fertile land. I will speak to you neither of the heat, nor of the fever . . . I will ask you simply to look at their faces. All the suffering of the Annamite farmer is there imprinted, and the slow labours of their fathers have marked them with deep creases, which inspire pity . . .

You and your good friends, who covet their lands, should make no mistake about it. It is all their toil, all their sufferings that you see in the magnificent rice.

You will say to them: 'French law has foreseen everything. Thus you will not suffer from this dispossession, should it take place. Your work will be evaluated by an expert, and you will receive its full value.'

But before that happens, they will have to start a lawsuit with the Council of Contentions and then have recourse to the Conseil d'Etat. Before the end of the legal proceedings they will be dead. And France, alas too distant, will cast over their tombs its great, sad shadow.

Thus the article-editorial that had begun as another exercise in sarcasm ended as a kind of dirge. Probably without noticing it, André Malraux had moved from irony to elegy, thus offering readers of *L'Indochine* a foretaste of the elegiac eloquence which later was to mark so many of his passionate speeches and funeral orations.

Nothing could have revealed more dramatically the bitterness felt by many Vietnamese over this new case of colonial skulduggery than the violent reaction of Hin, the stocky mountaineer from the highlands of Annam. One day, in Monin's living room, Hin got up and, standing very still on his two short legs, announced his intention of killing Maurice Cognacq during the military parade planned for the forthcoming visit to Saigon of the interim Governor-General, Monguillot.

There was a long moment of stunned silence, finally broken by the newspaper's publisher, Dejean de la Batie, who being himself half-Annamite, found it easier to reason with the grimly determined Hin. 'I don't see how you're going to pull it off.'

A long altercation followed, during which Monin, Malraux, and Hin's Vietnamese colleagues vainly sought to persuade him that trying to shoot Cognacq while masquerading as a press photographer during the ceremonial parade would only make things worse, unleashing an even more ruthless repression of the country's 'native' population.

Hin, however, remained inflexible. The dark shock of hair rising from the middle of the bronzed scalp made him look like an aggrieved cock. 'The important thing is to focus attention on us. If we do nothing, nothing will change.'

'Your gesture,' Monin reminded Hin, 'would assure the triumph of all the Darles of Cochin China.' After which he added the *coup de grâce*: 'You have no organization behind you, capable of exploiting the disorder and carrying on the struggle.'

'An organization! An organization!' spluttered Hin, glaring wildly around him like a cornered bull. 'To hell with it! To hell with it! To hell with it!'

As he stormed out of the room, he paused by the door and glowered at the other members of the team. To Clara his defiant glare needed no spoken words of explanation: 'We will free ourselves from you without your help.'

At that moment the telephone rang. Monin walked over to the one-legged table in the corner and lifted the receiver.

'There won't be a military parade,' he announced after exchanging a few words with his caller. 'Monguillot has changed his plans and is cutting short his stay in Saigon.'

Hin had gone to a lot of trouble for nothing to obtain a press photographer's pass. He had also provided Malraux with a first-hand insight into the mental make-up of the determined revolutionary, more dramatic in its intense immediacy than anything he had so far read in Dostoevsky.

Shortly after Monguillot's departure from Saigon, Monin, Malraux, and Dejean undertook a quick tour of the rich rice-producing areas of Camau. The trip might have ended in disaster but for the farsighted concentration of the driver, who slowed down and slammed on the brakes just in time. Across a level stretch of a road permitting a speed of 80 km an hour a taut rope had been stretched, tied solidly enough to overturn a fast-moving automobile. This was obviously the work of one of André Arnoux's Sûreté agents, if not of Governor Cognacq's sinister adviser, the former torturer, Darles.

Not long after their arrival in the Camau area they were surprised by the unexpected appearance of Cognacq's henchman, Eutrope. The Governor's Director of Political Affairs had been hastily dispatched to the scene to inform the desperate peasants that the planned auction had been called off and that they could keep the lands they had worked so hard to develop.

Monin broke the good news in the July 28th number of *L'Indochine* with a lead article headlined, 'First Victory in Camau!'. The next day Malraux rubbed more salt into the frustrated Governor's wounds by publishing another humiliating letter, this time addressed (in a most paternal tone) from that worldly wise *abbé*, Jérôme Coignard, to Lieutenant-General Cognacq, who was advised to act with greater prudence in the future.

There was good reason to exult. In six weeks Monin and Malraux had made *L'Indochine* the most controversial newspaper in southern Indochina. Despite harassment in the provinces and skulduggery in postal centres, where copies of the newspaper kept mysteriously disappearing, subscriptions as well as newsstand and individual vendor sales had never ceased to rise.

Next came the electrifying news that a prominent French socialist had been picked by the Painlevé government in Paris to replace the overly conservative Martial Merlin. It had taken a full year for the electoral victory of the coalition of left-wing parties to effect changes in the field of colonial policy; but with the appointment of an eminent liberal, Alexandre Varenne, to the post of Governor-General of Indochina, it did look as though the days of Maurice Cognacq's corrupt regime were numbered. With a favourable wind now blowing out of Paris, the skippers of *L'Indochine* had no reason to trim their sails or alter course. But, as Monin and Malraux were shortly to discover, their stormy voyage had only just begun.

11

Thunder Out of China

It is always dangerous to underestimate one's enemies, particularly when they are mediocrities. This was certainly the case of Maurice Cognacq, a graduate of the Faculty of Medicine of Hanoi's so-called 'university' whom an ill-advised French Minister of Colonies had appointed Lieutenant-Governor of Cochin China in 1922. It was even more the case with his mouthpiece and lackey, Henry Chavigny de Lachevrotière. Chavigny, as Malraux and Monin now invariably called him, divesting him of his aristocratic 'goat-tail' (*chèvre* in French means 'goat'), may have been clumsy and ham-handed; he may have been an arrant coward, an unfaithful husband, a heartless lecher, an unscrupulous blackmailer, a boot-licking *arriviste*, but he had the tenacity of a wire-haired terrier. Unable to match André Malraux's imaginative irony and sarcastic wit, he applied all his energy to an assault like a battering-ram, aimed at discrediting *L'Indochine* as an 'instrument of Bolshevism'.

This frontal assault was launched in the July 11th number of *L'Impartial* with a front-page editorial headlined: 'The Bolshevist Danger Threatens Us'. After praising Ernest Outrey, Cochin China's one and only deputy in Paris, for the 'great perspicacity' he had shown in denouncing the 'communist peril in the colonies', Chavigny raised his editorial trumpet and sounded the alarm: 'People of Indochina! The danger is real! The danger is imminent!'

Three recent developments in particular had helped to reinforce the widespread feeling that France and its colonial empire were threatened by a worldwide 'Bolshevist' conspiracy. The first was the 'war of liberation' that the Berber chieftain, Abd-el-Krim, had launched in the Rif mountains, first against the colonizers of Spanish Morocco, then against the French. In reality, this revolt was a strictly Muslim and tribal insurrection, comparable to Abd-el-Kader's fierce resistance to the French occupation of Algeria in the 1830s and 1840s.

The second development encouraging this particular mythology was the growing sympathy felt by Annamite intellectuals for Gandhi's nationalist movement in India. Although there was not a shred of evidence to suggest that Gandhi had ever been a communist – unless being a fervent admirer of Tolstoy was enough to make one a 'Red' – the Mahatma's bold opposition to continued British rule was enough to brand him as a dangerous subversive in the eyes of colonial diehards like Henry Chavigny or of sycophantic Vietnamese like Dr Lê-quang-Trinh.

The third and most significant international development was the growing unrest in China. Here the prima facie evidence of Soviet involvement was readily available. Soviet weapons were being smuggled across the Siberian border to warlords in Manchuria and northern China and were being shipped in even greater quantities to Canton, in the south. Russian officers had set up a military academy at Whampoa and were training a new army for the Republic of Southern China. Sun Yat-sen, who had interrupted the First National Congress of the Kuomintang in January 1924 in order to pay homage to Lenin – 'the saint and martyr of the revolution' – had entered into negotiations with Mikhail Borodin, a member of the Communist International's Executive Committee and the Comintern's chief agent in the Far East.

Geographic proximity, the existence of thriving Chinese communities in seaports like Haiphong and Saigon, and the fact that many educated Annamites could read and write Mandarin Chinese gave the dramatic events occurring within the Celestial Kingdom, to the north, enormous resonance throughout Indochina. On May 20, 1925 militant Chinese students, demanding an end to 'European imperialism' and foreign concessions, clashed with British police forces and a dozen of them had been shot dead. This provoked a wave of strikes and angry demonstrations. British and American citizens had to be hastily evacuated from inland China, while the British, US, Japanese, and French governments dispatched warships and marine infantry units to Shanghai and Canton. By June 17th, when Monin and Malraux brought out their first number of L'Indochine, the mainland strikes had spread to Hong Kong, while in Canton the demonstrations had degenerated into a chaotic tripartite conflict fought out between hastily armed workers and students, the remnants of a military rabble commanded by a Yunan warlord, and European forces entrenched inside the 'extraterritorial' compound of Shameen.

The reaction to these tumultuous events of Chavigny's L'Impartial was to play up their xenophobic, anti-Western, and, wherever possible, Bolshevik-fomented character. Quite different was that of Paul Monin who, though he had never been to China, had spent many hours discussing the Chinese situation with Kuomintang friends like Dong Thuan and Dang Dai. In the third issue of L'Indochine (published on June 19th) Monin had boldly expounded his 'heretical' views in the first of two articles. The British, he argued, had only themselves to blame for the wave of violent xenophobia that was now sweeping China, since they, above all, had been intent on maintaining the foreign concessions in Shanghai and Canton. It was a serious error to regard the present turmoil as essentially the work of Bolshevik agitators, for the Chinese masses knew next to nothing of Marxism and were motivated by a sense of nationalistic exasperation against foreign bankers and others who were bent on extracting as much money as they could without regard to the welfare of the Chinese people. The anti-Chinese sentiments now being fanned in metropolitan France and in Indochina were the result of misinformation supplied by Far Eastern *affairistes*, 'of whom M. Outrey is the hoarse spokesman'.

It was a full month before the French conservatives of Cochin China undertook to 'refute' Monin's lucid appraisal. The offensive was launched on July 15th by the 'hoarse-voiced' Ernest Outrey with a front page article published in Chavigny's *L'Impartial*. Once again the familiar colonialist clichés – the Rif rebellion, the turmoil in Shanghai, recent upheavals in Bengal – the 'red centre of India' – were trotted out as proofs that the Bolshevists were everywhere at work, like termites, gnawing away at the foundations of the imperial order.

Two days later Chavigny played his ace card, with a two-column diatribe, brazenly headlined: 'Paul Monin sold out to the Chinese Bolshevists.' The documents? The proofs, to support this accusation? The editor-in-chief of *L'Impartial* had all that was needed: the 'authentic minutes' of a Kuomintang meeting, attended by Monin, at which an orator (unnamed) had declared that 'the Chinese and the Annamites must prepare themselves to incite the yellow race to rise up against the imperialists and particularly against France'.

From then on, in daily front-page diatribes, printed under alarmist headlines – 'Bolshevism in Indochina: Paul Monin's Influence Trafficking'; 'Paul Monin's Usual Dirty Tricks'; 'The Bolshevik Movement: The Organization of the Class Struggle', etc – Chavigny kept up a drumbeat of vituperation, aimed at 'proving' that Monin was a paid agent of the Kuomintang and *L'Indochine* a propaganda organ bent on fomenting a revolutionary insurrection aimed at driving out the French and turning the country over to the Chinese Bolshevists.

Monin punched back fiercely, accusing Outrey of having sold out to the British, and Maurice Cognacq of having done everything he could to arouse the hatred of mistreated Annamites against the French, and the hatred of the misled French against the Chinese. Malraux, continuing his biting letters to 'M. Henry of Forward-March-to-the-Rear', ridiculed his 'documentary proofs', pointing out that the decision to launch *L'Indochine* had been made the previous January, long before the May banquet in Cholon.

This furious war of words reached a crescendo on August 11th, when *L'Indochine* published one more Malraux letter, addressed to the 'very poor, very noble, very loyal gentleman, Henry Chavigny of Forward-March-to-the-Rear, Former informer of the Sûreté'. The letter this time took the form of a solemn oration delivered by an imaginary 'President of Universal Moralists' on the occasion of the award of a prize for exemplary merit to

Chavigny. However, the butt of this letter was not simply *L'Impartial*'s despicable editor; it was also the inquisitorial Sûreté, whose unnamed boss, André Arnoux, was described towards the end of the 'encomium' as handing out 'bulging bags full of silver coins'.

That they were *personae non gratae* with the head of the Sûreté André Malraux and Clara had long known. They could not take a casual walk in Saigon without immediately being 'tailed'. All this, however, was routine – the standard operating procedure of a police state. More troubling was the suspicion that Arnoux had managed to infiltrate their small, closely knit team with the connivance of an informer.

By early August it had become clear to Maurice Cognacq and his cronies that they were involved in a fight for survival. If *L'Indochine*, now read by everybody, was allowed to continue its muck-raking assaults the new Governor-General, Alexandre Varenne, would almost certainly have Cognacq dismissed.

Monin and Malraux had planned an ambitious series of articles devoted to the crucially important question of France's colonizing effort, with a frank discussion of 'its virtues and defects, and the aspirations it has engendered'. The first article in the series, written by Malraux himself, appeared in the August 14th issue of *L'Indochine* under the curiously Barrèsian title of 'Sélection d'énergies'. It set the tone for what could and should have become a debate on the very highest level. Indeed, in its measured eloquence and historical sweep, it echoed Gibbon or Chateaubriand: a remarkable achievement for a young Frenchman who had never finished his *lycée* studies or attended a university. For example:

> Every power that feels within itself a will to expansion and that pent-up violence that distinguishes colonizing peoples fixes as its first objective the search for strength. Those whom Rome dispatched to the distant marches of the Empire, those whom Tai Tsong sent to the farthest reaches of the Gobi desert, those whom our kings sent to Louisiana were intent above all on ascertaining, among the scattered forces that opposed them, the qualities of resistance, of vigour, of energy that were there concealed, in order to bind them to their cause while recognizing, without uncertainty or contestations, their rights as masters. Never did a great king, never did a great statesman forget to discern this character of independence and loyalty, so easily revolted, which is the hallmark of the strong.
>
> At present our policy in Annam and Cochin China is quite simple: it states that Annamites have no reason to come to France, and it immediately stirs up, *against us*, a coalition of the finest characters and of the most tenacious energies. The political stupidities of petty clans or moneyed interests seem to be applying themselves with a rare perseverance to destroy what we have been able to achieve and to arouse in this

ancient land – sown with great memories – the slumbering echoes of more than six hundred revolts.

No matter what cultured Annamites here may say, the Chinese domination of Annam, for all the reservations that must be made, was carried out over centuries of history under the banner-sign of blood. Well do I recall the ancient streets of Florence, near the Arno; on each tawny or sunset-gilded palace is an inscription recalling a murder committed by some great family, in order to secure the domination of the city. The Inferno of the Divine Comedy is carved in full on the walls of those princely residences, but today the glory of the city sheds its mantle over the tumult of stilled struggles. Annam, when one travels through it from the estuaries of the Red River to the Mekong delta, evokes the same impression. The name of each illustrious town is that of a revolt; the most stirring of its plains bear the names of battles. The tomb of Lê-Loi is in ruins, but the songs that extol the sombre grandeur of its life of courage and adventures still hover on the lips of every woman and live on in the memory of every fisherman. At Quang-Ngai, at Thanh-Hoa, at Vinh, there are reserves of energy of which, in the Far East, we have a crying need and which are waiting to see realized the entente we had promised.

The main target of this editorial was an obtuse policy of geographical constriction that was forcing desperate Vietnamese to embark clandestinely on ships bound for foreign countries. The short-sighted folly of not allowing the Annamites to go to France could only precipitate the catastrophe its advocates were trying to avert: the wholesale disaffection of the country's native elite, with the fatal consequences this was certain to entail.

Five thousand copies of this August 14th issue had been rolled off the presses when, that evening, Louis Vinh informed Monin and Dejean that his typesetters had gone on strike and that the newspaper would not be appearing the following Monday. In reality, the 'strike' had been engineered by Governor Cognacq's henchmen and Sûreté agents, who had warned the typesetters and Louis Vinh himself that if they continued to bring out *L'Indochine* there would be a total cessation of further orders from the administration for the printing of official circulars, bulletins, leaflets, posters, reports, etc. Worse still, the Vietnamese typesetters and press-operators would be subjected to intensive police investigation and possibly incarcerated for their 'criminal' participation in 'subversive' activities. The *coup de grâce* was delivered by Chavigny, who with characteristic magnanimity – not for nothing was he a de Lachevrotière! – volunteered to 'rescue' Louis Vinh from bankruptcy by offering him and his workers steady employment with the incomparably more respectable *L'Impartial*.

Stunned though they were by this foul blow, neither Monin nor Malraux was in a mood to give up. Indeed, André for a while was in such a state of rage that he spewed forth extravagant proposals, more inspired by Alexandre Dumas novels than by a sober assessment of the possible. They must form a commando team of disguised and hooded 'robbers' and stage raids on other printing workshops to obtain the machinery they needed! Better still, they should boldly seize the presses of *L'Impartial*, whose 'liberated' Vietnamese typesetters would joyously be put to work printing *L'Indochine*!

With Alexandre Varenne due to arrive in a few weeks' time, it was essential that *L'Indochine* be somehow revived, so that the new, open-minded Governor-General could be informed of what was going on in Cochin China. But being dependent on administrative licences and contracts, not a single Saigon workshop dared take on the printing of *L'Indochine*. Annamite sympathizers employed in the bigger workshops smuggled out discarded pieces of machinery and spare parts, and with their help a makeshift printing press was screwed and bolted together under the verandah of Monin's house.

The assembling of this ramshackle machine was a miracle of mechanical ingenuity, but it still did not solve the problem. A printing press without sizeable quantities of type is useless. Finally it was decided that André and Clara would have to make a quick trip to Hong Kong, to see what they could pick up in that international market-place.

Having already been 'shadowed' during her three-day trip to Singapore, Clara had no reason to suppose that they would be much luckier in Hong Kong. All doubts on this score were dispelled on board the ship that was taking André and Clara there. An English doctor, who was returning from an 'absolutely ripping' tiger-hunt in the jungles of central Indochina, casually informed Clara that 'the reddest Bolshevik of all Annam' happened to be on board. The captain had radioed a warning message to the British authorities in Hong Kong.

The next morning, when the time came to disembark, they waved goodbye to the friendly tiger-hunter, whose Chinese 'boy' had failed to show up. Like the Crown Colony's dockworkers, bank clerks, and administrative employees, he too was participating in the anti-British general strike. To their surprise André and Clara found dockside coolies who were willing to carry their light suitcases to the hotel. A few Chinese members of the staff were still prepared to offer friendly smiles, but to make it clear that they too were 'on strike', André's and Clara's mosquito-netted beds were left unmade the next morning. In many Chinese shops potbellied owners sullenly refused to get up when they sauntered in. The sight of red-faced Britons in sweat-drenched shirts and shorts reduced to lugging home large chunks of meat from the butcher's shop was frankly comic.

The day after their arrival André and Clara chanced upon a small advertisement placed in a local newspaper by Jesuit fathers who had just received new characters for their printing press and who were ready to sell the old type. Their monastery was situated half way up the mountain. It would have been a hot, hard climb had Clara and André not come upon a rickshaw, which puffing coolies pulled and pushed up the steep roadway. Inside the walled enclosure a deal was quickly concluded. The delighted

Jesuits even undertook to have the crates delivered directly to the ship for the return voyage to Saigon. The rest of the type, which was not yet ready, would be shipped after their departure by normal freight.

The deal with the Jesuits was concluded so rapidly that André and Clara had time to make a quick trip to the Portuguese island of Macao. However, an excursion to the Chinese suburb of Kowloon, which would have permitted Malraux to set foot on mainland China, was called off at the last moment by an exhausted Clara.

At the hotel André and Clara soon noticed the discreet presence of the Chinese boy, usually dressed in black pyjama trousers, who each morning had been assigned to 'tail' them. Clara became so friendly with several of them that they ended up carrying her parcels. Like the coolies and the rickshaw-pullers, the obliging 'boys' of His Majesty's Intelligence Service were too dependent on this kind of employment to be able to forgo a week or two of tips and wages.

Curiously, it does not seem to have occurred to either André or Clara that this solicitous surveillance might spell trouble for the future. On the Hong Kong wharf they watched happily as a crane lifted half a dozen type-filled crates into the ship's hold. But when, a day or two later, they were lifted up by another crane and deposited on the dock at Saigon, several fussy French customs inspectors informed them that because the invoices had not been properly filled out and signed prior to loading, the crates would have to be regarded as 'contraband' and impounded.

At this point it looked as though they had lost the battle once and for all. But one week later a miracle occurred with the providential arrival of the two final crates of type, shipped from Hong Kong by ordinary freight. A strike had broken out among workers employed at the Naval Harbour's arsenal and the customs inspectors at Saigon's commercial port may have felt sympathetic to the cause of the underpaid – a cause Paul Monin was always ready to defend. The customs officers ignored the instructions telephoned by the commissioner of the port police, and let Monin and Malraux carry off the correctly invoiced goods.

There remained one final obstacle. The lead type bought from the Jesuits had been made for the English language. The French accents were missing. But here again they were saved by Vietnamese sympathizers working for officially approved newspapers. Malraux never forgot the dramatic moment when the first of these volunteer 'crooks' pulled from his pocket a bulging handkerchief the ends of which had been tied into two knots, resembling rabbit ears, and spilled out the accented type on to the table. If caught, he risked being tried and harshly sentenced for theft. 'If I am condemned,' he explained with touching matter-of-factness, 'tell people in Europe that this is what we did. Just so that they will know what's going on here.'

Not until early November was their resurrected newspaper ready to appear. It was renamed *L'Indochine enchaînée* – a title inspired by the satirical *Canard enchaîné*, a title aptly fitting their present, semi-gagged condition.

Forced by mechanical necessity and a sadly shrunken staff to reduce the eight-page format and limit publication to two numbers per week, *L'Indo-chine enchaînée* was a sickly skeleton compared to its robust predecessor. The good quality paper had to be replaced by gritty newsprint of a yellower hue, into which the French accents, being of different dimensions from the English-language type, punched holes – so that the surface of each page came to resemble (in Clara Malraux's words) 'the skin of a poorly fed woman'. The printing process became a painful ordeal because the makeshift press, which was installed in the basement, operated so unevenly that its clanking arms and levers caused the whole house to tremble.

It is a tribute to the stamina and the courageous tenacity of Paul Monin and André Malraux that they managed to bring out even a single issue, let alone the twenty-two that followed. They were handicapped by the departure of Eugène Dejean de la Batie, who agreed to resume his post as publisher for Nguyen-an-Ninh's weekly, *La Cloche fêlée*. No one could accuse Dejean of cowardly opportunism, but he had doubtless come to the conclusion that a bi-weekly publication, printed on shoddy, pockmarked paper was unlikely to impress the new Governor-General, Alexandre Varenne.

Dejean's misgivings were cruelly confirmed. During Varenne's two weeks in Saigon he was taken through a whirl of official ceremonies, bombarded with-deceitful compliments and flowery speeches, and kept in a dither of well-dined-and-wined entertainment – of the kind that clever politicans know so well how to organize for visiting strangers, presenting a 'Potyomkin village' of happy, prosperous, and contented subjects. Towards the end of his stay in Saigon he stunned Monin and Malraux by refusing to take a forthright stand on questions of fundamental principle – such as freedom of the press and rigged elections. Worse still, at a special meeting with the founder of the moderate Constitutionalist Party and some 600 leading Vietnamese from Saigon and the various provinces of Cochin China, the new Governor-General dumbfounded his expectant listeners by stating his hostility to any untrammelled freedom to publish newspapers in the native *quoc-ngu* language of Annam, on the specious grounds that Annamite journalists were 'as yet ill prepared to use it wisely'. 'If,' as Malraux pointed out in an article deploring the Governor-General's sad lapse into sophistry, 'freedom of the press is not granted to the Annamites, if censorship is maintained, one reform at least is essential: the elimination of prior authorization, the possibility for the Annamites to see their own ideas expressed by those they respect, rather than Mr Cognacq's ideas expressed by those they despise.'

So deep and widespread was the disappointment that when the time came for Varenne to move on to the 'imperial' capital at Hué, there was only one Annamite in the crowd of dignitaries gathered to see him off: Dr Lê-quang-Trinh, the obsequious inspector of Saigon's prostitutes and brothels.

The immediate present was bleak for those, like Monin and Malraux, who had fancied that Governor Cognacq's venal rule was about to end. In

September and October Cognacq and Chavigny had concocted a legal plot against Paul Monin on a bogus charge of bankruptcy and had tried to have him dismissed from the Colonial Council. The indomitable lawyer had fought off both attacks with his customary energy and talent. But now that Alexandre Varenne had come and gone, the conspirators felt free to make one final effort to silence the obstreperous trouble-maker.

One night, as he lay in bed beneath his mosquito netting, Paul Monin saw a shadowy figure approach. A hand began to draw back the netting. The other hand held an opened razor. Monin swung out his arm, then gave a violent kick that set the attacker off his balance. The would-be killer reached the paneless window in time and jumped into the garden below, managing to make a getaway without breaking any bones. The plotters had apparently intended to pass off the murder as an act of 'suicide', committed by a psychologically deranged Monin, reduced to despair by his impending 'bankruptcy'. The incident had an unexpected sequel eight years later when Malraux used a similar knife attack in the opening scene of *La Condition humaine*.

Reluctant though he was to admit defeat, Malraux soon realized that they were getting nowhere. Once again he and his wife were penniless, as unable to pay the bills at the Continental as they had once been at Manolis' hotel in Phnom Penh. And once again they were pariahs – this time as 'Bolshevist' revolutionaries and 'traitors' to the cause of France.

André and Clara, furthermore, had the distinct impression that they had overstayed their welcome – even with Paul Monin. The return of his wife, who had spent the summer and autumn months in France with their son and who was suffering painfully from phlebitis, did nothing to improve the situation. She was dismayed to see the ground floor of her house turned inside out to accommodate typewriters, files, and newspapers; the clanking monster in the basement was one more 'innovation' she would gladly have dispensed with.

The wild hopes for radical reforms which Monin and Malraux had done so much to encourage in the auspicious springtime of 1925 had since completely withered. The Vietnamese 'moderates' were now, among themselves, beginning to adopt the tougher vocabulary of revolt. Monin's and Malraux's failure was also a national French failure, one likely to confirm, according to the classic schema of self-fulfilling prophecies, the 'danger' (so essential to the alarmist rhetoric of the Outreys and the Chavignys) that Indochina might one day be 'Bolshevized'.

In late November a dispirited André said to Clara: 'Now there's only one solution left for me – to write.' Clara, who had long been convinced that this was her husband's real vocation, was in no mood to take issue with this sensible conclusion. But the question was – how to extricate themselves from the snake-pit of Saigon?

In the end it was the two wealthy Chinese compradores, Dong Thuan and Dang Dai, who came to the rescue by offering to pay their return voyage back to France. The number of eminent Frenchmen who had given interviews or had articles published in *L'Indochine* had led them to believe that André Malraux had enough contacts with influential Paris politicians and salon hostesses to be able to talk the new Minister of Colonies, André Hesse, into granting them permission to open a huge gambling hall – comparable to Shanghai's famous pleasure-dome, The Great Wide World – in the suburb of Cholon. Malraux did nothing to discourage this flattering confidence placed in his buttonholing talents.

When the time came to say farewell to Saigon and Indochina, Dong Thuan and Dang Dai were the only people who accompanied André Malraux and Clara to their liner. For someone who was hyper-sensitive to personal humiliation and who, as he once told his father, was not prepared to accept a setback, this second failure was a blistering defeat. But it is often in the fire of adversity that the strongest will is tempered. From his two escapades in the Far East André Malraux was bringing back a sackful of personal impressions and lived experiences: enough to fill four books, two of them destined to become novels of prime importance.

12

The Siren-Calls of the Orient

During the six busy months he had devoted to *L'Indochine* André Malraux had not forgotten that he was bound by a contract signed with a major publishing house in Paris. In early October 1925 he wrote a letter to Louis Brun, Bernard Grasset's managing editor, to say that the manuscript of the first promised book was almost finished. 'More than half,' he went on in the same confident tone, 'has been translated into Chinese and published in different periodicals and newspapers in Shanghai and Peking.'

In fact, André Malraux had not completed his manuscript. As for his extravagant claim that half of the text had already been translated into Chinese and published in a number of magazines and newspapers in Peking and Shanghai, this was simply a piece of fiction. How could it have been otherwise in a country now rent by revolutionary turmoil? But like the reference, in this same letter, to his 'current political role as head of the Young Annam Party', this was part of the 'image' of himself he was bent on projecting – as a recognized 'authority' on oriental matters and as a militant participant in the once-slumbering continent's turbulent awakening.

The idea of writing a book contrasting the legendary 'passivity' of the Oriental with the 'dynamism' of the Westerner was not a new one with Malraux. As far as can be judged from the diffuse manuscript material, he first began recording his random thoughts on contrasting oriental and Western attitudes to life, death, love, time, the soul, etc during his first four months in Saigon (July to October 1924), when he and Louis Chevasson were waiting for their second trial. The title he had first picked – *Conquêtes* ('Conquests') – suggests that his original intention was to concentrate on the complex, symbiotic relations existing between colonizers and their defeated subjects: more or less the theme that E. M. Forster later tackled in *A Passage to India*.

Malraux, however, soon abandoned this initial schema as too restrictive. It was the fascination exercised by Siamese Buddhist and Khmer art that had first lured him to the Far East, and he felt he had many novel things to say about deep-rooted differences of attitude in aesthetic matters. As a fervent admirer of Dostoevsky, he was naturally receptive to the theme of human humiliation – which loomed large in any discussion of colonial relationships. But as an equally fervent admirer of Nietzsche, he was obsessed by the notion of spiritual decadence – one which Oswald Spengler in Germany and Paul Valéry in France had applied to Europe's current condition.

The central question posed by Valéry, which became part of the intellectual *Zeitgeist* of the 1920s, was whether Europe was doomed by the very excess of its intellectual dynamism, spewing forth ideas that eventually degenerated into destructive ideologies. If such were the case, could it be that a dangerously frenetic, intellectually hyper-active Europe had much to learn from the age-old wisdom and spiritual serenity of the Orient?

One person who was convinced that Europe was spiritually sick was the Calcutta poet, Rabindranath Tagore, the first non-European to be awarded the Nobel Prize for Literature (in 1913) and who had been rapturously welcomed by a number of German university communities during a tour of Europe in 1921. Another person of the same persuasion was Tagore's friend, Hermann Keyserling, a cosmopolitan baron from Estonia who had set up a Platonic Academy (the so-called 'School of Wisdom') in post-war Darmstadt, and whose *Reisetagebuch eines Philosophen* (The Travel Diary of a Philosopher) had gone into a fourth edition by 1920.

Just how familiar Malraux was with the works of Spengler and Keyserling in 1925 is difficult to say. Keyserling's *Reisetagebuch* was not completely translated into French until 1929, and Spengler's *Untergang* had to wait for another two years. But we know from Clara's memoirs that she bought copies of both works during two trips she and André made to Berlin.

During the winter of 1924–5 the editors of a new Paris monthly, *Les Cahiers du mois*, decided to devote an entire issue to the topical questions of what, if anything, the 'perennial' wisdom of the East could contribute to the West. Of the more than forty articles and essays published in this special number, the longest and the most controversial was written by Henri Massis, with whom Malraux had taken issue three years before in an article devoted to André Gide. A militant Catholic who had teamed up with the arch-monarchist, Charles Maurras and the conservative historian, Jacques Bainville, to edit the fortnightly *Revue Universelle*, Massis in 1919 had helped to found a league of anti-Bolshevik intellectuals which had proudly advertised itself as the 'Party of Intelligence'. Not content to denounce the Red menace in Eastern Europe, Massis, who was not a French super-patriot for nothing, had denounced a Germano-Russian plot to subvert Europe's Latin heritage, long since undermined by Lutheran and other 'heresies'. Extending this analysis to include 'prophets of doom' like Spengler and 'fakir-like' *yoghis* like Tagore, Massis argued that a spiritually divided and decadent West was now confronted by an increasingly disoriented and spiritually unhinged East – a by no means stupid thesis and one Malraux undertook to explore in his new book. As a militant reactionary, however, Massis could not keep himself from ending his article with a blunt reiteration of the 'party line': the fear that

> pseudo-Oriental doctrines, enrolled in the service of the powers of disorder, will in the end serve only to revive the dissensions which, ever since the Reformation, have afflicted the spirit of Europe, and that *Asiatism*, like the *Germanism* of yore, will turn out simply to be the first message of barbarians. We must not wait until the storm thus announced has devastated civilization to denounce those who have made themselves the accomplices of that kind of Asiatism.

Having learned that Henri Massis was planning to develop his verbal assault on 'Asiatism' into a book called *Défense de l'Occident*, Malraux decided to scrap *Conquêtes* in favour of a new title, *La Tentation de l'Occident* (The Temptation of the West).

According to Clara, it was during their return voyage to France, in a 'comfortless second-class lounge, among chairs covered with false tapestry-work, where children hid under tables for the sole purpose, it would seem, of arousing the scolding irritation of the adults', that André Malraux wrote the first chapters of his *Tentation de l'Occident*.

They reached Paris towards the end of a wintry January (1926), and found lodgings in a *pension* on the Quai de Passy, near the elevated metro bridge spanning the Seine, with the Eiffel Tower visible to the left. To save money, they went every day to lunch in Grandmother Adrienne Lamy's uncarpeted apartment overlooking the railway yards of Montparnasse station.

There was, indeed, little room for fantasy or idle moments in their present impecunious condition. When Clara asked André if he was going to call on Marius Moutet, the influential Socialist deputy from Marseilles who was well known for his warm support of the Annamese of Indochina, he answered brusquely, 'I'm not crazy!' Forgotten overnight was Malraux's promise to do everything he could to persuade the French Minister of Colonies to allow Dong Thuan and Dang Dai to open a casino in Cholon. Forgotten too was his farewell editorial in *L'Indochine enchaînée*, in which he had promised to move heaven and earth to arouse French public opinion to the burning need for reforms in Indochina 'through speeches, meetings, newspapers, pamphlets'. In Paris the left-wing surge that had brought the Socialists and Radical Socialists to power in May 1924 had long since washed back from its high-water mark; the ebb tide of popularity increased steadily in momentum as the value of the franc kept dropping towards the unprecedented low of 50 francs to the dollar. With more and more Frenchmen calling for the return to power of the conservative Raymond Poincaré, Malraux knew that his personal efforts on behalf of the Vietnamese were foredoomed to failure.

At the Deux Magots café André presented Marcel Arland with a number of nearly finished 'letters' from his new book: letters written by a twenty-five-year-old Frenchman, cryptically named A. D., who was making a trip to the Far East, and by a slightly younger Chinaman named Ling-W.-Y., who was making his first trip to Europe. Malraux explained that he had composed these 'letters' in a great hurry and wished to make a number of revisions. However, given his precarious financial situation, his friend Marcel agreed to submit some of the finished material for prepublication to Jean Paulhan, who had succeeded the recently deceased Jacques Rivière as editor-in-chief of the *NRF*.

Given the haste with which it was put together, it is hardly surprising that *La Tentation de l'Occident* should have been a rather uneven work. The introductory section, written by Malraux's imaginary Frenchman on board the liner that is taking him to the Far East, was in effect a neo-Symbolistic tone-poem in which the author juggled with a kaleidoscopic succession of vibrant images evoking different aspects of a timeless Orient.

Malraux's original intention had been to construct a three-sided dialogue, in which the contrasting viewpoints of a Westerner visiting the Far East and a Chinaman visiting Europe were commented on by an Indian Hindu. For reasons of simplicity, the Indian 'commentator' was soon scrapped. Even so, the resulting 'dialogue' was patently unbalanced, at times reading more like an epistolary monologue (like Montesquieu's *Lettres persanes*) than the exchange of letters between a Frenchman and a Chinaman it was supposed to be. Twelve of the seventeen 'letters', including the first six, were written by Ling, and what they presented was a critique of the present state of Europe as viewed by a Chinaman who had visited Rome and Athens as well as Paris. Many of Ling's 'impressions' – the pomposity of Mussolini's Rome; the vulgarity of European brothels; the ugliness of French graveyards; the idea that civilization is a psychological rather than a social reality and that the further one seeks to penetrate the psychological rationale of one's actions, the more one comes up against the incomprehensible and the absurd – were sentiments any sensitive European could harbour without having seen the Far East.

A quarter of a century later, Wilbur Merrill Frohock, the first important American critic of André Malraux's work, pointed out that the author of *La Tentation de l'Occident* found himself 'in the predicament of a young and able composer whose head teems with more materials than he can use in a single piece of music'. None of the many themes proposed were properly developed, sounding at times like lapidary affirmations, which had to be accepted on trust. This is particularly true of the book's most important thesis: the post-Nietzschean idea that the death of God in the Western world was bound to result in the spiritual death of man, with all the psychic anguish this was certain to entail.

The book even ended on a gloomy note; Malraux suggested that a reliance on oriental values offered no ready-made solution, since China itself had become a gigantic 'Theatre of Anguish'. As he had a Shanghai mandarin explain to the visiting Frenchman, A. D.: 'China is shaking like a building in ruins, and the anguish comes neither from uncertainty nor from battles, but from the weight of the trembling roof. Confucianism has crumbled, the entire country will be destroyed.' This sentiment is echoed by Ling, who fears that out of this cultural débâcle – the Chinese having been 'despoiled of their culture, sickened by your own' – what is likely to emerge is not a triumphant and constructive new elite, but a wanton 'will to destruction'. A sombre prophecy dramatically fulfilled more than a quarter of a century later.

No less typically, the book's pessimistic conclusion was accompanied by a proclamation of defiance – not unlike that of William Ernest Henley in his famous poem, 'Invictus' – and a refusal to take the easy way out by embracing the Catholic faith – as Max Jacob had done, followed, more recently, by Jean Cocteau.

The exalted Barrèsian language and the occasional poetic nebulousness of the prose may have left many readers wondering just what Malraux's attitude was – other than one of bleak despair. But in an interview granted to the weekly *Nouvelles Littéraires* on August 31, 1926, a couple of weeks after the book's publication, he explained his attitude in forthright terms, assuming furthermore an almost oracular tone as a spokesman for his generation.

The entire 19th century, passionately linked to man, blossomed forth in a vehement affirmation of the pre-eminence of the Me. Well, this Man and this Me, erected on such ruins and which, whether we like it or not, dominate us still, do not interest us. Furthermore, we are determined to pay no heed to the summons of our weakness, which proposes a doctrine or a faith.

It has been said that no one can act without faith. I believe that the absence of conviction, like conviction itself, incites some men to passivity, and others to extreme action.

Having thus made it clear that, whatever happened, he himself intended to steer clear of these two extremes, Malraux concluded by declaring: 'The object of the search undertaken by the youth of the West is a new notion of Man. Can Asia perhaps offer us some teaching? I do not think so. One of the strongest laws of our mental make-up is that vanquished temptations are transformed into knowledge.'

But these words, which anticipated certain of Malraux's later writings, left unanswered the vital question: can knowledge, whether scientific or artistic, be a valid substitute for faith?

13

The 'Black Diamond' of the
Quai de l'Horloge

In viewing the life of an author it is always a mistake to suppose that everything was preordained and that genius was bound to triumph. In the spring of 1926 the twenty-four-year-old Malraux could not be absolutely sure of anything – least of all that he would soon become a famous novelist. Having previously made quite a bit of money publishing limited editions of elegantly illustrated books, he had every reason to return to an occupation with which he was thoroughly familiar.

One of the first things Malraux did on his return to Paris was to re-establish contact with his old Bondy friend, Louis Chevasson, and to propose that they found a rare-book publishing company of their own – without the help (or interference) of Simon Kra. The name chosen, A la Sphère, may have been partly inspired by a new travel book, *Rien que la terre* (Nothing but the Earth), which one of Grasset's best-selling authors, Paul Morand, had recently completed after a visit to the Orient. Their separate paths had actually crossed for a moment in Saigon, where Malraux had called on Morand, who was being treated for dysentery in the local hospital; and the first result of this chance encounter in Saigon was a de luxe edition of *Rien que la terre*, which André's friend, Demetrios Galanis, undertook to illustrate with fifteen copperplate engravings.

Malraux again demonstrated his expertise by persuading his influential admirer, François Mauriac, to let him bring out a luxurious edition of his little-known poems, *Orages* (Storms), which the Moravian-born artist, Otakar Coubine, was asked to illustrate. He had no trouble enlisting the talents of his friend Galanis to illustrate *Polyphème*, a two-act verse play by the Symbolist poet, Albert Samain. 'The printer offered credit, the authors were generous, and the engraver, Galanis, was a wonderful friend,' Clara later wrote of this publishing venture, adding, however, that the moment one debt was settled, another gaping financial hole developed, so that the important thing was to maintain the momentum – 'as on a bicycle, you have to keep pedalling to keep from falling'.

Although endowed with the instincts of a gambler, Malraux would not have embarked on such a risky venture if he had thought that *La Tentation de l'Occident* was going to be a bookselling success. But any illusions he may have had on this score were quickly dispelled by Bernard Grasset. The rather stilted form and meditative content of the letters exchanged between A. D. and Ling seemed too old-fashioned and ethereal for his taste, not at all what he had expected from the glamorous 'temple-robber of Angkor'. He agreed to publish these somewhat metaphysical ruminations about East and West as an encouragement for other books to come. But he refused to include *La Tentation de l'Occident* in the prestigious Cahiers verts series, which Grasset's associate, Daniel Halévy, had launched in 1921.

When *La Tentation de l'Occident* was finally published in late July 1926, Bernard Grasset's misgivings were partially confirmed. Neither Marcel Arland's advance praise of the book nor Malraux's own résumé, published in the July 31st issue of *Les Nouvelles Littéraires*, sufficed to overcome the puzzlement or lack of interest of many Paris critics. Not a word about the slim Grasset volume appeared in any of the capital's major newspapers.

This was not true, however, of certain weeklies and monthlies, nor, curiously enough, of the provincial French press and of French language newspapers in Switzerland and Belgium. The first significant review appeared in the August 14th issue of *Les Nouvelles Littéraires* and was signed J. P. (probably Jean Paulhan, editor of the *NRF*). What he had to say more than made up for the silence of so many others. For, after hailing André Malraux as a paragon of youthful audacity and as a young man of twenty-five who had 'divided his life between the Far East and Europe for the past ten years' – in other words, a kind of French Kipling – he concluded with a flourish by declaring that '*La Tentation de l'Occident* seems destined to occupy a place in France comparable to that in Germany of Count Keyserling's *Travel Diary of a Philosopher*'. An extraordinary encomium for a slim book containing seventeen not overly-long letters, compared to the 850 pages of the German philosopher's two-volume opus.

No subsequent reviewer was willing to go quite so far. But of the close to fifty articles and book reviews written about *La Tentation de l'Occident* over the next nine months the overwhelming majority were readier to praise than condemn it.

'A profound and delightful book' was the opinion voiced by Henri Mariol in the September 14th issue of *Le Progrès du Nord* (Liège). Geneva's *Revue Mensuelle* in its October issue called it 'a capital work and whose influence will be great'. One critic was so overawed by the philosophical subtleties of this exchange of letters that he roundly declared that 'Montesquieu's Persians look like simpletons compared to Mr André Malraux's Chinese'. The author's highly condensed, elliptic style was less appealing to another critic who, in the weekly *Revue des Lettres*, blamed the writer's youth for his 'disorderly taste for huge syntheses, for trenchant formulas which attempt to sum up whole millenia of history in a couple of lines'. But this was very much a minority opinion. As one of France's leading critics, Albert Thibaudet, put it in *Europe Nouvelle*: 'His sentences present that quality of poetry, synthesis, abridgement, and Chinese ideogram, which one finds in Claudel and Saint-John Perse.'

A number of reviewers took it for granted that the author had spent several years in China, and one, impressed by Grasset's extravagant publicity, boldly claimed that Malraux was the 'first living [French] writer to be translated into Chinese'.

In the meantime, André and his wife had moved out of the *pension* overlooking the Seine to a 'two-and-a-half-room' flat (Clara's description) on the Boulevard Murat, on the south-western periphery of Paris, not far from the green sward of the Auteuil race-track and the leafy Bois de Boulogne. It was totally bare of furniture for the first weeks of their occupancy, with a large crate and smaller packing cases serving as table and chairs. This humble abode also became the editorial office of Malraux's publishing company, which in September was renamed Aux Aldes – in honour of the celebrated Venetian typesetters of the sixteenth and seventeenth centuries who had invented the italic script and the in-octavo page format.

Although Clara was still blacklisted by other members of the Goldschmidt clan, she had chosen this location after learning that her mother had sold the Avenue des Chalets villa and was now living in a large five-room apartment in the same building. The move brought no immediate reconciliation. It did, however, effect a useful geographic rapprochement with André's family, when his mother, Grandmother Adrienne, and Aunt Marie left the noisy Montparnasse railway station area and moved into a nearby Boulevard Murat apartment, where the five of them continued to meet every day for lunch.

On the one hand Clara secretly disapproved of this excessively bourgeois arrangement. On the other hand, she was delighted to accompany André to the regular Wednesday evening dinner in 'Papa Fernand's' apartment on the Rue de Lübeck, near the Guimet Museum, where the table talk tended to be more lively. After four years of wedlock this all too charming *homme à femmes* had come to the conclusion that he was not made for a monogamous existence. Fourteen-year-old Roland and six-year-old Claude were thus left to the care of their mother, Marie-Louise Godard, whom Fernand Malraux had recently divorced.

The most influential of André Malraux's admirers at this moment of his life was Daniel Halévy, a close associate of Bernard Grasset. The son of the famous novelist and playwright, Ludovic Halévy – who had helped to write the sprightly librettos for Offenbach's *La Belle Hélène* and Bizet's *Carmen* – the young Daniel had known just about everyone worth knowing in the literary, musical, and artistic worlds of the pre-war *Belle Epoque*. He had made a name for himself as a biographer of Nietzsche and had been a close pre-war associate of the left-wing Catholic writer, Charles Péguy. Although in terms of literary output he was a lightweight compared to André Gide, the pole star of Gaston Gallimard's *NRF*, he had made Grasset's Cahiers verts books (so called because of their distinctive green covers) one of the most prestigious series in contemporary French publishing.

By the end of 1926 the fifty-four-year-old Daniel Halévy was beginning to feel the strain of having to bring out a new 'top-quality' book each month. He also felt a bit ashamed that his 'distinguished' list should have included so many literary celebrities and such a paucity of youthful 'talents'. The one salient exception was André Chamson, a hard-working young philologist who had mastered Greek and Latin, had developed a passion for Provençal poetry and had gained admission to the Ecole des Chartes, a venerable institution specializing in the training of 'medievalists' and scholars versed in the literature and monuments of classical antiquity. Chamson in the early 1920s had done most of his military service in Paris as a part-time teacher and officer cadet. This experience had inspired *Roux le bandit*, an artfully written novel about a religiously motivated peasant from the Protestant Cévennes region north of Nîmes who in August 1914 had 'taken to the hills' rather than let himself be drafted into an army where he would have been duty-bound to shoot other human beings. The novel's publication in 1924 had provoked a literary storm, being viewed by conservative critics as an apologia for draft-dodging.

Rejected by the Goncourt Prize jury, *Roux le bandit* did at least earn its author a significant *succès d'estime*. It also left a conscience-stricken Daniel Halévy with the feeling that he had so far done little to promote young authors. Chamson, as it happened, had just finished a philosophical essay entitled 'L'Homme contre l'Histoire', which by itself was insufficient to fill an entire Cahier vert volume. But it occurred to Halévy that he could make up for past omissions by publishing this essay next to other contributions from young 'writer philosophers' – like André Malraux – and thus refute the pessimists who were persuaded that the havoc of the Great War had irreparably crippled the powers of French thought.

It cannot in all honesty be claimed that the seventieth volume in the Cahiers verts series, published in March 1927 under the simple title, *Ecrits* ('Writings'), was a notable literary event, notwithstanding a kind of valedictory preface written by Daniel Halévy. However, Malraux's little essay – 'D'une jeunesse européenne' (the title implying that it dealt with the continent's thinking, as opposed to unthinking, youth) – was remarkable for its brevity, the lapidary concision of its formulations, the perplexed content of its 'message'. Everywhere in Europe (including Russia) people were trying to 'deliver themselves from their civilization', as others had once sought to free themselves from the constraints of the divine. The result had been to create a climate of anguish and a 'civilization of solitude'. For the hope entertained by nineteenth-century thinkers of having a cult of man replace the cult of God had turned out to be a vain illusion, simply because the 'Me', elevated to fill the void, is not something fixed and solid, but rather a confused welter of unfulfilled desires and ambitions. As Malraux put it more poetically: 'The Me, a palace of silence in which each of us penetrates alone, houses all the precious stones of our provisional madnesses, mingled with those of lucidity; and the awareness we have of ourselves is above all woven of vain desires, hopes, and dreams.'

More than one Malraux scholar has hailed this essay as a prophetic anticipation, since it suggested that the godlessness of modern times leads inescapably to the 'metallic' reign of the absurd – and did so, furthermore, almost ten years before Jean-Paul Sartre made the axiomatic absurdity of life the cornerstone of his philosophy. In itself the reiteration of this sentiment would not have been so forceful but for Malraux's parallel contention that the cult of psychological introspection, which Maurice Barrès, André Gide, Marcel Proust, and Sigmund Freud (none of them specifically named) had done so much to promote, could not dispel those 'constellations of despair' which, like 'disappointed loves', now hung over Europe's youth.

Years later, after re-reading her husband's short essay, Clara Malraux was struck by its almost religious tone, by

> the profound imprint of a Christianity one thinks one has rejected, but which does not keep it from being the medium through which one apprehends the world. A strange destiny, indeed, that of this Christian man abandoned by God; deprived of the aid afforded by confession, he is abandoned by his past, or modifies it according to his own desires.

In the context of the young Malraux's career the actual thematic contents of this essay were probably less important than its title – 'D'une jeunesse européenne' – which boldly staked out the author's claim to speak for the youth of Europe. Of even greater immediate significance were Daniel Halévy's generous words of introduction, in which André Malraux was described as the author of a first book, *La Tentation de l'Occident*, written after 'his return from China, where he had stayed for two years'. Halévy would never have dared to make such an affirmation if he had not thought it to be true; and the least that can be said is that Malraux made no attempt to undeceive him.

The winter of 1926–7 was a particularly trying one for both André and Clara. In early January he suffered a severe attack of rheumatoid arthritis. He remained virtually prostrate for three months, unable to get up unaided from the bed which occupied most of the tiny bedroom. Clara, herself affected by recurrent bouts of malarial fever, had to exert every ounce of strength to help her crippled husband drag himself into the modest living room, where there was now a small couch on which he could be propped up when receiving visitors. The medication needed to combat André's ailment came close to consummating their 'financial ruin', as did a rashly concluded contract for a rare-books edition of Paul Valéry's poems, which saddled Malraux with a debt of close to 20,000 francs (a debt it took him a year and a half to pay off).

They were sustained in these adverse times by the frequent visits of steadfast friends – beginning with Louis Chevasson, almost doglike in his fidelity to André, and the inventive Pascal Pia. Shortly after his return from Indochina, André had re-established contact with his eroticophilic friend, Pascal. The result was the hasty compilation of a two-volume anthology of salacious verse, published under the subtly ambiguous title, *La Quintessence satyrique du XXe siècle.* This heady satyrical brew was concocted from pornographic poems written by Baudelaire, Rimbaud, Alfred Jarry, Tristan Bernard, Laurent Tailhade, Guillaume Apollinaire, Jean Cocteau, Raymond Radiguet and Fernand Fleuret, along with a few bawdy samples composed by Pascal Pia himself.

For the mischievous Pascal Pia this kind of clandestine publishing was by now almost routine 'work'. In 1925, this accomplished literary joker had honoured the memory of his hero, Apollinaire, by bringing out a highly limited edition (exactly thirty copies) of his *Cortège priapique.* This was supposedly printed in Java (some copies claimed Cuba) – both of them were bogus locations probably protecting the Maastricht printer, A. M. Stols. Stols had been introduced to Pia by a curiously bohemian as well as affluent 'man of letters' answering to the francophonic name of Eddy Du Perron, who had been brought up in the East Indies. Pia was now preparing another 'strangely overlooked' collection of erotic poems by Apollinaire to which he gave the title, *Le Verger des amours* ('The Orchard of Love') – most of them were, in fact, his own concoction. Malraux, who probably first met the refreshingly unconventional Du Perron during the autumn of 1926, was almost certainly privy to this new Pascal Pia hoax. He is also thought to have had a hand in the fabrication of another literary hoax: the 'accidental discovery' by Eddy Du Perron of thirty-seven pages of diary notations which Baudelaire had 'casually left behind' at the end of his unhappy years of exile (1864–6) in the Belgian capital. Published in January 1927 under the title *Années de Bruxelles,* this extraordinary 'find' (limited to 150 de luxe copies) became a collector's item overnight. Indeed, so artfully were these diary entries composed – with a long introductory preface by Georges Garonne (one of Pascal Pia's many pseudonyms), a pen-and-ink self-portrait of Baudelaire (actually executed by Pascal Pia) and a few notes of explanation provided by a recently deceased Brussels printer named Féli Gautier (again Pascal Pia) – that years afterwards they were regarded as authentic by leading Baudelaire scholars and were later included in a more or less 'definitive' Gallimard–Pléiade edition of the poet's complete works.

The ingenious Pascal also helped in another clandestine enterprise which could have landed them in serious trouble had the secret reached the ears of the Paris police. One day Clara, enraged to see her husband casually reading a newspaper on the sofa while she was working in the kitchen, went to an employment bureau and hired a fifteen-year-old girl, Louise, to help her with the cooking. Clara had not the faintest idea how she was going to pay her, but this did not deter her, for she too had learned to live dangerously. The young Louise had an older sister named Fernande, a former model whose sweet disposition and shapely form had attracted a number of male admirers, one of whom had made her pregnant. When Clara, who in such matters was a militant feminist, discovered that Fernande did not wish to have the child, she appealed to Pascal Pia. He quickly found the right person for the job. Fernande was so delighted to be rid of the unwanted child that she discreetly spread the word to a number of embarrassingly pregnant friends, and for several months the little two-room flat on the Boulevard Murat became a consulting-room and informal clinic for illegal abortions.

In August 1927 the *NRF* began publishing long extracts from a highly provocative work, perhaps the most controversial book to have appeared in France during this first post-war decade. Written by Julien Benda, a fifty-year-old free thinker, *La Trahison des clercs* ('The Treason of the Intellectuals') was, in essence, a hammer-and-tongs assault on France's right-wing intelligentsia. Benda's thesis was that, unlike the great thinkers and philosophers of the past – Plato, Aristotle, Descartes, Leibniz, Kant, etc – who had always exhibited a certain elevation of thought, modern intellectuals were increasingly allowing partisan political passion to sway their minds and were thus betraying their sacred mission as objective searchers after truth. Although this rebuke was aimed at Marxist intellectuals of the Left as much as right-wing thinkers, it was chiefly with the latter that Benda was concerned – if only because at this moment in French history they enjoyed an incomparably superior prestige. Not only had these right-wing 'scribes' – led by the late neo-romantic Maurice Barrès, the fiery monarchist, Charles Maurras, and the caustic Léon Daudet – turned French nationalism into a fanatically intolerant creed, as had been demonstrated during the Dreyfus affair, but also they were now, in the same narrow-minded spirit, subverting the universalist ideals of truth and justice, once championed by Socrates and Plato – to whom they paid such hypocritical lip-service as among the founders of a timeless 'Mediterranean culture' – in order to give free rein to their petty, anti-democratic prejudices.

La Trahison des clercs was, in effect, the opening round in a bitter battle between left-wing and right-wing French intellectuals, which was destined to rage on through the 1930s and beyond. A battle into which André Malraux – in 1927 still relatively unknown – was to be inescapably drawn.

Julien Benda had long been a habitué of Daniel Halévy's literary salon, usually occupying a chair in one corner, where he maintained a watchful silence, not missing a word of what was said and only opening his mouth to utter some nasty comment: a highly 'intelligent, original, and unbearable' little man whom André Chamson's lively wife Lucie later likened to 'the twenty-four-hour guest who stays on for years and then leaves in a huff'.

A classically trained medievalist and lover of Provençal poetry, like her husband, Lucie Mazauric (to use her *nom de plume*) has left us a vivid description of Daniel Halévy's Saturday afternoon receptions, of which Malraux was soon to become a 'star'. The décor was unforgettable, for Halévy's salon walls were covered with a *fin-de-siècle* profusion of paintings and drawings by Degas, Forain, and other Impressionst artists. Indeed, there was an almost Whistlerian quality to this luxurious home, located in a seventeenth-century house on the Quai de l'Horloge, not far from the Pont Neuf's statue of Henri IV, which adorns the 'prow' of the Ile de la Cité.

A lovely pale light, filtering through the foliage of the big trees of the Quai, imbued it with a soft and as though muffled atmosphere, favourable to attentiveness and well-bred discussions. Very much a Paris peasant, Daniel Halévy fancied clothes made of a dark fustian fabric, which he wore with elegant nonchalance. His subtle face was framed by a short ring-beard, which made one think of a Clouet portrait. He steered the conversations without ever raising his voice. His wife, whose long robe was in harmony with the style of the house, moved silently about, overseeing the distribution of port, tea, and small dry cakes to the guests.

In addition to Julien Benda, the luminaries of the older generation included the lean, ascetic, and still astonishingly youthful-looking François Mauriac, with his sharply-chiselled El Greco features; the conservative philosopher, Gabriel Marcel; the short, imperious, and already grey-haired poet and essayist, Abel Bonnard, ever ready to pontificate on everything from the state of contemporary China to the love life of Stendhal; and the foppish Jacques-Emile Blanche, an eclectic portrait painter, novelist, and (often scathing) critic of the arts, whose elegant white spats seemed specially worn to underscore the feminine whiteness of his name. Among the younger generation were the disconcertingly haughty Henry de Montherlant, a neo-Nietzschean champion of virile values; the fervent pacifist and anti-Barrèsian Jean Guéhenno; the straight-shooting, strong-jawed André Chamson. A less determined young author might easily have felt overawed and tongue-tied in the presence of such literary heavyweights. But Malraux, who had long since learned that the best defence is attack, was not prepared to be a silent listener. Here, as elsewhere, he was going to shine, and, to judge by Lucie Mazauric's description of his first, almost comet-like appearances at these Saturday afternoon receptions, dazzle he did.

He spoke passionately of the 'destiny' of human beings, as religious souls speak of God, as though he knew that his, Malraux's, destiny was bound to be uncommon, Shakespearean, a destiny of glory and misfortune.

The photos of this period do not well portray his personal magnetism. He was neither Dr Caligari nor Professor Fu Manchu, nor the brooding, dark-haired hero of the cinema screen, as he has too often been portrayed. Lean, pale, with black eyes and fine features, an abundant mane of dark hair and a forelock falling over his brow (a typically Malraux˙forelock, having nothing to do with Hitler's), he had a highly personal, implacable way of tackling human beings and things and of voraciously snapping up passing words, like a hawk swooping down on its prey . . .

Everything about him was movement: his thought, rapid and elliptic . . . his fulgurant formulations, often of a dazzling intelligence and sometimes ferocious ('I don't argue with imbeciles'). He had a prodigious memory, scholarly references which were delivered like cannon-ball serves on a tennis-court (for he was always ready on any subject to cite the essential book, which almost no one else had read), jerky gestures betraying an almost sickly nervousnes, and a frantic desire to go immediately and always to the very heart of everything.

A charmingly dimple-cheeked brunette, Lucie Mazauric was also careful to add that, notwithstanding his imperious ways and his genius for lapidary formulas, this 'prodigy' did not belong to any political faction or literary clique, and that, in spite of everything, he remained 'accessible, courteous, and good company. Halévy was quite happy to be able to add this black diamond to the many-coloured garland of literary stars adorning his salon.'

14

A Dark, Dangerous Horse

In December 1927 André Malraux's precarious financial situation was slightly improved, thanks to the belated generosity of Bernard Grasset. A dashing, high-strung, temperamental man, whose lithe physique, good looks, and green eyes made him a redoubtable Lothario, Grasset was anything but a philistine. His love of audacious advertising *coups* had made him enemies as well as friends in Paris literary circles, but it had in no way diminished his love of handsomely-printed books. In the spring of 1927 Malraux, wishing to save his almost bankrupt Aux Aldes rare-books company, suggested to his publisher that he take over its commercial operations. The canny publisher, however, was in no mood to encourage Malraux's 'parallel' activities. Not until he was sure that the former 'temple-robber' had nearly completed the kind of 'exciting' book he had contracted for was he willing to relent. Finally, in December 1927, he agreed to pay him a monthly 'pension' of 4,000 francs. Relieved of the burden of trying to 'place' his rare illustrated books, Malraux could at last concentrate on the completion of *Les Conquérants* (The Conquerors).

Entire books, as well as articles and essays, have been written about the genesis and subsequent metamorphoses of this extraordinary novel. As Malraux wrote and rewrote it, a great deal of picturesque descriptive detail – concerning Singapore, Saigon, Cholon, and finally Hong Kong – was jettisoned, in order to concentrate the focus more exclusively on Canton. Radically banished was all trace of the exalted lyricism he had inherited from Maurice Barrès and the Symbolists, and more distantly from Chateaubriand, and which was still visible in *La Tentation de l'Occident. Les Conquérants* was intended to be, above all, a psychological-philosophical novel in which, as in Dostoevsky, the sparsely described surroundings serve essentially to enhance an atmosphere of lurking mystery and tragic gloom.

There was a similar drastic shrinkage in the time span, covering the dramatic summer months of 1925, when the Chinese nationalists of the Kuomintang in Canton had launched a general strike aimed at crippling British business and shipping activities. Rightly fearing that too detailed a description of those events would make the novel look like journalistic fiction, Malraux shortened the time span to seven weeks – from June 25th to August 12th.

The most revealing transformation, however, was that of the novel's central figure, Garine, the mysteriously motivated revolutionary whom Malraux had intended from the start to contrast with Mikhail Borodin, the Komintern's chief agent in China. In the first draft, this central figure was called Stavine – a name probably inspired by that of the disconcerting figure of Stavroghin, in Dostoevsky's *The Devils*. Stavine's ruthless efficiency, acting as kommissar for Propaganda for the Kuomintang, was contrasted with the wishful thinking of a Count Staloff, a White Russian émigré, acting as adviser to the dictator-warlord of Yunnan, General T'ang Chi-yao, whose chief weakness was a lack of theoretical conviction. Malraux, however, soon realized the danger of building up this particular contrast – which would have made *Les Conquérants* as much a Russian as a Chinese novel. Count Staloff was accordingly eliminated. His latent nostalgia for ancient values was then transferred to the Chinese character of Tcheng-daï, an old-fashioned mandarin brought up in the soft-spoken Confucian tradition who cannot bring himself to accept the need for pitiless revolutionary violence. He in turn was paired off (by way of contrast) with the terrorist, Hong – a character inspired not only by Hin (the nationalist from the mountainous regions of Annam who had wanted to shoot Governor Maurice Cognacq in July 1925), but also by the French Revolutionary figure of Marat (the quintessential 'hater').

But what role exactly was there left for Garine to fill, now that his natural foil or contrast had been removed from the scene? The answer, reduced to its simplest terms, is that he is an imaginative novice who learns the hard way just what it takes to become an effective revolutionary. Here is how Malraux chose to describe him in a key passage, as viewed by someone who had known him in his youth: 'He was generally thought to be ambitious. Ambition is never real except when the person it grips becomes aware of it in the form of acts to be accomplished . . . But within himself he felt a tenacious, constant need for power . . . "It's not so much the soul as it is the conquest that makes the leader," he said to me one day.'

These lines are immediately followed by a reference to Napoleon, remarking during his captivity on the island of St Helena that it is 'conquest which *maintains* the soul of a leader'. This, of course, is a truism – like saying 'nothing succeeds like success'. But what Malraux meant was that it is not childish daydreams, the wild imaginings of adolescence, or even a neo-Nietzschean will to power which make a revolutionary; it is the supreme pragmatic test, the revolutionary act itself. It was what Goethe had intimated when he had Faust say, contradicting the opening statement of the Gospel of St John: '*Im Anfang war die Tat.*' In the beginning was not the word, but the deed. All this might seem elementary, not to say self-evident. But it is interesting to reflect that those lines were written by a young French author who might not yet have heard of Martin Heidegger – the philosopher who, in *Sein und Zeit* ('Being and Time', published in 1927), had written: '*Das Wesen des Hammers ist das Hammern*' ('the essence of the hammer is in the hammering') – and who thus anticipated Jean-Paul Sartre's famous philosophical catchphrase, 'Existence precedes Essence', by fifteen or twenty years.

Although in later life Malraux habitually waved aside any suggestion that Garine's personality might have been partly modelled on his own, the resemblances are too striking to be casually dismissed. There is, to begin with, the fascinating passage, later scrapped because it was too obviously autobiographical, in which Garine is described as having been a devoutly religious youth, so addicted to making the sign of the Cross that it had become a kind of nervous tick; to say nothing of the adolescent sequel: his bitter disenchantment when, two years after his first communion (from which he had expected a spiritual transformation), he 'found himself in a world – of studies, friends, research – which paid no heed to religion'. Like the late-adolescent Malraux, the young Garine starts out in life with a fortune (inherited from his mother rather than brought to him by his wife) – a fortune he proceeds to lose, after using some of it for 'educational' trips undertaken for his personal pleasure.

Like Malraux, too, Garine admits that he is a gambler, adding that it was basically a love of the risks involved in dealing with turbulent situations which had made him a revolutionary. Garine's first great mishap befalls him when it is discovered that he has been secretly helping midwives to practise illegal abortions – a fate which fortunately did not overtake André and Clara during their months of poverty on the Boulevard Murat. Again, like Malraux, Garine is brought to trial and condemned for reasons he feels are grotesquely unreal and a travesty of 'justice'. Even Garine's seething impatience, betrayed by his nervous gestures and the 'jerky, staccato rhythm' of his speech, was an almost mirror-like reflection of Malraux's own high-strung temperament.

In matters of thought, attitude, and feeling, the similarities are no less striking. When, for example, he has Garine explain his preference for the proletarian underdogs of society, it was certainly his own sentiments that Malraux was expressing:

> I prefer them, but only because they are the vanquished. Yes, on the whole, they have more heart, more humanity than the others; virtues of the vanquished . . . What is certain is that I feel nothing but loathing and disgust for the bourgeoisie from which I come. As for the others, I know only too well how abject they would become once we had triumphed together.

It would be difficult to condemn the sacrosanct Marxist principle of the 'dictatorship of the proletariat' in more categoric terms.

In other passages Garine expresses a deep-seated suspicion of Marxist doctrine, which was certainly Malraux's own. 'He had few illusions as to the value of the theories he heard exposed or discussed. The strongest and most serious of them all, Marxism as it was then understood' – that is, by Bolshevik exiles in pre-1917 Switzerland – 'left him full of distrust, above all as regards its fatality.' Here, clearly, the romantic hero cult was openly at war with Marxist determinism.

Although nowhere near as rich in the number and diversity of its characters, it is clear that Malraux wanted *Les Conquérants* to be a kind of 'Asiatic miniature' of Dostoevsky's *The Devils*. Just as Dostoevsky's characters were fictional incarnations of the philosophical and political debates that raged in the provincial and urban salons of Russia in the 1870s, so in *Les Conquérants* many of the arguments as to the efficacy of revolutionary violence as a means for freeing human beings were fictional transpositions of the arguments Malraux had heard in Paul Monin's house or elsewhere in Saigon. In the novel, the assassination of the Confucian moderate, Tcheng-daï – at one point purposefully compared to Gandhi – symbolized the defeat of the spirit of moderate reform by the forces of revolutionary violence; and it can be regarded as a prophetic anticipation of the fate that awaited the overly hopeful Annamite moderates in French Indochina.

During the August vacation of 1928 André and Clara were invited to attend a ten-day literary conference (called a *décade*) at Pontigny, in western Burgundy, in an old Cistercian abbey where Thomas à-Becket had once sought refuge from the wrath of King Henry II of England. The pillared cloister, vaulted refectory and surrounding grounds had been bought in 1906 by a classical scholar and professor of rhetoric named Paul Desjardins, who had decided to use the venerable edifices for the holding of annual conferences.

At the railway station André and Clara were met by their sexagenarian host, Paul Desjardins, whose straggling beard and prominent cheekbones made him look a bit like a French Tolstoy. Also present were the pensive Roger Martin du Gard, whose many-volumed novel, *Les Thibault*, was to win him the Nobel Prize for Literature a few years later; the philosopher Léon Brunschwicg; and a number of others, later joined by André Gide and his friend and co-founder of the *NRF*, Jean Schlumberger.

The liveliest of the debaters during the daytime sessions were the two young Andrés – Chamson and Malraux. The theme chosen for this particular ten-day period – the contrasting attitudes of the post-war generations after the Franco-Prussian War and that of 1914–18 – was soon forgotten as Malraux brought the subject up to date by talking with his usual nervous volubility about revolutions past and present. Chamson, though anything but a conservative, undertook to contradict him. When they had first met in Daniel Halévy's literary salon, he had begun talking about Provençal poetry and poets – a subject on which he was an expert – only to be interrupted by Malraux with the peremptory observation that what he was saying disregarded 'the latest discoveries of the German school, which have shown that . . .' and so on. Chamson, who had never heard of such a school, was left speechless by this show of erudition, which struck him as suspect. (It was only years later that Malraux candidly explained his *modus operandi* at such moments: 'In an argument one must always win.') Now, at Pontigny, Chamson was determined not to let his young contemporary win again by default.

Roger Martin du Gard later noted in his diary that this *décade* was the

> liveliest and the most successful of all I have attended . . . The presence of two guests, André Chamson and André Malraux, contributed a lot to the proceedings. I took important notes about Malraux, who is one of the strangest and most appealing figures I have ever met. André Chamson . . . is a solid soul . . . who is still rooted to many generations on the land, an advanced free thinker, a partisan of certain social upheavals, but whose revolutionary spirit, attached to the past, was curiously opposed to the total nihilism, to the integral Bolshevism of the terrible, glacial Malraux.

On the final day Paul Desjardins made a little speech in which he singled out 'our two young friends, André Malraux and André Chamson, who most of the time seemed not to be in agreement. But at the heart of this disagreement, there is a profound accord.' This was too much for both Malraux and Chamson.

'No,' declared Malraux, getting to his feet, 'we are not in agreement, because for the past ten days I have represented the philosophy of the axe, and André Chamson the philosophy of the apple tree.'

Refusing to be upstaged, Chamson accepted the terms of the comparison but felt obliged to point out that 'to exist the axe needs the apple tree, whereas the apple tree can exist without the axe'.

When André and Clara returned to Paris, copies of *Les Conquérants* were already rolling off the presses. The serialized extracts, which had run through five successive issues of the *NRF*, had aroused enormous interest, and not only in France. In Germany Max Clauss, a connoisseur of French literature, was so thrilled by what he took to be an 'inside' account of the machinations and intrigues among Borodin's associates during the Canton upheavals of 1925 that he volunteered to translate it for serialization in the *Europäische Revue*, a recently launched Berlin monthly. The first extract appeared in the August 1928 issue under the arresting title, 'DIE EROBERER – *Ein Tagebuch der Kämpfe um Kanton 1925*' ('The Conquerors – A Diary of the Battles around Canton in 1925'). Nothing remotely comparable about the dramatic events in China had so far appeared in German, and Bernard Grasset had no trouble obtaining a book contract with the Berlin publisher, Kurt Vowinckel. Similar contracts were soon signed for an English-language edition of *Les Conquérants* with Jonathan Cape in London and Harcourt Brace in New York.

Just what Malraux had told his publisher about his experiences on mainland China during the summer of 1925, we do not know, but Bernard Grasset was not a man to quibble about such matters. This, after all, was a novel; it did not claim to be journalistic reporting, even if some of the dated entries made it look like a diary, kept by an active participant in the revolutionary upheavals of Canton. And if this intense young man, whose elliptic bursts of speech revealed an astonishing knowledge of the Far East, insisted that he was already known to book readers in China, who was Grasset to dispute the claim? Accordingly, the page facing the frontispiece of *Les Conquérants* carried this intriguing entry under the heading: 'By the same author' and under the listing of his first published work, *Lunes en papier*: '*La Tentation de l'Occident*, Chinese text, Shanghai-Peking; French text, Paris (Grasset).'

The serialization of *Les Conquérants* in the *NRF* also produced a windfall which Grasset was quick to exploit. This was an official ukase issued by the ideological watchdogs of Stalin's Communist Party, banning the importation of this 'subversive' novel into the USSR. Grasset immediately had a two-inch paper band wrapped around each copy. Printed on the bright-green streamer in bold black type were the electrifying words: 'INTERDIT EN RUSSIE ET EN ITALIE' ('Banned in Russia and Italy').

That the censors in Moscow should have reacted as they did was not surprising. The bosses of the Third International could hardly have relished Malraux's description of the heavy-handed ruthlessness with which Borodin and his associates had been operating in Canton, and the mere idea that he could employ a former Okhrana agent like Nicolaieff, or even worse, an unprincipled adventurer like Garine, to direct his propaganda efforts was nothing less than sacrilegious. But what motive, other than the inveterate 'professional stupidity' of the species, could have prompted Mussolini's censors to ban a book exposing Bolshevik propaganda methods in the Far East?

As it happened, *Les Conquérants* did not need such spectacular publicity to attract readers. The critical acclaim was overwhelmingly favourable – with phrases like 'a great book', 'a beautiful book', a 'breath-taking narrative', a 'masterly portrayal' being employed in article after article. Paul Souday, the influential critic of the conservative *Le Temps*, was predictably negative, devoting one short paragraph to this 'semi-novel, or novelised study of political history', which was marred by a 'somewhat confused and flickering abundance' of successive scenes. Even more negative was the anonymous reviewer in the French Communist Party's daily, *L'Humanité*. The novel, he wrote, provided a 'perfectly false picture of the immense Chinese revolution', and elevated certain figures – notably that of the 'impassioned dilettante' Garine – to grotesque heights of heroism, when the only possible hero of such turbulent events was the 'suffering Chinese people'. In short, *Les Conquérants* was 'definitely counter-revolutionary'.

Certain critics were dismayed by the absence of background information concerning the situation in China. But other critics felt, on the contrary, that the young author of *Les Conquérants* had invented a 'new conception' of novel writing. Albert Thibaudet, writing in the weekly *Candide*, concluded that Malraux had been right to proceed by 'a mass of impressionistic touches', since Western logic was out of place in China. The Swiss writer, Denis de Rougemont, went even further in the *Revue de Genève*, declaring that André Malraux had placed himself with this book 'in the front rank of contemporary novelists'.

In a long, three-column article the well-known novelist, essayist and poet, André Thérive, wrote in *L'Opinion* that André Malraux was 'a remarkable writer, a peerless narrator, without affectations of style. . . . Casualness . . . a secret love of disorder, or a Stendhalian scorn for "good rules" of writing and composition . . .' *Les Conquérants*, he wrote, was 'a book . . . of flesh and blood'. After quoting several examples of vivid passages in which an entire scene was described in one or two swift strokes, he added: 'An eye that knows how to choose so well is necessarily guided by a strong and intelligent brain.'

On October 6th Bernard Grasset emphasized the novel's importance by publishing a huge, eye-catching advertisement, filling a half page of *Les Nouvelles Littéraires*.

A
N
D
R
É

LES   CONQUÉRANTS

M
A
L
R
A
U
X

The four rectangles thus formed were filled with a clever montage of photos of Chinese scenes and of reproductions of the covers of the *NRF* and of the *Europäische Revue* – whose clearly legible Gothic script announced at the top 'Mit Borodin im revolutionären China' ('With Borodin in Revolutionary China'), and below 'DIE EROBERER' and '*Kampf um Kanton*', the words '*Tagebuch eines europäischen Kommunisten*' ('Diary of a European Communist'). In another rectangle, the reader was reminded that this book had been 'banned in Russia and Italy'. No less striking was a vertical sentence, indicating that here was revealed 'a new conception of the novel'.

Bernard Grasset may not have been the first to coin this arresting phrase, but he knew he was tossing out a bone of contention to hungry critics. They leapt on it with relish. Within a couple of weeks he had what he wanted: six juicy quotations, used to promote Malraux's novel in another large advertisement, under the heading: 'Les Conquérants et la Presse'.

Albert Thibaudet (*Candide*): A very curious, very lively, subtle book.

Auguste Bailly (*L'Intransigeant*): This book could immediately class its author among the greatest novelists of our time.

Göteborg Händelstiding (Sweden): *The Conquerors* is a prodigious novel.
André Billy (*L'Oeuvre*): One would not be turned off by novels if they all resembled this one.

Robert Kemp (*La Liberté*): Malraux is somebody.

Nieuwe Courant (Holland): One of the most curious works I have read in many a year.

Grasset was now convinced that he had a winner. A winner, furthermore, worthy to claim one of France's leading literary prizes – which, selected two or three weeks before Christmas, usually guaranteed the fortunate author a sale of 10,000, 20,000, or even 50,000 copies. His rivalry with Gaston Gallimard had by this time assumed the proportions of an epic battle between the two up-and-coming young 'titans' of French publishing. Although Grasset had come out with several sensational best-sellers, and though he was the proud publisher of the famous 'Four Ms' (Mauriac, Morand, Montherlant, and André Maurois), he had not fared well in the annual battle for the coveted literary prizes. Over the past ten years, Gallimard had won the Goncourt Prize five times, Albin Michel twice, but Grasset only once. All his hopes were now pinned on Malraux's *Les Conquérants*.

On November 10th Paul Morand joined the chorus of applauders with an article which raised the intriguing question: 'Where are these novelists taking us?' The first paragraphs were devoted to a cluster of French novelists who had confounded the pessimists by proving that in post-war France the novel was anything but dead. The rest of the article, however, was almost exclusively devoted to the young André Malraux. In August 1925, just when Morand found himself stranded in a strike-paralyzed Hong Kong, Malraux, he wrote, had headed for Canton. 'His destiny immediately carried him at the decisive hour to the neuralgic point; and since he is a great writer, a poet, and an artist, he was immediately able to "fix" that instant.'

How, after this, could anyone dare doubt that André Malraux had actually witnessed the scenes he had described? Whereas, Morand went on, others were content to dream or, being literary exhibitionists, indulged in the 'dandyism of the subconscious' (a barb aimed at André Breton's Surrealists),

Malraux had lived, had suffered. 'I saw him enter like a ghost, in the Saigon hospital where I myself was lying, looking pale, emaciated, harassed, infinitely more ill than the patients. He has personally been through the mill,' he concluded, and 'he can allow himself [to write] dangerous works because he has lived dangerously.'

This final Nietzschean tribute may have done the recipient more harm than good in the eyes of the more staid members of the juries. On December 1st Grasset again placed an advertisement in the *Nouvelles Littéraires* on behalf of his protégé – the darkest and most dangerous horse in this literary steeplechase.

The suspense lasted four more days as the now groggy jurors tried to make up their minds, which in some cases had long since been closed. Finally, on December 5th, at the traditional luncheon held at the Drouant restaurant, near the Paris Opéra, the doyen of the Goncourt jury let it be known that the coveted prize had been awarded by five votes (out of ten) to Maurice Constantin-Weyer's *Un Homme penché sur son passé*. At almost the same moment at the Club Interallié, next to the British Embassy on the Rue du Faubourg Saint-Honoré, the twenty-one ladies of the Femina jury cast thirteen votes in favour of Dominique Dunois for her novel, *Georgette Garou*. Not long afterwards, at the conclusion of another well-wined and brandied luncheon at Drouant's, it was announced that seven of the ten members of the Théophraste Renaudot jury had chosen to reward the well-known playwright, André Obey, for his short novel, *Le Joueur de triangle*.

Once again these arbiters of literary fashion had exhibited their almost infallible preference for novelistic mediocrity. On December 15th, when he had to review the three prizewinning books for *Les Nouvelles Littéraires*, Edmond Jaloux could hardly stifle his yawns. His praise for the Goncourt Prize winner was so luke-warm that, after noting that certain pages of his novel had reminded him of Jack London, he quoted three paragraphs from a 'powerful page', and left it at that. With Mme Dominique Dunois he was brusque, almost to the point of rudeness. 'One does not see the reason that prompted the Femina Vie Heureuse jury to give prominence to a work so lacking in significance. Each year there appear a good three hundred novels that are neither better nor worse than *Georgette Garou*.' As for André Obey's *Joueur de triangle*, Jaloux found it full of 'grace and charm. But don't ask me exactly what goes on in it.'

Having thus consigned these three nondescript works to the dustbin of future oblivion, the eminent critic gave full vent to his impatience: 'It is, indeed, most regrettable that no jury should have thought of rewarding the finest of the books written by a young author to have appeared this year – the most daring, the most powerful, and the most intelligent: Mr André Malraux's *Les Conquérants*.'

15

Farewell to Fantasy

A mere hundred metres from Bernard Grasset's editorial offices on the Rue des Saints-Pères were the equally congested premises of the *NRF*, located around the corner at no. 3, Rue de Grenelle. If anything, the available office space here was even 'tighter', since the monthly *NRF* had developed a prosperous book-publishing branch, managed by two enterprising brothers, Gaston and Raymond Gallimard.

André Malraux had first penetrated this temple of 'serious' literature in 1922, when his friend Marcel Arland had introduced him to the monthly's editor, Jacques Rivière. Three-and-a-half years later, when Malraux returned from Indochina, the often caustic and (in poetic matters) insufficiently original Georges Gabory had lost his reader's job with the *NRF*, whereas the conscientious, hardworking, and less opinionated Marcel Arland had risen steadily in the esteem of the *NRF*'s new boss, Jean Paulhan. The notorious 'temple-robber of Angkor' needed no special introduction, for in August and September 1924 Paulhan had agreed to sign several petitions for Malraux's release from captivity. He had even drawn Jacques Rivière's attention to the Phnom Penh court's stiff sentence, hazarding the opinion that 'prison can be a good school for reflection . . . Malraux will gain from it'.

This wry comment was typical of a man who was as reserved, enigmatic, and complex as his predecessor, Jacques Rivière, had been simple, forthright and direct. A master of lexicographical analysis, he had a horror of 'the obvious', of clichés and platitudes, of pat phrases and thinking, combined with a love of outrageous paradoxes, which those unfamiliar with his sinuous, questioning, sardonic cast of mind found most disconcerting. His skill in the art of suggestive reprimand made him (in the words of one admirer) a 'prince of acupuncture' capable of 'pricking men of letters at their most vital points'. This was accomplished with a diplomatic finesse belied by Paulhan's rough-hewn appearance, marked by big brown eyes surmounted by bushy eyebrows and an aquiline crest of faintly ruffled hair.

Paulhan's first impression of Malraux may not have differed much from that of Jean Prévost – a most unusual combination of athlete (sprinter, soccer player, boxer – even able to take on Ernest Hemingway) and brainy intellectual – who had become the *NRF*'s chief drama and film critic:

> He could not look you in the eyes, for his gaze followed the gyrations of an invisible bee. His shoulder blades were thrust together as though a dagger were pricking him in the back. His fingers flamed and flickered, they quivered, they sought to unknot themselves . . . He sought to shelter himself from others and from things behind a screen of compliments, doctrines, and fanciful reveries. Pen in hand, he tore at life and skinned it.

Those lines were probably written in 1928, because of Prévost's telltale use of the adjective *farfelu* (crazy, fanciful, comical) to describe Malraux's 'reveries'. For not until 1928 did Malraux manage to find a publisher for his final extravaganza in the magic realm of literary fantasy: a macabre tale entitled *Royaume-Farfelu* ('Crazy Kingdom').

Malraux would not have been Malraux – a young man with an insatiable curiosity for everything strange, outlandish, and exotic – if he had not, while still an adolescent, devoured most or perhaps all of the *Mille et Une Nuits* (*The Thousand and One Nights*). But it was not only those entrancing tales of the reign of the great Abbasid caliph, Harun al-Rashid, which fascinated Malraux; it was also the history of the entire Near and Middle East, including Byzantium, the Crusades, and not least the history of Persia, as far back as classical antiquity and those essentially tragic figures – tragic because their achievements never quite matched their wild dreams and ambitions – Cyrus (550–529 BC), Xerxes (519–465 BC) and Alexander the Great.

Theodore Mommsen, the great historian of monarchical and republican Rome, once remarked that when one surveys the landscape of the ancient past all one encounters are ruins. Malraux may never have read a single work by Mommsen, but he was fascinated by ruins and what, in their fragmented way, they tell us of vanished civilizations. One such ruin was the legendary city of Isfahan, which during the reign of the greatest of modern Persian rulers, Shah Abbas I (1557–1628), had become a royal capital of more than 600,000 inhabitants – a population greater than that of seventeenth-century Amsterdam, Genoa, or Venice – but which, one century later, suffered a vertiginous decline as the result of an Afghan invasion.

The idea of weaving a 'Persian fantasy' from the historical fabric of this once great but later derelict city seems to have occurred to Malraux as early as 1920, when he was putting the finishing touches to *Lunes en papier*. But whereas that kaleidoscopic 'fable', drawing its inspiration from romantic phantasmagoria, poetic metaphors, and medieval morality plays, was located in a kind of timeless wonderland, this new fantasy was linked to specific geographical regions and permeated with allusions to actual historical happenings. Clio, the Muse of History, thus joined her sisters, Calliope, Melpomene, Euterpe and Terpsichore in a curious *danse macabre*.

The first fragment of this 'Persian fantasy', entitled *L'Expédition d'Isfahan*, was published (under a pseudonym) in one of the last issues of *L'Indochine*, shortly before it was throttled to death in August 1925. In this short version the basic historico-fictitious ingredients were already present: the story of a disorderly march across an arid desert, followed by a curiously thwarted siege of the seemingly uninhabited 'ghost town', and culminating in an ignominious retreat across a parched wilderness in which most of the attackers perish.

After his return to Paris in 1926 Malraux decided to pad this skeletal outline with oriental flesh and add exotic trappings, casually borrowed from a variety of historical sources. What is most striking in this 'Persian fantasy' is the author's morbid delectation in scenes of violence, cruelty and terror. The narrator listens to another 'chronicler' describe the sacking and gutting of a palace ('one of the great nights of the world, one in which the exhausted gods yield the earth to the wild djinni of poetry'). This description (borrowed from Chinese history – Peking, 1860) is followed by another, even grimmer account of an 'exploit' perpetrated by the Byzantine Emperor Basil II, who crushed a Bulgarian revolt (in AD 1014), by having 15,000 prisoners blinded and then led back home by a few lucky soldiers who had been allowed to retain one eye. Then comes an account of another atrocity: the impaling of 20,000 Turkish and Bulgarian prisoners ordered, four centuries later, by the dreaded Transylvanian prince, Vlad III 'Tepes' ('The Impaler'), better known to posterity as Dracula ('the Devil'). As for the lethargic siege of what had once been the 'fairest city in the world' (Isfahan), but which is now eerily empty of inhabitants, it clearly owed much to one of the most famous stories of *The Thousand and One Nights* (the 'City of Brass' whose inert inhabitants have been petrified by some mysterious spell), and even more perhaps to the nightmarish obsessions of the author, born under the sign of Scorpio; for it is the terrifying sight of a lava flow of 'black pincers' engulfing the ghost city's empty houses which finally arouses the besiegers from their torpor and precipitates a flight across the barren desert, where most of them are devoured by vultures.

In the spring of 1927 these 'prose poems, which reek of literary opium' – as the writer Drieu la Rochelle later called them – were published in the prestigious quarterly, *Commerce*. Malraux, however, was still not satisfied. And so, after adding a few baroque touches borrowed from Kievan history, he offered this slightly longer text, now entitled *Royaume-Farfelu*, to the publisher, Gaston Gallimard.

In 1911, when André Gide and the other founding fathers of the *NRF* had decided to branch out into book publishing, their choice for a new, urgently needed partner had finally fallen on the thirty-year-old Gaston Gallimard because he seemed to offer a rare combination of virtues: he was rich enough to contribute the necessary capital, sophisticated enough to be genuinely interested in 'good' literature, competent enough to be able to 'run the shop' efficiently, and, not least, docile enough to heed the wishes of the founding fathers, led by Gide. However, with the passage of time this affable and affluent connoisseur of fine paintings and fine books had, thanks to his discriminating taste, sound judgement, and great personal charm, developed into a force and power of his own.

From the very beginning the *NRF* had been a collective enterprise. This was one of its great strengths, one which, when the monthly was revived in the summer of 1919, was given formal consecration by the establishment of a *comité de lecture* (a committee of readers) which met once a week in Gaston Gallimard's office to weigh the merits of new manuscripts. The book publishing branch's umbilical association with a prestigious literary monthly was also an enormous asset, since the *NRF* acted not only as a magnet for poets, short story writers, and aspiring authors, but also, thanks to the prior appearance of serialized extracts, as a sounding-box or amplifier for soon-to-be-published books.

Nothing remotely comparable existed in Bernard Grasset's editorial set-up, which from its earliest beginnings in 1909 had been essentially a one-man show. Of the relative merits and weaknesses of the two rival publishing companies – Grasset and Gallimard – André Malraux in the spring of 1928 was keenly aware. He had never really hit it off with Bernard Grasset. Much as he appreciated the early interest he had taken in the 'temple-robber of Angkor', Malraux knew that Grasset had been disappointed by the all too 'ethereal' *Tentation de l'Occident*, and he may well have suspected that his publisher, who was at heart a political conservative, had mixed feelings about *Les Conquérants*.

Thanks to the occasional book reviews he wrote for Jean Paulhan's *NRF*, Malraux was no longer a stranger to the House of Gallimard. One day, out of the blue, he received a note from 'Gaston' – as he was familiarly known to the members of the staff – asking if he would be interested in writing a 'Life of Edgar Allan Poe' for an NRF series of popular biographies. Malraux declined the flattering invitation on the grounds that he would do a poor job of it, adding: 'Among curious existences, there is one I might perhaps write fairly well, and that's my own; but given the title of your series, it would perhaps be premature?' However, Malraux took this opportunity to submit a copy of his Persian fantasy (as published in *Commerce*) to Gallimard.

On receiving Malraux's *farfelu* tale, Gallimard passed it on to his chief editor. Paulhan's answer, penned in the margin of Malraux's accompanying letter, was terse and to the point: 'Yes, if other books by him.' Although the NRF stood to gain little in terms of money and prestige from the publication of *Royaume-Farfelu*, the company was likely to profit greatly later on if the twenty-six-year-old author of *Les Conquérants* (currently being serialized in the *NRF*) wrote other books of exciting fiction based on his adventures in the Far East. Accordingly, a contract was drawn up granting Gallimard an option on five future novels once Malraux had fulfilled his contractual obligations to Grasset.

In signing this momentous contract, on April 12, 1928, Malraux was not putting an immediate end to his association with Bernard Grasset. But he was very definitely preparing a long-hoped-for transfer of allegiance. A series of extraordinary accidents – the stock market fiasco, the Cambodian foray, his arrest and trial, the crusade with Paul Monin, the surprise contract offer from Grasset – had imposed a long detour on his itinerary in the world of letters. But now at last he was nearly back on the highroad of his aspirations.

On January 11, 1928 reports reached Paris that Leon Trotsky and a number of other prominent 'opposition' figures had been banished to Astrakhan and distant Siberia by order of the Soviet Communist Party's Central Executive Committee. The news was predictably greeted by the servile Communist daily, *L'Humanité*, as a well deserved punishment for 'counter-revolutionaries', by the conservative press as one more proof that the Soviets were a dangerous and totally untrustworthy lot, and by the socialist trade-union organ, *Le Peuple*, with howls of protest and a denunciation of Stalin, whom it compared to Ivan the Terrible.

André Malraux's reaction, though at first privately expressed, was every bit as violent. But as the weeks passed and Trotsky's 'sojourn' in the Kazakstan capital of Alma Ata began to look like a permanent banishment, he grew increasingly impatient and began considering the possibility of recruiting a literary commando force, dedicated to 'rescuing' the former Red Army commander. Probably Malraux's hope was that he could enlist the co-operation of a few hardy souls – authors with a taste for adventure like Pierre Mac Orlan, Francis Carco, Joseph Kessel, and even the one-handed Blaise Cendrars (a veteran of trans-Siberian train travel) – have them apply for tourist visas, and then let the world know, once they had reached Moscow, that they had come to see Trotsky: an initiative certain to embarrass Stalin and his Party colleagues, who would not dare to incarcerate a group of prominent French writers. For it seems inconceivable that Malraux could have envisaged anything as foolhardy as trying to infiltrate the Soviet Union clandestinely via Afghan Turkestan or Kashmir and the Pamir plateau. In any case, Gaston Gallimard was in no mood to see some of his most popular authors exposed to the perils of such a risky venture, and the harebrained scheme was quietly buried.

Anxious to reinforce his still tenuous association with his new publisher, Malraux spent much of the summer of 1928 angling for a slot as a book reviewer on the *NRF*'s editorial staff, like his friend Marcel Arland. But Jean Paulhan's monthly had by this time acquired a formidable team of book reviewers, led by Albert Thibaudet, who was ably seconded by two first class critics – Ramon Fernandez and Benjamin Crémieux.

There was, however, another way of putting Malraux's talents to profitable use – by having him join the NRF's increasingly influential readers' committee. This decisive step, sealing his association with the House of

Gallimard, was taken in early October; by which time *Les Conquérants* – with its spectacular bright green streamer announcing that it had been banned in Russia and Italy – was being prominently displayed in booksellers' windows and was beginning to ignite heated discussions in every literary salon.

Most of the members of the important readers' committee – beginning with the forty-three-year-old Jean Paulhan and the forty-seven-year-old Gaston Gallimard – were considerably older than André Malraux, who had not yet celebrated his twenty-seventh birthday. If we exclude André Gide and Jean Schlumberger, who could (but rarely chose to) attend the regular weekly meetings of the readers' committee, the oldest-looking, if not actually the oldest, of these literary heavyweights was forty-year-old Benjamin Crémieux, whose thick spectacles and 'somewhat Assyrian' growth of beard – to quote Nino Frank – gave him a distinctly patriarchal look. After the Great War, during which he was wounded three times, he had been offered a senior newspaper reading post in the Italian service of the French Foreign Ministry – a daytime job which did not keep him from contributing a weekly article to the *Nouvelles Littéraires*, one or two articles a month to *Candide*, and a book review almost every month to the *NRF*.

An equally avid book-devourer and influential critic was Ramon Fernandez, a swarthy, dark-haired human dynamo whose passion for tango dancing had made him a favourite guest with the salon hostesses of the aristocratic Saint-Germain quarter. But with little doubt the most impressive member of this literary conclave – one of the most talented group of readers ever assembled by a publisher – was the forty-eight-year-old Bernard Groethuysen. The son of a Dutch doctor and a Russian mother, Groeth, as he was popularly called, had studied philosophy and art history in Vienna, Munich, and Berlin under Theodor Gomperz, Georg Simmel, Heinrich Wölfflin, and Wilhelm Dilthey, receiving his doctorate in 1904. In the early 1920s he had chosen to settle in Paris with his companion, Alix Guillain, a fervent communist who preferred a 'free union' to the old-fashioned constraints of marriage. The author of several books devoted to German philosophy, he had begun a controversial work (published by Gallimard) on *The Origins of the Bourgeois Spirit in France*.

However, it was not so much as an author that Groeth was an extraordinary phenomenon; it was even more as an oral performer. Unmistakably bohemian, with a wild shock of hair crowning his 'Socratic brow' and a muscular and partly bearded face, he looked a bit forbidding, with 'something stormy and violent' in his expression – as his close friend, Jean Paulhan, later described it. But this initial impression was quickly belied when the deep-set grey-green eyes lit up and he began to speak. For he was one of those human beings who live only for ideas. He could carry on for hours on almost any philosophical, historical, or aesthetic subject, and, being a chain smoker who had no time to look around for ashtrays, his rumpled suit or jacket would gradually change colour as it acquired a powdering of grey ash.

Of all the members of the NRF's readers' committee, it was Bernard Groethuysen who most attracted André Malraux. The feeling of friendship was fully reciprocated despite the marked difference in their ages, and it was not long before Groeth and Alix Guillain – at forty years still remarkably youthful-looking, pretty, and fair-haired – were leaving their Montparnasse studio apartment to come to dinner at 122, Boulevard Murat. After dinner, served on a collapsible bridge table, Malraux and Groethuysen would pace back and forth in the limited space available, each 'speaking his piece' – André in lyrical flights, Groeth in subtle interrogations – in a kind of dialogue-ballet which never ceased to fascinate Clara. Groeth, as she later recalled, 'did little contradicting, receiving the thought of his interlocutor and returning it to him enriched . . . Kafka was one of the presents he brought us. Previously there had been Freud, about whom he was careful not to speak with the casual irony encountered in the circles he frequented.'

At the weekly meetings of the NRF's readers' committee in Gallimard's office, literary merit was more highly prized than academic profundity. Here, just as he had shone in Daniel Halévy's salon, André Malraux flabbergasted his fellow readers by the brilliance of his interventions. 'Recreating in his own way the often unequal works . . . that were submitted to his judgement, he imbued them with such originality and intensity that his portrayals dazzled those who were not informed, just as they often dumbfounded those who had preceded him in the appraisal of that particular book,' wrote Robert Aron, who as Gaston Gallimard's personal secretary regularly attended these sessions.

During this same month of October 1928 Bernard Grasset terminated the generous monthly allowances he had been paying to Malraux. On the whole, André had good reason to be proud of the eight handsomely illustrated books he had brought out under the A la Sphere and Aux Aldes imprints. The tangible results so impressed Gaston Gallimard that he decided to demote his principal adviser for the arts – a lightweight poet and *bon vivant* named Roger Allard – and to replace him by Malraux. André was now offered a tiny garret under the eaves – quickly dubbed 'the Cabinet of Dr Caligari' – and as the House of Gallimard's artistic director he was at last able carry on his correspondence on paper carrying the prestigious NRF letterhead.

In early November Malraux was accorded the exceptional honour of being invited to have tea with André Gide in the new triplex apartment he had recently moved into on the Rue Vaneau, an easy ten-minute walk from the NRF's offices on the Rue de Grenelle. Wonderfully quiet, with an oblique view over the forecourt of what had once been the Imperial Austrian Embassy, it had been specially fitted out with an upstairs library for Gide's books, a studio for his photography-loving nephew, Marc Allégret, and a communicating door leading into the neighbouring apartment, occupied by

Gide's friend, Maria Saint-Clair, the widow of the Belgian painter, Théophile Van Rysselberghe. Her daughter Elisabeth had had a discreet affair with Gide and had given him a daughter (Catherine) in April 1923. Although her own relations with Gide had always been platonic, 'Mme Théo', as she was generally called, had for years been an almost inseparable companion, acting as a literary adviser and faithful scribe whose precious diary entries were intended to do for André Gide what Boswell had done for Dr Johnson.

Not unexpectedly, Mme Théo was present at this tea party, as was Jean Schlumberger. 'A free spirit and a demolisher', she noted in her diary of Malraux on this November 15, 1928,

> with, however, the balance that true culture provides; a monotonous, cold flow of speech, cut-and-dried opinions, formulated in extreme terms. He passes judgement on people and on things with very few words. His observations are very much his own, and always carried, on the most general plane, to their ultimate consequences. He displays neither waver nor hesitation.

The signal honour paid to André Malraux in being the first young writer of his generation to be invited to the Rue Vaneau was all the more remarkable since Gide, who was more than thirty years his senior, did not like *Les Conquérants* when he read it a few days later. 'I had trouble reading this book,' he admitted to Mme Théo. 'How unhistorically-minded I am! He [Malraux] is too young or too close to events. I will tell him this.'

Gide was as good as his word, explaining to Malraux when they next met that he had had trouble following the sequence of events in *Les Conquérants*, 'because I never know who is on whose side, who is winning or who is losing'. But this admission shed less light on the novel's composition and its 'faults' than it did on a particular blind spot in André Gide's mentality. During his one and only intervention at Pontigny, the previous August, Gide had explained that the group gathered around Mallarmé after the Franco-Prussian War – the only literary movement in France that really mattered – had sought to reduce everything, including religion and morality, to a question of aesthetics. What he did not say was the extent to which he himself, born in 1869, on the eve of the great Symbolist explosion, had been influenced by this school, notably in his indifferent attitude towards history. As André Malraux himself was to write forty-five years later, in a remarkable preface to Mme Théo's Journal:

> People have often been astonished by Maxime Du Camp's portrait of Baudelaire, even though he had published him in the *Revue de Paris*, before [the appearance of] *Les Fleurs du Mal*. If he didn't take him seriously, it was because high culture then implied a historical culture. Napoleon III had published a *Caesar*. Chateaubriand, Lamartine, Hugo

were obsessed by History ... . But Baudelaire, Mallarmé, Verlaine, and the second generation of the Symbolists knew nothing of this transfigured realm and of the development of History as destiny. Benjamin Constant, Balzac, and even Flaubert were aware of History, and regarded anyone ignoring it as a kind of amputated cripple. Gide brushed it aside, not out of ignorance – his culture was extensive – but because it was alien to his being.

The coming storms of twentieth-century Europe were to exact a cruel revenge during the sombre 1930s. For Gide during this period it would be the other, far younger, André who was destined to become the guide and mentor rather than a disciple.

16

The Royal Road to Success

The sudden change in their fortunes, due to the spectacular success of *Les Conquérants*, made it possible for André and Clara to leave their tiny two-and-a-half-room flat on the Boulevard Murat and move to a more spacious apartment on the Boulevard Berthier, situated one mile north of the Arc de Triomphe. The move put an end to the family lunches with Grandmother Adrienne and André's mother. It also made it more difficult for Clara to see her widowed mother, Mme Goldschmidt, with whom she had finally been reconciled.

Now that he had moved from his distant Auteuil villa close to the literary heart of Paris, Gide had decided to use 'Le Vaneau' (his new apartment) to hold informal discussions. André and Clara, among the first to be invited to these Wednesday afternoon and evening get-togethers, were again present on February 6, 1929 for a particularly lively debate during which Malraux, for once, was almost outshone by someone as vehement, articulate, and iconoclastic as himself: the thirty-seven-year-old writer, Emmanuel Berl. Several of Gide's friends had been invited, along with the rare-book publisher, Jacques Schiffrin, and the young Catholic novelist, Julien Green. Green, seconded by Schiffrin, argued that what mattered in novel writing was not the subject matter but stylistic artistry and the originality of the author's viewpoint. They were promptly challenged by Berl, who claimed that most contemporary French writers were still churning out conventional works of fiction, investing their characters with old-fashioned, stereotyped sentiments which bore little relation to present-day preoccupations. Malraux insisted that what was lacking in contemporary novels was psychological acuity in providing new insights into the hidden motivations of human actions – Gide being, he added, the only major writer with whom young authors could establish a rapport. As the heated debate progressed, illuminated by Berl's lightning sallies and Malraux's 'extraordinary eloquence', Gide found it difficult to keep up, later admitting to Mme Théo, with reference to Malraux: 'I am always put off by a kind of thinking which expresses itself with such precision. For my part, each time I feel a new idea burgeoning within me, I find that it has surprising trouble breaking through.'

A furiously nonconformist debunker, with the dark 'head of a fanatical Mephisto' (to quote André Chamson's wife, Lucie), Emmanuel Berl was ever ready to fulminate against the smug society in which he had been brought up. His *bête noire* was the well-heeled bourgeoisie from which he stemmed – he was distantly related to both Proust and Bergson – and his god at this particular moment was none other than Garine, the unorthodox revolutionary hero of *Les Conquérants*.

What André Malraux could not say in public was that he himself cared little for Julien Green's 'static' novels – of which the recently published *Adrienne Mesurat* was a typical example. As he wrote on April 20th to his adventurous Dutch friend, Eddy Du Perron, the poetry-loving son of a wealthy Javanese planter who had fled to Montmartre in 1922 in order to give free rein to his love of French literature and art:

> For critics (I am speaking of those who are not born idiots) the honest-to-god truth is that they like novels and that we don't like them. The longer I live, the more I realize our deep-seated indifference to what these fine fellows call 'the art of the novel'. *Adrienne Mesurat*, they tell you, is a masterpiece. This is unlikely, but even if it were true, it would have the same effect on me ... There are people who have something to express, and who never accomplish masterpieces (Montaigne, Pascal, Goya, the sculptors of Chartres) because one cannot dominate a passion that attacks the world; and there are those who 'produce objects'. But the critic, basically, is a man who likes 'objects' and not the expression of human beings.

Four years later, in a letter addressed to Edmund Wilson, Malraux candidly admitted that the 'role played by objectivity in my books is not of primary importance, and *Les Conquérants* is an "Expressionist" novel like, with all due allowances, *Wuthering Heights* and *The Brothers Karamazov*'. Malraux's meaning in the above letter to Eddy Du Perron would have been clearer if he had used the word 'intensity' rather than 'expression' as a contrast to routine 'objects' of fiction. In a revealing passage of *Les Conquérants* Garine is depicted as emerging from his literary studies at the age of twenty and wondering: 'What books are worth writing other than *Memoirs*?' If *Wuthering Heights* and *The Brothers Karamazov* were singled out as prototypes of 'Expressionist' novel writing, it was clearly, for Malraux, because Emily Brontë and Dostoevsky had personal and intense experience of the human temptations, torments and passions they had undertaken to describe.

In mid-June André and Clara were at last able to resume their travels – a pleasure they had had to forgo during three years of impecunious immobility. Their destination this time was Persia, the home of Zoroaster, the Magi, those proud Achaemenidian monarchs – Cyrus, Darius, Xerxes – the homeland of the legendary story-teller, Sheherazade, and of the great Shahs of Isfahan. It was also the alluring realm of desert mirages, amethyst domes and mountains, which Malraux had imagined so exotically in his recently published oriental fantasy, *Royaume-Farfelu*.

Still far from rich, they chose to embark at Marseilles on a cargo vessel in which they were the only passengers. The Black Sea port of Trebizond – now become the prosaic Trabzon of a fiercely Kemalist Turkey – must have seemed disappointing to the visionary author who, in *Royaume-Farfelu*, had peopled it with a mythological profusion of marine monsters, deathless birds and tiny dragons. But at Batum, where they finally disembarked, they were surprised to discover a Soviet port where noisy taverns, reeking of cheap tobacco and vodka, seemed unaffected by the triumph of 'scientific social-ism' and belonged more to the familiar world of Gogol, Dostoevsky, and Saltykov-Shchedrin.

They had trouble finding the railway station, and Clara had to use her German on a student they fortunately encountered before they could obtain two tickets for a 'hard' (wooden benches instead of cushioned seats) train journey through the mountainous Caucasus. But on their arrival in the Azerbaijan port of Baku, flanked by cohorts of steel scorpions busily sucking their 'black gold' from the bowels of the earth, they were informed by the suspicious hotel management and the local Intourist bureau that they should not have made this trip unescorted.

The next day, on a tiny steamship which took them across the green waters of the Caspian, Clara found herself seated next to the German ambassador, Count Friedrich von der Schulenburg, who explained to her in a correct but brittle French that Persia was a 'desert with small oases'. Not to be outdone by the forceful Mustapha Kemal, who had outlawed beards, turbans, and even the red fez in neighbouring Turkey, the new strongman of Persia, a former commander of the Cossack Brigade named Reza Pahlevi, had placed an official ban on the wearing of the veil. After they had landed at the port of Bander-e-Pahlavi, however, Clara was amused to see one of her shipboard companions slip her *rubandeh* over her head, in instinctive obedience to the age-old Islamic custom.

An automobile with huge wheels was waiting to transport the small group of foreigners to Rasht. From there they were driven up through the verdant valleys and narrow gorges of the Elburz mountain range over an untarred road, as crevassed and rocky as the craggy landscape, on to the parched highlands leading south to the ruined city of Isfahan.

The once thriving capital, which at the time of Shah Abbas had accom-modated more than 600,000 souls, 160 mosques, and 1,800 caravanserais, was now little more than a shell – with a single, rather squalid, inn kept by an Armenian for transient sightseers. Its one and only bathtub was located in a loft, reached by a ladder; the water had to be brought in buckets, since the connecting pipes were missing. But this discomfort was offset for André and Clara by the splendid view from their bedroom window down the once proud Chahar Bagh: the 'Four Gardens', which Shah Abbas I had lined with basins and fountains. The fountains and basins had disappeared, but wild rose bushes and sturdy sycamores had survived centuries of neglect.

Just as Schulenburg had told them, the French consul, Brasseur, was a most unusual character – a Jew, born and brought up in the Middle East and the head of the local Hebrew community. He maintained an 'open house' for Sufi mystics, Shi'ite theologians, Bahai heretics, sages and sceptics of every kind and creed, and even for a few 'free thinkers' who claimed to be Zoroastrians. In the evenings, after their chauffeur brought them back from a dusty excursion to one of the surrounding villages bordering the highway to Shiraz or to the legendary tomb of Darius, in the mountains, André would plunge into stimulating metaphysical discussions about life, death, man's purpose on this earth, and the nature of the supernatural. In this high-altitude climate of sun and moon-blessed exaltation beneath a timeless Babylonian sky, such topics seemed as natural to the unhurried participants as, in the West, an argument about the weather or the prospects for the next day's outing would have been.

One day, while lunching with the journalist Louis Martin-Chauffier, a jovial, pipe-smoking Breton with a disarming sense of humour, his wife Simone asked Malraux what he thought about when he had nothing in particular on his mind.

'It never occurs to me to think of nothing in particular.'

Simone Martin-Chauffier found this hard to believe.

'When, for example, I walk in the street,' Malraux explained, 'I reflect about a precise subject, chosen before I go out.'

'Yes, of course,' said Simone, 'one always thinks of something. But there are moments when it's imprecise, when one floats, when one daydreams.'

'I never daydream,' Malraux insisted. 'It's a waste of time.'

'Even when you are in the street?'

'I choose a subject to think about. When it's exhausted, and when some external reality imposes itself, I push it aside for a moment, then I take it up again.'

'Just where you left off?'

'Just where I left off, of course.'

Persia and all its marvels were still very much on André Malraux's mind when he and Clara returned to Paris on August 21st. From his tiny NRF office he telephoned to André Gide, who was about to leave for the annual literary get-together at Pontigny.

'What!' exclaimed Gide, 'It's you, Malraux? Just back from Persia this morning? And you absolutely want to see me before my departure? . . Ah, where the devil are you . . At the NRF?'

Gide, who was going to meet Roger Martin du Gard and two friends (Simon and Dorothy Bussy) for lunch at the Gare de Lyon, then suggested that Malraux join them there.

Accompanied by his faithful companion, Mme Théo, Gide had the taxi-driver stop in front of the NRF offices to see if, by chance, Malraux was still there. He was.

'Nimble, even thinner and paler than he had been ... he jumped into the taxi and wedged himself in among the suitcases,' Mme Théo later noted.

> The usual phrases about the journey and its fatigue were elbowed aside before they had been uttered, and, I believe, even before he was properly seated he was talking about the Persians' rapport with the divine.
>
> Malraux's conversation bounds across the centuries, history, and religions. The topic presented to you by his thinking is always so spare, so simplified and clear-cut that one would feel ungracious in not immediately taking up the subject, and thus one finds oneself adhering to things one has never thought about ... All through luncheon he was tireless, interesting, stupefying, and I could see by the faces of the others that he had made the same impression on them too.

It was probably in January or February of 1929 that André Malraux began seriously working on his next novel, *La Voie royale*. There are two important clues as to its development. The first is a letter, dated May 23rd and addressed to Roger Martin du Gard. Malraux had received the latest chapter in the forty-nine-year-old novelist's many-volumed chronicle of the Thibault family – *La Mort du Père* (describing Oscar Thibault's death) – but he had put the book aside for some weeks, being at that moment 'so violently obsessed by its subject, which impregnates all of the beginning of the novel I am writing, that I wanted to undergo a kind of [dis] intoxication cure and read nothing for a while that dealt with death'.

This letter corroborates Clara's later recollection of these months of tense gestation, during which André could hardly talk of anything but death – particularly with Bernard Groethuysen and Alix Guillain, both of whom, being Marxists, stoically rejected any notion of an after life.

A second clue regarding the composition of *La Voie royale* was provided years later by André Malraux himself, in his *Antimémoires* (published in 1967). During a 'radiant Italian morning', as he was pacing the deck of the cargo ship that was carrying them through the Straits of Messina on their way to Batum, he experienced an 'illumination' as to the character of Perken and the 'holocaust' he imagined as a climax for his novel.

From the three separate manuscript stages through which the novel passed it is clear that Malraux wanted to weave together at least four different themes or strands of personal experience. The first was his 'statue-robbing' adventure in the jungle depths of Cambodia. The second might be called the intellectual rationale for this archaeological 'raid', based on a philosophy of museology and art. The third was the obsession with the theme of death. The fourth constituent element, which soon dwarfed all the others, as the figure of a restless hero-adventurer, motivated by a sullen dissatisfaction with 'static' society, whose achievements (and even failures) are later magnified and transformed into folklore myth.

There is, of course, no compelling reason why a novelist should not weave disparate elements together to form a coherent whole. Indeed, life being essentially many-sided and complex, this is almost a *sine qua non* condition for any truly 'great' work of fiction. But in this particular case the inherent diversity in the aims created serious complications and problems of plausibility, which Malraux never fully overcame.

In the first, most clearly autobiographical version of the novel, the narrator, Claude Vannec, an enterprising young archaeologist interested in Khmer art, is accompanied by a friend named Dévy, obviously a combination of Clara and Louis Chevasson. After their stopover at Djibouti, where they visit a brothel, a mysterious passenger boards the ship: a 'legendary' English adventurer named Parker who, acting as adviser to the Court of Siam, had made himself a kind of viceroy in the wild eastern regions of that country. He had, however, finally fallen out of favour and been forced to leave the country after imprudently falling in love with a Russian *femme fatale*, who had previously seduced, married, and was thought to have poisoned, King Chulangkorn's second son. Although Parker himself was a fictional invention, this Russian lady had actually led an adventurous existence during the last decade of the nineteenth century, and her Siamese husband-prince had died in mysterious circumstances at the Raffles Hotel in Singapore: one more proof of how adept Malraux was in exploiting historical 'oddities' for the purposes of his fiction.

It did not take Malraux long to realize the inherent weakness of this plot construction. The colourless Dévy was accordingly eliminated, or rather metamorphosed, into a mysterious, world-weary adventurer named Radke, whose two principal obsessions are sex and a sense of the ultimate futility of human existence. Intrigued by the young Vannec's plan to unearth an undiscovered Khmer temple along the once proud 'Royal Road' leading from Angkor to the Dangrek mountains, Radke agrees to assist the novice explorer in his partly illicit enterprise. The expedition ends with their discovery of a temple half-buried in the Cambodian jungle. Claude Vannec is then left with the problem of getting his sculpted stones out of the country, to be sold to interested dealers in Berlin or elsewhere, while Radke, who had originally agreed to assist Vannec for pecuniary motives (he was in dire need of money), inexplicably continues on his way into the mountainous frontier regions inhabited by savage tribes.

Malraux had probably reached this unsatisfactory point in his narrative when he experienced his creative 'illumination' during the cargo ship's passage through the Straits of Messina. The problem confronting him now was how to splice together two basically dissimilar stories: Claude Vannec's jungle search for neglected Khmer statuary, and Radke's imperative need to return to the wild, 'unsubjugated' highlands, where he had carved out a kind of feudal fiefdom as the 'ruler' of a local tribe.

Malraux tried to solve this problem by introducing a new theme: that of individual loyalty. Accordingly Claude Vannec, forgetting his original aim of getting his precious Khmer stones out of Cambodia to be sold abroad, agrees to accompany his older, more experienced companion into the mountainous regions bordering Siam, inhabited by dangerously 'unsubjugated' tribes, such as the Mois, the Stiengs, and the Jarais. In strict terms of geography this made no sense, since these particular tribes had generally inhabited the thickly forested regions of the southern Annamese mountain range, bordering Laos *east* of the Mekong river. No Cambodian temple-robber, anxious to make it to Siam with his precious cargo of 'lifted' statuary, could conceivably have undertaken such an enormous detour from the 'Royal Way'; but Malraux figured (quite rightly, as it happened) that most French readers knew next to nothing of these ethnic problems, and that he could relocate the Mois, the Stiengs and other 'untamed' tribes several hundred miles to the west, in the uplands of the Dangrek mountains that marked the border between Cambodia and Siam.

In the final version of his novel, Malraux changed Radke's name to Perken – a name probably inspired by Malraux's friend, Eddy Du Perron, who, after his wealthy parents had sold their estates in distant Java and returned to Holland, had chosen to live a bohemian life, contributing poems and short stories to Flemish avant-garde reviews under the pen name of Duco Perken. Perken now absorbed some of the aura of mystery surrounding the 'legendary' Parker.

Of the nine or ten hero-adventurers who directly or indirectly influenced Malraux's fictional creation of Perken, at least five were prototypes of successful conquerors or rulers: Cortez, the conqueror of Mexico; Pizarro, the viceroy of Peru; Balboa, the explorer of Panama and 'discoverer' of the Pacific Ocean; Savorgnan de Brazza, the explorer and conqueror of the northern Congo region of Equatorial Africa; and the extraordinary James Brooke (1803–68), who not only set himself up as the 'Raja' of Sarawak (on the East-Indies island of Borneo), but established a short-lived dynasty. All of these men had been motivated, during the early stages of their adventurous careers, by aspirations of national aggrandizement as much as by personal ambition. This was not, however, the sort of character Malraux was bent on portraying. He wanted to create another Garine, another *révolté métaphysique* (as Clara aptly put it), a larger-than-life 'outlaw' and rebel against 'civilized' society, but one unmotivated by any patriotic sentiment or ideological conviction: another *aventurier raté*, a human failure or misfit, not unlike the strange derelicts or pathetic dreamers that people so many of Joseph Conrad's novels.

There was, as it happened, a real-life model for this kind of adventurer, at once heroic and pathetic: a Frenchman named Marie-Charles David, who had landed in Saigon in 1865 and had assumed the bogus title of Baron

David de Mayrcna – Mayrena being the name of his 'family castle' in the Savoie mountains of south-eastern France. During the 1920s several books were written about Mayrena, describing in detail how this garrulous adventurer had talked the French colonial authorities into letting him undertake a 'civilizing' mission among the 'unsubjugated' tribes of southern Annam. With the help of fancy uniforms, extraordinary self-assurance and brazen fearlessness, he had penetrated into this dangerous region and proclaimed himself 'King of the Sedangs'. Succumbing to the *folie de grandeur* which is apt to afflict this type of adventurer, Mayrena had enjoyed two years of 'regal' living (1888–90), during which he had mesmerized his native subjects by the feathered and medalled splendour of his imposing person. Finally disowned by the French colonial authorities, the spendthrift 'monarch' had been forced to return to France, where his vivid accounts of his exploits as a 'promoter of civilization' and an enemy of barbaric superstitions had enthralled the spellbound habitués of the cabarets and nightclubs of Montmartre, but had left hardheaded bankers in Paris and Brussels singularly unmoved.

At least one other Frenchman, of a less flamboyant but equally courageous mettle, influenced Malraux's description of the 'untamed' hinterland in the second part of his novel. An ethnologist, Prosper Odend'hal, had lost his life in 1904 after imprudently entering a sorcerer's hut during a search for the 'sacred' sword of the fierce Jarai tribe, which was supposedly invested with the talismanic power of being able to unleash fiery thunderbolts from heaven for the defeat and destruction of their enemies. Almost certainly this was the 'holocaust' André Malraux had in mind, as he paced the deck in the Straits of Messina, and which he later transformed, in the final pages of the novel, into a series of fires lit by the hostile Stiengs, desperately determined to halt the Siamese construction of a railway through their territory.

Literary, as well as real-life, models also influenced the composition of the novel's most mysterious and sketchily described character: Grabot, the swashbuckling deserter from the French Army who had helped the Siamese to establish their authority over the lawless regions bordering Laos – only to end up a pitiful human wreck, blinded by his 'subjects' and chained like a workhorse to a rotating millwheel bar. In inventing this somewhat spectral figure, Malraux may well have recalled a story the novelist Joseph Kessel liked to tell of how, one day, while walking along a Shanghai wharf, he had come upon a blind beggar, propped up against some sacks. Though clothed in Chinese rags, he was obviously not of Asiatic origin, and after questioning him in French and English, Kessel had switched to Russian. The limp body quivered and, raising his sightless eyes, the beggar, in a cavernous voice, uttered these extraordinary words: 'I was with Unberg-Sternberg, viceroy of Mongolia.' A trusted lieutenant of the flamboyantly anti-Bolshevik Baltic baron, this soldier of misfortune had been seized and cruelly blinded, by the local inhabitants of Urga, but had managed to make it to the

Pacific coast, aided by a devoted manservant. Kessel may well have told Malraux this story during the spring of 1928, as a warning of what might happen to him if he pursued his madcap plan to liberate Trotsky in distant Alma Ata.

One thing, at any rate, is certain: the strange 'mission' Perken assigns himself in wanting to find Grabot was directly inspired by Marlow's search for Kurtz, the initially 'inspired' prophet-ruler and later totem-captive of a savage Congolese tribe in Joseph Conrad's *The Heart of Darkness*.

After completing his novel in the late spring of 1930, André again left with Clara on a long trip to Central Asia. Their destination this time was Afghanistan, which they decided to approach via Moscow and Tashkent.

The previous year Afghanistan had been convulsed by an insurrection of fierce Shinwari tribesmen, enraged because King Amanollah had set out to imitate Reza Shah in Persia and Mustapha Kemal in Turkey by introducing Western reforms and freeing women from the compulsory wearing of the veil. The overly 'progressive' monarch had finally been forced to abdicate and flee from Kabul. A bandit chieftain, Batacha-Saquao ('the son of the water-carrier'), had taken advantage of the anarchy to occupy Kabul and to proclaim himself Emir Habibollah II. Soviet forces had occupied the northern town of Mazar-e-Sharif in the name of their pretender, Gholam-Nabi Khan. But the British, being closer to Kabul, had ended up the victors in this struggle for influence by supporting General Nader Khan, who had defeated and executed the 'bandit Emir' and proclaimed himself the turbulent country's new sovereign under the title of Nader Shah.

Kabul, in this month of June 1930, was definitely not a tourist attraction. This explains why André, Clara and a young Afghan were the only passengers in the stiflingly hot Tadjik town of Termès to board the small, single-engine monoplane bound for the Afghan capital.

In the narrow, crowded streets of Kabul, the twentieth century had suddenly ceased to exist. It was an unpleasant feeling for Clara to find herself conspicuously bare-armed among a surging throng of veiled women and turbaned brigands – for such they seemed – with eyes like burning coals and gleaming daggers thrust into their pistol belts and sashes. In the shaded alleys of the bazaar the atmosphere became dangerously tense, and André had to clutch the revolver in his pocket with ostentatious determination so that they could push their way past two rows of scowling mountaineers and out into the blinding whiteness of the sun-baked square.

Shortly afterwards they went to call on the French consul, who was surprised that none of his 'observers' at the airfield had informed him of their arrival. But of course, they had come from Moscow – which in itself was most unusual. 'Let me give you a piece of advice,' he said, wishing to be helpful. 'Don't venture alone into the bazaar. Particularly on a Thursday, like today, which is reserved for the Afridis' – a particularly wild mountain tribe.

'We've just come from there,' replied Malraux calmly.

The consul, informed that they were bound for India, offered to accompany them as far as Ghazni. The drive was rough and rocky and was finally brought to a halt by a puncture. All they could do was sit by the roadside and wait for another vehicle to come along. They had consumed almost half of their provisions when a small dust storm approached across the windswept plain.

An extraordinary jalopy – 'like something out of a Buster Keaton film' (as Clara later recalled) – drove up. The governor of Ghazni had dispatched his son along the road to find out what was wrong. The gubernatorial feast laid on for the distinguished guests could not have been more lavish – with seventeen different rice dishes served in unrelenting succession, which André and Clara would have found easier to consume had their stomachs been less full of chicken sandwiches.

Here, as in Kabul, Clara stubbornly insisted on asserting her prerogatives as a 'European woman' by walking about bare-armed as well as bare-headed – to the polite consternation of the governor who, to avoid an 'incident', had her preceded by an armed guard of six barefoot soldiers, with another, equally bootless, squad of swarthy riflemen protecting her from behind.

At Jellalabad they spent a restless night in a small royal pavilion, kept awake by the guttural war cries and invocations of Allah uttered by Afridi tribesmen. From there they growled their way around the umpteen curves and hairpin bends of the sinuous Khyber Pass as far as the frontier post, where a rough-hewn wooden barrier was raised for their entry into India. Looking back as they passed, they saw a large signboard on which were written the words: 'From here on we no longer guarantee the lives of Europeans'.

At Peshawar André suddenly decided to head east and upward across the verdant Vale of Kashmir as far as the 'floating city' of Srinagar. They rented a houseboat, moored to the river bank, and spent a few idle days, cared for by seven sahib-tending manservants and a versatile artisan, encountered in the bazaar, who carved a series of small teakwood dragons for André.

One day, while André was off 'exploring', two itinerant pedlars stopped by the houseboat and tried to interest Clara in their worthless artefacts. They spoke a pidgin English, enough to make it clear to her that they knew of a place in Rawalpindi where the kind of 'white heads' her husband was interested in were secretly sold. Malraux, on his return, carefully noted the address.

The long journey down from the flowered highlands of Kashmir to the scorching lowlands of Rawalpindi was made in a hired Ford, which idled to a halt a few miles short of the city, having run out of fuel. The final stretch was covered by a silent jalopy, ignominiously towed into town by a pair of bullocks. André and Clara were pleasantly surprised to find their two turbaned pedlars patiently waiting for them in the shade of a whitewashed wall. Guided through a maze of narrow streets into an inner courtyard filled with women and children, they were even more surprised to find themselves ushered through another door into a cool, dimly lit store-room. Here the dirt floor was lined with scores of Graeco-Buddhist heads of Buddhas and Boddhisatvas, princes and princesses, and their faithful retainers: some relatively small, others almost as big as water-melons.

André, after a rapid examination, decided that they were genuine terra-cotta specimens, at least 1,500 years old or more – the work of Central Asian sculptors who had been influenced by the Greek artisans Alexander the Great and his successors had introduced into this Buddhist region, not fully Islamized until the eighth century. They were not clever fakes, like the 'Chinese' dragons specially carved for him in Srinagar. The prices asked seemed astonishingly low, but still far exceeded their limited resources.

Malraux, now Gaston Gallimard's artistic director, decided to appeal to him for the necessary funds. The telegram took several hours to compose. It had to sound sufficiently exciting to elicit a prompt financial response, and yet be cryptic enough not to arouse the suspicion of British postal officials, since the export from India of such 'Gandhâra' heads was now strictly forbidden by the Colonial Office in London.

After five days of anxious waiting the sorely needed sum was cabled through by a perplexed but generous Gaston Gallimard. There remained the problem of getting the precious heads out of India without the crates being opened by suspicious customs officials. Fortunately one of the pedlars was distantly related to a senior customs official in Bombay. If he was double-crossed, Malraux could reimburse Gallimard out of future book royalties. He and Clara would leave India long before the crates reached Bombay, so there was no risk of local arrest and imprisonment. The agreed sum was paid out in advance for a first set of heads and arrangements were made for a second shipment, to be paid by a cabled money order once the first crates had been safely delivered.

Weeks passed and nothing happened. He and Clara had almost forgotten about the deal struck in distant Rawalpindi when one day a pink postal form was slipped under the door of their Boulevard Berthier apartment, informing them that 'archaeological objects prior to the XIIIth century' were waiting to be picked up, duty-free, at the Bercy goods station in eastern Paris.

André's and Clara's return to Paris coincided with Bernard Grasset's autumn launch of *La Voie royale*. Nearly 100 critics reviewed Malraux's new novel, yet not more than three or four were willing to place it above *Les Conqérants*. The vast majority felt that the narrative lacked the political *raison d'être* and revolutionary 'actuality' of the earlier novel, while generally praising (and in rare cases condemning) Malraux's 'masterly' delineation of Perken. The book critic of the reactionary *Action Française* condemned the novel as 'strange, grim, and as bristling as the Cambodian forest', while Jean de Pierrefu, of *Comoedia*, in an article entitled 'New Delirious Fits of Pride', compared Malraux's 'metaphysical adventures and virtuosos of physical sensation . . . uniquely concerned with their Me' to Kipling's far more energetic characters.

On October 11th Bernard Grasset launched his publicity campaign on behalf of *La Voie royale* with a long advertisement in *Les Nouvelles Littéraires* announcing this and three other novels. More than ever determined to win that year's Goncourt Prize, he followed this with another large, but this time horizontal, advertisement, almost half of which was taken up by a photograph of a monumental Khmer statue, proudly erect amid clumps of trees and tumbled stones.

One month later Grasset published an even more eye-catching advertisement, dominated at the top by the huge carved face of a Khmer god-king with, just below *LA VOIE ROYALE*, the challenging words: 'The most discussed novel of the year'. This was followed by two astutely printed columns:

First Opinions of the Press

Against　　　　　　　　　　　　　　*For*

Le Temps (André Thérive):
In one hundred years, who knows?, this may also appear as nice and romantic as the cries of Lord Byron

Le Temps (André Thérive)
The end is truly fine, with its violence, its blasphemies, its hymn to nothingness.

La Liberté (Robert Kemp)
I do not see very clearly just what Mr Malraux is driving at. Is all he wants to do to make us shudder with this black novel in a yellow country?

Le Matin (Joseph Kessel)
I thought back on the adventurers I have met, after closing *La Voie royale*, a very fine book which André Malraux has just brought out. Each page is nourished by the bitter, powerful juice of adventure. I found this terrible tone in Perken, in Grabot, two characters whom André Malraux has imbued with such a dense life against a background of tropical creepers, brutality, mysteries, and death.

La République (F. Lefèvre)
. . . to contradict a fundamental law of aesthetics, a vital exigency of the art of the novel.

L'Europe Nouvelle (René Lalou)
I regard *La Voie royale* as a veritable success; I see in it a work in which are durably expressed the personality, the carnal intelligence of a pioneer, and in which is also reflected the appearance that the genuine power of the human being has assumed in our time.

The comments printed under "For" were longer than those lined up under the "Against" heading – the blank spaces being calculated to suggest that what the adversaries of Malraux's novel had to say was trifling compared to the praise of his admirers.

Meanwhile, the ten members of the Goncourt Prize jury, who had long been irked by the Femina jury's habit of awarding its prize on the same Wednesday in early December, had at last prevailed on the ladies to advance the date of their award by one week. On Tuesday, December 2nd, they assembled in a specially reserved dining room of the Cercle Interallié, while a score of literary journalists were offered luncheon in another dining room. The twenty-one members of the Femina jury took a long time trying to obtain a clear majority. Finally the waiting newshounds began passing around slips of paper, to see which book they preferred. Within minutes André Malraux's *Voie royale* had won a clear 12–4 majority vote.

Four years before, another group of exasperated journalists had decided to protest at the length of these prize-awarding lunches by creating a Théophraste Renaudot Prize, named in honour of the seventeeth-century chronicler who had founded France's first 'gazette' in 1631. This time the impatient journalists chose to call theirs, more simply, the Prix Interallié. Thus, without at all wishing it, André Malraux and his *La Voie royale* had helped to generate a new literary prize.

The outpaced ladies of the Femina jury finally rose from their lunch table, after voting to award their prize to the forty-five-year-old 'front-runner', Marc Chadourne, for a lightweight novel rather giddily called *Cécile de la Folie*. Even before the dust had settled, more than one literary journalist felt Malraux should publicly refuse the accidentally begotten Interallié Prize, in the hope of winning the prestigious Goncourt Prize a few days later. Bernard Grasset, however, knowing how sensitive the Goncourt Prize jurymen were to 'affronts' of this kind, decided that there was no point indulging in wishful thinking. Instead, another advertisement was run in the December 6th edition of *Les Nouvelles Littéraires*. The Prix Interallié, it proclaimed, had just been awarded by twenty-two literary journalists to the novel they declared to be the best of the year:

LA VOIE ROYALE
by André Malraux

Underneath were two laudatory quotations: 'The evocation of the tropical forest equals in intensity the finest pages of Loti and Conrad' – Benjamin Crémieux (*Les Annales*); 'The atmosphere of the forest is comparable in beauty to certain of Baudelaire's poems' – André Maurois (*New York Times*).

Some critics had not yet published their reviews when overtaken by these events. But the day after the Interallié award, the last word on this subject had already been uttered by Bernard Lecache in an article published in the left-wing newspaper, *La Gauche*. After praising Malraux's description of the shuddering apprehensions a tropical forest can induce in a novice explorer, he concluded: 'The man who wrote it can rest in peace. All the prizes of the world can scorn him. He is too big for them.'

17

Literary Impasse

Shortly before Christmas of 1930, André's father Fernand put an end to his increasingly unhappy life by discreetly gassing himself. His second marriage to Marie-Louise Godard had finally ended, like the first, in divorce, and his stockbroking activities had ceased to be profitable. For years he had done well by administering the fortune of Marie-Louise's sister, Gabrielle; but the Wall Street crash of October 1929, followed by the short-sighted raising of tariff barriers and the onset of a worldwide depression, had had a devastating effect on the stock market quotations of the Paris Bourse. Holding Fernand responsible for the shrinking value of her assets, the wealthy widow had threatened to denounce the illegitimate birth of her two nephews, Roland and Claude, unless he relinquished control over her portfolio.

A few weeks later André found himself embroiled in an acrimonious controversy with several detractors who could not forgive the former 'temple-robber' for having had the gall to turn his artistic 'piracy' in Cambodia into best-selling fiction. As a gesture of gratitude towards Gaston Gallimard, Malraux arranged to have forty Gandhâra heads put on display in a ground-floor 'art gallery' set up inside the NRF's new premises at no. 5, Rue Sébastien Bottin. Ever eager to establish novel parallels, Malraux imprudently put out a small eight-page pamphlet, in which the Gandhâra heads were advertised as 'Gothico-Buddhist works from the Pamir'. The explanatory text – spiced with learned references to pre-Hittite bronzes, the bas-reliefs of Boghaz-Kheui, the demons of Mesopotamia, the 'periods of the Milandapanha or that of the Qizyl', and so on – was distinctly cryptic, as Malraux sought to weave ingenious parallels between the later development of Buddhist art in China and Japan and that of Gothic art in Europe. The text was accompanied, furthermore, by a brief notice indicating that the forty-two heads had been found in three sites located close to Tash-Kourgan (in the mountainous uplands separating Afghanistan from Chinese Turkestan).

Neither André nor Clara had ever been close to the Pamir, a wild region of windswept plains and valleys ridged by towering mountain ranges rising to over 20,000 feet. Although Alexander the Great had spent several years in Sogdiana and had married a Bactrian princess, he had never sought to penetrate, still less to colonize, the arid highlands of the Pamir. Nor so far had any historian or archaeologist claimed that it had once been the seat of a notable artistic culture.

The first to question Malraux about his extraordinary 'find' was Gaston Poulain, a journalist working for *Comoedia*, an eight-page daily devoted to belles lettres, music, drama, and fine arts. His published version of the interview – carried in the paper's January 21, 1931 issue under the title, 'The Writer Archaeologist', followed by the challenging question: 'Who sculpted the stones Mr André Malraux brought back from the Pamir?' – is worth quoting, not because every printed word was necessarily uttered, but because it shows how nimble Malraux could be in answering searching questions.

GP: How were the excavations organized?

AM: I left in June with my wife. I thought there would be something. I looked, I found.

GP: Did you undertake some special studies?

AM: I read Sanskrit. I am studying Persian.

GP: How long did you stay on the Pamir plateau?

AM: Three and a half months.

GP: And you found all this? Many scientists would be happy to have as much luck, excuse me, as much flair. Do you think that a scientific expedition would find many pieces?

AM: Why not? But the region is very dangerous. Sixty kilometres from Kabul, one would have to be equipped with machine guns.

GP: But you?

AM: For me it's not the same thing. I was a People's Commissar in Canton.

Did André Malraux actually make this extraordinary boast? Or was the myth he had himself created returning to mock its author, egged on by a malicious journalist? It is impossible to say. But Malraux's answer, by Gaston Poulain's own admission, left him momentarily speechless. After a pause he resumed his interrogation.

GP: Who helped you in your excavations?

AM: Some natives. There were no whites around other than my wife and myself.

GP: How come the heads you are exhibiting are all severed in the same manner?

AM: It was the desert wind which detached them. The sand then covered and preserved them. As for their decapitated bodies, they were destroyed by the Hephtalite Huns.

When he was approached by another journalist the next day, at first Malraux angrily refused to answer any questions. But after the reporter had pointed out that his silence could only cast doubt on the authenticity of all these busts and statuettes, Malraux calmed down and explained that the 'mystery' of these sculpted heads would soon be cleared up by an authoritative work on the subject, written by a certain Mr Strygowski (sic), which was soon due to appear in French, English and German.

Malraux had in fact vainly begged Josef Strzygowski to write a preface for his exhibition. Strzygowski, who occupied a chair in History of Art at the University of Vienna, could not speak French and could only communicate with him through Clara. And what Clara did not realize was that this scholar, who was something of a crank (later he became a proto-nazi), detested the classic art of Greece, reserving his admiration for the art of nomads, particularly when it tended towards abstraction.

The controversy aroused by these 'Gothico-Buddhist' heads had hardly abated when Malraux was confronted by another challenge, this time apropos *Les Conquérants*. His challenger this time was Leon Trotsky, who, after a few months of 'internal exile' at Alma Ata, had been allowed to leave the Soviet Union. From the island of Prinkipo, near Istanbul, he sent the *NRF* an extraordinary critique entitled 'The Strangled Revolution'. The critique was extraordinary because of its mixture of high praise for the author's literary talents ('By colourful little touches, following the method of the *pointillistes*, Malraux gives us an unforgettable picture of the general strike . . .') and severe condemnation of the author's 'condescending irony with regard to barbarians capable of enthusiasm' (the revolutionary Chinese masses) – a fault aggravated by 'excesses of individualism and aesthetic caprice', and even worse, by a 'little note of blasé superiority'.

For the figure of Borodin, whom Malraux had portrayed as a 'professional revolutionary', Trotsky felt nothing but contempt, pointing out that he was an 'accomplished representative of the State and Party bureaucracy' who had joined the revolutionary struggle after the victory had been won by others. For Garine, described as 'more original than Borodin', Trotsky felt more sympathy, but he could not forgive the author for letting Garine dismiss revolutionary Marxist principles as 'doctrinal rubbish'. The figure who found most favour in Trotsky's eyes was Hong, the single-minded revolutionary terrorist whom the opportunistic Borodin is finally forced to liquidate, in order to placate the bourgeois moneylenders, whose 'donations' he needs to finance the operations of the 'revolutionary armies'. A suicidal policy which made Borodin, and ultimately Stalin behind and above him, the 'strangler' of the Chinese revolution.

What was most remarkable about Malraux's elaborate rebuttal – filling five pages in the April 1931 issue of the *NRF* – was the extensive knowledge it revealed not only of China's revolutionary situation during the 1920s but also of the Bolshevik Revolution of 1917. He dismissed Trotsky's claim that

Borodin was not a 'professional' revolutionary as based on personal animus, and he defended Garine's sarcastic references to 'democratic twaddle' and 'doctrinal rubbish' as expressing spur-of- the-moment comments made by a different kind of revolutionary.

Trotsky's 'veritable adversary', Malraux continued, was the Third International and its opportunistic policies dictated from Moscow – and that meant by Stalin. But what other course could the Komintern have pursued, given the absence in China of a politically educated proletariat, and the ponderous handicap of a passive peasantry, which could only be galvanized by calls for war against the hated 'invaders' – ie, the British? It was the Kuomintang's nationalist character that had assured its success, and in joining forces with it, Borodin and Gallen were simply trying to develop a popularity which could not possibly have been acquired by a call for the immediate establishment of revolutionary soviets.

That the 'revolution' in China had ended in tragic defeat Malraux made no attempt to deny. But in a land where only two million out of some 50 million workers were employed in factories – one and a half million of them, furthermore, being women and children – and where most mechanics and skilled workers had joined the Kuomintang, the objective conditions for a communist victory simply did not exist.

In early May of 1931 André and Clara set out again, on the longest of all the trips they were to undertake together. Their first destination was Persia – not only Isfahan, but also Shiraz and nearby Persepolis. After that they moved on to India. At Jaipur – 'the most unreal town of Muslim India' (as Malraux later described it) – they climbed the monumental steps of the celestial 'observatory', admired the 'Palace of the Wind' ('an organ of pink stone, as strange for us as a cathedral is for an Oriental'), and wandered through an Arabian Nights décor of exotically painted façades concealing squalid dwellings, where most of the inhabitants seemed to be groups of 'melancholy monkeys'.

In the holy city of Benares, on the Ganges, all the hotels were closed during the mid-summer season. André and Clara were guided to a primitive guest-house, where aged women worked through the torrid night to keep the punkahs moving back and forth above their perspiring bodies. But the monsoon clouds enveloping the city in a twilight mist enhanced both the erotic spell of sculpted walls that glorified the fruit of lascivious undulations and the sombre splendour of the sacred river, lined by a jungle bank of half-submerged Brahmanic shrines and the flickering flames of funeral pyres.

To escape the heat of central India, they moved on to Patna and into the foothills of the Himalayas as far as Darjeeling – as close as they could get to Prince Siddharta's (Gautama Buddha's) birthplace in mountainous Nepal. Descending from these exhilarating heights to a sweltering Calcutta, they then took a boat to Rangoon.

Carefully avoiding Indochina – Paul Monin had died several years before, and most of their Annamese friends had by now been imprisoned or driven into exile – they sailed around the Malay peninsula and on to Hong Kong, once again a prosperous port city untroubled by a general strike. Now, for the first time, Malraux was able to set foot on the Chinese mainland and to visit Canton, so imaginatively described in *Les Conquérants*. All traces of the revolutionary fervour of 1925 had long since been driven underground, Borodin and Vassily Gallen (General Blücher) had been recalled to Moscow by a cautious Stalin, and the city was firmly under the control of Kuomintang conservatives. The animation of the crowded streets, the familiar coolie-cries and sounds of gongs, the smells of soy sauce and frying shellfish – all so reminiscent of Cholon – acted on Malraux like a heady stimulant. He suddenly felt the tug of a new literary inspiration: another novel based in China, and for which he had already found a title. 'What do you think,' he asked Clara, 'of my calling it *La Condition humaine*?'

Their next stop was the bustling city of Shanghai, where in 1927 Chiang Kai-shek's military forces had crushed a major communist-instigated insurrection, during which 400 workers had been killed and many more wounded. Here they paid a ritual visit to the Great Wide World casino, which had once aroused the envy of their Cholon friends, Dong Thuan and Dang Dai, and had a drink at what Paul Morand had described as the 'longest bar in the world'.

At Hangchow, once the seaside resort of the Imperial family, they said goodbye to the ocean and began a long train ride, which took them through narrow river gorges and past endless undulations of reddish loess hills. At last they reached Peking, which Chiang Kai-shek's Kuomintang troops had finally wrested from a northern warlord. They visited the huge walled compound of the no longer Forbidden City, as well as the Summer Palace, still haunted by the shrill tantrums of the last Dowager Empress, Tz'u Hsi.

Given its proximity, they decided to have a look at the Great Wall. It was already September, and the first chills of autumn made André and Clara shiver in their light summer clothes. They were also brought back abruptly to the harsh realities of the twentieth century when, during a stop at a railway station, they saw a score of young men on the platform jumping up and down and shaking their fists. 'War!' one of their fellow passengers explained to Clara. 'War between China and Japan.'

At Tientsin they boarded another ship and sailed on to Japan. From there the long voyage across the Pacific was probably more tedious for Clara than for André, who had by now discovered that ocean travel freed him from the visual distractions of overland trips and provided a fruitful stimulus for writing. America, which they reached via Vancouver, was something of a disappointment. The El Dorado frenzy of the late 1920s had given way to a climate of deepening gloom, aggravated by the grotesque constraints of Prohibition, which forced André and Clara to gulp down cupfuls of bootleg whisky in the speakeasies they visited.

On the homebound *La Fayette* they found themselves travelling with an already white-whiskered Marshal Pétain, whom they made no attempt to approach, and a distinctly bohemian 'man of letters', René Guetta – 'Toto' to his friends – whose black-bandaged right eye (disguising a purple bruise received during a bar room brawl) gave him a piratical look. His fund of droll stories about his shiftless past greatly amused Malraux, helping to inspire the character of Clappique, a minor but picturesque figure in the new novel he had begun.

Two days after his return to Paris, on November 16th, Malraux bumped into Bernard Groethuysen, who urged him to attend the Wednesday get-together in Gide's Rue Vaneau apartment. André's and Clara's unexpected appearance made it a memorable evening. For close to four hours, Malraux virtually held the floor, while Gide, Roger Martin du Gard, Groethuysen, Alix Guillain, Jean Paulhan and several others listened spellbound. Mme Théo once again found him 'stunning' and 'more Malraux than ever ... Everything in his speech is organized, without repetitions or corrections, with rapidity', she continued in her diary, in an effort to analyse the mental mechanism behind this torrential flow of words.

> There's not a relevance, not a comparison, not a distant consequence he misses, he really is prodigious. He poured it all out with a cold face, with a look of amused superiority, most of the time ironic. He talked of Persia and its marvellous gardens, all the more beautiful for lying so close to the desert, of masked women who accost you and make you think of Goldoni ... But of what didn't he talk? Later, it was all about America. We had hardly been introduced to his views – the predominance of women, the suppression of individuality, the search for sensation ... when already he was whirling off elsewhere ... He did, however, admit that he had no fixed opinion about America (what would it not have been if he had one!) ... He had expected to find a serious country, like Russia, but no, instead – alcohol, cheating, all the blemishes of the Old World, and worse ...

From late November of 1931 through to the end of 1932, André Malraux worked away at his new novel. He still occasionally contributed articles of literary criticism to the *NRF* – like the preface he wrote for the French edition of D. H. Lawrence's *Lady Chatterley's Lover*, whose publication in January 1932 provoked such a storm of controversy that the conservative Prefect of Police (Jean Chiappe) felt impelled to forbid its sale in sidewalk bookstalls and newspaper kiosks. As artistic director of the NRF, Malraux was given a slightly larger editorial den in the firm's cramped premises, further congested by Gaston Gallimard's decision to launch a new liberal weekly, *Marianne*, to compete with the conservative *Candide* and the increasingly pro-fascist *Gringoire*.

The editor-in-chief of this new publication was none other than the passionately anti-capitalistic Emmanuel Berl, whose small ground-floor office was only a few steps removed from that of his friend André. Aided by a highly intelligent art historian and film scenario writer, Janine Bouissounouse, whom Malraux had first met in 1927 in the company of Sergei Eisenstein, André and his friend Emmanuel developed a sixteen-page format; its distinctive features were a bold, usually caricatural photo-montage of prominent faces on the front page, and a back page pictorially illustrating the contemporary world's woes or (occasionally) delights. It was dramatically unveiled in *Marianne*'s first issue, on October 26, 1932, with a full page of photographs featuring striking workers, mounted policemen, and the face of Herbert Hoover, next to a mocking caption: 'Prosperity?'.

After a pleasant summer holiday spent in a friend's lakeside chalet in Switzerland, during which Clara startled André with the news that she was pregnant, they decided that the time had come to say goodbye to the Boulevard Berthier apartment. They moved to a more convenient, Left Bank flat in the very heart of the Paris publishing world. Located a mere hundred yards from the Gallimard offices, the three-room apartment at no. 44, Rue du Bac also placed them within easy walking distance of André Gide's top-floor apartment on the Rue Vaneau.

The move allowed Malraux to devote more time to *La Condition humaine*. His position, both as author and editor, was now solidly assured and he was not going to be rushed into premature completion of this new book; he was determined to profit from the criticisms that had been levelled at his first two novels by persons whose judgement he respected.

Of the dozens of articles devoted to *La Voie royale*, perhaps none had more dramatically combined implicit praise with incisive criticism than the one the *NRF* had published in December 1930 by Drieu la Rochelle. Eight years older than Malraux, Drieu was an authentic hero, thrice wounded in action at the front, whose courage under fire was fully matched by a fearless disrespect for the military hierarchy, which had found expression in an impertinent novelette, *L'Interrogation*, published in 1917 and promptly banned by an obtuse military censorship. A fervent admirer of Nietzsche – one of the reasons why he immediately hit it off with Malraux when they had first met in the offices of the NRF in the late 1920s – Drieu had developed a virile, but also pessimistic, philosophy, not unlike that of Henry de Montherlant or of Ernst Jünger in Germany, which made him particularly receptive to his younger contemporary's novels.

The flattering title Drieu had given to his *NRF* essay – 'Malraux, the New Man' – made it clear that here was a novelist whose literary aims and techniques differed radically from those of established 'masters' like André Gide and Roger Martin du Gard. But having made these flattering comparisons, Drieu took up Malraux's novelistic weaknesses.

His novels are fast moving, compelling, enthralling, but they are narrow and unilinear ... One has the impression that he hardly moves away from facts he has known ... A single line of events, and treading this line a single character, a hero. This hero is not Malraux, it is the mythical figuration of his Me. More sublime and concrete than himself. . . . Search your memory and you will find the greatest, flanked by their heroes: Byron and Manfred, Stendhal and Julien Sorel, Balzac and Rastignac, Dostoevsky and Stavroghin, etc.

In *Les Conquérants* this hero role was played by Garine, next to whom the conservative Tcheng-daï or the violent Hong were shadowy figures, almost reduced to the size of pygmies. Similarly, in *La Voie royale*, Perken had completely overshadowed the younger Claude Vannec, to say nothing of the evanescent Grabot. After expressing the fear that Malraux might prove unable to write complex novels, Drieu roundly declared:

He cannot adhere to his present procedure, which is to show us a hero, always alone, emerging from an obscure corridor towards a dazzling goal. Here there can be no progress . . . For the moment, Malraux's universe is the universe of a solitary person. He shows the Me, alone, engaged in a struggle against nature, against the crowd, against a mass of foes, 'against God', he may well say, but not against other Mes. Is this human?

Drieu's conclusion was that if Malraux was to make real progress as a novelist, he would have to choose between Stendhal's *The Red and the Black* and Dostoevsky's *The Brothers Karamazov*.

In effect, this was an invitation to Malraux to abandon the mythical hero–cult around which he had built his first two novels and to 'broaden the canvas' – much as Stendhal had done in *The Charterhouse of Parma*, or Tolstoy, on an even grander scale, in *War and Peace* and *Anna Karenina*. Almost certainly the two friends had discussed these literary problems during the long nocturnal walks they liked to take together. And the fact that Drieu should have held up *The Brothers Karamazov* as a challenging example was almost certainly no accident. When Dostoevsky had embarked on his last and greatest novel, he had gradually realized that he was labouring on the first panel of a triptych, the overall subtitle of which was to be 'The Tribulations of a Great Sinner'. In the process of composition, the kindly figure of Alyosha Karamazov had been completely overshadowed by those of the impulsive Dmitri and the diabolically intellectual Ivan. But while the novel had ended with the condemnation and disappearance from the scene of the violent Dmitri, Ivan Karamazov remained a force to be reckoned with for the later temptations and tribulations through which the 'saintly' Alyosha was to pass.

At the end of *La Voie royale*, Malraux had rashly announced that this was merely a 'tragic initiation' and the first volume of a longer work to be called *Les Puissances du Désert*. By the 'desert' Malraux meant a spiritual wilderness, the wasteland of a modern world bereft of God – one across which his surviving 'hero', Claude Vannec, would, like Alyosha Karamazov, have to find his way. But a godless wilderness – essentially a Nietzschean concept – was substantially different from the tumultuous universe of Dostoevsky's fertile imagination, teeming among other things with those tortuous incarnations of feminine passion and compassion, vanity, caprice, and sensuality: the Nastasya Philipovnas, the Lisas, the Julia Lembkes, the Grushenkas. In neither of Malraux's two novels had women played a part – other than as nameless prostitutes. Dostoevsky, furthermore, was, like Dante, a believer; and in such a universe women play their traditional role as daughters of Eve, as temptresses and consolers. But in Malraux's post-Nietzschean world, the very notion of sin – as he had already suggested in *Lunes en papier* – had lost its constricting force.

About the figure of Garine, who had thrown himself heart and soul into a cause greater than himself, there was a certain tragic grandeur, which could have provided the heroic stuff for later novels. But how was a rather insipid, self-seeking character like Claude Vannec to be transformed into a radically different type of socially motivated individual without straining the credulity of his readers? Was there not an inherent contradiction between Malraux's hero-worship – even if his heroes were embittered misfits – and the welfare of the downtrodden masses to which he was so passionately attached?

Such were the searching questions which André's good friend, Eddy Du Perron, had already raised even before Malraux had embarked with Clara on their long voyage to the Far East. *La Voie royale*, which was to have opened up new and grand vistas in its course across the wilderness of modern life, had turned out to be what Heidegger later called a *Holzweg*: one of those rutted paths that lumberjacks carve into a forest for timber-collecting and which peter out surrounded by tree trunks. In short, *La Voie royale* was a fictional dead end.

It is a tribute to Malraux's lucidity that he should have faced up to these disagreeable implications, even if the decisive 'illumination' did not dawn on him until after he and Clara had set foot on mainland China. Its sights, sounds, and smells immediately suggested a Chinese setting for his next novel. But this time the scene would be shifted from Canton to Shanghai, and the tumultuous events moved two years later to the tragic crushing of the first Chinese Revolution during the crucial months of March and April 1927. Like Alexander the Great, who never ceased to fascinate him, Malraux thus cut the Gordian Knot that had been paralyzing his literary efforts. Momentarily forgetting his rash promises about the 'powers of the desert', he would simply start out again from scratch, envigorated by new sensations and the still lively stimulus of unforgotten struggles.

18

Storm Clouds Over Europe

On January 31, 1933 the capitals of Europe learned with varying degrees of stupefaction that in Berlin the eighty-five-year-old president, Field Marshal Paul von Hindenburg, had appointed Adolf Hitler Chancellor of Germany. The news, all the more disquieting since it coincided with the collapse of yet another Third Republic government, surprised André Malraux, as it did André Gide, Roger Martin du Gard and many other Frenchmen. In its New Year's Day issue, *L'Humanité*, the French Communist Party's newspaper, had boldly announced in a front-page article that in Germany 'fascist crimes and internecine struggles are accelerating the disintegration of the Hitlerian party' – which was on the verge of collapse.

Just ten months before, in March 1932, Roger Martin du Gard had made a two-week trip to Berlin, which so thrilled him that he had been moved to write an enthusiastic note in a quaintly ungrammatical German to his '*Lieber Freund*' ('Dear Friend'), André Gide, to tell him '*wie gût* [sic] *schmeckt mir Berlin*' ('how much Berlin is to my liking'). Oblivious to the mounting tension between Communists and National Socialists, Martin du Gard had been swept off his feet by the natural friendliness of the people he talked to in the bars, by . . . 'the way in which the young generations of this nation, which has been suffering almost without let-up for seventeen years, have managed to replace the costly pleasures of the former bourgeoisie by free-and-easy, natural joys, sport, bathing, free love, games, a truly pagan, dionysiac freedom . . . Perhaps' he concluded in the same ecstatic tone, 'the light will come to us from the East. Not from that Slavic East, so strange and with such unassimilable formulas. But this East that is so close, and also so Western.'

It would be easy to hold up this rhapsodic letter as a model of the self-deception to which so many travellers succumb in judging foreign countries on the basis of random contacts in hotels, bars, parks and sailing clubs. But in one significant respect Roger Martin du Gard was not mistaken. Berlin – the culturally vibrant city which was the chosen home of Albert Einstein, George Grosz, Käthe Kollwitz, Kurt Weill, Otto Klemperer, Wilhelm Furtwängler, Fritz Lang, Friedrich Murnau, Georg Pabst,

Erwin Piscator and Max Reinhardt – had lost none of its infectious dynamism. This was in striking contrast to the acrimonious climate of a sullen, defensive-minded France, epitomized by André Maginot, the Minister of War, who had died in January 1932.

Nor was Roger Martin du Gard the only Frenchman to feel this way about Berlin. During the spring and summer of 1932 his friend André Gide, who could read and speak German reasonably well, made three trips to the city, telling Mme Théo on his return to Paris in August that the German capital seemed to him 'prodigious'. Indeed, curious to know if he wasn't being overly influenced by – for him – the heady atmosphere of sexual licence, Gide made two further trips to Berlin. On October 31st he had breakfast with Harry Graf Kessler, often referred to as *der rote Graf* (the Red Count) for his progressive views. The conservative *Journal des Débats* had recently published an article predicting that the Hohenzollern dynasty would soon be restored by the monocled Junkers of the German General Staff. Was this, Gide asked, a serious probability? No, answered Kessler, for the German 'masses' were revolutionary-minded as well as anti-capitalistic. The present crisis was far more dangerous, since it more closely resembled the birth of a new religion.

One week later German voters were again summoned to the polls, this time to elect a new Reichstag. To the surprise of many Germans, including Harry Graf Kessler, Adolf Hitler's nazis suffered a significant reverse, losing 2 million votes and 34 parliamentary seats (from 230 to 196 out of a total of 608).

In Paris this startling development was hailed by French newspapers as a sure sign of the 'disintegration' of the National Socialist Party, fatally rent by the antagonism of its two chief rabble-rousers, Gregor Strasser and Adolf Hitler. In a December 28th editorial, summing up the salient events of this 'sombre year' – marked by financial scandals, the 'suicides of millionaires', hunger marches in Washington and London – Malraux's friend Emmanuel Berl noted certain favourable developments. The year 1932, he wrote in *Marianne*, had 'rid Germany of Hitler, America of Hoover, France of the [reactionary] governments of Mr Tardieu and Mr Laval. Mr Herriot did not go to Washington; and it is not impossible that eventually the question of the debts may be settled . . . The failure of the Five Year Plan, Stalin's downfall, the overthrow of the regime had been announced for 1932 . . . None of all this happened.'

In painting such a rosy picture, this fervently anti-bourgeois pacifist was speaking for many French liberals – like his friend André Malraux, Roger Martin du Gard, and not least André Gide, who was beginning to shock readers of the *NRF* by the candour of his pro-communist sympathies. What, indeed, was one to think of a system of *laisser-faire* economics, which had unleashed a fever of get-rich-quick speculation, followed by a catastrophic slump in the United States, where 12 million able-bodied Americans were now unemployed; a system that had generated a similar industrial collapse in Germany, with 6 million jobless workers; a pitiless system in which, at a time when millions were close to starving, thousands of tons of coffee beans were being dumped into the ocean and huge quantities of wheat were being burned, to keep the prices of basic foodstuffs from dropping any further? Gone was every trace of the euphoria generated by the Locarno Pact of 1925 and the Kellogg–Briand Pact of 1928, now replaced by a climate of crass selfishness in which it was *chacun pour soi*. Shortsighted governments were now raising tariff barriers, US Congressmen were insisting that France go on repaying 'war debts' incurred in what had once been hailed as a common struggle 'to save democracy', while their parliamentary colleagues in Paris continued to clamour, like twentieth-century Shylocks, for another pound of reparations flesh from a prostrate Germany. Never had the 'internal contradictions' of capitalism been so glaringly apparent, even for those who had never studied Karl Marx; and there were many among the French intelligentsia – beginning with André Gide, Roger Martin du Gard, Jean Schlumberger, Emmanuel Berl, and André Malraux – who were convinced that this system was on its last legs and that the sooner it was done away with, the better.

That this was also the prevailing sentiment in Moscow was hardly surprising. For Stalin and his colleagues in the Kremlin, the Weimar Republic was essentially a creation of the German bourgeoisie. Its mainstay all along had been the Social Democratic Party, repeatedly denounced by Lenin, Trotsky, and the leading figures of the Komintern for its 'reformist', 'anti-revolutionary', and even 'social-fascist' tendencies. Since the eagerly awaited 'crisis of capitalism' had now entered its 'final stage' in Germany, the moment had come to deal a death blow to this bourgeois republic by destroying its Socialist mainstay. When, in the immediate wake of the November 6th elections, the crestfallen nazis chose to flex their muscles by launching a public transport strike, they were joined by the communists – acting on orders from Moscow. The purpose of this unholy alliance was to discredit the city of Berlin's Socialist administration and to hasten the collapse of this deplorably 'reformist', neo-bourgeois party, which had been betraying the true interests of the revolutionary proletariat. Unable to interpret international events in non-Marxist terms, Stalin and the other 'masterminds' in the Kremlin had decided that all of the 'objective' conditions now existed for a communist triumph in Germany. It was simply a question of time – of three to six months.

There was at least one fatal flaw in this deterministic reasoning: a grave underestimation of the importance of individual initiative in revolutionary crises. Several years later André Malraux was provided with a rigorous explanation of these grotesque miscalculations by Manès Sperber, an ardently communist psychoanalyst who was then living in Berlin. But Malraux had already anticipated this revolutionary dilemma when, in *La Condition humaine*, he had had Kyo object to the Soviet apparatchik, Vologhin: 'There is in Marxism a sense of fatality, and the exaltation of a will. Each time fatality takes precedence over will-power, I am wary.'

In the dramatic clash between the two in Germany, it was not the 'objective' forces of Marx's 'scientific socialism' which had triumphed. It was the highly subjective, neo-Nietzschean 'will to power' of a demagogue of genius: Adolf Hitler.

On February 28th, a bare month after Adolf Hitler had been appointed Chancellor, the French were again startled by the news that in Berlin the 'imperial' parliament, the Reichstag, was in flames and that the 'arsonist' responsible for the blaze, a Dutch communist, had been arrested.

The brazen attempt to 'frame' the German Communist Party by blaming it for this fire was greeted sceptically by most Paris newspapers and denounced in the communist organ, *L'Humanité*, as a monstrous provocation. The arrest of more than 100 German communists, including the Party's leader, Ernst Thaelmann, and one of its leading deputies, Ernst Torgler, along with the closing-down of the mass-circulation communist newspaper, *Berlin am Morgen*, and of the Socialist Democrats' *Vorwärts* (Forward), made it patently clear that the Reichstag fire was a put-up job, intended to cripple Germany's two left-wing parties on the eve of new parliamentary elections.

Over the next few weeks Paris, like Prague and Vienna, was inundated with German refugees fleeing the nazi reign of terror – some of whom, like the composer Kurt Weill and the film director Fritz Lang, arrived with little more than the clothes they were wearing. Among them were a number of communist or 'fellow-travelling' authors – the poet Anna Seghers, the Prague-born but German-speaking journalist, Egon Erwin Kisch, the novelist Theodor Plivier – who set up a *Schutzverband deutscher Schriftsteller* (an Association for the Defence of German Writers), which, like so much else, was communist-controlled.

Their French colleagues had not waited for this moment to form a league of 'revolutionary' authors, which was quick to take up the cudgels for their persecuted 'comrades' from beyond the Rhine. Their inspirer was a dynamic German activist named Willi Münzenberg, next to Lenin probably the most resourceful promoter of communist-front organizations the world has so far seen. Shortly after the Japanese invasion of Manchuria in November 1931, he had decided to found an International League against War and Fascism, which had held a huge congress, attended by more than 1,000 delegates, in Amsterdam in August 1932. Parallel with this effort, on a more literary plane, was the establishment in Paris of an Association des Ecrivains et Artistes Révolutionnaires (Association of Revolutionary Writers and Artists, or AEAR), designed to mobilize authors, painters, actors and composers for the support of left-wing causes: these being in 1932 the promotion of peace, the struggle against Italian and Hitlerian Fascism, and whole hearted support of the USSR.

The two prime movers in the establishment of the AEAR were both veterans of trench warfare who had emerged from the hideous slaughter of the 1914–18 war with the bitter feeling that the Socialist Party of Jean Jaurès (assassinated on the eve of the great conflict by a chauvinist fanatic) had betrayed its original international ideals by patriotically supporting the wartime Union Sacrée forged by Clemenceau and Poincaré. The first, Henri Barbusse, was a bilingual poet (his mother was English) who had made himself famous by writing a best-selling novel about a squad of infantrymen, which was awarded the Goncourt Prize in 1916. The second, Paul Vaillant-Couturier, was, like Emmanuel Berl, a product of the well-to-do middle class – his mother, Marguerite Vaillant, had been one of the stars of the Opéra-Comique – who had developed a keen sense of solidarity with the mud-splattered *poilus*, later rising to become editor of *L'Humanité*.

The Association des Ecrivains et Artistes Révolutionnaires cannot properly be said to have been a 'communist-front' organization, so transparent was the façade. But the launching of this 'revolutionary' authors-and-artists' league was admirably attuned to the anti-capitalist mood of many prominent French writers. Romain Rolland, who agreed to become one of the AEAR's sponsors, was a particularly prize 'catch'. By the early 1930s the once ardent pacifist, who had chosen a comfortable exile in Switzerland in order to remain 'above the fray' during the Great War, had been so lavishly praised and courted by the Soviets – notably with six-figure print orders for Russian translations of his books and plays – that by the early 1930s he had to all extents and purposes become a Stalinist.

André Gide proved less easy to snare. Unlike Romain Rolland, he had never been actively engaged in a political crusade. Increasingly outspoken in airing his admiration for what the Soviets were trying to achieve, he had a deeply ingrained distaste for all forms of dogma, and he was afraid, as he put it one day (in March 1932) to Mme Théo, of becoming an *agité* – which in his case would have been a 'form of senility and of folly too'.

In early March 1933 Gide returned to Paris from a brief vacation on the Côte d'Azur to find his new secretary – none other than the twenty-year-old Roland Malraux (whom André had persuaded Gide to hire) – being besieged by frantic telephone calls begging Gide to preside over a public meeting which the Association of Revolutionary Writers and Artists was planning to hold on March 21st. Gide gave in to the 'sympathetic' Vaillant-Couturier's entreaties, then tried to backtrack, claiming that he was a wretched orator and had no stomach for 'tirades on liberty' and that kind of claptrap. But it was too late. Vaillant-Couturier had already publicized the fact that Gide would be presiding over the meeting, at which a number of writers he knew well would also take the floor.

That André Gide had this time been skilfully 'lassooed' – with considerable encouragement from both Malraux brothers – there can be no doubt. The meeting, held in a Right Bank hall which was filled to overflowing, was opened by Paul Vaillant-Couturier with a lengthy preamble outlining the objectives of the AEAR – which had so far assembled 550 'non-conformist' members from the fields of literature, plastic arts, architecture, music, theatre, cinema and photography, for a common struggle 'alongside the proletariat'. Gide, though elated by a sense of cordial *camaraderie*, must have felt relieved not to have been included; for before he was through his introductory speech, Vaillant-Couturier had trotted out almost every platitude in the communist lexicon, promising the birth of a truly 'proletarian literature', a 'proletarian art', and even the advent of a 'proletarian culture' made possible by an eventual 'seizure of power'. There could be no such thing as 'neutral literature', he asserted, 'any more than of a neutral State in a régime of the class struggle', and so on.

Gide, looking like 'an Ibsen preacher' (as *Izvestiya*'s correspondent, Ilya Ehrenburg, later put it), was greeted with a thundering ovation when he rose to speak. He explained apologetically that he was no orator, adding that 'in the great historical conflict of which Nazism in Germany is nothing but an execrable episode', he had decided to place himself firmly on the side of 'the working class'. The gist of his short speech was summed up in a single controversial sentence: 'We know that the only way to "wage war against war" is to wage war against imperialism' – including of course French imperialism.

André Malraux, one of the last to address this audience of 'intellectual workers', made a brief, largely 'unintelligible' speech (so at least it sounded to Ilya Ehrenburg), which was more noteworthy for what was allusively suggested than for what was clearly enunciated. He began, with a poetic flourish, by describing how over a period of ten years Fascism had 'spread its big black wings over half of Europe'. He bluntly declared that 'German Fascism' posed a threat of war, denounced the existing French regime as a *gouvernement de sourds* (a government of deaf people), and concluded with a dramatic peroration by asserting that threats must be met by threats. 'We will always be able to find those who truly serve the proletariat; in case of war, even if Russia is not involved, we will turn in our thoughts towards Moscow, we will turn towards the Red Army.' And to show the audience that he really meant it, he raised a clenched right fist amid a tumult of applause from the 'proletarians' in the hall, who understood this gesture, if little else, in what was obviously a fighting speech delivered by a bourgeois intellectual.

In his introductory address Paul Vaillant-Couturier had taken pains to emphasize that the Association of Revolutionary Writers and Artists was not the 'annex of a Party'. However, all doubts on this score were dispelled at the end of the meeting when André Gide was asked to read a resolution, which was unanimously endorsed by all those present:

We denounce in Fascism the desperate effort of a bankrupt civilization, which is trying to survive, to escape its ineluctable ruin through violence and bloodshed. Fascism is trying to chain the masses to the decrepit body of capitalism . . . But German fascism . . . was made possible only by the criminal policies of French imperialism, which sought to truss up the German people, which it has despoiled, humiliated, reduced to despair. French imperialism is responsible for the coming to power of Hitler and his gangs of hired assassins . . .

Two days later *L'Humanité* devoted a lot of space to this AEAR meeting, under the headline: 'André Gide speaks: the Press keeps silent.' The complaint, at least as regards the weekly press, was premature. For before the month was over, Gide's 'conversion' to Communism and his performance at the AEAR meeting were subjected to a searching critique published by the conservative essayist, Alfred Fabre-Luce, in a new political weekly, *Pamphlet*. The article, written by a Frenchman who had actually visited the Soviet Union, gently reminded Gide that Soviet Communism was essentially a modern form of puritanism, in which the State imposed 'horrible constraints' on its subjects, infinitely more tyrannical than those of 'family and religion' (two of Gide's *bêtes noires*). Gide had managed to preserve his idealized vision of the USSR by wisely not going to look at it at close hand – a sagacious attitude which was to be dramatically justified three years later.

Fabre-Luce was no less critical of the simplistic slogans Gide had endorsed at the AEAR meeting, in which 'French imperialism' was placed alongside 'Hitlerian Fascism' as an evil to be combatted. 'Let us rub our eyes. We are in March 1933. There is a danger of war. Does it, properly speaking, come from French imperialism, that is to say, from a desire of our government to acquire foreign territories? No one can seriously claim that.'

Fabre-Luce then trained his guns on André Malraux. He found it not a little 'ironic' that he could exhort those 'who defend human dignity' to turn toward Moscow and the Red Army, precisely at a moment when General Maxime Weygand, Inspector-General of the French Army, was, on behalf of a government Malraux had castigated, forging military ties with this same Red Army.

The March 21st meeting, like most of those that followed, was a classic example of how a critique, which may at one moment be well-founded, can become a paralyzing anachronism ten or twelve years later, when the international context has dramatically changed. In December 1920, when a majority of French Socialists chose to shatter the unity of Jean Jaurès' old party by joining Lenin's Third International, it made sense to criticize the Treaty of Versailles as a product of short-sighted vindictiveness likely to rekindle the resentful belligerence the young Communist Party was most anxious to avoid. John Maynard Keynes, whom no one could accuse of sympathy for the October Revolution, had criticized the treaty for roughly the same reasons in *The Economic Consequences of the Peace*. It had also made sense in 1923 to oppose Raymond Poincaré's heavy-handed decision to occupy the Ruhr in order to force a financially stricken Germany to continue paying reparations. But ten years later, when the peoples of Europe were beginning to reap the whirlwind from such casually sown seeds, it no longer made sense to keep mouthing the same old slogans and to put all the blame for Hitler's rise to power on the Treaty of Versailles – that typical product of 'French imperialism'. Like the attacks on Léon Blum's Socialists and on social democracy in general, which Vaillant-Couturier's *L'Humanité* kept up throughout this year of 1933, this inane slogan-mongering could only weaken France when it needed to be more united, in order to deal effectively with an increasingly militaristic and bellicose Nazism on the other side of the Rhine.

André Malraux, it should be said in his defence, rarely indulged in simplistic slogan-mongering, forever trying – as the German Communist writer, Gustav Regler, later noted – to 'elevate the level of the debate'. Nor did Malraux, whose Rue du Bac apartment soon became an 'open house' for German and Italian refugee writers, limit his political 'activism' to rhetorical phraseology. In early April Albert Einstein, who had announced his intention not to return to Germany, established temporary residence in the seaside resort of Ostend. At a Rue Vaneau dinner, held on the 5th, Gide brought up the subject with his friends Bernard Groethuysen and Alix Guillain, saying what a shame it was that nobody should have had the idea of having new teaching posts for German refugee professors set up at the Collège de France, with a special chair in physics for Albert Einstein. Indeed, he now regretted not having made this proposal at the recent AEAR meeting and of having had it voted by acclamation, instead of 'barking with the others'.

If the idea had not already occurred to Malraux, it was probably because his attention at this moment was distracted by pressing domestic problems. But on April 7th, when Gide mentioned the subject, Malraux volunteered to take the matter up with Anatole de Monzie, the liberal-minded Minister of Education in Edouard Daladier's government. Unfortunately, by the time Malraux contacted Monzie, it was too late. On April 11th the news reached Paris that the universities of Brussels and of Madrid had both offered Einstein a special chair in physics.

Suddenly aroused from their lethargy, the prestigious academics of the Collège de France met in emergency session and offered Einstein a chair in mathematical physics. The same day (April 12th) Anatole de Monzie made a similar proposal at an evening session of the Chamber of Deputies.

The French, once again, had been taken by surprise. But the two Andrés (Gide and Malraux) could at least congratulate themselves on having done their belated best to shake their drowsing countrymen out of their complacent slumbers.

19

A Romantic Intermezzo

For André Malraux the first months of 1933 were vitally important for other, more personal reasons. In January Jean Paulhan's *NRF* began the publication of *La Condition humaine*, serialized in five successive issues (as had been done for *Les Conquérants*). Although the first reviews did not begin to appear until after Gallimard had brought out the novel in book form in late April, these first serialized extracts aroused enormous interest.

Asked for her reaction, Malraux's *NRF* neighbour, Janine Bouissounouse, said that, whereas *Les Conquérants* had struck her as being a dynamic 'novel in the making', the reader being forced to follow the various characters without knowing just where they were going or what they really wanted, in *La Condition humaine* 'everything is so finished, so definitive that one feels oneself confronted by something immobile, immutable'.

André Gide, after reading the first two instalments, told Mme Théo that it was all a bit 'stunning, all in all a success', even though he had found it difficult to sort out the characters. But in early May, after reading the novel from start to finish, he noted in his journal that the text now seemed to him 'perfectly clear, well ordered in its confusion, of an admirable intelligence, and in spite of that (I mean, despite the intelligence), profoundly embedded in life, deeply committed, and gasping with a sometimes unbearable anguish'.

The opinion of André Thérive, who had succeeded the dreaded Paul Souday as book reviewer for *Le Temps*, was more reserved than Gide – which was not surprising, given the dyed-in-the-wool conservatism of this newspaper. He praised the novel's 'inexpressible richness', perfectly mastered by the author, declared that *La Condition humaine* was 'an exceptional, indeed a great book', and congratulated Malraux for having 'rid himself of that obscurity which encumbered his previous narratives'. He had to admit, however, that he had lost his footing amid the welter of strange historical circumstances in a distant Shanghai. But what most irked Thérive was the excessive verbosity of the novel's 'enraged intellectuals', whom he termed 'pedants'.

In *L'Oeuvre*, a liberal daily, André Billy expressed similar reservations. After declaring that 'we have in Mr André Malraux a story-teller of an assuredly uneven but exceptional vigour', he regretted that the author of *La Condition humaine* should not have succeeded better in 'disciplining his gifts: they are magnificent, and a wiser, cleverer utilisation of them would probably deaden their impact. What is weak in his novels is the technique' – by which he meant the 'classic' mode of novel writing – adding with a sigh of resignation: 'We know that the new generation does not care two hoots about it. It spurns preparations, explanations, transitions.'

For that pathetically tormented Christian, Jean Guéhenno, the main trouble ·with the novel was of a different order. 'The essential tragedy in this book lies in the efforts made by various heroes – Tchen, Katow, Kyo – to escape their human condition, to become gods. The revolution is at once an occasion for, and the result of, this prodigious effort. And therein, I believe, lies the true greatness but also the limitation of this work.' Why? Simply because, as he wrote in *L'Europe*, 'I have come to regard the daily life of mediocre human beings as being far more heroic than that of heroes. Heroes are lucky: they can rely on bombs, revolvers, opium, adventures. Not so most human beings.'

The same 'fault' was denounced, but with ten times more virulence, by Robert Brasillach in the vehemently monarchist daily, *L'Action Française*:

Blood is André Malraux's master. It is what explains his sensuous fury and likewise his destructive fury. Therein lies the basis of his heroism. Those who have read *Les Conquérants* will doubtless never forget the scenes of horror with which that book ends, the atrocious tortures and the dead ones whose eyelids have been cut off. *La Condition humaine* ends with pages that are just as dreadful, even though the author spares us the sight of flaming bonfires.

Malraux's crime was, in the eyes of this intransigent Catholic, his resort to novelistic melodrama in order to inculcate an 'unhealthy taste for heroism'.

This critique provoked a prompt reply from Malraux. In a personal letter to Brasillach he wrote: 'I did not have to choose savagery, for I encountered it. Every man draws his values from the life it has been given to him to live, and I lay claim to both, not as objects of smug satisfaction but as something on which to build.'

More eloquent, however, than the dozens of review articles devoted to *La Condition humaine* was the studied silence of Edmond Jaloux. Whereas, in his weekly column in *Les Nouvelles Littéraires*, the noted critic discussed André Chamson's latest opus (*Auberge de l'abîme*), Drieu la Rochelle's *Drôle de voyage*, and many other novels, he did not breathe a word about *La Condition humaine*. Having in 1928 criticized the various literary juries for snubbing *Les Conquérants*, he now prudently held his peace, thus averting any suspicion that he might be trying to impose *his* favourite by too loudly trumpeting his extraordinary talents.

Two other developments further complicated André Malraux's existence at a moment when the alarming events in Germany were dragging him into a maelstrom of politico-propagandistic activity. The first was Clara's pregnancy. On March 28th she gave birth to a daughter. 'She will at least have done one intelligent thing at the start of her existence, by being a girl and not a boy,' was André's sardonic reaction. 'I would not have endured a caricature of myself.' After three days of suggestions and counter-suggestions he finally hit on a satisfactory name for the 'object': Florence – 'in memory of the city where we were happy.' And so Florence, later shortened to 'Flo', the baby girl became.

In giving André a child, Clara may have wished to reinforce a union which was beginning to erode. But her hopes in this respect were soon to be severely dashed. It is probably fair to say that André Malraux was basically monogamous, despite his keen interest in erotic matters, and that he was a theoretical or vicarious, rather than a practising, libertine. If he indulged in infidelities, it was more than anything else because Clara continued to insist on her 'right' to have occasional extramarital adventures. This, after all, had been the 'pact' they had agreed to during their Italian 'honeymoon'. But to this 'pact' André had never wholeheartedly subscribed. The kind of 'free union' Jean-Paul Sartre was later to practise with Simone de Beauvoir – with, in the language of Leibniz, a single, 'necessary' love, unaffected by 'contingent' affairs – was utterly alien to Malraux's psychological make-up.

At the heart of the 'misogyny', of which he was already beginning to be accused by some because of the minor role accorded to women in his novels, there was probably an idealization of marriage and indeed of Woman – as a being differing radically from Man – paralleling his tendency to idealize the revolutionary process. It one day found expression in an outburst which dumbfounded Clara: 'Will you never understand that for a Christian the woman he loves is always the Holy Virgin'. He himself had long since abandoned Christianity, but not, deep within him, the chivalrous ideals which had given birth to the great medieval romances and *chansons de geste*. For Malraux, the ideal wife was one who could be placed upon a pedestal and revered as a model of irreproachable behaviour. Each of Clara's 'parallel' adventures further undermined this exalted notion, inflicting a searing wound on his highly vulnerable masculinity and self-esteem. Nor did Clara's insistence on 'loyally' informing him of what had happened after each escapade in any way lessen the sense of injury. On one such occasion André was so exasperated that he told her bluntly that he was not the least bit grateful for her frankness, 'for it is impossible for you to keep something to yourself'. Nettled, she promptly had another affair, this time without telling her husband, just to prove that she was 'as capable of dissimulation as any other woman'.

Even the most monogamous can be subject to temptation. In 1926 René-Louis Doyon's wife Marcelle had told Clara that she found her husband 'a bit lanky, on the thinnish side, rather pale, made of bits and pieces, but you'll see, at the age of thirty he will be very handsome.' Now, at the age of thirty-one, André Malraux had matured, physically as well as intellectually, and he did not need to 'turn on the charm' to fascinate the women who crossed his path.

At Pontigny, the previous August, a woman intellectual attending the ten-day colloquy had conceived such an overpowering 'passion' for the tall, dapper author of *La Voie royale* that, on her return to Paris, she began boasting to all and sundry that she had managed to lure André Malraux away to a secluded spot . . . A fancied 'rape' which had greatly amused André and Clara.

This time the 'overture' took an entirely different form. In early January Malraux had received a telephone call from Louise de Vilmorin, an aristocratic young lady whom he had once glimpsed in the Paris salon of her distant cousin, Yvonne de Lestrange (a close friend of André Gide). The painter Pierre Roy and the aviator and author Antoine de Saint-Exupéry were urging her to complete a recently begun novel. She was returning to the United States, where she wanted to rework what she had so far written. Would he care to look at her manuscript, once it was ready, with the idea of bringing it to Gaston Gallimard's attention? Malraux said he would gladly read what she had written and give her an honest answer.

In early May Malraux received sixty pages of manuscript, which she had sent from her American home in Las Vegas. Although far from being 'great literature', Malraux agreed with André de Vilmorin that these pages were full of charming fantasy and humour, despite the absence of a 'plot' and a total disregard for accurate spelling and punctuation. Drieu la Rochelle and André Gide, to whom he showed the manuscript, both felt as he did that Louise de Vilmorin had created a fanciful universe of her own, which was quite enchanting. Malraux transmitted the good news to André de Vilmorin, then wrote to 'Loulou' – as she was known to family and friends – a long, handwritten letter in which the vain efforts of cowboy-booted American adventurers to find the 'golden treasure' hidden in the 'Isle of Hearts' were contrasted to her own, eagle-winged exploratory flights over vanished cities and cathedrals buried in the prickly depths of cactus forests whose 'lamp-like fruits light up at night' – a *farfelu* way of expressing his personal appreciation. 'Above all', he concluded, 'don't wrack your brains to find a plot.'

Leaving her three daughters in Nevada, Mrs Henry Leigh-Hunt (who had decided to divorce her American husband) left New York and reached Le Havre on June 8th. And it was probably once again in Yvonne de Lestrange's beautifully located Quai Malaquais apartment (opposite the Louvre) that the veteran author of *La Condition humaine* met the novice author of a still far from finished fantasy, amusingly entitled *Sainte-Unefois* (St Onetime).

Tall, with lovely auburn hair and hazel eyes, Louise de Vilmorin, whose teeth were a shade too equine, may have lacked the facial perfection of her mother Mélanie, one of the great beauties of pre-1914 (and post-1918) Paris. But no one would have thought for a moment of holding this against her, so irresistibly did she radiate a captivating mixture of spontaneous verve,

174 · André Malraux

caustic wit, and irreverent whimsy. Born into an aristocratic family who had

174 · André Malraux

caustic wit, and irreverent whimsy. Born into an aristocratic family who had managed to survive the turbulent upheavals of the French Revolution by developing the foremost seed-producing enterprise in France, Louise, along with an older sister and four younger brothers, had been brought up at Verrières-le-Buisson (south of Paris) in a seventeenth-century country house which Louis XIV had built for Mlle de La Vallière. Casually entrusted to the care of a governess and an erudite *abbé*, the six Vilmorin children had not received any formal schooling during their early years – an anomaly that had helped to generate a clannish spirit or *esprit de famille*, causing them to look upon the grown-ups of the outer world with varying degrees of ironical amusement. This was particularly true of Loulou. Spared the scholarly chores of memorizing Greek and Latin verbs or of having to grapple with algebraic equations, she was left free to cultivate her private garden of poetic reverie. She was totally free of bogus erudition, and it was precisely this absence of cultural pretense, the surprise and zest she brought to the discovery of every novelty, the carefree spontaneity with which she seemed to say and do whatever happened to cross her mind, which made her so irresistible. No one, perhaps, has better captured this extraordinary feminine combination of ingenuous gaiety, *joie de vivre*, and wit than Jean Cocteau, who, writing not long after the completion of *Sainte-Unefois*, portrayed her as being

> a tall, ravishing girl with a husky voice and somewhat loose jointed schoolgirl gestures, a laugh which wrinkles the skin of her nose and lifts a cruel lip above flashing teeth . . . a perfect, trusting, uncultured simplicity . . . and genius . . . Madame de Vilmorin has a red balloon which lifts her up from the earth and then carries her wherever she wants to go.

Ardently wooed and adored by a succession of young 'hopefuls', she had had a number of love affairs and had even been engaged for a while to a distant cousin, as prone to poetic daydreaming as she was: the aviator and future novelist, Antoine de Saint-Exupéry. Later she had drifted into marriage with an old friend of the family, Henry Leigh-Hunt, an American descendant of Keats' poet-friend, who had come to France as a wartime volunteer in 1917. Smitten by her charm, Henry Leigh-Hunt had forgotten all about the business trip he was supposed to make to Brazil; instead, he had married Loulou and carried her off to Las Vegas, which his father was busily developing. Forced to spend two years in a Santa Fe sanatorium, she had fought off boredom by playing the guitar, painting watercolours, dreaming up poems for the future, as well as giving birth to three daughters.

That André Malraux was 'smitten' in his turn, there can be no doubt. But it was probably not until early September of this crucial year of 1933 that they finally became lovers – and intermittent lovers at that – so pressing were Malraux's political and literary activities, and so distracting Louise de Vilmorin's other amorous entanglements.

In early July André decided to offer himself and Clara a three-week cruise up the Norwegian coast and on to Spitzbergen, returning via Iceland and Scotland. Shipboard travel and sea air always acted as sedatives for his tense nerves and enabled him to concentrate his mental energies on his literary projects, which were now in a state of disarray. He still wanted to write a novel designed to illustrate the inherent conflicts between individual volition and the demands of collective action, but the 'solution' he had come up with – of having the role of the 'masses' played by the petroleum workers of Baku – posed enormous problems. He had never lived in Russia, and he had made only one brief visit to the capital of Soviet Azerbaijan.

Nor was this the only thing that troubled him. On May 10th bonfires had been lit in half a dozen German cities for the public incineration of 'decadent' or 'Bolshevik' works, particularly those written by German-Jewish authors. This fanatical ferocity generated in Malraux a feeling of intense frustration. Here were new outrages that needed to be denounced – and how more forcefully than in a novel? But here too the vitally needed first-hand experience was lacking.

Hoping to find a solution to these problems, André and Clara boarded the French cruise ship, *Colombie*, on July 19th, bound for the fjords of Norway. From the northern port of Hammerfest he sent Jean Paulhan a playful note, saying that he had come upon a street full of white bears – all of them, alas, stuffed, and exhibited in the display windows of fur and animal-hide merchants. When the cruise ship reached Spitzbergen he was even more disappointed by the absence of penguins. It was no use going to the North Pole, he pointed out in another, longer letter,

if it's to see penguins. One arrives in a great glacial landscape with black rocks, in front of a mine where 160 Russians do nothing while listening to 40 of them playing balalaikas. 'My penguins!' one says in a firm tone. 'But, Monsieur,' says the fellow, much embarrassed, 'you've got the wrong Pole . . . The penguins are to be found at the South Pole.' And it's true. Which proves that it's not only at Beaune-la-Rolande that one encounters disappointments.

This letter was not addressed to Jean Paulhan, nor was it written until mid-September. For shortly after Malraux's return to France on August 10th, he learned that Edouard Daladier's Radical Socialist government had granted political asylum to Leon Trotsky. The moment the news reached Paris that he had left Turkey the Stalinist *L'Humanité* began denouncing the 'traitor', the 'renegade', the 'counter-revolutionary boyard', the *agent provocateur*, the 'veritable agent of Fascism', and so on. Indeed, to keep Trotsky from being lynched by communist dockworkers, the French authorities had him and his wife secretly removed and taken by tugboat to the little port of Cassis before their liner docked at Marseilles.

Just where Trotsky was hiding was a closely guarded secret. But thanks both to André Chamson, who now occupied an important post in Daladier's secretariat, and to one of André Gide's Trotskyist friends, Malraux was able to obtain an appointment with the illustrious revolutionary. In Paris he was picked up by a stranger who only identified himself after they had driven well beyond the city's southern suburbs as Trotsky's son, 'Lyova' Sedov, who had managed to escape from Berlin shortly after the Reichstag fire. It took them a full day to cover the 500 kilometres, and it was long after sunset when they finally drew up in front of a seaside villa situated in the village of Saint-Palais, near Royan, on the northern shore of the Gironde estuary.

Brilliantly illuminated by the two headlight beams, Trotsky came out to greet the visitor, dressed in light summer attire of white shoes and trousers. Malraux was struck by his taut thin lips and small 'extraordinarily young teeth' in the bespectacled face which reminded him of an 'Asiatic statue'.

Without wasting a moment, Trotsky led Malraux into his study. On the desk a revolver was placed like a weight on a sheaf of papers. The interview which followed – to judge from Malraux's later published version – was as remarkable for the questions that were not raised as for those that were. No mention was made of recent events in Germany. Instead, Malraux bombarded Trotsky with questions of a philosophical or aesthetic order, some of which clearly disconcerted the veteran Bolshevik. What did he think of Pasternak and contemporary Russian poetry? Trotsky replied rather lamely that all young Russians were mad about Pasternak, but that he himself cared little for his poetry. 'I don't have much taste for the art of technicians, art for specialists.'

But what of the cinema, which, Malraux suggested, was the 'veritable expression of communist art'? Here too Trotsky found himself placed on the defensive. Although it was Lenin's belief that Communism could be artistically expressed in films, he himself had seen neither Eisenstein's *Potyomkin* nor *The Mother*, simply because when they were first projected he was with the Red Army at the front. When they were shown later, he was in exile.

Then came a question of capital importance – at any rate for Malraux. Trotsky having declared that: 'Humanity does not abandon what once it has conquered', Malraux pointed out that the Europe of the Middle Ages had for 800 years turned its back on the artistic ideals of Periclean Athens, only to rediscover them later. Wouldn't it be possible to 'admit the persistence of individualism in Communism, a Communist individualism as different from bourgeois individualism as, for example, the latter was from Christian individualism?' Trotsky, who was not a Marxist for nothing, replied that 'Christian individualism' had to be placed in its economic context; it meant little to those who were impoverished, and in fact 'the spirit of primitive Christianity' was inseparable from 'a very great poverty'. For the time being, the Communists of the Five-Year Plan were forced to sacrifice individualism in order to build the future; but once the period of these Plans was over, Soviet Russia would apply the same energy to itself (by which Trotsky presumably meant Soviet society's moral and intellectual improvement).

When Malraux returned the next day from his Saint-Palais hotel, he was pleasantly surprised by the view from Trotsky's study window – with a foreground of parasol pines silhouetted against a vast expanse of sky and ocean. To Trotsky's considerable relief, Malraux now abandoned the domain of art to discuss more pragmatic questions – such as the likelihood of a war between Russia and Japan.

As dusk fell, after dinner, Trotsky and Malraux went for a stroll past the wave-splashed rocks, accompanied by the German shepherd dogs that had been added to the 'security forces' of the household. Malraux chose this moment to raise a crucial question. Did his host expect communism to produce a new type of human being, or did he expect 'a certain continuity in this domain?'

'A new man? Certainly,' replied Trotsky, adding that as far as he was concerned, the possibilities of communism were 'infinite'.

And what about death? the author of *La Voie royale* could not help asking. Once mankind had freed itself from what he called a 'religious, national or social mobilization', enabling it to act instead of simply thinking, wouldn't 'the presence of death necessarily regain its force?'

This question must also have startled Trotsky. But his answer showed that, despite a recent illness and his fifty-six years, he had lost none of his mental agility. 'I think,' he answered gravely, 'that death is above all a disparity in a process of deterioration. On the one hand, there is the deterioration of the body, on the other, that of the mind. If the two were combined, or moved at the same tempo, death would be simple. There would be no resistance.'

So ended an encounter which for Malraux was so memorable that, after recording it for *Marianne* a few months later, he added several wistful paragraphs, regretting that the thousands who turned out to listen to speeches on behalf of Ernst Thaelmann or Dimitroff never heard a word spoken in Trotsky's favour.

Trotsky, for his part, was so impressed by his visitor that he wrote to his New York publishers, urging them to bring out an American edition of *La Condition humaine*. 'Only a great superhuman purpose, for which Man is ready to pay with his life, gives meaning to personal existence. This is the final import of the novel, which is free from philosophical didacticism and remains from beginning to end a true work of art.'

Not long after this quick trip to Trotsky's 'hide-out', André Malraux picked up his pen and wrote a letter, describing some of the things he had seen during his mid-summer cruise to the Arctic Circle. As they were approaching Reykjavik he had seen a huge flight of seagulls eat one of the nonchalant rainbows which were accompanying us. It's true that a seaman had just tossed a sack of bread into the sea; but nothing was left of the rainbow, all the same. Young Icelandic girls come out in rowboats (four boats with room for twenty equal eighty young girls) to be kissed by the officers, and then return demurely home in the same boats to another month of embroidery. They are tall and blond.

The recipient of this letter was also tall and blond. Indeed, with her aquamarine eyes and her lithe, Diana-the-Huntress figure she was striking enough to have been mistaken more than once for a 'Miss France' beauty contestant. Her name was Josette Clotis, and she lived with her parents at Beaune-la-Rolande, a provincial town in the flat, wheat-growing country north-east of Orléans, where her father was a tax inspector. Both her parents came from south-western France, and she herself had preserved the quaint Languedoc accent of the Rouergue and a feeling for rural life which had inspired several short stories. Encouraged by an Auvergnat writer, Henri Pourrat, she had written a novel, *Le Temps vert* ('Greentime'), which he had recommended to Gaston Gallimard.

Gaston, who had a keen eye for feminine beauty, insisted on personally looking over this 'prodigy' of lovely looks and youthful talent, whose age, for the press releases, was reduced from around twenty to eighteen. For the launching of the novel, in the late spring of 1932, she was uprooted from the provincial boredom of Beaune-la-Rolande and installed next door to the NRF's offices at the Hôtel Montalembert, so as to be able to autograph copies of her book and exercise her charm on inquisitive reporters. She was introduced to Gallimard authors and literary critics, and finally, as a supreme treat, she was luxuriously transported in Gaston's chauffeur-driven limousine to his large seaside villa near the fashionable resort of Deauville, on the coast of Normandy. Here, in the intimidating company of Marcel Arland, Drieu la Rochelle, Antoine de Saint-Exupéry, his ebullient wife Consuelo, and other literary 'stars', she felt completely overwhelmed and out of place.

Not quite knowing what to do with this lanky beauty who was being encouraged to write a second novel, Gaston turned her over to Emmanuel Berl, who promptly nicknamed her *la pucelle d'Orléans* (the Maid of Orléans), because of her intellectually gauche, unsophisticated ways. She was given the honorific title of 'general secretary' of Gallimard's new weekly, *Marianne*, and offered a regular column, *Sous la Lampe* ('Under the Lamp'). Here she was supposed to demonstrate her literary gifts by wittily interviewing famous men and women, as the scintillating Odette Pannetier had been doing all too successfully for the rival weekly, *Candide*. Unfortunately, Josette Clotis' contributions revealed so little trace of wit that by mid-January of 1933 an exasperated Emmanuel Berl had to entrust her column to more talented journalistic veterans.

The lovely newcomer's insistence on being smartly clothed in dresses which the *couturière* Jeanne Lanvin offered to her virtually free of charge was another source of annoyance to radically-minded members of the staff – like the hard-working Janine Bouissounouse. But this particular 'weakness' did not put off André Malraux, who kept bumping into Josette Clotis on the staircase or in the crowded corridors of the NRF. Clara, who had once taken great pains to be elegantly dressed, now paid less attention to such sartorial details, the better to emphasize her anti-bourgeois sentiments and her militant attachment to left-wing causes. Completely different in every respect was this tall blond beauty, with her refreshing naïveté and guileless-ness.

According to Josette Clotis' diary, André Malraux first began to pay serious attention to her during a luncheon in a restaurant where a number of other people were present. He was amused by her youthful impetuosity in denouncing chastity (an obstacle to intelligence!) and in affirming a twenty-year-old girl's right to take physical risks – even that of contracting syphilis – in order to escape from the hypocritical 'comedy' within which a young girl finds herself imprisoned.

The next day Malraux sent her a note asking if she would like to have lunch with him – an invitation she accepted with alacrity. He took her to a first-class restaurant and was delighted to discover that she had sound gourmet tastes, like his own, and was quite prepared to devour sea-urchins, venison, or garlic-flavoured dishes with the same relish. Other lunches followed. Emboldened by the interest he seemed to take in her journalistic woes, she told him how unhappy she was working for *Marianne*. He approved her decision to resign. Since she was already working on a second novel and had a third in mind, Malraux urged her to stick to writing fiction.

Reluctantly Josette Clotis agreed to follow this advice. Deprived of her journalistic salary, she had to give up her one-room flat on the Rue du Dragon and return to her parents' house at Beaune-la-Rolande. And it was here, in mid-September, that she received André Malraux's letter, describing his Arctic voyage. 'Give me news of *La Clé des champs*' – the name of the novel she was wrestling with – 'and write me frivolous things or, which would be even better, come and tell me about them.'

Thus encouraged, she bought a cheap rate, multiple-trip railway pass on the Paris–Orléans line, enabling her to make weekly visits to Paris. This casual flirtation might never have gone further than such weekly lunches, had Clara not chosen this moment – late November 1933 – to carry out the boldest of her extramarital escapades. It is probably no accident that it should have taken place during the crucial fortnight when the jurors had to select the annual awards of the Goncourt and other literary prizes. No other French novel, during the preceding eleven months, had aroused as much favourable acclaim as *La Condition humaine*. If he didn't walk off with the Goncourt, André Malraux was certain to be awarded the only slightly less prestigious Femina Prize and be mobbed by journalists and admirers for days on end. This was one spectacle Clara was quite willing to forgo.

For years a feeling of intense frustration had been building up within her because of her inferior status as a kind of female 'satellite', obliged to look on in more or less silent admiration while her more brilliant husband 'shone' at public meetings. Nothing did more to stoke a smouldering resentment against this 'inferior' status than Malraux's insistence that she stick to translating work and not try to rival him by becoming an author herself. 'It is better to be my wife than a second-rate writer' was his sharp rebuke on one occasion. Such repeated humiliations sometimes erupted in weird outbursts of self-deprecation, as happened in 1931 during a trip to Cologne, when, referring to her husband, she said to Leo Spitzer, organizer of a symposium for French writers: *'Er hat sich eine kleine Jüdin geheiratet'* – a vulgar way of saying, 'he took himself a little Jewess for a wife'.

Now, in late November of this eventful year of 1933, Clara told André that a young Zionist painter had invited her to spend a week or two with him in Haifa. Since André had felt free to have an affair with Louise de Vilmorin, Clara gave him *carte blanche* to continue it. All she asked, in a spirit of comradely loyalty, was that this liaison should not exceed the two-week period of her own trip to Palestine.

The idea of once again being cuckolded by his wife can hardly have overjoyed a hyper-sensitive André. But what was even more galling at this moment was the shattering discovery that he was also being 'cuckolded' by Louise de Vilmorin, who had started an affair with a handsome 'man about town' named Friedrich Sieburg. The Paris correspondent of the *Frankfurter Zeitung*, Sieburg several years before became famous with a book (*Glücklich wie ein Gott in Frankreich?* – (As Happy as a God in France?) – a best-seller on both sides of the Rhine – in which he had propounded the thesis that France was a charmingly old-fashioned, epicurean, and basically 'static' country, whereas Germany was a truly 'dynamic' land, geared to the needs and interests of the twentieth century. In itself, this interesting thesis would not have been so objectionable had Sieburg not chosen the spring of 1933 to bring out a 'sequel', *Es werde Deutschland*, which appeared in France under the provocative title, *Défense du nationalisme allemand*. That the lovely Loulou should have started an affair 'on the side' with a German who had made himself an apologist for German nationalism in general and for Adolf Hitler in particular (in an interview published in the Paris daily, *L'Excelsior*) infuriated Malraux. He may at first have wondered if such a thing could be true, for his informant was none other than Consuelo de Saint-Exupéry, a flamboyant Latin-American mischief-maker, who had begun cuckolding her husband 'Tonio' (Saint-Exupéry) almost from the moment she had invaded the Paris scene. But having herself been one of Sieburg's mistresses, Consuelo was in a position to guess what was going on in the handsome Friedrich's de luxe suite at the Hôtel Ritz.

André took the jolting news of this betrayal very badly. He abruptly terminated his affair with a disconcerted Loulou, upset by the fear that this rupture would fatally doom her literary brainchild, *Sainte-Unefois*. But this messy dénouement to a romance that had begun so charmingly probably explains what now ensued: a new affair, destined to last much longer.

On November 7th, after Clara had left for Palestine, Josette Clotis came up to Paris, accompanied by her prim mother and her father, who had business to attend to at the Ministry of Finance. They had arranged to dine together and to spend the evening at the theatre. But when M. Clotis joined them inside the restaurant, a bit late because of his appointments, Josette got a shock. On the front page of the evening paper her father brought with him was an article announcing the winner of this year's Goncourt Prize: André Malraux. Throwing caution to the winds, she hurried to the telephone and called his Rue du Bac apartment number. Above the background uproar, caused by a throng of friends and admirers, André told her to join him a little later at the Brasserie Lipp.

The dinner over, Josette Clotis let her startled parents go on to the theatre without her, while she headed for the Boulevard Saint-Germain. The famous Brasserie was so crammed that she could hardly push her way in through the revolving door, and had to abandon all attempts to reach the Goncourt Prize winner. She did, however, bump into his half-brother, Roland, who, after two semesters at Marburg University to perfect his German, had returned to Paris and worked for a few months as Gide's private secretary. Gide, to André's dismay, had finally decided that he could dispense with Roland's services, but this had in no way dampened the natural cheerfulness of this tall, slim, and singularly handsome twenty-one-year-old man, who was already beginning to outdo his father's achievements as an accomplished lady-killer. Elbowing his way through the mob, 'Kysou' – the childish nickname used by his family and friends – brought Josette Clotis a glass of champagne so they could drink to the inaccessible André's good health and future literary triumphs.

Explaining that she had to stay on in Paris for another day or two for the final fittings of a new dress, she let her parents return to Beaune-la-Rolande, while she again took a room at the Hôtel Montalembert. Here, after a day of nervous expectation, she received a telephone call from André, who invited her to join him for lunch the next day at the Ritz. She turned up elegantly clothed in a fox-fur coat and *haute couture* dress. While she listened distractedly, André treated her to a monologue about the present state of the world, finally remarking, after a glance around the dining room, that 'all this is threatened by death. Everything must be resolved, and doubtless soon, by Fascism or by Communism.'

Later, while they were waiting for the cloakroom attendant to fetch their overcoats, André suddenly turned and, deliberately averting his gaze, he said, 'If a man asked you to spend a month with him without any follow-up, would you be capable of doing it, without a desire to obtain more? I know of no woman who would do so honestly . . . The essential thing,' he added in the next breath, 'is that it be a month of thirty-one days. The first day, in any case, one thinks one can do it.'

In the taxi, André suddenly turned and kissed Josette on the lips, a kiss disturbed by the thick fox-fur collar of her winter coat. But then, just as unexpectedly, he asked where he could drop her off, since he had to return to his NRF office. There was no mention of another rendez-vous.

In despair at being so abruptly 'ditched', Josette Clotis called up 'Mico' (Michel) Gallimard, Raymond's son, an uncomplicated adolescent whom she had befriended at various family luncheons and weekends and who was always ready to accompany her to a movie, or – as now happened – to an *argenterie* shop, where she wanted to buy a silver chalice for her parents' twenty-fifth wedding anniversary. Dutifully she returned to her provincial 'exile' at Beaune-la-Rolande, while André Malraux continued to be hounded by journalists eager to interview the country's latest literary 'star'.

Josette Clotis returned the following weekend and spent a boring Sunday – once again with her friend, Mico Gallimard – feeling too abashed, even in Clara's absence, to ring the doorbell of the Rue du Bac apartment. But on Monday, December 18th, André telephoned to say that he would be dropping by to pick her up. This time he took her to the Hôtel Crillon, where he treated her to a champagne lunch and talked gaily of the Dutch East Indies island given to him by his friend Eddy Du Perron. Later, in the taxi, they saw little of the Place de la Concorde as they exchanged a far longer kiss, untroubled this time by the tickling of fox fur.

The lobby of the Hôtel Montalembert seemed embarrassingly full of curious eyes, so they fled down the Rue du Bac as far as the Quai Voltaire and took a comfortable suite in the far larger and more anonymous Hôtel Palais d'Orsay. Dazed as well as thrilled to realize that the unbelievable was happening at last, Josette Clotis felt paralyzed with fright at the idea that she might spoil everything by making a wrong, indelicate gesture, but André calmed her apprehensions by saying to her softly, 'Don't do anything you don't want to do.'

Outside it had begun to rain, the drops trickling down the window-panes like tears. Night had fallen over the Seine and the shadowy rooftops and chimneys of the Louvre when André finally left. She had to return for Christmas to her parents' home at Beaune-la-Rolande and he had decided to hurry down to Marseilles to meet Clara's returning ship. New international and other challenges loomed, and he could not tell Josette exactly when they would next meet. Little could he guess that more than two months would pass before they saw each other again. Nor probably did it occur to him that he had started a casual romance which was to dominate the rest of Josette Clotis' life.

20

The Activist

Throughout the autumn and winter of 1933 André Malraux was kept busy by the demands of his 'anti-fascist' activities. At first he was more a literary symbol of his generation's mounting concern than one of the driving forces behind the anti-Hitlerian movement, whose most effective behind-the-scenes operator was the German Communist, Willi Münzenberg.

Within weeks of his arrival in Paris (early March 1933) this energetic propagandist – a kind of real-life Garine, but unaffected by any of the metaphysical torments of the hero of Les Conquérants – had established a World Aid Committee for the Victims of German Fascism, headed by a liberal British peer (Lord Marley); he had forged links with a Paris publishing company for the translation into French of works by his exiled compatriots; and he had launched a fortnightly (later a weekly) entitled Der Gegen-Angriff ('Counter-Assault'), designed to counter the vitriolic bilge being poured out by Goebbels' newspaper, Der Angriff ('The Assault').

'A shortish, square, squat, heavy-boned man with powerful shoulders, who gave the impression that bumping against him would be like colliding with a steam-roller' (as Arthur Koestler later wrote), this Saxon of dubious aristocratic and indubitably peasant extraction was a human dynamo it was difficult to resist. In August of 1932 he had personally masterminded the Amsterdam Peace Conference, and in September had persuaded Vaillant-Couturier and Henri Barbusse to organize a follow-up meeting in Paris.

Münzenberg's most spectacular anti-Nazi achievement took a little longer to prepare. In a cramped old house on the Rue Mondétour, near the market area of Les Halles, he put together a research team whose job it was to expose the 'mystery' of the Reichstag fire. The team was headed by his assistant, Otto Katz, a Czech-born polyglot who had once served as business manager for the Berlin stage director, Erwin Piscator. It also included the Hungarian-born journalist, Arthur Koestler (he had not yet become a novelist), and a distinctly 'odd duck' named Gustav Regler – originally a Catholic Saarlander who in January 1919 had helped the German Socialists defend the Reichstag against the Spartakists, only to be so sickened by the ensuing slaughter of the naive young supporters of Rosa Luxemburg and Karl

Liebknecht that he had developed a strong sympathy for communism. A gifted story-teller, Regler, during his flight from Germany, had passed through Strasbourg, where, posing as a student of late-nineteenth-century 'Wilhelmian' architecture, he had persuaded the university librarian to let him photograph the basement ground plan of the Reichstag. Clearly shown on the plan, which he brought to Münzenberg in Paris, was an underground tunnel leading from the Reichstag building to the home of its presiding officer – none other than Hermann Goering. It was probably through this tunnel that the real arsonists had moved with their incendiary devices during the fateful evening of February 27th.

While Otto Katz was sent to Holland to look into the curious past of the Dutch 'arsonist', Marinus Van der Lubbe, the rest of the team worked overtime, compiling a *Brown Book*, which contained a detailed analysis of how the Reichstag fire had been started. Its primary purpose was to establish the innocence of four arrested 'culprits': Georgi Dimitrov, an important Komintern official; two fellow Bulgarians; and Ernst Torgler, the German Communist Party's parliamentary leader in the Reichstag.

On September 11th, ten days before Van der Lubbe, Torgler, Dimitrov, and the other two 'arsonists' were due to go on trial before the German High Court in Leipzig, the Comité international d'aide aux victimes du fascisme held a large meeting at the Salle Wagram. Inside the crammed hall, capable of accommodating 10,000 spectators, André Malraux found himself seated on the podium along with Georgi Dimitrov's sister Elena, Rabindranath Tagore's nephew (found 'undesirable' in Hitler's Germany), Henri Barbusse, several German writers, and two of France's most famous lawyers, Henry Torrès and Vincent de Moro-Giafferi. The latter stole the show with a devastating indictment that rose to a thundering crescendo with the ringing accusation: '*L'assassin, l'incendiaire, le criminel, Goering, c'est toi!*' ('The assassin, the arsonist, the criminal, Goering, is you!')

This meeting, and the even more effective 'counter-trial' in London, helped to show up the Leipzig trial for what it was: a grotesque parody of justice. However, Dimitrov's spectacular success in baiting a furious, insult-barking Goering and a venomous Goebbels began to alarm the communist leadership in Paris. Hitler, who in October had boldly flouted international opinion by withdrawing Germany from the League of Nations, was capable of anything – even of having Torgler, Dimitrov, Popov, and Tanev beheaded, shot, or hanged. Once again Gide's patronage was needed. Louis Aragon, the former Surrealist who was fast becoming the French Communist Party's most dogmatic intellectual, asked Gide to preside over a 'monster meeting', due to be held shortly before the Leipzig Court delivered its verdict on the Reichstag 'arsonists'. Gide, who had gone to Lausanne to oversee the staging of a play, was forced to bow out. Malraux, however, was more than happy to attend.

On December 19th '30,000 proletarians' – as *L'Humanité* proclaimed the next morning – crowded into the huge Luna-Park auditorium near the western outskirts of Paris, to applaud the dozen speakers who demanded the acquittal of Torgler and Dimitrov, and the release from prison of the German Communist Party's leader, Ernst Thaelmann. Seated on the platform with Malraux was his friend André Chamson, the actor Charles Dullin, and two of France's most distinguished scientists: Paul Langevin, who might have been the first to formulate the Theory of Relativity had Einstein not done so before him, and Lucien Lévy-Bruhl, a philosopher with a keen interest in primitive mentalities. Malraux must have been flattered by the special attention accorded by *L'Humanité* to his presence on the stage. For in two successive issues of the paper the name 'André Malraux' was followed (in parenthesis) by 'Prix Goncourt 1933'.

Three days later *L'Humanité* was able to inform its readers, in banner headlines, that:

> Under the pressure of the worldwide proletariat
> THE NAZI HANGMEN HAVE RETREATED.
> TORGLER, DIMITROV, TANEV, POPOV
> HAVE BEEN ACQUITTED

The jubilation was premature. The blubbering Van der Lubbe was promptly executed, but Goering, still smarting from Dimitrov's mocking taunts, blocked the release of the other 'culprits'. Angry manifestos were issued; indignant telegrams were dispatched to the Third Reich's Ministry of the Interior; Dorothy Woodman, a Labour Party MP and leading member of the British Committee for the Victims of German Fascism, travelled to Leipzig to lodge a formal protest. All to no avail.

Willi Münzenberg, however, was in no mood to give up. What was needed was a streamlined 'Dimitrov Committee', headed by non-communists. And who was better fitted for the post than France's most prestigious author, André Gide, aided by his younger, no less committed colleague, André Malraux? The two were asked to fly to Berlin to talk to Joseph Goebbels and possibly to call on President Hindenburg, in order to obtain Georgi Dimitrov's release.

The pros and cons of this curious mission were still being debated when, after dinner on December 28th, André Gide brought his friend Jacques Copeau over to the Malrauxs' apartment on the Rue du Bac. The famous theatre director was not impressed by the 'things of the Orient' cluttering the small vestibule, and even less by Clara, who, with a 'superlucidity' heavily spiced with cynicism, told him candidly that she was leading an 'atrocious life . . . She said she had smoked eight or nine pipes (of opium, I think) during the day.' As for Malraux

He talks non-stop, his back somewhat arched, the head bent forward, continually using a finger to push back the tuft of thin hair which keeps slipping over his forehead. He explains, he demonstrates, he classifies: 'First', 'Second', concluding each part of his explanation with 'Fine', on which he steadies himself while catching his breath before launching out again. While he speaks, his eye never leaves you. He treated me to a lecture on sovietism, compared to Hitlerism and Fascism. There is nothing he doesn't know about the doctrine and the historical facts in their logical sequence. One is astonished that so much intelligence and lucidity, backed by so much ardour, leave one with an overall impression of disorder and confusion.

If confusion there was, it was in the very conception and planning of the harebrained scheme of sending the two Andrés to the German capital to 'reason' with Hitler's Minister of Propaganda. When Gide and Malraux reached Berlin by airplane, on January 4, 1934, they were told that Goebbels and other members of the cabinet were attending a Nazi gathering in Munich!

Gide and Malraux had hardly returned to Paris when their country was plunged into a new political crisis, more serious than any France had experienced since the end of the Great War. The root causes of the trouble, here as in pre-1933 Germany, were a combination of political instability and growing economic distress.

This is not the place to describe the various phases of ths anti-parliamentary agitation, maintained above all by various right-wing leagues of 'patriots' and war veteran associations, which reached its bloody climax during the Place de la Concorde riots of February 6, 1934. Suffice it to say that, like their left-wing friends, André and Clara took part in the huge counter-demonstration, which was organized on February 12th by the Socialist Party leader, Léon Blum, by Léon Jouhaux, head of the powerful CGT (Confédération Générale du Travail – France's largest trade union organization), and by Paul Langevin.

The February 6th riots had at least one immediate as well as several long-term consequences. They stimulated the formation of new anti-fascist movements and associations, all of which up till then had been more or less communist-controlled. On January 31st Paul Langevin had been scheduled to preside over a large meeting at the Salle Wagram to protest against the continued incarceration of Torgler, Dimitrov and the two Bulgarians. Langevin was forced to bow out because of illness. Malraux was then asked to preside over the meeting, which he did with his usual incisive brilliance. However, some of the speeches heard on this occasion made it sound as though the orators were less interested in the fate of their imprisoned comrades in Germany than in carrying out in France the revolution which had so spectacularly failed beyond the Rhine.

Paul Langevin himself may not have fully shared these revolutionary sentiments; nor, unlike his wife, his daughter, and his son-in-law, was he yet a member of the French Communist Party. But he was very much a fellow-travelling admirer of the Soviet Union. Now, alarmed by the events of February 6th, he felt that something had to be done on the home front to combat what seemed to be a fascist threat to the Republic. The result was the creation of a far more ecumenic organization, the CVIA (Comité de Vigilance des Intellectuels Anti-fascistes), which was headed by a triumvirate: Langevin, the Radical Socialist philosopher, Alain, and the eminent ethnographer, Paul Rivet.

Embracing intellectuals of all kinds – and not simply writers and artists, like Barbusse's and Vaillant-Couturier's AEAR – this 'Anti-Fascist Vigilance Committee' attracted an enormous number of adherents, several thousand strong, among whom were to be found men like Julien Benda and Roger Martin du Gard, who were allergic to all forms of political extremism, or who were frankly non-political, like the bohemian *noctambule*, Léon-Paul Fargue. Similar Vigilance Committees quickly mushroomed all over France. The national headquarters of the Socialist and Radical Socialist parties were bombarded with telephone calls from the mayors of provincial towns declaring their readiness to come to Paris fully armed, and *Izvestiya*'s correspondent, Ilya Ehrenburg, was both relieved and amused to see peasants turning up in the suburbs armed with shotguns and hunting rifles, who kept asking, 'Where are the fascists?' The Third Republic might look potbellied and effete compared to the jack-booted dynamism being exhibited beyond the Rhine and the Alps, but the vast majority of the French were clearly in no mood to accept the establishment of one more European dictatorship.

On February 27th Hitler yielded to the international clamour aroused by his government's refusal to abide by the verdict of the Leipzig High Court. Released from prison, Dimitrov, Tanev, and Popov were flown to Koenigsberg and Moscow. André Malraux, however, was unable to celebrate this triumph with his anti-fascist colleagues, for he had ill chosen this moment to embark on a new adventure of 'archaeological exploration' – almost as crazy as the madcap Cambodian foray of 1923.

21

Over the Deserts of Arabia

In December, three days after the Goncourt Prize award, André Malraux was about to enter the NRF–Gallimard building on the Rue Sébastien-Bottin when he bumped into Carlo Rim, a versatile cartoonist, essayist, and magazine editor who shared his own left-wing inclinations. Rim congratulated Malraux, whose radiant spirits made him look more youthful than ever. 'The prize, well –', said André, with a casual shrug. 'What counts is the money. But this time it's clinched. We're now going to be able to buy our propeller.'

This propeller was intended for an aeroplane he needed to make a flying trip to Arabia. Three years before, during their trip to Afghanistan and Persia, André and Clara had met a German adventurer who had recently visited Mecca disguised as a Muslim *hadji* (pilgrim). He had given them a glowing description of treasures which lay buried beneath the ruins of the Queen of Sheba's legendary capital, located at Mareb, near Sana'a, in the rocky, 'off-limits' kingdom of Yemen. Had he actually visited the site, or was he simply repeating what he had heard from others? One thing is certain: this adventurer (named Jacobsthal) possessed an extraordinary 'gift of the gab'. His lyrical descriptions of seventy ruined temples, of 'crumbling palaces more beautiful than the Parthenon, hidden behind golden dunes', enthralled Malraux.

Irresistibly attracted by everything exotic, he had long been fascinated by the legendary figure of Queen Balkis (or Bilkis), the only recorded queen of biblical antiquity – with her 'elephants crowned with ostrich feathers, her green horsemen on piebald mounts, her honour guard of dwarfs, her blue-wood fleets, her chests covered with dragon hides, her ebony bracelets (but dripping with gold jewels!), her enigmas, her slight limp and a laugh which has travelled across the centuries,' as Malraux later wrote in *Antimémoires*, probably adding with poetic licence at least one trait (the laugh), inspired by Louise de Vilmorin, to what he had gleaned from the Old Testament and the Koran, Strabo and Pliny. His attention may also have been drawn to the presence among the statues of Chartres Cathedral of a lovely Queen of Sheba, shown standing on a crouched Abyssinian dwarf between the angel-guided soothsayer Balaam, with his talking ass, and a majestic King Solomon. The mysterious queen's beauty is said to have been marred by a physical deformity. One of her feet, according to oriental legend, was an ass's hoof, but, according to European legend, it was the webbed foot of a goose: whence the name given to her in medieval France – *la Reine Pédauque* (Queen Goosefoot).

If the kingdom of Sheba – Shabwa in Arabic – had so long inflamed the imagination of explorers, it was due to its difficulty of access, protected to the west by the gaunt crags of Yemen (some of them 3,000 metres high) and to the north and east by the vast Rub'al Khali desert of southern Arabia. But it was precisely this dangerous inaccessibility which made the legendary queen's ancient capital so alluring to Malraux. He and Jacobsthal had spent hours discussing how, properly disguised of course, they could join a Bedouin caravan and thus reach the 'forbidden' city.

There were at least two major stumbling blocks impeding the fulfilment of this extraordinary pipe dream. The first was the length of time it would take to carry out such an expedition, which even the euphoric Jacobsthal reckoned would take two years. The second was the problem of linguistic preparation. Richard Burton, whose *Pilgrimage to al-Medina and Meccah* Malraux had almost certainly read (either before or after his 1930 trip to Persia), was an extraordinary linguist who had mastered Persian, Arabic, and at least five Indian vernaculars, before undertaking his 1853 *hadj* disguised as a Pathan. Malraux, notwithstanding his phenomenal memory, had never tried to become a linguist.

At the Société de Géographie, on the Rue de Grenelle, he was received by Jean-Baptiste Charcot, a celebrated Antarctic explorer and the son of the even more famous founder of modern neurology. Charcot warned Malraux that only three Europeans had actually seen Mareb and lived to tell the tale. But the story of the first – a French regimental pharmacist named Thomas Arnaud who had travelled to Sana'a with a Turkish column and had made copies of more than fifty 'inscriptions' at Mareb, before making it back to the Red Sea port of Jeddah thanks to his 'talismanic' companion, a hermaphroditic donkey – was so fabulous that it merely whetted Malraux's appetite.

The idea of undertaking an expedition to the sun-baked ridges and arid deserts of Yemen would never have got beyond the stage of speculative fancy had Malraux not been introduced one day to a former airforce captain, whose nonconformist restlessness was as keen as his own. Several years older than Malraux, Edouard Alfred Flaminius Corniglion-Molinier was the turbulent son of a Nice notary who, during the first months of the Great War, had enlisted in the French Army when he was barely sixteen years old by cheating over his age. Sent to Italy as an airman after the 1917 German breakthrough at Caporetto, he had distinguished himself by shooting down a number of Austro-Hungarian warplanes. Discharged with the rank of captain, he had reluctantly yielded to parental pressure and had obtained a law degree so as to be able to take over his father's notary business.

We have Clara's word for it that Corniglion-Molinier, 'though a resourceful fellow possessed of a lively rather than critical intelligence', was not as crazy as his adventurous past might lead one to suppose. He proved it one evening during the autumn of 1933 when, for the third or fourth time, he heard Malraux begin to talk in lyrical terms of the Queen of Sheba, announcing his extravagant intention of travelling overland to Sana'a and Mareb, disguised as a Persian merchant. 'I find it perfectly ridiculous', broke in the former airforce captain, 'to lengthen the list of scholars and romantic adventurers who have been killed in expeditions of this kind, since today there exists a far surer way of finding this city, if it exists.' The means for not joining the list of killed adventurers was, quite simply, the aeroplane.

Reduced to peevish silence, Malraux turned the matter over in his mind. The next morning he rang Corniglion-Molinier, to find out if he had seriously meant what he had said about the feasibility of organizing aerial expeditions of archaeological reconnaissance. 'Absolutely serious,' was the aviator's prompt reply. For the past five years a Jesuit from Beirut named Poidebard had been using aerial reconnaissance photos to complete a historical map of the Near East indicating ancient forts and highways once built by the Romans.

Several meetings followed. Corniglion-Molinier said he would contact Paul-Louis Weiller, a former Great War aviator who now ran the Gnome & Rhône aero-engine company, to see if he could obtain an aeroplane capable of rising to 4,000 metres, so as to be able to clear the highest peaks of Yemen. Malraux said he would take care of the photographic equipment, relying on the advice of Carlo Rim, who had achieved such marvels with the illustrated weekly, *Vu*.

When they heard of this new archaeological foray, many of Malraux's friends – including Janine Bouissounouse, Mme Théo and André Gide – refused to take it seriously, relegating it to the visionary wonderland of *Royaume-Farfelu* fantasy. They underestimated the thirty-two-year-old author's psychological need to live dangerously – so clearly expressed in a letter sent on January 7, 1934 to Edmond Jaloux: 'What you say of the adventurer who seeks to find himself through the metamorphoses called for by adventure seems to me very penetrating, but it is far truer of me than of my characters.'

The person most violently opposed to this wild Queen of Sheba project was, not unnaturally, Clara. It was, she objected, an indefensible exercise in escapism at a time when explosive threats and pressures were building up beyond the Rhine. This madcap venture, she was convinced, was motivated above all by a secret desire to avenge the recent humiliation she had imposed on her husband by making her amorous 'pilgrimage' to Palestine. Furious arguments ensued. One day, after a violent quarrel, Clara, still fuming with rage, put on her winter coat, took a train to Rennes in Brittany and then headed for Bordeaux. The constantly changing scenery gradually calmed her nerves and brought her to her senses. From Bordeaux she telephoned to find out if her daughter Flo was all right; then she took the next train back to Paris.

By this time Paul-Louis Weiller's initial scepticism had been overcome. The wealthy aero-engine manufacturer was not going to be a spoilsport. What was needed was an engine robust and powerful enough to propel an aeroplane capable of carrying at least three passengers over a distance of 2,000 kilometres. The British, who at this time controlled Aden and the southern emirates of the Arabian peninsula, took a jaundiced view of aerial adventurers. The airborne 'archaeologists' would therefore have to take off from the French port of Djibouti, on the western coast of the Red Sea, adding several hundred kilometres to their flight plan.

On January 27th Carlo Rim was invited to have tea with Corniglion-Molinier. He had already been tipped off about the highly 'confidential' expedition, which Malraux and the former airforce captain had planned to keep 'top secret', in the hope of being able to pull off a journalistic scoop. Corniglion-Molinier was jubilant. He wouldn't, after all, have to rely on his old *zinc* (crate), since Paul-Louis Weiller was lending them one of his own machines – a Farman 190, powered by a 300-horsepower Gnome & Rhône engine.

A little later Malraux appeared, with (in Carlo Rim's words) 'a suspicious glint in his eye, an aggressive lock of hair, and the secretive air of a conspirator'. He rid himself of 'his overcoat and a few facial ticks' before announcing the good news: 'It's a deal with *L'Intransigeant*' – a liberal daily. 'We'll give them exclusive rights to our in-flight record, as well as the best pictures. But there'll be some photos left for you,' he reassured Carlo Rim.

There were a number of last-minute delays, partly caused by the need to fit new fuel tanks into the body of the plane to make it capable of achieving ten hours of uninterrupted flight. But finally, on February 23rd, the Farman 190 took to the air, with Captain Corniglion-Molinier at the controls, Malraux seated next to him as navigator, and, wedged in behind them next to the extra fuel tanks, Paul-Louis Weiller's personal mechanic, Maillard.

On reaching Cairo, Corniglion telephoned to *L'Intransigeant*'s local correspondent. Several days before, Gabriel Dardaud had received a cryptic cable informing him that the 'aviator Corniglion-Molinier' would soon be arriving 'plus passenger and mechanic. Stop. Grateful facilitate pursuit of their trip.' No signature, or further explanation. At the Hotel Continental, Dardaud finally located 'Monsieur Cornichon' ('Mr Pickle', as the porter had chalked up the name on a portable slate), leaning on a terrace balustrade overlooking the Opera Square and enjoying the spectacle of noisy altercations between *arbadji* cab-drivers, *drogman* interpreters, and street urchins, all offering their services to clients emerging from the lobby.

Dardaud couldn't understand why he hadn't been informed of André Malraux's arrival. Why all this mystery? After a moment of hesitation, the two pranksters – for such they seemed to Dardaud – let him in on the secret.

Holding a cigarette in his right hand and weaving smoky arabesques, Malraux launched into a lyrical description of the 'prodigious' civilization of the Shebans, a golden age for the spice-traders of *Arabia felix*, situated at the confluence of three worlds – 'the Asia of the Yellows, the Africa of the Blacks, the Europe of the Whites'. Misinterpreting Dardaud's smile, he stopped and said, 'Obviously, the Queen of Sheba means nothing to you.'

'On the contrary,' replied Dardaud, 'she was the Bedouin who invented the finest skin-smoother for pretty women.' He then offered Malraux the standard Arabic version of the legend, according to which the quick-witted Daughter of the Desert, realizing King Solomon's initial displeasure during her visit to Jerusalem, had used a magic ointment to decapillate her hairy legs.

Corniglion-Molinier's present preoccupations were less ethereal. Paul-Louis Weiller, he explained, had lent them his private aeroplane for a brief month, along with his personal mechanic. In Paris they had lost a lot of precious time refitting the interior of the cabin to accommodate the extra fuel tanks. They hadn't had time to obtain proper clearance and they had fooled the aeronautic police by saying that they were going up on a test flight, no more. If it became common knowledge that they were now in Cairo, they might find themselves grounded.

There remained the troubling inaccuracy of their fanciful maps. Malraux wondered if there wasn't someone in Cairo who had made a study of the ancient kingdom of Sheba. No problem, said Dardaud. He knew just the man they needed for a bit of sound advice: Henri Munier, secretary-general of Egypt's Société Royale de Géographie, an archaeologist-historian whom King Fuad had chosen to head a prestigious research centre.

The next morning Malraux, Corniglion-Molinier, and Dardaud were ushered into Henri Munier's office, where they were offered Turkish coffee and cigarettes. Malraux had barely opened his mouth when he was abruptly interrupted by Munier. 'The Queen of Sheba, Monsieur Malraux, but let's be serious! A figure of legend, no more. For thirty centuries she has made millions of men dream; but nothing, absolutely nothing – I am speaking here as a historian – has been established to link the Woman of the Desert who went to haggle with Solomon and Yemen, where, you say, you would like to find her capital, her palace and her temples.' Malraux couldn't help wincing. Henri Munier, with his one eye (the other was whitened by leucoma), must have looked to him like a hideous gnome, behind his rampart of books and folders, intent on tearing his cherished dream to pieces. 'But the people of Sheba had a long, well-known history,' Malraux protested. 'They built temples for their gods, dams to irrigate their valleys. They had a language, a kind of proto-Arabic, I've been told, which has been deciphered on monumental inscriptions.'

'All that has nothing to do with the legendary Queen of Sheba,' retorted the pitiless Munier. 'She met Solomon during his reign, nine hundred years before the start of our era, but it was three hundred years before any mention was made of the passage of this female traveller in the Book of Kings. Three hundred years provide plenty of time for daydreaming, particularly for those who wish to magnify the wisdom of a deceased monarch. Solomon was not the only one to have met the Shebans. We encounter them in the cuneiform chronicles of the kings of Assyria . . . As for the inscriptions of southern Arabia, the oldest date from the first centuries AD, and while they furnish us with the names of Sheban kings, never have we found one of a queen.

'While you're at it, why not try to track down the Three Kings who came to Bethlehem to pay homage to the Christ Child in the manger?' continued Munier, deaf to Malraux's protests. 'They too were merchants of gold, frankincense, and myrrh, so the Gospels tell us. Legend gave them the names of Melchior, Caspar, and Balthazar, and how many different names were not given to Solomon's lady friend – Balkis or Bilkis for the Arabs; Makeda for the Ethiopians; Nikaule for the Greeks? She existed, but could have belonged to some ethnic group from the north or centre of Arabia, far removed from Mareb and the Yemenite hinterland. The Shebans were always to be found near the borders of Israel.'

'But how are we to find Mareb?' asked the pragmatic Corniglion. Henri Munier stood up and from a bookshelf he pulled the latest number of the *Revue de la Société Royale de Géographie d'Egypte*. 'Here's an excellent study on the journey to Mareb made by a Jesuit Padre, Pedro Paez. Captured by pirates and sold as a slave, he followed his masters over the caravan routes of Arabia. He was the first European to see Mareb, and later, after he was freed, he described its ruins. But that was in 1590.'

Munier pulled out several maps, as lacking in precision as those Malraux and Corniglion-Molinier had obtained in Paris. He urged them, when they reached Djibouti, to contact the Egyptian airman, Anis Pasha. He also felt it to be his duty to offer them a word of warning. Recently a number of Sudanese merchants from the Nile valley had been massacred, stout Muslims though they were. The present Imam, Yahia, was a senile, morbidly suspicious opium-addict, who felt himself threatened by the British to the south, by the Saudi Arabians to the north, and by the Italians on the western shore of the Red Sea. His rabid xenophobia had been exacerbated by the recent death of his favourite son, Mohammed, who had been devoured by a shark during a fishing expedition. The irascible monarch now took it out on his victims, and regularly, every Friday, a few of his subjects, suspected of plotting to overthrow him, or simply of being 'bearers of misfortune', were publicly beheaded before the city gates of Sana'a.

The return to the hotel was not exactly joyous. 'I could do with a stiff whisky,' announced Corniglion. Left alone with him at the bar, *L'Intransigeant*'s Cairo correspondent asked the airman how on earth he had got himself involved in such a risky venture. 'A simple sandstorm, or a blanket of fog could ruin all your plans.'

'Maybe it's crazy,' Corniglion admitted, 'but it's a kind of bet, or, if you prefer, a challenge between André and myself. It all began one evening last autumn, after a good dinner at a friend's home. You know how it is, he spends his time dreaming his life out loud. One day, he talks of the sturgeons of the Caspian, carved up alive for their caviar. The next, he leads you past the smoking funeral pyres of the Ganges, or takes you on a night hunt for the marvellous butterflies that settle on rotting toadstools in the jungle depths of Malaya. . . . I think' Corniglion concluded, 'that Malraux was fed up with the kitchen-sink politics that were poisoning the atmosphere on both banks of the Seine, and that this prompted him to talk of his forthcoming trip to Yemen, disguised as a Persian.'

Malraux, meanwhile, had been lured to an impromptu book-signing ceremony, secretly organized by Gaston Gallimard, who had had several hundred copies of La Condition humaine quietly shipped to Cairo in advance. The book-signing ceremony quickly turned into an informal press conference, during which, as Etienne Deloro, of La Bourse Egyptienne, later described it, Malraux's sentences were fired off 'like rockets in massive salvos, the words raining down on us like spent fireworks'. The lid was thus blown off their 'top secret' enterprise, even before the two adventurers and the pith-helmeted Maillard had taken off from the Almaza airfield for Port Sudan.

At Djibouti, Corniglion-Molinier was warmly welcomed by two French Air Force officers. The three airmen and Malraux spent two days comparing their own sketchy maps with one that was kindly lent to them by the Egyptian aviator, Hassan Anis Pasha.

Shortly after dawn on March 7th, the Farman 190 took off from Djibouti and headed out over the Gulf of Tadjourah. Corniglion-Molinier carefully skirted the island of Pirim, declared off-limits by the British, and headed north toward Moka. The famous coffee-trading town was shrouded in a blanket of russet fog which hid the western rim of the Arabian peninsula all the way to Hodeidah, 200 kilometres farther north. The Red Sea port loomed out of the shoreline mist like an 'Algerian fort' (as Malraux later described it), but Corniglion was careful not to overfly it, reckoning that it was probably linked by wireless to the Yemen capital of Sana'a. Only after they were well beyond it did he alter course, banking to the right in the direction of the rising sun. It was 8 o'clock. They had been flying for three hours.

Ahead of them, jutting up through the layer of tawny fog, loomed a 'gigantic prehistoric troupe' – the first jagged peaks of mountainous Yemen. Below them, the fog slowly dissipated into wisps, revealing villages, lurking 'in their holes like crabs' (Malraux's description once again). Valley after valley followed, but where on earth was Sana'a? As they overflew one more ridge, they spotted a lonely fort – and there suddenly was Sana'a, directly below them, with its circumference of inclined ramparts built of white and reddish rock enclosing a patchwork of sun-baked roofs and verdant gardens. Fortunately the irascible Imam had no anti-aircraft weapons, or he would have ordered his gunners to open fire – too late – on the insolent intruder.

Once again Corniglion banked, this time towards the north. Although there was no longer any ground fog, the Kharid river had vanished –

underground. But 2,000 metres above it they could follow its subterranean course by a thin green line of trees and vegetation winding across the increasingly flat, chalk-white, yellow, and ochre-coloured wilderness, which a merciless sun had cracked and fissured into fantastic patterns like the palm of an ancient hand. They had left Yemen behind them and were venturing out over the great parched deserts of southern Arabia, where, twenty centuries before, the thirsty, heat-crazed legions of Aelius Gallius had lost their way and had had their bones picked clean by vultures.

As the minutes passed the wilderness below grew desperately flat and featureless. The ruins they were looking for were located near Mareb, but Mareb itself was nowhere to be seen. Seated behind Malraux, Maillard, the mechanic, was increasingly restless. They had been flying for five-and-a-half hours, and if they continued much longer, they would not be able to make it back to Djibouti. But then, suddenly, Malraux and Corniglion spotted a gleaming patch of white in the tawny desert. A geological accident? No. For as they watched the patch grow larger ('much as a famished man eats', as Malraux later put it), they could make out ruined walls and towers – or such at least they seemed to be. There could be no further doubt. They had reached their destination. This was what they had been so avidly searching for – the Queen of Sheba's city!

Putting the Farman into a 45-degree bank, Corniglion reduced speed and began circling the ruins so that Malraux, next to him, could start his filming. Trying to land here was out of the question; on one side were treacherously soft dunes, on the other tips of volcanic rock jutted up through a covering of sand. As they lost altitude, Malraux could see the shadow of their tilted plane racing across the sand, followed by a smaller, more slowly moving shadow – that of a desert bird of prey with fully outspread wings. From the shadows of the ruined walls, some of which must have been forty to fifty metres high, there flashed tiny dots of orange flame. They were being fired on by Bedouins, who had pitched their tents in the shade.

The return trip was almost as tense and nerve-wracking as the outbound flight. Malraux had persuaded Corniglion to adopt an irregular flight plan, enabling them to overfly the 'Valley of the Tombs' (the traditional burial ground of the kings of Sheba). Corniglion now put the Farman on an almost due south course. As they approached what they took to be the famous valley, Maillard leant forward and pointed to the fuel gauge. Most of the narrow canyon was already hidden by a reddish sandstorm. A moment later they were hit by a furious wind which flipped the Farman over several times and then catapulted it away 'like a slingshot' (as Corniglion later described it).

Relying on his compass readings, Corniglion altered course to a south-westerly direction. Everything now depended on the force of the tailwind. If they were lucky, it could increase their speed to 210 kilometres an hour; if unlucky, its weakness might force them to ditch in the shark-infested Red Sea.

Corniglion began a slow descent over the lowlands of Yemen, where once again tiny bursts of flame told them that they were being fired on by antique Mausers. Finally, to their intense relief, the first hint of blue appeared on the horizon. Their fuel reserves were now so low they could no longer make it back to Djibouti. Instead, Corniglion headed across the Red Sea towards a point situated some distance to the north, on the French Somali coast. He brought the Farman safely down on an airstrip next to the fort of Obok. Here they were warmly welcomed by a French colonial sergeant, who put them up for the night inside the local prison – the coolest building in that godforsaken outpost.

The day after their return to Djibouti, the Consul-General of neighbouring Ethiopia informed them that His Majesty, the King of Kings, would be delighted to receive them. Climbing to more than 2,500 metres, the Farman 190 covered the distance in two hours and fifty minutes, compared to the three days it took the steam train to wind its way up to the central highlands of Addis Ababa. As Corniglion came down to land, he saw riders galloping up and down the field engaged in a polo match.

In the Ethiopian capital the two aerial explorers were first welcomed by the foreign minister, and then accorded a private audience in a small pavilion by the 'imperial' descendant of King Solomon and his legendary desert queen.

From Addis Ababa they flew north to Massawa, and on to Port Sudan. But it was in Tripoli that they were accorded an unforgettable welcome by Marshal Balbo. Mussolini's most celebrated aviator refused to let his two French guests go before he had copiously wined and dined them. He had probably never heard of Malraux, but even if he had known that the thirty-two-year-old author had been making anti-fascist speeches, he would probably have shrugged off the news as unimportant. The Duce at this moment was more worried than pleased by Hitler's dramatic rise to power and the pro-*Anschluss* agitation that his noisy Brownshirts were stirring up in Austria. He was eager to improve Italy's relations with its Mediterranean neighbour, France, and this too was Balbo's sentiment. Malraux, as far as he was concerned, was an archaeologically-minded 'tourist'. But the former French Air Force Captain Eduardo Flaminio Corniglione, who had come to his country's rescue in 1917 and had shot down a number of enemy warplanes, was a comrade-in-arms who deserved a hero's welcome.

The rest of the trip would not have been particularly eventful had they not run into a violent hailstorm over the mountains west of Tunis. Their Farman 190 was bounced up and down like a ping-pong ball for twenty nerve-wracking minutes, which Malraux was persuaded would be their last.

After making a detour via Fez, whose magnificently walled medina is one of the wonders of the Muslim world, they flew up Spain's Mediterranean coast to Barcelona, and from there, to Lyons. Here, on March 20th, the three airborne adventurers were greeted by a select welcoming committee:

Clara and 'Uncle André' (Gide), who had been trying to console her during the spells of worrying silence between laconic telegrams.

In December, when Gide had sought to dissuade him from undertaking this crazy venture, Malraux had simply answered, 'Yes, I'm too impatient.' He proved it once again the next morning when the five of them returned to the Lyons airfield. Heavy clouds darkened the horizon and they were informed that no aeroplanes were currently landing in the Paris area. After hours of tiresome waiting and a frugal lunch, Malraux got up and announced that he was going to check with the meteorological office. He soon returned, saying, 'Let's be off. The weather's lifting, it's fine over Paris.' But shortly after the take-off the Farman 190 plunged into another storm, so violent that at one point André Gide's bald head hit the cabin's low ceiling. It did not take a grim Corniglion long to realize that Malraux's report on 'fair weather' over Paris was sheer bluff. After he had brought the Farman safely down on the Orly airfield he told Clara to sit up front next to him in his car: 'If your man' – he meant André – 'was seated there, I couldn't keep myself from slapping him in the face.'

This, as it happened, was not the final storm the two adventurers had to weather. The next day, when Corniglion flew Paul-Louis Weiller's Farman from Orly to the Le Bourget airfield, the former airforce captain was informed that he faced disciplinary action for having left on a long flight without the proper clearance.

Their archaeological 'raid' had also given rise to a diplomatic 'incident'. News of the two adventurers' discovery of the Queen of Sheba's 'capital', prominently headlined in the March 10th issue of *L'Intransigeant*, had aroused the ire of Imam Yahia. An official protest from the Ministry of Foreign Affairs at Sana'a had been lodged with the British authorities at Aden, to be transmitted to the Quai d'Orsay in Paris. The territory of Yemen, the note declared, had been overflown without prior authorization by two aircraft – one piloted by a certain Corniglion, the other by an aviator named Molinier.

Nor was this the end of the hubbub. Six weeks later *L'Intransigeant* began publishing its series of exclusive articles – seven written by Malraux, three by Corniglion-Molinier – under the rivetting title, 'ABOVE THE DE-SERT OF ARABIA – Overflying the Queen of Sheba's mysterious capital'. These were accompanied not only by photographic illustrations, but also by drawings by André Hardy; on one of his drawings ramparts, gates, 'vast terraces', oval towers, 'temples or palaces' and monumental columns were specifically identified. The sheer effrontery of Malraux's claim that these were the ruins of 'the Queen of Sheba's mysterious capital' could not pass unchallenged. And sure enough, in the April 6th issue of *Le Temps*, Malraux's 'discovery' of the Queen of Sheba's 'capital' was challenged by a gentleman named Beneyton, who claimed to have spent thirteen years exploring the Red Sea coast and the Yemen hinterland on horseback.

Exactly what the ruins were André Malraux had photographed is something of a mystery. One thing is certain: they were not those of the Queen of Sheba's capital, or more exactly of the capital of the kings of Shabwa, which all archaeologists now identify with the town of Mareb (or Marib). In the early 1960s, when a French Air Force Colonel, Edmond Petit, undertook a painstaking study of this question, he found that all of the original maps, flight plans and drawings had disappeared. He then consulted Jacqueline Pirenne, a recognized authority who had carefully mapped the Yemen hinterland and the deserts of southern Arabia. From Malraux's descriptions of his and Corniglion's flight, she concluded that the 'city' they had discovered was an immense oasis, located on the Ragwhan Wadi, north of Marib, composed partly of ruined buildings, partly of still inhabited hamlets (Asahil-Rymn, Duraïb, Kharib) – which would explain why it seemed to the two adventurers 'five times bigger' than the other sites they had overflown.

22

Four Months in the USSR

In early June André and Clara set out on yet another trip. Their destination this time was not one of the exotic lands of a more or less timeless Orient, but the new twentieth-century mecca of communists and fellow travellers: Moscow. Moscow, where the recently renamed Union of Writers had decided to hold an international congress.

Malraux's active participation in anti-fascist meetings had brought him into contact with Ilya Ehrenburg, a talented novelist who, as correspondent for the Soviet government's newspaper, *Izvestiya*, had recently returned from Central Europe, upset by Chancellor Dollfuss' ruthless crushing of a socialist 'insurrection' in Vienna. Almost everywhere – in Admiral Horthy's Hungary, Marshal Pilsudski's Poland, King Alexander's Yugoslavia – reactionary regimes were throttling the revolutionary aspirations of their working classes and restive peasantries. Even in Moscow it was now glaringly obvious that the Komintern's extremist line – with its relentless attacks on 'bourgeois capitalism' and the 'social–fascist' betrayers of the proletariat – had merely weakened the partisans of parliamentary democracy and encouraged the emergence of vehemently anti-communist, dictatorial regimes. The time had come to soft-pedal the emphasis on the class struggle and the dictatorship of the proletariat, and to forge new tactical alliances with 'anti-fascist' authors in the West.

As one of the organizers of the August congress, Ilya Ehrenburg had decided to return by boat to Moscow well in advance of the event. The prospect appealed to Malraux. He and Clara accordingly joined Ilya and his wife Lyuba in London. The leisurely voyage to Leningrad on the SS *Djerzhinsky* was uneventful, giving Malraux time to work on a Baku petroleum workers novel.

With its magnificent granite quays, painted rococo palaces and Hermitage Museum, the former capital of Peter the Great and his successors had lost none of its imperial grandeur. Leningrad, the site of three twentieth-century revolutions, struck Clara as being a 'big, very big Versailles'. But for André it was, in its poorer quarters – with 'endless iron steps lost in the haunted shadows of canals' – the city of Raskolnikov and his creator, Dostoevsky.

Not long after André and Clara had registered at the Hotel Astoria, a high-powered journalistic team turned up to interview Malraux for the *Literaturnaya Gazeta*. It was led by the famous historical novelist, Alexei Tolstoy, and included Paul Nizan, an ardently communist pamphleteer and author of didactic fiction who had been sent to Moscow to edit the French edition of the monthly, *Mezhdunarodnaya Literatura* (International Literature). Malraux impressed his questioners by his rapid replies and flashes of mordant wit. Satires of capitalistic society were fine – there was no dearth of material in this respect – but satire, he maintained, was 'always "conditioned", schematic, when we should aim at a complete artistic representation of reality, the creation of finished literary portrayals'.

As for his own literary projects, he was working on his novel about petroleum. 'My novel will take place in Persia and Baku, where I intend to go.' He also spoke of his intention of making a film version of *La Condition humaine* for the *Mezhrabpom* (International Workers Aid) film-making concern. 'Soviet films have a very considerable influence on French intellectuals. For us, the history of the cinema is divided into two parts: before and after Soviet films.'

'But I am not a pacifist, not at all,' he protested, in answer to another question. 'If war breaks out, and I think it's Japan that will start it, I will be the first to work for the formation of a Foreign Legion, and in its ranks, rifle in hand, I will defend the Soviet Union, the land of freedom.'

In Moscow André and Clara were given a red velvet suite, with a window looking out over Red Square, Lenin's Mausoleum, and the multi-coloured onion domes of St Basil's Cathedral. They were at first allowed a surprising amount of free time before being taken on guided tours of model factories, clinics, and institutions for the 'rehabilitation' of wayward orphans. The old-fashioned trams were everywhere filled to overflowing, with passengers bulging out over the crowded steps like clumps of grapes, but empty taxis were instantly available each time they stepped out of the hotel lobby. Clara was struck by the fact that no children could be seen skipping or playing in the streets. The explanation was simple: they had all been sent away to summer holiday camps, financed, like so much else, by a beneficent, omnipresent, all-supervising state. Yet Clara and André could not help noticing the crowds of beggars who gathered every Sunday near the entrance to St Basil's Cathedral – proof that the 'opium of the people' still enjoyed favour with poor, 'backward' souls.

Exactly what went wrong with Malraux's plans to have *La Condition humaine* made into a film is anything but clear. The Dutch film director, Joris Ivens, was also in Moscow at this moment, working with the German writer, Gustav Regler, on a propaganda film about daily life in Soviet Russia (which they had great trouble persuading the Komintern's cultural boss, the Hungarian Communist, Bela Kun, to accept). Ivens, a most likeable as well as imaginative director and, like Regler, a dedicated Communist, would almost certainly have been delighted to make a film version of Malraux's novel. But the ultimate decision lay not with him but with the bureaucrats of the *Mezhrabpom*-Film organization, where the ideological screws were being tightened by Stalin's *apparatchiki*.

André and Clara were invited out to Bela Kun's dacha, where she wore herself out translating her husband's machine-gun bursts of French into German, and Kun's equally rapid affirmations from German into French. With the illustrious theatre director, Vsevolod Meyerhold, there were no such problems since he spoke fluent French. Not only did he receive André and Clara in his suburban dacha, but he personally took them to see the old Moscow house where Dr Mikhail Dostoevsky had lived and in which the young Fyodor Mikhailovich had spent his earliest years.

Malraux had some long conversations with Eisenstein, who made several visits to his and Clara's hotel suite. The celebrated director, who seemed genuinely interested in making a film of *La Condition humaine*, had lost none of his originality, so pithily expressed in French; but he was no longer the same carefree Serghei Mikhailovich whose wry wit and brilliance in answering technical questions had enchanted his Sorbonne fans in February 1930, when an obtuse police ban had prevented the projection of *The General Line* in Paris. The blue eyes, beneath the massive, Beethoven-esque brow, were still astoundingly vivacious, the wit was as keen as ever, but the creative drive was absent. Even as he sketched on the sheets of paper in front of them, Eisenstein knew, and Malraux should have guessed, that all of their vividly imagined scenes, syncopated contrasts, symbolical hints, and startling montage effects belonged to the realm of dreams. In 1930 Eisenstein had made a deal with Paramount for the production of four films. Since then only one of them, a hymn of praise to the revolutionary Mexico of Pancho Villa and Lázaro Cárdenas, had been even partially completed. The reason was not hard to find. Anatoly Lunacharsky, who as Lenin's Kommissar of Enlightenment (ie Education) had been the leading advocate of a genuinely 'proletarian culture', had been 'sent abroad', like Trotsky. His recent death – at Menton, on the French Riviera – had symbolized the end of a creative era. For his infinitely less tolerant and more dogmatic successor as the ideological watchdog of the Arts in Stalin's Soviet Union was a narrow-minded *apparatchik* named Andrei Zhdanov. Implacably opposed to all forms of 'abstract', non-literal experimentation, he had joined forces with the novelist and playwright, Alexander Fadeyev, the real boss of the new Union of Writers, to have 'socialist realism' officially prescribed as a method to be followed 'in art, literature, and literary criticism'.

Shortly before the start of the International Writers Congress, due to open on August 17th, André and Clara had to move to the less centrally located, but equally plush, late Victorian Metropole, in whose vast dining rooms those who wished could waltz and tango in the evenings to the guitars and violins of a gypsy orchestra. The hotel was now entirely reserved for congress participants – from forty different lands representing 'fifty-two languages'.

Malraux by this time was no stranger to the USSR's intelligentsia. On June 12th his friend Paul Nizan had introduced him to readers of the *Literaturnaya Gazeta* with an incisive article, one of the most penetrating ever to have been written about him. Of contemporary French writers Malraux, according to Nizan, was the most anguished and death-obsessed. It was a mistake to compare him to Pascal, for in his books the problem was not linked to any specifically ethical or theological conception; it simply underlay 'the anguish, the despair, the irremediable solitude which characterize man'. Rather, Malraux reminded him of

> that great thinker and contemporary philosopher, Martin Heidegger, for whom, as for Malraux, the essence of human life is to be found in despair and anguish. This rapprochement is very symptomatic of the present historical period. In this hour of decline of bourgeois civilization, great thinkers have suddenly discovered that, face to face with nothingness, anguish and despair constitute a reality for man . . . To the fundamental question: 'How is one to deliver oneself from anguish and death?', they offer dissimilar solutions. Heidegger has found an answer in the complete and unconditional acceptance of National Socialism. Malraux, for his part, has been trying to overcome this anguish. He has discovered in action, any kind of action, the strength to overcome it or simply to draw a curtain across it. Action can protect man against despair and against anguish . . . its supreme form is revolutionary heroism.

For Malraux, Nizan went on, revolution was simply a remedy against anguish, it was not, 'as for the masses of the people, a historical necessity'. As a result, Malraux did not understand what a revolution really was, underestimating the role of the masses in the revolutionary process. 'Malraux is not a revolutionary writer; he is one of those renowned young writers who, born into the bourgeoisie, doom this class to a natural death and rally to the side of the proletariat.'

If the ideological watchdogs who were now trying to formulate a universal doctrine to which all 'revolutionary' authors could and should adhere had been as intelligent as Paul Nizan, it is just conceivable that Malraux would have joined their ranks. But the most powerful among them, Stalin, had probably never heard of Heidegger, still less tried to read a page (even in translation) of *Sein und Zeit*. The simplistic slogan he had coined as a kind of *mot d'ordre* on the eve of the congress – 'Writers are the engineers of the soul' – and which was parroted by the Moscow press throughout the congress's duration, was a minor masterpiece of deceptive fatuity. While it paid lip-service to the existence of an individual 'soul' or 'psyche', it embodied the preposterous assumption that from the untapped, subterranean riches of what Jung later called the 'collective unconscious' new masterpieces could be mined or dredged by intellectual *udarniki* (shock-workers), applying themselves with unremitting zeal to the fulfilment of Five-Year Plans of Cultural Production.

The Stalinist slogan adorned the square facing the Trades Union building (formerly the Assembly Hall of the Russian Nobility), in which the congress was to be held. Huge posters had also been put up of Lenin, Stalin, and the doyen of Soviet letters, a most unsexagenarian Maxim Gorky, 'his features unmarked by age, his hair cut short, looking rather like a fox-terrier' (as Gustav Regler later described him).

The Writers Congress was formally opened in the Hall of Pillars on August 17th with an interminable, three-hour harangue delivered by Gorky in a cracked, reedy, increasingly hoarse voice. The veteran author, who in 1928 had been lured back to Moscow from his comfortable 'retreat' at Sorrento and Capri, had spent weeks in his suburban dacha labouring on the text. It was little wonder it had given him such trouble. For the speech was nothing less than an attempt to put world literature – from the earliest myth-makers of ancient Greece and Egypt down to the 'corrupting' literature of recent times – through the ideological wringer of dialectical materialism. Gorky got his first laugh from the packed rows when he declared that Immanuel Kant would never have worried his head about 'the thing in itself' if he had been a primitive man clad in skins. 'Primitive man,' Gorky declared, 'was a materialist.'

Seated between Malraux and Regler, their French interpreter, a full-bosomed, highly perfumed lady named Bola Boleslavskaya, had difficulty keeping them properly informed of the latest Gorkyan banalities. After stripping Prometheus, Tantalus, and Icarus of their mythological significance – like Hercules, the 'first hero of labour', they were basically shock workers who in their misguided ways had sought to improve the dismal lot of the cavemen workers of primitive antiquity – Gorky went on to demolish the Christian concept of God as 'an artificial summing-up of the products of labour'.

'*Quoi?*' asked Malraux.

'*Généralisation des résultats du travail*,' answered Bola Boleslavskaya with a luminous gleam in her dark grey eyes.

The shorthand answer amused Malraux, who leaned forward and said to Regler, '*Ils le font travailler*' – the 'they' being Gorky's proletarians, who were forcing a lazy God to work.

'*Je préfère Nietzsche*,' answered Regler, whose highly subjective communist sympathies had never affected his undergraduate fondness for Hölderlin and Goethe's lyric poetry.

Seated nearby was Thomas Mann's son, Klaus, who was drawing strange pictures on a scrap of paper; the German novelist Theodor Plivier had fallen asleep; the anarchist Oskar Maria Graf, who had turned up in Moscow in a colourfully strapped pair of Bavarian *lederhosen*, was smiling contentedly though he did not understand a word; while the former Surrealist rebel and now faithful Party-liner, Louis Aragon, was picking up each worn pebble in the master's fatuous speech as though it were a precious gem on which he bestowed his smiling benediction.

Few of the later speeches reached such heights of tortuous fatuity. But the relentless multiplicity of the 'popular' pressures that were brought to bear on the two-week congress soon turned it into a demagogic carnival, at once 'moving, naive, and pathetic', as Ehrenburg later put it. At 9 am, when they gathered for the morning session, and even more so after the lunch-time break, the writers found themselves besieged by 'spontaneously' formed delegations of textile workers demanding novels dealing with spinning and weaving, miners demanding works of fiction set in the Donbass region, construction workers demanding poems and short stories describing the marvels of the Moscow subway system, kolkhoz peasants demanding a 'new literature' extolling the radical 'dekulakization' of the country.

Meanwhile, inside the Hall of Pillars, where 700 novelists, poets, essayists, critics and miscellaneous literary hacks were assembled, speech followed speech. Some were vehemently partisan, like that of the noted critic, Viktor Shklovsky, who declared that if Dostoevsky were still alive he would have to stand trial before the tribunal of the Revolution and be condemned as a 'traitor'. The vodka-loving Yuri Olesha, who in a moment of drunken exasperation had startled his neighbours in the dining room of the Hotel Metropole by declaring that Stalin was an 'old pederast', made a poetic confession of his past aberrations and announced his literary 'resurrection' in a highly emotional, self-lacerating speech. Mikhail Koltsov, one of *Pravda*'s editorial stars, amused the auditorium with random anecdotes, as did the gifted story-teller, Isaak Babel; while Willi Bredel, recently released from a Nazi concentration camp, won himself a standing ovation after describing the harrowing tortures inflicted on the pacifist-novelist, Ludwig Renn, and on Carl von Ossietzky, the courageous Berlin editor of the left-wing weekly, *Die Volksbühne*.

The most significant speech heard at this congress was the one delivered by the senior Komintern official, Karl Radek. Devoted to 'bourgeois literature and proletarian literature', it set out to differentiate the two. Radek's thesis was that the 'literature of a moribund capitalism' could only be regarded as a form of 'intellectual degeneration'. 'Bourgeois art' was no longer capable of the 'realism of Balzac'. All it could now produce was the introspective ruminations of a Marcel Proust – likened by Radek to a 'mangy dog, incapable of action', which, basking in the sun, 'ceaselessly licks its sores' – or an indigestible Irish brew, like *Ulysses*, whose 800 pages were dismissed as a 'dungheap crawling with worms', the petty wrigglings of which Joyce had subjected to a microscopic inspection.

Having thus demolished two of the twentieth-century's greatest authors as typical specimens of a capitalistic culture which, like 'capitalistic science', was in an advanced state of 'putrefaction', Radek proceeded to define what the proletarian literature of the future should and must be. He urged the comrade writers in the hall to turn their backs on the capitalistic world's morbid interest in 'the irrational, the unconscious, and the subconcious' – an indictment which not only swept the pioneering works of Freud, Jung, and Adler into the 'dustbin of history', but which implicitly condemned virtually everything that had been truly innovative in twentieth-century literature and art. The way forward, for proletarian writers, was in effect a return to the past, as exemplified by the robust realism of Balzac. What was needed was an 'active, positive, combative' literature, a 'literature filled with hatred for a rotten capitalism'.

André Malraux's speech did not immediately follow Karl Radek's. This was just as well, for Malraux's short, pithy speech was, in effect, a blunt rebuttal of Radek's on several vital points. He began, diplomatically, by congratulating Soviet writers on their good fortune, since they could already work 'for the proletariat', whereas 'we revolutionaries of the West work against the bourgeoisie'. He expressed his admiration for what the Soviet Union had achieved by liberating women, by giving confidence to children (including the hundreds of thousands of *byesprizorny* orphans who had been made homeless and parentless by a cruel civil war).

But having made this ritual offering of compliments, Malraux got down to brass tacks by raising one or two pointed questions. Had recent Russian literature produced a positive image of the USSR? The answer could hardly have been more bluntly stated: 'In external facts, yes. In ethics and psychology, no.' And the reason? 'Because the confidence you accord to everyone, you have not always accorded to writers.'

At a congress convened to endorse the new gospel of 'socialist realism', this was close to blasphemy. But it was quickly followed by a second hammer-blow, aimed at the very foundations of the USSR's new literary ideology. 'Comrades,' Malraux warned, 'America is there to show us that in expressing a powerful civilization, one does not necessarily produce a powerful literature, and that it will not be enough to photograph a great epoch for a great literature to be born.'

Culture, he went on, is always a process of education. 'But, comrades, those from whom we learn, where did they themselves learn? We read Tolstoy, but he himself had no Tolstoy to read. What he brings to us, he had first of all to discover.' Then came the ringing words which exposed the fatuity of the Stalinist *mot d'ordre*: 'If "writers are the engineers of the soul", do not forget that the highest function of the engineer is to invent.' To which was immediately added a second defiant affirmation: 'Art is not a submission, it is a conquest.'

Lest anyone should have any doubts as to what he meant, Malraux delivered another hammer-blow. To the question: how could this conquest be expressed, he replied that one had to rely 'on the unconscious, almost always; on logic, very often'. And, as though that were not enough, he added one more sentence, perhaps the most heretical of all: 'Marxism is the consciousness of the social; culture is the consciousness of the psychological.' In other words, the teachings of Marx and Engels were valid for the solution of social and economic problems, but were not a recipe for 'cultural progress'.

No less heretical was the tenor of replies made by Malraux to an interviewer from the *Literaturnaya Gazeta*: 'I consider that what matters in art is not the representation of something but the expression of someone. The affirmation – that the artist is entirely subordinated to the world surrounding him – is worthless. In itself the world is without form, and the first duty of the artist, of the painter, consists of giving it form, of choosing the necessary materials. And this choice is conditioned by ideology, which provides the glasses through which the artist observes the world . . . The ideology determines the field of vision.'

Even if the final words had a Marxist ring, the earlier sentences, affirming the sovereignty of the artist over the circumambient world, and, even more, that 'the world, in itself, is without form', were unmistakably Kantian. This was the kind of 'detestable' idealism which Hegel had inherited from Kant and which Marx, in the name of 'scientific materialism', had sought to purge from his historico-deterministic 'system'.

This interview, added to his incisive speech, explains why, long before the Writers Congress had ended, André Malraux had become a kind of twin-action magnet – attracting those, like Gustav Regler, who detested mind-numbing formulas, while repelling exasperated dogmatists like Karl Radek.

The Writers Congress would not have been a truly Russian event if it had not been concluded by a lavish banquet. In Gorky's dacha near Moscow a huge horseshoe table had been set up in a long reception room, with windows looking out on birch trees and bushes. There was barely room for the plates and glasses, so crowded was the table top with platters of cold meats, Russian salads, smoked fish, creamed herrings, caviar and every imaginable form of *zakuski*. Gorky, who presided over the gargantuan spread with unassuming simplicity, was seated at the bottom of the horseshoe, flanked immediately to his right by a stiff, pince-nezed Molotov. Ehrenburg was two seats further down, next to the red-bearded Nikolai Bukharin, who kept glaring contemptuously at Klimenti Voroshilov, Stalin's Minister of War. The latter, on the other side of the horseshoe, repeatedly emptied his vodka glass almost as soon as the waiter filled it. Gustav Regler and his artistic wife, Marie-Louise, were seated next to Bukharin, while André Malraux and Clara had been placed some distance further on, next to the 'classic', non-Communist writer, Leonid Leonov, who, like Yuri Olesha, had learned to drown his personal chagrin in alcohol.

After a number of toasts, the *Pravda* editor, Mikhail Koltsov, who was acting as master of ceremonies, asked for silence, since Oskar Maria Graf wanted to make a speech. Graf, who had endeared himself to many at the Writers Congress by his unconventional bohemianism, now stood up with a tumbler full of vodka in his hand. He had, he informed the assembled comrades, a serious proposal to make in the name of peace: that the annual November 7th festivities commemorating the glorious October Revolution should not include a military parade – here he looked pointedly at Voroshilov, by now too drunk to understand a word, even in translation – and should instead be given over to singing and dancing. Indeed, it would even be a good idea to advance the annual date to a warmer season of the year and to make the celebrations a fresh air spree, so that the 'wenches' and their boy friends could wander off and disport themselves in the bushes. Having made this droll suggestion, the uninhibited baker's son from Bavaria thanked Bukharin for having urged those attending the Writers Congress not to be afraid to portray life and human problems in all their inherent complexities. After that he raised his tumbler and said, 'Try to remain good socialists!'

The embarrassed interpreters seated behind the Party bigwigs – the glacial Molotov, the drunken Voroshilov, Moscow's rough-hewn mayor, Lazar Kaganovich – were understandably relieved to see the unconventional, *lederhosen*-clad Bavarian empty his glass and resume his seat. But then, looming out of the fog of cigarette smoke like a ghost, appeared Bukharin's friend, Karl Radek, who had been bitterly attacked and blamed for the German Communist Party's failure to carry out a successful revolution in 1923. The Nazis' triumph ten years later had done nothing to lessen his inner bitterness at being made the scapegoat for collective errors of appreciation. Radek, too, was almost certainly drunk but, unlike Voroshilov, he was still remarkably articulate. Pacing up and down, Radek launched into a Dostoevskian speech, full of ecstatic confession and self-flagellation, made all the more pathetic by the diabolical gleam in his eyes and the ugly fringe of beard dirtying his chin. His speech was a paen to the Party, a hymn of praise to the collective system, an exaltation of the 'voice of the people', which, properly guided, must always be listened to. His voice grew increasingly shrill as he worked himself up to a first rhetorical crescendo, declaring that the Revolution was no pleasure trip or safari and that 'executions must be evaluated, not made mysteries of' – a critical reference to past, present, and future purges, intended to 'purify' the Party. 'We are all still petty bourgeois!' was his challenging conclusion.

Then, turning towards the German writers present, the polyglot Radek launched into a bitter attack in fluent German on the 'comrades' of the Ruhr valley, of industrial Silesia, of Berlin, who had betrayed the Revolution by adapting themselves so readily to Hitler's National Socialism. After which, looking more grotesque than ever with his shirtfront hanging out over his belt, he stopped in front of André Malraux. Why, he wanted to know, had Malraux, during his meeting with young *Komsomol* members, asked them what they thought about death? 'Why does he adopt this unfruitful attitude in a century in which the individual has at last been given the chance to fulfill himself in community with others?' The rhetorical tirade then rose to a second climax with another ringing affirmation: 'Comrade Malraux, too, is still a petty bourgeois!'

But Radek was still not finished. Certain of Malraux's statements during his congress speech – 'Your classic writers give a richer, fuller picture of the inner life than is to be found in Soviet novels. . . . If one eliminates psychology, it simply means that those who have seen most deeply withhold their experience from others' – had remained stuck, like fishbones, in his throat. Such sentiments were unworthy of a revolutionary writer, and were proof again that Malraux was not what he claimed to be, but simply one more 'petty bourgeois'. After which, lapsing back into Russian, he completed his increasingly incoherent speech with mumblings of self-accusation, before disappearing like a spectre through the cigarette smoke.

It was probably at this moment, when the confusion was at its height, that Malraux rose to his feet to propose a toast in his turn. He had probably understood little of Radek's diatribe, but, having already incurred his displeasure during the pompous congress proceedings, he realized that he was again coming under fire. Raising his glass, while a series of nervous twitches creased his cheek muscles, Malraux announced: 'I drink to the health of an absent one, whose presence makes itself felt here at every instant, I drink to the health of Leon Davidovich Trotsky.'

This astonishing toast was greeted by an 'ashen' silence, as Clara later described it. But it is probable that few of those present grasped the meaning of the French words, even if they caught the final name; for Gustav Regler, a fervent Malraux admirer, would surely have recorded this dramatic moment if he had heard the toast.

So ended, in cacophonous and discordant confusion, a memorable banquet which, though neither Malraux nor Regler could have guessed it, was to be the last of its kind. If Stalin himself had not deigned to attend it was because the paranoiac dictator would have exposed himself to general ridicule by coming accompanied by his official food- and wine-taster. Within two years Maxim Gorky was dead, poisoned – so it was later 'confessed' by Stalin's secret-police chief Yagoda – and before four years were up, Bukharin, Zinoviev, and Radek had also been 'flushed out' in a series of new purges. And this time it was not simply a few 'rotten branches' that were being lopped off; it was the very tree trunk of the Party which was being savagely attacked with axes.

23

The Revolutionary Mirage

The four months André Malraux spent in Stalin's USSR were a serious disappointment in at least one respect. His original intention had been to visit Baku, in order to soak up local atmosphere for his 'Caucasian' novel on the conflict between the petroleum workers of Azerbaijan and their 'imperialist' exploiters during the turbulent months immediately following the October Revolution of 1917, when Baku, like the Turkish port of Batoum, had been occupied by British forces. Instead, Malraux accepted the Soviet authorities' proposal that he and his wife should spend a week or two in an official guest-house located at Novosibirsk, near the Altai mountains of Siberia. Was his desire to return to Baku quietly sabotaged by the powers-that-be in Moscow, less than pleased by his heretical pronouncements during the Writers Congress? Or had Malraux come to the conclusion that a slightly different version of *Les Conquérants*, in a new Caucasian setting, would look too much like a 'historical novel' with little relevance to present problems? Clara's memoirs unfortunately shed no light on this enigma, focusing instead on a number of rows she had with André during their trip to Siberia, which prompted her to pack her bags and return to France alone, a good week before he was ready to leave Moscow.

By the time Malraux reached Paris in early October, he had decided to scrap his petroleum workers novel and to choose a more topical, anti-nazi theme. We have Clara's word for it that it was Willi Bredel's speech at the Writers Congress which prompted Malraux to write a novel about life in a nazi prison: one which, inspired by Rimbaud's *Le Temps des Assassins*, he called *Le Temps du Mépris* (literally 'Times of Scorn', but later translated into English under the title, *Days of Wrath*).

Willi Bredel's novelistic account of the thirteen months he had spent in a concentration camp near Hamburg differed radically from Malraux's *Temps du Mépris* in at least two significant respects: it was a thinly disguised autobiographical fragment and a piece of didactic fiction designed to contrast the aggressive brutality of the nazi jailers – end-products of 'capitalistic-bourgeois decadence' – with the collective will to resist of men who, prior to their arrests, had been strangers or political adversaries. The main theme of Malraux's novel, on the other hand, is human solitude. It was the closest he ever came to writing a partly oneiric novel.

It was precisely at this moment that Malraux met another German-speaking author who had spent some weeks in a Berlin prison. A short, intensely serious and introspective man whose entire being exuded a sense of gritty determination, Manès Sperber was a Central European intellectual consumed and sometimes torn by three conflicting loyalties: to communism, to his Jewish heritage, and to individual (which is to say, non-Freudian) psychotherapy. From the largely Jewish town of Zablotow, in what was then Austrian-ruled Galicia, he had moved at the end of the Great War to Vienna, where, at the precocious age of sixteen, he had become a disciple of Alfred Adler and a practising psychoanalyst. In 1927 he had agreed to move to Berlin, in an effort to keep the Adlerian movement there from 'drifting to the right'. He had thus lived through the final years of the giddy 1920s, when Berlin was a culturally pulsating capital. This experience was particularly enriching, for his public lectures and his therapeutic sessions brought him into contact with anarchists, Mensheviks, and even secret agents of the GRU (Soviet Military Intelligence), who were subjected to terrible psychic stresses because of their feelings of loyalty to their former Red Army boss, Leon Trotsky. Several of Sperber's clients had tried to warn him of what was happening inside Stalin's USSR, but they had left his communist allegiance unshaken, so glowing was his revolutionary conviction that Berlin was going to be the scene of fantastic happenings, of 'very imminent decisions of world-historic scope'. Highly critical of Freudianism because it implicitly promised a truly 'free' and 'uninhibited' life, with a shifting of responsibility from one's own psychic woes to to one's parents and the circumstances of one's infancy, he had crossed swords with his fellow communist, Wilhelm Reich, the neo-Freudian prophet of 'sexual liberation' and 'orgasmic happiness': short-cut recipes for 'perfect happiness' which struck Sperber (a pessimistic realist) as being 'one of the most tenacious, deceptive, and fateful illusions mankind has ever had'. His own feeling about such matters was summed up in a single sentence, made to appeal to André Malraux since it aptly combined the collective and the individual: 'Each being infinitely resembles all; nobody is identical with another.'

The onset of the Depression in the early 1930s had merely reinforced Manès Sperber's radical inclinations. 'In this capitalistic world, each day shaken by the general economic crisis,' as he later wrote in his autobiography, 'we were millions, and in Germany tens of thousands of young intellectuals, who were persuaded that the world could not be freed once and for all of poverty, oppression, humiliation, and war save through a revolution.' This belief, combined with the conviction that Hitler's Nazism was the last-gasp symptom of a moribund capitalism, had acted as a kind of soporific, numbing the reactions of an astounding number of prominent German Communists, who, like their plodding leader, Ernst Thaelmann, had let themselves be rounded up during the night of the Reichstag fire.

Arrested by a squad of *Sturm-Abteilung* Brownshirts and herded with thirty other 'culprits' into a truck, Sperber had spent five grim days with fellow captives in a dark cellar before being locked up in a tiny police cell, where he was repeatedly interrogated. Finally, released as a 'special favour' on April 20th, the *Führer*'s birthday, because he was an Austrian citizen, he was allowed to proceed by train to Prague. Much the same thing had happened to the popular journalist, Egon Erwin Kisch, who had been arrested because of his communist affiliations, and who had later been released because of his Czech origin.

Kassner, the 'hero' of *Le Temps du Mépris*, may not have been of Czech origin – he is variously described as being from Munich, and of being the son of a Silesian coal miner – but he has somehow managed to develop a 'Pilsen accent' and he too ends up in Prague. A veteran Communist, Kassner is arrested by a squad of *SA* Brownshirts, is taken to a police station for interrogation, then flung into an almost lightless cell, where he is savagely punched and kicked by the prison guards before being dragged, unconscious, to another gloomy cell. These 'external' tribulations soon give way to inner torments and an internal monologue, in which Kassner tries to keep from going mad by regulating his stream of consciousness. It soon becomes apparent that what interests the author are the fears and obsessions, bordering on madness, which solitary confinement can induce. Malraux's short novel is in reality a fictional meditation on human solitude and on the autonomy of the human spirit, even when the body is enchained. It is also a meditation on human servitude, inflated at times to heights of lyricism which certainly owe more to Pascal and Rilke than to Willi Bredel.

Differing in its construction from Malraux's previous novels, essentially based on the Dostoevskian dialogue technique, *Le Temps du Mépris*, with its reliance on flashbacks, was clearly the first cousin of *Royaume-Farfelu*. It was also filled with autobiographical references. Kassner was basically an *alter ego*, the veteran revolutionary Malraux would have liked to be had he been born ten years earlier and been able to join the 'Reds' during the turbulent post-1917 period of Russia's civil war. Like Malraux, Kassner is married and has a child. Indeed, the sixth chapter of the novel, describing Kassner's implausible escape from Germany in a small monoplane, which runs into a violent storm during its flight to Czechoslovakia, was directly inspired by the terrifying hailstorm Malraux and Corniglion had encountered west of Tunis on their way back from Djibouti.

The brevity of this *nouvelle*, as Malraux himself termed it, and its narrowness of focus puzzled Paris critics. But the surprising thing about most of the reviews was, on the whole, their mildness of tone. As André Gide, who was frankly disappointed by Malraux's *nouvelle*, remarked to Mme Théo on June 18th, three weeks after its appearance, it was as though critics 'on the right are afraid of being accused of a *parti pris*, and those on the left of being accused of jealousy'. In the conservative *Le Temps*, André Thérive felt obliged to add a flattering epithet in describing 'a beautiful disorder of frenzy and pain', while the equally conservative Thierry Maulnier could find in this anti-nazi novel 'nothing that is properly Marxist'.

The sourest note of all was sounded some weeks later by the left-wing Catholic, Emmanuel Mounier, who had recently founded a monthly, *Esprit*, designed to propagate a new 'personalist' philosophy. After noting that Malraux was 'the only Marxist writer' in France who enjoyed favour with 'right-minded' bourgeois critics, he declared that *Le Temps du Mépris* belonged to the realm of

> minor art. The exasperated introspection remains exasperating, even if it involves a prisoner of the Nazis; the pity merely accentuates the embarrassment. And when it turns to hallucination, we find no joy in again coming upon Malraux at his worst, the mythomaniacal, lyrically enraged Malraux, with a wilful, concentrated grandiloquence . . . It is only when the hero emerges from these stylized depths and is amazed to rediscover the familiar habits of everyday life that the Malraux we like awakes once more. Let's say that he too had a bad dream.

In Moscow, the previous August, Jean-Richard Bloch, a self-styled believer in historical materialism, had replied to Karl Radek's 'petty bourgeois' charges by inviting him to attend a first 'Congress of Soviet Writers in the French Language', to be held in Paris after the coming Communist revolution there had triumphed. From the seed sown in this speech an ambitious new project soon sprouted: the idea of holding another International Writers Congress, this time in France. The idea was enthusiastically embraced by André Malraux, who became one of the Congress' chief organizers, along with Louis Aragon, acting on behalf of the Komintern.

This International Writers Congress – more cosmopolitan than the first, since it included several prominent English authors (E. M. Forster, Aldous Huxley), Robert Musil, Kafka's friend Max Brod, and the former Italian foreign minister, Count Carlo Sforza – finally opened at the Left Bank's Salle de la Mutualité, on June 21st. It was a distinct improvement on its predecessor in several significant respects. Limited to five days, it was shorter and less tedious. It was not convened to endorse a single *mot d'ordre* or slogan, but to discuss a number of topics, such as 'the individual and individualism', 'humanism', 'the nation and culture', 'the dignity of thought', the nature of 'artistic creation', and how culture could best be defended. Not least, it was addressed by men who were genuine writers or poets (rather than ideological watchdogs like Karl Radek), several of whom were not particularly sympathetic towards communism. The credit for all these improvements must go to Malraux – without whom, as Janine Bouissounouse later wrote, 'nothing would have been done', and who wound up the congress on its final day with a speech which raised him 'literally to an apogee'.

The five-day congress generated two moments of genuine drama. When his turn came to address the audience, Gustav Regler launched into an impassioned speech, directed above all against the ineptitude of communist propaganda, which had contributed so much to the victory of nazism in Germany.

'We were combatting the false "Theodocy" of Hegel,' he began dramatically,

while they were mass producing busts of the new God, Hitler . . . We insisted too much on the need to deal with purely proletarian themes . . . Millions of petty bourgeois had left their bowers, their sofas, and their shops. They had become politically minded, they carried the victorious fetish [he meant of course the swastika] into the working districts where our literature was not well enough distributed . . . By replacing positive criticism by mechanical discipline, one creates bad writers, bad literature and, besides, a mentality which neither suits the working masses, whose humour and natural intelligence we are supposed to have, nor that agility of the mind, without which one cannot live.

Regler then cited three examples of what the Nazis considered to be 'culture'. After which, he held up two leaflets, from a batch of 3,000 which had recently been smuggled into Germany, each containing quotations from forty anti-fascist exiles.

They are being circulated at this very moment! [cried Regler]. And none of the spies seated among us has been able to prevent it. I now address myself to that spook of the German Gestapo in Paris who follows us around as the shadow follows the sun. And this I say to him: 'You can block the borders, but our literature will still get through. You could kill Mühsam [the bohemian Berlin poet who had been strung up by the Nazis from a hook in a concentration camp latrine]! You hold Ossietzky and Renn! But you will not stifle our voices, you will never stifle our love for the working people, nor the doleful flame of our passion for the truth!

Suddenly, as though the speaker had raised an orchestral baton, every person in the hall stood up and spontaneously began to sing *L'Internationale*. In the wings a dim figure beckoned imperiously to Regler. It was the Expressionist poet, Johannes Becher, now a rabid Communist, who had come from Moscow with other members of the Russian delegation.

'You must be mad!' hissed Becher.

'Mad?' exclaimed Regler breathlessly. 'Can't you hear what they're singing?'

'That's just it!' cried Becher, to make himself heard above the chanting voices in the hall. 'The *Internationale*! You've ruined everything. You've given us away. This Congress can't pretend to be neutral any more. *Lieber Gott*! You'll be turned out of the Party.'

The second dramatic moment came on the fourth day of the congress, when the Italian historian, Gaetano Salvemini, delivered a trenchant speech, in which he denounced all forms of dictatorship, whether fascist or proletarian. He cited the case of Victor Serge, a French-language novelist, brought up in Brussels by his exiled Russian parents, an ardent Communist who had gone to the USSR after the Bolshevik Revolution, had befriended Trotsky and many other prominent Soviet leaders, and who had finally been banished to Siberia without even the semblance of a trial as a suspect 'counter-revolutionary'. The uproar aroused in the Mutualité hall by the mention of Victor Serge's name – with a number of Trotskyists, led by Magdeleine Paz, the Belgian novelist Charles Plisnier, and Henry Poulaille, the proletarian author of *Les Damnés de la Terre* – was such that Gide insisted the question be discussed the next day, since it involved the basic issue of freedom of expression.

This unscheduled 'hearing' took place the following afternoon at an even more tumultuous session, over which André Malraux presided. From the rostrum Magdeleine Paz read a lengthy report on Victor Serge's arbitrary confinement in Siberia, over the vehement protests of Ilya Ehrenburg, *Pravda*'s Mikhail Koltsov, the popular playwright Vladimir Kirshon, the poet and faithful Party-liner, Nikolai Tikhonov, who had the gall to pretend that he had never heard of Victor Serge, even though he had translated some of Tikhonov's rousing ballads into French. When Mme Théo reached the scene, some time after 4 pm, the tumult was at its height, with the Stalinists in the hall whistling, booing, and heckling in an effort to keep Magdeleine Paz from completing her report. 'With a trenchant energy,' as she noted in her journal, 'Malraux, who was presiding, imposed silence and restraint.' The tumult rose to new heights when another French Trotskyist, Edouard Peisson, again castigated the Soviet regime for its mistreatment of Victor Serge. 'People whistled and shouted,' (to quote Mme Théo once again) 'and somebody who had lost all self control had to be forcibly ejected . . .'

The incident, a typical example of Stalinist intolerance (secretly encouraged by Louis Aragon), illustrated what was to become a 'friendly disagreement' between the two Andrés (Gide and Malraux) in their respective attitudes towards the USSR. Whereas Malraux was annoyed by this troublesome 'diversion', Gide responded to Magdeleine Paz's appeal by calling on the Soviet ambassador and handing him a letter in which he deplored the flimsiness of the 'evidence' the Soviet delegation had produced in an effort to denigrate Victor Serge's credentials as a writer.

Malraux's concluding speech, delivered on the last evening of the congress, was deliberately unpolemical, in marked contrast to those that had immediately preceded it. Never, so it seemed to Mme Théo, had the Mutualité's main hall been so jam-packed. Louis Aragon delivered a

blazing, acid, authoritarian speech, demanding realism with a madman's frenzy . . . Gide, who had stepped down into the hall, to be able to hear him better, was leaning against the wall next to Thierry Maulnier. I could see him shaking his head, with an exasperated air . . .

Was it Guéhenno who followed him? Perhaps. Frankly deplorable. He paced back and forth, speaking in bursts, as though seized by fits, comically brandishing a clenched fist and pausing pointedly . . . for the expected applause . . . Then came Malraux's turn; a polished speech, with beautiful images developed with strong, decisive eloquence, but which seemed a bit superfluous.

Mme Théo was not the only one to be mystified by Malraux's speech. It was essentially a continuation of the meditations on art and museums he had begun in *La Voie royale*, and which were to blossom forth later in *Les Voix du Silence*. 'Every work of art is created to satisfy a need, but a need passionate enough to bring it forth. Then the need withdraws from the work, like blood from a body, and the work begins its mysterious transfiguration. It enters the realm of shades. Only our need, our passion can bring it back.'

For Gustav Regler this was sheer music, 'the level on which we wanted to fight for a new art. But it was difficult to maintain so high a level. The Soviet writers present did not understand one word, though they excelled at boasting of their five-year plans.'

No less fascinated by Malraux's rich but often elusive mode of speech was the playwright, Henri-René Lenormand. Malraux's eloquence, he later wrote, was particularly extraordinary in that it was

the integral and direct expression of the sublest kind of thinking I have ever known. The rapidity of his associations and of his delivery, his indifference as to whether or not he was being understood, his scorn of all concessions, of any adjustments to mediocrity, to the foreseeable sloth of his listeners, made each of his interventions seem like a magical operation. With his long body erect behind the table of the *praesidium*, his head slightly bent toward the microphone, he spoke in a low, hurried voice. A nervous tick occasionally creased his face with a lateral twitch, a fleeting jerk of negation. The crowd received the message in deep silence, then erupted into ardent applause. An act of love saluted these obscure, glacial incantations. After him, the loftiest intellects of the century, a Gide, a Huxley, seemed like professors embarrassed by their trains of thought and the difficulties of diction.

This International Writers Congress, though well covered in *L'Humanité*, received relatively little attention in other Paris newspapers. One reason for this lack of interest was the fiery controversy raging at this moment over the repeated demands of France's left-wing parties that the para-military fascist 'Leagues' be officially disbanded, and the Laval government's reluctance to take this measure.

Equally equivocal, however, were the auspices under which this Writers Congress was held. Six months before, the assassination of Serghei Kirov, the popular Communist Party boss in Leningrad and next to Stalin the most powerful figure in the Soviet leadership, had been followed by mass arrests of suspects, scores of summary executions, and the incarceration of two of the country's veteran Bolsheviks – Grigori Zinoviev, who had once headed the Komintern, and Lev Kamenev, a former *Pravda* editor. Both were accused, incredibly enough, of complicity in this assassination. The rapidity and ruthlessness of Stalin's response to this new 'plot' was disturbingly reminiscent of the switfness with which Hitler's Nazis had acted in the immediate wake of the Reichstag fire. 'The misfortune of this Congress,' as Henri-René Lenormand later summed it up,

> was to defend humanism and culture by relying on Bolshevism. The preparatory committee reports, the public greetings, the speeches were transformed into veiled or direct expressions of homage to the Russian revolution, looked upon as the safeguard and refuge of civilization. More than one hundred writers from all sorts of countries . . . had either come or given their adherence. The result was that in the eyes of the world the most famous poets and novelists of the time became the defenders of Communism . . . The men who expended so much talent and eloquence to assert the rights of liberating thought must, I am sure, have felt some embarrassment when they realized that the Congress was a trap constructed by revolutionary propaganda to snare the world's intelligentsia . . . For, if to the Congress participants at the Palais de la Mutualité, Hitler appeared as the Enemy Number 1 of freedom of thought, Stalin was explicitly designated as the defender of the independence of the mind.

This International Writers Congress was soon followed by another far more massive demonstration of left-wing 'solidarity'. On Bastille Day Léon Blum's Socialists, Maurice Thorez's Communists, and many of Edouard Daladier's Radical Socialists joined forces in a huge parade. André Malraux and Clara were once again part of the human tide which surged through the traditionally radical Faubourg Saint-Antoine, brandishing fists and banners and singing the revolutionary *Carmagnole*.

If political and social problems could be solved by popular demonstrations of this kind, the country's immediate woes could have been fairly quickly overcome. Unfortunately this has seldom been the case. France at this moment was governed by a clever Auvergnat politician named Pierre Laval who, like most of his parliamentary colleagues, understood little about economics and was willing to promote the maintenance of an overvalued franc and the pursuit of a deflationary policy at home. The result was a climate of permanent unrest – for if there is one thing that workers and employees resent, it is to see their salaries reduced because the cost of living has gone down.

A canny lawyer who cultivated sartorial sloppiness, Laval was a hard-headed pragmatist who had no use for ideology or pacifistic sentimentality. Alarmed by the increasing belligerence of Nazi Germany, he had chosen to pursue a policy of diplomatic and military rapprochement with the Soviet Union, which the Radical Socialist Minister for Air, Pierre Cot, and the president of the Chamber of Deputies, Edouard Herriot, had inaugurated in 1933. In May 1935, a few weeks before Malraux's International Writers Congress, Laval had gone to Moscow as foreign minister to negotiate a Franco-Soviet pact, which had as yet to be ratified by the French parliament. As a cynical *Realpolitiker*, he had refused to adopt an openly anti-fascist attitude towards Mussolini. He was grateful to the *Duce* for having massed four Italian divisions along the Brenner Pass and for having ostentatiously travelled to Vienna in July 1934 in order to keep Hitler from absorbing Austria through a pan-Germanic *Anschluss* after his Nazi Brownshirts had murdered Chancellor Dollfuss.

Maintaining cordial relations with Soviet Russia and Fascist Italy was bound to involve a lot of tricky tightrope walking, particularly in a country increasingly split by vehemently anti-Bolshevik nationalists, on the right, and friends of the USSR, on the left. But Laval, who had an unlimited confidence in his own cleverness, was persuaded that he was dexterous enough to be able to maintain this extraordinary balancing act. Unfortunately, he had not reckoned on the sanctimonious obtuseness of the British, who quietly torpedoed the resolutions of the tripartite (Anglo-Franco-Italian) Stresa conference (April 1935) by authorizing Hitler's Reich to increase its naval tonnage to one third of Great Britain's. There were sharp protests from Paris and Rome, which were received in London with supercilious hauteur. This hasty concession to Hitler's demands for 'equality of armaments' encouraged Hitler to carry his defiance of the continent's 'collective security' one step further by dramatically increasing the size of Germany's ground and air forces. Since Hitler – that 'sexual degenerate', that 'dangerous fool', that 'abominable murderer', as Mussolini had called him after the Night of the Long Knives (June 30th) and Dollfuss' assassination (July 25, 1934) – was being allowed to get away with it, the *Duce* too could thumb his nose at the League of Nations and mock the myth of 'collective security' by expanding the 'Italian Empire' to include a dismally backward and 'barbarous' Abyssinia.

On October 3rd, the day after Italian troops massed in Eritrea began invading neighbouring Ethiopia, the French historian Louis Madelin, writing in the ultra-nationalist *Echo de Paris*, expressed his surprise that the British, who had been so passive over the question of German rearmament, should now be working themselves into a righteous rage over the far less dangerous problem of Ethiopia. 'What are one hundred thousand Italians threatening Ethiopia, next to ten million German soldiers who are being drilled between the Rhine and the Niemen, and to what end? To defend themselves? Who is threatening them?'

In a far more emotional editorial, published in the same newspaper, Henri de Kerillis, a fearless Great War airman, wrung his hands in anguish at the prospect of the 'universal catastrophe' that was about to unfold. If the sanctions against the Italian aggressor now being talked about in Geneva were to have any practical effect, they would have to be imposed by force, leading, he feared, to a war between Italy and Great Britain. And if the French refused to support the British against the Italian aggressors, the British would have a ready-made excuse for not lifting a finger to help the French in case of future trouble with Germany.

That there was a lot of rhetorical exaggeration in this doomsday scenario cannot be denied. But Kerillis' fear that France's lukewarm support of sanctions against Italy might persuade the British to let the French fend for themselves the next time Hitler made an aggressive move was dramatically confirmed when, six months later, *Wehrmacht* troops reoccupied the Rhineland – in flagrant violation of the Locarno Pact and the Treaty of Versailles.

Paradoxically, the death-blow to Pierre Laval's tortuous diplomacy was delivered by the very conservatives who were most sympathetic to his brand of amoral *Realpolitik*. On October 4th the conservative newspaper *Le Temps* published a 'Manifesto of French Intellectuals for the Defence of the West' which was a monument of reactionary sophistry. The title alone was enough to suggest that its author was the arch-Catholic Henri Massis. Signed by forty-four writers and literary critics – including the vitriolic monarchist Charles Maurras, the waspish deputy Léon Daudet, the novelists Henry Bordeaux and Pierre Drieu la Rochelle – the manifesto condemned the imposition of sanctions on Italy on the grounds that it was ridiculous to punish the Italian people 'on the pretext of protecting in Africa the independence of uncultivated tribes'. It was deplorable that 'great countries' like France and Great Britain, whose ... 'colonizing work remains one of the loftiest, one of the most fecund expressions of their vitality', should now be trying to keep Rome from doing what they themselves had so gloriously achieved in the past.

This grotesque apologia of a flagrant military aggression, practised by a country that was accomplishing its lofty 'civilizing' mission by dropping bombs on Ethiopian towns and settlements, merely sharpened the disagreements inside of France, which Pierre Laval had been trying to paper over. Inevitably it provoked a forceful reaction from other French intellectuals. On October 5th several Paris newspapers published the text of a 'reply', hastily prepared by Louis Aragon, the novelist Jules Romains, the left-wing journalist Luc Durtain, and the book-selling patroness of Left Bank authors, Adrienne Monnier. Within the space of a few hours, thanks to feverish telephone calls, the text was approved by no fewer than 203 signatories, headed by André Gide, Romain Rolland, Paul Langevin, Paul Rivet, the philosophers Alain and Lévy-Bruhl, Emmanuel Mounier, the Swiss writer, Denis de Rougemont, Jean Prévost, and, it is hardly necessary to add, André

Malraux. This 'reply' challenged Henri Massis' 'notion of the West' and his colleagues' absurd claim to be speaking in the name of French intellectuals.

Malraux's contribution to the debate, which had already split France's Catholics into two opposing camps, took the form of a speech, delivered on November 4th at the first 'Assizes of the International Association for the Defence of Culture'. A few passages are worth quoting, even if his assertions on the subject of European colonialism have not all stood the test of time.

Directly challenging the 'reactionary intellectuals' who had heeded Henri Massis' call, Malraux attacked the facile notion that a 'Latin Order' (daily propounded by Charles Maurras' *Action Française*) was the foundation stone of Europe:

This Latin Order to which you tirelessly entrust the destiny of Europe is one it has given up. Who and what does the West mean – in Shanghai, Singapore, Manila? On the one hand, England, the United States – Protestants. On the other hand, the Soviets. And the entire thrust of your ideology is nothing but a promise that a triumphant Italy will perhaps become what the England you attack has been for one hundred and fifty years.

The Western culture whose prestige you are bent on maintaining in the world is unknown to the world. The West, for the world, is everything you are not. And for the others, you know that France is not Racine, it's Molière; not Joseph de Maistre, it's Stendhal; not Napoleon III's fascist poets, it's Victor Hugo; it's not one of your eleven academician signatories, it's André Gide and Romain Rolland.

The conquests of Western technology are evident. But if technical superiority implies a right of conquest, the United States would begin by colonizing Europe . . .

What are the countries which today are being the most rapidly Europeanized? Precisely those you do not control. Muslim women in Morocco, Tunisia, Tripolitania, India, are veiled. Persian women have virtually ceased to be so, and Turkish women not at all. What is the only country where the mandarinate still exists? Not China, not Japan, but Annam. What a free Siam has been trying to abolish is being preserved in Cambodia and Burma . . .

These economic sanctions which France has agreed to apply, is it in the name of the ancient Rome which made Western civilization that you combat them? What Rome bequeathed to Western civilization was not its disintegrating empire, it was not the interminable series of local wars which made a desert of the West, it was the Roman law which put an end to them. Not war, but the regulation of war. The voice which in this debate drowns out yours is precisely that of ancient Rome. You know how Roman law used to be defined: fidelity to pacts . . .

No civilization, whether white, black, or yellow, began with the warrior; it began when the lawmaker or the priest undertook to civilize the warrior.

It began when discussion took precedence over deeds. Every civilization implies the awareness of and respect for *others* . . . The creative virtues of the West are born of the death of what you, reactionary intellectuals, defend. From the weakening of the notion of hierarchy; the end of ancient society, so much less 'Western' than our own, so much closer to Asia. Your insistence on hierarchy is not the West, it is not Rome; it is India . . .

It is impossible to read some of these sentences today without a smile. Liberia, the one country in Central Africa that was never colonized, is not exactly a model of either progress or of 'civilization'. The women of Iran today are veiled, as are those of a 'liberated' Afghanistan, although neither country was ever truly colonized, either by the West or by Soviet Russia.

But these are trifling quibbles. All in all, it was a splendid speech, and what Malraux had to say against his old enemy, Massis, and his ilk badly needed saying. The only trouble was that it was just one more 'anti-fascist speech'. For what the international situation demanded at this moment was not words but deeds. The sanctions against Mussolini's Italy, which the British had been so vociferous in demanding, were never seriously applied; above all not by Stanley Baldwin's Conservative government which, fearful of antagonizing its pacifistic electorate, casually 'neglected' to close the Suez Canal to Italian ships bound for Eritrea.

In late January 1936 the embittered *Realpolitiker*, Pierre Laval, was forced to resign. He was thus spared the test of having to react forcefully when, six weeks later, Hitler decided to 'remilitarize' the Rhineland. Laval's successor, the Radical Socialist, Albert Sarraut, wrung his hands, like Pontius Pilate, delivered a long radio speech in which he defiantly declared, 'We are not prepared to allow Strasbourg to be placed under the fire of German guns!,' and then allowed Hitler to get away with his military gamble without a shot being fired. All in the name of peace, if not of 'collective security'.

But the prize for dialectical futility on this occasion was carried off by Léon Blum who, in a front-page editorial published in *Le Populaire* on April 7th (one month after Hitler's *fait accompli*), congratulated his countrymen on their sagacious passivity.

The literal text of the Locarno Pact leaves no room for doubt. The military occupation of the Rhineland zone is formally likened to an unprovoked aggression and an invasion of the national territory. The French government would thus have a strict right to consider the crossing of the Rhine by the *Reichswehr* as a flagrant blow, as an act of war, and, I repeat it, as an invasion. It did not do so. I do not believe that it would have thought for one instant of doing so [in which, as it happened, Blum was mistaken]. Instead of handing the German ambassador his papers, of mobilizing, of demanding that the guaranteeing powers should immediately carry out their incontestable military obligations, it took the matter to the League of Nations. Between a direct settlement through arms and a procedure of peaceful settlement through international action and mediation, neither the French government nor French opinion hesitated. Let there be no mistake about it, this is a sign of the times.

It was indeed. A sign that from now on words could replace decisive action as a means of dealing with international threats. Several months later Léon Blum's fellow Socialist, Paul-Henri Spaak, drew the logical conclusion. Since France was a weak reed and could no longer be relied upon to defend its vital interests and to uphold the Locarno Pact, which Belgium too had signed, it was high time for Brussels to cut its military links with Paris and to adopt a policy of strict 'neutrality'. Passivity had become contagious, spinelessness the fashion in diplomacy. Confronted by a bellicose Third Reich, 'collective security' (the latest opiate of the masses) had given birth to a new monster: the myth of 'individual neutrality'.

As Raymond Aron later wrote in his *Memoirs*, explaining his own refusal to join the others, when the time came to act concretely all that Rivet, Alain, Langevin, and Jean Guéhenno, of the Comité de Vigilance des intellectuels antifascistes, could do was, like Polonius, to spout 'words, words, words'. They too had succumbed to the revolutionary mirage of decadent societies: the belief that, being 'indivisible' (as the overly clever Maxim Litvinov had put it), peace could comfortably be assured by rhetorical reprobation and collective passivity.

24

From Moscow to Madrid

In March 1936, shortly after Hitler's military occupation of the Rhineland, André Malraux decided to accompany his half-brother Roland to Moscow. After mastering English and German, Roland had been encouraged to learn Russian, so as to be able to replace Gide's friend, Pierre Herbart, as editor of the French edition of the Moscow monthly, *Mezhdunarodnaya Literatura* ('International Literature'). André could help Roland by introducing him to journalists like Mikhail Koltsov of *Pravda*, and writers like Isaak Babel. Besides, he very much wanted to see the *Mezhrabpom*-Film people and Serghei Eisenstein, to find out why no progress had been made on the filmed version of *La Condition humaine*.

From Warsaw, where the international express stopped for several hours, he sent a 'hideous' postcard (showing two Polish hooligans dancing a polka) to Josette Clotis. For several years now they had been meeting secretly in various Paris hotels, but these intermittent trysts had merely exacerbated her simmering frustrations at being treated like a 'backstreet' mistress, while André continued his outwardly 'normal' married life with Clara. 'I am travelling with Kysou, who is in the other bunk,' Malraux wrote in a playful mood, 'and when I daydream, I fancy it is you who are up there. The austere reality sets things straight, despite the Polish stations, where military bands strike up as the officers climb down on to the platform, causing the cabmen's horses to raise their ears in time to the music.'

We know next to nothing about the writers and journalists Malraux called on during this second trip to the USSR – beyond the fact that he saw Eisenstein again (without being able to advance the filming of *La Condition humaine*). Isaak Babel, however, agreed to accompany him to the Crimea to visit Maxim Gorky. The main purpose of this pilgrimage was to discuss the feasibility of holding another International Writers Conference, this time in London. Stalin and his chief ideological watchdog, Andrei Zhdanov, had already embarked on the rewriting of both Russian and Soviet history; 'patriotic' films extolling heroic figures of the Russian past were beginning to be produced; and it was almost certainly with encouragement 'from above' that Gorky proposed that the writers who had formed an International

Association for the Defence of Culture should undertake to bring out a new 'encyclopaedia' – doubtless intended (in the eyes of the Soviet leadership) to combat Goebbels' Nazi propaganda and to emphasize the progressive, peace-loving policies of the USSR.

On his return to Paris in late March, Malraux found his countrymen in the grip of an intense pre-electoral fever. The German occupation of the Rhineland had been completely forgotten. A 'Popular Front' of left-wing parties had become a political reality – with Communists, Socialists, and Edouard Daladier's Radical Socialist supporters agreeing to unite their forces during the second round of the parliamentary elections. The result was a political earthquake. Léon Blum's Socialist Party forged ahead of the hitherto dominant Radical Socialists – with 149 seats to the Radicals' 109 in the Chamber, while the number of Communist Party representatives soared from a mere 11 to 72 deputies.

The 'political explosion' was immediately followed by a 'social explosion'. The frustrations and resentments generated by years of deflationary wage cuts now erupted into a contagious movement of anti-managerial defiance, as workers everywhere staged sit-down strikes and occupied their plants and workshops. All over the country red flags blossomed from the flagstaffs of provincial town halls. Hotels and restaurants, and even the Opéra-Comique in Paris, were temporarily 'seized' by radical committees, and in the Marseilles dockyards a few ships were boarded by seamen and stevedore 'soviets' in histrionic imitations of a Petrograd October.

André Gide was so astounded by the pacific rather than acrimonious nature of what had turned into a huge, nationwide *kermesse* (splurge) that he wrote to his friend, Roger Martin du Gard: 'No jubilation, no shouts; a surprising "decorum". People accost you in the streets, you can talk to anybody; the passers-by stop, take part in the discussion; a thick throng forms under the amused eyes of the policemen.'

The capitalistic world might be tottering to its collapse, as the left-wing Socialist, Marceau Pivert, proclaimed in a May 27th article in *Le Populaire*, entitled, 'All is Possible'. Trotsky, now writing from distant Norway for his disciples' *Lutte Ouvrière*, could urge the French to form armed committees composed of 'unemployed workers, peasants, and soldiers' in order to seize power, as he and his fellow Bolsheviks had done in 1917; but few Frenchmen were prepared to listen to this violent advice. 'People danced in the occupied factories . . . everyone forgot that the Fascists beyond our borders were victorious,' as Clara later put it. Indeed, so infectious was the atmosphere that she and her friend Madeleine Lagrange one day light-headedly let the menfolk continue their earnest discussions in the Quai Malaquais apartment. Descending to the river barges moored to the Left Bank, they joined the idle boatmen – they too were on strike – for some crazy waltzing on the wooden decks.

In mid-May Malraux persuaded his colleagues to send him to Madrid, along with the Hispanophile Jean Cassou, an ardent admirer of Unamuno and a personal friend of President Manuel Azaña, and the dramatist, Henri-René Lenormand. Their mission, as representatives of the International Association of Writers for the Defence of Culture, was to convey the warm feelings of friendship expressed by members of the Front Populaire in France for the writers and politicians of the Frente Popular, which had been swept into power by the electoral triumph of left-wing parties in the Spanish elections of February 1936.

Malraux, however, had other, more personal reasons for wishing to make this trip. He wanted to have a good look at the Prado Museum's magnificent collection of Velazquez paintings for an essay on aesthetics he was trying to write in rare moments of spare time. He also wanted to offer an increasingly fretful Josette Clotis another outing, comparable to the clandestine trip they had made to Bruges the previous August.

Although generously inspired, this new touristic 'treat' for Josette was an act of sentimental rashness he would have done better to forgo. The moment they reached Madrid, Malraux was caught up in a whirl of official receptions and meetings with Spanish writers, which kept him occupied for a good part of each day and sometimes far into the night. While Josette was left to languish in her hotel room, Malraux and his two companions were besieged by reporters and dragged off to meetings with the left-wing Catholic writer, José Bergamín, the Communist poet, Rafael Alberti, and others.

On May 22nd Malraux, Cassou, and Lenormand were driven out to the royal estate of El Pardo, beyond the northern outskirts of Madrid, to be received by Manuel Azaña, who had been an *homme de lettres* before becoming involved in politics. Indeed, for most of their afternoon conversation the president of the Spanish Republic refused to discuss the worrying political situation – so tense that left-wing revolutionaries were already engaged in almost daily gun battles with right-wing monarchists and 'nationalists' – preferring to talk instead of literary matters.

The three French delegates were then driven to the Ateneo Club in Madrid, where Malraux delivered a fighting speech attacking ivory tower intellectuals: 'We know that our differences with the Fascists will one day have to be resolved with machine guns.'

So hard pressed was Malraux that he barely had time to visit the Prado with Josette. Her presence in Madrid was duly noted by the left-wing French journalist, Georges Soria, who lost no time bringing the news back to Paris. Of the rash promises André had made to Josette – he would take her to Seville, he would show her the fountained gardens of the Alhambra – not one could be kept. He did, however, find time to take her to nearby Toledo, where she was strangely unmoved by the stark beauty of the ochre battlements, the sweeping view over the Tagus, with its delicately arched Moorish bridge, the scent of jasmine and ripe apricots perfuming the pure air of Castille. As they ambled up and down the narrow streets, visiting chapels and small museums, he talked to her in lyrical terms of the *Cid*, of

El Greco, and was annoyed to find that she was hardly listening. She was in a sulky mood and made no attempt to hide it.

There was little let-up in the tempo when Malraux returned to Paris. To the dismay of Josette – now installed with a journalist friend (Suzanne Chantal) in a suburban apartment, where André tried to join her at night – Malraux had to prepare another trip, this time to London, where the 'secretaries' of the International Writers Committee for the Defence of Culture were meeting to discuss Gorky's project for a new, 'progressively inspired', Twentieth Century Encyclopaedia.

From London, in mid-June, Malraux sent Josette another playful note: 'Whitechapel salutes you, with all the shadows of Charlot [i.e. Charlie Chaplin] in the doorways, real bobbies in the streets, and thirty or forty cats in the light of greenish gas-lamps. *Bonjour.*' What he did not bother to add was that, after crossing the English Channel, the International Encyclopaedia scheme had totally collapsed. During a 'plenary meeting' attended by Ilya Ehrenburg, Julien Benda, John Strachey, John Lehmann, José Bergamín, Gustav Regler, Ernst Toller, Bertolt Brecht, Manès Sperber and others, the redoubtable H. G. Wells had walked in, deposited his hat on a side table, and then proceeded (in Ilya Ehrenburg's words) 'to pour a bucket of cold water over our heads. He explained with lucidity that we were neither Diderots nor Voltaires, that we had no money, and that, in general, we were entertaining illusions. He told us the story of the three tailors who had the preposterous idea of speaking up in the name of the British Empire. Having spoken, he picked up his hat and walked out.'

This four-day trip was not a total waste of time, at any rate for Malraux. To an enlarged forum, mostly composed of British intellectuals and exiled writers who had taken refuge in London, he delivered a speech devoted to the question of 'cultural heritage'. This speech was full of seminal ideas, which were to be more fully developed later – in speeches, essays, and books devoted to problems of artistic creativity.

Yielding at last to the entreaties of his friends, André Gide left Paris on June 16th, bound for Moscow. He was accompanied by the once ardently communist journalist, Pierre Herbart, who had gratefully turned over the frustrating job of editing *Littérature Internationale* to Roland Malraux.

Three days after Gide's departure, the news reached Paris that Maxim Gorky had died. An entire page of the June 21st edition of *L'Humanité* was filled with tributes from a score of prominent French authors, journalists, and artists paying homage to a man whom Jean Cassou described as having been a human as well as proletarian prodigy, a *'force de la nature'.* If Malraux's name did not figure alongside those of Romain Rolland, Julien Benda, André Chamson, and Paul Nizan, it was simply because he was away in London. But after his return to Paris, Malraux agreed to speak at a commemorative meeting, held at the Mutualité hall on June 29th.

Although *L'Humanité* described it as 'gripping and profound', this does not seem to have been one of Malraux's best oratorical performances. His friend, Janine Bouissounouse, who was seated up front in the second row of the auditorium, was struck by his sickly look. 'He was pale, nervous, full of ticks, and gave one the impression of speaking while thinking of other things, of not always being the master of his phrases.' After the meeting she approached him, and they agreed to meet the following day at the NRF–Gallimard building on the Rue Sébastien-Bottin.

The news that her friend André had been seen walking arm-in-arm with Josette Clotis on the Gran Vía in Madrid had left her thunderstruck and unbelieving. But she had been assured by a woman reporter working for *Cinémonde* (another Gallimard publication) that this affair had been going on for quite a while. The reporter had even tried to persuade Josette Clotis to give up her liaison, pointing out that there was no future in it. To which Josette had replied: 'I prefer a liaison with a fellow like him to a marriage with a tax collector.'

In the sun-filled garden of the NRF building, Janine Bouissounouse was unusually aggressive in bringing up the subject. She wanted to know why André, with whom she had long been on such frank and friendly terms, should have kept this secret from her. Why had she had to learn the news in an editorial office rather than from him directly? She was answered by a singularly evasive Malraux, quite different from the one she had previously known.

'Let people talk. What difference does it make to me?' And, a moment later; 'Stories about women, I suppose. I've already been attributed fifteen mistresses. Why not one more?'

'I don't have to count your mistresses. You're not, after all, going to deny Josette.'

'I'm denying nothing.' he insisted, adding a little later, 'people never know what you commit yourself to when you go to bed. You can't know what's involved. Content yourself with what people say.'

What Malraux did not wish to say was that his relations with his wife had been steadily deteriorating, and that with Josette Clotis he had found a restful solace which Clara was no longer capable of providing.

Five days later Janine Bouissounouse returned to the NRF building with a book she wanted to give Malraux. In the authors' waiting room she ran into Groethuysen's companion, Alix Guillain, who asked her how well she knew 'that woman who takes up so much of his time'.

'Not much,' answered Janine Bouissounouse, 'and I have no desire to know her better.'

'What does she do?'

'She writes.'

'She has talent?'

'Reasonably so.'

'What's she like?'

'Very beautiful, very affected, very elegant,' came the crisp reply.

'Ah,' said Alix Guillain, 'Groet keeps saying, "With André we must watch out for the elegant woman, she'll flatter his vanity." He would like to divorce. Groet thinks this divorce won't take place, even though the tension between André and Clara keeps growing, because he remains too grateful to Clara for what she did for him during his [Saigon] trial.'

A few minutes later, as they started down the stairs, they passed Josette Clotis, seated on the top step. 'A High Mass style,' as Janine Bouissounouse noted in her diary, 'a chestnut-brown two-piece suit of a remarkable respectability, and a hat as broad-brimmed as a parasol.'

'That's her?' asked Alix Guillain, as they reached the ground floor.

'Yes.'

'Won't be easy to call her "Comrade", will it?'

25

The Lyrical Illusion

On the evening of Saturday, 18th July, André and Clara were seated in a theatre box watching a play with their friends, Madeleine and Léo Lagrange (recently appointed Under-Secretary for Sports and Leisure in the Front Populaire government) when a messenger opened the velvet-padded door and whispered to Lagrange that M. Pierre Cot, the Minister for Air, who was seated in a nearby box, wanted to see him. Several minutes later Lagrange returned to say that a military insurrection had broken out in Spanish Morocco, led by army officers who had proclaimed their intention of overthrowing the Republican government in Madrid.

During the next few days Malraux had several talks with Pierre Cot, whom he had already met at several anti-fascist meetings. A former law professor, enthusiastic supporter of the League of Nations, and an idealistic believer in 'collective security', Cot was one of the 'Young Turks' of the Radical Socialist Party's left wing, and as such a fervent supporter of Léon Blum's Front Populaire. His heroism in action during the Great War of 1914–18 had won him the steadfast support of former Captain Edouard Daladier, who as an almost permanent Defence Minister had had him named Minister for Air in three successive Radical Socialist governments. Pierre Cot had never been a wartime airman, but he had overcome this handicap by obtaining a civilian pilot's licence. In September 1933 he had headed a French delegation, sent to Moscow to study the possibilities of technical co-operation with the USSR: the first step in a rapprochement between the two countries, which had led to the signing of a Franco-Soviet pact in May 1935 and to its ratification by the French parliament in March 1936. Cot's pro-Soviet sentiments had not endeared him to conservative French Air Force officers. Indeed, it had made him, almost as much as Léon Blum, the *bête noire* of many right-wing journalists and politicians.

Shortly before his resignation, Prime Minister Pierre Laval had signed a trade agreement with Madrid, entitling the Spanish government to buy arms and military equipment from the French up to a value of 20 million francs. Accordingly, on July 19, the new Spanish government, headed by a left-wing Republican, José Giral, put in an urgent request for weapons – in particular for a score of Potez 54 bombers, a few 75 mm howitzers, and sizeable quantities of bullets, shells and aerial bombs. In June 1935 a Potez 54 had been flown to Madrid and the Spaniards had been much impressed by its flexibility, since – with three machine gun nacelles (above, below, and up front, in the bulbous, glassed-in nose) – it could be used for bombing, combat, or reconnaissance (BCR). Their own Bréguet 19 – a single engine, two-seater biplane more resembling a fighter – was so antiquated that it could only carry several hundred kilograms of bombs, whereas the Potez 54 could carry two tons.

In principle, the delivery of the twenty Potez 54s posed few problems, since the Spanish government had contracted to pay for them. But there remained the question of how they were to be manned. The Spaniards, who lacked competent pilots and bombardiers, were hoping that French pilots could be recruited not only to fly the bombers and a certain number of fighters to Barcelona, but also to go on piloting them in Spain.

Malraux immediately volunteered to fly to Madrid on an exploratory mission. If Pierre Cot could provide him with an aeroplane, he had a crack pilot capable of flying him over the Pyrenees: former Air Force Captain Edouard Corniglion-Molinier.

Malraux had long been persuaded that airpower would play a major role in any future conflict. A year and a half before, during a December 1934 dinner at Mme Théo's Rue Vaneau apartment, he had amazed André Gide, Bernard Groethuysen, and Alix Guillain by launching into a 'visionary' description of the next war, which, he claimed, would primarily be won by airpower. The idea had been developed in a number of books by Giulio Douhet, an Italian airman who had been condemned and imprisoned in 1916 for venturing to criticize his High Command's conduct of the war. He had later been released after the Austro–German breakthrough at Caporetto had confirmed the validity of his blistering critique. No one had done more to promote the autonomy of military airpower, and if Corniglion-Molinier had not actually met Douhet during his period of service in northern Italy in 1917–18, he had certainly read at least one of his books and talked to Malraux about it.

As an amateur airman who was trying to run a restive ministry, Pierre Cot immediately grasped the utility of sending Malraux to Madrid. There was everything to be gained by operating 'out of usual channels', for of Malraux's loyalty to the Front Populaire there could be no shadow of doubt.

Malraux had originally intended to make this trip alone. But Clara, feeling that a show of 'joint solidarity' in a common cause might help to re-cement a fissured marriage, made such a fuss that André reluctantly gave in to her entreaties.

The five-hour flight to Madrid had to be made in two laps, so that the twin-engine Lockheed could be refuelled. But when they reached the military airfield of Forgas, near Biarritz, they were held up by the wary base commander, who insisted on checking with the Air Ministry in Paris to make sure they had the proper clearance. (All flights to Spain from Pyrenean airfields had temporarily been banned.) Thinking he was doing them a service, he awoke them in the middle of the night with the cheering news that Madrid had fallen to the rebels. Malraux dismissed this rumour as right-wing wishful thinking, and the next morning they took off in a south-westerly direction.

They had hardly cleared the westernmost crest of the Pyrenees when Corniglion off-handedly observed that the aeroplane's compass had stopped functioning. 'I always know if I am headed in the right direction,' he reassured a nervous Clara. This doubtless explains why, after several hours in the air, there was still no sign of Madrid. Spotting an old city perched like a golden crown on a sunbaked plateau, Corniglion lowered altitude in an attempt to identify it. As they overflew the railway tracks near the towered walls, they saw the name spelled out for them by a large bed of flowers on the station square: AVILA. They were 60 kilometres off course, west of the Guadarrama range, when they should have been approaching the airfield of Barajas, 10 kilometres east of Madrid.

The angry puffs of smoke provoked by their rude overflight of Santa Teresa's venerable city probably meant that Avila too had fallen into rebel hands. But how were they to know? Not until they approached Barajas and could see a red flag floating from a mast were they sure that Madrid had not yet been captured by one of General Mola's columns.

Waiting to greet them, in front of a ragged 'honour guard' of armed militiamen, was the beaming, broad-shouldered, surprisingly fair-haired figure of Julio Alvarez del Vayo, who had attended the International Writers Congress of June 1935. A left-wing Socialist who was doing everything he could to encourage the conversion to Marxism of the popular Socialist leader, Largo Caballero (already a ripe 67!), Alvarez del Vayo hastened to reassure them about the present situation. Although the rebels, with the help of troops from Morocco, had established a foothold in the south, with the capture of Cadiz and Seville, most Spanish cities had remained loyal to the Republic. Particularly spectacular had been the collapse of the insurgency in the country's two largest cities, Madrid and Barcelona, where local militiamen were now in complete control. The Navy too had remained loyal, the crewmen refusing to take orders from rebel officers. What Alvarez del Vayo did not say – perhaps not realizing how widespread was the disaffection – was that the majority of the Army's officer corps had gone over to the rebels, while the *Guardia Civil*, established by the monarchy as a rampart of the State, was disintegrating into murderously hostile factions. But these were 'subterranean' realities, obscured by the euphoria generated by the Republic's first 'Battle of the Marne' – the defeat just inflicted on a rebel column from the north, which had vainly tried to break through the line of the Guadarrama mountains via the Somosierra pass.

The city of Madrid was now in the grip of a wild, popular exuberance, starkly dramatized by the multitude of rifles, carbines, and cartridge belts, which (in Clara's words) had been distributed 'like presents' to women as well as men, all uniformly dressed in blue denim overalls. The Cortes was still in emergency session, the Giral cabinet was still in office, Manuel Azaña was still installed in the presidential palace, but the real power had 'descended into the streets', rendered more tumultuous by the incessant sound of radio loudspeakers blaring through open windows the announcements of new governmental victories. Red flags had sprouted everywhere, even from the baroque campaniles of recently gutted churches, and there was not a major intersection which did not have its checkpoint barricade erected to intercept suspect 'fascists' or other 'enemies of the people'. Save for the bell-ringing trams, the traffic was now limited to trucks filled with gun-brandishing 'soldiers' in shirtsleeves and red sashes, and to requisitioned automobiles – Renaults, Citroëns, and Fords, and an occasional Hispano-Suiza, commandeered from a wealthy Madrileño who had fled the city, while his luxurious home became the headquarters of some labour syndicate or vigilante group.

Even for a much-travelled Malraux, this was an extraordinary experience. For the first time he was actually living what he had so vividly imagined in his novels, what he had read about in Michelet and Taine, with overalls replacing the striped pantaloons of the *sans-culottes*. But this was not a Chinese, nor a Russian, still less a German revolution; it was a Latin and, even more, a quintessentially Iberian revoluton – cruel yet light-hearted, grim yet jocose, something wild, anarchic, and untamed, far closer to Proudhon and Bakunin than to Engels or Marx. As Gustav Regler later described it, in words it would be difficult to better: 'There was a spirit of intoxication in the people, an infectious eagerness for sacrifice, a hot-blooded unreason and fanatical belief in freedom, which could never lead to the constitution of an orderly State on any earlier pattern.'

Loyal Air Force officers, Malraux soon discovered, had played a key role in securing the capital's three main airfields. At Getafe, south of Madrid, a light artillery regiment, commanded by rebellious officers, was getting ready to bombard and seize the airfield, on which a sizeable number of Air Force planes were parked, when their barracks were surrounded during the night by militiamen and about sixty Air Force gunners and mechanics armed with rifles.

Another large barracks, in the southern suburb of Carabanchel, had also surrendered after being hit by fighter planes and small bombers. The last rebel stronghold to fall – after a four-hour assault, later described by Malraux in his novel, *L'Espoir* – was the garrison of La Montaña, a vast military compound located not far from the royal (now presidential) palace on the western periphery of Madrid, overlooking the sluggish Manzanares river.

The overall picture was less clear-cut. Most of the major airbases in the country were still in loyalist hands, but the government had suffered two important losses. The first was that of León, in northern Castille, where two groups of small Bréguet 19 bombers (eighteen in all) were normally based. The second, even more serious loss was that of the Tablada airbase, near Seville, which had been overrun by General Queipo de Llano's forces. The Spanish Air Force, moreover, had just lost its highest ranking officer, General Miguel Nuñez de Prado. In a brave attempt to persuade a hesitant General Cabanellas, commanding the 5th Division, to remain loyal to the Republic, he had flown to Zaragoza, and had not been heard of since.

On July 26th, after being received by President Manuel Azaña, Malraux sent a telegraphic dispatch to Paris, which was published in the next morning's edition of *L'Humanité*. He flatly denied reports that the Spanish capital was surrounded by 'fascist groups . . . Madrid has been completely cleared as far south as Andalucia, to the east as far as the sea, to the west as far as Portugal. It is only in the north that the rebel army has sent out small advance guards, which have been beaten and pushed back beyond the hillsides of the Sierra de Guadarrama.'

When André, Clara, and their friend 'Eddy' (Corniglion) returned to Paris on July 27th, they found that the Popular Front government was being buffeted by a new storm, violent enough to shatter its fragile cohesion. On Friday, July 24th, Léon Blum and Foreign Minister Yvon Delbos had returned from a quick trip to London, where they had been dismayed to discover that Stanley Baldwin's Conservatives were anything but sympathetic to the idea of aiding the Spanish 'Reds', who had shocked British public opinion by their fiery readiness to put churches to the torch and to shoot priests, bishops and even nuns. These sentiments were fully shared by the French ambassador in London and by many senior diplomats in the French Foreign Ministry, now controlled by the rabidly anglophile Alexis Léger (the poet, Saint-John Perse). When Pierre Cot, as a matter of routine, had telephoned the Quai d'Orsay to say that, in accordance with the Prime Minister's instructions, he was having twenty Potez bombers delivered to the Spanish Republic, there was an explosion at the other end of the line. Confronted by mutinous subordinates, Yvon Delbos had begun to question the wisdom of aiding the Spanish Republicans, as had Pierre Cot's superior, Defence Minister Daladier, who was upset to learn that the presidents of both parliamentary chambers – Edouard Herriot, of the Chamber of Deputies, and Jules Jeanneney, of the Senate – were appalled by Léon Blum's 'overhasty' response to the Spanish government's request for arms.

The right-wing press campaign, which had been launched on the eve of Malraux's departure for Madrid, had quickly assumed the force of a typhoon, and he now found himself in the eye of the storm. On Saturday, July 25th, Henri de Kerillis, the editor-in-chief of *L'Echo de Paris*, had opened fire on Pierre Cot, demanding to know when the French planes he was having 'delivered' to the Spanish were going to leave for Barcelona. What made this and subsequent attacks so serious was Kerillis' prestige as a much decorated Great War airman and now a parliamentary deputy, whom no one could seriously accuse of being a 'fascist'. An outspoken enemy of

Hitler's Germany, he was an admirer of Eduard Beneš of Czechoslovakia, whom he had recently visited in Prague. However, Kerillis' hostility to Hitler's Nazis was matched by his detestation of Lenin's Bolsheviks, who (unlike Kerensky and his Mensheviks) had betrayed France in 1917–18 by reneging on Russia's alliance and wartime pledges and by negotiating the separate peace of Brest–Litovsk. The mere idea that a Popular Front government, with the active support of the French Communist Party, could think of supplying bombers to the 'communo-anarchistic soviet' which had taken over in Madrid was enough to make Kerillis foam at the mouth.

The next morning Kerillis had followed up with another scorching editorial, which began dramatically: 'As I write these lines, an American Lockheed aeroplane, belonging to France . . . , has been delivered to Spain and has reached Madrid. It was piloted by Mr Corniglion-Molinier, mounted by a sergeant-mechanic from the Air Force, and carried as a passenger the novelist André Malraux. On board were two crates of gold sent by "International Red Aid".'

The language used by Maurice Pujo, managing editor of *L'Action Française*, was infinitely more vicious, and his campaign against Pierre Cot more insistent and sustained. By July 24th Charles Maurras' arch-monarchist newspaper had coined a new name for the once pacifist prime minister: he had become '*Blum-la-Guerre*' (which can be roughly translated as 'Blum-for-War'). On Tuesday, July 28th, Pujo in his turn was able to report that 'a big aeroplane belonging to the State, piloted by a reserve officer', had been used to carry 'the special correspondent of *L'Humanité*, Mr André Malraux' to Madrid, 'in order to bring back the new Spanish ambassador'. The same day the normally staid *Journal des Débats* joined the baying chorus by labelling Malraux 'an agent of Moscow'.

The storm of protests worked up by France's right-wing press aroused increasing concern in London, where the prevailing sentiment among many Conservatives was summed up in this cynical comment, attributed by some to Prime Minister Stanley Baldwin: 'We hate Fascism. But we hate Bolshevism just as much. If, therefore, there is a country where Fascists and Bolsheviks kill each other, it is a boon for mankind.'

Léon Blum now found himself in an acutely embarrassing position. He was sympathetic to the Frente Popular, a number of whose leaders were personal friends. He was determined to honour France's commitments to provide a legally elected Spanish government with military assistance, for the last thing he wanted was one more Fascist regime installed next to another of France's borders. But Blum was equally loath to antagonize the British, without whose diplomatic co-operation there could be no hope of containing an aggressive Nazi Germany. If, furthermore, he made an issue of massive military aid to Spain, the more conservative Radical Socialists in the cabinet would walk out, precipitating the collapse of his Front Populaire government. The only way out of this dire dilemma was to resort to subterfuge in supplying arms to Republican Spain, while trying to limit the damage by persuading the major European powers – above all, Hitler's Germany and Mussolini's Italy – to respect a policy of 'non-intervention' in the Spanish Civil War.

Of one thing Malraux was convinced. Since the arms race in the Iberian peninsula had in fact begun, it was up to France to win it. This was no time for making speeches, or, as he put it in an interview granted to the Swiss correspondent of the *Basler Rundschau*, for sitting around 'with folded arms' waiting to see what was going to happen next, since this was the surest way of offering 'indirect support to the Spanish generals . . . As for the prospects, it should be realized that the military outcome will be decided during the next fourteen days.'

In the meantime, Pierre Cot had not waited for Malraux's return to start rounding up bombers and fighter planes for the Spanish Republicans. His *chef de cabinet*, Jean Moulin, had prepared a list of Air Force reserve officers who could be approached, and arrangements had been made to facilitate the granting of 'leave of absence' permits to Air Force officers or non-commissioned officers on active duty willing to interrupt their regular service. Cot's Radical Socialist colleague, Lucien Bossoutrot, who headed the Chamber of Deputies' Aeronautics Commission, had even opened a bureau for the hiring of pilots willing to fly French warplanes to Barcelona. Such overt recruiting activities now became a risky business for a politician committed to supporting Léon Blum's Popular Front and its officially proclaimed 'non-intervention' policy. The job was accordingly turned over to André Malraux, whose Rue du Bac apartment was transformed overnight into an annex of the Spanish Embassy and an informal recruiting office.

If this particular chapter of Malraux's life is still shrouded in mystery, it is not only because of the semi-clandestine nature of the enterprise; it is also because it was difficult for Malraux, and later for a host of hagiographic admirers, to fit certain setbacks he suffered into the composite image of his 'heroic' legend. For the truth of the matter is that in this hastily improvised undertaking Malraux started out with two handicaps. Unlike Lucien Bossoutrot, who had served as an airman during the 1914–18 war and had later worked for the Farman aircraft company, or Pierre Cot, the holder of a civilian pilot's licence, Malraux had never flown an aeroplane and knew next to nothing about aviation technology. His Queen of Sheba spree had done nothing to enhance his reputation with many professional airmen, who had tended to regard it as a sensation-seeking stunt. This explains the brush-off he received when he approached Adrienne Bolland, a daredevil airwoman who had rocked the *macho* world of South America in 1921 by overflying the Andes between Argentina and Chile. He received an equally cool reception from former Aéropostale officials, like Roger Beaucaire, who, though himself a rabid Socialist, felt that Malraux's plan to recruit an international squadron composed of pilots and bombardiers was 'lacking in seriousness'.

It must in any case have been a daunting task. The managers of the Potez company, like those of virtually every other French aeroplane manufacturer, were still fuming over the recent strikes, which had crippled production for weeks on end, and, feeling no fondness for Léon Blum, they were in no hurry to help his Frente Popular friends in Spain.

Of the fifty to sixty warplanes that Pierre Cot – assisted by the head of his secretariat, Jean Moulin, and by Léon Blum's personal factotum, Jules Moch – was able to turn over to the Spanish Republicans, only three – a Bloch 210 bomber, first put into service in 1934, and two Dewoitine 510 fighters, powered by Hispano-Suiza aero-engines – were in any real sense 'up-to-date' warplanes. The rest – the Dewoitine 37s (dating from 1934), the Potez 54 bombers, and the Potez 25 observation planes (first put into service as far back as 1926) were already superannuated aircraft. For fear of further offending the hostile diplomats of the Quai d'Orsay, Pierre Cot was forced to have the fighters stripped of their machine guns – a concession to diplomatic hypocrisy which had catastrophic consequences in Spain. When the Dewoitines finally took off from the Montaudran airfield, near Toulouse, each pilot was supposedly going up for a 'trial flight', although the gendarmes on the ground knew perfectly well that the warplanes were headed for Barcelona. The MAP (Manufactures d'Armes de Paris) machine guns were supposed to follow separately by train, along with the necessary bullets. They were in fact dispatched, but never reached their intended destination, having been seized by Spanish anarchists who during the early weeks of the Civil War controlled many of the frontier posts along the Pyrenees. Days later, when the Dewoitine fighters were flown from Barcelona to Madrid, they were still unarmed.

The multiple task, which Malraux had assumed as unofficial go-between, paymaster, and recruiter, of finding truly qualified airmen capable of handling these Dewoitines proved so difficult that thirteen of them were still lined up on the airfield at Pau, in the foothills of the Pyrenees, on the morning of August 7th, the day on which the Blum government was due to announce that, in agreement with the British, it was henceforth adopting an attitude of strict neutrality.

Of Malraux's hectic activities during these early August days, we know precious little, beyond the fact that fabulous sums of money were offered to aviators willing to fly warplanes to Spain. The remuneration finally decided on for pilots willing to stay on in the service of the Republic was of the order of 50,000 francs per month – 150 times the monthly pay of a Spanish Air Force second lieutenant.

Among the first to respond to these lucrative offers were, inevitably, adventurers of one kind or another, quite willing to sign up as mercenaries. Some were veteran airmen of the Great War. Typical of the breed was the 'jovial and athletic' François Bourgeois, who, after shooting down several German warplanes in 1917–18, had emigrated to the United States, where he had worked for the notorious John Dillinger – for a long time America's

Public Enemy No. 1 – flying bootleg liquor over the Canadian border. Yet another was the elegant (he always wore a tic), phlegmatic, aloof Jean Darry, a forty-one-year-old Great War airman who had also crossed the Atlantic, married an actress, divorced, and then returned to Europe, where his 'distinguished' salesmanship of beautifully disguised – as well as stolen – automobiles had come close to landing him in prison. Two outstanding exceptions, on the other hand, were an Alsatian named Hantz, who had been a German Air Force pilot during the Great War, and Abel Guidez, an anarchistically inclined fighter pilot of Catalan extraction. Because of the genuineness of his commitment – he was emphatically not a mercenary – Guidez was chosen to command the fighter group of what came to be called the *escuadra España*.

It was probably on August 6th that André Malraux finally left Paris. He was accompanied once again by Clara, but this time they boarded a Potez 54 bomber, which flew them to Barcelona. Waiting to greet him at the Prat de Llobregat airfield was Abel Guidez, whose dark, sunburnt features enhanced the toothy whiteness of his smile.

The situation in the capital of Catalonia – which had been taken over by half a dozen 'anarcho-syndicalist' or other left-wing groups – was, if anything, even more chaotic than in Madrid. It was impossible to move around without being provided with three or four different 'passes', each one officially sealed and stamped by 'officials' of Durruti's FAI (*Federación Anarchista Ibérica*), Garcia Oliver's CNT (*Confederación Nacional de Trabajo*), or Andrés Nin's anti-Stalinist but still Marxist POUM (*Partido Obrero de Unificación Marxista*). Here too all the hotels had been requisitioned, beginning with the once luxurious Colón, now occupied by Civil Guards.

By the time Malraux reached Madrid, a day or two later, the situation on the 'northern front', extending along the partly wooded, partly rocky slopes of the Guadarrama range, had settled down to a kind of static warfare. General Mola had had to abandon his attempt to 'capture' Madrid – among other reasons, for lack of ammunition. The capital was still in the grip of an exuberant revolutionary fever. The holstered pistol, often suspended from a makeshift strip of canvas, had become a badge of loyalty, a conspicuous emblem of one's determination to defend the Republic. Everywhere fists were still being raised and the comradely greeting *Salud!* exchanged whenever trucks or requisitioned automobiles filled with soldiers or militiamen careered past each other in the streets.

Two requisitioned hotels – the Florida and the Gran Vía – had been placed at the disposition of the foreign airmen who were beginning to reach Madrid. At this basic level of board and lodging there was little to complain of. But Malraux must have had a shock the first time he visited the War Ministry, in the middle of Madrid. Surrounded by pleasant gardens, with a proud statue of Gonzalo de Córdoba ('*el Gran Capitán*' of fifteenth-century Spain) adorning the forecourt, this grandiose edifice with marble staircases, palatial halls and Gobelin tapestries had become an 'open house'. It was full of gesticulating and sometimes querulous civilians, many of them dressed in zip-fastened overalls: parliamentary deputies or delegates from this or that provincial town or region, who had come to beg for 500 soldiers, 300 rifles, or a dozen machine guns to defend a few sacred acres of Republican territory. The easy-going Casares Quiroga, who had been premier when the uprising had erupted on July 18th, had acted as his own defence minister – something that had not helped the orderly running of the Army. His successor, Martínez Barrio, who had remained in power for half a dozen hours, had at least tried to bring in a military man, General José Miaja, to run the ministry. But Miaja had decided that his presence was badly needed in the south, where Republican forces were trying to recapture Córdoba. The actual running of the ministry had been entrusted to a Colonel Hernandez Sarabia, who spent most of his time on the telephone, calling this or that battalion or column commander in the field, so that he could relay the latest information to Manuel Azaña in his presidential palace. The Air Force, if such it could be called – its official title was the General Directorate of Aeronautics – was still without a commanding officer; and, like the Army, it did not seem to possess even the semblance of a General Staff.

At Barajas, where he was assisted by the invaluable Abel Guidez, Malraux discovered that they had to begin virtually from scratch, improvising as they went along. The first Dewoitine fighters had been flown up from Barcelona unarmed, and it was more than a week before they could be fitted out in the workshops of Cautro Vientos with antiquated Lewis machine guns, capable of firing only 400 rounds per minute. Indeed, it was while piloting two antiquated Nieuport 52s that Jean Darry and his fellow 'mercenary', Gouinet, scored the first two victories for the squadron by shooting down two small Bréguet 19 'bombers' over the Sierra de Guadarrama.

That same day (August 14th) Madrid was shaken by the news that General Franco's forces had stormed Badajoz, an important Extramaduran town located near the Portuguese frontier. Two days before, Colonel Yagüe had occupied Mérida, some 60 kilometres to the west. It had taken Franco's forces just two weeks to make an advance of 200 kilometres from Seville. While the Republicans were hypnotized by events on the 'northern front', along the Sierra de Guadarrama, the rebels were winning the war in the west.

Malraux now received an urgent message from the War Ministry in Madrid. A motorized column, advancing westward from Mérida, had been spotted near the town of Don Benito, south of the Guadiana river. Thousands of Extramaduran peasants had armed themselves with shotguns and carbines, but what could they do against armoured cars and the automatic rifles of Moroccan infantrymen? Could Malraux's group send out several of its Potez 54s on an urgent bombing mission?

For Malraux and his squadron mates this was a perilous challenge. The first fully armed Potez bomber had been flown up from Barcelona just four days before. Teaching a fighter pilot to handle a new warplane effectively was already no easy task, as Pierre Cot must have explained to Malraux in Paris. But it was child's play compared to the training needed to get a Potez 54 bomber crew to act as an effective team, since it required the well-co-ordinated efforts of two pilots, a navigator bombardier trained to handle the forward machine gun (in the bulbous nose) in the case of a head-on attack, as well as a radio technician and a mechanic, each capable of handling the machine guns in the fuselage turret and underbelly nacelle. In theory, this meant a crew of five well-trained men: an operational ideal never attained in Malraux's bomber squadron, where the crew normally numbered no fewer than seven men.

It was little short of miraculous that by August 16th as many as four Potez 54s could be readied for action. With a typical disregard for strategic priorities, the 'High Command' at the Ministry of War in Madrid decided to divert two of the Potez 54s to bomb targets near Teruel, north-east of Valencia. To reinforce the bombing force headed for Extramadura, a twin-engine Douglas DC-2 was ordered to accompany the two Potez 54s. This Douglas was one of a number of Spanish civilian mail carriers which ground crews at Getafe and Cuatro Vientos had been working overtime to transform into warplanes. These rudimentary 'bombers' were so ill-designed for the job that the 8- or 10-kilo bombs they were capable of carrying had to be heaved out manually through the cabin door or window. Being something of a braggart and even capable of fiction (as he later proved), Corniglion-Molinier may well have been the person who first spread the story – which hardened overnight into legendary 'fact' – about his Spanish wartime exploits, overflying rebel trenches while his friend André Malraux heaved bombs out of the cabin window on to the fascist troops below.

Malraux himself did not take part in the August 16th raid over Extramadura – contrary to the impression given in his later novel, *L'Espoir*, where two different raids were, for the purposes of fiction, telescoped into one. The pilots of the Potez 54s finally spotted the rebel column they were looking for: a long line of small red squares stretched out along a kilometre of yellowish highroad between Mérida and Medellín: the uncamouflaged bonnets of a convoy of trucks, whose sun bleached canvas coverings were virtually invisible against the dusty roadway. Not all of the bombs hit their targets. This was hardly surprising, given the limited training of the crews, and, in the case of the transformed Douglas, the improvised nature of the bomb-drop – through the evacuation chute of an enlarged toilet bowl! But a number of trucks were hit, enough to halt the column and to send the khaki-clad soldiers and turban-wearing Moroccans scurrying like frightened ants across the arid plain.

When Mikhail Koltsov disembarked at Barajas, on August 18th, he found the airfield swarming with officers and soldiers. Bustling about in the midst of them was André Malraux, looking 'tired, thin, and irritated. He has gone for many days without sleep,' noted *Pravda*'s roving correspondent. The challenges to be met seemed to be growing by the hour. Two days before, on their way back from their bombing mission in the region of Teruel, the two Potez 54s had been attacked by several formidable Fiat SR–32 fighter planes. Flying an old Nieuport, a young French fighter pilot named Adrien Matheron had managed to down one of the Italian fighters, while the former French Air Force captain, Victor Véniel, chased off the others; but in the course of this dogfight Thomas, a naturalized Frenchman of Polish origin, had gone down in his Nieuport.

On August 20th Malraux's bomber squadron was again asked to intervene, in another attempt to halt the rebels' westward progression in Extramadura. Despite his weariness, Malraux insisted on flying as an 'observer' in one of the Potez 54s. This bombing mission proved even more successful than the first. The two Potez 54s and the converted Douglas DC–2 took Franco's forces completely by surprise. A number of trucks were parked in the main square of Medellín, while others were half hidden in the shadows of the neighbouring streets. Slowly circling, the three Republican bombers flew over the town at an almost 'suicidal' height of 300 metres. Malraux was able to distinguish the different hues – salmon pink, pale blue, pistachio green – of individual house walls beneath the tiled rooftops. The bomb-shutters were opened and, glinting briefly in the sunlight, the 50-kilo bombs 'continued on their way with the independence of torpedoes'. A moment later the square was violently disrupted by a series of orange flashes, as though set off by mines. The dark toylike outline of a truck seemed to shoot up against a whitish jet and then disappear beneath a cloud of dirty smoke.

The bombers had hardly overflown the town when the lead pilot saw what looked like three Douglas DC–2s flying towards them, followed at a slightly higher level by another trio. Since this was more than the Barajas base possessed, he instantly realized that they were not Douglases . . . but three-engine Junkers 52s. The pilots of the approaching warplanes must have been equally surprised by the sudden appearance of the Republican Potez 54s. There were brief bursts of machine gun fire as the opposing bombers passed, a few bullets slammed through the fuselage of Malraux's Potez, and he himself was slightly wounded in the arm.

This raid, one of the group's most notable achievements, did little to halt the tempo of the rebels' advance – which might possibly have been halted for a while had Malraux's bomber group had a dozen or more Potez 54s able to operate around the clock, with twice that number of Dewoitines to escort them. But, in cruel fact, at no time did his unit have more than five Potez 54s in operational condition.

Malraux's bold prediction (made to the *Basler Rundschau*) that the war in Spain would be won during the first fourteen days was now coming true. Taking advantage of Britain's passivity and France's half-hearted inertia, Hitler and even Mussolini were now providing Franco and Mola with the weapons and above all the warplanes they needed.

On August 23rd the increasingly daring Nationalists staged a bombing raid on the airfield of Cuatro Vientos, south of Madrid, where Guidez's fighters were based, and damaged several Dewoitines. Four days later they returned for a second visit, damaging several more. To halt Colonel Yagüe's forces, the Republic's High Command should long before have weakened the overmanned Guadarrama front and rushed some artillery batteries to defend the key road junction of Talavera de la Reina, on the Tagus, 80 kilometres from Toledo and a mere 120 from Madrid. Even if they had been properly dug in and camouflaged, however, these batteries would have been exposed to aerial bombardment, unless assured of overhead protection. But by this time – late August – it was already too late. With each passing day the rebels' strength in the air was being dramatically increased – with the delivery of more Fiat SR–32s (usually piloted by Italians), more Junkers 52 bombers and Heinkel 51 fighters, almost all of them piloted by Germans, to keep them from being wrecked by insufficiently experienced Spanish airmen. The Republicans, who had started out with a numerical superiority in warplanes, had already lost this advantage and were beginning to show themselves incapable of properly defending Madrid.

On August 26th Malraux and his squadron-mates were heartened by the arrival at Barajas of a Bloch 210, piloted by a dynamic Air France captain, Lionel de Marmier, who was working overtime in Paris trying to find warplanes and pilots for the Spanish Republicans. But the excitement aroused among Malraux's 'internationals' by the addition of this truly modern bomber was short-lived. For the very next day Antonio de Haro, one of the Republic's best pilots, was 'jumped' by several Fiat fighters as he was coming in to land at the Getafe airfield, and his precious Dewoitine 372 was completely destroyed.

On August 28th, Adrien Matheron, piloting a Dewoitine, shot down a rebel Bréguet bomber near Talavera de la Reina. However, this victory was marred by an incident which caused an uproar among the outraged officers of the Republic's High Command. As the young Matheron was flying home over the Sierra de Gredos, his companion, 'Captain Vic' (Véniel), saw what he took to be a rebel detachment marching a number of prisoners along a country road. Swiftly banking, he came down to almost tree top level and fired a machine gun burst in order to give the Republican prisoners a chance to escape. A number of prisoners did inded 'take to the hills' as a result of this 'providential' strafing; but, as Véniel later learned to his dismay, they were Franco Nationalists, while the captors he had intimidated with his gunfire were Republican militiamen.

When news of this unsolicited 'assistance' got back to Madrid, it aroused a storm of indignation inside the Ministry of War. Particularly outraged by this 'breach of discipline' was Antonio Camacho, who had been serving as Under-Secretary for Aviation. From this blow to its prestige, and in particular to its trustworthiness in Spanish eyes, Malraux's fighter-and-bomber group never fully recovered.

André Malraux, aged four.
(Collection F. Malraux)

Berthe Malraux, née Lamy
mother of André.
(Collection F. Malraux)

André, dressed as a musketeer,
about nine years old.
(Collection F. Malraux)

Marie Lamy, André's aunt.
(Collection F. Malraux)

Fernand Malraux with his son André
in 1915.
(Collection F. Malraux)

André, as a *lycée* student
in 1915.
(Collection F. Malraux)

Malraux and his wife, Clara, after their marriage in 1921.
(Collection F. Malraux)

Malraux with Vsevolod Meyerhold and Boris Pasternak in 1934.
(Collection F. Malraux)

Malraux in 1933.
(Photo Germaine Krull)

Louise
de Vilmorin playing
the guitar in 1933.
(Photo *Vogue*)

Malraux and his deputy, Abel Guidez, in 1936.

Malraux and Josette Clotis in 1938.
(Collection F. Malraux)

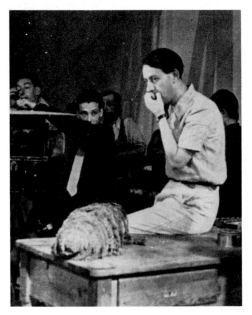

Malraux in Barcelona, during
the filming of *Sierra de Teruel*.
(Collection F. Malraux)

'Colonel Berger', Commander of
the Alsace-Lorraine Brigade in 1944.
(Collection F. Malraux)

Florence Malraux, daughter of André
and of Clara. (Collection F. Malraux)

Malraux and his second wife
Madeleine.
(Collection F. Malraux)

Malraux and Charles de Gaulle.
(Photo Gisèle Freund)

Malraux with one
of his cats in the garden
of 'La Lanterne'.
(Photo Gisèle Freund)

Malraux and Louise de Vilmorin in the garden of Verrières.
(Photo Pierre Lelièvre, *Le Figaro*)

Nor, for that matter, did the War Ministry recover from the ridicule heaped on it the next evening, when a Nationalist bomber calmly overflew Madrid and dropped a couple of bombs in the gardens of the Ministry of War. This essentially symbolic raid dramatically exposed the Spanish capital's vulnerability and the reckless insouciance of its inhabitants. Not only had no effort been made to dim the garish neon signs outside cinemas and theatres, but also no major edifice could have been more perfectly targeted at night than the Ministry of War, located at the intersection of the brilliantly illuminated Calle de Alcalá and the long, double row of street lamps lining the Paseos.

That same evening Mikhail Koltsov happened to be dining in a small Basque restaurant near the Gran Vía with a delegation of anti-fascist politicians led by the French Socialist, Jean Zyromski, and Jacques Duclos, of the French Communist Party. When Duclos heard that the Fascists had dared to bomb the centre of a 'peaceful' Madrid, he went into a tirade, saying that this was an intolerable outrage, that he was going straight back to Paris to arouse French public opinion. If Paris took the lead by acting, then everyone would follow – Copenhagen and Stockholm, Prague, Vienna, even distant Bucharest!

How Koltsov would have liked to believe him! But as he noted sadly in his diary:

For the moment, the reality is that no more than a dozen lads of the international squadron [he was referring to Malraux's] represent the military aid of the other countries. At 4 o'clock in the morning Guidez and two other pilots hied themselves out to Barajas to mount guard over the fighter planes. The rest, accompanied by ladies, remained seated here in the lobby, offering commentaries on the form a future war might take.

On September 1st, Malraux's bomber group chalked up a new victory by staging a surprise attack on a secret airstrip which Mola's Nationalists had established near Olmedo, some 40 kilometres south of Valladolid. A local peasant, who had observed it being used by four big aeroplanes (presumably bombers) and two smaller warplanes (fighters?), had managed to infiltrate his way across the 'no-man's land' of the Guadarrama front, passing from rebel-controlled to Republican territory. After being intensely interrogated, to make sure that he was not conniving in a Nationalist trap, he was placed up front in the bulbous nose of a Potez and was able to guide the lead pilot and those of the following Potez 54s to the target. The surprise raid caught the rebels off guard. Three Nationalist warplanes were destroyed on the ground, an ammunition dump was blown up and a fuel tank set ablaze. All of the Potez 54s made it safely back to Barajas, thanks to the escorting Dewoitines, which successfully fought off several rebel fighters.

On September 2nd the Dewoitines escorted the modern Bloch 210 bomber on its first wartime raid. It was made against Colonel Yagüe's forces, which were now besieging Talavera de la Reina, overlooking the banks of the Tagus, and several bridges on the Lisbon–Madrid highway – which, as Mikhail Koltsov pertinently remarked after a visit to this crumbling 'front' – was a good bit closer to Madrid than to Lisbon. But neither the Bloch's 50-kilo bombs nor the lighter ones dropped by several old Bréguet 19s from the Getafe group could keep Yagüe's tough troopers from storming this key town the next day.

The lyrical illusion had lasted eight long weeks. The rude awakening had only just begun.

26

The Ordeal

Malraux had chosen this moment to return to Paris for several days of badly needed rest. For weeks he had been working at a furious tempo. As he had written to Josette Clotis in mid-August, 'I sleep three hours a night amidst a mixture of heroism and imbecility.' In Paris they arranged another clandestine tryst, this time at the Hôtel Elysée Palace, from whose windows they could admire the sparkling fountains of the Rond-Point des Champs-Elysées 'spreading their First Communion veils' in the sunshine.

The little time he spent with Clara was anything but calm. During her trips to Madrid Clara had tried to make herself useful by occasionally accompanying André out to the airfield and by keeping a 'journal' for the squadron. As Malraux's wife, she had naturally shared the *Comandante*'s bedroom at the Hotel Florida – a physical proximity which had exacerbated the growing *mésentente* between them.

Now, in Paris, André told Clara that her departure from Madrid had helped him to act with greater efficiency. Though nettled, she managed to control her temper. When André Gide turned up at the Rue du Bac apartment, he found young Florence seated on the floor, happily stripping the petals from a large dahlia (removed from a bouquet), with which she was preparing a 'salad'. Pleasantly surprised, Gide found Malraux looking less haggard than he had expected. 'His face is even less creased by ticks than usual,' he noted in his journal, 'and his hands are not too feverish. He speaks with that extraordinary volubility which often makes it so difficult for me to follow him. He depicts their situation, which he would regard as desperate if the forces of the enemy were not so divided.'

When Malraux returned to Barajas three days later, he learned that on September 3rd the squadron had lost another pilot: the Alsatian Hantz, shot down by four Fiat fighters, while his fellow fighter pilot, Issart, had barely made it back to Cuatro Vientos in his old, seriously riddled Nieuport.

On September 4th – perhaps its busiest day yet – the squadron had made several bombing raids on Talavera – one of which was later vividly written up by Malraux's intellectual friend, Nicola Chiaromonte, a former Italian artilleryman who had felt it to be his anti-Fascist duty to leave his wife in

Paris and to volunteer for service as an airborne gunner. Piloting a converted Dragon Rapide, the former bootleg smuggler François Bourgeois had managed to bring his lightly hit 'bomber' back to Barajas, but an aged Lioré 21 (a long-winged bomber dating from 1927) had failed to return. At the airfield of Cuatro Vientos, the normally cheerful Abel Guidez was in a state of shock. He had just lost two more pilots, as well as an ace mechanic, and never had they been so sorely needed. For Malraux, just returned from Paris, this was a bitter blow. The next day, it was dramatically compounded when a squadron of Junkers 52s, piloted by Germans, overflew the Cuatro Vientos airfield, destroying three Dewoitine 37s and three old Nieuport fighters, and damaging several other warplanes. The 'miraculous' reappearance of Lioré's crash-landed crew, all given up for 'lost', did little to lessen the magnitude of the disaster.

This serious setback crippled Malraux's squadron for most of the month of September. It occurred at a moment when the Spanish Republic was again in the throes of a political crisis. José Giral's 'cabinet of radical intellectuals' was replaced by a broad-based coalition government (in which for the first time two Communists were included), headed by the Socialist Party's most popular, most radical, most unpredictable politician, Largo Caballero. In mid-August, when Giral had proposed that the Republic set up training schools for infantry, artillery, cavalry and engineer officers, Largo Caballero had threatened a general strike, angrily declaring that the last thing the Republic needed was the re-establishment of a 'military caste'. But an army without officers – 'cadres', as Malraux had put it in his interview with the *Basler Rundschau* – is not an army; it is simply a military rabble. This was what Colonel Yagüe's forces found 'facing' them during their triumphant, 250-kilometre advance from Mérida to Talavera.

On September 10th, when Mikhail Koltsov returned to the western 'front', he had a talk with Colonel Asensio Torrado, the forty-four-year-old 'prodigy' who, from a safe distance of 7 kilometres, was preparing a shattering counter-attack aimed at reconquering Talavera. *Pravda*'s correspondent was amazed to see that, whereas Yagüe's Moroccans and Legionnaires were invisible, there was no trace of a trench on the Republican side. The colonel smiled condescendingly, pointing out that his men had neither the special units, nor the 'instruments', nor the patience for such work. Trenches, the new premier and Minister for War had imperiously declared, were not suited to the mentality of the Spanish soldier. If he had to, when under fire, the Spaniard sought refuge behind a tree; but he found it most offensive to place himself in a ditch.

Had this attitude continued to prevail in the land of Don Quixote, there is little doubt that, as Koltsov wryly noted, the Nationalists could have piled a few soldiers on to a single tank and ridden triumphantly into Madrid. But meanwhile, more or less spontaneously, certain 'veterans' of the Guadarrama front had taken matters into their own hands. With the active support of the Communist Party leadership, they had formed a 'Fifth

Regiment' of well disciplined militiamen, who had made the sobering discovery that the surest way of surviving an artillery bombardment was to dig oneself in.

The international fame soon acquired by the *Quinto Regimiento*, which became a training centre for militiamen from other units, was not long in reaching Paris, where its exploits were extolled by *L'Humanité* and other left-wing organs. They aroused great enthusiasm at the *Maison de la Culture* and among prominent members of the Women's League against War and Fascism, providing Clara Malraux with a good excuse for returning to Madrid. She found the mood of the city singularly altered, with little trace of the intoxicating euphoria of the revolutionary apocalypse (as Malraux was to call it), which they had encountered during their first visit in July. In certain suburban streets stone barricades were being erected, while trenches were being dug around Madrid's southern and western extremities. Meat, bread, and oil – traditionally supplied from verdant Galicia, the wheatfields of Castile, and the olive orchards of Andalucía (all now in rebel hands) – were in short supply, and the shocked Madrileños had even had to accept a stringently enforced nocturnal blackout.

For several days Clara found herself billeted once again with her husband at the Hotel Florida. This enforced cohabitation was irksome to both of them. True to her militantly feminist philosophy and probably also to avenge herself for André's infidelities with Josette Clotis, Clara chose this moment to indulge in another 'parallel' adventure, one so blatant that it was the talk of the hotel the next day. This insult to the *Jefe*'s virile prestige was something he never forgave her.

The 'relaxed' atmosphere of this 'terribly red and terribly revolutionary centre' – Mikhail Koltsov's sarcastic description of the Hotel Florida – seems to have encouraged adventures of this kind.

Here [Koltsov noted in his diary] live the aviators and engineers of the international squadron, who wear unbuttoned sport shirts and carry knives and revolvers in wooden sheaths attached to their belts. At first they wanted to bring their wives, but they were not granted permission. Now they no longer make this request – for women they have found in Madrid. At night there are noisy scenes, with sudden exits in the corridors – so much so that correspondents and foreign Socialist deputies have complained to the manager. Among the flyers there are valiant and loyal men: they are grouped around Guidez; they are seldom to be seen at the hotel, and often spend the night at the airfield. There are ten men who unquestionably are spies, and a dozen loafers who, seated at the bar, spend their time scandalously intriguing against André [Malraux] and Guidez. They have been given slow-moving 'tubs' instead of planes, they complain.

That Malraux's squadron might have been infiltrated by 'spies' is, of course, quite possible. But it is more likely that this accusation was a product of Mikhail Koltsov's inflamed imagination, haunted by the Stalinist witch-hunt against Trotskyists and 'saboteurs' now raging through the Soviet Union and which had prompted him to seek refuge in Spain, along with his German mistress, Maria Osten, a 'war correspondent' like himself.

Altogether, this was a dismal month for most members of Malraux's squadron, condemned to idleness for lack of warplanes in operational condition. On September 10th one of the unit's Potez 54s, piloted by a German, was sent out to bomb Talavera, but this was the last mission of its kind for several weeks.

On the 28th a rebel column, commanded by Colonel José Varela, stormed Toledo, scattering its panic-stricken militiamen. This humiliating finale to a grotesque siege – in which quantities of ammunition, tons of dynamite, and tank-loads of fuel were uselessly expended in vain attempts to topple and even incinerate the rock-hard fortress of the Alcázar – inevitably increased the vulnerability of Madrid's two southern airbases at Getafe and Cuatro Vientos.

Two days later Malraux's squadron lost its first Potez 54, shot down over the Sierra de Guadarrama. The French Air Force pilot emerged unscathed, but three of the crewmen, including the Italian bombardier, were killed, and three others, including the co-pilot, were so seriously injured that they had to be retired from active service. That Malraux's squadron should have lost only one Potez bomber in six weeks of operation is little short of miraculous. It is unquestionably a tribute to the versatile talents of its 'mercenary' pilots and volunteer machine gunners (like the Czech, Jan Ferak, who later became a crack pilot with another unit). The record is doubly impressive when compared with that of another Republican bomber squadron, commanded by the Spaniard, Martín Luna, which over a similar period lost five Potez 54s. When, on July 19th, the well intentioned José Giral had put in an urgent request for twenty Potez 54s, he was asking for relatively sophisticated bombers which it was folly to entrust to inexperienced Spanish airmen. But it is no less true that it was craven hypocrisy on the part of Daladier's Defence Ministry to have delivered these Potez 54s to the Spaniards without the rapid-fire Darne machine guns that were supposed to equip them. This helped to make them *ataúdes volantes* (flying coffins) in Spanish eyes.

On the evening of October 5th Mikhail Koltsov had himself driven out to Barajas in his luxurious, chauffeur-driven Autoplán. He found officials and mechanics in an unusually nervous state. A Potez 54 had been sent out to bomb an armoured column advancing eastward from Talavera, but it had failed to return and one of its escorting fighters had been shot down in an unequal dogfight against nine Fiat SR–32s. For a moment it was feared that Abel Guidez was the one who had been downed, but his fighter landed safely after an acrobatically steep descent. As he rolled to a stop, he shouted to the ground crews to get the ambulance ready. His normally beaming features and dazzling white toothed smile were now glum. Not long afterwards the Potez 54, listing drunkenly to one side, landed with a thud and rebounded several times before rumbling slowly to a halt. The cabin door remained closed. Only after the ground crewmen had yanked it open did they understand the reason. The floor of the bulbous cabin cockpit was awash with blood. The German pilot, his hands still clutching the controls, pierced by bullets in shoulders, arms, and legs, was so weak he could no longer move.

'It's not the personnel we lack,' Guidez explained to Koltsov, after the ambulance had raced off with the wounded crewmen. 'The trouble is we have more gunners than machine guns, more pilots than machines. We are doing what we can. France has not helped us. The Spaniards are brave lads, but somebody has to be next to them to shake them up a bit. In August they were dropping bombs from three thousand metres or higher, but now with us they have come down to five hundred.'

On October 8th Varela's forces overran the important road junction of San Martín de Valdeiglesias, on the main road to Avila, putting them a mere 60 kilometres due west of Madrid. One week later – in itself an indication of how weak Malraux's squadron had become – a single Potez 54, escorted by three Dewoitine fighters, was sent to bomb the castle of San Martín de Valdeiglesias, where a tower used by anti-aircraft gunners was successfully demolished. But this 'exploit' was more than offset by the Republicans' loss of three more Dewoitines, based at Barajas, leaving Madrid increasingly defenceless against daily assaults by German Junkers 52s and the even more formidable Italian Savoia 81s. Nor did this 'pin-prick' assault on Valdeiglesias have the slightest impact on operations on the ground, where Franco's forces made a major breakthrough on October 17th by occupying Illescas, on the main Toledo highroad, a mere 25 kilometres south-west of Getafe. Inexorably, an iron ring of hostile forces was being forged around Madrid, leaving the capital with but two connecting lifelines to the Mediterranean coast – one along the highroad via Alcalá de Henares and Guadalajara to Lérida and Barcelona, the other via Arganda and Tarancón to Albacete, Cartagena, Alicante, and Valencia.

It was precisely at this moment, when the Republicans were preparing to evacuate the threatened bases of Getafe and Cuatro Vientos, that their sagging hopes were buoyed by a momentous new development. On October 16th a telegram from Joseph Stalin assured the Central Committee of the Spanish Communist Party that the workers of the Soviet Union would do their utmost to help the revolutionary masses of Spain. The message, given enormous publicity in the next morning's edition of *Mundo Obrero*, created a sensation in Madrid. The Spanish Republic was no longer isolated and ignored by a largely indifferent world; it could count on the material support of at least one friend.

The first train-load of foreign volunteers for the International Brigades had in fact already reached the provincial capital of Albacete as early as

October 14th. Located on a sparsely populated plateau roughly half-way between Don Quixote's La Mancha and the eastern seabord provinces of Murcia and Alicante, Albacete had been chosen as an assembly point and training centre because it was strategically located at the intersection of seven highroads and two railway tracks, linked to the vitally important Mediterranean ports of Valencia, Alicante, and Cartagena, where the Soviets were already beginning to unload guns, tanks, and unassembled aeroplane parts.

Among the first contingent of volunteers for the International Brigades, as Malraux knew, were French aircraft factory workers, some of whom could be transformed overnight into invaluable mechanics for his squadron. After several days spent at Albacete, where the long Los Llanos airfield was soon to become the Republic's foremost training base, Malraux decided to make a quick trip to Paris to find out if the Blum government might now choose to follow Moscow's lead. During the afternoon of October 21st he had a long talk with André Gide, who told him that he had been writing up his impressions of his two-month stay in the Soviet Union, which had ended shortly before Lev Kamenev and Grigori Zinoviev were brought to court, condemned, and executed in the most sensational and troubling 'show trial' Moscow had yet witnessed. When Gide heard that Bernard Groethuysen and the ardently communist Alix Guillain had been invited to dinner at the Rue du Bac apartment, he found a pretext for declining Clara's invitation, probably afraid of being bluntly told that this was no time to be bringing out a book criticizing the Soviet system.

Mme Théo found Malraux unusually glum, and resigned for once to let others do the talking.

He . . . spoke little and his hope of winning seems very relative. Ehrenburg was there, pasty-faced, talkative, indulging in pathology in speaking of the Spaniards, with a certain finesse and glibness, but with too amused, too detached an air, displeasing in someone who has just come back from there . . . This impression of unseemly frivolity was reinforced by Clara Malraux's odalisk-like attitude, receiving her visitors stretched out on her bed and speaking with extraordinary volubility and animation, pathetically magnifiying the dangers run by Malraux and then talking without transition of her feminine successes on the Spanish front – all very embarrassing. The Groets seemed as ill at ease as I was.

There were solid grounds for Malraux's pessimism. When he returned to Madrid on October 22nd, he found that the situation had not improved. An ambitious counter-attack aimed at recapturing Illescas had been repulsed by Franco's Nationalists, and 15,000 Republican soldiers had been pushed back beyond their starting line, so that gunfire could now be clearly heard in the Spanish capital. Yielding to the clamour of his cabinet ministers, Largo Caballero had been forced to remove Asensio Torrado – 'kicked upstairs' as

Under-Secretary for War – and to replace him by General Sebastián Pozas, former commander of the Civil Guard, and by General Miaja, made personally responsible for the defence of Madrid.

Meanwhile Indalecio Prieto, Minister for both Marine and Aviation, had been putting together an Air Force general staff. One result of this belated initiative was the wise decision to shift several of the *escuadrilla*'s bombers from the vulnerable field of Barajas to the long Los Llanos airbase near Albacete. It was from here that three of the squadron's best pilots – Abel Guidez, Victor Véniel, and Jean Darry – took off on October 24th in two Potez 54s and the Bloch 200 for an unescorted night attack on Talavera de la Reina. The operation, calculated to bring the three bombers over the target area just as dawn was breaking, was a total success, resulting in the 'plastering' of the Nationalists' field headquarters and the destruction of a number of Fiat 32 fighters on the ground. But this long-distance blow – the last major victory scored by Malraux's squadron – was answered by a crushing riposte two days later, when a dozen Junkers 52s, escorted by Fiat fighters, smothered Barajas under an avalanche of bombs, destroying five precious Dewoitines and blowing up a fuel tank.

On October 29th Malraux made another quick trip to Paris, probably to see if he could smuggle out a few French machine guns and the necessary ammunition for the Dewoitines. This time Gide was more forthcoming about the controversial book he was preparing for publication under the title, *Retour de l'URSS*. His distinctly negative feelings about the worst aspects of Soviet life, he explained, had been fully shared by all those who had accompanied him to Moscow. However, news about its critical contents had leaked out, and Louis Aragon and Ilya Ehrenburg were moving heaven and earth in an attempt to block its publication. Malraux scoffed at this harassment – 'They've been giving you a bad time, haven't they?' – and urged Gide not to yield to this kind of pressure.

Gide and Mme Théo were both struck by the remarkable change in Malraux's mood. He seemed extraordinarily 'light-hearted, relaxed, smiling' (as she noted in her diary).

What is happening is rather pathetic [he explained to Gide]. Stalin, by having the USSR come out at last for Spain, has stolen Trotsky's thunder and cut the grass out from under his feet. The truth is that in Russia people are absolutely convinced that war is unavoidable, and since the German airforce for the moment is very inferior and the Russian airforce very strong, Stalin thinks the moment would not be ill-chosen for a war.

If this was Stalin's thinking, which is anything but certain, he was unquestionably right. But he was as powerless as was Malraux to budge Léon Blum's Front Populaire government from its paralytic inertia.

On November 4th the Republicans' main fighter airbase at Getafe was overrun by Moroccan soldiers and Spanish Legionnaires, and so too was the second airfield of Cuatro Vientos, on the capital's south-western periphery. Nothing, it seemed, could now save the capital from its fate. General Mola again informed the world that he would soon be riding into Madrid on a white horse. Those who had cars piled suitcases on the roof racks and hurriedly left with as many kin or friends as could be crammed into each vehicle. They included virtually every member of Largo Caballero's government, and even several generals, who now headed south-west on the main road to Valencia. Many Madrileños were wondering why Franco had not cut the road to Arganda and Tarancón, thus blocking the escape route to Valencia. The witty explanation was simple: the route had deliberately been left open to facilitate the exodus of '*los conejos*' (the 'rabbits' of Republican officialdom), fleeing for their lives.

Franco's Nationalists, simultaneously assaulting Madrid from the south, west and north-west, were now so close that they could track the heavy Potez bombers from the moment they took off from their new airbase at Alcalá de Henares, 35 kilometres to the north-east. The attacking forces, furthermore, were protected by formidable anti-aircraft batteries. After seeing a Republican bomber ahead of him split in two by an anti-aircraft burst, spilling out its helpless crewmen like seeds from an overripe pomegranate, François Bourgeois, the erstwhile bootleg smuggler, decided he had had enough. Slipping into the clouds to elude the deadly flak, he returned to Alcalá with both his bomber and his bombs intact.

Malraux's relations with his squadron-mates had up till now been pleasantly informal. There was no saluting, no drillwork, no standing at attention, no raising and lowering of flags, there was no 'rank pulling' – the form of address used by most being the comradely *tu* rather than the more formal *vous*. Nor was there anything remotely resembling a court martial procedure for misdemeanours. The only sanction was immediate repatriation. This was the punishment Malraux now had to impose. Faced by a mutinous recalcitrance which threatened to demoralize the squadron, Malraux sent the mulish pilot and his crewmen straight back to France – a scene melodramatically described in his later novel, *L'Espoir* (where the disgruntled Bourgeois became the sheepish as well as insolent Leclerc).

On the evening of November 5th the American journalist, Louis Fischer, was walking past the large plate glass window of the Gran Vía Hotel when he saw Malraux seated alone inside, a frown furrowing his forehead, a cigarette dangling from his lips.

'What's the situation?' asked Fischer, who as the European correspondent for the left-wing weekly, *The Nation*, had met André and Clara during their stay in Moscow in 1934.

'The enemy is at Carabanchel Alto,' (a southern suburb of Madrid) answered Malraux crisply.

'How do you know?'

'We bombed them there this morning.'

'What do you think I should do?' asked Fischer, loath to abandon the Madrileños at this desperate moment.

'Get out quickly,' advised Malraux. 'Get a car. If you can't get one, I'll fly you out to the provinces tomorrow morning. But first, you'll have to go bombing with us.'

Louis Fischer finally declined the invitation, preferring to leave Madrid by car, along with the former *Reichswehr* officer, Ludwig Renn, who after his release from a German prison had decided to volunteer for service with one of the International Brigades.

From Alcalá de Henares, now a Soviet airbase, Malraux and his squadron-mates were reassigned to Albacete, from there to another airfield, and finally to La Señera-Chiva, located amid orange groves 30 kilometres west of Valencia. In effect, the squadron was being downgraded to employment on fronts of secondary importance. The aerial defence of Madrid was hence-forth entrusted to Soviet fighter planes and bombers, which had shown what they could do on October 30th, when three swift SB-2 ('Katiuska') bombers, with a top speed of 400 kilometres per hour (90 kph more than the Potez 54), pounded the rebels' airfield at Talavera, outracing the Heinkel and Fiat fighters, which vainly sought to intercept them.

The Soviet military advisers could now call the shots as they pleased. They had little trouble persuading Antonio Camacho, the Under-Secretary for Air, to have the *escuadrilla España* dissolved and then incorporated under another name into the Spanish Air Force. Although *el coronel* retained his lieutenant-colonel's rank and his position as the unit's official commander, the squadron lost all of its previous freebooting autonomy. From now on, all foreign pilots, machine gunners, and bombardiers were paid monthly wages closer to those of their Spanish counterparts. Malraux was not surprised to see a number of 'mercenaries' quit. But one or two of them – including Jean Darry, the distinguished stolen-car disguiser – loyally opted to stay on as less lavishly paid 'volunteers'.

Towards the middle of December the Thirteenth International Brigade began an offensive in the wild, mountainous country around Teruel with the aim of reducing the military pressure on Madrid. Malraux's squadron was called upon to support this Republican offensive by effecting daily missions over Teruel.

For ten days or more all went well, but two days after Christmas the stretch of good luck was abruptly terminated by a double catastrophe. As one of the Potez 54s was taking off from the airfield of La Señera, an engine failed and Jean Darry had to make a crash landing, which wrecked the bomber. All members of the crew were injured, including Malraux, a self-appointed gunner, who suffered cuts on his nose, throat, and chest.

The other Potez 54, which had no trouble getting off the ground, successfully unloaded two tons of bombs on its Teruel targets. But as it was returning to its base, escorted by Russian fighters, it was pounced on by a group of Heinkel 51s, which riddled it with bullets, killing one of the gunners, wounding several others, and knocking out a motor. Beneath the stricken bomber was an awesome landscape of yawning gorges and rocky slopes, from which there seemed no escape. But spotting a patch of snowy summit, the pilot, Marcel Florein, headed for it. The crunchy snow cushioned the shock of the crash-landing, as the disintegrating fuselage ploughed its way across the expanse of whiteness. The bombardier and two gunners were severely wounded, and one of them, Raymond Maréchal, whose passion for the Spanish Republic was equalled only by his passion for members of the fair sex, was so disfigured – with a fractured jaw, a smashed nose and a hideously bloodstained face – that Florein had great trouble dissuading him from blowing out his brains with his Spanish Army pistol.

Back at La Señera, Malraux and his squadron-mates were alarmed by the Potez bomber's failure to return. Finally he received a call from Spanish Air Force officials, saying that the Potez 54 had crashed in the mountains somewhere in the region of Mora de Rubielos, 40 kilometres south-east of Teruel. Malraux immediately set out in a car to see if he could locate the wreck and possibly rescue any survivors. The drive took him past orange groves and cypress trees and up the coastal road from Valencia as far as the ruined fortress walls of Sagunto. Turning inland, they then headed up into the mountains, the orange groves soon giving way to clumps of hardy oaks. Stopping in several towns to make telephone calls, Malraux learned that there were indeed survivors and that they had been located by shepherds from the mountain village of Valdelinares, which was virtually inaccessible except by mule.

His subsequent account of this rescue operation, involving a three-hour ascent over rocky pathways with peasant stretcher bearers – into the very heart of a 'timeless Spain' – was, in terms of scenic description, one of the finest sections of his novel, *L'Espoir*. The expedition, which enabled him to rescue the two pilots, the bombardier and the gunners – including the hideously disfigured Raymond Maréchal, destined to become one of his most loyal companions in other crisis situations – also provided epic material for an extraordinary film. But the simultaneous loss of two Potez bombers left the squadron crippled and was enough to convince Spanish Air Force officials (not all of whom were admirers of Malraux) that he could best serve the Spanish Republic in other ways.

27

Sierra de Teruel

At 3 o'clock in the morning of January 5th, 1937, André Malraux was being driven from the War Ministry in Valencia back to La Señera when, briefly illuminated by the headlights, an extraordinary menagerie loomed out of the darkness: fantastic shapes which, in their spectral gaiety, seemed to sum up the eery unreality of this war. It was the Epiphany, as he later wrote, 'the Feast of the Three Kings, the great festival of the children of Spain . . .' For the past week workshop artisans had been busy every night making card-board figures inspired by traditional playing-card characters, along with twelve-foot figures of Mickey Mouse and Felix the Cat.

As Malraux soon discovered, the phantasmagoric unreality of life in Valencia was matched by the make-believe unreality of the political atmo-sphere in Paris, where, in a New Year's Eve broadcast, Prime Minister Léon Blum had expressed the pious hope that 1937 might be a 'peaceful year' and 'prepare long peaceful years after it' – without once mentioning the inter-national conflict now raging in Spain. Britain's Conservative government had just reached a 'gentlemen's agreement' with Mussolini's Italy to respect the 'status quo' in Ethiopia, in the apparent belief that this would prompt a grateful *Duce* to withdraw his airmen and soldiers from Spain. Not to be outdone, the French government was about to introduce a resolution banning further recruitment and dispatch of volunteers to Spain, on the grounds (explained by Blum to the Chamber of Deputies' Foreign Affairs Committee) that what had been started in the chivalrous spirit of a La Fayette, a Lord Byron, a Garibaldi, had assumed such proportions that it seriously threatened the peace of Europe.

The Left Bank, meanwhile, was in a state of uproar, occasioned by the recent publication of André Gide's less than rhapsodic *Retour de l'URSS*. Overnight the former intellectual idol of *L'Humanité*, who had refused to follow the example of Romain Rolland, George Bernard Shaw, Julian Huxley, Upton Sinclair, Sean O'Casey, Harold Lasky and so many others in expressing a slavish admiration of the Soviet Union, the iconoclast who had dared to assert, 'I doubt that in any country today, even in Hitler's Germany, the spirit is less free, more cringing, more fearful (terrorized), more vassalized,' had become an apostate, a 'traitor to the cause', a Judas Iscariot.

On January 16th Malraux had lunch with Gide and the now vehemently anti-Stalinist Pierre Herbart, whom Gide had all too casually sent to Spain in November with the proofs of *Retour de l'URSS*, which he wanted Malraux to read. The mere fact that Herbart had accompanied Gide to Moscow had made him so suspect in Madrid that the omnipotent Soviets had virtually placed him under house arrest at their Palace Hotel headquarters. The impetuous Herbart now asked Malraux point-blank what he thought of Gide's book on the Soviet Union. Embarrassed to be asked this question in the presence of the master, Malraux felt forced to agree with those who felt that the book's publication was inopportune at a moment when Stalin and the Soviet Union were coming to the rescue of the Spanish Republic.

His return to Paris also coincided with two troublesome developments. The first was a highly partisan press campaign launched by the arch-conservative writer, Robert Brasillach, against Malraux and the *escuadrilla España*, accused of having in early December shot down a French embassy mail-plane on a routine flight from Madrid to Toulouse. Malraux could have shrugged all this off as cheap journalistic froth, had he been able to leave, as planned, for the United States, where he was due to make speeches on behalf of the Spanish Republic. But on January 17th he was notified by the US Consulate in Paris that his visa application had not been approved by the State Department in Washington. He had to cancel his transatlantic steamship reservation and dash off a telegram to *The Nation*, which had invited him to be the guest of honour at a banquet due to be held in New York on January 28th. The outraged editors of *The Nation* promised to take the matter up with the Secretary of State, Cordell Hull.

The second troublesome development – for those, like Malraux, who felt grateful to Stalin for his support of the Spanish Republic – was another thunderbolt from Moscow, announcing the start of a new show trial – this time involving Grigori Sokolnikov, a former Commissar of Finance and ambassador to London, and Karl Radek, who was accused not only of being a Trotskyist but also of having maintained a criminal correspondence with Hitler's associate, Rudolf Hess!

Throughout these hectic autumn and early winter weeks André had been trying to reassure a worried Josette by sending her hastily scribbled notes and telegrams dispatched from Albacete, Valencia, Barcelona. Once or twice he had arranged to see her for a few hours in Toulouse. Like Clara, Josette had been pestering him to give up his perilous life in Spain. She wanted him to return to writing – without which, she felt, he would 'go mad'. She had suggested that they find a 'little inn in a lovely spot with a river' somewhere in the Périgord region of south-western France, where he could work in peace.

Malraux, however, was in no mood to relax. The dream of rustic tranquillity was impatiently brushed aside. Instead, André offered Josette something quite different: a semi-clandestine trip to the United States, where he had to give lectures and speak at fund-raising dinners on behalf of a volunteer American ambulance corps, to be recruited for Spanish Republican forces in the field. If eyebrows were raised or questions asked, he could pass her off as his secretarial assistant.

Although this was not quite the 'holiday' she had been looking forward to, Josette was elated at the prospect of having André to herself for a few weeks. Both seem to have derived an almost childish delight from the concoction of a little plot designed to keep Clara in the dark. Josette's accomplice was her journalist friend, Suzanne Chantal, who agreed to accompany her as far as Southampton on the *Paris*, which was to sail from there to New York. They took an early train to Le Havre, preceding the more elegant boat train by several hours. André's accomplice was his friend 'Eddy' Corniglion-Molinier, who, unaware of this wise precaution, accompanied Clara and André to the Gare Saint-Lazare in Paris with some anxiety, afraid that the two women – the lawful wife and the clandestine mistress – might meet on the station platform and create a hideous scene.

On February 26th, two days after his arrival in New York, Malraux delivered his first major speech at a banquet thrown for him by the left-wing weekly, *The Nation*. The dinner was attended by liberal and left-wing luminaries of Manhattan's intelligentsia, who, unlike the vast majority of indifferent, uncomprehending, or frankly hostile Americans, were fervent supporters of the Spanish Republic.

In this, as in other speeches, Malraux relied on anecdotes and brief descriptive scenes to dramatize the message he was intent on getting across. The young critic, Alfred Kazin, who heard him speak at a large meeting sponsored by the North American Committee to Aid Spanish Democracy, was left spellbound by the evocative force of Malraux's imagery in conjuring up 'the suffering and heroism of Spanish Republicans in stabbing phrases that had driven the agony of Spain like nails into our flesh . . . He spoke with such fire that his body itself seemed to be speaking the most glorious French.'

On March 12th – after five public appearances in New York, one in Washington, another in Philadelphia, and one at both Harvard and Princeton universities – Malraux and Josette Clotis left the eastern seaboard, flying across the continent in giant grasshopper leaps from city to city in Douglas' latest model: the DC–3. In Los Angeles he gave two speeches, one of them at a fund-raising dinner attended by many film directors, scriptwriters, actors and actresses. Lillian Hellmann threw a party for him in her Beverly Hills home. Josette, who had hoped to catch a glimpse of Greta Garbo or Joan Crawford, was bitterly disappointed. Edward G. Robinson and a curiously timid Boris Karloff ('Malraux scares me!') were, as far as she was concerned, unappealing substitutes.

From Los Angeles they flew north to San Francisco, returning to the eastern seaboard via Montreal. In all, Malraux managed to raise close to $40,000 – enough to finance the purchase of forty ambulances for his Spanish Republican friends.

This otherwise successful trip was jarred by an unpleasant clash with his former idol, Trotsky. Malraux provoked it by most imprudently declaring during his speech at *The Nation*'s fund-raising banquet: 'Trotsky is a moral force in the world, but Stalin has lent dignity to mankind; and just as the Inquisition did not detract from the fundamental dignity of Christianity, so the Moscow trials do not detract from the fundamental dignity of Communism.' For once his love of dazzling associations had got the better of his common sense; for this justification of Stalin's inquisitorial methods in the name of a 'fundamental dignity' so lofty that it could not be affected by even the most shocking travesties of truth and justice was bound to offend everybody, including orthodox Stalinists, less than pleased to see their Kremlin idol compared to Torquemada.

On March 1st Malraux agreed to be interviewed in the office of his Random House editor, Robert Haas, by a journalist working for Mexico City's *El Nacional*. Nettled by the reporter's insistence on questioning him about Trotsky, he finally lost patience: 'I want to tell you that the fate of mankind is at present being decided in Spain and that we must set intellectual considerations aside, so as to devote ourselves wholeheartedly to defending and assisting the Spanish people. It is almost criminal to waste hours, entire months speculating on matters that can wait until later . . .'

The moment Trotsky read the Spanish text of this interview and in particular the sentence in which the Moscow show trials, intended to destroy him, were dismissed as being purely 'intellectual considerations', he erupted. The result was a long United Press dispatch in which Malraux was accused, among other things, of being responsible for the

> strangling of the Chinese Revolution. Malraux is organically incapable of moral independence; he is official by birth. In New York he issued an appeal to forget everything except the Spanish Revolution . . . Malraux himself left Spain for the purpose of conducting a campaign in the United States in defense of the judicial work of Stalin and Vyshinsky.

These wild accusations, issued by an embittered Old Bolshevik who had been forced to flee from a hostile Europe to seek refuge in distant Mexico, were so absurd that there is no need to quote any of André Malraux's rebuttal, published alongside an abridged version of Trotsky's fulminations in the March 27th issue of *The Nation*. The acrimonious debate honoured neither of the two participants, and it had the unfortunate result, in Malraux's case, of closing his mind to the outrages being committed, not only in Stalin's USSR, but also in Largo Caballero's helpless Republic by an increasingly omnipotent swarm of NKVD agents.

On April 19th, when Malraux returned to Paris, casually dropping off a mortified Josette at the Hôtel du Louvre while he returned to his 'home' on the Rue du Bac, André Gide found himself confronted by an 'integral Stalinist, even in the matter of the [Moscow] trials'. However, Josette Clotis' fear that she was again going to be relegated to the role of a 'backstreet mistress' turned out to be exaggerated. On May 5th, when 'Oncle André' lunched with his younger namesake, he begged him to concentrate on his new novel and not to get sucked into new Spanish adventures, like that of his bomber squadron, which might cost him his life. 'But haven't you understood,' Malraux immediately retorted, 'that one of the reasons that kept me in Spain was a desire to flee my home?'

Limited to secret trysts at the Hôtel du Louvre, André's double life would have been a source of continuing exasperation for Josette had she not re-established contact with her journalist friend, Suzanne Chantal. Suzanne, as it happened, was in a similar emotional predicament. The two of them decided to set up house together with a third woman partner named Jeanne, an unhappily married Belgian who had begun an affair with a man who, like Malraux, could only make periodic visits to his beloved. Much amused by this ingenious solution to a common problem, André found an exotic name for their well cushioned habitat: it was, he explained, a '*zenana*' – the Persian equivalent of the Arabic or Turkish harem.

It was in this relatively tranquil nook that André Malraux began writing his Spanish Civil War novel. As usual, he wrote it in longhand, in a small and sometimes almost undeciferable script, which Josette then typed up for him, chapter by chapter.

Through much of the month of June, however, there were multiple distractions. It had been decided that the next Congress of the International Writers Association for the Defence of Culture would be held in Spain. To the Spanish members of the executive committee, José Bergamín and the Communist poet Rafael Alberti, it seemed vitally important that the congress should not be postponed, notwithstanding the civil war and even though the Republican government had moved from Madrid to Valencia.

A convoy of requisitioned automobiles was waiting to transport the foreign authors to Barcelona, and from there to Valencia, where they were welcomed by the new prime minister, Juan Negrín, the influential Alvarez del Vayo, and his successor as foreign minister, José Giral. The intended aim of the congress was to discuss the attitude that responsible intellectuals should adopt toward the anti-fascist war in Spain. The most trenchant reply to this question was delivered by the former *Reichswehr* officer, Ludwig Renn: 'The role of writers fighting for Liberty does not consist of writing stories but of making history' – a recommendation he was entitled to make as the recently appointed commander of an International Brigade, but which, Malraux perhaps excepted, no other writer present could subscribe to. Nor did they make much of an effort in this respect. As was later noted by Ilya Ehrenburg, who turned up with two of the Soviet Union's most skilful literary opportunists, Alexei Tolstoy and Alexander Fadeyev, 'at times it seemed that the war did not exist and that we were attending an ordinary PEN-Club congress'.

Indeed, the congress's primary purpose was soon overshadowed by another preoccupation: the need to flail the scandalous apostasy of André Gide. His *Retour de l'URSS* was, predictably, condemned by Tolstoy and Fadeyev, lampooned with clever parodies by the sharp-witted Mikhail Koltsov, and denounced, along with its successor (*Retouches à mon "Retour de l'URSS"*), as an attack on the Russian people by José Bergamín.

The outstanding figure at the congress, at any rate for the English poet Stephen Spender, who found him a spellbinding conversationalist

was undoubtedly André Malraux. In 1937 he had the air of a battered youth, with a face jutting pallidly over his intently crouching body as he looked at his audience. He wore a tweed suit into whose trouser pockets he thrust his hands . . . He made an art of exposition. He could take ideas, express them as images, and set them before the mind's eye.

Although Spender was delighted to be able to meet men like Rafael Alberti, 'a kind of baroque Communist', the whimsical José Bergamín, and the 'pure' poet Antonio Machado, he soon came to feel that

the Congress, with all its good qualities, had something of a spoiled children's party, something which brought out the worst in many delegates.

This circus of intellectuals, treated like princes or ministers, carried for hundred of miles through . . . war-torn towns, to the sound of cheering voices, amid broken hearts, riding in Rolls-Royces, banqueted, fêted, sung and danced to, had something grotesque about it.

For from Valencia the congress soon moved to Madrid – so rapidly, indeed, that Malraux and Ehrenburg were almost killed by their reckless Spanish driver.

In Valencia the July heat had been tempered by sea breezes. But in Madrid there was no relief from the scorching sun, which beat down mercilessly on the rubble-strewn streets. Even the nights, spent behind drawn blinds or curtains because of the wartime blackout, were suffocatingly torrid, and disturbed by thumps and rumblings of not-so-distant artillery fire.

Another disturbing factor was the recent exposure in Moscow of yet another anti-Stalin 'plot' – this time hatched by Marshal Tukhachevsky, Yakir, Uborevich, and other high-ranking Soviet officers, with the incredible connivance of Nazi agents and members of the German General Staff. Like well trained parrots, the Soviet writers present (with but one exception) proceeded to denounce these 'traitors' and 'enemies of the people'. The Spaniards were understandably perplexed, saying to Ehrenburg: 'We believed that twenty years after the Revolution the generals were marching side by side with the people, but now we see that it's the same with you as it is with us.'

From Madrid the 'travelling congress' of writers moved on by road to Barcelona. Here there was another big meeting. Each delegate's speech was followed by a Catalan translation and preceded by the playing of the orator's national anthem – with the comic result that when it was Stephen Spender's turn to speak, the orchestra played 'God save the King' while all present rose to their feet brandishing clenched fists.

This was not, as it happened, the finale to this tragi-comic exercise in intellectual fatuity. It had been decided that this Second International Writers Congress should be concluded in Paris, where the Association had been founded two years before. Leaving their requisitioned Rolls-Royces and Hispano-Suizas at the frontier town of Port-Bou, several Spanish writers accompanied the other delegates to the French capital in a special luxury train composed entirely of *wagons-lits*: one more shocking contrast with the sorrows and sufferings being endured by the stoic Spanish people, whom these itinerant intellectuals had come to encourage . . . once again with words.

Taking leave of his anti-Fascist 'comrades', Malraux took the train back to Perpignan, where he found Josette Clotis waiting for him with her friend Suzanne Chantal. They had found a chalet in the small Pyrenean watering-spa of Vernet-les-Bains, 65 kilometres inland from the Mediterranean, in a landscape of verdant hills, pine trees, gushing streams and mountain torrents, dominated to the south-east by the soaring summit of the 2,780-metre-high Canigou. And it was in this secluded, idyllically sylvan retreat that André Malraux wrote *L'Espoir*.

Of all his novels, *L'Espoir*, which he had virtually completed by the end of September, was the longest, the richest, the most varied and diffuse, but also, it must be said, the roughest, the most uneven, and in some places, the most clumsily written. But these were not accidental flaws; they were deliberately willed by an impatient author who had a tough message to deliver and who was not interested in the stylistic perfection and 'objectivity' of Flaubert. Based on a wealth of personal experiences far exceeding any he had previously possessed, this was a *roman de combat* (a fighting novel), in which the frantic horrors of modern industrialized warfare were expressed in sharp, brittle sentences. Whence the fairly frequent resort to vulgarisms – like *gueuler* (to yell), instead of the tamer *crier* or *hurler* (to cry or to shout) – used not in speech but in descriptions of men in action. The warlike world of *L'Espoir* was not that of Tolstoy; it was far closer to that of Louis-Ferdinand Céline's *Voyage au bout de la nuit*.

According to Wilbur Frohock (perhaps the first to make a detailed count), *L'Espoir* was composed, almost cinematographically, of 146 scene-units, grouped into 58 chapters. We have Suzanne Chantal's word for it that

Malraux had already thought of making a film out of his Spanish Civil War experiences before he began the novel. But what was perhaps even more significant, offering a foretaste of the non-novelistic works that were to follow, were the revealing traces of artistic, rather than simply cinematographic, influences. Here, for example, is a dense description of the visual impression made by a cigarette lighter ignited for a barely visible peasant in the evening gloom: 'From the neighbour to his right the short flame pulled a bean-like face, the nose and mouth ill-defined between the jutting chin and forehead.' This suddenly illuminated profile, which is what Malraux meant by 'bean-like face', almost certainly owed more to Gérard Dou or Caravaggio than to Charlie Chaplin, Max Linder, or Dovzhenko.

At times, with an exasperating intermingling of the concrete and abstract, the complex imagery was left deliberately tangled and obscure, leaving the reader to unravel the various elements, as in a Cubist painting:

Up there, in the shadows, the Spanish palaces of banks and insurance companies, and a little further down all the colonial pomp of ministries set sail into time and into the night, with extravagant hearses, the chandeliers of clubs, the girandoles and the galleon-flags suspended in the courtyard of the Navy Ministry, immobile in this airless night.

Just what the 'extravagant hearses' were doing in this kaleidoscopic jumble is not clear, but this is how a Robert Delaunay or a Juan Gris might have recorded nocturnal impressions of Madrid if either had chosen to live there.

When to these visual impressions was added the element of noise, the results were at times so convoluted as to sound almost like parodies of Malraux's worst stylistic 'ticks'. Consider, for example, this sentence describing the former statue-and-armour-filled Museum of Santa Cruz in Toledo, transformed into a guard-room and makeshift military hospital with brick walls pierced by bullets: 'The sound of radios lost somewhere in the depths of the dazzling light from outdoors seemed to enter through the bullet holes and to wrap itself around Pancho Villa, asleep in the middle of the rifles under his extraordinary hat.' In sentences like this one has the feeling that Malraux the aesthete was waging a secret war against Malraux the *écrivain engagé* (the committed writer), and that the message he wished to get across – the need for revolutionary discipline if the Spanish Republic was to survive – could have been more powerfully conveyed by paring away some of the sophisticated dross.

In August or early September – by which time a large part of the novel had been written – André left Josette and Suzanne Chantal in the Pyrenees and went to see Clara, who was spending the summer with Florence near the seaport of Toulon, east of Marseilles. He felt the need to read the text to someone who was truly interested in politics, who shared his left-wing inclinations, and who was intelligent enough to understand the novel's philosophical nuances. By this time most of their wild hopes were shattered.

Léon Blum's Front Populaire government had been replaced by one headed by Camille Chautemps, the Radical Socialist who more than any other had imposed the flagrantly violated policy of 'non-intervention'. The Soviet-inspired offensive against Brunete had proved a costly failure, and Franco's Nationalist forces were now snuffing out the last pockets of Republican resistance in Asturias and Bilbao. More than ever, the Spanish Republic's hope of survival depended on Soviet aid. Clara, however, was frankly dismayed by what she read. This was not the work of the questioning, obstinately nonconformist, courageously Trotskyist André Malraux she had known; this was a novel about the war in Spain, viewed through the eyes of an orthodox Communist. Her own feelings resembled those of Nicola Chiaromonte, who had one day said to her that the Spanish anarchists were troublesome enough, but that the Communists were even more insufferable. Malraux was so shaken by her arguments – so at least she claimed in the fifth volume of her memoirs – that he prolonged his stay in Toulon by four days, remarking wistfully, during their last meal together, that he couldn't spend all of his life 'with a woman who has no taste for ideas' – by which was clearly meant Josette.

In late September Malraux returned to Paris with a typed manuscript. André Gide, who went to see him in his small NRF office, found him 'kinder, more affectionate than ever', and in one respect unchanged – 'speaking four times too fast, four times too intelligently', with the result that Gide had trouble understanding why José Bergamín had attacked him at the Writers Congress in July, whereas the Dutch Communist Jef Last had refused to do so.

In October Malraux made another quick trip to Barcelona and Madrid, to find out if he could still call his novel *L'Espoir*. From Toulouse he imprudently put in a long-distance call to Josette, to say that he would be back in Paris in a day or two. Deaf to the objections of her friend Suzanne Chantal, Josette hastily packed a bag. She had just discovered she was pregnant and wasn't going to let another day go by before announcing the 'good news' to André. At the station she was told that there were no places left in the *wagons-lits*, and she had to make the long night trip seated uncomfortably. The next morning she reached Toulouse, looking clearly unwell. André rushed her back to Paris. At the Hôtel des Grands Hommes, near the Panthéon, where Stendhal, Balzac, Blasco Ibañez, and André Breton had once lived, her friend Suzanne found Josette looking deathly pale. She had just suffered a haemorrhage. Several hours later she was driven to a clinic in the western suburb of Neuilly, where she underwent a curretage.

Her father had chosen this moment to come to Paris and he very much wanted to see his daughter. Weak though she was, Josette was hastily brought back to the Hôtel des Grands Hommes, where Malraux was posted at the entrance to intercept M. Clotis before he could ask for Josette at the porter's desk (where she was not registered under her own name). 'We're playing *The Marriage of Figaro*,' André remarked with a wink to the real-life Suzanne. With an ingenuity worthy of Count Almaviva's resourceful major domo, he steered M. Clotis past the porter's desk and up to Josette's room, where he found his daughter looking unnaturally pale but seemingly contented, amid a casual welter of women's magazines, books and perfume bottles.

In terms of emotional stress this November, when the first prepublication extracts from *L'Espoir* were serialized in Louis Aragon's afternoon daily *Ce Soir*, was one of the most painful André Malraux had ever endured. To pacify Josette he informed Clara that he no longer wished to live with her and wanted a divorce. They went to see a lawyer, but came away appalled by the sordid 'evidence' (incriminating letters, etc) needed to satisfy the magistrate. Clara, for her part, was not yet psychologically resigned to the idea of losing André forever. Throughout this troubled period she kept bombarding him with desperately worded notes, attesting to a mood of deep depression. Far from keeping her marital woes to herself, she made them an open secret. Languidly stretched out on the living room couch of the Rue du Bac flat, she assumed the tragic air of a recently bereaved widow, or, as Henriette Nizan later put it, 'of one of Louis XIV's abandoned mistresses'.

To keep Josette distracted, André persuaded her to accompany her friend Suzanne Chantal on a journalistic assignment to Scandinavia. He himself remained behind in Paris to ponder the reviews of *L'Espoir*, which began falling like thick flakes of snow throughout the wintry month of January 1938. Almost invariably, the novel was judged according to the reviewer's political orientation. Writing in *Ce Soir*, Malraux's friend Paul Nizan declared categorically that *L'Espoir* was a 'great book'. The Stalinist Georges Friedmann was equally unstinting in his praise: 'If, in his previous novels and even in *La Condition humaine*, Malraux revealed a too purely intellectual, at times Nietzschean tension, his new book, which makes no concession to facile emotions, resounds with fraternal echoes that were already announced in *Le Temps du Mépris*, but which are here far more sustained.'

In the conservative *Le Temps*, the novelist André Thérive, often critical in the past, was torn between his irritation with Malraux's 'elliptic speeches', his 'peremptory dialogues', certain of the characters in *L'Espoir*, and his admiration for the words exchanged between old Alvear and Scali in a scene which is unquestionably one of the high points of the novel: 'There is nothing in them that is not brilliant, original. An exceptional talent and an anything but mediocre mind are here revealed . . . The ideas sparkle and crackle in all directions . . . The pleasure is very lively when Malraux lets his thinking, always sharp and subtle, foam and fizz.'

In a second book review devoted to *L'Espoir* in France's leading literary weekly, *Les Nouvelles Littéraires* – in itself an indication of the novel's explosive impact – Louis Gillet expressed stylistic reservations about this strange and beautiful book . . . I cannot say that it really delights me as a work of art, or that I much care for its incoherent and jerky manner, the tough, wild characterizations, the gallopade of jostling images, as on a cinema screen . . . Yet how can one escape the strange impression of fervour, the arid fever emanating from these pages? . . . One is amazed, in this book of communist inspiration, by the total absence of questions of interest, of questions of wages, in short, of the paraphernalia of Marxist thinking . . . The famous 'historical materialism', which is the warhorse of Party doctrinaires, has been returned to the stable, like a puffing nag . . . It is exclusively a question of honour. It is a question of a revolt of human dignity, of an insult that must be avenged; the class struggle (another word Malraux does not use) is not so much the conquest of power as the revolt of long humiliated conscious beings, who can no longer endure scorn.

The most caustic review of all came from the pen of Robert Brasillach. In the ultra-monarchist *Action Française* he rubbed his hands gleefully over the frankness with which the author of *L'Espoir* had exposed the dissensions between anarchists and communists, thereby proving that 'the revolutionary cause . . . is a lost cause . . . Just between ourselves, if this novel had been composed by a Hitlero-Japanese, a lubricious viper, a Trotskyist dog, a jackal of the POUM, or by an anarcho-fascist, it could certainly not be more harmful to the cause it wishes to defend.'

Amid this blizzard of reviews André's half-brother Roland returned from Moscow with several pieces of bad news. He had been unable to persuade Eisenstein to continue working on a filmed version of *La Condition humaine*. Like every other creative artist in the Soviet Union, Eisenstein was now trying to make himself as inconspicuous as possible, in the hope that Yezhov's NKVD would not find some criminal 'flaw' in his work warranting his arrest and interrogation. Stalin, who had never much cared for his films of the 1920s, had recently vetoed the projection of *Byezhin Looki* (The Meadows of Byezhi), in which Eisenstein had wanted to express his strong anti-nazi feelings. He had managed to redeem himself in the paranoiac dictator's eyes by finding a suitably 'heroic' subject – the story of Alexander Nevsky's great victory over the Teutonic Knights at the battle of Lake Peipus in the thirteenth century – which suited his own anti-German feelings as well as the aims of Soviet foreign policy. The fact that Malraux had publicly quarrelled with Trotsky was a point in his favour, but it had not escaped the vigilance of the watch dogs in Moscow that, unlike Louis Aragon, José Bergamín and many others, he had not uttered a word of public protest against Gide's anti-Soviet books.

The second piece of bad news was that Vsevolod Meyerhold, who had so cordially received André and Clara in his home during their Moscow stay in 1934, had just had his famous TIM theatre company dissolved on the grounds that the plays he had been putting on were 'alien to Soviet art'. Overnight anti-Meyerhold committees had sprung up 'spontaneously' in virtually every theatre in the Soviet Union. Boris Pilnyak, who had tried to write a conformist novel (*The Volga Flows into the Caspian*), to save his skin, had been attacked the previous May for 'counter-revolutionary writing' before being arrested; since then no one knew what had happened to him. Isaak Babel was now afraid of suffering the same fate. When he heard that Roland Malraux was getting ready to leave Moscow – where the handsome Roland had made many glamorous 'conquests' in the world of actresses and ballerinas – he had hurriedly left his dacha in the writers' village of Peredelkino and come to see him. Stalin's drinking pal, the swashbuckling ex-cavalryman, Semyon Budyonny, had never forgiven Babel for the rollicking short stories he had written about his Civil War experiences while serving in his cavalry army. Nor apparently was Stalin any readier to forgive him for having written up the life of a certain Caucasian revolutionary for whom Yosif Vissarionovich Djugashvili felt a strong antipathy: so strong indeed that he had bluntly told the author: 'This will be published in thirty years, but not before.' Babel had come to the conclusion that his only chance of surviving would be to be allowed to 'take a trip abroad' (like Yevgheny Zamyatin, author of the unorthodox novel, *We*). He therefore had a message he wanted Roland Malraux to transmit orally to his half-brother. Could André please write a personal letter to Stalin, urgently requesting Babel's presence at some kind of pro-Soviet conference in Paris?

When Roland's friend, Abidine Dino, a Turkish artist who had left Moscow a week or two before him, called on André at his NRF office with this message from Babel, Malraux assured him that he would write, as requested, to Stalin. In Spain, and not least in *L'Espoir*, serialized in Louis Aragon's Stalinist *Ce Soir*, Malraux had, in the name of military efficiency, clearly favoured the Communists over the undisciplined anarchists. But he may equally well have decided that a personal intervention, given his well-known friendship with Gide, might do Babel more harm than good.

The news from Moscow did, however, have one immediate effect. It spurred Malraux's determination to make a film of his own. In his small, often smoke-filled den, on an upper floor of the NRF–Gallimard publishing company, he had carefully preserved several film reels – notably of Robert Wiene's *The Cabinet of Dr Caligari* and F. W. Murnau's *Nosferatu* – two silent masterpieces of German Expressionist experimentation which he had managed to obtain during a trip to Berlin with Clara. Forming a metallic pedestal for one of his 'Graeco-Buddhist' heads, they were tokens of his passion for avant-garde films. Now, he decided, was the time to take the plunge.

When Josette Clotis returned from her brief tour of Scandinavia, she found André already engrossed in the preparation of a scenario for his planned film on the Spanish Civil War. Since filmed battle scenes are prohibitively expensive, Malraux had decided to concentrate on two specific episodes in the wartime history of his squadron: the bomber attack on the secret rebel airfield near Olmedo, discovered by a humble Castilian peasant, and the crash-landing on the snow-covered mountain top near Teruel – two events which, in reality, were chronologically separated by several months, but which, in *L'Espoir*, Malraux had welded into a single sequence.

Over the Easter holidays he took Josette to the town of Moulins, north of Vichy, where seven copies of the shooting script were typed up by a wonderfully co-operative, though often harassed, Josette.

The problem of finding a producer was quickly solved thanks to Edouard Corniglion-Molinier, who had set up a film production company with the help of two gifted professionals: Roland Tual, deputy director of Pathé Films, and his script-writing wife, Denise. Close friends of Emmanuel Berl, they also became good friends of André Malraux. Corniglion, at this moment, had invested all of his capital in a curious scenario, adapted by the talented Denise Tual from an English novel and involving an extraordinary trio: an ageing, less than innocent 'scientist', his eccentric wife, and a lecherous Anglican prelate, who was making advances to her – in, of all places, a Soho hotel. With Michel Simon slated to play the role of the crackpot 'scientist', Louis Jouvet that of the scheming prelate, and Françoise Rosay that of the eccentric wife, Corniglion felt that he had a 'winner', particularly since the comic dialogue was being written by a gifted young poet – Jacques Prévert. All Corniglion and Tual could offer Malraux for his film was their professional expertise. For the financing he would have to approach the Spanish government.

One day, without a word of warning to Josette, Malraux left Paris for Spain. In Barcelona, now the capital of Juan Negrín's Communist-dominated regime, Malraux was told that the hard-pressed Spanish Republican government was prepared to invest 100,000 francs and 750,000 pesetas towards the financing of the film, provided it was shot in Spain with Spanish actors.

Malraux had to improvise almost everything from scratch. Finding a studio proved no easy matter. The Spanish film industry was a good ten years behind the French. Of the three studios available in Barcelona, Malraux chose one located on the heights of Montjuich, five kilometres from the centre of the city. But it was so poorly equipped that almost everything, including floodlight lamps, had to be brought in from France.

Malraux's chief Spanish assistant, recommended to him by the Ministry of Public Education, was the invaluable Max Aub, a playwright who had served as secretary-general for the Republic's Central Council for the Theatre, and who was fluent in French. It was in fact Max Aub who recruited the most important Spanish actors – beginning with a local vaudeville star, José Sempere, chosen for the role of the squadron commander, whose name, to assuage Spanish susceptibilities, was changed from Magnin to Peña.

The original script had to be modified as they proceeded, for, among other things, Malraux was informed that not a single tank could be lent to him, even for a day, since they were all badly needed at the front. A wooden mock-up, fashioned by Catalan carpenters, was constructed for simulated in-flight sequences showing the Potez 54's cockpit cabin and the corridor running back along the fuselage.

When the filming finally started, during the first week of August, there was only enough cellulose film on hand for eight days of shooting. Almost every foot had to be imported from France, with exasperating delays at custom-control points on the border. Worse still, none of the film could be developed on the spot. Not a day passed in Barcelona without at least one Nationalist air raid, during which, even in broad daylight, all electric power was cut off for an hour or two. Since a momentary interruption in the supply of current could ruin the chemical process, every inch of shot film had to be sent to the Pathé laboratories in Paris. Sometimes it was three weeks before Malraux, Max Aub, and Louis Page (the cameraman) could check the developed film, to see if this or that scene had been properly shot.

Extraordinary ingenuity was needed to carry out the aerial photography. Malraux had to wait three months before General Ignacio Hidalgo de Cisneros, a recently converted Communist who now headed the Spanish Air Force (and who felt an airman's scorn for Malraux, the amateur), agreed to lend them a skilled pilot and one of the Republic's few remaining Potez 54s for the filming of a night-time take-off from an airfield illuminated by the headlights of carefully positioned automobiles. The other aerial scenes – of mountain ranges, of burning villages, of smoke billowing up from bombed targets – were all shot from an old converted Latécoère 'bomber' whose machine guns were removed to make room for the installation of the cameras.

In early June André sent several telegrams to Josette, inviting her to join him in Barcelona. A rude shock awaited her. Barcelona's Ritz Hotel bore no resemblance to that of Paris. 'For breakfast', as she wrote to her friend Suzanne Chantal, 'we have a darkish water (called tea or coffee), the tasteless taste of which is horrid. No sugar, nor milk, nor bread, nor butter. At noon we ate some cat. No tobacco . . . We dream of cold chicken and of *soles Mornay*.'

A week or two later the devoted Suzanne turned up at Barcelona's Ritz Hotel with requested items (Guerlain soap bars, skin tonic, Listerine shaving cream), fortunately supplemented with Roquefort cheese, sausages and cigarettes for André. Casually dressed in sandals, Catalan fisherman's trousers and a loosely laced shirt, Malraux seemed to Suzanne to have lost ten years of age. Here, far from the parochial shop-talk of Saint-Germain-des-Prés, far too from the reproaches and complaints of a desperately unhappy Clara, he was once again in his element, doing something worth while.

Suzanne Chantal, who seems to have been as efficient as Josette tended to be improvident, lost no time returning to Paris. Here she took charge of the alimentary logistics. M. Clotis was asked to contribute, which he did with his customary bonhomie. With the help of Raymond Valière, a travelling salesman and the fiancé of Suzanne's Belgian friend Jeanne, foodstuffs were brought to the frontier town of Cerbère and a smuggling ring organized via the Perthus pass to Figueras.

Josette's letters to Suzanne offered revealing glimpses of the steadily increasing hardships Malraux and his cinematographic team-mates were forced to endure as slowly, inexorably, Franco's victorious forces tightened their stranglehold around what was left of the Republic, soon to be abandoned to its fate by the Soviet Union.

'We returned yesterday from Tarragona, where we have just spent two weeks,' Josette wrote on September 22nd, at the height of the Sudetenland crisis, which was to culminate six days later in the Munich capitulation of Chamberlain and Daladier. 'The bombardments are far more impressive than in Barcelona. The town is small, the defences are insufficient, we hear the bombs whistle as though they were about to drop on our heads.'

Two weeks later (October 7th): 'André and I have reached a kind of Munich accord . . . So we are living an idyll. He is very kind, as long as I don't pester him. "I won't let myself be eaten by you, Ogress."

'André is more and more famished. So am I . . . We are slowly poisoning ourselves . . .'

Five days later (October 12th):

We have been filming the descent from the mountain top, at Montserrat. They had lent us the monastery, where there were 1,700 beds for our 2,500 'extras'. But then the wounded arrived and occupied all the beds. The soldiers are thus camping out at Colbato. We had to answer the bugle call at 5.30 a.m. We remained on the mountainside from 7 in the morning until 5.30 in the evening, without eating in order not to lose a minute of daylight . . . My arms are black, my face is wrinkled and sunburnt . . . Then we eat whatever we have, along with monstrous salads made of pimentos and onions. You can't imagine how a Spanish rosé wine, a spicy salad, and herring slices can get you drunk . . .

The 2,500 extras are soldiers from the mountain battalions, a newly called-up group who have come to be filmed by us before going to the front . . .

(November 15th): We made a quick trip to Perpignan and ate some partridge *à la catalane*. A fantastic invention, partridges in a garlic stew laced with brandy . . .

(November 26th): For some time there has been no let-up in the bombings. They cause a terrible tensing of the nerves. You wait for the sound, you hear it all night long, all through the morning, in the evening. Six times a night, three times in the morning. We spend long evenings in the dark, with only a single candle . . . There are twenty dead and two hundred wounded with each bombing raid. The day before yesterday I saw some rather disgusting things.

In early January 1939 Josette returned to Paris, looking absolutely dreadful, with (in Suzanne Chantal's words) 'tufts of lovely hair falling in fistfuls' from her head. To Suzanne's astonishment, she paid no visits to any *haute couture* houses and wasted no time in perfume shops. Her one desire was to return to Barcelona as soon as possible, but this time properly supplied with foodstuffs. Packets of rice, noodles and spaghetti, kilograms of potatoes, tins of salad oil were crammed into several bulging sacks, along with a variety of goodies – everything from canned duck *à l'orange* to caviar and Dijon mustards – which were added by her friend Suzanne before being entrusted to the care of the competent Raymond Valière. Miraculously, the sacks all reached their destination via the smugglers' network.

So pleased was Josette by this little triumph of logistics that on January 19th she put through a long distance call to Suzanne, telling her not to believe the newspapers and to come join her in Barcelona. Two days later she had to send a second telegram: 'Don't come.' Bursts of flame and puffs of smoke could be seen along the mountains to the south, where the advance guard of Franco's forces were fighting their way down the slopes. 'The Persians!' said Malraux to Max Aub, as they gazed over the parapet at the disheartening spectacle.

It was, inevitably, a disorderly exodus over roads clogged with refugees, in several trucks and cars piled high with suitcases, sacks, metal drums, and carboard boxes, into which some of the precious film-reels had been carefully stacked. One or two suitcases were lost in transit, as well as Josette's make-up case, inadvertently heaved overboard to make room for a crippled Spanish soldier.

And it was thus, seated in an open truck next to his cinematographic gear, with a beret, a woollen neckpiece, and a duffelcoat to protect him from the February wind, that André Malraux returned to Paris, looking distinctly glum. Barely recovered from the rigours of the trip, he hurried out to the film studios of Joinville, east of Paris.

Now, for the first time, he was able to see a fairly complete projection of his work. In the semi-obscurity of the small hall, Denise Tual could sense his mounting impatience by the way he chain-smoked, pointing an accusing finger each time a screen image was prematurely cut, and grumbling whenever he realized that a vital connecting frame was missing. 'That's only one third of what I need,' was his irritated comment when the ceiling lights were switched on.

Slinging his overcoat over his shoulder, Malraux strode out and down to the nearby Seine, where he was joined by Roland Tual. They paced up and down, smoking, gesticulating, and discussing what could be done to save this 'shipwreck'. 'Nonsense,' Tual kept repeating. Enough had been shot to convey the essential message of human fraternity. The rest of the filming could be done in France. And the money? asked Malraux. He couldn't ask his Spanish sponsors for another peseta. No problem, Tual reassured him. Corniglion, though financially hard pressed, would provide the necessary funds, once he had seen for himself that the film had the makings of a 'masterpiece'.

Corniglion's response, just as Tual had predicted, was positive. A day or two later Malraux and his team went to work amplifying and revising various sequences of *Sierra de Teruel*. For an *al fresco* luncheon under the welcome trees of the Pomme d'Api restaurant, they were often joined by Josette Clotis, her friend Suzanne Chantal, and Raymond Maréchal, the facially scarred but indomitable survivor of the Teruel crash-landing, who, with a truly dog-like fidelity, was now ready to follow '*le patron*' to the ends of the earth.

In April Malraux and his team travelled down to Villefranche-de-Rouergue, in south-western France. The old stone, tile-roofed houses, and even more, the shawled women and swarthy men in black, all speaking the *langue d'oc* vernacular, bore an astonishing resemblance to what could be seen in Catalonia. Here a number of missing frames were shot.

To stress the climactic solemnity of the descent-from-the-mountain sequence, Malraux had first thought of a voiceless finale. It was also intended to provide a kind of catharsis, a dramatic contrast to the earlier scenes, in which wartime noises – wailing sirens, exploding bombs or shells, frantic machine gun fire – played a major role. However, eleven minutes of total silence, coming after so many dialogues and noisy scenes of war, would have been difficult to endure and seemed too deliberately willed. Malraux then decided that a musical accompaniment was needed. Chopin's *Funeral March* was rejected precisely because as a march it was ill attuned to a halting, irregular descent over rocky paths and roads. Denise Tual then suggested that Malraux approach the composer, Darius Milhaud. Though disconcerted by the earnest intensity of Malraux's explanations (punctuated by facial spasms, sneezes, hiccups, and nervous coughs), Milhaud agreed to compose a moving dirge for the finale.

The first private showing took place on June 3rd. Malraux was so pleased by the enthusiastic response that he invited his friends to share a huge *paella valenciana* with him at a Spanish restaurant. In July the film was again projected at a private session for Juan Negrín and other members of the Loyalist government in exile. On August 11th Corniglion-Molinier unveiled it at the Rex cinema on the Champs-Elysées, for a select group of *aficionados* and critics, including Louis Aragon, who hailed it as a 'masterpiece'. A masterpiece, however, which French film fans were not able to see for another five, singularly momentous, years.

28

Sitzkrieg

In early August Malraux surprised Josette by buying her a Ford V–8 convertible, which he had specially painted bright red. The high-strung André had never learned to drive a car, but Josette had obtained her driving licence at the wheel of her father's bulky Renault, and she had little trouble getting used to this new automotive marvel, which was immediately dubbed *el coche estupendo* (the fabulous car).

Their first long trip was made to Chartres. From there they drove on to Angoulême and Brantôme, to Les Eyzies, Sarlat, and other picturesque towns in the Dordogne and Quercy regions of south-western France. On August 27th they reached Montpellier, where they realized that a new international storm was looming. The first thunderbolt had fallen four days before, with the signing in Moscow of a cynical 'non-aggression pact' between those two arch enemies – Hitler's Third Reich and Stalin's USSR.

It was at Nîmes, as he sat waiting for her in a pleasant restaurant near the old Roman arena, that André was informed by Josette, who had gone to have the car greased in a garage, that early in the morning of this fateful September 1st the German armies had invaded Poland.

When they reached Paris three days later it had assumed a semblance of wartime readiness. Above the suburbs of the capital anti-aircraft balloons rode leisurely at anchor. Everywhere windows were being sealed with strips of blue paper to keep tell-tale shafts of light from filtering out behind closed curtains or shutters. Cars, trucks, buses and taxis all had, or were supposed to have, their headlights dimmed, and in the almost lightless streets at night the once proud *Ville Lumière* now looked like a ghost town.

André and Josette rented a small suite in an apartment-hotel located on the Rue Le Marois, not far from the Seine and the Boulevard Murat where he and Clara and their respective mothers had once lived. In reprisal for the diabolical alliance recently concluded between Hitler and Stalin, the Daladier government had closed down the Communist Party's daily, *L'Humanité*, as well as its evening organ, *Ce Soir* (in which Louis Aragon had cravenly justified the infamous Germano-Soviet pact). It had also ordered all unmarried men among the tens of thousands of Spanish Repub-

licans who had taken refuge from Franco's forces in the region of Perpignan to be rounded up and forcibly conscripted into the French Foreign
Legion. Given the wave of anti-Communist hatred now sweeping through
all echelons of French officialdom, there was not much Malraux could do
to help his former comrades-in-arms, victims of the latest, cruel twist in
international events.

For reasons of wartime comradeship Malraux refused to break all ties with
the French Communist Party, even after its leader, Maurice Thorez, had
deserted from the French Army and made it clandestinely to Moscow. One
evening André and Josette met for dinner with Suzanne and Raymond Aron;
Aron was now serving with a meteorological unit; fed up with Stalin's
USSR, Aron vainly tried for three hours to persuade Malraux to make a
public break with the French Communist Party.

While the French Army divisions deployed along the Rhine and the Saar
rivers maintained a prudent *Sitzkrieg*, the authorities in Paris were making
up for this inertia in the field by launching a furious war of words against
the enemy. An ad hoc Commissariat of Information, luxuriously quartered
at the Hôtel Continental on the Rue de Rivoli, had promptly been established under the joint control of Jean Giraudoux and an affable general
named Chardigny. While the German eagle, soon to be joined by the Russian
bear, was tearing Poland to pieces, several writers, led by André Maurois
and Georges Duhamel, had already gone on the air to denounce the *Führer*
and his legions. André Malraux, however, was not interested in this kind of
verbal activity. His one passionate desire was to join the French Air Force.
Unfortunately, Pierre Cot was no longer Minister for Air. Nor did Malraux's
'exploits' as the former commander of the *escuadrilla España* cut any ice with
the Air Ministry professionals he talked to. Unlike Edouard Corniglion-
Molinier or Antoine de Saint-Exupéry, Malraux had never learned to fly an
aeroplane, still less a fighter or a bomber.

Summarily rejected by the Air Force, Malraux visited the nearest recruiting office and said he wanted to volunteer for service, preferably with a
mechanized tank unit. He was given a form to fill out and told that he would
be notified if his services were needed.

This second rebuff, aggravated by the refusal of the wartime censors to
authorize the distribution of *L'Espoir* (the French title of his recently
completed film), plunged him into a state of deep dejection. Suddenly
rendered idle, after years of feverish activity, he grew strangely listless, rising
late in the morning and remaining in his dressing gown until lunch or even
later. Often he would stand in front of the window for minutes on end, his
hands clasped behind his back, saying not a word and so intimidating Josette
and her friend Suzanne that they would cease their whispering. Particularly
infuriating was the fate that overtook a number of prominent anti-fascists;
Arthur Koestler, Gustav Regler, and Willi Münzenberg, who had all broken
with Moscow and the Komintern, were picked up by the Paris police and
forcibly interned.

Even the normally generous Gaston Gallimard seemed powerless to relieve Malraux's despondency, courteously declining 'in these difficult times' to grant him an advance for the neo-Conradian novel he proposed to write, based on the singular life of that swashbuckling adventurer, Baron Marie-David de Mayrena, self-proclaimed King of the Sedangs.

Meanwhile Clara had driven six-year-old Florence down to south-western France and had found a wartime home for her with a friendly schoolmaster and his wife in a village near Cahors. Afterwards she returned to Paris, determined to do her little bit for the war effort by making occasional broadcasts.

Malraux was by now in such a state of combined shame, alarm, and personal frustration – shame because an inert French Army had made no attempt in September to relieve a stricken Poland by attacking the Germans along the Rhine, alarm because Hitler was now massing his victorious divisions in the West, personal frustration because he had been rejected by the French Air Force – that in early December he decided on a desperate gamble. It was a wild project, crazier than his Queen of Sheba spree and even more daring in its ambitious scope than his 1928 scheme to liberate Trotsky from his place of confinement in Siberia.

Among the writers Malraux had befriended during the 1930s was André Beucler, a gifted journalist-author whose first novel Gallimard had published in 1925. Like André Salmon, Beucler had been brought up in St Petersburg, where he had learned Russian. In September 1939 Jean Giraudoux had offered him a job as head of the editorial department of his General Commissariat of Information. One frosty morning in late November Beucler was working at his desk when an orderly on duty at a side entrance came up to say that a stranger who refused to identify himself or to sign the registry insisted that Major Beucler leave his office for a moment because he had something of vital importance to tell him. From the description he was given of the stranger's nervous manner and facial ticks Beucler realized who it was.

Sure enough, at the Rue Rouget-de-Lisle entrance a highly agitated André Malraux was waiting impatiently for him. Taking Beucler by the arm, he led him around the corner to a taxi. 'Your hotel, your set-up,' Malraux explained once they had climbed inside, 'is stuffed with spies, deceitful gossips, and prying busybodies of every kind – which is why I didn't come upstairs. What I want to tell you, or rather propose to you, must not be overheard by anybody. I'm going to take you to a quiet spot, to the Café de la Régence, which is usually empty in the morning.'

The select Café de la Régence, located near the square in front of the Comédie Française, was, as Malraux had predicted, almost empty. The moment they were seated, he outlined his plan with his usual torrential fluency. The West had so far managed to avoid the 'horrible massacre' and partition that had overtaken Poland – which was both 'a good and a bad sign. But we still have time to avoid the worst. I don't know what people are thinking at the very top, if one still exists, or in your Commissariat, but what I know, from information reaching me from Germany, is that we are seriously threatened. However, we can still cheat fate and react unexpectedly in order to disorient the enemy and change an ending which nobody in France seems to be thinking about and which can only be an appalling disaster.'

Beucler assured him that a number of his colleagues in Giraudoux's information set-up shared these apprehensions. But given the general indifference of the French and a feeling of disgust for the war, what could be done?

'By getting Stalin to intervene . . . ,' began Malraux.

'But, despite what is commonly thought, you are secretly against Stalinism?'

'Everybody's against it,' Malraux insisted. 'But in the present case what counts is the very might, symbolic if you like, of Stalin's person. He can raise a fist and mobilize his army.'

'But what about the Germano-Soviet pact?' Beucler objected, once again.

'The two signatories don't give a damn about it, and are ready to bury it from one day to the next.' Stalin, Malraux went on, carried greater weight in the West than was generally thought. The important thing was to reverse the present tendency, to make Stalin realize that it was in his country's interest to get involved in the war now.

'And who will get him to make such decisions, so contrary to what we know of him?' asked Beucler.

'You and I,' answered Malraux.

Beucler stared at him open-mouthed.

'Exactly. You and I,' went on Malraux, with the same earnest insistence. 'We leave for Moscow in an aeroplane and go see Stalin in the Kremlin. Once there, I'm sure of being able to get in. I have the aircraft, the personnel, the funds, everything needed for this undertaking. If you agree, and I'm counting on it, we'll take off at the end of the week – naturally, in the utmost secrecy.'

The aeroplane Malraux spoke of was almost certainly to be piloted by his daredevil friend, Edouard Corniglion-Molinier. Malraux probably figured that they could escape detection by overflying Germany by night. But, Beucler promptly pointed out, there remained the likelihood of their being shot down by Russian fighter planes. Nor was that all. As ill luck would have it, Beucler was due to leave by train for Rome on an official mission in a day or two.

Beucler then asked why, given his international reputation, Malraux couldn't make the trip without him. To this Malraux replied that Beucler was indispensable, since he occupied a senior post in the Commissariat of Information, itself directly subordinated to the prime minister's office. This gave him an official status, vitally important for impressing Soviet functionaries in Moscow. Without the help of someone able to speak Russian he,

Malraux, would be helpless. As for the timing, the trip could not be postponed till later, after Beucler's return from Rome, for reasons Malraux did not elaborate, but which probably had to do with the availability of the aeroplane Corniglion-Molinier was due to pilot, or – who knows? – was preparing to 'borrow' from some French Air Force unit.

When the two 'plotters' parted a little later, after a quick lunch, it was, as Beucler later noted, with the feeling of sadness that follows a shattered dream. A dream which, had it been been carried out without a fatal crash, might well have landed both of them in a Soviet prison.

During this same month of December 1939, André and Josette moved to an attractively furnished ground-floor flat on the Rue Berlioz, not far from the Porte Maillot, west of the Arc de Triomphe. Here they enjoyed an unbelievably white Christmas as snow settled softly on the handsome lamps, lawns, and railings of Boni de Castellane's *Palais rose*, on the nearby Avenue du Bois. But the purity of all this whiteness, coinciding with the Soviet Union's assault on little Finland, only made the unreality of this 'phoney war' more difficult to endure.

One of those Malraux tried to help during this period of enforced inactivity was Koestler's companion, the twenty-year-old sculptress, Daphne Hardy, who for three months had been trying to survive in a tiny maid's room. Finally released from his internment camp in the foothills of the Pyrenees, Koestler went on a drunken binge, followed by a twenty-four-hour siesta. Josette was fascinated by his youthful zest but a bit appalled by the leathery ugliness of his features, with an 'air of bestiality' which she sententiously attributed to his Magyar origin.

Another anti-Nazi expatriate for whom Malraux displayed a particular solicitude was Jenka, the blond Latvian companion of his friend Manès Sperber, who had volunteered for service with the French Foreign Legion. As reassuringly calm as the short, taciturn Manès tended to be irritable, tormented, and depressed, Jenka was a much appreciated lunch or dinner guest at the Rue Berlioz apartment. One day Josette confessed the troubles she was having with her own unmarried 'mate' – for Sperber too was legitimately married to another. Jenka, who had not studied Adlerian psychology for nothing, urged her to write about her frustrations to her closest friend rather than trying to bottle them up inside her, where they were likely to erupt one day with such violence that it might fatally damage her relationship with André. Heeding this sound advice, Josette now released her feelings not only in her diary but also in her letters to Suzanne Chantal, who had been sent to Portugal on a journalistic assignment. In a typical outburst to her friend she complained of this 'too superior man' – she meant of course Malraux – of 'his exasperations, his silences, to say nothing of his harshness. Certain of his words are like a cutting stone, a blade widening an open sore. Yet he has brought me such fascination that I cannot see life without him.'

At the root of these bitter grievances was the nagging feeling that for André she was little more than a playmate he had never seriously thought of marrying. For three years he had been fending off her questions, claiming that it was Clara who was refusing a divorce.

The simmering suspicions soon rose to a furious boil. During a visit to the Hôtel Continental Malraux had met André Maurois, who introduced him to General Chardigny. Impressed by Malraux's earnest desire to be inducted, if possible in the tank corps, the sympathetic general had used his influence in high places. In early April Malraux finally received an official notification, ordering him to report for duty with a 'mechanized cavalry' regiment based at Provins, some 80 kilometres south-east of Paris.

On April 14th Josette saw André off at the Gare de l'Est in an atmosphere of tension aggravated by the realization that she was pregnant. Not only was she going to be separated from her beloved André – quite prepared to court a heroic death in action – but she would also be giving birth to an illegitimate child, to the horror of her shocked parents. The long-discussed divorce between André and Clara was no longer a theoretical question; for her it had become an urgent, obsessive necessity.

The DC41–E1 detachment, to which Private Georges Malraux had been assigned, was an ad hoc training unit composed of conscripts and volunteers who were supposed to learn the rudiments of armoured warfare on turretless 'tanks': one more symptom of the lamentable unpreparedness to be found at almost every level of the 'finest army in the world'. The detachment occupied a barracks compound on the edge of the 'new' or lower town of Provins, the older, hilly part of which had once been a Roman stronghold.

In his first letter to Josette, André did his best to reassure her – at least as regards the likelihood of his being dispatched to a wartime 'front'.

Theoretically, we are here for three to six months. General training on tanks, armoured cars, etc. Specialization later. We can therefore make an arrangement with a hotel or rent something [he meant of course in Provins]. We won't be given uniforms until tomorrow, and in the meantime are doing nothing. At first sight all this is bearable and even very human. Very instructive too. Intelligence, as artists understand it, is a very small thing on the surface, but what one finds beneath, when there is no collective or individual passion, is like the prehistory of the human being. Even so, tanks can only be defended if climbed into, not simply by being greased and numbered. I am writing in the *Foyer du Soldat* [a kind of recreation hall] and the radio has started to bellow again. I have the impression of having begun to learn the meaning that happiness could have, when I was there and didn't see it. Above all since the taxi drive to the station.

In a brief note to his former schoolmate, Louis Chevasson, the 'apprentice *tankeur*', as he called himself, wrote that 'all is fairly well, save for the possibility of writing'. To Roger Martin du Gard, who had sent him the final volume of his *Thibault* series, just published by Gallimard, Malraux wrote in a more philosophical vein to say that

> the questions posed by Antoine are raised every day before me by each of the men of my barracks room . . . I am a simple private and thus see my buddies close at hand. They [ie those questions] are posed in such a rough, if not in a still more fundamental, manner that everything we [intellectuals] think is made to look bizarrely superficial – without what I hear and see, alas, becoming profound.

The *maréchal des logis* – the wonderfully old-fashioned term still used in the French cavalry to designate a 'corporal' – under whose orders Private Georges Malraux was placed was a rugged patriot with roots in the Franche-Comté (the same mountainous region from where André's maternal grandfather had come) who had lost his father during the first months of the 1914 war. An excellent pianist, Albert Beuret had wanted to pursue a musical career, but after his mother's death when he was only sixteen, he had stoutheartedly bid farewell to his artistic hopes in order to take over the running of her hairdressing parlour. Later he had had a modestly successful career in banking. A fervent nationalist who had even adhered for a while to Charles Maurras' ultra-conservative *Action Française*, he must have greeted the arrival of the 'Bolshevik' *plumitif* (pen-pusher) with some suspicion, along with secret envy for the artist who had so brilliantly fulfilled his ambition. But grudging envy was not part of Albert Beuret's make-up, and he could not but feel genuine admiration for a 'veteran' – Malraux was eleven years his senior – who in Spain had risked his life for the cause he believed in and who had now *volunteered* for active service as a simple private.

Meanwhile, in Paris, Josette had gone to see a doctor, who had confirmed her ten-week pregnancy. This was a worrying prospect. The news from Provins, however, sounded reassuring. André had been assigned to a platoon of officer cadets, but, as he wrote to Josette, 'I shall probably be shunted aside because of age. All of thirty years already . . . Poor "Psychologie de l'Art",' he went on, referring to another manuscript on which he had been working. His personal relations with his regimental 'buddies' were excellent. He felt perfectly at home with the peasants and artisans serving with him. 'Whence a truly great solidarity. I have to sew and sweep. I didn't know that sweeping made one feel so hot.'

The next Saturday Josette arrived with a suitcase full of men's underwear, toilet water, and other 'goodies' for André. They spent the night in a hotel, but were so appalled by the size of the bill that they decided it would be better to rent a room in the 'old town'. Meanwhile, from the Mediterranean town of Hyères, near Toulon, to which her husband had recently been transferred from Beaune-la-Rolande, Mme Clotis, eager to spoil her 'dragoon', was now sending generous parcels of sardines, potted pâtés, almonds and jars of strawberry jam.

In Paris Josette had just been joined by Suzanne Chantal, who volunteered to accompany her to Lisbon where, far from the eyes of scandalized relatives, Josette could give birth to her child. This would indeed have been a sensible solution to her predicament had Suzanne Chantal's proposal been promptly acted on. Unfortunately it was not. For Josette had gone to see Malraux's lawyer, Maurice Garçon, a distinguished member of the Paris bar, who had assured her that divorce proceedings were not as complex as she seemed to think. In this case, however, the preliminaries had not even been initiated. This shattering discovery threw Josette into a towering rage, unleashing a particularly reproachful letter to André.

In early May Josette made a second trip to Provins, accompanied this time by her friend Suzanne. Over the lunch table Malraux painted an amusing picture of his life as a 'trooper'. But that night, in the room next to the one André and Josette had rented in a house of the picturesque old town, Suzanne Chantal couldn't help hearing Josette's tearful accusations against a lover who for years had been 'stringing her a line' about divorce proceedings.

At the root of this bitter quarrel was the old conflict between his desire to take up arms in defence of his country and her desire to found a home. For Malraux it was inconceivable that the ideal of domestic bliss could take precedence over patriotic duty. Getting himself exonerated from active military service on grounds of age would have been nothing less than cowardice. Since nobody could predict what might happen during the coming months, the face-saving formality of a marriage would not solve the fundamental problem of how Josette was going to subsist as a mother, since the father of her child might be killed in action tomorrow. In short, this was no time to bring a baby into the world.

A tearful Josette finally accepted this cruel decision, but with grudging bitterness. The next morning, as André hurried back to his barracks while the two friends returned to the rented room in the old town, Josette said to Suzanne: 'Malraux is going to fight like a lion, and it will be excellent for his glory. I find it more worthwhile to live cleanly and simply than to die like a hero.'

29

The Débâcle

On Friday, May 10th, two days before the Whitsun holiday which Josette had been hoping to spend at Provins with André, Hitler launched his *Blitzkrieg* against the West. A neutral Holland and a neutral Belgium were invaded. Malraux and his 'buddies' were immediately consigned to barracks.

In Paris Josette went to see a doctor whom Maréchal had recommended, but he categorically refused to carry out an abortion. Josette felt shattered. The swift collapse of Holland and Belgium unleashed a wave of panic-stricken Belgian refugees, who poured into northern France by the hundreds of thousands. The Portuguese embassy in Paris was suddenly swamped with visa applications, and when Suzanne Chantal turned up with Josette's French passport, she was told that the government in Lisbon had halted the issue of new visas.

Josette chose this moment to make a quick trip to Beaune-la-Rolande, to sort out some personal belongings in the house her parents had abandoned when they had left for Hyères. On her return to the Rue Berlioz apartment, she found she had missed André, hurriedly dispatched from Provins to the Val-de-Grâce military hospital in south-eastern Paris for a medical examination in which, belatedly, he was found fit for military service.

This contretemps was quickly followed by another. When, accompanied by her friend Suzanne, Josette went to see a Spanish abortionist her courage failed her. As she stared in horror at the bare table on which she was to lie down, she imagined herself bleeding to death from a uterine haemorrhage.

Two days later Suzanne Chantal said goodbye, giving her friend as much money as she could before boarding the train for Lisbon. Josette now felt trapped and abandoned. Obsessed by the prospect of giving birth to an illegitimate child, she wrote an anguished letter to André, wondering if his half-brother, Roland, would be willing to assume this troublesome paternity. 'Kysou' had once impertinently remarked, 'my sister-in-law resembles the Loire – long, blonde and lazy.' But this was no time to quibble. The only trouble was that Roland Malraux was now serving with a Chasseurs Alpins unit based above Menton, close to the frontier of Mussolini's Italy, which was expected to declare war on France at any moment.

Meanwhile, in the French capital tens of thousands of scared Parisians had locked up their apartments, piled everything they could on to the roofs of their crammed cars, and were heading slowly southward. André had long urged Josette to waste no further time and seek refuge with her parents at Hyères, but with maddening obstinacy she continued to cling to their Rue Berlioz apartment. Not until June 12th, the day Premier Paul Reynaud declared Paris an 'open city', did she finally leave the doomed capital. She made it to Beaune-la-Rolande in her luggage-crammed *coche estupendo*, so exhausted by the snail-like progress of the bumper-to-bumper column of fleeing automobiles, trucks, delivery vans, horse-drawn carts and wagons that when she reached the mayor's house in Beaune-la-Rolande she barely had the strength to drag out the suitcases before collapsing on to a mattress in the attic, which was full of refugees.

At Provins, on June 14th, the remnants of the 1st Training Squadron of Cavalry Depot 41 were ordered to evacuate the barracks in a hurry. At the river crossing of Pont-sur-Yonne, 35 kilometres further south, the machine-gun-mounted *chenillettes*, with their caterpillar treads, were sent on ahead with the duffel-bags and heavier gear (which included some of Malraux's notebooks), while the tankless 'troopers', armed with rifles, slogged their way south and west on foot. On June 16th, a motorized *Wehrmacht* detachment caught up with them near the village of Prunoy, south of Courtenay, in the *département* of the Yonne. There was a brief exchange of gunfire and Malraux was slightly wounded in the foot – after which he, Beuret, and their footslogging 'tankmen' were taken prisoner.

Embarrassed by the number of prisoners they were taking, the Germans herded their captives back to Sens, some 45 kilometres to the north-east. For a hobbling Malraux this must have been a painful 'march', which ended, almost blissfully, when they were pushed through the sculpted Gothic portal and into the nave of the cathedral. Here Malraux had his foot treated by a German medical unit. They were then marched out of the cathedral's cool interior into the sun-baked square, already filled to overflowing with thousands of other prisoners-of-war, and led north to an empty building lot on the edge of the Yonne river.

Inside the shadeless lot, hemmed in by palisades and hastily erected barbed wire, and guarded by helmeted *Wehrmacht* soldiers armed with menacing machine-pistols, the afternoons were unpleasantly hot; it was not until evening that the faintly murmuring poplars lining the Yonne river began to cast their shadows over the ragged multitude of KGs: *Kriegsgefangene* – prisoners-of-war. 'Sleep and dysentery filled our daily twenty-four hours,' the future journalist and author, Jean-Baptiste Jeener, later recalled. With nothing to eat but a truly 'iron ration' of three soldiers' biscuits and a quart of boiled water every day, the sole, obsessive topic of conversation was FOOD! FOOD! and DRINK!

André Malraux began to look around to see if he couldn't find a kindred soul capable of carrying on a less tedious form of conversation. Spotting another soldier who was stepping gingerly over the prostrate prisoners-of-war sunning themselves or otherwise 'taking it easy', Malraux hailed him: 'Hey there, what do you think? Why did we lose the war?'

The stranger, Jean Grosjean, does not recall exactly how he responded to the question. But the discussion thus begun lasted until nightfall, when each had to return to his particular 'corner'. The next day they met again and continued their discussion, walking up and down between rows of listless bodies. The following evening a Belgian prisoner-of-war said to Grosjean: 'Do you know who that fellow is you've been walking around with? It's the novelist, Malraux.'

Jean Grosjean was, like Malraux, no ordinary fellow. An ardent Catholic poet with a particular affinity for mysticism, he had interrupted his seminary studies during the mid-1930s in order to visit the Holy Land. Passionately interested in biblical antiquity and the historical conditions recorded in the various books of the Old and New Testaments, he had served for a while as secretary to a judge and had completed his military service in Syria, then a French mandate established by the Treaty of Versailles. Given his interest in religions and his first-hand knowledge of the Middle East, this ascetic scholar-mystic who had taken the trouble to learn Arabic as well as Hebrew was bound to hit it off with André Malraux.

Unlike Malraux, whose make-believe 'tank regiment' had hardly moved from its training camp during the ten months of the 'phoney war', Grosjean had been assigned to the 101st Infantry Regiment, which had been ordered to 'show the flag' by occupying swampy ground north-east of the Maginot Line where the Germans could have wrought havoc by simply flooding the area. The colonel commanding the regiment was a sword-waving blusterer who had repeatedly boasted that the French Army would soon finish off 'that fanatical monk, Hitler'. Being a man of peace rather than a man of war, Jean Grosjean had developed a profound antipathy towards all things military. When, towards the end of June, he heard that a rebellious French general had defied Marshal Pétain and was carrying on the struggle, Grosjean was not at all impressed – particularly since the message broadcast from London by the BBC had begun with the words: '*Moi, Général de Gaulle . . .*' Radically different was the reaction of Albert Beuret and André Malraux, both of whom were elated to learn that at least one heroic Frenchman had refused to throw in the towel. It can be said, without exaggeration, that André Malraux's 'Gaullism' was born at this particularly bitter moment, when a dazed, demoralized, profoundly disheartened people were still reeling from the shock of a humiliating defeat.

On June 25th Malraux and his fellow prisoners-of-war learned that an armistice had been signed with Germany and Italy. All of France north of the Loire river became occupied territory under German military administration, but most of southern France and the colonies of the French Empire were allowed to maintain a nominal independence, provided that they adhered to a strict neutrality during the continuing war with Britain. The demarcation line between the two zones ran from the Atlantic coast some distance south of Nantes and the Loire river in an easterly direction, before curving south towards Switzerland. Almost all of Burgundy, including the provincial capital of Dijon and the town of Sens, ended up in the zone of German occupation.

Most of the prisoners-of-war in the Sens camp greeted the armistice with a feeling of relief, bordering on euphoria. Now that France had been officially 'neutralized' and removed from the war, they would soon be demobilized and allowed to go home. In an informal 'Gallup Poll' undertaken among his fellow prisoners-of-war, the former Foreign Legion officer, Jean-Baptiste Jeener, found that the optimists believed they would be released promptly, while the most pessimistic felt their liberation might require sixty to seventy days, no more.

There was, however, one notable exception: a legendary figure, already referred to by some as 'the Great Man', who was sombrely predicting that the Germans had no intention of releasing them. Intrigued, Jeener decided to meet this extraordinary phenomenon. He found him walking up and down along the barbed-wired river-front, so emaciated that his uniform seemed to hang around his body, a nervous tick giving an occasional pathetic twist to his peaked features. Possessed of an inexhaustible energy, he never stopped talking, punctuating his rapid-fire commentaries with disconcerting questions as he moved from one subject to another: from God . . . to women . . . to cigarettes . . . to the latest rumour . . . and even (incredible as it sounded to Jeener's ears) to what would happen if the Mongols were suddenly to appear out there, beyond the barbed wire and the German sentinels, on the highroad to Paris bordering the river!

The 'Great Man' was André Malraux. The setbacks he had experienced during the Spanish Civil War had generated a sobering sense of realism most of his fellow prisoners lacked. The 2 million or more French soldiers who had managed to make it to the south could now be discharged by officials of Marshal Pétain's new ad hoc administration. Like some 8 million civilians and hundreds of thousands of Belgian fugitives, they could return to their homes in the north without being molested. But for the 2 million French soldiers who had been captured by *Wehrmacht* units north of the demarcation line, there was but one eventual destination: prisoner-of-war camps in Germany. They were political hostages, whom the *Führer* could choose not to release, to make sure that the Pétain government did not stray from its officially proclaimed neutrality.

In July the camp authorities slightly relaxed the stringent conditions of the first weeks. The prisoners were allowed to communicate with next-of-kin and friends by writing brief messages on 'family cards', to be distributed by the Red Cross. Malraux filled out dozens of these postcard-size forms with his tiny script, sending them to all the addresses he could recall, in the hope that one or two of them at least might reach their destinations. Some were signed 'Georges', a few with his playful signature – the half-completed silhouette of a cat. The militant anti-Fascist who had spoken up for Dimitrov, denounced Hitlerism, and had written *Le Temps du Mépris* could not risk the use of his usual name.

The first person to respond to one of these 'family cards' was André's aunt, Marie Lamy, who had been unable to leave Paris before it was occupied by the Germans. She took the train to Sens, where she found herself among a throng of mothers, wives, and sisters, all vainly seeking to gain admission to the prisoner-of-war camp. She spent seven wearying hours tossing scraps of paper over the wooden palisade, addressed to Private Georges M. of the 3rd Group's 132nd Company. One of these scraps of paper finally reached its destination, and for a few minutes André was able to talk to his aunt through a narrow gap between the slats. He still had no idea as to Josette's whereabouts, but he asked his Aunt Marie to send a 'family card' to Josette's father's address at Hyères.

Josette, meanwhile, had finally made it to her parents' new home on the Côte d'Azur. Paul Cabanis, the mayor of Beaune-la-Rolande, and his wife Denise had shaken her out of her lethargy, filled her Ford V–8 convertible with emergency cans of petrol and advised her to avoid the clogged highways and to zigzag her way south over secondary roads. At Hyères, which she finally reached looking haggard and in hideously rumpled clothes, Josette was at first warmly welcomed by her indulgent father and prim mother, despite their acute embarrassment at her clearly pregnant as well as unmarried state. The atmosphere of not always silent reproach – 'How could you do this to your father?' (whose reputation as a respectable tax inspector would now forever be tarnished in the eyes of the local bourgeoisie) – became so unbearable that Josette finally sought refuge with a friend at Sanary, on the other (western) side of Toulon. But before she left Hyères, she and her father received the two 'family cards' André had sent from the Sens prison camp on July 17th.

One week later she received a second, longer letter – probably the one he had entrusted to his Aunt Marie – in which he wrote:

The camp life is tolerable. If I had news of you, it would be fine. So far, only farmers have been liberated. I think we shall stay in this region. It has started to rain once more. I am going to find shelter in a tiny lair. I walk around with ridiculous shoes' – [he had had to shed one boot because of his foot wound] – 'but I no longer limp and I now have an [Anthony] Eden moustache, which I will keep until the time when you can see it.

'I'll have to reconstitute the *Mayrena* chapter (the one about art). Everything was lost. The last day we were ordered to put everything into the half-tracks. All I have left is what I had in my pockets: the small, foldable fork and the *cigarette-lighter* . . . I now see what the ex-novel about gas attacks and other Spains is going to be. For the moment, my American publisher is neither threatened nor inaccessible. We will have one year in which to find ourselves, and the film is not yet outdated. I think that the liberation [he meant of course his own] will require a stay in occupied territory. But first I must know your [physical] state. No matter what, we'll arrange that too. Write. But here 1,500 letters are waiting to be distributed to the prisoners and may well never be. I think back on the snow, which made the Rue Berlioz look like a street in Vienna . . .

The signature was the familiar outline of a cat.

The film mentioned in this letter was, of course, *Sierra de Teruel*, a copy of which had been entrusted the previous autumn to Paris representatives of MGM (Metro-Goldwyn-Mayer). They had promised to take care of its distribution in the United States. The American publishers were Random House and also *Life* magazine, which before the débâcle had asked Malraux to write an article describing life in the French Army.

Inside the prisoner-of-war camp Malraux had not been idle. 'Believe me,' he explained to Albert Beuret and Jean Grosjean, now inseparable companions, 'in such a situation, acting on one's own is pointless. We already form a trio, but that's not enough. If we can form a larger group – let's say a Group of Ten – we'll stand a better chance of impressing the discipline-loving *Boches*.'

The idea made sense, and the job of recruiting was immediately begun. One of the first to sign up was Jean-Baptiste Jeener. The next two recruits were ecclesiastics – one of them named Martin, the other (Magnet) a bearded friar from the Jura mountains with 'a heart as big as his stomach', who had not hesitated to divide his meagre biscuit rations with his hungry fellows. To provide for better social balance they next recruited a truculent peasant named Boulmé, who made no secret of his contempt for intellectuals but who agreed to follow Grosjean because he had once worked as a metal fitter. The others were André Clavier, a delivery van driver who had once belonged to the right-wing *Jeunesses Patriotes*; Paul Pluche, a fair-haired house painter from northern France with a rollicking gift of pungent speech; Voiselle, a Protestant garage owner from Nice whose Provençal accent was a permanent delight; and finally, a landscape painter, Petitjean, who came from Bayonne, near the Pyrenees. About the last-named, Malraux had certain reservations, privately confiding to Beuret and Grosjean his belief that he would one day 'cheat' by not heeding group discipline and striking out on his own. 'But never mind,' added Malraux, with Judas Iscariot in mind. 'If it isn't him, it will be someone else.' Such being the case, the eleven might as well go on calling themselves *le Groupe des Dix*.

The utility of this group became apparent when the German camp authorities let it be known that they were ready to release French prisoners-of-war of peasant stock on parole to local communes for work in the fields, where there was now a dire shortage of farmhands for bringing in the harvest. Soon the mayors of nearby villages were queueing up outside the offices of the camp *Kommandantur* with their requests for sorely needed manpower. One of the *Wehrmacht* officers in charge was a Lieutenant Metternich, from an Austrian branch of the illustrious family. There was something about Jean Grosjean's otherworldly air which had inspired confidence, and whenever Metternich was on duty, the former seminarist was allowed to leave the camp on parole for 'walks' in the country. Encouraged by Malraux, Grosjean visited several villages, offering them the help of able-bodied 'volunteers'. Several apprehensive mayors refused, but finally, in the village of Collemiers, seven kilometres south-west of Sens, he found a more courageous mayor named Courgenet, who was willing to assume responsibility for ten 'amateurs' along with half-a-dozen authentic peasants, provided they gave their word that they would not try to escape.

The friendly lieutenant – Count Wolff Metternich, to give him his full name – was no fool; being a cultivated gentleman whose views about this 'fratricidal' war probably resembled Grosjean's, he turned a blind eye to the un-peasant-like appearance of Grosjean's 'team' and allowed them to leave the Sens prisoner-of-war camp and to be billeted in the nearby village.

At Collemiers the friendly mayor offered them a choice of three empty houses, one of them belonging to a French general. Beuret and Malraux declined this tempting offer, deciding that the villa was likely to arouse envious mutterings among the villagers. Instead, they chose a ramshackle farm house in such a state of disrepair that they had to sleep on straw. One day Lieutenant Metternich rode up on an inspection tour. He was presented to various members of Grosjean's 'team', including Private Georges Malraux, who informed him that in civilian life he had been a professor at the Collège de France. The lieutenant made no comment, but later he reappeared with the mayor and other town council members. '*Messieurs*,' he said to them in perfect French, 'look at the situation of your countrymen. I wouldn't let my horses lie down in a place like this.' One hour later, Malraux and his fellow prisoners-of-war all had beds and mattresses to sleep on.

While Boulmé, an authentic peasant, went out early each morning to help bring in the harvest, Courgenet, the mayor, was often at a loss as to how to keep the others usefully employed. Malraux, the self-proclaimed Collège de France 'professor', was one of those chosen, along with Jeener, to catalogue the books in the little town's public library.

Every evening, when they gathered for supper, Malraux would select a topic for discussion. 'Do you believe in eternal life? . . . What do you think of women? . . . Do you like sunsets?' One evening, while the exhausted Boulmé was drowsing, worn out by a full day in the fields, Malraux challenged his companions to name the 'loveliest love poem in the French language'. To everyone's surprise, the full-bearded 'Father Hugo' (with a bit of prompting from Malraux) walked off with the prize.

Altogether, it was not a life of hardship. Petitjean, often stripped to the waist, was able to set up an easel and to paint pastoral landscapes, while Malraux worked away at his 'Tanks' (intended for *Life*). 'Except for the boils (for the past month, unfortunately, I've had thousands of them), things are all right,' André reassured Josette. 'The healthy food, I hope, will sort that out too. I have got rid of the dysentery and the lice.'

In September Malraux, Beuret, and Grosjean were given saws and axes and dispatched each day to the nearest wood to chop down trees and collect faggots for what threatened to be a winter largely without coal. During these forest excursions, made particularly pleasant by the 'golden light of autumn' (as Grosjean later put it), Malraux regaled his companions with fragments from his new work of fiction. Their critical comments were singularly pertinent. Thus the description of a nocturnal tank attack – inspired by something his father Fernand had actually experienced during the 1914–18 war – did not culminate, as Malraux had originally intended, with a mystical appearance of Chartres Cathedral, but with a pastoral eclogue, largely inspired by the old peasants of Collemiers.

With the resumption of the school year, Malraux was entrusted with the task of tutoring certain of the village's more advanced pupils. He could now devote almost half of each day to his writing. He was even rash enough to suggest that, if Josette could return to the German-occupied zone, she would be able to see him four or five times a month.

Josette needed no further encouragement. At this particular moment – late September 1940 – obtaining a German *Ausweis* for inter-zonal travel was a fairly easy matter, since millions had reluctantly decided to return to their homes in the north, encouraged by the Vichy government, which lacked the means to offer them lodging and employment in the desperately over-crowded 'free zone'.

Josette Clotis reached Collemiers on a stormy day in early October. The unexpected arrival of this tall and obviously pregnant blonde beauty aroused the sympathy of the villagers, open-mouthed with admiration at the stubborn stamina displayed by this loving wife. A room was found for her in the local inn, where André was able to join her at night.

Malraux's plight, as a prisoner-of-war, was compounded by the fact that he would soon have two children to support at a moment when his financial situation was increasingly precarious. Gaston Gallimard and Jean Paulhan, along with their families, had taken refuge near Carcassonne, in south-western France; but even if the Germans did not purely and simply occupy the NRF building at 5, Rue Sébastien Bottin, no further royalties could be expected from any of Malraux's past books. Some of the Graeco-Buddhist statuary he and Clara had acquired had been moved for safekeeping to his Aunt Marie's apartment. Other pieces had been entrusted to the care of

Dr Jean-Marie Sotty, an art enthusiast whom André and Clara had be-friended at a Pontigny *décade*. Sotty, who had been demobilized in the region of Cahors with the help of one of Clara's friends, had decided to return to his home in the Burgundian capital of Dijon. Clara, being desperately short of money, asked Sotty to get in touch with André and to obtain his permission to sell one or two of their Graeco-Buddhist heads. The good doctor kept his word, bicycling from Dijon to Collemiers (some 240 kilometres to the north) to see Malraux. Shortly afterwards, Clara received an uncensored letter, which a friend of Sotty's had posted in the Vichy 'free zone'. Her husband, the helpful doctor warned, was going to be transported with his fellow prisoners-of-war to Germany, unless ways were quickly found to facilitate his escape.

Clara, who at this chaotic moment was living with seven-year-old Florence in a hillside farm hut not far from Cahors, had meanwhile been visited by Roland Malraux, looking handsomer than ever in his dark blue beret and Chasseur Alpin uniform. He had then returned to Marseilles to get himself demobilized. Clara immediately wrote to Roland, asking him to contact Dr Sotty in Dijon, who could help him to facilitate Georges' escape. Back came a letter wondering who this 'Georges' could be. 'Instead of Georges, read André,' was Clara's telegraphed reply.

The danger threatening Malraux was, in fact, even greater than Clara feared. According to a news broadcast emanating from Switzerland, the German authorities in Paris were said to be actively searching for the 'bolshevik' writer, André Malraux. This meant one thing: his ultimate fate, if the Nazis ever caught up with him, would not be an uncomfortable train ride to a prisoner-of-war *Stalag* in Germany, but intensive interrogation by the Gestapo and confinement in a concentration camp.

The exact sequence of events during the next few days – late October, early November 1940 – may never be precisely known. The main organizer was Roland Malraux, who borrowed 500 francs from Edouard Corniglion-Molinier and 800 more from one of his Paris friends, Philippe de Guns-bourg (who later became important in the Resistance in the *département* of the Lot under the code name of 'Philibert'). Thus aided, Roland made two trips to Collemiers, bringing with him the civilian clothes André needed. He was accompanied on the second trip by Josette, who with characteristic light-headedness had not thought of buying André a pair of shoes. Roland (reduced to wearing sandals) generously gave him his own shoes, which, though he was almost as tall as André, were one size too small.

By this time each member of the 'Group of Ten' had prepared an escape plan. With the tacit agreement of Mayor Courgenet, resigned to seeing his 'farm hands' disappear discreetly one by one, it had been decided that only those whose homes were located in the Vichy 'free zone' had a right to seek their freedom when the moment came. The one exception was Malraux, given his prominence on the Nazis' black list.

The last night of his 'confinement' at Collemiers, his fellow 'foresters' Albert Beuret and Jean Grosjean came over to the inn and threw pebbles against Josette's window. André came down and for a few minutes they strolled up and down in the moonlight, wondering what was likely to happen next, since the German 'victors', despite Goering's grotesque boasts, had not yet destroyed the RAF nor crossed the English Channel.

The next morning he left the village and at Sens boarded the train for Paris. André and Roland figured that the controls on passenger movements would be less stringent during the long Toussaint (All Saints' Day) holiday, when French parents and children traditionally visit cemeteries to lay bouquets of chrysanthemums on the tombstones of their loved ones. The top priority was to get André across the demarcation-line as fast as possible. Roland, now domiciled in Marseilles, could return there any time he chose. Josette's gynaecologist had assured her that the child she was carrying would not be born until December. She thus had plenty of time to obtain a German *Ausweis*. The three of them would meet in Avignon, where Josette would bring her child into the world and have it registered in the presence of Roland Malraux, who would act as official father.

The first part of the programme was carried out without a hitch. Roland had discovered a place for crossing the demarcation-line in a wooded area south of Bourges. The long walk from the station in his half-brother's tight shoes caused André such agony that he sought refuge in a cinema, where he could relieve the pain by taking off his shoes in the darkened theatre.

Later, as he approached a wood, he was followed by a friendly black cat, which must have sensed Malraux's passion for the feline species. However, he crossed the wood without attracting the attention of the slowly patrolling German guards, and continued on to Montluçon in the Vichy 'free zone'. From there he telephoned Josette's parents at Hyères to tell them that he had escaped from the prisoner-of-war camp near Sens. Josette, still in Paris, would be following shortly.

At Hyères, on the Mediterranean coast, which he reached after an exhausting trip on packed trains, Malraux was warmly greeted by the indulgent M. Clotis and his censorious wife. He was offered Josette's bedroom, and for the first time in weeks was able to enjoy a moment of genuine relaxation. But not for long. Two days after his arrival, a telegram from Paris informed a dismayed André that at 3 pm on November 5th Josette had given birth to a baby boy.

30

The Struggle to Survive

Several weeks before, Josette Clotis had gone to see Dr Vignes at his clinic in the western suburb of Neuilly. The obstetrician who had taken care of her at the time of her 1937 miscarriage had told her that her child would probably be a boy and that there was no urgency, since the birth would not take place until December. However, on the morning of November 5th she was suddenly seized by the first telltale pains. Putting on her fur coat, she decided to take the subway to Neuilly. But on the way she suddenly collapsed in agony, and an ambulance team had to be summoned with a stretcher to drive her post-haste to Dr Vignes' clinic. The birth was not an easy one; forceps were used, and the number of nurses in attendance had to be doubled. She had hardly recovered from the ordeal of bringing a baby boy into the world when she found she already owed the clinic 2,000 francs.

Though almost penniless, she had one or two friends in Paris on whom she could still count. One of them, Raymond Valière, went to the local town hall to have her son officially registered. The child was given the first name of Pierre, followed by Guillaume Valentin, before the terminal Clotis – *né de père inconnu* (born of an unknown father): precisely the humiliation she had wanted to avoid.

The faithful Raymond Maréchal came to see her at the clinic. All he could offer her was a handful of francs obtained from the sale of Josette's portable typewriter – barely enough to buy a few nappies and badly needed babywear items. Equally helpful was 'Mico' Gallimard, who persuaded his mother (now divorced from Raymond) to offer Josette a place to sleep – on the living room sofa of her Montmartre apartment. Dr Vignes finally let her leave his clinic, but because she could not pay the various bills, she had to leave her baby boy with the nurses. Not a day passed without 'family cards' being dispatched to Hyères with desperate requests for money, which Joseph Clotis tried to intercept before his wife erupted into a new tantrum. Between them, he and Malraux sent Josette 7,000 francs during the second half of an increasingly glacial November.

One thing was clear. André had to find a new home for himself, Josette, the baby boy, and the official father, Roland, who had agreed to adopt the child, so that he could be called Malraux. Given Mme Clotis' temperament and opinions, the prolonged presence at Hyères of an unmarried 'son-in-law' and an illegitimate grandchild would fatally wreck the fragile harmony of the Clotis household.

It did not take Malraux long to re-establish contact with literary friends who either lived or had taken refuge on the Côte d'Azur. One of them was Roger Martin du Gard, who years before had moved to Nice. Through him Malraux learned that the painter Simon Bussy and his English wife, Dorothy (a sister of Lytton Strachey), had hastily left Roquebrune, near Monte Carlo, in anticipation of an Italian invasion. Still distrustful of Mussolini's intentions, they had decided to remain in Nice and were happy to let Malraux occupy their empty villa.

On November 14th he paid a surprise visit to André Gide, who had found refuge with his friends, Mme Théo and Aline Mayrisch, in the village of Cabris, near Grasse. Malraux looked 'very thin, tanned, as though passed through fire', as Mme Théo noted, having lost the 'puffed and whitish' complexion he had so often had in Paris. He had, however, lost none

of his internal fire . . . nor the dizzying rapidity of speech with its implacable logic, which functions as pitilessly as a sub-machine-gun and leaves you bewildered, astounded, exhausted, like a film unfolding itself too quickly for the capacity of sight . . .

He talked practically the whole time [she went on, once again attempting to analyse the inner workings of this torrential delivery], the infernal pace at which he smokes cigarette after cigarette allows of no respite. Everything was poured out: what he did, what he endured, what he saw, what he heard, technical and ideological notions, his personal experiences, general reactions, all of it too cut-and-dried, too trenchant, without possible hesitations or uncertainty, illustrated by neatly pinned anecdotes, requiring no repetitions.

It was probably Gide's intimidating presence – he was after all more than thirty years his senior – which kept Malraux from relaxing, even for a moment. For, as Mme Théo also noted

One has almost no human contact with Malraux save for a faint fleeting smile which, for the fraction of a second, pushes aside the world of thought; this smile, moreover, is his only form of politeness, for, notwithstanding his self-assurance, Malraux is completely lacking in natural ease . . . There is never a gap between his judgements and his line of conduct, or rather his personal ethic – so much so indeed that one would like to be more certain that it is not a concern for his attitude which determines his judgements.

From Cabris it was a short hop to Cannes, where André looked up his friend, Emmanuel Berl, and his musically gifted wife, Mireille. This impenitent pacifist had hailed the Munich accords of September 1938 and praised the down-to-earth language of General Pétain during the dark days of 1917 as an example to be followed by his country's long-winded politicians. On June 22nd he was summoned to Bordeaux in an attempt to repair the verbal havoc caused by the eighty-four-year-old Marshal's second speech, which called on his compatriots to cease fighting, even before an armistice had been signed with the Germans. Berl had rewritten two particularly difficult speeches – a feat of oratorical tightrope walking so deft that he had managed to avoid attacking Winston Churchill. His honeymoon with the Vichy régime had barely lasted one month, finally wrecked by Pierre Laval's diabolical scuttling of parliamentary rule and the first discriminatory measures against refugees and Jews introduced by the virulently xenophobic and anti-republican Minister of Justice, Raphaël Alibert.

Particularly poignant, because of their long friendship, had been Berl's encounter with Drieu la Rochelle. For two hours they had strolled under the venerable trees lining the river bank of the Allier, while Drieu explained that England would be conquered by the autumn of 1940, Bolshevik Russia crushed by the spring of 1941, and the United States defeated in 1942. When Berl repeated the warning against collaboration with the Germans he had given to his fellow pacifist, Jean Luchaire, Drieu looked at him with friendly commiseration: 'You say that because you are a Jew.' Berl, appealing to Drieu's chivalrous instincts, then asked him if he was ready to deliver the tens of thousands of refugees who had sought refuge in France – Spanish 'Reds', the Jews of Poland and Central Europe, etc – into the hands of the Nazis. 'I know the SS,' replied Drieu. 'They are not a party, they are not an army; they are a religious order . . . I want to save France, no matter what.'

They parted company on the spot, without a final handshake and, Berl felt, probably forever. But when Malraux asked Berl if he thought that Drieu, who was now back in Paris seeking to revive the *NRF*, could extricate Josette from her plight by helping her to obtain an *Ausweis*, Berl immediately answered 'Yes'. There was no reason to suppose that every spark of human feeling had been extinguished in the desperate pessimist who had decided, for better or worse, to collaborate with the conquerors.

In Paris, Josette Clotis' problems had been compounded by the fancy explanations she had to provide for surly officials, curious to know why she should have chosen to return to Paris after the débâcle. She could not openly admit that it had been to see her captive lover, now more than ever on the 'wanted list' of the German occupants. In despair, she finally called on Drieu la Rochelle at his NRF–Gallimard office. The Germans had already taken over the Havas news-service and the Hachette newspaper-distributing agency, and they might well have moved into the *NRF*'s premises as well, had Drieu not persuaded the German ambassador, Otto Abetz, to let the publishing company and the monthly review continue operating under the supervision of the *Propaganda-Staffel*. Gaston Gallimard had endorsed the agreement, not out of any love for Adolf Hitler and the Nazis, but simply because the grim alternative – to close the shop and move to the 'free zone' – would have resulted in the immediate occupation of the premises, the dismissal of the staff, and the freezing of the bank accounts of all Gallimard authors. As it was, 153 NRF books – including André Gide's two books on the USSR and his *Journal*, Malraux's *Le Temps du Mépris* and *L'Espoir*, all of the translated works of Sigmund Freud as well as those of Julien Benda, had been placed on the German 'Index' and withdrawn from circulation.

Drieu la Rochelle had already informed Gide that he was trying to have the ban lifted on his *Journal*. He could do nothing for Malraux's two novels. But as a friend who placed loyalty in moments of duress high on his list of human virtues, he was more than willing to help Josette Clotis by using his influence with the Paris Prefecture of Police. Shortly before the end of November Josette finally obtained the precious inter-zonal pass and was able to telegraph the good news to her father at Hyères.

André, dressed in an unfamiliar chestnut brown suit, was waiting on the platform when Josette's train steamed to a halt in Monte Carlo's cliff-flanked station. He had no time to examine the four-week-old baby as he lugged Josette's suitcases out of the compartment. But a moment later all three were seated in an open taxi-cab with a striped canopy, which laboured up the mountainside to the village of Roquebrune.

Hidden from the road by a screen of olive trees and shrubs, La Souco (the Bussys' luxurious villa) dominated a steeply inclined garden, filled with orange trees and tamarisks. The spacious five-windowed living room commanded a spectacular view over the Mediterranean coastline, stretching from the Italian Riviera on the left to the rocky promontory and fawn-coloured citadel of Monte Carlo to the right. A single cypress stood over the rocky garden, like a solitary sentinel. An even more martial note was struck by the crossed cavalry sabres adorning the long, cool vestibule – weapons said to have belonged to a colonel of the Bengal Lancers. But the villa's most valuable element, as Josette quickly realized, was the Bussys' versatile butler, a jovial, curly-haired Italian named Luigi who could cook, wait on table in white gloves and jacket, and, above all, sneak across the nearby frontier on his bicycle to bring back a precious Italian ham or salami.

It was Luigi who solved the thorny problem of what Malraux Jr should be called. Since the parents seemed unable to agree on a suitable first name, Luigi called him 'Bimbo', and so Bimbo he became. Officially adopted, thanks to Roland's generous co-operation and unmarried status, Bimbo could now quite legally carry his real father's family name.

Roland, who had developed a remarkable flair for under-the-counter deals, had already obtained ration cards for André, Josette, and their son.

But the ration tickets meant less and less during this grim winter of 1940–41, when the authorities in Vichy were forced to reduce the monthly quotas to 300 grams of margarine, 100 grams of rice, 250 grams of noodles, 200 grams of cheese, 1.4 kilograms of meat, 400 grams of animal fats or vegetable oil, and 500 grams of sugar for every adult. The British, to punish the Pétain government for having made peace with the Germans, had imposed a stringent blockade against all merchant ships headed for French ports, and it was not until a Canadian diplomat had been dispatched to London on a secret mission to Lord Halifax that the Churchill War Cabinet finally agreed to ease a blockade that was reducing most of southern France to a condition of starvation. Many were the lunches and suppers at which all André and Josette could offer their guests was a main course of swedes, the coarse taste of which Luigi sought to disguise in a variety of garlic sauces. It was a 'great day' when Luigi was able to pay a local fisherman for a *dorade* or a few *rougets*. Bimbo, like many other children of his age, was kept alive by flour and powdered milk, supplied by UNRRA (the United Nations Relief and Rescue Administration).

Equally troublesome was the shortage of cigarettes. Although Josette could do without, André would go through one month's ration in a single week. Extraordinary ingenuity was used in the fabrication of home-made 'brands'. Residual tobacco, rescued from blackened stubs, was mixed with finely ground grasses or dried oleander blossoms: alchemical experiments which never ceased to fascinate Malraux, even when the 'weeds' thus manufactured produced an acrid smoke and led to fits of coughing.

If André, Josette, and the other members of the household were able to survive – at a time when (as Victor Serge later wrote) even the sea-gulls of the now famished port of Marseilles were so 'hungry that they came hovering around windows they knew to be charitable' – it was thanks to a chance encounter which enabled Malraux to re-establish contact with his New York editor, Robert Haas. The 'Fall of France', proclaimed in glaring newspaper headlines, had come as a shock to many Americans, naturally sympathetic to the land of Lafayette. Among the dozen agencies that sprang up to help the stricken country was an Emergency Rescue Committee, organized to facilitate the passage across the Atlantic of threatened writers.

In December, shortly before Christmas, Malraux was in a tram in Nice when he was accosted by a stranger named Varian Fry, an ardently anti-nazi American who had attended one of his fund-raising meetings for the Spanish republicans in New York in 1937. Fry, who headed the Emergency Rescue Committee's office in Marseilles, explained what his group was doing: he would gladly help Malraux leave France if he wished to emigrate.

It did not take Malraux long to find out – through Gide, and Simon and Dorothy Bussy – that the Emergency Rescue Committee was a bona fide organization. Reassured, Malraux made a quick trip to Marseilles to talk to Varian Fry. He explained to the young American that he had written to his Random House editor, Robert Haas, asking him if he couldn't be paid some of the royalties (more than $15,000) that had accrued from sales of *Man's Hope*. Haas had arranged to have monthly payments of $50 made to him, this being the limit that the administration in Washington had imposed on dollar transfers to persons living in countries occupied or threatened by Nazi Germany. However, if Malraux could find other, less official channels for such transfers, Haas would gladly send him larger sums of money. This would pose no problem, Fry assured him. Many refugees, before leaving France with passport visas obtained by the Emergency Rescue Committee, left considerable sums of money in his safe-keeping, to reduce the risk of their being robbed by unscrupulous *passeurs* or venal customs inspectors during the hazardous trip through Spain. In New York an equivalent sum in dollars was given to them by Fry's wife, acting as a private bank.

On January 14, 1941 Malraux sent Robert Haas two fragments from a future novel – one of them called *La Fosse aux chars* (The Tank Ditch), another recording conversations among French prisoners-of-war. They were entrusted to Varian Fry for clandestine shipment to New York. They took months to reach their destination. But on April 22, 1941 Haas wrote that he had found them most interesting, 'The Tank Ditch' attesting a 'real inspiration'. Unfortunately, he had been unable to 'place' any of this material with an American magazine.

Mrs Varian Fry, for her part, was warmly received by Robert Haas. Together they arranged to have the franc equivalent of $500 immediately made available to Malraux in Marseilles – in addition to the regular Random House royalty payments, which were soon increased to $75 a month.

Although, thanks to Roland, the question of Pierre Gauthier's parentage had been officially resolved, allowing him to carry the name of Malraux, the problem of obtaining a divorce from Clara had assumed a greater urgency than ever. In mid-January, André sent Clara a telegram, asking her to meet him at the Café Lafayette in Toulouse. Clara turned up at the appointed place and hour, overjoyed at the prospect of soon being able to leave for the United States with seven-year-old Florence. She was in for a shock.

'We must divorce,' declared André, after kissing Clara lightly on the forehead. 'I don't want an illegitimate son.'

'How I wish my daughter were illegitimate and did not have a Jewish mother!' was Clara's retort.

She explained that the art historian, Henri Focillon, who had made it to the United States, had sent her an affidavit for herself and Florence, making it possible for them to obtain visas from the US consular officials. 'When everything is in order, I will file my request for a divorce.'

'I must have this divorce request immediately. Nothing proves that you will make it at the moment of your departure.'

'I thought I had given you sufficient evidence for you to have confidence in me.'

At the heart of this bitter quarrel was Clara's unwillingness to start divorce proceedings while she was still in France, since they were bound to focus a highly embarrassing attention on herself and her Jewish origins. On the other hand, André was afraid that once she reached the United States she would not grant him a divorce, so as to be able to go on calling herself Clara Malraux, rather than Clara Goldschmidt. This fear was, indeed, confirmed after the conclusion of the war, when she signed all of her future novels under her married name instead of adopting a *nom de plume*.

The upshot was an *échec vociférant*, as André put it in a two-word telegram to Josette. According to Clara, Malraux even accused her heatedly of wishing to leave France in order to join a young Scottish lover she had befriended in 1938. But exactly what was said on this occasion we shall never know, since Clara's version, written in a spirit of bitterness thirty-five years after the event, is the only one we have. André did, however, promise to help her and Florence once he had obtained some money – which, he assured her, 'will happen soon'.

On this point at least he was not mistaken . . . and was able to keep his promise.

31

The Galley Slave of the Pen

In February 1941 Malraux re-established contact with his old friend, Pascal Pia, who spent several days with him at Roquebrune. To escape the stringent vigilance of nazi censorship and any taint of 'collaboration', the textile magnate Jean Prouvost had moved his daily, *Paris-Soir*, down to Lyons, which was fast becoming the centre of resistance sentiment in Vichy France. The newspaper's dynamic editor-in-chief, Pierre Lazareff, had emigrated to the United States, and Pia, deprived of the editorial help of his friend, Albert Camus (who had returned to his native Algeria), was now working twelve to fifteen hours a day in an overheated workshop trying to keep the paper going with a sadly reduced staff.

This intense activity, however, did not satisfy Pascal's patriotic sentiments. Since many Gallimard authors were unwilling to contribute to Drieu la Rochelle's collaborationist *NRF*, Pia wanted to launch a new, 'untainted' monthly – to be called *Prométhée* (Prometheus) – in the 'free zone'. Malraux promised his wholehearted support. Roland, already an 'old hand' in clandestine border-crossing, was sent to Paris to pick up manuscripts and to find out what had happened to two copies of *Sierra de Teruel*.

In the end, nothing came of Pascal Pia's *Prométhée* initiative, which was blocked by suspicious censors in Vichy. But his visit to Roquebrune had one immediate practical consequence for Malraux. He had discovered that the half-tracks, sent on ahead at Pont-sur-Yonne with the DC–41's duffel-bags, had made it to a town near Tarbes, in the foothills of the Pyrenees. When he heard that two friends had taken refuge in south-western France, he asked Pascal Pia to get in touch with them and to see if they could find out what had happened to his 'gear', which must have contained 'more papers than the entire dormitory' and, specifically, 'two typed chapters of the *Psychologie de l'Art*, ditto for a chapter of a novel, and all of my war notes'.

In early March Dorothy Bussy curtly informed them that she was having all the furniture, as well as curtains, carpets, and silverware, removed from the Souco villa. Finding another furnished house posed no problem, so massive had been the panicky exodus of villa owners from the Côte d'Azur.

But it was with genuine regret that André and Roland, Josette, Bimbo, the nurse, and the invaluable Luigi said goodbye to the tamarisks, the orange trees, and the eagle's nest of Roquebrune, and moved to a spacious villa, Les Camélias, located on the promontory of Cap d'Ail, west of Nice. This villa was so ostentatious, with a cascade of flowered terraces and a lift for indolent inhabitants, that André took an instant dislike to it.

A few days after this irksome move Malraux made another trip to Marseilles to see Varian Fry. During one of his inter-zonal trips to Paris the resourceful Roland had managed to retrieve a complete set of *Sierra de Teruel* film reels. André wanted to know if Varian Fry could have them smuggled out of France via the US diplomatic pouch. Fry invited him to a Marseilles restaurant, where Malraux was introduced to his old Trotskyist adversary, Victor Serge, and to Fry's ERC deputy, Daniel Bénédite and his British-born wife, Theodora. Bénédite, a once ardent Trotskyist who had met Malraux six years before at a meeting sponsored by the Anti-Fascist Vigilance Committee, found him greatly changed.

He was bothered by embarrassing twitches, breathed heavily through the nose, and with constant head shakes and audible snorts he flicked back the lock of hair that kept falling over his forehead. But the atmosphere was pretty relaxed. Malraux, who had distanced himself from the Communists, listened attentively to Victor's [Serge's] reproaches and agreed that 'many errors were committed during the May 1937 repression in Catalonia'. After dinner he took us to a hall which had been turned into a clandestine movie theatre, and there he showed us and several friends some of his *Sierra de Teruel* film reels.

The next day Malraux returned to Fry's office and gave him a note addressed to General de Gaulle, in which he indicated his readiness to join him and to participate in the organization of a Free French Air Force. Fry turned the letter over to his secretary, Theodora Bénédite, telling her to take precious care of it until she could contact an escaping RAF airman willing to carry the message to London. What, one wonders, would have happened if this handwritten note had ever reached de Gaulle? It certainly would have touched off an explosion from a furious Josette, had she ever got wind of it. The letter, however, never reached its destination. Several weeks later (April 5, 1941), during a demonstration by a joyous crowd, thrilled with the news that Yugoslavia had denounced its alliance with Nazi Germany, Theodora Bénédite was arrested by a Marseilles police squad and bundled into a police van, where she bravely munched and swallowed André Malraux's compromising letter.

In early April, shortly before Josette's twenty-ninth birthday, they were joined by her friend Suzanne Chantal, who, after marrying a Portuguese journalist, José Augusto de Santos, had decided to give birth to her first child in France. The days passed in an often jolly atmosphere, thanks to the presence of Roland, whose good humour and native wit never ceased to delight André. While the 'girls' made their way down the rocky path to the sun-baked cove, André – *le forçat de la plume* (the galley slave of the pen), as he called himself – remained upstairs on the terrace among the rose bushes, before retiring indoors.

The title he had chosen for his new novel – *La Lutte avec l'Ange* (The Struggle with the Angel) – reflected his own struggle not only with literature but with life. All the progressive causes he had so passionately embraced – on behalf of the Annamese in Indochina, against the Fascists in Europe and Ethiopia, with the revolutionary Republicans of Spain – had ended in defeats, crowned by the most humiliating of them all: France's collapse in a campaign which had barely lasted five weeks. The very titles he had chosen for his novels – *Les Conquérants, La Voie royale, L'Espoir* – now had a hollow ring, since each was in reality the chronicle of a shattered hope.

Malraux had come to the conclusion that there was no point in writing the kind of follow-up novel on the Spanish Civil War of which he had rashly spoken in a letter to Robert Haas in June 1939. He would have to write something radically different from a *roman de combat*: something more in the nature of a meditation on the many themes that were dear to him.

Of all André Malraux's novels, if it can be called a 'novel', *La Lutte avec l'Ange* (better known by its later title, *Les Noyers de l'Altenburg* – The Walnut Trees of Altenburg) turned out to be the most fragmented and disconnected. It lacked a central figure (like Garine of *Les Conquérants*, Perken of *La Voie royale*); it lacked unity of place (as in the Shanghai of *La Condition humaine*); it lacked a precise historical context (like the Spanish Civil War, binding together the three parts of *L'Espoir*). This new work was less a 'novel' than five rather diverse prose pieces, strung like beads on the thread of Malraux's personal reminiscences: reminiscences not only of what he had actually experienced, but of what he had often dreamed.

In the first pages Malraux conjures up with extraordinary realism the reactions of prisoners-of-war crammed into a cathedral, which, for the purposes of fiction, becomes that of Chartres, instead of Sens. He then transports us to the pre-war Istanbul of Enver Pasha and the 'Young Turks'; after which we join a group of scholars in a vaulted library (inspired by the Cistercian abbey of Pontigny) who carry on a learned debate about civilizations, psychology, the 'fundamental man', eternity, God. Malraux then carries us on his magic carpet – not towards a terrestrial paradise, but to an earthly hell: the eastern front in 1915, where, on hideously scarred Polish soil, German troops launch a lethal gas attack against their Russian enemies. In the fifth and final sequence – incongruously entitled 'The Chartres camp' (though neither the city nor the cathedral play any part in the narrative) – the author has us take part in a nocturnal tank attack against the Germans, somewhere in Flanders. This was the fragment, then called *La Fosse aux chars* (The Tank Ditch), which he had sent to Robert Haas early in 1941.

The third section of what came to be called *Les Noyers de l'Altenburg* was clearly intended to be the intellectual *pièce de résistance* of this loosely formed five-part work, since among the subjects debated at the Altenburg symposium were the historical theories of Oswald Spengler and Leo Frobenius. However, the section immediately preceding it was, from the psychological (as opposed to philosophical) point of view, no less fascinating. The 'hero' of this section, Vincent Berger, who is also the narrator's father, clearly owed far more to André than to Fernand Malraux. As a professor appointed to head his (German) embassy's propaganda service as well as the trusted adviser and *éminence grise* of Enver Pasha, Vincent Berger was clearly an imaginary *alter ego*, projected on to the history of the Ottoman Empire during the first two decades of the twentieth century: the prototype of the intellectual turned warrior, playing the combined role of thinker and man of action which Malraux himself had sought to fill as an informal representative of Léon Blum's government and as the organizer of an 'air force' during the Spanish Civil War.

Enver Pasha, like Lawrence of Arabia, was an inspired dreamer: one whose romantic vision of an 'empire' stretching from Adrianople and Gallipoli in the Balkans to Samarkand and Bokhara in Central Asia, culminated in disaster. He and Lawrence (as well as Alexander the Great) clearly belonged to a particular human category – that of 'tragic destinies' – which had long fascinated Malraux. But without a library, Malraux seems to have found the story of Enver Pasha difficult to sustain at any length. This may explain the increasing attention he devoted to Lawrence of Arabia, whose *Seven Pillars of Wisdom* had been translated into French as early as 1936 and republished by Payot in 1940. Malraux, who was likely to launch into an inspired monologue at the mention of Lawrence's name, had in fact already begun making preparatory notes for a work later called *Le Démon de l'Absolu*. But there were two practical reasons for concentrating first on the intellectually less fascinating figure of Enver Pasha. During the First World War Enver had been an ally of the Germans, whereas Lawrence had played the role of a Middle Eastern *dinamitero*, blowing up stretches of Ottoman railway track. Malraux knew his only chance of being published was in some foreign country; but a 'novel' or biographical essay extolling the exploits of Colonel Lawrence, an important member of His Majesty's Intelligence Service during the Great War of 1914–18, could only be regarded by the authorities in Vichy, and even more by the Gestapo in Paris, as highly 'provocative' literature. Enver Pasha, on the other hand, was an irreproachable pro-German 'hero'. However, for those wishing to heed the unspoken implications, the collapse of Enver's pan-Turanian fantasy could be regarded as a reminder of what happens to 'empires' when their over-hasty architects – Adolf Hitler being an egregious example – seek to realize their lunatic ambitions.

We have Manès Sperber's word for it that never during these disheartening months, when Britain had its back to the wall and Roosevelt's United States was still smugly attached to a policy of 'absolute neutrality', did Malraux doubt for a moment that the war would end with Hitler's defeat. Adler's former disciple and practitioner of 'individual psychology' had managed to escape the fate that had overtaken Arthur Koestler and Gustav Regler – both imprisoned in the scandalous camp of Le Vernet (in the foothills of the Pyrenees) – by enlisting in the Foreign Legion. Demobilized at Aix-en-Provence after an exhausting series of forced marches, he had miraculously re-established contact with Jenka, thanks to a friend living in' Auguste Renoir's old village of Hauts-de-Cagnes, perched on its rocky, thyme-and-lavender-scented summit west of Nice. They had been among the first 'old friends' to visit the Souco villa; and whenever Manès Sperber appeared, André would immediately abandon his writing and, sometimes carrying Bimbo on his shoulders, repeatedly walk up and down the garden slope, speculating on what was likely to happen next. On one point both of them, as military 'veterans', saw eye to eye: the pointlessness of trying to fight the German occupants with defiant tracts and leaflets. The only vitally import-ant question was (as Sperber later wrote) when the resistance (which did not yet deserve a capital 'R') 'would cease to be a movement of propagandists hostile to collaboration and transform itself into the well-organized and coherent combat groups of a clandestine army'.

Throughout this momentous spring and summer, which saw Yugoslavia overrun, the British ignominiously chased out of Greece and Crete, and Stalin's USSR invaded by a seemingly invincible *Wehrmacht*, Malraux kept receiving visits from curious 'emissaries' and old friends, who wanted to find out what he personally proposed to do. The answer, differing only in the vocabulary used, was invariably the same: 'For the time being, nothing. Let's not play at being boy scouts.' It was the answer he gave to Jean Cassou, who had accompanied him to Madrid in June 1936 (and who went on to found his own Musée de l'Homme resistance network in Paris). It was the answer he gave to Emmanuel d'Astier de la Vigerie, who came to see him with Edouard Corniglion-Molinier, both of them determined to found a resist-ance network unambiguously called Libération (and which later led to Corniglion's arrest and incarceration in a Marseilles fort, from which, like the Count of Monte Cristo, the ebullient 'Eddy' managed to escape). It was the sobering advice Malraux gave, even more bluntly, to the all-too-young, eager, and idealistic Claude Bourdet, who had been enrolled in the COMBAT network.

'Do you have any money?'

Bourdet could only stammer that well, no, not yet, but . . .

'Do you have any weapons?' was the second, no less pointed question. It elicited the same vaguely hopeful reply.

'All right,' said Malraux, as a twitch of impatience creased his face, 'come back and see me when you have money and weapons.'

The ease and rapidity with which Hitler's Panzer divisions advanced across the plains and rolling hills of Russia and the Ukraine during the weeks following the fateful June 22, 1941 depressed Malraux only momentarily. He refused to abandon his conviction that Hitler would be defeated in the end, reminding his young admirer, Roger Stéphane, of what had happened to Napoleon. 'One day,' he assured him, 'anti-tank guns will conquer the tanks' – a prophecy soon to be fulfilled with the invention of the *Panzerfaust* and the Bazooka, the tank-destroyers of the US army, and British Typhoon attack planes. When, in late September, Roger Stéphane came to tell him that he was about to go 'underground' and to join a resistance network, Malraux shrugged his shoulders: 'If it pleases you to play the little soldier.' And when Stéphane asked if he had ever thought of joining de Gaulle in London, Malraux was equally caustic: 'What would I do among the *Action Française* officers who surround de Gaulle? Why not try to join the Red Army?'

In July Suzanne's husband, José Augusto de Santos, reached Cap d'Ail, after an interminable four-day train trip across Spain and southern France, during which he had half starved himself in order to preserve the precious foodstuffs he was bringing from Lisbon. Rushing down the steps to greet the former correspondent who had covered the Spanish Civil War with Franco's forces, André seized him by the arm, dog-tired and dirty though he was, and led him out on to the road. There they spent an hour exchanging reminiscences about a strife-torn Spain, which each in his own way had come to love.

Like Suzanne, who was already knitting warm woollen clothes to carry Bimbo (and her own, soon-to-be-born infant) through another winter without fuel, José Augusto proved to be a useful addition to the household. He went to work translating Malraux's 'novel' into Portuguese – in which language it appeared, two-and-a-half years later, under the title of *A Luta com o anjo* (The Struggle with the Angel).

In August André Gide turned up at the Camélias villa, dressed in an exotic brick-red suit, made of a material which, he explained, had been offered to him by Stalin. A good part of the villa's reserves – sardines, dried sausage from Alentejo, a bottle of port wine, several bottles of Montrachet, a crateful of cherries offered by M. Clotis, a juicy chicken sent by one of Josette's aunts – were consumed to keep the distinguished visitor happy. This privileged treatment did not, however, soften the severity of Gide's critical judgement of the long passages of *La Lutte avec l'Ange* (later retitled *Les Noyers de l'Altenburg*) which Malraux read to him behind closed doors in a number of private sessions, from which André emerged looking paler than ever. Once he had recovered from this literary shock therapy, however, he was honest enough to admit that many of Gide's criticisms were justified and that a lot of rewriting needed to be done.

Gide's departure was soon followed by that of José Augusto, forced to return to Lisbon in early September, shortly before the birth of their baby daughter (Marie-Chantal).

In early September Malraux learned to his dismay that Varian Fry, the courageous director of the Emergency Rescue Committee's Marseilles office, had been expelled from France – after having facilitated the departure to America of more than 1,000 refugees – including Max Ernst, Marc Chagall, the sculptor Jacques Lipchitz, the harpsichordist Wanda Landowska, the painter André Masson, Victor Serge, André Breton and many others. Fry's hard pressed assistant, Daniel Bénédite, and his equally brave wife Theodora could no longer arrange for unofficial transfers of dollars from Malraux's account with Random House. Fry's expulsion was equally upsetting because Malraux had been planning, with his assistance, to have the film reels of *Sierra de Teruel* shipped to the Library of Congress in Washington.

In October 1941 André and Josette chose to leave Cap d'Ail and return to Roquebrune. Malraux had to interrupt work on *La Lutte avec l'Ange* to help Roland comb the shops of Cannes, Nice and Menton for furniture and furnishings which they needed to bring a little warmth and life back to the glacial rooms and bare walls of the Souco villa, which Simon Bussy and his wife were willing to rent to them for a pittance. They found the sloping garden sadly gone to seed, the rocky ground covered with wild mint and citronella, the persimmons laden with over-ripe fruit, but the air was full of all the dry scents of Provence, and the view from the Italian coast to the promontory of Monaco was as breathtaking as ever.

On November 3rd, huddled around an electric radiator in a room wanly heated by the autumn sun, they celebrated André's fortieth birthday. This was followed two days later by an equally frugal repast honouring the first anniversary of Pierre-Gauthier's (Bimbo's) birth. They had acquired a cat, which found it easy to outrun the wobbly Bimbo as he tottered around, with outstretched hands, in a pair of tiny felt boots. This furry acquisition could not make up, however, for the void created by Roland's departure for Toulouse, where he had found employment. André's *La Lutte avec l'Ange* became increasingly grim; but he emerged from it triumphant, having finally found a way of expressing the brutal irruption into the twentieth century of the demonic forces of absolute evil, with a hallucinating description of a gas attack made by German forces on the eastern front in 1915.

When, towards the end of November, Malraux reappeared in Nice, André Gide and Mme Théo could hardly believe their eyes. Never had he seemed more relaxed, without a trace of nervousness, nor even the faintest spasm of a facial twitch.

A few days later the Japanese bombed Pearl Harbor, and Hitler committed the ultimate folly of declaring war against the United States. Almost simultaneously, Marshal Zhukov's forces began a powerful counter-offensive, which forced the *Wehrmacht*'s perilously exposed divisions into a humiliating retreat from the outskirts of Moscow. The war, as Malraux had been predicting, was going to be won by Russian tanks and American warplanes.

Suzanne's departure with her child on the last day of December reduced the hitherto animated household from seven to four. It made Josette's cohabitation with André more difficult, since they were now thrown back on their sole resources at a time when Malraux – with his 'green face', as she called it – seemed increasingly remote, absorbed as he was by the novel he was wrestling with.

Pierre Laval's dramatic return to power in April 1942 was a further irritant, hastening André Gide's departure for Tunis. On June 22nd Laval chose to celebrate the first anniversary of the *Wehrmacht*'s invasion of the USSR by making a radio address in which he called on his compatriots to join the common struggle against Bolshevism, forthrightly declaring, 'I hope for the victory of Germany because, without it, Bolshevism would triumph tomorrow everywhere.'

Just two days before, Jenka Sperber had given birth in a Cagnes clinic to a baby boy. The child – named Dan, followed by André (in Malraux's honour) and Faber (his mother's maiden name) – could not have come into the world at a more perilous moment for both parents. For Laval's despicable radio speech was soon followed by another abject capitulation to German pressure, with a massive round-up in July 1942 of close to 20,000 French men and women of Jewish origin in German-occupied France, and during the months of August and September of 10,000 Jewish 'foreigners' (most of them refugees from Nazi Germany) who had fled to the 'free zone'. Already suffering from a painful stomach ulcer, Manès Sperber was now forced to spend each night in a nearby barn. With the aid of friends he obtained false identity cards for himself and for Jenka, in which they were presented as being Alsatians. Sperber, like Malraux, had been working on a novel, passages of which he had read to his friend André during visits to the Roquebrune villa. 'If ever you have to run for it,' Malraux had advised him, 'have your manuscript delivered to Roger Martin du Gard in Nice. Having never been politically *engagé*, like Gide and myself, his books have never figured on a Nazi blacklist, and your papers will be in far safer hands with Martin du Gard than with me.' Sperber decided to try to get his family to Switzerland.

It was not until weeks later that Malraux learned of the safe arrival in Switzerland of his two friends. For by the mid-summer of 1942 the village of Roquebrune had become so insufferably hot, the nights so plagued by mosquitos, and the waterless garden so dessicated that Malraux decided that they could do with a change of scenery. He was also worried by the fate of another Jewish friend, Emmanuel Berl, who had prudently left Grasse and taken refuge in the *département* of Corrèze. Emmanuel Arago, a descendant of the famous astronomer, had found a perfect hide-out for Berl in the town of Argentat, located at the junction of three rivers 30 kilometres southeast of Tulle. His 'host', who answered to the humble name of Bouyou, had two rooms to rent. An anti-German patriot who had lost an arm during the Great War of 1914–18, he was the postman, and as such a unique source of local news, since he had privileged access to every household, farm, and grotto in and around the town.

Of all André Malraux's friends none, not even the formidable Bernard Groethuysen, could match the rapidity of speech and startling diversity of mental associations better than Emmanuel Berl. Their interminable discussions had the suspense and vivacity of ping-pong matches. Seated on a stool, Berl's wife Mireille would watch with admiring incredulity, her head moving back and forth from one speaker to the other until her neck muscles began to ache. But the two weeks spent at Argentat proved to be engrossing for other, non-intellectual reasons – with fateful consequences for the future. For thanks to Berl, Malraux met Emmanuel Arago, the first to talk to him of Major Pierre Jacquot, twice wounded while leading his infantry regiment in a fighting retreat from the Somme to Bergerac, who was now trying to co-ordinate the anti-German resistance efforts of professional Army officers in the Corrèze region.

It was also at Argentat that André Malraux first came to realize one enormous advantage possessed by the Massif Central over the Côte d'Azur. At Roquebrune Josette and Bimbo had been trying to survive on a sparse diet of tomatoes, courgettes, boiled eggplant, and the inevitable swedes. But here, in the verdant Corrèze, butter, eggs, and milk, to say nothing of sausages and meat, could be obtained from local farmers.

The surprises, agreeable as well as disagreeable, of this summer of 1942 were mild compared to those that awaited André and Josette during a momentous autumn. Even before returning to Roquebrune in late October Josette discovered that she was pregnant once again, and at a time when André's unexplained absences seemed to be growing more frequent and prolonged. The loneliness Josette dreaded soon surpassed her direst apprehensions. On November 8th an Anglo-American expeditionary force began landing at various points along the shores of Algeria and Morocco. Three days later the Germans retaliated by invading the 'free zone'. Taken completely by surprise and above all commanded by a spineless Minister of War (General Bridoux), Vichy's small *armée de l'armistice* (100,000 men) collapsed with hardly a shot being fired at the German invaders. The Italians, who by the terms of the Armistice of June 1940 had been granted a 'zone of influence' embracing Nice, now invaded the Côte d'Azur. Luigi chose this moment to decamp to Monte Carlo, where he opened a restaurant. This 'desertion' and Josette's pregnancy made it imperative that they find another habitat in a less rocky, more verdant part of France.

On November 16th Malraux left Roquebrune, stopping briefly at Toulon, where the battleships of Admiral Jean de Laborde's Mediterranean fleet were still calmly moored to the docksides as though nothing had happened. He then continued on to Toulouse, to see how Roland was faring in his new job with a local tax inspector. There was also another reason. Roland's younger brother Claude – at twenty-two the most impetuous of the three Malraux brothers – had long since given up his boring studies in agronomy, preferring to enlist as a cavalryman with a regiment of Moroccan *spahis*. From Algiers, where he had been demobilized in December 1940, he had returned to Paris, not quite knowing what to do with himself. A lover of adventure and no enemy of the fair sex, he had gradually drifted into a curiously penumbral, semi-bohemian world of 'let's-live-for-the-moment' opportunists who lived off their wits and kept the wolf from the door by indulging in black market deals, often with the connivance of French 'collaborators' and their protectors among the seedier elements of the Gestapo and nazi officialdom. To extricate his younger brother from these quicksands of cynical immorality, Roland had introduced Claude to Philippe Liewer, who was able to offer the sybaritic daredevil a far more challenging and useful life. A thirty-year-old journalist, Liewer had been engaged in anti-nazi resistance activities from very early on, together with Pierre Bloch, a Socialist deputy from Dordogne. With the help of Bloch's enterprising wife, they and eight others had made a spectacular escape from a Vichy prison camp at Manzac, 12 kilometres south-west of Périgueux, and had made it across Spain and Portugal to London. Here Liewer had been recruited by Colonel Buckmaster's SOE (the British Special Operations Executive) and assigned the task of setting up a sabotage network in the Rouen–Le Havre region of the lower Seine. One of the first people Philippe Liewer had looked up after his clandestine return to Paris was his widowed aunt, Alice-Jean Alley, a friend of Roland and André Malraux. It was thus, on Roland's initiative, that Claude had been integrated into the SOE's SALESMAN network. Since SOE agents were always looking for 'safe' hide-outs where radio operators, sabotage technicians, automatic-weapons instructors, or downed airmen could spend a night or two, Roland had rented an apartment on the ninth floor of the Rue Lord Byron, not far from the Arc de Triomphe.

In Toulouse Roland introduced André to a dark-haired, dark-eyed piano virtuoso named Madeleine Lioux, whom he had recently been courting. Without wasting a moment, André subjected her to a peremptory examination. Did she like poetry? Yes, was the reply.

'What do you know of Apollinaire?'

'*Le Pont Mirabeau*,' she answered, and proceeded to recite it.

'Ah', said Malraux, favourably impressed. 'But what of Claudel's *Oratorio*?' With this too she was surprisingly familiar.

'You must marry Madeleine,' he told Roland. And to prove to both of them that he meant it, he went out and bought a copy of Claudel's text, put to music by Honegger, offering it as a gift to the future bride.

From Toulouse Malraux headed north to Brive-la-Gaillarde and Argentat. At the postman Bouyou's house, he explained to Emmanuel Berl and Mireille that he wanted to leave the Côte d'Azur, now overrun by Italians, and find some quiet, out-of-the-way spot nearby, little frequented by the Germans. Informed by telephone of this (for her) unexpected move, Josette packed her bags in a hurry, said goodbye to the orange trees and cypress of La Souco, and made the wearying two-day journey on crowded trains, accompanied by the toddling, two-year-old Bimbo. By the time they reached Argentat, on or around December 12th, André had found a new home for them: three rooms in a freezingly cold château overlooking the rustic village of Saint-Chamant, six kilometres north-west of Argentat, on the road to Tulle.

'I am writing on the terrace of my château,' Josette wrote a few days later to her friend Suzanne, as though she already owned it, 'with guinea fowls dressed in tulle and my child dressed in red cackling around me. We are above a lovely valley . . . Everything is of a russet hue . . . We have towers galore, we are living in one tower, our room is round, like the study, where we eat in front of a big log fire.'

In another letter Josette wrote, almost ecstatically: 'You cannot imagine what our life is like in Corrèze. But it's PEACE! We don't see a single German. Never . . . We suffer from restrictions . . . that is, we can't find Paris mushrooms, nor caviar, nor choice goodies from Hédiard, but we make our omelettes with fresh truffles and Armagnac . . . A farm is attached to the château and we have all the food in the world.'

In early January of the new year (1943) Roland Malraux and Madeleine Lioux came up from Toulouse, and on the 9th they were married in a civil ceremony held at the town hall of Tulle. Emmanuel Berl acted as witness for Roland, André as witness for Madeleine. Josette, who had never forgiven Berl for the way he had treated her when she was working for *Marianne*, peevishly refused to attend the ceremony. Fortunately she found her new sister-in-law 'absolutely charming . . . Sweet, shy . . .', as Josette wrote to her friend Suzanne in Lisbon, 'black, very deep-set and gleaming eyes. A radiant smile, and above all a ravishing expression.'

For Madeleine, as for Roland Malraux, this was the beginning of a strange new life. Three days a week – Tuesday, Wednesday, Thursday – she remained in Toulouse, where she gave piano lessons to students of the music conservatory. Thursday evening she took the night train to Paris and was able to spend the four remaining days – Friday through to Monday – in the small Rue Lord Byron apartment, where there was barely enough room for an Erard piano.

Although perfectly aware of Roland's clandestine activities, André took no active part in them, preferring to wait for the 'decisive' moment when the Allies finally invaded France. That moment, he was convinced, was now only a few months off. As he wrote to Roger Martin du Gard on January 2nd, 'I feel sure, and a fairly good prophet for my forecast of May 43, as to the decisive hours.'

In the meantime, the all-important problem was how to keep body and soul together at a moment when a new Malraux baby was about to be born – one for whom Josette had already found the name of Corinne. André's attempt to have a typed copy of Part I of *La Lutte avec l'Ange* sent to Robert Haas via Suzanne's husband, José Augusto de Santos, in Lisbon, failed. Malraux had better luck in Europe. Probably with the help of François Lachenal, a diplomat serving with the Swiss legation in Vichy, he had another copy of the text smuggled out of France and published by the Editions du Haut-Pays in Lausanne.

He had been saved momentarily from his financial predicament thanks to an advance Gaston Gallimard had been willing to make for his book on Lawrence of Arabia. But the deeper Malraux delved into this fascinating subject, the more difficult he found the task. The main problem, as he admitted in several letters to Roger Martin du Gard, who had replaced André Gide as his chief literary confidant, was 'the impossibility to write with precision' of a mysterious figure about whom he possessed inadequate documentation. No less troubling was the basic biographical data he found himself obliged to supply, and which ran counter to his natural penchant for fictionalizing reality. 'My "Lawrence" is becoming a big book. And I am more and more attracted by the novel since I have been separated from it,' he wrote on February 2, 1943. 'So much so that I find that the subtlest parts of Lawrence's adventure would be rendered far more intelligible by fiction than by the analysis I am making.' Two months later he wrote again:

I am completely intoxicated by Lawrence. In one month I have completely checked, corrected, and partly rewritten close to 300 pages. What a strange kind of monster is a book where the only art is in the narration, where one can invent nothing . . . When I am speaking, it's all right. But in 150 pages I have to cover what he [Lawrence] described, with the advantage of personal experience, in 800 . . . L[awrence] finished, I will give it to Gaston, and I will try to become a human being again.

But alas, the time for relaxing had not yet come. For during a trip to Paris in June – where he found the capital filled with a surprising number of 'women in flowered dresses', while the morale of the German occupants was steadily sinking – he visited the Bibliothèque Nationale. 'Sinister,' as he wrote to Martin du Gard. 'But so much a record that I must begin part of my book all over again.'

Meanwhile, in early March, almost one month before the expected date, Josette was seized by violent birth pains and had to be driven through the night to Brive, where a frantic André finally found a clinic capable of handling emergency cases at 4 o'clock in the morning. The painful labour was so rapid that Josette gave birth stretched out in the corridor.

This first shock was followed by another, when she discovered that instead of a Corinne, she had given birth to an ugly, chinless boy, who reminded her of Pierre Renoir, of Harry Baur, of Sainte-Beuve!

A day or two later André brought her back to Saint-Chamant, carrying her up two flights of stone steps to their bedroom in the tower, warmed by a crackling and spitting fire. A new name had to be found. Vincent was finally chosen, in honour of Vincent Berger, the 'hero' of the central section of La Lutte avec l'Ange..

It did not take Josette long to be reconciled to the unexpected presence of this second son, particularly since he had inherited his father's and grandmother's (Berthe Lamy) gleaming, marble-like eyes. 'Heavens, what lovely eyes they have in this family,' she wrote to Suzanne, adding, a trifle prematurely: 'I am so calm that I can think of Clara without caring a damn. Never have I been more authentic than in this little neck of the woods. We came here because of the Berls and we never see them. Since we are alone in the world, with no intellectuals in sight, we get on well.'

Given her dislike of Emmanuel Berl, another godfather had to be found. Drieu la Rochelle, whom Josette liked as much as she disliked Berl, agreed to be Vincent's godfather, when Malraux called on him in Paris some time in June. The godmother was Rosine Delclaux, the wife of the village notary who had arranged the rental lease for 'their' turreted château.

All of Malraux's optimistic forecasts about 'decisive events' taking place in May 1943 were disproved by the slowness of the Allies' advance up the Italian 'boot', by the tenacity of the *Wehrmacht* in Russia and the Ukraine, by the manifest reluctance of the US High Command to risk another abortive invasion on the coasts of Normandy comparable to the Anglo-Canadian fiasco at Dieppe in August 1942. And so, as the green of summer gave way to the russet of autumn, a restive Josette had to abandon the novel on which she had fitfully been working in order to prepare for another cruel winter.

'I have never liked the autumn,' she wrote to Suzanne, 'but here it suits the countryside, with a wealth, with a wild splurge of riches. Woods filled with chanterelles, boletus mushrooms, *clavaires*, with chestnuts and walnuts rolling underfoot among dead leaves.' The chestnuts, in particular, were precious – for the soups that could be made of them. No less valuable were the nuts: pounded with a hammer and then crushed, they provided a crude vegetable oil for cooking and preparing salads. From the pig they had bought, Josette had been able, with the help of the local butcher, to make all sorts of *pâtés*, *terrines*, and pots of lard and animal fat. For someone who had always been beautifully groomed and perfumed, the 125 grams per month of soap were a dire hardship; but so too was the total absence, in this corner of the Corrèze, of anything resembling shoes – with the result that Bimbo was reduced to stumbling around in heavy wooden clogs.

He keeps falling and crying like a desperate little seal, his nose in the air. He has a pair of ugly shorts cut from old woollens, which we make ourselves and which are badly made. He looks like a ragged tramp going out to keep an eye on the cows, but [he is] of a breathtaking beauty, talkative, bold, rambunctious, wilful, but tender and protective with his brother. Vincent, for his part, is draped in the robe of an infanta. He is as black as a prune. He laughs all the time, like a music-hall comedian. A model child.

Before they knew it, winter was upon them, covering the chestnut trees, the walnuts, the firs and birches with mantles of snow. Despite the cold,

Josette could thank her lucky stars that André had had the sense to bring her here, thus sparing her and her two infants the near starvation to which Roger Martin du Gard and his wife Hélène were reduced in Nice, with nothing to keep them weakly alive but noodles, a thin *entrecôte* for two once every fifteen days, and an egg every six weeks.

32

The Resister

Among the ardent patriots Malraux had met in this region of Corrèze was a Brive businessman, Maurice Arnouilh, who had set up an enterprise for the manufacture of charcoal-operated *gazogène* boilers. Mounted on trucks, vans, and private cars, these enabled them to go on functioning in the absence of tightly rationed fuel. As expansive as he was resourceful, Arnouilh was delighted to discover that Malraux shared his anti-nazi sentiments. One day, in late September 1943, he drove to Saint-Chamant in his *gazogène*-operated Chevrolet and informed Malraux that he had hired an associate, one Henri Chevalier, to act as a travelling salesman for his Bloc-Gazo company. But this was simply a 'cover' for activities of a more exciting nature.

Just where André Malraux first met Major Henry Peulevé, of the SOE, we do not know. But they immediately hit it off. An Englishman descended from Huguenot expatriates, Harry Peulevé had lived for several years before the war at Menton and spoke excellent French. Affable, good-humoured, witty, he seemed the very prototype of the clean-cut Briton, in whom one could place a total trust. He was also a man of exceptional stamina and courage. On his first mission to France, in 1942, he had been parachuted out of an RAF plane at too low an altitude and had broken a leg. Transported by members of a Resistance network to Mougins, near Cannes, he had later limped his way across the Pyrenees and made it back to London. This time, he had been flown over in a small, single-motor Lysander aeroplane and deposited at night on a secret field with the mission of organizing an effective Resistance network in the *département* of Corrèze.

Impressed though he was by André Malraux's combative temperament, Peulevé knew that his mission was not to recruit prestigious individuals; it was to find suitable sites for the parachuting of weapons and explosives, and to establish contact with the two main Resistance networks in the Corrèze–Dordogne region – these being the AS or *Armée secrète* (the military branch of the COMBAT and LIBERATION networks) and the communist-dominated FTP (FRANCS-TIREURS et PARTISANS).

By January of 1944 Peulevé had found at least three good 'drop-zones' for the parachuting of containers in the Dordogne. He had recruited a helpful assistant, Charles Delsanti, a former police commissioner from Ussel (northeast of Tulle), who in turn had enlisted the talents of a competent technician, Louis Bertheau, a former French Air Force radio operator who could tap out coded messages to London. Malraux, for his part, had tried to help Peulevé by recommending his faithful liegeman, Raymond Maréchal, who, as a former Air Force gunner, was well qualified to serve as an instructor in the handling of Sten guns for present and future *maquisards*.

During this same month of January 1944 Peulevé was joined by a younger SOE officer named 'Jack Peters'. His French was so perfect that he could easily have passed for a Frenchman – which in fact he was, though this was a carefully concealed secret to keep him from being involved in the petty intrigues and in-fighting between rival Resistance movements. Not yet eighteen at the time of the débâcle, Jacques Poirier had been too young to serve in the French Army, but this had only made him more determined to avenge the defeat of 1940. Introduced to Peulevé in a Nice restaurant in 1942, he had insisted on having him lodged at his parents' nearby villa. This was the start of a firm friendship, sealed in the late autumn of 1942 when the young Poirier had accompanied Peulevé across the Pyrenees.

It was at the Moulin du Cuzoul, a farm located near Daglan (in the Dordogne), that 'Jack Peters' first met Raymond Maréchal. After three sleepless nights spent on the Domme plateau waiting for a parachute drop of twenty containers, the robust 'Jack l'Anglais' (as he was promptly dubbed by other network members) had contracted pneumonia – cured by the application to his chest and back of old-fashioned cupping glasses. The cure had been effected by Georgette, the courageous wife of the farm's owner, Paul ('Poulou') Lachaud, who had become an expert in the art of night-time parachute-drop 'receptions' and one of the pillars of Peulevé's AUTHOR network. The strip of metal that had been slipped under the skin of Maréchal's forehead, to cover the hideous wound he had received near Teruel gave him an almost brutal appearance. But, as 'Jack l'Anglais' was not long in discovering, this fearless fighter was a wonderfully warm-hearted *force de la nature*.

Jack l'Anglais was first introduced to André Malraux at a country inn near Tulle, where he had gone to meet George Hiller, organiser of an SOE network (FOOTMAN) in the neighbouring department of the Lot. Briefly pausing to greet the newcomers – simply introduced as 'George and Jack' – Malraux resumed a monologue in which, as far as the new SOE officer could tell, brief allusions to Braque and the siege of Stalingrad were woven into a discourse on Lawrence of Arabia. Although spellbound, Jacques Poirier shared Peulevé's misgivings. With his mobile features, a watery eye, and incessant ticks, a man like Malraux could not go unnoticed, and if allowed to join their ranks, the AUTHOR network could be tracked down within a week or two by the Gestapo.

Malraux himself must have been aware of this handicap. Towards the end of the meal he dismissed Colonel Lawrence and spent a few earnest minutes vaunting the linguistic merits of his half-brother Roland and his experience in clandestine activities. He then devoted several minutes to extolling the loyal fearlessness of Raymond Maréchal.

Maréchal, already well known to Peulevé, Poulou and Georgette Lachaud, needed no further introduction. But André had to go to Paris and bring back Roland Malraux, so that Peulevé and 'Jack l'Anglais' could judge for themselves. Both found him quite different from his half-brother – more relaxed, more elegant, somewhat worldly, but a most likeable fellow whom it would be easy to integrate into their group.

During the second week of March Roland Malraux returned to his Rue Lord Byron apartment in Paris, where he was joined by his wife Madeleine. Here, on March 9th, a young SOE courier, Violette Szabo, brought them the news that Roland's brother Claude had disappeared. The Germans were clearly bent on dismantling Philippe Liewer's SALESMAN network, which had blown up an electricity-generating plant near Rouen, and had sunk a recently refitted minesweeper.

Alerted by his half-brother, André turned up the next day at the Rue Lord Byron apartment and told Roland and Madeleine to clear out immediately. He then returned to his château at Saint-Chamant. The next day Roland and Madeleine left on the same train, but instead of accompanying Madeleine to her parents' home in Toulouse, Roland got off the train at Brive. She was to continue giving piano lessons at the Toulouse Conservatory and not to move until she heard from him.

The AUTHOR network's transmitter had been set up at Brive in a small two-storey house rented by the technical director of the Bloc-Gazo enterprise, a M. Lamaurie. It was from the first floor of this house that on March 12th a coded message was flashed to London informing SOE headquarters that Claude Malraux had disappeared, probably trapped by the Gestapo, that his radio operator, 'Pierre', had been arrested, and that 18 tons of hidden ammunition had been seized by the police.

In the meantime, Peulevé's AUTHOR network had acquired an astonishing new recruit who had left his home in the Savoie mountains to offer his services. He was Robert Poirier, a French Air Force major who turned out to be Jacques' father. His services were joyfully accepted by Harry Peulevé – on the strict condition that his kinship with his son 'Jack' be kept a closely guarded secret from all other members of the network.

Struck by Harry Peulevé's weary look – he had just returned from a tiring trip to several *maquis* leaders – Robert Poirier suggested that he offer himself a 'breather' by coming to spend a few days with him at his Savoie villa. But Harry Peulevé insisted that Jacques be the first to make the trip.

The next morning, March 21, 1944, Jacques Perrier (the false name inscribed on a new identity card issued to him by the Mairie of Brive) boarded the train for the long overland trip to Savoie. A few hours after his departure two black front-wheel-drive Citroëns drew up in front of La-maurie's house and out piled four German soldiers and their leader, an SD (*Sicherheitsdienst*) agent named Walter. Intrigued by the frequent visits made by strangers to this little house, a neighbour who happened to be a member of the pro-nazi *milice* had gone to inform Walter that no. 117, Route de Tulle had become a centre of black market activities. Unfortunately for those inside the house, Harry Peulevé had momentarily abandoned his watch-post by the window, probably because his radio operator, Louis Bertheau, was having trouble tapping out a coded message to London. The German soldiers, whom Peulevé and Delsanti could have mowed down with their Sten-guns, caught the SOE team completely by surprise. Opening the unlocked front door and hearing voices on the first floor, the Germans stormed up the stairs and burst into the small room, shouting, '*Hände hoch!*' When Walter walked in, he could not believe his eyes – or his good fortune. Instead of four wretched black marketeers engaged in haggling over the price of a goose, a few kilograms of cheese, sausages or butter, he had just caught an important Resistance team, who, in addition to a radio trans-mitter, had several Sten-guns with them and a cupboard filled with plastic dynamite. The four 'terrorists' were pushed down the stairs at gunpoint. Harry Peulevé and Charles Delsanti were forced to curl up inside the boot of one of the Citroëns. Louis Bertheau was then given a seat in one of the Citroëns, Roland Malraux in the other. They were immediately driven to Tulle.

This misfortune would have been a total disaster but for a stroke of luck. Maurice Arnouilh was on his way to join the other members of the team when he spotted the two black Citroëns and saw Peulevé and his companions being pushed out of the house at gunpoint. Walking quickly back to the car parked in front of his nearby house, Arnouilh headed for the road junction of Quatre-Routes, 25 kilometres to the south, where he knew he could contact Jean Verlhac, a member of George Hiller's SOE network. Hiller's radio operator, Cyril Watney, promptly transmitted the news to London. The evening of Jacques Poirier's arrival at his parents' chalet in Savoie, his mother turned on the radio set and suddenly, over the airwaves of the BBC, came the words: '*Message important pour Nestor. Jean très malade. Ne retournez pas à Bloc-Gazo.*' 'Nestor' was Jacques Poirier's SOE code-name, Jean that of Harry Peulevé. Five minutes later the BBC message was repeated.

Jacques Poirier's holiday in the Savoie mountains was of short duration. The next day he took the train back to Corrèze, accompanied by his father. When the train reached the next-to-the-last stop, at Quatre-Routes, both hastily got off and headed for Jean Verlhac's *fromagerie*. Here, after a brief argument with a suspicious, white-haired lady, Jacques Poirier was admitted to a back room office, where George Hiller was warming himself in front of a blazing fire. The SOE major informed him that he had received strict instructions from London ordering 'Nestor' to disappear from the Corrèze area, since the Germans had obtained a photograph of him (fortunately a poor one) and were beginning to paste it up in railway stations and on town hall notice boards. Poirier had no intention of compromising Hiller's FOOTMAN network, but he was determined to rebuild Harry Peulevé's SOE network after 'disappearing' for a while.

Malraux decided that he too had better vanish for a few days. Leaving Josette at Saint-Chamant, he headed for Paris. Early on March 25th he stopped to see his friends Bernard Groethuysen and Alix Guillain in their 'artist's garret' near the Boulevard Montparnasse. He had just escaped arrest by the Gestapo, he told them; could they find a hide-out for him for the next couple of days? Groet and Alix hurried over to the Rue Vaneau, where, in the absence of André Gide, Pierre Herbart had moved in, next to his mother-in-law, Mme Théo. There could be no question of refusing to shelter a friend in danger.

Early in the afternoon Malraux appeared with Groet and Alix and, as Mme Théo noted in her diary, immediately took

possession of his room with energetic simplicity. He went straight to the balcony, walked along it, inspecting with the eye of a practised connoisseur the gutter, the roof, the footholds on the façade – for, after all, who knows? . . . All of it done rapidly, without one word too many. He would not have done a better job if he had been acting in a *Malraux* film.

While Malraux was in Paris, Jacques Poirier and Maurice Arnouilh had been constantly on the move, driving around the *département* of the Lot in the *gazogène*-propelled Chevrolet. They had several narrow escapes – enough to convince Jacques Poirier that he and Maurice Arnouilh's overly conspicuous automobile would have to go their separate ways. After re-establishing contact with Hiller's radio operator, Cyril Watney, who transmitted his latest recommendations for drop-zone sites, 'Jack l'Anglais' returned to Lachaud's farm at the Moulin du Cuzoul, near Daglan, to organize the parachuting of more weapons. While there, Raymond Maréchal had him meet his chief 'lieutenant' (René Coustellier), an exuberant hot-head from the Côte d'Azur who had adopted the dazzling code-name of 'Soleil'.

At the Verlhacs' *fromagerie* in the little town of Quatre-Routes, Jacques Poirier again met George Hiller, who handed him a message just received from Colonel Buckmaster in London. 'Nestor' was informed that he was being placed in charge of a new network, DIGGER, which was to replace the decapitated AUTHOR. As soon as he could indicate an absolutely secure drop-site, two assistants would be parachuted down to help him. He was further informed that he had just been promoted to the rank of captain.

That same evening, as 'Captain Jack' was preparing a radio message for SOE in London, Georgette Lachaud turned up at the Verlhacs' *fromagerie* in a state of bewilderment and shock. 'Raymond,' she announced in a trembling voice, 'has been caught by the Germans. They assassinated him by the roadside.' Thus died the fearless gunner, the 'Gardet' of *L'Espoir*, the 'hot rabbit' who had wanted to shoot himself after the crash-landing in the mountains near Teruel, persuaded that no woman would ever want to kiss his hideously disfigured face. Accompanied by other members of his 'team', he had run into a German road block, not far from Domme. Most of his companions had been killed on the spot. He himself had been seized. His German captors had pressed his hands down on the red-hot coals of his *gazogène* burner, and had then finished off the 'terrorist' with a burst from a machine-pistol.

When 'Captain Jack' turned up at the Lachauds' farm, at the Moulin du Cuzoul, he found André Malraux waiting for him. 'This is another tough blow for all of us,' said Malraux. 'But it is from such tragedies that hope will finally be born, for we will succeed. I can bring you a great deal, thanks to my connections. I am not universally liked, but people will listen to me. I enjoy the confidence in Paris of members of the CNR [National Council of the Resistance]. You, Jack, enjoy the confidence of London . . . I think that a close association between us can only be of benefit to the Resistance. I propose that we go spend a week in Paris. For you this is indispensable. If you remain here, you will get yourself arrested – that much is obvious. As for myself, I must clarify my situation with the Resistance leaders in Paris.'

Captain Jack was all for closer co-operation with André Malraux. He was even prepared to spend a few days with him in Paris. He had discovered that Harry Peulevé, after being interrogated and probably tortured by the Gestapo in Limoges, had been sent to Paris and incarcerated in the suburban prison of Fresnes. He was eager to see if ways could be found to help him escape. But first, as he explained, he had to oversee the parachuting of two badly needed SOE assistants: an arms instructor ('Basil'), and a radio operator ('Casimir').

By this time Poulou Lachaud had acquired such a mastery in the techniques of flashlight signalling that he and his men could have taken care of everything unaided. But to avoid a repetition of the Brive catastrophe, Captain Jack needed an absolutely safe place from which his radio operator could maintain permanent contact with London.

The problem was solved with the help of Raymond Maréchal's deputy, 'Soleil', who had fortunately escaped the roadside massacre near Domme. He introduced Captain Jack to a rugged carpenter who had assumed the *nom de guerre* of 'Charles le Bolchevique'. Installed with his wife and three children in a huge stone edifice known as the 'castle' (which he shared with the local *curé*) in the very centre of Siorac-en-Périgord, he had transformed this little town, located some 25 kilometres downstream from Domme near the southern bank of the Dordogne river, into a bastion of anti-German resistance. Thanks to a system of surveillance set up with the co-operation of post office employees and telephone operators in several nearby villages, no 'strangers' could approach the town without their presence being immediately signalled to 'Charles le Bolchevique' in his 'castle'.

As canny and resourceful as he was resolute, 'Charles le Bolchevique' soon became one of the pillars of Captain Jack's network. He knew exactly who could be trusted to offer emergency shelter to X, Y, or Z; who could be relied upon to be a discreet as well as hardy leader of a combat or sabotage group; which sites were suitable for parachute drops, and so on.

In early April, after another meeting with Malraux, Captain Jack returned to 'Charles le Bolchevique' 's 'Castle', where he found Georgette Lachaud in tears. The Germans, who had been combing the Domme region for other 'terrorists' like Raymond Maréchal, had driven up to the Moulin du Cuzoul, and finding it deserted had set the mill on fire, then savagely cut the throats of all the ducks, hens, and other animals they could lay their hands on.

The next day, Easter Eve, the BBC transmitted the anxiously awaited message. That night, illuminated in a cloudless sky by an embarrassingly bright full moon, 'Basil' and 'Casimir' came floating down on parachutes, along with fifteen containers filled with arms, munitions, explosives, cigarettes and money, on to a narrow stretch of ground not far from Limeuil, some 15 kilometres north-west of the anti-Boche bastion of Siorac.

A shy, bespectacled Englishman, with the thoughtful look of a scholar, 'Casimir' (in normal life Ralph Beauclerk) demonstrated his skill as an expert radio transmitter by establishing contact with London within hours of his landing. Quite different in looks and personality was his younger companion, a small wiry fellow whose no-nonsense disposition was fortunately relieved by a wry sense of humour. Promptly divested of the exotic code-name ('Basil') given to him in London, he was renamed 'Jean-Pierre' (closer to his real name of Peter Lake) for French members of the network.

Captain Jack was now ready to accompany Malraux to Paris. They had agreed to meet in Limoges and to travel in the same train, but as an added precaution Malraux had decided to bring along one of the network's couriers, a pretty girl named Flora who would pretend to be Captain Jack's fiancée. As Malraux had reckoned, the railway trip to Paris passed off without a hitch – the German *Ausweis* examiner even wishing the young couple a 'Pon voyage!'

Malraux had explained that in Paris they would be taking the metro to the Gallimard offices. At the Gare d'Austerlitz Captain Jack wished Flora a *bon voyage de retour* and asked her to tell 'Jean-Pierre' that all had gone well. From then on Captain Jack had trouble keeping up with his nervous guide.

On the Rue de Beaune, Malraux told Captain Jack to take a walk and to come back in twenty minutes. Entering the familiar NRF–Gallimard building, he walked up the stairs to Albert Camus' tiny office, one he himself had once occupied. Camus, whose *L'Etranger* manuscript Malraux had received from Pascal Pia and which he had warmly recommended to Gaston Gallimard, was, thanks to Pia, now closely associated with Henri Frenay's

COMBAT resistance movement. He was someone Malraux could trust. In a few words he explained the situation: he needed a hide-out for an English major he had brought with him and who was arranging to have weapons parachuted to the *maquisards* of the Dordogne. Camus explained that he himself had no room and that, like Jean Paulhan, he was closely watched. But he would see if he could find someone else in the building willing to take the risk.

While Malraux disappeared down the stairs, Camus walked into Paulhan's office, where one was almost certain to find a fellow 'plotter' connected in some way with the Resistance. Among the half-dozen people in the room he spotted Jean Lescure, who had been running circles around the German censors by smuggling manuscripts out of France with the help of the Swiss diplomat at Vichy (François Lachenal), who then had them published in Switzerland. Like Paulhan and the Surrealist Communist poet, Paul Eluard, Lescure was now helping to edit *Les Lettres Françaises*, a clandestine review put out by the anti-collaborationist CNE (Comité National des Ecrivains). Taking him over to the window, Camus asked Lescure in a low voice if he could lodge somebody for one night. Lescure was embarrassed. On the Gestapo's 'wanted' list, he had not returned to his own apartment for the past two months. His wife, moreover, had recently given birth to a baby and they were presently living a cramped existence in a room offered to them by relatives who knew nothing of his clandestine activities.

'I had forgotten,' said Camus apologetically.

As he started down the stairs, Lescure caught up with him. 'Is it important?' he asked.

'Pretty much,' replied Camus. 'It's the fellow who's been managing the parachuting of weapons to Malraux's *maquis*. An English major.'

'If he's English, he must have lived through the Blitz. And if he's with the *maquis*, he must have learned how to "rough it". Which means he can sleep on the floor. All right,' nodded Lescure.

Outside, Malraux and Captain Jack were waiting at the corner of the Rue de Beaune and the Rue de l'Université. Impressed by Captain Jack's rosy cheeks – here obviously was a lover of roast beef – Jean Lescure was even more impressed by the 'Briton' 's fluency in French. A nation capable of producing young men with such a perfect command of French could not fail to win the war.

That evening Captain Jack had no trouble finding the Sablons metro station in the western suburb of Neuilly, where he had spent the first years of his life. Upstairs, in his fifth-floor bedroom, Lescure, aided by Captain Jack, lowered the mattress to the floor for his wife to sleep on, while the two men stretched out on the covered springs. It proved to be a memorable night, at any rate for Lescure and his wife, who hardly got a wink of sleep. For around midnight several hundred Allied bombers, greeted by a spectacular display of exploding bursts and criss-crossing searchlights, ploughed up the railway marshalling yards of Villeneuve-Saint-Georges in the eastern suburbs of the capital. Untroubled by the angry barks of anti-aircraft guns and the repeated thuds of exploding bombs, Captain Jack slept through the uproar without hearing a sound.

The following afternoon Malraux joined his friend Jack at the tiny Neuilly hide-out, and as a token of his gratitude he offered Jean Lescure two tins of *pâté de foie gras* – a rare luxury during these painfully 'lean' months. Lescure's polite protests were imperiously overruled. 'Taken from the enemy!' was the peremptory explanation. Malraux took a quick look at a small painting hung over a chest of drawers, immediately identifying it as by Bazaine. He asked Lescure if his 'guest' could stay one more night.

'Of course,' was the brave reply.

The next morning, when Malraux and Jack met on the *quais*, Malraux was in high spirits. He explained, as they walked towards the metro station, that the Conseil National de la Résistance (CNR) was giving serious consideration to his scheme for coordinating the activities of the various Resistance movements in the *départements* of the Lot, the Corrèze, and the Dordogne.

When they reached the Concorde stop, Malraux suddenly decided to get out: 'Let's have a good lunch, let's go to Prunier.'

'But you must be well known there?' Captain Jack objected.

'No, not too well known,' was the casual reply.

When they walked into Prunier's, the *maître d'hôtel* beamed: '*Bonjour, Monsieur Malraux*'. The dining room was filled with German officers and French collaborators. A nervous Captain Jack had trouble swallowing the first delicious mouthfuls, but after a glass or two of wine his initial apprehensions dissolved in a pleasant glow of confidence.

'I have a rendez-vous near here on the *quais*,' said Malraux, after they had finished a first-class meal. But instead of leaving his friend to fend for himself for an hour or two, Malraux brought him along, saying, 'This will interest you.'

It did – beyond Captain Jack's wildest expectations. The man Malraux was to meet was Camus, who gave the 'British major' a warm handshake and asked how things had gone *chez* Lescure.

For the next couple of hours Malraux, Camus, and Captain Jack strolled up and down the *quais*. Most of what was said was way above the young man's head – with passing allusions to Lenin, China, Stalingrad, Algeria, interspersed with comments on the absurdity of life and the mystery of human existence.

Finally Camus put an end to the two-hour dialogue: 'It's time. We must go *chez* Paulhan, on the Rue des Arènes.'

Jean Paulhan, who was expecting them, opened the door. After briefly greeting Malraux and Camus, but without inviting them in, he led Captain Jack upstairs: 'All this is very dangerous. I am watched by the Germans. I myself risk being arrested. But anyway . . .'

On the third floor he had his visitor climb a narrow staircase leading to a kind of attic, where there was a bed in one corner. Against the walls were stacked a large number of canvases.

'Yes,' sighed Paulhan. 'I have to hide all this because of the Germans. These are paintings by Braque and Fautrier. If the Germans come, you can leave by the hatch and over the rooftops and "Good luck!" But my paintings . . .'

'You perhaps find me too prudent,' went on Paulhan, who, as Malraux had explained, had been playing a subtle game as the official literary director of the House of Gallimard and an unofficial promoter of clandestine literature. 'But I have been arrested already, in 1941 . . . I was freed, but it was no joke . . . Now I must leave you . . . Tomorrow your friends will come to fetch you. You will go to Gide's place.'

The next morning Malraux came to pick up Captain Jack. He said nothing about the the CNR, adding that he would not be able to see his friend Jack for the next two days. After which he proposed that they take the Monday train back to Limoges. Shortly afterwards, they met an unnamed man who guided Captain Jack to André Gide's apartment.

What Malraux was careful to hide from the SOE officer was Josette Clotis' totally unexpected arrival in Paris. Exactly what happened while Malraux was on his way to Limoges is anything but clear from Josette's diary jottings, which became increasingly erratic during this hectic year of 1944. André apparently became frightened when he heard rumours in a café that the Germans were planning a big 'clean-up' operation. The hideous fate that had recently overtaken Poulou and Georgette Lachaud's farm at the Moulin du Cuzoul made him fear the worst if the Germans were to turn up at Saint-Chamant and find a pretty young mother alone with two young children and unable to explain convincingly what had happened to the father.

Over the telephone André could not risk suggesting exactly where she should go 'underground'. All he could do was plead with her to leave the château for a few days. This unexpected telephone call completely unnerved Josette, who no longer had the resourceful Roland nor the loyal Raymond Maréchal to offer her advice, help and encouragement. Her one real friend in the region was the wife of the notary at Saint-Chamant, Rosine Delclaux. This gave her an idea. She would leave one-year-old Vincent with his godmother at Saint-Chamant, and then head for Paris with three-and-a-half-year-old Bimbo (Gauthier). In Paris at least she had several reliable friends – beginning with 'Mico' Gallimard and Drieu la Rochelle.

After dropping off Vincent with his godmother at Saint-Chamant, Josette took a circuitous route, reaching Paris via the Gare de Lyon. There were no directories in the public telephone booths, and she did not even have the number of the Gallimards' family house on the Rue Saint-Lazare. Accompanied by the porter, to whom she had to pay an enormous tip of 350 francs to carry all her luggage, she took the métro across half of Paris, finally turning up at no. 56, Rue Saint-Lazare at 9 am.

The door was opened by a suspicious maid who grudgingly admitted the dishevelled beauty and her blond child. Josette's friend Michel had to be aroused from bed. Finally his Aunt Jeanne appeared in a multi-coloured dressing gown with a blanket thrown over her shoulders. 'You haven't changed, you are still a young girl!' were her first, hospitable words, followed by, 'And André? What's André up to? Where is he?'

The answer to this question was not long in coming. Shortly before noon, after she had taken a bath and put Bimbo to bed, Josette was called to the telephone by Michel Gallimard, speaking from his NRF office. He passed the receiver to Albert Camus, who said, 'Hold on, don't hang up.' A moment later she heard André's unmistakably husky voice: 'Métro Censier–Dauberton, in twenty minutes.'

Malraux probably knew that there was not one chance in a million that Josette could in twenty minutes reach Censier–Dauberton, a dozen stops away on the other side of the Seine. But he probably wanted to arrive well ahead of time to see if any 'undesirables' were also going to turn up.

André was waiting for her outside the Censier–Dauberton métro station with a bouquet of tulips in his hand. He took her to a little bistro, where he spoiled her with a *pâté* as an hors-d'oeuvre, a main course of fish, an assortment of small cakes for dessert and a bottle of fine wine. The conversation took an acrimonious turn, however, when she said she had telephoned to the NRF and had arranged a meeting with Drieu la Rochelle. But this was mild compared to the violence of André's reaction when she added that Gaston Gallimard thought it would be easy to arrange the validation of the false identity card Roland had prepared for her under the name of Josette Malraux. Turning green (Josette's description), Malraux said, or rather hissed: 'You couldn't possibly do anything worse!'

His fury was understandable. At a time when the name Malraux was certain to attract the attention of the police – two persons of that name had recently been arrested by the Gestapo – here was Josette wilfully seeking to abandon the innocuous name of Clotis in order to become Mme Malraux, on the strength, furthermore, of a bogus identity card.

Before they parted, both in a huff, Malraux explained that she was under no circumstances to tell Drieu la Rochelle that he was in Paris, or that his half-brother Roland had been arrested, or that she had had to leave their temporary 'home' in Corrèze in a hurry. When, late for her appointment, she returned to the Gallimards' house on the Rue Saint-Lazare, an impatient Drieu was visibly perplexed as he listened to her embarrassed explanations as to why she had been so anxious to see him.

Meanwhile, in the fifth-floor apartment at 1 bis, Rue Vaneau, 'Jack l'Anglais' was growing restless. Much as he appreciated the wealth of books lining the shelves of André Gide's library, a well stocked alcove reached by a narrow spiral staircase, he began to find the long hours of enforced confinement increasingly tedious, particularly since he was under strict instructions not to open the shutters in daytime or to let a ray of light filter out at night. (He did, just once, hazard a quick glance outside and was flabbergasted to see that the window overlooked the forecourt of the Hôtel Matignon where a row of *Gardes Républicains*, in full-dress uniform, were drawn up to greet the arrival of Prime Minister Pierre Laval.) Every few hours an ageing, white-haired lady (probably Mme Théo van Rysserberghe herself) brought in a tray of food for breakfast, lunch, or dinner, but this was virtually his only contact with the outside world.

After forty-eight hours of involuntary confinement, Captain Jack decided that he had had his fill of great literature. He was anxious to find out how 'Casimir' and 'Jean-Pierre' were making out at Siorac-en-Périgord, with the help of Poulou Lachaud and 'Charles le Bolchevique'. As their boss, he should be sharing the perils they were exposed to in the Dordogne. When the stranger who had acted as his guide turned up, as he did once a day, the SOE officer told him to inform André Malraux that he was returning the next day to Limoges.

The next morning he found Malraux waiting for him on the platform of the Gare d'Austerlitz. 'I understand you,' were André's first words. 'I have a lot of things to tell you.'

'From now on, my dear Jack, I am "Colonel Berger",' declared Malraux after they had installed themselves in an empty compartment. 'I saw all the members of the CNR. I have received a mandate from them. I am to co-ordinate Resistance activities in the Lot, the Corrèze, and the Dordogne . . . You can help me in many ways. First of all, by keeping me informed of the Allies' main objectives, in order to make the *maquis* groups very effective. Then, with your assistants, by setting up a kind of military training school, and, of course, by organizing the parachuting of weapons. The other weapon-parachuting systems are non-existent.'

Had Malraux really received some kind of 'mandate' from the CNR in Paris, now headed by Georges Bidault? Probably not. Captain Jack, for his part, was careful not to ask any searching questions. He was frankly impressed by Malraux's indomitable determination, his infectious enthusiasm, his charisma, his boldness, his willingness to take risks. The rest, as far as he was concerned, was of secondary importance. As he later explained (writing under his real name of Jacques Poirier):

I did not raise questions about Malraux's mandate. We were living through a very peculiar period. How many were the brave, dynamic men I met at that time who had proclaimed themselves leaders of this or that group. And why not, if they were capable of shouldering the burdens they had assumed? We were waging war. The problems of hierarchical advancement, so dear to our administrative functionaries, no longer counted. 'Colonel Berger' at the outset may not have carried much authority. But General de Gaulle had perhaps had even less in 1940.

33

The Alsace–Lorraine Brigade

On their return to the Dordogne, 'Colonel Berger' and Captain Jack were relieved to discover that no new disaster had occurred during their absence. The German 'sweep' had not taken place. Poulou Lachaud and 'Charles le Bolchevique' had done a remarkable job scouring the countryside for parachute drop-sites. 'Casimir', lodged with a Luxembourg doctor, had established a daily radio contact with London. 'Jean-Pierre', thanks to a happy mixture of wry humour, commonsense, and technical competence, had spent a useful week training 'Soleil' 's Resistance fighters.

'Soleil' rendered Captain Jack one more invaluable service by recommending him to a school-teacher bearing the magnificently Gascon name of Fernande Vidalie de Castelnaud-Fayrac, whose husband was a prisoner-of-war in Germany. The splendid country house in which she was living with her young son and fervently anti-nazi mother commanded a sweeping view of the Dordogne valley. La Treille Haute, furthermore, was surrounded by a thick stone wall and was close to a wood into which the members of the SOE team could escape if the Germans showed up. The day after his return from Paris, Captain Jack had 'Jean-Pierre' join him in this spacious house, while 'Casimir' set up his transmitter in an adjoining barn.

For the next two weeks Malraux and Captain Jack were constantly on the move, avoiding large towns and using the many unpaved roads of the region. The purpose of these perilous trips was to establish contact with local *maquis* chiefs and to decide just how reliable each Resistance group might be if supplied with arms and explosives. Wherever 'Colonel Berger' went, his bogus identity was unmasked, and it was as André Malraux, the maverick left-wing writer, that he was judged. Of the four main Resistance movements in the Corrèze–Dordogne area the least co-operative were the *maquisards* of the FTP, controlled with an almost Stalinist severity by members of the Communist Party. In certain cases the hostility was so blatant that Malraux bowed out of further meetings. 'They are *curés*, my dear friend,' he would say to Captain Jack, describing an aerial square with his finger in order to stress their dogmatic intransigence. 'Go see them alone, they are your friends.'

Thus, little by little, tenuous links were established with various Resistance groups, while the close-knit team at La Treille Haute began to acquire the look of a military command post. The job of protecting it was entrusted to a vigilant 'Major Robert' (Poirier's father), who quickly built up a commando force of bodyguards, sentinels, and scouts. Malraux himself was responsible for the addition of two important members to this informal 'headquarters staff': 'Colonel' Charles de Rochebouët, an intelligence expert who had previously served with the French Navy, and a Captain Bernhardi, who had been brought up in North Africa.

It was here, in the ad hoc 'fortress' of Castelnaud, that Malraux one day received a visit that was to have far-reaching consequences for his wartime career. The visitor was a Lieutenant 'Ancel' (the code name for Antoine Diener), a twenty-eight-year-old school teacher from Lorraine who had had to 'take to the woods' after his brother-in-law had fallen into a Gestapo trap. For months he and his companions had been 'roughing it' in various forested areas south of Périgueux. Like so many other *maquis* chieftains, he had been clamouring desperately for weapons; but, aside from what his men had been able to wrest from ambushed Germans or traitors working for the pro-nazi *milice*, all he had so far received were a few Sten-guns, turned over to him by his superiors of the AS. The existence of an *état-major interallié* reported to maintain radio contact with London naturally intrigued him.

Although his own zone of operations had never extended south of the Dordogne river, Lieutenant 'Ancel' decided that it would be worth making the 60-kilometre trip to Castelnaud to find out more. Accompanied by his trusted deputy, Adelphe Peltre, he persuaded 'Major Robert' 's sentinels to admit him to the ad hoc fortress. They were ushered into a bare room, unadorned save for a wooden desk. Here they were greeted by a tall, slim officer, dressed in an elegant uniform and holding a gold-tipped cigarette (obviously of British origin) in his hand. The dark wisp of hair falling over the pale forehead was unmistakable – at any rate to the two men from Lorraine, both of them schoolteachers by profession.

'I am "Colonel Berger",' said Malraux, a bit surprised at the unkempt look of the two visitors in their leather jackets and ragged leggings, who did not even have proper holsters for their pistols.

'Ancel' (Antoine Diener) explained that he commanded several hundred men and that they badly needed weapons.

'What organization?' asked the colonel crisply.

'The Alsace–Lorraine movement,' answered 'Ancel'. 'But in the *maquis*, we mostly have local lads from Périgord.'

'Alsatians?' said Malraux, visibly surprised.

Malraux apparently did not realize that Périgueux had been inundated by Alsatians, hastily moved in 1939 from towns and communes close to the Rhine and the German border. Save for a few doctors, nurses, police officials and firemen, the entire city of Strasbourg – 200,000 souls – had been evacuated from Alsace and relocated in the Périgord and adjacent regions, stretching from Limoges to the north all the way to Toulouse, several hundred kilometres to the south. Périgueux had in fact become a duplicate Strasbourg-in-exile – with a bishop, a municipal council and administration, Alsatian restaurants, Alsatian hairdressers, an Alsatian fire-brigade.

Intrigued to learn that a sizeable number of German-speaking Frenchmen in the area were motivated by a strong *esprit de corps*, Malraux and Captain Jack sent 'Jean-Pierre' to have a look at 'Ancel' 's forest hide-out and to give his *maquisards* some initial training in close combat, the use of plastic explosives, and the proper care and handling of automatic weapons. A little later Malraux and Captain Jack decided to see for themselves what this Resistance 'unit' looked like.

The short, stocky 'Ancel', who came out of the woods to greet them, explained that their aim had been to create a Groupe Mobile Alsace–Sud. They had begun by forming *centuries*, each made up, on the Roman pattern, of 100 men. By April 1944 no fewer than eight *centuries* had been created: two of them in the region of Limoges, three in the Dordogne, and three more in the region of Toulouse.

As he approached the forest clearing where 'Ancel' 's ragged 'warriors' were drawn up in military squares, Malraux noticed the presence of a central flagpole. This was clearly a serious camp, run by an efficient, no-nonsense officer. 'Ancel' ordered his men to snap to attention, and a tricolour flag was run up the mast. At this point the visiting 'colonel', clad in riding breeches, leggings, a sheepskin jacket, and a beret, stunned the assembled *maquisards* by not giving a military salute. Instead, he raised a clenched fist.

These preliminaries completed, Malraux/Berger delivered a 'pep-talk' which was brief and to the point. 'You want weapons?' he cried in his rasping voice. 'You will get them! You want to fight? You will fight!'

At the end of his short harangue, in which not a word had been wasted, he again raised his fist. Then, turning on his heel, he walked briskly back up the forest path.

So frequent were the comings and goings in and out of La Treille Haute that sooner or later the Germans were bound to be alerted. And so, to spare the hospitable Castelnaud-Fayrac family the fate that had overtaken Paul and Georgette Lachaud's mill near Daglan, the SOE team reluctantly evacuated the country house with the terrace and the splendid view. At Bernhardi's urging the entire command-post – now dubbed (probably by Malraux) *'le Q. G. interallié* (the Inter-Allied Headquarters) – moved some 30 kilometres further west to the château de La Vitrolle, located near Limeuil, where the Vézère river flows into the Dordogne. The château, in accordance with what 'Charles le Bolchevique' had achieved for Siorac, was promptly fitted out with telephonic 'antennae' – activated by the switchboard operators in the post offices of Le Bugue and Limeuil, on the Vézère, and (downstream on the Dordogne) of Trémolat and Lalinde.

On the evening of June 1st, Malraux, Major Robert (Poirier), Colonel Charles de Rochebouët, Captain Jack, and several others were seated in the drawing room of the château de La Vitrolle when an excited 'Casimir' burst into the room. Taking Captain Jack upstairs to the radio-room, he showed him a 'super-coded' message he had had trouble deciphering: 'Important message for NESTOR. Major operation foreseen in next few days. You will be alerted by a BBC message 24 hours before the start of operations. This message will be: "The giraffe has a long neck." '

When Captain Jack returned to the drawing room, to say that a message from London had indicated an important operation due to take place in the next few days, Malraux exclaimed, 'It's the landings!'

The next day Malraux had himself driven to Saint-Chamant. Josette had become increasingly upset by his prolonged absences, and to humour her André had decided to find another hide-out for her, closer to his head-quarters in the Dordogne. Vincent, now fourteen months old, was once again entrusted to the care of his godmother, the notary's wife, Rosine Delclaux. Then, with Josette and Bimbo, André boarded the train for Toulouse. They were met that evening at the station by Roland's wife, Madeleine, now in an advanced state of pregnancy.

Exactly what happened during Malraux's two days (June 3–4) in Toulouse is something of a mystery. The city, long a bastion of French radicalism, was wholeheartedly committed to the Resistance struggle, and the FTP and other Communist-controlled groups were solidly implanted in the region. To control this restive area, Hitler and the *Wehrmacht* High Command had stationed a sizeable number of German troops, including the SS Panzer Division, *Das Reich*. Malraux probably imagined that the moment the inhabitants of Toulouse heard that the Allies had landed, the city would explode. The Resistance groups would rise *en masse*, try to seize key buildings and installations, the Germans would react with ferocious fury, and the result would be a bloodbath, as had happened twice in Warsaw – first with the Jewish ghetto, then with General Bor-Komarowski's Polish resisters.

Using his formidable powers of persuasion, André insisted that Madeleine must leave Toulouse, along with Josette, Bimbo, and himself. It was folly to impose a train journey on his pregnant sister-in-law, but André was adamant. He and Roland had made a solemn promise that if ever something happened to the other, the survivor would take care of his brother's 'widow' and children. No power on earth was going to make him shirk his duty. Accordingly, on June 5th, André, Madeleine, Josette, and Bimbo left Toulouse and headed north for the town of Souillac, on the right bank of the Dordogne.

They got off at Souillac, where André accompanied them in a *gazogène* taxi over winding roads to the old walled town of Domme, perched on a dramatic cliff-face overlooking the Dordogne. Josette, however, was in no mood to enjoy the three-star panorama. Accustomed to the *vie de château* she had enjoyed at Saint-Chamant, she was horrified by the hide-out André had found for Madeleine, Bimbo, and herself in an old *hospice* run by two nuns for old age pensioners. She considered herself a prisoner, abandoned by her lover, whose name she was not allowed to use, and 'locked up' in a gloomy 'convent' with a legitimate Malraux wife, even though (thanks to Roland's shrewd insistence) the latter had retained her pre-marriage identity card as Madeleine Lioux.

Meanwhile, at the château de La Vitrolle, the eagerly awaited BBC message – 'The giraffe has a long neck' – had been received by 'Casimir'. Two hectic nights followed for Captain Jack and Poulou Lachaud. Travelling in their *gazogène* car, they drove from one *maquis* command-post to the next, alerting the leaders they had helped to arm and instructing them to go into action by blowing up railway lines, attacking German warehouses, destroying fuel dumps, preparing roadblocks and ambushes.

Early on Tuesday morning, June 6, 1944, the inhabitants of Corrèze, Dordogne, and the Lot were electrified by the news that the Allies had landed at last on the coasts of Normandy. The *maquis* groups now erupted into full-scale action against the Germans. The three main railway lines crossing the region – Bordeaux–Périgueux–Brive, Agen–Périgueux–Limoges, and the north–south Toulouse–Cahors–Brive–Limoges line (over which Josette and Madeleine had travelled the previous day) – were promptly sabotaged by well-placed dynamite charges.

The primary objective of the Resistance groups in the region was to delay the northward progression of the *Das Reich* SS Panzer Division, which, in terms of numbers of soldiers (20,000) and tanks (97 'Tigers', 52 medium tanks, 77 self-propelled 88 mm guns) had the strength of an armoured corps. From its headquarters in the region of Agen and Montauban, the division on June 7th was ordered to move north up Route Nationale 20 (through Brive and Uzerche) and the more circuitous RN 140 (via Figeac, Saint-Céré, and Tulle), in order to join the German armies on the Normandy front. Lacking anti-tank guns and bazookas, the inadequately armed *maquisards* of the Lot and Corrèze could do little to stop the tanks except to blow up bridges (at the risk of seeing an entire town or village destroyed in reprisal). They did their best, however, to attack the truckborne *Wehrmacht* troops accompanying the tanks.

Das Reich, however, was not the only German division in the area, as Captain Jack and other members of the '*Q. G. interallié*' discovered on June 23rd. Towards evening a woman telephone operator in the post office of Lalinde laconically informed Paul Lachaud (who had picked up the receiver), 'They are arriving with tanks. *Bon soir.*' The German column was moving along the main road from Bergerac. Since Lalinde was some 18 kilometres to the west of Limeuil, there was time to evacuate the château de La Vitrolle – an emergency operation so well rehearsed by Major Robert

(Poirier) that almost all the members of the staff, and in particular the invaluable transmitter, were safely out of sight by the time the German column approached the château.

The resourceful 'Charles le Bolchevique' soon found them a new home. It was another château, La Poujade, located near the hamlet of Urval, three kilometres west of Siorac. Its owner, the marquis de Commarque, had been arrested and shot by the Germans in 1942. His British-born widow was delighted to have the '*Q. G. interallié*' set up shop in her château, which she no longer inhabited. It was a large austere edifice with ochre walls and tall sloping roofs, which had been erected on an upraised spur of land, well screened by conifers.

Throughout this hectic period Malraux had been harassed by other, highly personal worries. By removing his sister-in-law from her home town of Toulouse in order to spare her the horrors of street warfare, he had not imagined that the battles he feared were going to move inexorably northwards and engulf the little town of Domme. On June 11th, five days after the first Normandy landings, Madeleine gave birth to a baby boy. At the start of her pregnancy Madeleine and Roland had decided that if their child was a boy, he would be called Alain André Roland Claude Montgomery Malraux; and it was indeed with this garland of names that the baby boy was officially registered at the town hall of Domme.

This act of patriotic defiance could have had grave consequences for Madeleine and Josette. For one week after little Alain's birth, the sleepy town of Domme was suddenly invaded by a German unit. The obstetrician who had been looking after Madeleine vanished, leaving the two abandoned mothers to fend for themselves. The presence of the turbulent Bimbo did nothing to help matters, for he spent his time crying (like his mother, Josette) and demanding to be allowed to go out to play in the streets with other children his age. There was even a moment of tense crisis when the *hospice* was invaded by German soldiers bent on searching the cellars for 'terrorists'. A German officer entered the gloomy, ground floor bedroom. Having made sure that no terrorists were hiding under the beds, he was about to walk out when Bimbo, fascinated by the binoculars hanging from the neck-strap, went to look at them.

'*Joli garçon!*' said the officer as he contemplated the blond boy, a magnificent specimen of future Aryan manhood. Lifting up the child, he asked him his name. Petrified, the two mothers held their breath.

'I am called Gauthier...' began André's and Josette's son, adding a moment later, 'Bimbo... Bimbo Malmo...' Even if the family name had been correctly pronounced, it is by no means certain that it would have meant much to the German officer, who was not working for the Gestapo.

Belatedly realizing the vulnerability of their position – by blowing up several bridges, the 'terrorists' could have trapped them inside Domme – the Germans evacuated the old town after two days of noisy occupation. The day after their departure Malraux sent Raoul Verhagen, a Belgian officer who had joined his '*Q. G. interallié*' staff, to Domme to see how Josette and Madeleine were faring. The former Air Force captain made the trip on a bicycle, accompaned by a Belgian nurse, Hélène Huffman, who was seriously alarmed by Madeleine's weak condition and the state of her undernourished baby (for several days, all the two mothers had found to eat were apricots and peaches). Josette kept cursing her 'miserable' state and was manifestly incapable of looking after Madeleine. Verhagen decided to take her to a manor house at Fayrac (near Castelnaud), occupied by several members of the Huffman family. It was a painful journey for the jovial Belgian captain, who had to carry the weight of Josette, uncomfortably seated on the rack behind him, for ten wearying kilometres, while Hélène Huffman pedaled more easily with Bimbo, wedged into the handlebar basket. Leaving Bimbo with his mother, she pedalled courageously back to Domme to take care of Madeleine and the tiny Alain.

By late June the pressure on 'Jean-Pierre' had grown so intense that Captain Jack accepted London's offer of a second arms and sabotage instructor. He was dropped by parachute during the night of July 1–2nd at a spot with the chilling name of Coupe-Gorge (Cut-Throat), some 15 kilometres south of Périgueux. Given the code-name of 'Gilbert', the newcomer was Marc Gerschel, a young history student from Calais and early anti-nazi resister who had spent time in four different Vichy prisons before masterminding a spectacular escape with fifty-three other 'convicts' from a penitentiary near Agen. By the next morning 'Gilbert' 's real identity must have been known to a few 'insiders', for when he was introduced to 'Colonel Berger' Malraux improvised a vivid description of the penitentiary break-out, as though he had taken part in it himself. 'Never, more than at that moment,' Marc Gerschel later liked to recall, 'have I ever had such a tactile impression of genius.'

Meanwhile, an ambitious SOE project was being secretly prepared, intended to make the forthcoming national holiday an unforgettable July 14th. Captain Jack was asked to explore the possibility of a *daylight* parachute operation in which large numbers of containers would be dropped, not by a single, low-flying warplane, but by high-altitude bombers. What was needed was a stretch of ground 3 kilometres long by 3 kilometres wide, capable of receiving more than 400 parachuted containers. The nearest flak batteries had to be at least 20 kilometres away and local Resistance forces strong enough to repel German attacks.

Captain Jack decided that the group best equipped to support such an operation was the AS *maquisards* of the Corrèze, commanded by two able captains, René Vaujour and Marius Guédin, whose men on June 8th had boldly attacked elements of *Das Reich* at several Dordogne river crossings. An enthusiastic Malraux insisted on accompanying Captain Jack and 'Jean-Pierre' to René Vaujour's ('Hervé's) *maquis* command post, on a height overlooking the Dordogne river between Argentat and Beaulieu. Here they were introduced to a short, stocky, fair-haired major, Pierre Jacquot, of whom Malraux had already heard from Emmanuel Berl and Arago.

Unlike the garrulous 'Hervé' (Vaujour) and the more discreet 'Georges' (Guédin), Jacquot had never used a pseudonym and was not a member of the AS. A native of the Vosges and a graduate of the Ecole Supérieure de Guerre who had served on Edouard Daladier's military staff, Jacquot was no armchair strategist, content to let others fight the battles he had planned. As a battalion commander serving with the 109th Infantry Regiment on the Somme, he had been twice wounded in 1940 while leading his men in a fighting retreat. Closely associated with General Frère, who in 1942 had been trying to develop a spirit of resistance among the 100,000 officers and soldiers of Vichy's small *armée de l'armistice*, Jacquot had vainly sought to persuade the general to seek refuge in a convent of the Corrèze; but Frère, a model of military rectitude, had refused to 'go underground' and had paid the price by being arrested by the Germans and sent to a concentration camp.

Unconventional, quick-witted, often peppery, Pierre Jacquot, who was one year younger and almost a full head shorter than Malraux, made up in nervous energy what he lacked in physical size. A military professional, he was quite willing to forgive Emmanuel Berl's pre-war pacifism; an anti-clerical radical, he was ready to befriend a Mother Superior whose patriotism matched his own. It was doubtless this open-mindedness and quick-wittedness which impressed Malraux, giving rise to a conversation which went on for hours. For while he and Jacquot were 'batting the breeze', Captain Jack, 'Jean-Pierre', and Poulou Lachaud drove off with Vaujour and Guédin to examine what they considered to be a 'perfect site' for the massive parachute drop being planned by the SOE. It was a long stretch of level ground located just north of the Dordogne at Moustoulat, a mere six kilometres west of Argentat.

When Captain Jack and the others returned from their exploration, elated by the ideal nature of the terrain, they found André Malraux and Pierre Jacquot still engaged in an animated conversation, as though they were old friends who had known each other for years. 'Jean-Pierre' was left behind with Vaujour and Guédin, to oversee the preparations on the ground, while Captain Jack, Poulou Lachaud, and Malraux drove back to Urval. As they approached the firs and pines screening the château de La Poujade, Malraux asked Captain Jack what he thought of Jacquot.

'André,' came the answer, 'I only caught a glimpse of him. I really don't have an opinion.'

'Ah!' said 'Colonel Berger', probably relieved that his friend's reaction was not negative. 'I've just named him my deputy.'

A few days later, a BBC message indicated that the allied bombers carrying the containers would be overflying the chosen site at 6 o'clock on the morning of July 14th. Three huge bonfires, placed 200 metres apart to form a triangle, were lit, and as the allied bombers flew over, 432 containers filled with arms, munitions, explosives, and cigarettes came drifting down and were retrieved without Vaujour's and Guédin's *maquisards* having to fire a single shot. Later they learned that this was not an isolated operation. George Hiller's FOOTMAN network had been similarly honoured with a shower of parachuted 'gifts', which came floating down near Loubressac in the Lot.

There were other worries on André Malraux's mind when he reached the Moustoulat plateau on the morning of July 14th. During his long talk with Pierre Jacquot a few days before, they had agreed that their primary task from now on should be to help trap the remaining German forces in south-western France, of which there were still tens of thousands. This they would do by establishing a 30-kilometre 'front' south of the Dordogne, backed up by a 50-kilometre 'front' immediately north of it, aimed at making it impossible for any *Wehrmacht* units to cross the river. Accordingly, on July 20th Colonel Berger informed a meeting of *maquis* leaders, who had been invited to his headquarters at the château de La Poujade, that a 'Mission interrégionale FFI' was being established to co-ordinate military activities of *maquis* groups in the three departments of Corrèze, Dordogne, and Lot.

Of the three *départements* named, it was in the Dordogne that Malraux's position was strongest, thanks to the solid rapport he had established with 'Ancel' and his *maquisards*, while it was weakest in the Lot. Since the Lot lay outside the perimeter assigned to Captain Jack's DIGGER network, Malraux decided to re-establish contact with George Hiller and his FOOT-MAN network, to the immediate south. He was also irritated by the attitude of blatant defiance being manifested by the communist-controlled FTP, who seemed more interested in using the weapons they had received from the SOE to strengthen their political power than to fight the Germans.

George Hiller, who was facing the same problems, had offered to intro-duce Malraux to a colonel named Vincent, whose 'Veny' group (mostly composed of socialists) had been generously provided with weapons, thanks to the recent, massive parachute drop. On July 21st Malraux left Urval and had himself driven south to Hiller's clandestine hide-out in the Lot. With a chauffeur, Marius Loubare, a bodyguard, Emilio Lopez, and Henri Collignon, one of the leaders of the 'Veny' group, George Hiller and Malraux set out in a front-wheel-drive Citroën for the Tarn, sticking as usual to secondary roads. After meeting Colonel Vincent, they returned via Cajarc. From there they set out across the Causse (limestone plateau) in the direction of Gramat, not realizing that it had just been occupied by the Germans. At around 5 o'clock in the afternoon of July 23rd, as they were rounding a bend they ran straight into a road-block. The jittery Germans opened fire, killing the driver and blowing out one of the car's front tyres.

Skidding out of control, the Citroën turned over into a ditch. Collignon and Lopez managed to get out unharmed, but George Hiller was seriously wounded in both legs. Crawling along the bloodstained ground, he made it to a cornfield. The bodyguard, Lopez, tore a tourniquet from his shirt, and then, borrowing a bicycle, pedalled frantically to bring the news to the radio-operator 'Michel'. (It took Cyril Watney twenty-four hours to locate the gravely wounded Hiller. He was saved by a local doctor, with the help of hastily parachuted anti-gangrene serums.)

'Colonel Berger' was less fortunate. Extricating himself with difficulty from the overturned Citroën, he tried to run across the nearby field, had one of his leggings partly ripped by a first bullet, and was then hit by a second one in the leg. He briefly lost consciousness. When he came to, he found himself on a stretcher. Two German soldiers picked it up and carried him towards the town. But for the fact that he was wearing a uniform, his captors might well have finished him off on the spot as one more 'terrorist'. Instead, they carried him past a row of tanks to a garage on the outskirts of Gramat. Asked for his papers, he handed the *Feldwebel* a wallet containing a bogus identity card. 'They are false,' Malraux declared, a phrase which was translated into German without eliciting either comment or surprise.

A little later he was transported on the same stretcher to a German infirmary, where his leg wound was cleaned and firmly bandaged. From there he was carried to the local *Kommandantur*, established in the Hôtel de France, where he was interrogated by a *Wehrmacht* second lieutenant and then by a white-haired colonel. Making no attempt to conceal his identity, he boldly explained that he was 'Lieutenant-Colonel Malraux' (the rank he had held in the Spanish Air Force) 'alias Colonel Berger', that he was 'the military head of this region' and was working for de Gaulle. This was a fib, but far safer than admitting that he had been working with the British SOE. Questioned about his profession in civilian life, he brazenly declared that he was a 'professor and a writer', adding for good measure that he had delivered lectures at the universities of Marburg, Leipzig, and Berlin. He was thus able to concoct an intriguing 'dossier', making it clear that he was an important 'catch'.

From Gramat he was driven in an armoured ambulance to Villefranche-de-Rouergue, where he had no trouble recognizing the 'almost Spanish' church, which had been used as part of the décor for the filming of *Sierra de Teruel*.

At Revel, some distance south of Albi, he was seated in a staff car and blindfolded during a ten-minute drive to a 'rather ugly' château, where, in a scene worthy of Curzio Malaparte's *Kaputt*, he was 'interrogated' by a despondent German general, who in the same breath condemned 'the brutes from the East' (the Russians), 'the sellers of automobiles and canned goods who have never known how to wage war' (the Americans), and 'England, which follows its Shakespearean drunkard'.

He was next driven to Toulouse in another armoured ambulance, where he spent several hours in a once luxurious hotel, later discovering it was the local Gestapo headquarters. He was then transferred to the Saint-Michel prison, where he ended up in a kind of dormitory with ten other prisoners. His appearance, in uniform, created a sensation, particularly when the poor devils discovered that he was a *maquis* leader who had been working for de Gaulle. Led across a courtyard to a special sector of the prison, Malraux was spared immediate torture. The interrogation that followed was almost surreal in its absurdity. It turned out that the 'dossier' his jailers had requested from Gestapo headquarters in Paris was that of his brother Roland – a bureaucratic mix-up which threw his methodical interrogator into a fit of Teutonic rage.

Brought back to his dormitory without having been tortured or shot, 'Colonel Berger' was greeted with joyous incredulity by his cell-mates. Something was beginning to crack in the Gestapo's efficient set-up. The next morning Malraux and his cell-mates were galvanized by the sound of female voices in the courtyard below, chanting the *Marseillaise*. Not only were the Germans evacuating Toulouse, the prison guards had fled – along with the keys. The captives were still imprisoned behind solid oak doors.

And then, suddenly, as though faintly rocked by an earthquake, the entire prison seemed to tremble under the impact of dull reverberating thuds – quite unlike falling bombs or shells or cannon-fire. The prisoners in the other cells were trying to break down their locked doors.

Malraux and his cell-mates gripped the heavy table in the middle of their 'dormitory' and did their best to use it as a battering ram. Boom! The door seemed to bend slightly under the impact, but held fast. They tried again. As Malraux later recalled, 'We were in a very weakened condition, but hysterically exalted.'

Finally, on the fifth attempt, the heavy table smashed through the splintered door. Outside in the courtyard there was a joyous pandemonium, followed by shouts and screams. The first prisoners who rushed through the front gate were greeted by machine gun bursts from tanks advancing implacably upon them. The front gate was hurriedly closed to keep one of these monsters from spraying the prison courtyard. Only after the last tank had passed could the gate again be opened, allowing the human tide to pour into the street.

Tottering from weakness and fatigue, 'Colonel Berger' felt himself borne forward on a collective wave of hope, as he trudged towards the apartment of M. and Mme Lioux, the parents of his sister-in-law, Madeleine.

Paradoxically, 'Colonel Berger' 's capture by the Germans did more to enhance his military prestige than had any of his previous actions as a self-proclaimed co-ordinator of *maquis* activities. Overnight it transformed him into a near-martyr, a victim of his own restless intrepidity, a Resistance hero. Strenuous efforts had been made to find out where he was being held. At the Château de La Poujade, Colonel Charles de Rochebouët and Captain Bernhardi sent goodwill emissaries to find out if his German jailers could

332 · André Malraux

be bribed into letting him escape. These efforts were financed with borrowings from a huge haul of Banque de France notes, seized in early July during a daring train robbery carried out near Périgueux by two Resistance groups, one of them commanded by Diener-'Ancel'. The SOE in London arranged a special parachute drop of money to facilitate the rescue operation. Accompanied by Bernhardi, Major Robert (Poirier) even bicycled to Toulouse to see what could be done, as did 'Captain Arthur' (Raoul Verhagen's *nom de guerre*), who spoke German fluently. All in vain.

Meanwhile, Paris had not yet been liberated and the war was not yet over. When Captain Jack and 'Jean-Pierre' drove down to Vaujour's *maquis* command-post to inform the AS officers of Major George Hiller's and Malraux's misfortune, they again met Pierre Jacquot. On hearing the sad news of 'Colonel Berger' 's capture, Jacquot said calmly, 'In these circumstances, it's up to me to assume command.'

Visible from miles away, the massive daylight air-drop of July 14th had given an enormous psychological 'lift' to the morale of French patriots and *maquisards*. It had also led to a fortuitous meeting which, by an extraordinary concatenation of events, was to catapult 'Colonel Berger' to a post of real military significance. That evening the short, wiry 'Ancel' had driven over to the Moustoulat plateau in order to obtain his share of the parachuted containers. To his utter delight he discovered that 'Hervé', the leader of the AS forces in Corrèze, was none other than René Vaujour, who had been his company commander during his period of military service in 1937. 'Hervé' was no less staggered to discover that 'Ancel', of whose exploits he had heard from AS colleagues in Dordogne, was none other than the former Lorraine schoolteacher, Antoine Diener, whose best man he had been for his wedding.

Two weeks later, on July 27th, a dog-tired cyclist reached 'Ancel' 's *maquis* camp near Saint-Alvère, so sore and stiff that he could barely walk. Bernard Metz was a former medical student from Strasbourg who had just pedalled 60 kilometres through the night from an FTP camp in the hills north of Figeac, where he had been acting as an ad hoc supply officer.

The first, and for a long time the sole, serious Resistance movement in Alsace had been launched shortly after the signing of the Armistice, at Thann, the only Alsatian town to have been recaptured by the French in 1914 and subsequently held against all subsequent German attacks for four long years. Its leaders were three dynamic and fearless Francophiles: Paul Dungler, the ultra-conservative owner of a small machine-tools factory; a thirty-two-year-old ex-artillery sergeant, Marcel Kibler, who in civilian life was the technical director of an enterprise specializing in printing natural and synthetic fabrics; and the Mulhouse industrialist, Paul Winter, whose innumerable friends later organized General Giraud's sensational escape from the Saxon fortress of Koenigstein, on the Elbe. In September 1940 they had founded the Septième Colonne d'Alsace, dedicated to the liberation of their homeland. In December 1940, after Kibler's expulsion and

Dungler's hasty departure from Alsace (to escape arrest by the Gestapo), they had re-established a clandestine headquarters in an old people's home run by nuns in a northern suburb of Lyons. One of the Septième Colonne's earliest recruits was a young seminarian named Pierre Bockel, whose father had been a notary in Thann. Bockel in turn had recruited the deceptively placid, bespectacled Bernard Metz, who had agreed to give up his medical studies and serve full time as the Septième Colonne's chief courier and liaison officer.

To put together an effective force capable of taking part in the liberation of Alsace the Septième Colonne needed a military leader. The officer best qualified to fill this role was a certain Dirringer, who had made his mark working for the French Army's clandestine intelligence department in Lyons before going to London to join the SOE. But not a word had been heard from Dirringer since his departure for London.

Such was the situation on July 27th, four days after 'Colonel Berger' 's disappearance, when Bernard Metz turned up at 'Ancel' 's *maquis* headquarters near Saint-Alvère. Metz was told that he could contact Dirringer in London by going to see 'Casimir' at the château de La Poujade. A coded message was duly transmitted to Dirringer and the SOE in London, but it elicited no response.

By August 15th it was clear that time was running out. Dirringer could no longer be counted on. Some other leader would have to be found. Tony Diener, whose *maquisards* were now besieging Périgueux, suggested that Metz bicycle to the region of Argentat and contact 'Hervé', under whose orders he had served in 1937. If he was willing to take over, he would make an excellent commander.

On August 23rd, after making a quick bicycle trip to the region of Toulouse, Bernard Metz finally tracked down 'Hervé', who had installed his command-post in a school building in a small village near Argentat. 'Hervé' explained that he was forming his own Corrèze column for the AS, with which he intended to join the First French Army that had recently landed in Provence. 'However,' he added, 'I have just the man for you. Major Jacquot, a regular Army officer. Ecole de Guerre, the works. It was he who negotiated the surrender of the German garrisons at Brive and Tulle. But he's a leader without troops.'

Climbing on to a motorcycle – his means of transporation had improved – the indefatigable Bernard Metz zigzagged his way over rough roads to Aubazines, a town overlooking the gorges of the Coiroux, north-east of Brive. Here he found Jacquot established in a modern villa near the convent, whose Mother Superior had so courageously offered to shelter General Frère.

Pierre Jacquot welcomed Bernard Metz's flattering proposal. But as a military professional he was frankly daunted by the prospect of assembling a mass of Alsatians and Lorrainers scattered over an area of several hundred kilometres without proper means of transport. He had no intention of leading an armed rabble across France to take part in the liberation of Alsace.

It would have to be a well organized military force equipped with trucks and radios and acting in permanent liaison with General de Lattre and his First Army.

'Perfect,' said Bernard Metz, pleased to realize that at last he had found a serious substitute for Dirringer.

Returning to Toulouse, Metz found the city in a state of post-liberation turmoil, the streets filled with armed *maquisards* and trucks everywhere decorated with red as well as tricolour flags. In a café on the Place du Capitole, his friend Pierre Bockel, now a fully ordained priest, and Captain Charles Pleis explained that they had assembled 300 Alsatian *maquisards* who were burning to take part in the liberation of their homeland. Moreover, they had found an Alsatian capable of commanding their Groupe Mobile Alsace–Sud: a stoutly Catholic, patriotic colonel named Noetinger, whose credentials were impeccable.

Bernard Metz then explained that he too had found a good candidate: a Lorrainer from the Vosges, Major Pierre Jacquot, a graduate of the Ecole Supérieure de Guerre, twice wounded during a fighting retreat in 1940.

By the time Bernard Metz was back in Dordogne, Périgueux had been liberated. Now installed with his staff at the Hôtel Fénélon, Tony Diener was busy organizing a battalion of 600 men, ready to take part in the liberation of Alsace and Lorraine. Virtually all of the Périgourdins who had 'roughed it' in the forests had decided to stick with him. As for the overall commander of the GMA–Sud, 'Ancel' didn't care whether it was Jacquot or Noetinger.

Climbing back on his motorcycle, Bernard Metz headed once again for Pierre Jacquot's 'command-post' at Aubazines. Here he was in for the surprise of his life.

From Toulouse, where he had been generously housed by Madeleine's parents, André Malraux had managed to telephone to the manor house of Fayrac, to find out how Josette, Bimbo, Madeleine and two-month-old Alain were doing. Josette was immediately offered a car, and several days later she brought André back to Fayrac.

He himself decided to make a quick trip to Paris. He didn't want to miss the extraordinary spectacle of a recently liberated capital. He was anxious to find out what had happened to his Aunt Marie. (André's mother had died in the early 1930s, several years after her husband Fernand's suicide, and Grandmother Adrienne had died in 1940.) He also wanted to find out what had happened to Harry Peulevé and his half-brother Roland.

During this brief visit to Paris Malraux heard that Ernest Hemingway had arrived with the US Fourth Infantry Division and had flamboyantly 'liberated' the Hôtel Ritz. This was too much for Malraux, who decided that he was not going to be upstaged in his home town by the author of *For Whom the Bell Tolls*. Crossing the Tuileries Gardens, he headed for the Place Vendôme. In his bedroom, at the Ritz, Hemingway had just removed his army boots and was busy stripping some weapons with several 'bodyguards'

(FFI 'patriots' he had picked up on his way in to the festive capital), when the tall, lean figure of André Malraux appeared in the doorway. He was in uniform, with the five distinctive silver bars of a colonel's rank on his shoulders.

'*Bonjour*, André,' said Hemingway, as affably as he could.

'*Bonjour*, Ernest,' replied Malraux.

It is not recorded if they shook hands, but since Hemingway's were smeared with oil, it is quite possible that they dispensed with this formality.

'How many men have you commanded?' Malraux asked.

'*Dix ou douze*,' answered Hemingway casually. '*Au plus, deux cents.*' Since he was supposed to be a war correspondent, he could not reasonably boast of having commanded more.

'*Moi, deux mille*,' announced Malraux, whose look of triumph was ruined by a facial tick.

This was an affront Hemingway was not prepared to take lying down, particularly from a Frenchman who had rushed to the support of Republican Spain months before his own tardy appearance on the scene, and whose novel, *L'Espoir*, had outpaced his *For Whom the Bell Tolls* by several years.

'*Quel dommage!*' said Hemingway with icy sarcasm, 'that we didn't have the assistance of your force when we took this small town of Paris!'

If 'Colonel Berger' winced, Hemingway later did not bother to record it, any more than he bothered to record Malraux's rejoinder. The conversation, in any case, must have been lacking in cordiality. For we have his word for it – it became one of Ernest's favourite dinner table stories – that one of his bodyguards beckoned Hemingway into the bathroom and asked, '*Papa, on peut fusiller ce con?*'

From Paris, Malraux first headed for the town of Tulle, where he commandeered a car and had himself driven to Saint-Chamant to have a look at his second son, Vincent. The dark-haired boy seemed to be cheerful and happy and was obviously doing well in the care of his godmother, Rosine Delclaux.

Reassured, Malraux moved on to Argentat, where he was joyously received by his old friend Emmanuel Berl ànd his wife Mireille. After briefly describing his adventures with his German captors, André explained that he wanted to re-establish contact with the '*Q. G. interallié*' he had helped to set up with the help of Captain Jack and, more recently, of Berl's friend, Pierre Jacquot. Berl then told André that they had been telephoning to each other almost every day and that Jacquot was now living in a villa in the town of Aubazines.

The next morning (August 30th) the two friends set out with Mireille for Aubazines. Here they were invited to lunch by Pierre Jacquot. An hour or so later, Bernard Metz made his unscheduled appearance.

'You've arrived just at the right moment!' cried Jacquot, 'Everything has changed. Malraux has returned.'

Dragging the young 'liaison agent' into the dining room, Jacquot introduced Bernard Metz to André Malraux, whose novel, *L'Espoir*, had enormously impressed him. He was then introduced to Emmanuel Berl and to the famous singer, Mireille, who, he now discovered, was also Mme Berl. Feeling very humble and little more than a 'messenger-boy' of the Resistance, Bernard Metz listened enthralled as Malraux and Berl kept up a ping-pong match of lively sallies and repartee. But what most amazed the former medical student was the tacit accord that had been reached between Malraux and Jacquot. It was Malraux, the military amateur, not Jacquot, the professional, who was to command the GMA–Sud.

Towards the end of the meal, Malraux turned to Bernard Metz and said, 'You've been chased out of your homes. You want to return, but not empty-handed. By fighting. It's a symbol, to be sure.' And with that he launched into a lyrical description of 'Ancel' 's camp near Saint-Alvère, of the sufferings his brave *maquisards* had endured.

Bernard Metz needed little persuading. Malraux had put his finger on the nub of the problem when he had spoken of the *symbolic* value of their battle to free their homeland. Jacquot, with his professional proficiency, could offer them his invaluable military experience; he could never provide them with the additional *élan* of an epic mystique.

Bernard Metz soon returned to Toulouse to sound out the terrain with the Alsatians of the region, who had been formed by Captain Charles Pleis into four companies. The GMA–Sud's hobnailed title – Groupe Mobile Alsace–Sud – had already been scrapped, replaced by the more fleet-footed 'Brigade Alsace–Lorraine'.

In Toulouse Metz was joined by Jacquot and Malraux. While Malraux went to call on General Maurice Bertin-Chevance, a leader of the COMBAT movement who had been appointed to head the FFI forces in south-western France, Jacquot, Pleis, and Metz went to see his deputy, a co-operative Alsatian colonel, Georges Pfister.

'What is it you want?' asked Pfister. 'An order naming "Colonel Berger" head of the Alsace–Lorraine Brigade? Here, write it out yourself.' Jacquot scribbled out the order on a scrap of paper, had it typed up by a secretary and promptly signed by Pfister. A second *ordre de mission* was then typed up, authorizing Captain Pleis to group together all the Alsatians and Lorrainers in the region of Toulouse.

The basic formalities were thus taken care of. There was only one problem. Pleis had not been told that 'Colonel Berger' was none other than André Malraux. When he learned the truth all hell could break loose.

Bernard Metz was offered a foretaste of the looming storm when he went to see his friend, Pierre Bockel, who, he decided, was the person best fitted to influence Pleis. When Bockel heard that the person chosen to command the Alsace–Lorraine Brigade was not to be Jacquot or Noetinger, but Malraux, he was appalled: 'What!' he exclaimed. 'How do you think we're going to be received by the people of Alsace when they see us returning behind the man of the International Brigades?' No, he insisted. This was out of the question, impossible!

Bernard Metz had taken the precaution of bringing along Antoine Diener's deputy, Adelphe Peltre, who vividly described the electrifying impact made on 'Ancel' 's *maquisards* at Saint-Alvère by Malraux's first appearance. Metz had also brought along Emile Baas, a professor of philosophy from Strasbourg, who insisted that Malraux had never really been a Communist and that there was more humanism than Communism in his books. Pierre Bockel himself was a liberal Catholic, like Emmanuel Mounier. Impressed by the solid confidence displayed by Bernard Metz, Adelphe Peltre, and Professor Baas, Pierre Bockel finally agreed to take up the question of Malraux's leadership with Charles Pleis.

Bernard Metz, as it happened, had another weapon of persuasion. A week or two before, at Souillac, he had been introduced to André Chamson, who had served as one of General de Lattre de Tassigny's aides-de-camp during the campaign of 1940. Their meeting had given Chamson an idea. De Lattre was bound to need infantry support to protect the left flank of his troops as they moved up the Rhône valley. At the Hôtel du Roi René, in Aix-en-Provence, where Chamson managed to intercept de Lattre, the general had been impressed by his former aide-de-camp's claim that a battalion of 700–800 Alsatians and Lorrainers was as ready to join his First Army. He agreed to offer him sixteen GMC trucks, filled with valuable jerry cans, and protected by armed Moroccans, to keep the precious fuel from being 'requisitioned' at gunpoint by some *maquis* commander. And so during the first days of September Major André Chamson drove into a barracks compound at Montauban, where Captain Pleis had assembled his four companies.

On the evening of their arrival Pleis and his officers sat down to dinner. This was the moment chosen by their chaplain, Pierre Bockel, to reveal the dreadful truth. 'Colonel Berger', who had been appointed to head the Brigade Alsace–Lorraine on official orders from the FFI commander in the south-west, was André Malraux. There was an immediate explosion.

'Communism doesn't exist in Alsace!' thundered an almost purple-faced Pleis. 'It's not up to us to introduce it. Don't count on me to endorse this mess!'

The fifteen other officers seated at the table all approved. Thus supported, Pleis was categoric. He was going to Toulouse the next day to see Pfister, and have him cancel the order placing him under Malraux's orders. His so-called 'Brigade' could carry on without him.

At that moment Bernard Metz turned up and was violently attacked. What a grotesque idea – that of 'parachuting' a former 'colonel' of the Spanish Reds to head the future liberators of Alsace! 'You are delivering Alsace to the Communists. Own up, admit it, you've double-crossed us!' they shouted at him.

Once the first furious wave of invectives had subsided, Bernard Metz suddenly displayed a gutty resolution no one would have suspected in a 'messenger boy'. No, he declared firmly, Malraux was not a Communist and he was not going to introduce Communism into Alsace. He, Metz, knew what he was talking about. During his weeks of service with 'Colonel' Georges' FTP *maquisards* he had heard Malraux's name cursed as a rene- gade, a traitor. If ever they seized power, the first thing the Communists would do would be to shoot him.

'Those trucks outside in the courtyard,' he went on, 'I was the one who asked Chamson to bring them. If you don't want to join us, I'll take them back. The boys in the Dordogne with nothing but old lorries and jalopies won't spit on them, that I can assure you.'

Finally, in a state of exaltation induced by the very fragility of his position, he cried, 'Believe me, for heaven's sake, believe me! If after the war you regret having served under Malraux, I authorize you to have me shot!'

This culminating plea, this impassioned *cri du coeur*, was met by silence. Pleis looked at his officers. They had to hand it to him. This nondescript civilian who had never taken part in a battle had tenacity and guts. He also had the sense to obtain what they all desperately needed – modern trucks to carry them east towards Alsace. And what a sorry bunch of cowardly idiots they would seen, if they now bowed out and found themselves stranded and left behind in south-western France, while the others took an active part in de Lattre's campaign to liberate Alsace!

Two days later, at the river-crossing of Cornil, a few kilometres north-east of Aubazines, sixteen modern GMC trucks, carrying the four companies of Major Charles Pleis' battalion, caught up with an extraordinary caravan of *gazogène* lorries, patched-up ambulances, and front-wheel-drive Citroëns whose doors had been removed to enable their *maquisard* occupants to 'hit the ditch' if they had the misfortune to run into a German roadblock. They were carrying 'Ancel' 's raggle-taggle 'soldiers', most of them without helmets or uniforms, but all armed, if not to the teeth, at any rate with an imposing array of Sten-guns, German machine-pistols, rifles, hammer- shaped *Wehrmacht* grenades, and bayonets.

On September 17th, one week after this momentous meeting, Malraux and Jacquot reported to General de Lattre's headquarters, now luxuriously installed in the Hôtel de la Cloche, in the Burgundian capital of Dijon. Here they were surprised by the arrival of three Alsatian officers – a Captain René Dopff and two lieutenants, who had come from the region of Annecy with 300 *maquisards* from the mountains of Savoie.

Malraux was impressed. 'You Alsatians always manage to find one another!' he exclaimed. 'But what's your trick?' he asked. 'There must be something behind all this – some kind of underlying structure. A political party? A workers' union? A religious sect? Or perhaps a secret society?'

'None of them,' replied Captain Dopff, who came from one of the finest wine-growing families of Alsace. 'Patriotism, the love of one's homeland, no more.'

That evening they all went to dine together at Les Trois Pigeons. They talked about the historic woes of Alsace, torn between two cultures; about how 100,000 of its sons had been forcibly enrolled into Hitler's *Wehrmacht*; and about many other problems. Stimulated by the fascinating talk, inspired by the glowing wine, Malraux launched into a lyrical forecast of the future as he saw it, in which a liberated Alsace would find its rightful place, at last, in a finally reconciled and peaceful Europe.

'Fine,' said Captain Dopff, at the end of the meal. 'I'm your man.'

The Brigade Alsace–Lorraine had just acquired a new battalion, destined to be called 'Mulhouse'. Malraux and his 'soldiers' were still far from the figure of 2,000 he had casually given to Ernest Hemingway in Paris, but the Brigade Alsace–Lorraine was no longer a dream or a vision; it had become a military reality.

34

Triumph and Tragedy

Nothing better illustrates the special style of André Malraux's leadership of the Alsace–Lorraine Brigade than a phrase which, curiously combining the elegiac and the exalted, made an indelible impression on all who heard it. Antoine Diener first heard 'Colonel Berger' utter it during a 'pep talk' in a school classroom at Nolay in Burgundy: 'I salute, among you, your dead of yesterday, and among you here those who will die tomorrow.' Others heard it repeated by their colonel in a bistro at Corravillers, in the foothills of the Vosges, where they had crowded together in search of warmth and shelter after four rainy nights and days spent in muddy foxholes on the fog-bound mountain slopes.

The first serious engagements of the eleven-day 'Battle of the Vosges', which lasted from September 27th to October 7th, were fought among the evergreens and ferns of Bois-le-Prince, one of the crests of an almost unbroken chain of mountain forests curving south-east for several hundred kilometres as far as the Swiss border. The 'conquest' of this sector of the front had been assigned to a Combat Command of the French First Armoured Division, whose tanks had been stopped by *Wehrmacht* infantry-men armed with *Panzerfaust* bazookas. It was thus left to Malraux's 'brigands' (so named by their commander because of the initial lack of helmets and proper uniforms) to flush the Germans out of the dense underbrush and from behind the protecting pines.

Early every morning a meeting was held in the 'operations room' (it might be in a schoolroom or farm), where the battalion commanders and their officers were briefed on their respective missions. Malraux, in his hoarse, rapid-fire diction, would begin the session with a quick review of the strategic situation on the western and eastern fronts, explaining in general terms what was expected of them by General de Lattre de Tassigny. Pierre Jacquot would then take over, assigning precise tactical tasks to each company commander in the terse language of the military professional. Although of strikingly different backgrounds, the two men formed a remark-able pair – Malraux galvanizing his subordinates with winged words and philosophic exhortations, while Jacquot (rather like Abel Guidez, of the *escuadra España*) contributed his professional expertise.

On the fourth day of battle the drenched 'doughboys' in their front-line foxholes were surprised to see their 'colonel', in his black beret and sheepskin coat, walk out ahead to a little hummock, from where, puffing calmly at a cigarette, he gazed across the clearing to the well-concealed enemy beyond. This was an almost reckless gesture since it exposed him to machine gun fire or a sniper's bullet, but it raised the spirits of the weary front-liners, whose often sagging morale had so far been sustained above all by their brave chaplains – the Catholic padres, Bockel and Bonnal, their Protestant counterparts, Frantz and Weiss – who bounded like squirrels from one foxhole to the next.

The eleven days spent clearing the wooded heights of Bois-le-Prince were costly for the 'greenhorns' of the Brigade. Indeed, on October 7th, the Brigade came close to losing its most experienced officer on the final mountain ridge overlooking the Moselle river valley. Pierre Jacquot was trying to straighten out an ill-co-ordinated advance when he was laid low by a German machine gun burst. Wounded by a bullet that pierced his armpit, the intrepid lieutenant-colonel was still cursing his ill luck when a stretcher was brought up and he was driven in a jeep to the hospital at Luxeuil.

Shortly thereafter the Brigade was ordered to withdraw for a badly needed rest to Remiremont. During the last week of October, Malraux used the respite to make a quick trip to Paris to see Josette, who had recently found an apartment she was trying to have furnished. He was accompanied by Pierre Bockel, who had greatly intrigued 'Colonel Berger' when they first had a chance to engage in a long conversation. In the *España* squadron, essentially composed of adventurous mercenaries and left-wing anti-Fascists, there had never been any chaplains to provide encouragement or solace to pilots, bombardiers and gunners; for Malraux it had been a revelation to discover the extraordinary rapport that was quickly established in the Alsace–Lorraine Brigade between Catholic and Protestant chaplains and non-believing combattants.

In the chauffeur-driven car 'Colonel Berger' and Chaplain Pierre Bockel talked at length of Victor Hugo, some of whose verses Malraux recited. In Paris they parted. On the day set for their return Pierre Bockel turned up at the little apartment and was dazzled by Josette's beauty. She accompanied them downstairs, and it was on the sidewalk that the Catholic chaplain witnessed the last kisses exchanged between André and Josette.

On their return to the Vosges Malraux and Bockel learned that the Brigade was due to leave Remiremont. De Lattre's offensive in the Vosges mountains had bogged down; he had decided to try a breakthrough at the southernmost point of the front, near the Swiss border. 'Colonel Berger' 's soldiers climbed back into their GMCs, their smoking *gazogène* trucks, their jeeps and front-wheel-drive Citroëns, now equipped with doors adorned with the Brigade's coat-of-arms: the combined crests of Alsace and Lorraine. Heading south, they took up new quarters in seven villages on a wintry plateau, 30 kilometres west of Besançon.

Malraux set himself up in the château of Montagncy, a curious structure with pointed rooftops located in the centre of the town and inhabited by an old pro-Pétain lady. It was here, in a large ground-floor hall warmed by a huge fireplace, that Malraux in the evening entertained the members of his headquarters staff at '*la popote du colonel*' (the Colonel's mess). When the coffee was served at the end of the meal, 'Colonel Berger' once again became André Malraux. No subject seemed beyond the bounds of his universal ken. He seemed as much at ease with the Protestant chaplain, Fernand Frantz, discussing St Augustine's influence on Martin Luther, as he was with his chief of staff, a former camel riding *méhariste* named Brandstetter, in explaining the manoeuvre that had enabled King Artaxerxes of Persia to defeat his brother at the battle of Cunaxa (401 BC).

The serious staff work was accomplished at the schoolhouse of Montagney, where at 9 o'clock every morning the various unit commanders reported for their daily assignments. And it was here that on November 11th an orderly brought 'Colonel Berger' a most upsetting telegram. Josette had been in a serious accident and was in hospital at Tulle. One hour later Malraux left Montagney with his chauffeur, shaken by the premonition that he would not see Josette alive.

From Paris Josette had returned to stay with her friend Rosine Delclaux, the notary's wife, at Saint-Chamant. Her mother, who had not yet seen her grandsons Gauthier and Vincent, had chosen this moment to visit her daughter. As censorious as ever, Mme Clotis criticized the extravagant *vie de château* her daughter had been living. There were stormy scenes, so stormy indeed that Mme Clotis decided to cut short her stay. Furious, Josette lugged her mother's suitcase to the railway station at Saint-Chamant and pulled it up the steps into the 'local': a small steam locomotive and ancient carriages which would take Mme Clotis north to Tulle. Severely afflicted by arthritis, her mother had trouble heaving herself up into the carriage and her ill humour did nothing to ease the final leave-taking. The stationmaster blew his whistle and the tiny train began to move. Rosine Delclaux leapt nimbly on to the platform, but Josette jumped out carelessly in the wrong direction, lost her footing and rolled over. Her legs, extending over the rail, were hideously mangled by the carriage wheels.

There were shouts, the whistle blew, the engine driver braked – but it was too late. A horrified Mme Clotis climbed unsteadily down the steps. An ambulance was summoned to take Josette to the hospital at Tulle, where, still alive and able to speak, she had her friend Rosine sit by her bed. Crushed and grief-stricken, Mme Clotis was forced to wait in the corridor outside.

When André Malraux reached the hospital at Tulle late in the evening of November 12th, Josette Clotis, the mother of his two sons, was already dead. 'I never thought dying would be like this' were among her last words, accompanied by the request that her friend Rosine put some make-up on her face, so that for the last time she might look beautiful.

Years later, writing of Lawrence of Arabia, André Malraux wrote that 'he does not seem to have experienced the death of the woman one loves. It is . . . a thunderbolt.'

After the funeral he went to Paris where, barely able to conceal his grief, he looked up his old friends Pascal Pia and Albert Camus, who had installed themselves at no. 100, Rue Réaumur (*L'Intransigeant*'s old premises) as editor-in-chief and managing editor of a new two-page daily called *Combat*.

On the evening of November 16th, Malraux climbed the five flights of 1 bis, Rue Vaneau, to call on Mme Théo. André Gide was still in North Africa, but his daughter Catherine was there, joyously pregnant. For both women it was a strange Malraux who now appeared before them – 'tight-lipped, contracted, his face ravaged', as Mme Théo noted in her journal. 'One senses that one must not in any way approach his suffering.'

On the eve of Malraux's return to Montagney the soldiers of the French First Army took Montbéliard and pierced the German front at Delle. The leading tanks stormed into Alsace and headed for Mulhouse and the Rhine. Five days later – November 23rd, the day when General Leclerc's tankmen reached Strasbourg – the 1,160 footsloggers of the Alsace–Lorraine Brigade were at last able to leave their austere plateau, transported in 75 new Dodges as well as their old '*gazo*' trucks, several ambulances, and a Paris bus, now turned into a mobile kitchen. Held up for several days by a gigantic bottleneck caused by a single, precarious bridge spanning the Allaine river, the soldiers of the Brigade were jubilantly welcomed when they finally entered the first Alsatian villages.

Malraux's troopers were now attached to the Fourth Combat Command of the French Fifth Armoured Division and assigned the task of clearing the German-held village of Ballersdorf and the town of Dannemarie, so as to open up a second, more direct supply route for de Lattre's vanguard units, which had reached Mulhouse.

The two battles that followed were probably the toughest fought by the infantrymen of the Brigade. At Ballersdorf every farmyard and cellar had to be 'cleaned out' with sub-machine-gun bullets and grenades.

Dannemarie proved an even tougher 'nut' to crack. It was defended by a number of formidable 88mm anti-tank guns. 'Colonel Berger' made a point of going out for a morning stroll with Pierre Jacquot, prior to the start of the assault across frozen ground chilled by wisps of freezing fog. The effect on the morale of the attackers was excellent, for a number of newly arrived soldiers were amazed to hear the two colonels carrying on a lively literary argument some distance *beyond* their outposts. The attacking infantrymen, however, were thrown off their stride by several artillery salvos, one of which severely wounded Diener–'Ancel'. Other shellbursts knocked out two of his company commanders. Jacquot, who as usual was out in front, would have found himself without officers to lead the decapitated companies had Major

René Dopff (now a battalion commander) not made an unscheduled appearance and gone on to direct the attack.

At the end of that freezing day, so cold that the sentries had to be relieved at their guard-posts every fifteen minutes, the bruised and battered footsloggers of the Brigade found that for the first time they had captured 100 German prisoners. That night – it was November 28th – the kirsch and the Gewürtz-Traminer flowed in abundance.

No one has described the singular atmosphere of this day in its strange mixture of wintry beauty and destructive fury more eloquently than their commander, 'Colonel Berger'. The account he later gave is as fine a description as any he ever wrote. The elegiac tone, a wintry landscape worthy of a Ruysdael, a hymn to the solidarity of warring men, an evocation of the doleful eternity of Evil, ever ready to burst the fragile crust of civilization – everything is there:

> Perhaps on my dying day, I may recall that road disappearing off to the left in the darkening dusk. Then, it was hardly a road: a straight line of frost, reddened by the glow of fires, burrowed its way between bumpy furrows towards a blazing Dannemarie. Villages and hamlets were no more than the names of flames. And when the sharp wintry wind lifted the veil of light, out loomed a positioned tank, which the white frost of eternity was beginning to cover . . .
>
> Along with the war, it was more than war, it was the intermittent flare-up come from the depths of the ages: the Scourge. Once again, the old, death-drenched earth was sounding in the night its old Saturnian cry. There, where there was still a stable, our wounded lay stretched out next to the warm animals . . . They it was who had roughed it in the snow, in Resistance hide-outs among the stunted trees of Dordogne and Corrèze, where one could advance only on all fours . . . The ones who had crossed half of France, including the Massif Central, in crazy *gazogène* trucks. The ones who had wrested half of their weapons from the enemy. The same who, from time immemorial, have pinched farmyard chickens. Those who, as soon as they stopped shaving, resembled farm labourers of the Middle Ages . . .
>
> They were simply waiting. Together. And their fraternity sprang from the depths of ages past, as far back in time as the first smile on the lips of the first child. As profound, as invincible as the sourge that was shaking the earth. For all the millennial crackling of the flames, the Eternity of Misfortune could not cover that of a fraternal silence.

From Mulhouse, where German troops were still holding out, as they were at Colmar, the Brigade was moved yet again – this time to Strasbourg. It was a long displacement, taking all of two days. The bizarre caravan of modern Dodges and old *gazogène* trucks had to make a long detour, skirting the western slopes of the Vosges as far as Sarrebourg, where, turning east, they descended on Strasbourg through the Saverne pass. There followed several weeks of joyous carousing, the local lads being welcomed as liberators in every town and village, stuffed with sauerkraut and *kugelhopf* pastry, copiously plied with Sylvaner and kirsch.

On Sunday, December 16th, a solemn Mass was held to celebrate the reopening of Strasbourg's cathedral, which had remained closed for four long years on orders from the *Führer*. The gloom caused by the sand-bagged windows accentuated the soft flicker of the candles. This was the church of the early Christians, the church of the catacombs – reborn after four years of ferocious, Nero-like persecution. Standing in the front row, between the Bishop of Strasbourg and several US army generals, Malraux listened with emotion to the vibrant sermon delivered by Pierre Bockel. The Brigade's chaplain spoke with moving simplicity of Alsace's Patron Saint, Saint Odile, the blind daughter of Duke Athich, who had recovered her sight at the moment of her baptism – just as, it was hoped, the madmen of this world would recover their sight and sanity once the tempests of unreason which had shaken Europe and the world were calmed.

On December 24th, just as the men of the Brigade were getting ready to celebrate their first truly merry Christmas in four years, they were brutally jolted back to earth. The war was far from finished. The *Boches*, commanded by one of their ablest generals, Gerd von Runstedt, had just pierced the American front north of Luxembourg. General Leclerc's tankmen were moved north to plug a 'hole', while the defence of Strasbourg was entrusted to US army units, various French Resistance groups, two squadrons of *gardes mobiles*, and the Alsace–Lorraine Brigade. Its soldiers were dispatched south to occupy a number of villages, the furthest being 35 kilometres south of Strasbourg.

During the night of January 2–3, 1945, René Dopff, whose battalion covered the northern stretch of the 'front', discovered to his stupefaction that the Americans had decamped. They were later found at a road intersection near Molsheim, where they were chopping down trees to construct a road block, 25 kilometres *west* of Strasbourg. The Alsatian capital had been abandoned to its fate . . . and to the sole protection of several Free French Resistance units, the *gardes mobiles*, and the 1,000 'doughboys' of the Alsace–Lorraine Brigade.

Surprised by the initial success of the German offensive in the Ardennes, General Eisenhower had decided to shorten the Allied front by pulling his US army troops back to the 'rampart' of the Vosges mountains, leaving Strasbourg uncovered. And this precisely at the moment when the *Führer*, having failed in his bold attempt to capture Liège and Antwerp, had decided to stun the world with another 'master stroke' by seizing Strasbourg.

If the Germans had still had enough reserves to cross the Rhine in force, the under-armed infantrymen of the Alsace–Lorraine Brigade could not have prevented them from investing Strasbourg. But the battered *Wehrmacht* no longer had the necessary means in inflatable dinghies and well trained soldiery – which is to say, something more formidable than the teenage youngsters and pathetic sexagenarians who were now being forcibly enrolled in so-called *Volkssturm* units.

Even so, Strasbourg was seriously threatened for a few tense days. On January 5th, German soldiers managed to cross the Rhine and to establish a beachhead at Gambsheim, 20 kilometres north of the Alsatian capital. The panic-stricken inhabitants hastily erected barricades by overturning a few trams to block snow-covered avenues and streets. The temperature kept dropping – to 10, 12 and even 15 degrees below zero (centigrade), adding to the hardships of the Brigade's shivering soldiers in their snow-rimmed fox holes, barns and unheated rooms.

On Sunday, January 7th, the German forces to the south decided to break out of the 'Colmar pocket' by advancing north towards Strasbourg with Tigers, Panthers, and huge tank-destroyers. They bypassed a number of villages held by soldiers of the Brigade's right wing (facing the Rhine), who could now feel the enemy breathing down their necks. As it approached a key bridge spanning the Rhine–Ill canal in the town of Krafft, the leading German tank-destroyer, a 70-ton monster armed with a formidable 128mm gun, had one of its treads torn off by a 57mm anti-tank shell fired by French marines, backed up by one of the Brigade's commandos. The three following tanks hesitated long enough to enable French sappers to dynamite the bridge, which collapsed with a crunch into the frozen canal. Strasbourg was thus saved, almost miraculously.

On January 20th Malraux had to leave Strasbourg to attend the first congress of the MLN – Mouvement de Libération Nationale – which had been set up the previous year in an effort to co-ordinate the activities of different Resistance networks. The majority of those present, including Henri Frenay, the founder of the important COMBAT network, were opposed to the proposal put forward by delegates from the Communist-Controlled networks that the various Resistance organizations be welded into a single National Block. The reason was simple. The French Communist Party at this moment of its history was sailing with the wind behind it. It felt itself borne forward on a mighty surge of sympathy for the Soviet Union, whose citizens had suffered so terribly and whose heroic armies were now marching from victory to victory. In contrast with the western front, where the Allies were painfully nibbling away at the German defences, if not actually beating a retreat, the Soviet armies were advancing with giant strides. On January 17th, four days after the start of their offensive, Marshal Zhukov's soldiers occupied Warsaw, while Koniev's men seized Cracow. Further north, Rokossovsky's forces smashed through the German lines and invaded East Prussia. Before the MLN Congress in Paris had completed its debates, the Russians had reached the Oder and were only 170 kilometres from Berlin.

Never had the prestige of the Red Army been so high. And it was precisely at this moment that Stalin decided to exploit the patriotic fervour engendered in several European countries from their experience of a Nazi occupation by setting up a 'national front' in each. A masterpiece of the genre was the one that was established for Czechoslovakia and endorsed by Eduard Beneš – the result of which was a provisional government where Communist Party members or sympathizers were awarded six out of twelve cabinet posts.

Such was the international context when Malraux reached the Mutualité Hall in Paris. His colonel's uniform, so different from the civilian suits worn by most of the delegates, created a sensation. On Thursday, January 25th he mounted the rostrum and delivered a speech which his friends at *Combat* published *in extenso* – the only MLN Congress speech to be so honoured. It was a curious speech, at once exalted, precise and vague. He began by praising the 'movement of national liberation' as being 'one of the forms of the country's consciousness'; he described the exploits of weaponless Resistance fighters – 'we were a France in rags'; he praised 'English parachuting', going as far as to declare that without the English 'we would really not have had anything'. (It was the plain truth, but how many French 'patriots' were prepared to admit it?)

Then, employing a vocabulary worthy of Maurice Barrès, he defined the Resistance as a 'general mobilization of French energy' and bluntly insisted that General de Gaulle's government was 'not only the government of France, but the government of the Liberation and the Resistance'. He reminded his listeners that the war was not yet over. 'But,' he immediately added, raising a warning finger, 'if it is indispensable that it [ie the problem of the revolution] come only afterwards, it is indispensable that it should come afterwards.' He thus endorsed the political ideals of the newspaper *Combat*, whose motto was: 'From Resistance to Revoluton'. Malraux added that 'a fundamental ingredient of the revolutionary will is the end of capitalism'. Which meant what? That 'capitalist credit' must be destroyed 'in an orderly fashion'. In other words, the banks needed to be nationalized, but without the country's financiers having to be guillotined, since this would stir up 'revolutionary disorder'.

Then came the most curious passage of this astonishing speech. To remain 'pure and hard', the Mouvement de Libération National would have to take its cue from the Communist Party.

The Communist Party, for example, is not a nexus of means of persuasion, but a nexus of means of action. Now all of us here, let's not forget that together we too are a nexus of means of action. Consequently, if we wish to maintain our mobilization of energy such as it was in the past, it is according to a technique similar to that of the Communists that we should act; that is, we should, within our Movement, maintain a discipline equal to that Communist Party's, with all the tough hardships that this implies.

It must be admitted that Jacques Baumel, one of the pillars of the COMBAT movement, who had been entrusted with the task of defining the MLN's immediate goals, was both briefer and clearer in advocating a 'grouping-together of the Resistance into a union on specific points . . . but not one of organic unity' – which was what the Communists were after – 'which would swallow up in an artificial unanimity the great spiritual tendencies that were manifested in the Resistance and which constitute the richness of a country like France, whose unity rests on a relative and freely accepted diversity'. This was the prevailing view with a majority of the delegates to the congress, who at the final session rejected the proposed 'fusion' of French left-wing parties and splinter-groups by 250 votes to 119.

This vote, defending individualism of thought and opinion against a monolithic unity of action, in effect sounded the deathknell of the MLN. If, all things considered, André Malraux's speech was not as decisive as has sometimes been claimed, it nevertheless marked a crucial date in his career as a man of action. Without quite realizing it, he had just delivered his first big Gaullist speech.

On May 22, 1945 Antoine Diener's brother-in-law, Gustave Houver, reached Paris. A member of the same Resistance group in Périgueux, he had fallen into a Gestapo trap in early April 1944, had been tortured and then deported to a Nazi concentration camp at Neuengamme, 20 kilometres south of Hamburg. In this camp he had met Roland Malraux.

During the last days of April 1945, as British and Canadian forces were approaching the Elbe estuary, the SS commandant at Neuengamme had ordered the camp to be evacuated. The famished prisoners were transported to the port of Lübeck, where they were herded like cattle into several ships anchored in the bay. The terrestrial hell of Neuengamme was thus replaced by the floating hell of Lübeck bay. The stinking holds were soon piled high with corpses, dead from hunger or typhus, which the SS jailers threw overboard by the hundreds every day.

Towards midday of May 3rd, two of the German ships opened fire with anti-aircraft weapons on a low-flying RAF reconnaissance plane. Several Allied fighter-bombers were sent out to work the ships over with bombs and torpedoes. Gustave Houver managed to extricate himself from his stricken cargo ship (the *Thielbeck*) by plunging into the cold waters of the Baltic. Another bomb struck the 26,000-ton liner, *Cap Arcona*, which began to burn as slowly it tilted over on one side. Of the 6,500 prisoners trapped in its holds and cabins, only 150 managed to make it to the shore. Later; one of them, a Pole named Owczarek, whom Houver had met in the Neuengamme camp, told how he had caught a glimpse of Roland Malraux amid the smoke before managing to squeeze his way out through a porthole.

At the Gare du Nord, in Paris, Gustave Houver was met by a welcoming committee and taken to the Hôtel Lutétia, on the Left Bank, which had been turned into an emergency relief centre for repatriated Frenchmen. There he met several former inmates of the Neuengamme concentration camp who told him that two women had been trying to find out what had happened to Roland Malraux. On May 23rd, after a number of telephone calls, André Malraux turned up at an apartment on the Rue de Caulaincourt where Gustave Houver was staying with relatives. With Malraux was a woman who seemed very worried.

After hearing Gustave Houver's sad tale, Malraux asked him bluntly: 'Is Roland alive or dead?'

'I didn't see him dead,' Houver answered, adding reluctantly, 'but I think that he is dead.'

Madeleine Malraux, for it was she who accompanied André, burst into tears.

35

Two Months in Power

André Malraux must have felt dazed, disoriented and dismayed when he returned from the front to the humdrum routine of civilian life in the spring of 1945. He had to find a new home and remake his life on several levels. He had lost the woman he loved, the mother of his two sons, and he had 'inherited' a sister-in-law, Roland's widow, who also had a son to take care of. From the pre-war figure of three, the household had suddenly increased to five, not counting Clara and young Florence, for whose upkeep he was still financially responsible.

On 23rd January, during his brief stay in Paris for the first MLN Congress, Malraux had dined with his old friend Marcel Arland. He told him how, the previous November, when de Gaulle and Churchill were making a front-line visit to General de Lattre's First Army, he had been linked to the rear by telephone. He had been drowsing when suddenly he saw a woman's face loom up before him and announce: 'I am your third wife.' Several hours later he learned that Josette had suffered a serious accident.

After a long moment of silence, he said to his friend Marcel: 'During the Occupation, I used to tell myself that after the war I would live with Josette and the children, perhaps far removed from everything in order to work. Now I no longer know, I'm hesitating.'

'Between . . .?'

'Being a writer, making films, and engaging in action.'

'You've always needed action, conquest, power,' Arland pointed out. 'Even for your books you needed it . . .'

'But what action? To be . . . Minister of Information? Can that satisfy men like us?'

Already in 1936, during the Spanish Civil War, Malraux had said to Marcel Arland: 'I can only live with human beings in relations of friendship or of command.' But if this latter urge found its natural fulfillment in times of war or during revolutionary convulsions, it was much harder to satisfy in times of peace, when politics-as-usual was once again the order of the day.

On the literary level he found himself momentarily stymied, simply because a sword of Damocles was now suspended over the head of his publisher, Gallimard. Accused by super-patriots of having 'collaborated' with the Germans, Gaston at this point was anxious above all to exonerate himself in the eyes of the reading public by bringing out books that had been banned by the German censorship. Books that could be promoted by striking advertisements – like Louis Aragon's *Aurélien* ('a clandestinely composed work'); Saint-Exupéry's *Pilote de Guerre* ('book published in 1942 and seized by the Germans'); or *Le Temps du Mépris* ('a book banned by the Germans'). On the other hand, *La Lutte avec l'Ange*, not having been clandestinely published in France nor banned by the Germans, did not serve Gaston's immediate interests. While waiting for better times, Malraux offered his text to the Swiss art-book publisher, Albert Skira, who in October brought out a de luxe edition, with a limited print order of 5,000 copies.

Although the *NRF* had fallen into silence from June 1943, it was condemned in advance simply because it had been relaunched in December 1940 and had appeared for two-and-a-half years under the editorial direction of Drieu la Rochelle (who had finally committed suicide in March 1945, after naming Malraux the testamentary executor for his literary works). Malraux could have looked for other outlets. But he did not do so. When Jean-Paul Sartre asked him to contribute to his new monthly, *Les Temps Modernes*, Malraux refused the offer. Sartre, several of whose plays had been performed during the Occupation before audiences that included German officers, was, in Malraux's eyes, the very prototype of the comfortably 'hidden', 'flabby' Resistance fighter. Nor did he care much for Sartre's writing – he had said as much to André Gide prior to 1941 – perhaps because he already foresaw the subtle ways in which Sartre was going to exploit the existential preoccupations that he, Malraux, had begun to air as early as 1926. Besides, as he explained to Roger Stéphane, nothing exasperated him more than the verbosity of Sartrian prose, already manifest in essays written by the author of *La Nausée*: 'Yes, I've seen the trial number [of *Les Temps Modernes*], it's extraordinarily non-literary, anti-literary, and it's going to be a bore. To seem worthy of publication by Sartre, an article must be at least 400 pages long.'

Malraux's first concern, on a practical level, was to find a proper home for his new family; for the apartment on the Avenue d'Orsay where he lived with his sister-in-law Madeleine and the three boys – Bimbo (Gauthier), Vincent, and Alain – was far too small. This problem was solved in June, when he found a villa in the south-western suburb of Boulogne. Built in the 'art déco' style of the 1920s, with curious alcoves, staircase balustrades and halfway landings, it had the advantage of being large and light, with a front entrance facing the leafy horse-chestnuts of the Avenue Victor Hugo. The ground floor was occupied by the owners, so Madeleine and the three boys took possession of the second floor, while Malraux made himself at home on the first. Sparsely furnished for the first few months, this floor was large enough to accommodate the 'Graeco-Buddhist' sculptures, which André was at last able to recover from his Aunt Marie and Dr Jean-Marie Sotty, who had hidden a number of them in his Burgundy home during the war. Later, an enormous grand piano was added, as a gift for Madeleine.

There remained the still unsolved problem of what this 'father' of a suddenly enlarged family was going to do in the immediate future. Malraux was once again tempted by the cinema. He must have discussed the idea of shooting a film based on the wartime exploits of his comrades of the Alsace–Lorraine Brigade with his friend 'Eddy' Corniglion-Molinier when they met again in Paris. But Corniglion at this point had no time for film-making. After all sorts of hair-raising adventures, which had taken him to North Africa, then to Egypt and Libya, where he had commanded two FAFL (Free French Air Force) bomber groups, he had returned from London with de Gaulle. As an Air Force general and an honoured *Compagnon de la Libération*, he was now a member of Charles de Gaulle's military household and occupied an office at the War Ministry, on the Rue Saint-Dominique. It was here that Malraux came to see his old chum each time he returned to Paris from the front. Their conversations were often continued in Corniglion's apartment near the Champs-Elysées, where the airman amused his colleagues – including Lieutenant (later Captain) Claude Guy, an aide-de-camp, and Gaston Palewski, the head of de Gaulle's secretariat – by reading extracts from the hilarious Franco-British dialogues which Corniglion had begun writing in the desert sands of Libya. 'Colonel Berger', soon reconverted to civilian life as André Malraux the writer, thus penetrated the entourage of the president of the GPRF (Provisional Government of the French Republic).

One evening in early August the telephone rang in Malraux's suburban villa. An hour or two later an official car drove up, and, hurrying up the steps, Claude Guy said to Malraux: 'General de Gaulle wishes to know if, in the name of France, you would be willing to help him.'

'There's no need to ask' was the immediate reply.

The next day Malraux was driven to the town house on the Rue Saint-Dominique where de Gaulle had installed his secretariat and his personal military staff. From Gaston Palewski's office he was led to the other side of the grand staircase. A moment later he found himself in de Gaulle's office, which was dominated by the portraits of two illustrious predecessors: the Comte de Saint-Germain, who had served as Minister of War under Louis XVI, and Lazare Carnot, the 'organizer of victory' for the First French Republic's revolutionary forces who had helped to end the Terror of 1793–4 by promoting the downfall of Robespierre.

Malraux was less startled by the General's great height than by the small-ness and darkness of his moustache. But what struck him most was the density of Charles de Gaulle's heavy, brooding look. Equally surprising was the brevity of the General's first three words: '*D'abord, le passé*.' (First of all, the past.)

There was, obviously, much to be explained, even if these three words did not contain an implicit reproach: 'How is it that you did not join me before?' As had, for example, André Gide and many other French writers. But Malraux chose to interpret this question as embracing his entire past as a revolutionary. This he proceeded to summarize in a few sentences of lapidary brevity.

'It's very simple. I engaged in a struggle for, let's say, justice. Perhaps, more exactly, to give human beings a chance. . . . I served as president of the World Anti-Fascist Committee with Romain Rolland, and I went with Gide to deliver to Hitler – who did not receive us – a protest against the trial of Dimitrov and the so-called arsonists of the Reichstag. Then there was the Spanish War, and I went to fight in Spain. Not in the International Brigades, which did not yet exist; for the Communist Party' – ie, Stalin's Politburo – 'took its time deciding . . . Then came the war, the real one. Finally came the defeat, and, like many others, I espoused [the cause of] France.'

Whether subtly calculated or prompted by a spontaneous *élan*, this was the kind of Gaullist vocabulary that was made to appeal to the General. 'When I reached Paris,' Malraux went on, 'Albert Camus asked me: Will we one day have to choose between Russia and America? For my part, it's not between Russia and America, it's between Russia and France. When a weak France finds itself confronted by a powerful Russia, I no longer believe a word of what I believed when a powerful France was confronted by a weak Soviet Union. A weak Russia wants popular fronts, a strong Russia wants popular democracies.'

The purpose of this meeting being to test his 'guest', it is hardly surprising that de Gaulle should have allowed him to talk at such length – with passing references to Marx, Victor Hugo, Michelet, Nietzsche, Clausewitz, Clemenceau, Mirabeau, Hoche, Saint-Just, Diderot, Catherine the Great, etc, served up as naturally as if Malraux had been conversing with André Gide at some literary get-together.

Dazzling as this demonstration of intellectual virtuosity on the part of a brilliant 'young man' of forty-three (twelve years less than the General) may have been, it was almost certainly the acuity of Malraux's analysis of the political ambitions of the different Resistance groups that most impressed de Gaulle.

'The National Front is para-Communist, while waiting to be Communist. My comrades are para-labourites, while waiting for a form of "labourism" that does not exist, and about which they don't know whether to expect it from themselves, from the Socialist Party, or from yourself.'

'What do they want to *do*?' insisted the General.

'As in 1848, as in 1871, [they want to] play out a heroic drama called Revolution. Nobly, for the real ones, for those who did not come out from under the cobblestones after the army had arrived . . . Without a state, any policy is in the future tense and becomes more or less a kind of ethics.' This, clearly, was the language of the former admirer of Lenin and Trotsky, who in Spain had condemned the anarchistic disciples of Proudhon, Bakunin and Kropotkin, and who could just as easily have spoken out in the name of Richelieu or Napoleon.

'. . . The Communist Resistance leads to the Communist Party, or to communism with a phoney nose. The other leads . . . anywhere you wish . . . The resisters were, on the whole, liberal patriots. Liberalism is not a political reality; it is a sentiment, and a sentiment can exist in several parties, but cannot found a single one. At the Congress of the MLN I discovered that therein lies the present drama of the Resistance.

'Its members are not opposed to communism. In terms of economic doctrine, 50 per cent of them prefer it. They are against the communists; perhaps, more exactly, what is Russian in French Communism . . . The secret dream of a good part of France, and of most of her intellectuals, is a guillotine without guillotined victims.'

That General de Gaulle should have been subjugated by this brilliant improvization, like so many others before him – from Gide to Bernard Groethuysen, from Mikhaïl Koltsov to Gustav Regler, from Stephen Spender to José Bergamín, from Emmanuel Berl to Pierre Jacquot – is hardly surprising. De Gaulle, after all, was the son, not of an Army officer but of a school-teacher who, furthermore, had been a firm supporter of Dreyfus.

Yet how is one to explain this spontaneous and unconditional rallying of a former revolutionary to the person of Charles de Gaulle? Nine months before – so his nephew Alain has claimed – Malraux, on hearing Corniglion-Molinier sing the General's praises, had exclaimed: 'What! That Fascist?'

This dramatic 'shift' can be explained by three reasons or motivations of a purely tactical nature, linked to specific actions. The first was the firmness displayed by de Gaulle after the liberation of Paris in insisting on the prompt dissolution or forcible incorporation into the French Army of the Communist-controlled FTP groups and of the lawless gangs of eleventh-hour 'resisters' who in certain regions had gone on a rampage, terrorizing the local populace and looting the châteaux. The second action was the risky trip to Moscow General de Gaulle had undertaken in December 1944, in defiance of the 'Anglo-Saxons', in order to have a 'man-to-man' talk with Stalin. The third action was de Gaulle's intransigent refusal to abandon Strasbourg in January 1945.

In June 1940 André Malraux may not yet have read anything written by Charles de Gaulle. But later on he had taken the trouble to read *L'Armée de Métier* and *Le Fil de l'Epée*, both of them reprinted in 1944. Now the second chapter of this latter work (the thinly disguised autobiography of an ambition), which is entitled 'Of Character', is, quite simply, a portrayal of the political hero, the military hero, the inventive hero, the rebellious hero. Consider these extracts:

Challenged by events, it is upon his own resources that the man of character relies. Far from seeking shelter beneath the hierarchy, hiding behind texts, shielding himself behind reports, he draws himself up, digs in his heels and faces the challenge . . . Difficulties attract the man of character, for it is by embracing them that he realizes himself. [A sentence Nietzsche could have written.] 'Proud, undisciplined', is what mediocrities say of him, treating the thoroughbred with the sensitive mouth like the mule that refuses to budge, not perceiving that ruggedness is the gut-lining of powerful characters, that one can lean for support only on that which resists, and that it is better to prefer firm, gruff hearts to flabby, spineless souls.

To these words Drieu la Rochelle could have subscribed without an instant's hesitation. And they were followed by this astonishing apologia for disobedience which must have thrilled the former rebel student of the Rue Turbigo, the brazen adventurer of the jungles of Cambodia:

For, after all, if one must, according to Cicero, 'study each thing in the most perfected examples we possess of it', where was a great human work ever realized without there being revealed thereby a passion for action on the part of a man of character? Alexander would not have conquered Asia, nor Galileo demonstrated the movement of the earth, nor Columbus discovered America, nor Richelieu restored the authority of the king, nor Boileau have established the rules of classical tastes, nor Bismarck realized the unity of Germany, nor Clemenceau have saved the country, if they had yielded to the counsels of a petty prudence or to the suggestions of a cowardly modesty. Such was Pélissier at Sebastopol, pocketing the Emperor's accusatory dispatches and reading them only after the matter had been settled. Such was Lanrezac, saving his army at Charleroi by breaking off the battle despite the order he had received. Such was Lyautey, preserving the whole of Morocco in 1914 notwithstanding the instructions of his superiors. After the naval battle of Jutland during which the English had bungled the chance to destroy the German fleet, the First Lord of the Admiralty, Lord Fisher, exclaimed, after receiving Admiral Jellicoe's report: 'He has all the qualities of Nelson, save one: he does not know how to disobey.'

It was thus, after a conversation which had barely lasted half an hour, that André Malraux entered the service of Charles de Gaulle. Was he given any specific assignments? Probably not. At the urging of his aide-de-camp, Claude Guy, de Gaulle had added Claude Mauriac to his staff, in order to be kept informed of what 'people were thinking' (of him and his government) in the liberal Catholic circles to which his illustrious father (François Mauriac) belonged. With Malraux, however, de Gaulle acquired an 'antenna' situated a good deal further to the left.

'I must admit I can't get used to seeing you in this official setting,' Claude Mauriac said to him one day. He had begun a book about the author of *La Condition humaine* in which no allowance had been made for the inclusion of an 'official' or 'bureaucratic' Malraux. Malraux sensed it, growling in reply:

'But it's to the General, to him personally, that I'm attached.'

During the elections of October 21st, one French elector in four (26 per cent of the total) had voted for the Communist Party. With 5 million votes and 160 seats in the Chamber, the French Communist Party had a slight edge over Georges Bidault's moderately Catholic MRP (Mouvement Républicain Populaire – 4.9 million votes, 152 seats) and Léon Blum's Socialists (4.7 million votes, 142 seats). With an absolute majority of 50.7 per cent of the votes and 302 seats in the Assembly, France's two left-wing parties – Maurice Thorez's Communists and Léon Blum's Socialists – could have formed a coalition to rule the country. But this was out of the question. The gunfire of criticism to which his Front Populaire government had been subjected by the Communists throughout its eighteen months in office in 1936–7 was still too painful a grievance to be forgiven by Blum, who had returned from the concentration camp of Buchenwald six months before, whereas Thorez had quietly sat out the war in Moscow.

What excited Malraux in the present situation were not the behind-the-scenes manoeuvres in the corridors of the Assembly; it was the smell of gunpowder in the air, prior to the looming battle. 'The fear of all these yellow-bellies surrounding us . . . is ridiculous. One must dare to stand up to the Communists – it's neither all that difficult, nor vain . . . There's going to be a lot of turmoil and excitement, believe me. It's my only excuse, my sole *raison d'être* for being in this office.'

On November 21st, after protracted negotiations because of General de Gaulle's stubborn refusal to entrust one of the three key cabinet posts – Foreign Affairs, Defence, or the Interior – to a Communist deputy, a new government was formed. Alongside Christian Democrats from Georges Bidault's MRP, Socialists and Communists, it included three 'pure Gaullists': René Pleven, a Breton resister who became Minister of Finance, the ethnologist Jacques Soustelle, named Minister for France's Overseas Possessions, and André Malraux, appointed Minister of Information.

From his office on the Rue Saint-Dominique Malraux now moved across the Seine to the provisional quarters which Jacques Soustelle (the controversial ex-boss of de Gaulle's secret services in Algiers) had found for the Ministry of Information on the Avenue Friedland, not far from the Arc de Triomphe. For lack of funds and also time, Malraux was unable to realize any of the grandiose schemes for visual information-spreading – the introduction of cinema into classrooms, for example – which he had outlined to Gaston Palewski with such fiery enthusiasm. As Raymond Aron (chosen by Malraux to head his secretariat) later wrote: 'The Ministry of Information wielded few powers, and the director of his secretariat even fewer.'

The ministry's primary task was to authorize the appearance of new newspapers and to settle disputes in which 'collaborationist' publishers were arrayed against 'patriotic' journalists who, in many cities, beginning with Paris, had seized printing presses and editorial offices, to the fury of the former owners who were noisily demanding the return of their 'property'.

This situation could not last; and it was with a sigh of relief that one day they received a directive from the prime minister's office inviting them to do away with such authorizations. 'A praiseworthy initiative,' Aron later noted, 'but which did not remove the real obstacle to a return to a normal regime of freedom: shortage of paper.'

It was what Malraux pointed out, on December 29, 1945, in defending his ministry's budget before the deputies of the Assembly. For the time being, the allocation of newsprint was a sad necessity. Otherwise, he explained, a black market in newsprint was bound to spring up, with small fortunes being made by speculators – all of which would 'amount purely and simply to re-establishing capitalism in this country'. For it is worth noting that if Malraux – not officially registered with any political party and considered a 'technician' – was now a Gaullist minister, he had not ceased to 'have his heart on the left'. Whence his scheme for having reproductions printed up of 100 masterpieces of French painting – such as Renoir's *Moulin de la Galette*, Watteau's *L'Enseigne de Gersaint*, Cézanne's *Château noir* – and displayed in thousands of schools all over the country: an initiative he justified in the same speech by declaring: 'It seems to me indispensable that culture should cease to belong to people who are lucky enough to live in Paris or to be wealthy.'

As the official spokesman for the government, which is to say for General de Gaulle, André Malraux was obliged to receive a never-ending stream of claimants and complainers of every kind. For a person of his temperament this must have been a trying chore. Particularly so, since when he took over the ministry (to quote Aron again),

> Malraux knew even less than I did about the functioning of the administrative system: the distinction between a law, a decree, and an administrative directive. But he learned what he had to in a few hours and managed with the same rapidity to plough through the files concerning subjects of interest to journalists. He set himself a rigorous schedule and received the newspapermen punctually, never varying more than a minute or two from the pre-arranged time. He replied to precise questions with pertinent answers, which impressed ordinary journalists . . . Notwithstanding his nervousness, I cannot recall his ever having raised his voice in dealing with a member of his staff.

Exasperated by the manifest determination of most deputies to draft a Constitution similar to the Third Republic's, where once again the president would be no more than a figurehead beside an omnipotent parliament, de

Gaulle decided suddenly to put an end to his mandate. Malraux was one of the few 'insiders' to be informed of his decision on Thursday, January 17, 1946, along with Adrien Tixier, the Minister of the Interior, and Edmond Michelet, the heroic former inmate of Buchenwald whom the General had put in charge of the armed forces to keep a Communist from taking over the Ministry of Defence.

Three days later, on Sunday 20th, de Gaulle convened an emergency cabinet meeting in the 'Hall of Arms' of the Defence Ministry, which was still adorned with the tapestries and draperies hung there one year before to honour Winston Churchill's visit to Paris. Shortly after midday the General strode into the hall and informed his ministers, who received the news standing, that, disappointed by the behaviour of the various political parties, which had continued to bicker and squabble among themselves, he preferred to retire, his mission accomplished.

Later in the afternoon Malraux was summoned to the General's home in Neuilly, to help him prepare a radio address in which he intended to explain to the men and women of France why he had decided to resign. We may be sure than Malraux, with his customary ardour, was all for making this speech as trenchant and 'muscular' as possible. But the mere idea that the General was going over their heads to address directly the people of France so alarmed certain ministers that the Socialist leader, Vincent Auriol, sent the outgoing premier an urgent letter begging him not to deliver a speech which would sow the seeds of discord and antagonize French 'republicans'.

Half an hour after midnight (of January 21st) a telephone call from the prime minister's office informed the Agence France-Presse that General de Gaulle would not after all be delivering a radio address. But for the next twenty-four hours Paris buzzed with wild rumours, as if a *coup d'état* were being planned.

Of Malraux's role in all these doings we know next to nothing. But, like Claude Mauriac, he must have thought that the 'liberator' had muffed his exit from the political stage by sending to his interim successor, Félix Gouin (president of the Constituent Assembly), an overly complaisant, self-congratulating letter in which the present circumstances of France and its Empire – 'Economic activity is reviving. Our territories are in our hands. We have set foot again in Indochina. Public peace is not disturbed' – were portrayed in singularly rosy hues.

36

Herald of the RPF

The year 1946 marked a 'pause' in André Malraux's career as a man of action. In the spacious suburban villa of Boulogne he could at last resume work on the illustrated book devoted to the psychology of art he had begun preparing in 1936 but had been prevented from completing by two successive wars.

This was also the year in which he was finally able to settle the painful problem of his relations with his wife. Clara, who had managed miraculously to elude the clutches of the Gestapo and the French pro-Nazi *milice* and to keep from starving by moving frequently with Florence from one village to the next between Montauban and Toulouse, had returned to Paris in September 1944. From a tiny apartment, which did not even boast a bathroom, on the Rue Berthollet, not far from the Latin Quarter, she wrote to her husband to say: 'I am ready to divorce where, when, and how you wish.'

André took his time replying. He first wished to meet his daughter, whom he had not seen for six years. A rendez-vous was arranged near the Gare Saint-Lazare. 'Flo' was waiting on the sidewalk in front of a shoeshop when she saw a black front-wheel-drive Citroën draw up to the kerb, driven by a smartly capped chauffeur. She had difficulty recognizing the man who climbed out, for he was dressed in military uniform. He advanced towards his daughter, held out his hand, and then asked: 'What are you reading just now?' The reply given to him by his daughter, who was only twelve years old, must have come as an agreeable surprise: '*The Brothers Karamazov*'.

The prickly problem of the divorce was at last happily resolved in a lawyer's office: a meeting (as Clara ironically described it later) between 'Monsieur le Ministre' – this was in January 1946 – and 'a nondescript lady'. To facilitate a settlement, both agreed to recognize their 'reciprocal wrong-doings', while a financial agreement was drafted to cover the costs of Florence's education.

From the moment he left his ministry right through to the end of 1946, André Malraux devoted most of his time to the preparation of his *La Psychologie de l'Art*. He paid close attention, however, to what was happening politically

360 · *André Malraux*

in France and Europe. He continued to see Gaston Palewski at weekly meetings of former members of General de Gaulle's secretariat.

On May 6th Malraux, like other Gaullists, was elated by the news that, in a national referendum, 53 per cent of French voters had rejected a proposed constitution which officially consecrated the supremacy of the legislature over the presidency, thus reduced to a purely ceremonial role. Six weeks later, on June 16th, he was one of the 'faithful followers' who accompanied General de Gaulle to Bayeux, in Normandy, to commemorate the second anniversary of the historic day when the leader of the Fighting French forces had at last set foot on the soil of the *patrie* after four frustrating years of exile. The important speech delivered by the General on this occasion must have impressed Malraux – not only because of its explicit condemnation of dictatorial methods of government, but also because it strikingly revealed how much de Gaulle's emphasis on his 'legitimacy' owed to Jean-Jacques Rousseau's mystical conception of a 'General Will', as expounded in his *Social Contract*.

It was, however, the increasingly tense international context, as much as the scorn he felt for the petty intrigues and 'kitchen politics' of France's post-war parties, which throughout this period placed Malraux very firmly in the Gaullist camp. The ruthless sovietization of Romania, Bulgaria, and Poland, followed in December 1945 by Marshal Zhukov's rejection of a Western proposal aimed at eliminating barriers to the free circulation of goods and human beings between the four occupation zones of Germany, made it clear that, as Winston Churchill put it in a historic speech delivered at Fulton, Missouri, in March 1946, Stalin's USSR was lowering an implacable 'iron curtain' across all of Eastern Europe.

In October 1946 a new French Constitution was narrowly approved by 9 million registered voters (35 per cent 'Yes' votes, 33 per cent 'Nos'). Several of de Gaulle's faithful followers chose this moment to set up the first embryonic office of what, a few months later, became the publicity and propaganda bureau of the RPF (Rassemblement du Peuple Français). The initiative was taken by Jacques Soustelle, Jacques Baumel (who had joined Pascal Pia and Albert Camus as one of *Combat*'s editorialists), the banker Alain Richemont (a resister who insisted on retaining his wartime code-name of 'Bozel'), and several 'veterans' of the Gaullist Resistance networks such as Jacques Foccart and Brigitte Friang. The latter, a plucky female member of the BOA (Bureau des Opérations aériennes – the 'Thomas Cook Agency' for the clandestine transport of money and agents between Britain and France) – had been wounded while trying to escape a Gestapo trap near the Trocadéro and had survived two terrible years in the concentration camps of Ravensbrück and Zwodau (in the Czech Sudetenland).

In January 1947 vague speculation began to give way to practical action. A radiant Jacques Baumel was at last able to inform Michel Debré (a Gaullist super-patriot) that the General, leaving his country retreat at Colombey-les-Deux-Eglises, in Champagne, was coming to Paris to weigh the pros and cons of his forceful return to the political arena. A few days later, the 'plotters' met in a 'simply furnished Paris apartment' with the General, Jacques Soustelle, Gaston Palewski, Alain Richemont and André Malraux. All felt that it was imperative that the General emerge from his self-imposed political retirement. It was the only way of halting the process of national 'decadence, which, in the view of prevailing world tensions, could culminate in a disaster'. A great lover of striking contrasts, as Michel Debré later wrote in his memoirs, Malraux 'for the first time developed the theme: there are two realities in France – de Gaulle and the Communists. The rest is simply a décor peopled with phantoms who can no longer fool anyone.'

This first meeting was followed by others, equally 'secret', as Michel Debré later admitted. He soon found himself outstripped by his 'companions, untroubled by any doubts . . . Palewski was fired by a total sense of fidelity: once again the General would succeed . . . Soustelle and Baumel dreamed of engaging the parties, whose intrigues and manoeuvres they pitilessly described'. Malraux, for his part, 'was Malraux – that is, he espoused the General's analysis regarding the risks of an impending conflict, while firing them with a romanticism which later readily made him see plots being hatched everywhere. This atmosphere of conspiracy, culminating in an immense appeal to the people, warmed his heart and imagination.'

Naturally inclined to expect the worst, *l'Homme des tempêtes* ('the man of the storms', as the General conceived himself to be) was none the less persuaded, as he told a visitor who came to see him at Colombey on February 2, 1947, that France had been saved by the American atomic bomb – 'without which the Russians would already be in Paris'. On this point there was no notable divergence between de Gaulle's view and Malraux's – except that Malraux was convinced that America's omnipotence in the atomic field was presently so crushing that it was capable of paralyzing Soviet advances in Europe for several years to come. This, at least, was what he maintained to Cyrus Sulzberger when the *New York Times* columnist called on him at his Boulogne villa on February 21, 1947.

Sulzberger found him 'even more nervous than the last time I had seen him. He smoked one cigarette after the other, without the slightest let-up. He grunts, he sniffles, he makes all sorts of strange noises while he talks. Apologizing because an old wound bothered him when he sat down, he spent an hour pacing up and down the room.' Malraux concluded his monologue with a melodramatic 'act' of political forecasting. Vincent Auriol, the first, recently elected, president of the Fourth Republic, having failed to find a suitable prime minister, would be forced by a ground swell of popular support to appeal to General de Gaulle.

De Gaulle will then spell out his conditions . . . He will declare to Auriol that he must have an absolute majority for two years in order to realize certain precise objectives, which he will expose in black and white, in a fifteen-point programme. This will first have to be submitted to the French people in a referendum, and if he wins the referendum, he will come to power as a dictator.

In uttering the word 'dictator' – eloquently rejected by de Gaulle in his Bayeux speech – Malraux, with his habitual *élan*, was galloping far ahead of the General's announced intentions. But this was unquestionably the scenario he envisaged to speed de Gaulle's return to power. The mature man of 1947, who had taken part in the 'reconquest' (of Lorraine and Alsace) alongside young Resistance fighters, was no longer the ardent leftist who had scornfully mocked the super-patriotic neo-fascist 'leagues' of the 1930s. The new 'veterans', heroes of the Second World War, merited the greatest respect – provided they were mobilized behind the banner of the Cross of Lorraine.

The campaign was finally launched on March 30th 1947, with a major speech delivered by Charles de Gaulle atop the Normandy cliffs of Bruneval, where in February 1942 a score of Free French soldiers had joined British and Canadian commandos in destroying a big German radar centre. More solemn still was the major speech the General delivered on Easter Monday (April 7th) from the balcony of Strasbourg's town hall, before a huge crowd of enthusiasts who clapped and cheered him on, with shouts of '*De Gaulle au pouvoir!*' ('Power to de Gaulle!') While certain phrases, praising the re-establishment of the Republic, must have pleased Malraux, who was standing behind him on the same balcony, what can he have thought when he heard the General also declare: 'At the present hour our soldiers, who are restoring peace in Indochina, are displaying as much courage and devotion to duty as ever soldiers did'? Was that France's 'civilizing mission', the one the young Malraux had defended with such eloquence and perspicacity in his 1925 editorials in *L'Indochine*? Almost certainly not. In the long interview granted to Cyrus Sulzberger a few weeks before, he had not beaten about the bush in bluntly declaring that 'the colonial phase of history is over'. In Clive's day, in eighteenth-century India, he had pointed out, the imperial nations enjoyed a great moral advantage. 'They were convinced that they were spreading civilization and they were convinced of the rightfulness of their conquests. But how can a government in London, which cannot even prevent a strike, hope to retain its hold on India? How can a government in Paris, which cannot even prevent a strike, hold on to Indochina?'

Did he suspect that the General's patriotic bluster was going to plunge France into a new and particularly disastrous Indochinese war? Possibly. What is certain is that once the RPF – or so-called Rally of the French People, for the word 'party' had to be avoided at all costs – was launched, Malraux began to be worried by the kind of supporters it was attracting. On May 17th, while lunching with Cyrus Sulzberger and in the presence of

Jacques Soustelle, he predicted that the RPF would fail if it was unable to attract left-wing elements, adding: 'We are embarrassed by certain of our right-wing adherents.' He even declared that if, in present-day France, there existed a Trotskyist movement that stood a chance of succeeding politically, then he, Malraux, would be a Trotskyist and not a Gaullist.

Fine words, betraying a troubled conscience. But at a moment when France was living through a particularly turbulent period of its history, this was no time to abandon *l'homme des tempêtes* and the surging movement of 'national renewal' he had helped to launch. It was even in Malraux's villa, in the suburb of Boulogne, to which de Gaulle came with his aide-de-camp, Claude Guy, a day or two after the Strasbourg speech, that he drafted the statement announcing the creation of a *Rassemblement* of the French People. With a rare humility and a serene confidence, which astonished Claude Mauriac, the General allowed Malraux and Guy to improve the rough draft he had personally prepared and which he subsequently rewrote by hand, so that the handwritten version of this 'Appeal of April 14' might appear, next to the printed text, in the first number of *L'Etincelle* (The Spark), intended to be the 'Internal Weekly Bulletin of the Rally of the French People'.

While Jacques Baumel, its editor and publisher, and Jacques Soustelle, its chief editorialist, were the principal artisans of this four-page newssheet, Malraux was none the less the inspirer of *L'Etincelle*, whose title recalled the *Iskra* (Spark), which Lenin and Plekhanov had founded with other Russian revolutionaries in Munich in 1900.

From this moment on Malraux devoted himself heart and soul to the Gaullist crusade. On May 15th, Ascension Day, he went to Bordeaux, where de Gaulle delivered another major speech before a huge crowd. This Bordeaux speech, in which the General sought to define his vision of the post-imperial French Union of tomorrow, did not please Claude Mauriac, still less his illustrious father.

> I was put off by the reactions of the public in the official grandstand, who made it clear that this hateful and, alas, eternal extreme right wing has, by hook or by crook, made de Gaulle its own. My father reacted even more negatively than I did – something that was foreseeable, given his distrust of the Rassemblement du Peuple Français. It was, to put it mildly, curious to see Malraux defend de Gaulle's movement against charges of Fascism and to plead with Mauriac to *remain on the left* of the Rassemblement, where he is so badly needed. When one thinks of Malraux's background and where my father comes from, one can only ponder the unexpected course sometimes taken by the destiny of men.

François Mauriac's reservations were all the more pertinent since at no time did he betray the slightest sympathy for Communism, whether Soviet or French. Throughout this particularly hot summer of 1947 he never ceased denouncing the French Communist Party and the policy of enslavement pursued by Moscow in Hungary and other 'satellite' countries.

In France itself the social tension kept steadily rising from May 5th on – the day on which the Socialist premier, Paul Ramadier, decided to expel the Communist ministers from the government. But it was the announcement of the Marshall Plan, offering American financial assistance to *all* European countries – even the USSR was not excluded – which brought things to a boil. Without waiting for the signal from Moscow, the Bulgarians and the Yugoslavs reacted negatively. On July 8th in Moscow, an icy Stalin made it clear to Czechoslovakia's foreign minister, Jan Masaryk, that acceptance of the American offer would lead to the immediate repudiation of the Soviet–Czech alliance. The same day, to put an end to any further shillyshallying, Radio Moscow announced that Poland and Romania had 'refused' to participate in the forthcoming Paris Conference. Prague then capitulated in its turn.

In France strikes and street demonstrations erupted everywhere – among railway workers, public utilities employees, factory hands, and even among bakers, infuriated at receiving corn instead of wheat flour from the Middle West, out of which they had been trying to bake singularly dense *baguettes*. In Paris, which was paralyzed for a good part of October by a bus and métro strike, the new Prefect of Police requested reinforcements; 750 steel-helmeted *gardes mobiles* from the provinces and 1,000 gendarmes serving with the French occupying forces in Germany were rushed in to reinforce 21,000 hard-pressed policemen.

It was in this climate of incipient civil war that Charles de Gaulle launched the mighty offensive that was intended to restore him to power. On July 27th, during a tour of Brittany, the municipal council of Rennes refused to receive the General. His speech, delivered in a nearby suburb, was blunter, more uncompromising than ever, aimed directly at the 'separatists' of the French Communist Party, pliant tools of the Kremlin and its organs of subversion:

> Among us, on our soil, are men who are taking their orders from a foreign force of domination, directed by the masters of a Slavic power. Their aim is to achieve a dictatorship in our country, as those like them have been able to do elsewhere with the aid of this same power ... This block of close to 400 million people now borders Sweden, Turkey, Greece, Italy. Its frontier is separated from our own by no more than 500 kilometres, which is to say by barely two laps of the Tour de France ...

The text, like that of all the other major Gaullist speeches that year, was published on the front page of *L'Etincelle*, which had in effect become the 'memory' and the 'official record' of the RPF.

It is by no means certain that Malraux approved of de Gaulle's hasty decision to put up RPF candidates for the municipal elections of October

1947. However, the spectacular result – a tidal wave which, with 40 per cent of the vote, swamped the country's thirteen largest cities and placed the RPF at one stroke ahead of all the other political parties in France – could not but delight him.

During the month of November the turmoil reached new heights. Communist elements in the leadership of the country's largest trade union federation – the CGT – issued general strike orders to factory workers everywhere. In Paris gas and electricity supplies were frequently cut, adding to the choas caused by periodic stoppages in the normal function-ing of the métro system. On November 19th, the Ramadier ministry was overthrown and for four days France was without a government. Robert Schumann, an Alsatian who replaced him, was greeted in the Chamber with shouts of *'Boche!'* from Jacques Duclos and cries of *'Heil Hitler!'* from other Communist deputies. Jules Moch, the Socialist Minister of the Interior, became a 'French Goebbels'. An insurrectionary wind began to sweep the country, and in certain regions Communist hotheads decided to resume their Resistance activities of 1944 by sabotaging rail-way lines.

In the southern seaport of Marseilles, long a hotbed of French radicalism, a furious mob invaded and ransacked the Palace of Justice, then proceeded to transform the town hall into a *Maison du Peuple* (a 'House of the People') after having beaten up and ejected the newly elected mayor (Carlini, a member of the Gaullist RPF). A tough, new Prefect was hastily dispatched to the scene to restore order.

But what, in the midst of these upheavals, was Malraux doing? Curiously enough, not much. He was working in the shadows, awaiting the decisive moment, much as he had with the Resistance movements during the Occupation. His task, once again, was not so much to organize as to galvanize and inspire, to improvise brilliant pep talks, and generally to lift the level of discussions to those historic heights where Charles de Gaulle, that Alpine-climber of politics, could breathe the vivifying air of the summits. Experienced enough in military matters to know that no modern army can function without a system of supplies, the General, as a theorist of warfare and of *Realpolitik*, could not help being a bit scornful in his attitude to the 'subaltern' problems of logistics. It was for this unstated reason that in June 1947, when the Executive Committee of the RPF met in its new premises at no. 5, Rue de Solférino (not far from the National Assembly, on the Left Bank), André Malraux was placed on de Gaulle's right – Palewski having already been relegated to his left – while the Party's chief organizer, Jacques Soustelle, sat opposite him, in the place where, twelve years later, the General's most trusted executive agent, his prime minister, would be seated.

Many years later, in 1967, when Janine Mossuz asked him if the 'epic dimension' he had wanted to give to the RPF didn't mean that the movement should purely and simply seize power rather than 'follow the neatly indicated paths of parliamentary democracy', Malraux replied without hesitation that, as far as he was concerned, the 'RPF was an insurrectionary movement'.

There was, however, another, purely practical reason why his propaganda work, at this moment, was so discreet. *L'Etincelle*, with its small four-page format, was a wretched newssheet. What the RPF needed was something bigger, more varied, more interesting.

Curious indeed was the destiny of this man of letters whose written works seemed to have anticipated the circumstances – one might even say the metamorphoses – of his life. For if Jacques Soustelle, the organizer, the industrious file shuffler was a bit the Borodin of the Gaullist movement, Malraux was its Garine, the fiery propaganda chief ever ready to curse routine. At the risk of exaggerating, one might even say that he was a bit the Vincent Berger of the movement, playing the role of adviser to a French Enver Pasha, obsessed by dreams of bygone grandeur. And this was all the more curious since Malraux-'Berger' was perfectly aware of how hollow and inflated this dream of grandeur was. He had said as much to Claude Mauriac in March 1946, in a moment of pessimistic lucidity:

> We are no more than a country of forty million inhabitants (for our colonies no longer belong to us), confronted by monstrous empires. A vassal status is thus inevitable, and absurd is a policy that pays no heed to new realities. France will continue absurdly to think and to pretend to act as a great power. But she is already no more than a pawn in a game that does not concern her.

These words, admittedly, had been uttered two months after General de Gaulle's resignation. France, like a frail caravel, had just lost its skipper. But everything was changed the moment he resumed his position at the helm. What is forbidden to 'dwarfs' can be granted to a demigod.

There are human beings who are truly fired only by a longing for the impossible. Malraux was one such, Charles de Gaulle another. And for someone as *assoiffé de l'absolu* – yearning for the absolute – as was André Malraux, nothing could inspire greater admiration than the absurd claims of this Tom Thumb of a Frenchman, refusing every form of vassaldom and determined to stand up to the two world giants, between whom a terribly weakened Europe was painfully trying to rebuild its strength. In the face of this epic challenge, this grandiose defiance, all one could do was acquiesce, bury one's scepticism . . . and follow.

This is what Malraux did in February 1948 – the month of the Prague putsch which culminated in the tragic defenestration of Jan Masaryk. The modest *L'Etincelle* flickered out after its forty-third number, immediately replaced by a larger weekly called *Le Rassemblement* (white letters against a red background). The very first number, dated February 21st, included a front-page article by Malraux ('To Companions of the Resistance'). On February 28th Arthur Koestler made his entrance with an article devoted to a 'sizing-up of Gaullism'. One week later Malraux returned to the fray, this time tackling the problem of 'Europe and Russia'. On March 13th, under the headline, 'The Technique of the Lie', the first part of the major speech ('An appeal to intellectuals') appeared which Malraux had delivered one week before in the concert hall of the Salle Pleyel and which was later added, as a kind of epilogue, to a new edition of *Les Conquérants*.

Albert Ollivier, a *Combat* editor, was now regularly contributing commentaries, while the equally pro-Gaullist Pascal Pia amused himself parodying the styles of French politicians in a series of 'Imaginary Editorials' – In the manner of . . . Léon Blum ('A government headed by Communists'), etc. A column of literary criticism also made its appearance, along with an occasional cartoon. In a word, without ceasing to be an organ of Gaullist propaganda, *Le Rassemblement* began to look like a genuine weekly.

Now that the financial backing was assured, the 'pioneers' were able to set up shop in offices rented from Swissair, on the second floor of a building located at 19, Boulevard des Capucines (between the Madeleine and the Opéra). From then on Malraux came every day to run his Propaganda Service, displaying the same regularity that had so impressed Raymond Aron during their brief association at the Ministry of Information. Each morning, six days a week, a small chauffeur-driven Simca car would bring him from Boulogne to the Boulevard des Capucines around 9.45 am. Having worked for part of the night on *La Psychologie de l'Art*, Malraux would start reading the morning papers while commuting from Boulogne. Sometimes he brought along pages from *La Création artistique* (the second volume of *La Psychologie de l'Art*, which Albert Skira brought out in Geneva in July 1948). Fascinated, his press attachée, Brigitte Friang, would watch as he handed his secretary 'pages that were entirely crossed out, streaked with blue lines made by his small, neat hand-writing, rough drafts that had been typed and corrected, along with isolated phrases which he himself inserted into his text with the help of a pair of scissors and a pot of glue . . . as indispensable as his pen to his method of creation'.

But it was as a public platform speaker, far more than as an *engagé* journalist, that André Malraux shone, electrifying crowds at big RPF rallies. His speeches were rarely written in advance, for they were usually lyrical outbursts which he improvised on the spot, aided only by brief notes and shock slogans scribbled on tiny scraps of paper. Brigitte Friang vividly described such moments when, before an audience, he seemed to enter a trance, as though 'beside himself', not so much speaking as living what he was saying with an intensity which caused his entire body to vibrate and his nervous hands to fly up and puncture the air. 'The surge of the successive waves of his forceful delivery imbued them with a fascinating power, as though one were listening to the sea . . . Only someone who was present at some of the Vélodrome d'Hiver meetings during the years 1947–1950, when the galleries were dangerously jam-packed, can appreciate the ecstatic trance that his incantations could induce in crowds of listeners . . .'

François Mauriac, who attended one of these big meetings in February 1948, was reminded, as he listened to Malraux, of Maurice Barrès' declamatory style. He added, however, that

> it is against Stalin that this ageless David is waging his battle. He is fighting against Stalin much more than he is fighting for de Gaulle . . . Yesterday evening, trembling all over, he told us that a new Stalinist offensive was about to be launched. It was with relish that he was already anticipating those sabotage actions, those simultaneous train derailments – with the excitement of the player who is beginning to be bored by the slowness of the game and who at last sees the moment approaching when he'll throw all he has on to the table; for it is only in such brief moments that he feels he is really living, when he can stake his destiny on a single gambler's throw.

Three weeks later, this 'ageless David', speaking at the Salle Pleyel, issued his 'Appeal to intellectuals' – several paragraphs of which are worth quoting, since they show how greatly the Malraux of 1948 differed from the 'internationalist' Malraux of 1935, who was ready to denounce 'the Roman, the German' in the name of 'Man'.

> From the mighty voice of Michelet right down to the mighty voice of Jaurès, it was almost self-evident throughout the last century that the less one was linked to one's homeland, the more one became a man. It was neither cowardice nor an error; it was then a form of hope. Victor Hugo believed that the United States of Europe would be constituted of their own accord, and that they would be a prelude to the United States of the World. But the United States of Europe will be born in pain, and the United States of the World are a long way off . . .
>
> What we have learned is that the gesture of disdain with which Russia has discarded the chant of the *Internationale* – which will remain, whether she likes it or not, linked to the everlasting human dream of Justice – has at one blow dispelled the dreams of the nineteenth century. From now on we know that one will not be more of a man, the less French one is, but that one will merely be more Russian. For better or for worse, we are tied to the homeland.

37

Return to Art

In March 1948 André Malraux decided to 'regularize' his family situation – which for some time past had shocked 'Tante Yvonne' – the nickname bestowed by Paris wits on Madame de Gaulle – by marrying his sister-in-law Madeleine. The place chosen for the wedding was the town of Riquewihr, on the eastern slope of the Vosges mountains, of which René Dopff, the former commander of the 'Mulhouse' battalion of the Alsace–Lorraine Brigade, was the mayor. The marriage took place in the town hall. Antoine Diener acted as witness for Malraux, but there was no religious ceremony, despite the presence of Pierre Bockel, who came specially from Strasbourg to greet the man who had so inspired and encouraged him in his priestly vocation in 1944 and 1945.

Back in Paris, Malraux continued to direct the propaganda bureau on the Boulevard des Capucines, to see his Gaullist friends, and to make speeches on behalf of the RPF, all of them published in *Le Rassemblement* and in *Carrefour*, a weekly ardently devoted to the General's cause. Malraux, however, could not help noticing the stagnation of the RPF, which after its landslide triumph of October 1947 descended to 35 per cent, and then to less than 25 per cent in the senatorial and municipal elections of 1948 and 1949. More and more, the RPF came to resemble the other political parties of the Fourth Republic, and for a person of Malraux's fiery spirit – whose motto could have been Danton's: *'De l'audace, encore de l'audace, toujours de l'audace!'* – this sensation of getting bogged down into the perennial quagmire of business-as-usual politics could only engender boredom.

What most surprised the literary critics, and with them many Malraux admirers, was the 'disappearance' of the great pre-war novelist. They had expected him to use his adventures in the Resistance and during the 'reconquest' to compose a second and even more magnificent *L'Espoir*. But they misjudged the man and also his work as a novelist. First of all, Malraux was hamstrung by a sense of impropriety with respect to his comrades-in-arms of the Alsace–Lorraine Brigade, whose character traits and battlefield achievements he would have been forced to exploit for fictional purposes.

L'Espoir, in this respect, was justified, for it was a *roman de combat* written in white heat to uphold the cause of a still unvanquished Spanish Republic. *Les Conquérants* and *La Condition humaine* had explicitly denounced the exploitation of the Chinese masses by capitalistic managers and reactionary generals. But what, after the collapse of nazism in Europe, was there left for Malraux to condemn when as a novelist he had always felt closer to Joseph Conrad than to Emile Zola?

There remained *Le Démon de l'Absolu* – the book on Lawrence of Arabia he had begun during the Occupation. Why, once the Second World War was ended, did he not try to finish it? There are several answers to this enigma. First of all, as we have seen, Malraux felt ill at ease in the biographical genre, and to recreate an essentially fictitious Lawrence according to the whims of his restless imagination would have made him a target for hostile critics. More important were two considerations of political expediency. A book praising a colonel who had worked for the British Intelligence Service during the First World War could hardly please de Gaulle, who was in no mood to forget his wartime battles in London with Claude Dansey and other IS chiefs. To this must be added a second, unexpected factor: the establishment in 1948 of the state of Israel – something that transformed the political landscape of the Near East and which relegated the Lawrentian dream of a great seven-pillared Arab realm to the attic of historical curiosities. As a vehement anti-nazi who had married a Jewish woman, as someone who numbered Jews, like Emmanuel Berl and Manès Sperber, among his best friends, André Malraux had not the slightest desire to seem to be harbouring anti-Israeli or anti-zionist sentiments.

The rough drafts of *Le Démon de l'Absolu*, mostly typed on Josette Clotis' typewriter and filling seven cardboard boxes, attest once again to the pyrotechnic brilliance of his intellect. Each step taken during his reading of *The Seven Pillars of Wisdom* ignited thoughts that rocketed off in all directions. Almost everything is to be found here – passages recalling the Malraux of *Royaume-Farfelu*, others which anticipate *La Métamorphose des Dieux*. Reflections on the adventurer, on the nomad as compared to the sedentary human being; on 'time, space, and work', these being the 'three fundamental bondages of man'; on the 'psychic instability of the Slavs'; on Ignazio de Loyola; on the soldier and the sailor, compared to the civilian; on the place of morality in different religions ('faults, for a Muslim, for a Hindu, are faults, not sins . . . Were Christianity to lose its genius for crypts and cathedrals, it would become moral'); on tourism, expressed in this pithy aphorism: 'Travel is always a liberation: even tourism, which is to travel what prostitution is to love, experiences it and battens off it.'

The same profusion of ideas, exploding everywhere like rockets, marked the books on art Malraux began to publish eleven months before his marriage to his sister-in-law Madeleine and which he continued to bring out until 1957 at the average rate of one per year. If *Le Musée imaginaire* – the first volume of a trilogy ambitiously entitled *La Psychologie de l'Art* – caused a sensation when it was published, it was not only because of the wealth of illustrations (20 colour plates and 66 black-and-white photos), which filled almost half the 156 pages of a luxurious book. It was the extraordinary range of the author's erudition, which seemed to embrace all cultures and styles, and, even more, the peremptory nature of his affirmations. For the most startling thing about this 'dilettante', who was neither a recognized scholar nor a professor of art or history such as Hippolyte Taine, Elie Faure and Henri Focillon had been, was the tranquil audacity with which he made his assertions without bothering to back them up with the slightest bibliographic footnote or reference.

In a remarkable article ('Malraux the fascinator') published in October 1948 by the monthly review, *Esprit*, Claude-Edmonde Magny pointed out that the 'discontinuism' which characterized his novels was even more evident in his essays, but with less satisfactory results. She confessed that in *Le Musée imaginaire* the many flashes of brilliance 'leave us blinded as much as dazzled'. The point was well taken. But one could go further and say that nowhere in all of Malraux's works was his penchant for 'cubistic' composition more strikingly exhibited than in the three volumes of *La Psychologie de l'Art* (the other two being *La Création artistique*, published in July 1948, and *La Monnaie de l'Absolu*, which appeared in June 1950). These three books were written during the years when their author was profoundly engaged in a campaign of political propaganda. A certain symbiosis between those two distinct activities seems to have occurred, the political propagandist in Malraux coming to be shadowed by a propagandist in the field of art. As Robert Payne pointed out astutely, this even affected his singularly aggressive vocabulary, with the frequent use of words like 'conquer', 'impose', 'tear away', 'annex'. We know – thanks to Brigitte Friang's precious testimony – that the first two volumes of *La Psychologie de l'Art* were composed almost like a mosaic or a Matisse collage, with paragraphs and even sentences cut out with scissors and pasted on to blank pages with glue. While this method of work suited the author's aphoristic style, it also resulted in singularly disorderly texts. Even so admiring a critic as the American scholar Wilbur Frohock felt obliged to point out the incoherences, the frequent repetitions, and a style that was so 'breathless, oracular and elliptic' that it misled some French commentators, who concluded that André Malraux had wanted to compose a 'Spenglerian' work, whereas his fundamental aim was precisely the reverse.

Even if he had tried to discipline himself, it would have been difficult for someone of such an impatient temperament to write a prose of classic limpidity. The stylistic landscape of *La Psychologie de l'Art*, at any rate, is anything but classical; it is a romantic landscape, like those Nietzsche loved, a landscape bristling with superlatives, but also fissured with crevasses into which a supercharged prose slips towards powdery platitudes or plunges headlong into hyperbolic blizzards.

Here is an example, culled from *Le Musée imaginaire* (curiously translated into English as 'The Museum without Walls'):

Poussin drapes his characters, Rembrandt illuminates his, in order to raise them above the level of ordinary human beings, just as the mosaic-maker of Monreale stylizes his own [figures] in order to make them enter into his magic universe.

The language of Phidias' forms or of those of the pediment of Olympia, humanistic though it is, is also as specific as that of the masters of Chartres and Babylon or of abstract sculptures, because, like that of the great Italians of the fourteenth to the sixteenth centuries, it simultaneously modifies the representation and its style.

There is in the David of Chartres, in the *Roncalli Pietà*, something *other* than there is in Maillol, in Bach something other than in Ravel, in Shakespeare something other than in Mallarmé.

And when it is not a slow slide toward a truism, it is only too often a free fall into a maelstrom of vertiginous comparisons. Thus, in speaking of Cézanne: 'Between his *Still Life with Clock*, which strives only to be painting, and his canvases which have become a style, there resurfaces the call which raises up Bach over and against negro music, and Piero della Francesca over and against barbarian arts – the art of mastery, as opposed to that of the miracle.'
Similarly, in the second volume, we learn that 'genius is inseparable from what it springs from, but like the fire from what it burns'. The idea would doubtless not have occurred to the ordinary mortal, but the author of *La Création artistique* makes a point of warning us that

It is as vain to confuse the imitators of Raphael with Poussin as it is to mix up the interchangeable Gallo-Romans with the sculptor of the architrave of Poitiers, the flock of chisel-wielders of the cemeteries of Palmyra with the unknown artist who anticipated Byzantium, the faithful followers of the Byzantine canon with the author of the mosaics of Santa Sophia, the artisans of the blue schists of Gandhara with the prophets of Wei art.

Does the *Roncalli Pietà* differ more from an 'antique' than a Byzantine bas-relief from an Achemenidean bas-relief? When, the warlike chants of Sargon's palace having died away, Persia was at last delivered of Assyria, the treasures of the Iranian past, having reappeared with the Sassanides, will deliver Byzantium from its babbling, and the vultures perched on the Towers of Silence will, through the smoke of sacred fires, watch the Christianity of the Orient petrify itself according to old familiar forms . . .

This, to be sure, is neo-Barrèsian poetry; but is it an adequate answer to the question raised?

Forty years later, one of his admirers, Jacques Gaucheron, noted sadly: 'Art and works of art unquestionably dazzled the writer and from them he produced some dazzling pages. But dazzling only . . . I am still wondering what meaning one can give to this remark about Chardin's *Pourvoyeuse*: "a Braque barely clad enough to fool the spectator". '

It would of course be absurd to claim that everything André Malraux wrote in *La Psychologie de l'Art* was simply glittering tinsel. It would probably be fair to say that no previous theorist was so fascinated and obsessed as was Malraux by the essential 'relativism' of artistic perception – not for nothing was he a member of the first post-Einstein and post-Pirandello generation – and the extent to which one's appreciation of artistic 'greatness' is governed by a contemporary 'perspective': one which varies from one epoch to the next, creating what might be called 'black holes' in the cosmography of art, sometimes lasting centuries. (For example, the medieval Christian's blindness to the beauties of Hellenic art, or the three centuries of indifference which followed El Greco's death, until he was 'rediscovered' by Renoir.) No one prior to Malraux had so strongly insisted on the impact made on the artistic sensibility of twentieth-century painters, sculptors, and art lovers by the broadening of the cultural horizon due to the prodigious development of photographic reproduction. The 'Museum without Walls' – now accessible to anyone ready to leaf through illustrated art books – has become a reality of contemporary life.

Every written work, even if it aspires to attain a 'deathless' value, is to some extent the creature of the circumstances in which it was born. This explains certain exaggerations in *La Psychologie de l'Art*, which doubtless 'dumbfound the bourgeois', but which hardly illuminate the true nature and motivations of the will to create. Malraux has been credited with having in effect formulated a 'liberational' philosophy of artistic creation – something that naturally appealed to the man who had previously fought for the emancipation and advancement of the Annamites of Indochina, the humiliated and oppressed of Republican Spain, and in general all the 'damned of the earth'. According to Malraux, the 'true' artist is the one who first experiences the influence – one can even say the domination – of a certain style or school *against* which he subsequently asserts himself. The genuine, active creator, as opposed to the imitator or passive 'copier', is thus necessarily a rebel, if not a revolutionary. This notion, which unquestionably contains a solid kernel of truth, is, however, so obsessively promoted that it leads Malraux to assert – almost *urbi et orbi* – that the real artist *never* copies nature, since this would constitute an occult form of submission.

At Collemiers, during the summer and early autumn of 1940, the prisoner-of-war Georges Malraux used to startle his comrades of the 'Group of Ten' by declaring: 'Seamstresses like sunsets; painters like pictures.' The same phrase is repeated, almost word for word, in *La Création artistique*.

However, expressed so crudely, nothing is more debatable. Would Claude Gellée (better known as 'Lorrain') have taken the trouble to paint sunsets if he had not appreciated their luminous effulgence? Would Leonardo da Vinci and other Tuscan painters have chosen to embellish their portraits by giving them 'Alpine' backgrounds if they had been blind to this form of beauty? And would Turner, of whom Malraux, curiously enough, hardly ever speaks, have started painting fog, clouds of smoke, and weeping suns if he had been insensitive to their misty beauty? To uphold the contrary, simply to 'score a point', can only lead to the formulation of a masochistic theory of art – which was certainly not Malraux's intention.

The simplistic idea that 'genuine' artists never copy nature, but revolt against an already established style, in effect rules out any rational explanation of the origins of art. Even Malraux never dared to say that the people who painted bisons and stags on the rocky walls of Altamira and Lascaux were not genuine artists. Yet they had no predecessors to teach them a style. But these faults of emphasis are easily enough explained when it is remembered that the three volumes of *La Psychologie de l'Art* were composed between 1946 and 1950, at a time when the Cold War was particularly bitter and when Malraux was deeply engaged in an anti-communist campaign. His somewhat summary rejection of all forms of realism did not simply betray the preference he had always, from adolescence on, accorded to Cubist and avant-garde art, as opposed to '*l'art pompier*' of Bouguereau, Bonnencontre and other academic painters; it in effect perpetuated the struggle he had begun in Moscow in 1934 in opposing the 'socialist realism' preached by Karl Radek, Andrei Zhdanov, and their terrifying master, Joseph Stalin.

That Malraux, on this 'front', should not have lowered his guard is altogether praiseworthy, as was his rejection of Spenglerian determinism. Wilbur Frohock was one of the first, if not the very first, to grasp the fact that the three volumes of the *Psychologie* were designed to provide a philosophy of art capable of attacking a philosophy of history – precisely that of Oswald Spengler. In *The Decline of the West*, the key word around which everything else is articulated is 'morphology'. Each civilization, according to Spengler, has its own morphology; each is to a certain extent programmed in advance, follows the curve of its ascension, attains its apogee and then begins to decline according to an innate rhythm and laws which could almost be described as organic and which determine the 'closed field' of its cultural development.

To this mythology – which it partly is – Malraux boldly opposed another key concept: that of 'metamorphosis'. Men die, it is true, but not civilizations – contrary to what Spengler and Paul Valéry claimed. Thus, as the history of art attests, the rigid, static, mortuary art of ancient Egypt was gradually metamorphosed into the freer, more flowing and more joyous style of Greece, which itself gave birth to Roman culture. The latter was itself metamorphosed by the Christianization of the Roman Empire under

Constantine, the result being two new cultures: that of Byzantium and that of the Gallo-Roman and later Gothic world of Western Europe.

In 1950, just when the third volume, *La Monnaie de l'Absolu*, was being printed, André Malraux and his wife Madeleine were incapacitated by a mysterious illness. It may have been some kind of typhoid fever, although the symptoms were also those of an acute attack of jaundice. A nurse was installed in the Boulogne villa, and it was only after three months of painful fevers that the two invalids could resume a normal life. Malraux used this enforced retirement from his career as a Gaullist activist to weld the diverse fragments of his trilogy into a single tome, for which he found a more poetic title, *Les Voix du Silence* (The Voices of Silence). Essentially it was the same heady wine, but poured into four amphoras – the fourth recipient, thrust in between the first and the second, being a section called 'The Metamorphoses of Apollo'. The title, like the contents, showed that Malraux had lost none of his audacity. More than ever he was persuaded that it was the sculpted figures of Gandhâra – like those he had 'discovered' at Rawalpindi in 1930 – which had given birth to Buddhist art. Thus Apollo, promoted to the rank of God of Wisdom – something he had never been among the deities of Olympus, where this honour was reserved for a woman – became the sculpted precursor of the meditative Buddha. This metamorphosis in the inter-pretation of Greek mythology was doubtless inspired by the Nietzsche of *The Birth of Tragedy*.

These improvements did little to alter the essence of the message André Malraux wanted to get across. And it was the essence of this message which one of the greatest art historians of our time, Ernst Gombrich, dared to challenge in an eight-page article published in 1954 by the *Burlington Magazine* in London. It was a devastating article which created an uproar when, several years later, it was translated and published in the left-wing weekly, *France-Observateur*.

What irritated Gombrich, a brilliant product of the Viennese school of *Kunstgeschichte* (art history) who had been forced to take refuge in London during the mid-1930s, was to find, in *The Voices of Silence*, an almost delirious romanticism and an apology of the myth – of the kind that had so ravaged Central Europe in the 1930s. At the start of his essay, Gombrich quoted several sentences from *The Voices of Silence* devoted to the past:

> For a very small number of men, keenly interested in history, the past is a complex of riddles asking to be solved, whose progressive elucidation is a series of victories over chaos. For the vast majority it comes back to life only when it is presented as a romantic saga, invested with a legendary glamour . . . it is art whose forms suggest those of a history which, though not the true one, is the one men take to their hearts.

'There is no better way,' wrote Gombrich,

of describing what Malraux's book is about, than to say that it is about the 'romantic saga' suggested by art. At times he succumbs to its spell and relates it as though it were a fact, at times he holds himself in check and probes into the forces that gave rise to it, but in his style and presentation he never renounces the 'legendary glamour' which this saga can lend to rhapsodies about art . . . Malraux tries to do for the anti-classical styles of Europe and Asia what Winckelmann did for the ancient Greeks and Ruskin for the Age of Faith. But even here there is a fundamental difference in stature. These giants created the myths they propagated: they were the founders of an aesthetic religion. Malraux is, at best, an apostle. His message is derived from that of the expressionist critics most *en vogue* in Central Europe in the 1920s. Moreover, he gives the impression of an apostle who wrestles with the very faith he preaches. While Winckelmann and Ruskin passionately believed in their visions of the past, Malraux recognizes such visions for what they are – projections of our own preoccupations and desires. But he would rather have faith in an illusion than have no faith at all, and so we find him extolling the notion which has proved so fateful and fatal to our time – the Myth.

In his essay, *Saturne*, published in 1950, there was less emphasis on metamorphosis and more on a radical break or rupture with existing styles. More violently than any other painter of his period, Goya was the one who slammed the door on the 'charming' art of the eighteenth century: that of Fragonard, Nattier, Guardi, Boucher, Gainsborough. His paintings and drawings tore away the veil of current hypocrisies, announced the end of the genteel illusions which had graced the Age of the Enlightenment, and presaged the convulsions and anxieties of the morrow. What they amounted to was the forceful return of Satan and of all those subterranean forces that had so long fascinated Malraux: the irruption into the modern world of the *domaine démoniaque* (the domain of the demonic), which had haunted *Les Noyers d'Altenburg* and of which he had spoken in *Le Musée imaginaire*: 'From war, a major demon, to complexes, minor demons, the domain of the demonic – more or less subtly present in all barbaric arts – has entered the stage. The demonic demon is that of everything which, in man, aspires to destroy him. The Demon of the Church, that of Freud and that of Bikini have the same face.'

It was through this book about Goya that André Malraux became fully reconciled with Gallimard, who had been somewhat stunned by the dazzling pyrotechnics of *La Psychologie de l'Art*. Gaston no longer opposed the publication, under a Galerie de la Pléiade imprint, of a series of lavishly illustrated books by the man who now resumed his place as the artistic director of the NRF.

In 1952 two handsomely illustrated monographs were published – one devoted to Leonardo da Vinci's paintings, the other to Vermeer's. Three years later, encouraged by his former 'trainer' and fellow prisoner-of-war,

Albert Beuret, and with the aid of the Louvre curator, Georges Salles, Malraux persuaded Gaston Gallimard to give him a free rein. Thus was born *L'Univers des Formes*. Originally designed to be a collection of forty illustrated volumes, each one devoted to a specific culture and prepared by recognized authorities, this monumental project (undertaken in co-operation with four other publishing companies in England, Italy, Germany) was, thirty-five years later, still far from completed, the number of scheduled volumes approaching seventy.

Then, in 1957, Malraux published his last major book on art, *La Métamorphose des Dieux*. For those who had not already understood, it confirmed the importance he attached to religious art and man's relation to the divine. Once again it expressed his conviction that art, in an increasingly tormented and agnostic century, was the only thing solid enough to serve as a substitute for religious faith.

Malraux had already revealed his deepest thoughts on the subject in answering a questionnaire which the Copenhagen newspaper, *Daglig Nyheter*, had sent to him in 1955. Here, in his written replies, it was clearer than ever that the sombre anguish of Blaise Pascal had triumphed over the tranquil 'futurism' of René Descartes. Insisting on the fact that our modern civilization had merely substituted a 'phantom for the profound notions of man which the great religions had elaborated', he added:

Each of these in its own way conveyed a vision of human greatness. Science, no: it does not tend toward a notion of Man but to the knowledge of the Cosmos. The Unified Field Theory would not become false if Man no longer existed. The drama of the civilization of the century of machines is not to have lost the gods, for they have been less lost than people say; it is to have lost all sense of a profound notion of Man.

Such a notion alone would make it possible to answer your question, by rendering intelligible the 'devotion' you call in question, and in specifying just how it is one of the renascent powers of human beings – not as are instincts, but such as heroism is. For the past fifty years psychology has been reintegrating the demons in Man. Such is the serious record of psychoanalysis.

I believe that the task of the next century, in the face of the most terrible threat mankind has ever known, will be to reintegrate the gods.

38

Minister of Culture

André Malraux was visiting Venice in May 1958 when he learned that a military putsch had just been staged in Algiers. From the balcony of the main government building, a paratrooper general named Massu had uttered the three electrifying words, *'Vive de Gaulle!'* to a delirious crowd, mostly composed of Europeans. Thus the seething crisis, which had long been expected to put an end to the iniquitous 'system of the parties', had finally exploded.

The author of *Les Conquérants* lost no time leaving the shimmering city of the Doges. Forty-eight hours after his return to Paris, he was summoned by Charles de Gaulle to the Hôtel de La Pérouse, near the Arc de Triomphe. The General outlined the principal aims of his policy. The state was to be 'refashioned' and a new constitution was to be prepared, clearly separating the executive from the legislative power. The currency was to be stabilized. What was left of the Empire was to be transformed into a French Community of Nations. He did not go into details – why should he, since President René Coty had not yet asked him to form a government? – but he already knew that in his new government the brilliant 'herald' of the RPF would be named Minister of Information.

This was not what André Malraux craved. For this activist, this man of incandescent temperament, this was a moment for acts, not words. To restore order in a seething Algeria a two-fisted man was needed. Above all, someone was needed who was lucid enough not to have been deluded by the crazy mirage of a 'French Algeria', organically linked to metropolitan France and incorporated into a greater national entity stretching 'from Dunkirk to Tamanrasset', which Léon Delbecque and other Gaullist hotheads were now promoting. As a Resistance fighter who had managed to raise himself in a couple of months to the rank of colonel, Malraux was not afraid to take on the wealthy French settlers who, by exploiting a people of second-class citizens, were repeating in Algeria the fatal errors which the Cognacqs, the Chavignys and their ilk had committed in Indochina. A Ministry of Algerian Affairs? Why not? And why not even the Ministry of the Interior? Carnot, after all, was not yet forty years old when he assumed responsibility for the defence of France in 1792. He, Malraux, was already fifty-six – more than enough to be regarded as experienced and 'mature'.

This, of course, was wishful thinking. In the end Malraux had to content himself with an honorific title as 'Minister delegated to the Prime Ministry' and the post of Minister of Information. Once again he installed himself in the offices of the Avenue de Friedland, along with the faithful Albert Beuret and Brigitte Friang who, after the 'pioneer' years with *L'Etincelle* and *Le Rassemblement*, had distinguished herself as a war correspondent in Indochina, even making a number of perilous jumps with French paratroopers.

Malraux must have experienced a strange feeling of *déjà vu* in taking his cabinet seat at a premier's table, next to so many 'men of the system' whose 'incompetence' Charles de Gaulle had so often mocked and excoriated in the past. Indeed, Malraux was backed up by only two veteran Gaullists: Michel Debré, named Minister of Justice, and Edmond Michelet, Minister for the *Anciens Combattants* (war veterans).

Already, as a 'left-wing Gaullist', Malraux had had to swallow many misgivings in loyal silence. Since he had not at that time become a member of de Gaulle's entourage, he could not be held even remotely responsible for the bloody crushing of a nationalist uprising in eastern Algeria in May 1945, during which at least 6,000 Algerians were massacred by Senegalese and Foreign Legion soldiers. And then there was Indochina . . . What would the General have done if he had still been in power in November 1946 and had had to face the defiant taunts thrown at the French by Giap and Ho Chi Minh?

This explains the astounding display of verbal fireworks ignited by Malraux on the occasion of his first press conference on June 24th. Some 500 journalists turned up, curious to know how a former anticolonial 'leftist' could take his place in a government next to Michel Debré, whose *Courrier de la Colère* (The wrathful courier) had been a weekly propaganda organ on behalf of French settlers in North Africa and elsewhere. Without wasting a moment, Malraux assumed the offensive, spicing his replies with incredible comparisons.

A dictator, de Gaulle? Come now! 'General de Gaulle is not yet Napoleon III . . . A paralytic France wants to walk. It's not a question of giving her one more form for her paralysis. She is not trying to recover her weakness of yesterday, but her hope . . .'

What did the Minister of State think of the slogan, *'Algérie française'*? Reply: 'For the first time a revolution in the Islamic world is not being conducted against the West, but in its name, and people are now shouting "French Algeria!", whereas they did not shout for an "English Pakistan!" '

Did these replies satisfy most of his listeners? Probably not. But they could not help admiring the virtuosity displayed by the man whom Pierre Viansson-Ponté, of *Le Monde*, called the Minister of the Word delegated to the Prime Minister's Office:

In a fluttering, jerky charge and to the rhythm of a syncopated pathos, which mixed lyrical eloquence and elliptic sobriety, André Malraux seemed to be plagiarizing André Malraux. He viewed the political agitations of the hour through the binoculars of history and the electronic telescope – that 'marvel of French genius' – galloping in three sentences from the djebels of the Aurès to Valmy, from the Crusades to Nasser, from 1789 to fraternization in Algeria, with a detour via Moscow, a brief halt at the Palais Bourbon [ie, the French Assembly], a parenthesis on Louis XVI, and an allusion to NATO.

Towards the end of this harassing ordeal, Malraux had to answer the inevitable question concerning various tortures practised by French officers and non-coms on the rebel *fellaghas* who fell into their hands and who were 'encouraged to talk'. The reply: 'To the best of my knowledge and of yours, no act of torture has occurred since General de Gaulle's arrival in Algeria. None should occur henceforth.' After which, throwing caution to the winds, he added: 'In the name of the government I invite the three writers on whom the Nobel Prize has conferred a particular authority and who have already studied these problems to form a commission to go to Algeria.'

Not surprisingly, nothing came of this spectacular proposal. The first of these prestigious writers, Roger Martin du Gard, was seriously ill and declined the invitation, while congratulating himself on the uproar created by the protest he, as well as Sartre, Mauriac, and Malraux had signed six weeks earlier. The second Nobel Prize winner, François Mauriac, prudently let it be known that if General de Gaulle asked him personally to undertake such a trip to Algeria, he could not refuse. The third laureate, Albert Camus, was off on a cruise in the Aegean Sea and thus spared the embarrassment of having to say no.

To spare him other ordeals of this kind, de Gaulle decided to send his brilliant State Minister responsible 'for the expansion and diffusion of French culture' on a propaganda tour of the country's overseas possessions in the Caribbean. This enabled the General to entrust the Ministry of Information to Jacques Soustelle, for whom the French settlers of Algeria and activist officers had for weeks been demanding a cabinet post. It was also, for Malraux, a new challenge: an occasion to exercise his gifts as a magician of the word on overseas French subjects, by persuading them to vote for the new constitution which General de Gaulle had been preparing with the aid of the head of his secretariat, Georges Pompidou, and his Minister of Justice, Michel Debré.

The trip to the Caribbean, where he visited Guadeloupe, Martinique, and French Guyana, provided Malraux with an opportunity for delivering several impassioned speeches and, later, for adding several anthology items to his autobiographical mosaic, *Antimémoires*. At Cayenne, the capital of

French Guyana, where he had to face a hostile crowd brandishing posters – 'DOWN WITH FASCISM! . . . DOWN WITH DE GAULLE! . . . DOWN WITH FRANCE!' – he spent the 'zaniest night' of his life: a night vaguely haunted by voodoo spirits, which later inspired several ironic pages of description worthy of Graham Greene.

This trip was crowned by a delayed-action triumph. For, in the referendum of September 27th, 80 per cent of the electors of Martinique, Guadeloupe, and a supposedly hostile French Guyana voted for the 'great sorcerer', Charles de Gaulle. In France, 79 per cent of the voters (with only 15 per cent abstaining) approved the new constitution. As for Algeria, where for the first time Muslim women (most of them illiterate) were granted the right to vote, there was a tidal wave of yeses: 96 per cent in favour, compared to a meagre 4 per cent (118,000) who dared to hold out against the 'Nasserians' – the name coined by Malraux for the French colonels of Algeria.

This victory, however, turned out to be a trap. The vast majority of the Muslims of Algeria voted 'yes' for de Gaulle the peacemaker, whereas the French settlers voted no less massively for a 'French Algeria', indissolubly linked to metropolitan France. Having failed to present the French with a coherent, long-term political programme for the future, de Gaulle allowed the vociferous partisans of a 'French Algeria' to fill the void. In the parliamentary elections of November 1958 more than 200 deputies belonging to the General's new party – the UNR (Union pour la Nouvelle République) – swept triumphantly into the National Assembly, to the dismay of de Gaulle, who realized that it was against their conservative, neo-colonial inclinations that he would henceforth have to struggle.

Feeling more affinity for general (and generous) ideas than for 'kitchen politics', Malraux held himself aloof. His ministerial colleagues had already been struck by his unusual silences during cabinet meetings and by the curious monsters and devils he sketched on sheets of paper while others did the talking. He stubbornly refused to run for office, as Jacques Soustelle did by getting himself elected UNR deputy for Lyons.

De Gaulle, realising that on this point he could not budge him, finally decided to dispatch his Ambassador Extraordinary for French Culture to New Delhi, to reassure Nehru, who, like many other Indians, viewed the recent Algiers putsch with a jaundiced eye. Malraux had little difficulty persuading him that Charles de Gaulle, already sixty-nine years old, had no desire at this late date to become a French Mussolini.

From Jawaharlal Nehru's India, Malraux continued on to Japan, where he was received by Emperor Hirohito in person.

After his return from Asia, in January 1959, André Malraux was given a new task: that of managing France's 'cultural affairs'. At cabinet meetings, which were now held at the Elysée Palace, on the Right Bank rather than in the prime minister's Left Bank town house, he henceforth occupied a place of honour, on Charles de Gaulle's right, the new prime minister, Michel Debré, being seated opposite.

Malraux now moved back across the Seine, installing his staff on the first and second floors of one of the Palais Royal's two wings – opposite the theatre which Richelieu had built while he lived there. Faithful as ever to his old friendships, he again picked Albert Beuret to be his chief trouble-shooter and 'technical adviser', giving him two assistants – his old school friends Louis Chevasson and Marcel Brandin.

To run the important Directorate of Arts and Letters, he chose Gaétan Picon, a literature professor from Bordeaux and the author of a remarkable *Panorama of French Literature*. To assist him in the domain of the plastic arts, Malraux enlisted the services of Jacques Jaujard, a former aide to Paul Painlevé who, as director of the historical monuments department at the Ministry of Education, had managed, during the wartime Occupation, to hide away in various French châteaux an impressive number of masterpieces which those voracious 'art lovers', Reichsmarschall Hermann Goering and the 'philosopher' Alfred Rosenberg, might have been tempted to 'add' to their personal collections.

To understand the formidable challenges André Malraux had to face, one must recall that until then the Comédie Française, with its two theatre halls (the Salle Richelieu and the Odéon), the Paris Opéra and the Opéra-Comique, the various national conservatories, the Ecole Nationale des Beaux-Arts, the Louvre and a galaxy of smaller museums in Paris and the provinces, as well as various commissions created for the safeguarding of monuments, palaces, and historic sites, all depended administratively on the Ministry of Education. This corresponded to a more than century-old notion of 'culture' as something of educational value to be acquired by unremitting efforts towards aesthetic as well as intellectual improvement. In actual practice, however, these cultural institutions were abandoned to the petty tyranny of bureaucratic services and sub-departments which the Minister of Education, harassed by 'more urgent' problems of schooling and teacher training, oversaw with a distracted eye.

The French state, in its cultural allocations, had long shown that it could be as miserly as a Norman peasant. Only too often it chose the easy way out. Thus, during the inter-war period from 1919 to 1939, it simply turned the Paris Opéra over to the care of a wealthy Maecenas, Jacques Rouché, whose largesse plugged the annual deficits and whose despotic taste for young ballerinas earned him the nickname of 'Divan the Terrible'.

It was to put an end to such 'abandonments' that André Malraux was chosen to be the first official overseer of France's cultural activities. In practice, this meant there were a number of cultural 'Bastilles' – a prime example being that fortress of 'academicism', the Ecole des Beaux-Arts – which needed to be stormed.

The frontal assault André Malraux chose to launch in the spring of 1959 against one of the most prestigious of these fortresses of *haute culture* – the almost 300-year-old Comédie-Française – was so hastily conceived that it culminated in a fiasco. In 1946 an enlightened Minister of Education had decided to reward the actors and actresses of the Comédie-Française by offering them a second theatre hall: that of the Odéon, a marvel of acoustics equipped with a large stage built during the last years of Louis XVI's reign. This regal gift had allowed the company to flourish on both sides of the Seine under the astute management of Pierre Descaves. Seldom, indeed, had the box-office receipts been as good and the theatre halls so well filled as during the six years of his mandate, which was due to expire in April 1959. Impressed by this record of commercial success, a commission of inquiry recommended that the two theatre halls – the venerable Salle Richelieu and the neo-classic Odéon – continue to function as national theatres under the overall aegis of the Comédie-Française.

Malraux, however, paid no heed to this wise recommendation. He saw an opportunity for killing three birds with one stone – first, by punishing the Comédie-Française, guilty of having recently performed too many comedies and not enough tragedies; second, by rewarding Jean-Louis Barrault; and finally, by imposing on the actors and actresses a 'tough', new administrator, capable of reorienting a company which, beguiled by the supple charm of Jean Meyer, an actor gifted above all for comedy, had forgotten its noble vocation and had meandered off into the by paths of frivolity.

By mid-March, rumours concerning the projected 'reforms' had begun to circulate, arousing great concern among the sixty actors and actresses of the Maison de Molière. They were particularly dumbfounded to learn that the man Malraux had chosen to lead them back on to the proper path was a certain Claude Bréart de Boisanger, a veteran diplomat and until recently French ambassador in Prague.

The name, though resonant with the sound of autumn hunting horns, fell on uncomprehending ears. Why this choice of a diplomat of whom nobody in the Paris theatre world had ever heard? One of the first to express his astonishment was the writer Jean de Beer. In a sensationally headlined article – 'Must the Comédie-Française be destroyed?' (published in the April 8th issue of *Le Monde*) – he alluded to previous crises that had rocked the world's oldest repertory company, adding: 'It is as great an error to place at their head someone who does not know them as to place there someone who is one of their own. The time has passed when the Comédie-Française could afford itself the luxury of an enlightened amateur.'

The next day, in the same newspaper, Robert Kemp, the doyen of Paris drama critics, picked up the cudgels in his turn. In an article entitled 'The House on Fire', he vigorously defended the existing situation – two theatre halls for a company of players with an enormous repertory going all the way back to Molière, Corneille, and Racine – praised Pierre Descaves' astute administration, and concluded with this stinging admonition: 'An old proverb says, "He who gives and takes away, a serpent is in every way".'

It was in this tense atmosphere that Malraux summoned the press to his ministerial offices on April 9th. He began his exposé, in a neo-Gaullist style, by reminding his listeners that in matters of culture 'the doctrine of the Fifth Republic is to make the loftiest works of mankind, and first of all of France, accessible to the largest number of French men and women'.

Malraux aimed his next remarks at the (unspecified) administration of Pierre Descaves. The repertory of the Comédie-Française being part of the 'uncontested patrimony of French genius', the essential problem was one of knowing how this treasure was being placed at the disposal of the public. The answer was – badly. 'We have wandered far from the path . . . Up until February 28th, taking the last period of the Comédie-Française, there were sixteen performances of Racine, out of 556, and not one of Greek tragedy. Nothing of Victor Hugo.'

What had happened? Malraux's answer: 'The Comédie-Française is no longer administered. A group of actors, not without talent but dedicated by their roles to comedy,' – here he was pointing an accusing finger at Jean Meyer, not named – 'have substituted their authority for that of the administrator.' As a result, the Comédie-Française, over the same period, had played Labiche 113 times, Racine only six.

Malraux then exploded his two bombshells. Henceforth, the Comédie-Française would be deprived of its second theatre hall – that of the neo-classic Odéon – which would be entrusted to Jean-Louis Barrault, 'a first-rate stage director', thereby establishing a 'competitiveness which is more than ever necessary'. Then came the second bombshell. The management of the House of Molière, from now on deprived of one hall, would be entrusted to Monsieur Claude de Boisanger, until recently French ambassador in Prague.

Malraux was promptly avalanched with questions. Astounded, the journalists wanted to know the reasons for this surprising choice of a French ambassador of whom no one, save a few insiders at the Quai d'Orsay, had ever heard. To calm the yelping of the journalistic pack, Malraux took refuge behind an aphorism of Delphic ingenuity: 'Monsieur de Boisanger was a diplomat in Prague. I thought that, if he could cope with the Iron Curtain, he would be able to cope with the red curtain', ie, that of the proscenium.

Clearly targetted, Jean Meyer sent two letters of protest – one to the President of the Republic, the other to Prime Minister Michel Debré, who by a curious coincidence was also the promoter of an association calling itself 'The Friends of Labiche'. Meyer went even further. He asked to see various ministers. Those who deigned to receive him said: Nothing doing. 'Malraux is mad, but he amuses the General.'

The choice of Jean-Louis Barrault to manage the Odéon – now pompously renamed the 'Théâtre de France' – could be defended on the grounds that he had once been a Comédie-Française actor, while his wife, Madeleine Renaud, had played for the company for twenty-two years. A talented mime, as he had brilliantly proved in Marcel Carné's film, *Les Enfants du Paradis*, Barrault had later created several unforgettable stagings, notably of Paul Claudel's *Partage du Midi* and of Kafka's *The Trial*. But how did an outsider like Claude Bréart de Boisanger come to be involved in this imbroglio? According to his own account (published five years later), it was during a visit made to Prague by a former actor-member, Julien Bertheau, and by Denise Noël, a Comédie-Française actress, that this veteran diplomat took it into his head to volunteer to succeed Pierre Descaves. The news soon reached the ears of André Malraux. What a gift from the gods! An experienced diplomat who had never had any links with the Comédie-Française, a man capable of rising above the company's internal squabbles and intrigues. In short, the perfect instrument, the 'joker' that would enable Malraux to crush Jean Meyer and everything he represented in the realm of theatrical 'facility'.

Even Malraux's most fervent admirers must have been nonplussed by the impetuous insouciance with which he threw himself into this adventure. His first meeting with Claude de Boisanger did not take place until the evening of March 22nd, a mere two weeks before the official announcement of his appointment. According to Boisanger, Malraux simply indicated the general line of the reforms he wanted to introduce and apply: a revision of the programmes, with more emphasis on tragedy – more Racine, less Labiche and Feydeau; invitations to talented stage directors from outside the company to prepare new plays; a strengthening of the powers of the administrator of the Comédie-Française.

'Everything up till then, though often not very clearly expressed, seemed logical,' Claude de Boisanger later wrote. 'But things changed when the minister moved on to questions of persons, as though he had ceased to feel at ease . . . He spoke to me at length and with mounting nervousness of the excessive influence wielded by Jean Meyer, of the urgent need there was to put this actor in his place.'

It would be tedious to detail the various disagreements between André Malraux and Claude de Boisanger which built up over the next nine months. From the start there was a fundamental incompatibility between two radically different temperaments. Calm, courteous, unhurried, Boisanger had been disagreeably struck by André Malraux's 'uncertain look, an absence in his remarks of humour, of naturalness, of simplicity, his love of striking phrases and effects, his way of expressing himself, at once recherché and obscure'.

On New Year's Eve (December 31, 1959) Boisanger was summoned to the Ministry of Cultural Affairs, where Malraux curtly informed him: 'In agreement with the Prime Minister, I am leaving you the choice between resignation and dismissal.' The urbane administrator of the illustrious repertory company was even more surprised when he discovered, a few hours later, that the Prime Minister (Michel Debré) knew nothing of this ultimatum.

There followed a curious duel, fought out with journalistic allegations and denials in the press, which would have delighted Molière or Alexandre Dumas had they been around to watch the fun. From the Rue Valois side of the handsomely colonnaded court came 'well informed' reports that M. de Boisanger was going to offer his resignation at any moment. A bare hundred yards away, in his administrator's office overlooking the Place du Théâtre Français, an astonishingly serene Claude Bréart de Boisanger parried each thrust with the cool nonchalance of an Athos. But no, what nonsense, he had no intention of resigning. He was even ready to submit this quarrel to the Council of State (which he later did). In the backstage corridors and in their dressing rooms, the actors and actresses of the House of Molière laughed and sniggered to see a farce worthy of Beaumarchais descend from the stage out on to the street.

The 'scandal' moved all the way up to the Elysée Palace. René Brouillet, who headed the President of the Republic's secretariat, tried to patch things up, and on January 15, 1960 there was even talk of a 'summit meeting' between General de Gaulle and this rebellious functionary. But the meeting, for reasons left unexplained but not hard to fathom, did not take place; and on January 21st Claude Bréart de Boisanger learned from the newspapers that the Council of Ministers had just put an end to his functions.

The next day Boisanger finally abandoned the administrator's office, from which he was being illegally expelled. It was not the end of the Comédie-Française, which had ridden out many another crisis of the sort. To smooth the ruffled feathers of the cackling brood on the other side of the colonnaded court, Malraux judiciously chose Maurice Escande, the doyen of the company, to administer the House of Molière. This he did, without further fuss or scandal and with a great deal of diplomatic skill right up until his resignation ten years later.

On April 9, 1959, the day on which he outlined his programme of reforms for the Comédie-Française, Malraux also announced that he had picked André-Maistre Julien to direct the Paris Opéra and its smaller and less prestigious satellite, the Opéra-Comique. It seemed a judicious choice. A disciple of Jacques Copeau, a former assistant to Alberto Cavalcanti and Charles Dullin, Julien was above all the stage manager who had organized the first International Festival of Dramatic Art in 1954 and who, at the renamed Théâtre des Nations, had offered Parisians the chance of seeing foreign masterpieces performed by first-rate theatre troupes from other countries. It was thus a veteran of the stage and the very opposite of an 'outsider' whom Malraux chose to 'reform' Paris' two opera houses – which did not keep a new row from blowing up three years later, precipitating Julien's 'downfall'.

It must be said, in all fairness to Julien and Malraux, that the problems posed by Paris's two opera houses were well-nigh insoluble. Both had long been plagued by repeated strikes. If to this we add the absence of discipline displayed by so many Paris instrumentalists, with many of them refusing to rehearse more than four days a week, it becomes clear why it takes a superman with the courage of a lion-tamer (like the Swiss composer-conductor, Rolf Liebermann) to overcome the innumerable obstacles involved.

The three years of Julien's 'reign' produced two 'unforgettable moments' of a truly grotesque 'grandeur'. The first was a luxurious production of *Carmen*, presented to the public on the huge stage of the Opéra (instead of the smaller Opéra-Comique). Intended to rival the splendour of Rameau's *Les Indes galantes* (which Maurice Lehmann had lavishly staged in 1955), this new version of *Carmen* was transformed into a cavalcade, with (to quote from Charles Dupêchez's *Histoire de l'Opéra de Paris*) 'an incredible menagerie for each performance: fifteen horses, two donkeys, mules, a piebald dog, a monkey, and parrots . . . The opera required a cast of 473, as many costumes, and one hundred female wigs fashioned with hair obtained from Italian convents.'

The second 'great moment' was, or should have been, provided by the staging, for the hundredth anniversary of Claude Debussy's birth (1862), of a sensational new version of *Pelléas et Mélisande*. Usually this opera is presented with everything nebulous and painted in soft pastel shades. But for this version, against Malraux's advice, a décor of such brazen modernism was created that tenors and sopranos had to display the acrobatic skills of ballet dancers in order not to lose their balance when ascending and descending platforms that were suspended like 'magic carpets' twelve or fifteen feet above the stage. Unveiled in April 1962 for the Venice Biennale, this *mise en scène* – a catastrophic accumulation of 'nonsensical absurdities' (as René Dumesnil wrote in *Le Monde*) – could all too easily have put an end to Denise Duval's singing career if she had missed her step – which fortunately she did not. It did, however, put an abrupt end to A.-M. Julien's lacklustre 'reign'.

Malraux was well inspired in choosing to replace Julien by the composer Georges Auric. Affable, lucid, disinterested, Auric nevertheless failed – even though, with the help of André Masson (for the backdrops), Jean-Louis Barrault for the *mise en scène*, and the composer–conductor Pierre Boulez (who obtained 36 preparatory rehearsals), he succeeded in having Alban Berg's *Wozzeck* performed by the Opéra, which for a few brilliant evenings was able to raise its waning prestige. But alongside the rare 'triumphs' must be chalked up many fiascos and failures, which heaped further ridicule on the Opéra and caused its finest singers – like Régine Crespin and Mady Mesple – to seek employment in other countries. As Charles Dupêchez later summed it up: 'Protected by inextricable collective agreements, the personnel were a law unto themselves. Strikes became a permanent operatic hiccup. They carried on as usual, heedless of the tons of dust covering the backdrops, the advancing age of paunchy choral singers with creaking voices . . .' etc.

Personally, no less than professionally, the years 1960 and 1961 were occasionally sad, often trying, and finally tragic ones for André Malraux. In January 1960 he thought he had obtained one of his objectives: finding a theatre for Albert Camus. One of his assistants, Pierre Moinot, was drafting a letter to announce the good news to the author of *Caligula* and *La Peste* when Albert Beuret opened the door to say that Camus had just been killed in a terrible car accident with Raymond's son, Michel ('Mico') Gallimard.

The month of June 1960 brought Malraux another, even more disagreeable shock. For some time his numerous left-wing critics had been wondering how the author of *Les Conquérants, La Condition humaine*, and *L'Espoir* – the man who, along with François Mauriac, Roger Martin du Gard, and Jean-Paul Sartre, had signed a 'solemn address' to President René Coty in April 1958 – could go on pretending to believe that all forms of torture had been banished from Algeria since General de Gaulle's return to power. The controversy had heated up again with the publication and prompt seizure by the French police of a new book, *La Gangrène*, written this time not by a notorious French Communist but by several Algerians. In a long letter published by *Le Monde* on June 23rd, Graham Greene reminded Malraux that they had once sat on the same literary jury which, each year, 'granted a prize honouring the memory of a French heroine who had died in the [concentration] camp of Mauthausen for the defence of French liberties . .'. Outraged by a trial at which the public prosecutor had demanded that a lawyer for the defence be hauled before the court for having dared to challenge 'facts' presented by the prosecution, the famous novelist added: 'It is difficult to believe that such a law court can exist when the leader of the Free French heads the government and the author of *La Condition humaine* is one of his ministers.'

Three months later the tribulations of the Minister of Cultural Affairs became even more acutely painful when, in September 1960, more than 100 writers, literary critics, composers, film directors, actors and actresses signed a 'Manifesto of the 121', condemning the pursuit of the war against the *fellaghas* and upholding the right of 'non-submission' for young draftees obliged to complete their term of compulsory military service in Algeria. André Malraux was in his wife's bathroom when Madeleine brought him a copy of the newspaper listing the names of the signatories. They included a number of celebrities – Simone Signoret, Françoise Sagan, Pierre Boulez, François Truffaut, Jean-Paul Sartre, Simone de Beauvoir . . . and Florence Malraux. After working for a while (in photographic research) for Gallimard's *NRF*, and later as editorial assistant on the weekly *L'Express*, 'Flo' had developed a keen interest in films and had left for Munich as an assistant to Alian Resnais, who was filming *Last Year in Marienbad*.

André Malraux's reaction, after a long moment of silence, was hard and categorical. 'This time I've seen enough of her' – followed a few seconds later by this cry of indignation from a wounded father: 'What book has she written, what picture has she painted, to be able to sign this text? When we have made peace in Algeria, a fine lot they'll look, these great revolutionaries who tell me what I should do in the name of what I've done. Sartre has stepped into my slippers.'

Appalled, neither Madeleine nor her son Alain – now a sixteen-year-old *lycée* student – dared say a word, knowing only too well from experience that the more they put in a good word for someone against whom Malraux had developed a grudge, the more bitter became the grudge. If his reaction was so violent, it was also, as Alain well understood, because Florence was the daughter of Clara, who in the past had so often wounded his self-esteem. Once again, he felt himself 'threatened from inside' by an act of female defiance.

Six months later, as the fog began to lift on Charles de Gaulle's veritable intentions, four 'factious' generals in Algeria again raised the standards of revolt. The astonished citizens of metropolitan France now saw, or rather heard, their Prime Minister, Michel Debré – once a fervent champion of a French Algeria – effect the most spectacular about-face of his career by broadcasting an appeal to his countrymen to get themselves to Orly airport by any means available – by car, on bicycle, on foot or even 'on horseback' (as cabaret wits promptly added) – in order to 'dialogue' with the paratroopers, who were about to drop at any moment.

Malraux responded to this appeal by heading for the Ministry of the Interior. There, in the pale glow of the courtyard lamps, he harangued a few intrepid souls crying in a hoarse voice, 'This night, everything depends on you! If the paratroopers are not here in an hour, they will never come.'

When he returned the next morning (April 22, 1961) to the Boulogne villa, André Malraux could not have guessed that one month later he would be confronted by a far graver crisis for himself and his family. During the intervening years his two sons – Gauthier (the erstwhile 'Bimbo') and above all Vincent (two-and-a-half years younger) – had been causing him many headaches. The younger son had grown increasingly hostile to all forms of scholastic discipline. A past master in the art of 'disappearing', he had become such a nuisance that his father had sent him to a Swiss boarding-school, from which the skilful truant had lost no time escaping. After a number of such escapades, Malraux had his bodyguards seize the lad and 'intern' him in a Catholic boarding-school in Metz, from where Pierre Bockel later rescued him, taking him to Strasbourg. Realizing that the only 'discipline' the young Vincent respected was drawing – for which he displayed an unquestionable talent – his amiable tutor had him admitted to the School of Decorative Arts, and allowed him to 'let off steam' by buying a powerful motorcycle. On this the young daredevil staged 'hit-and-run' raids on the capital.

During one of these quick trips Vincent met and befriended a charming young woman with the fateful name of Clara (Saint) who, like the one who had so generously helped to finance the young André Malraux, was older and wealthier than Vincent. She showered the lucky adolescent with presents, offering him a small black-and-white car, soon replaced by a swifter bluebird – an Alfa Romeo Giulietta.

Tamed at last, the seventeen-year-old student agreed to return to his Paris *lycée*. Now willing to 'cram' for his baccalaureate exams, Vincent had proposed to his older brother Gauthier that he accompany him to the Mediterranean island of Port-Cros. Isolated in the old off-shore port, they could spend the long Whitsun holiday in perfect peace, without being disturbed.

On the evening of May 23rd, André Malraux and Madeleine had just returned from an Italian restaurant when the telephone rang in the Boulogne villa. It was Albert Beuret, calling from the Ministry of Cultural Affairs: Gauthier and Vincent had had an automobile accident on their way back from Port-Cros. Other telephone calls followed. And then, at last, came the dreadful news, this time definitive: Gauthier and Vincent had both died in a terrible collision not far from Beaune.

Dazed with grief, Malraux had a call put through to Pierre Bockel, asking him to join him at Beaune's Hôtel des Hospices. He then left for Burgundy with Albert Beuret. Pierre Bockel arrived some hours later.

André Malraux had decided to have his two sons buried next to their mother in the little graveyard of Charonne, in north-eastern Paris. Alerted by telephone, Florence arrived from Thann, in Alsace, where she had been helping François Truffaut film *Jules et Jim*. The little graveyard could hardly contain all those who came to express their sorrow and their sympathy.

As evening approached, Malraux took Bockel by the arm and led him down a path to one side, then asked him, almost timidly: 'Would you agree to celebrate a Mass for them, as we used to do when burying our comrades-in-arms, struck down beside us?'

'Of course,' was the reply of the former chaplain of the Alsace–Lorraine Brigade. Malraux then let it be known that the Mass was being postponed until 11 o'clock the next morning.

That night, momentarily forgiven for the 'Appeal of the 121' she had signed, Florence was able to spend the night at the Boulogne villa, where, a little later, General de Gaulle and his wife came to express their condolences. Malraux himself said nothing, suddenly frozen into a silence which seemed to have rid him of his facial ticks as well as his gift of speech. But in a single sentence he summed up the grief he had bottled up within him: 'With them, it's all of Josette's part that is reduced to nothingness.'

Tragic though it was in personal terms, this year of 1961 nevertheless ended with a first small triumph for the Ministry of Cultural Affairs: the approval by the Debré government of a long-term programme tending towards the protection and restoration not merely of individual edifices but of entire urban quarters. It was soon followed by the 'Malraux Law' of August 1962, which made it possible to 'classify' as of historic interest and thus to protect not only urban quarters – like the threatened quarter of La Balance, at Avignon – but entire towns, like Senlis, Sarlat, and the old centre of Bourges. (By 1976, no fewer than fifty-seven French cities had old quarters thus safeguarded against the neglect of indifferent citizens and the destructive rapacity of property developers.)

Early in 1962 a particularly odious act earned Malraux a sudden renewal of favour, particularly among left-wingers. Shortly after midday of February 7th, a bomb – almost certainly laid by some fanatic member of the anti-Gaullist OAS (Organisation Armée Secrète), which was struggling tooth and nail to preserve a 'French Algeria' – exploded, pulverising the window panes of the façade and the broad picture window of the first-floor salon where, a moment before, Alain Malraux had been practising on his mother's piano. André had long since left for his ministerial office at the Palais-Royal, but the four-year-old Delphine Renaud, who lived on the ground floor with her parents, had one of her eyes blinded by a splinter of flying glass.

Malraux now realized that he would have to look for a new home. The solution was found in April, thanks to Georges Pompidou, who had just replaced Michel Debré as prime minister. Among his 'secondary residences' was a little jewel of a Louis XVI château called La Lanterne, whose garden bordered the park of the palace of Versailles. Pompidou graciously offered it to André Malraux. It was to remain his main residence until 1969.

The year 1962 should logically have marked a turning point in the early youth of the Ministry of Cultural Affairs. Up till then the Ministry of Finance had justified the meagreness of the annual allocations granted to the fledgling ministry (0.43 per cent of the national budget) by the high military costs the French state had to bear to pursue a policy of 'pacification' in Algeria. Now that the war was over, many people expected to see this tiny percentage increased. Not at all. The end to hostilities in Algeria was followed by the panicky exodus of one million French settlers, who needed financial assistance to make new homes for themselves in France. The Finance ministry thus had a ready-made pretext for not loosening the purse strings – particularly since General de Gaulle was determined to forge an atomic *force de frappe*, which turned out to be a huge devourer of public funds. In short, Charles de Gaulle's policy of military grandeur took precedence financially over the policy of cultural grandeur which the General was simultaneously trying to promote by sending Malraux out to make vibrant speeches in Africa, Latin America and the United States.

Placed in such a delicate situation, a more experienced politician would have carefully avoided launching into spectacular and costly ventures, which did a lot to sour his relations with an increasingly critical French press. In this long-drawn-out quarrel André Malraux was the victim of his own legend. For the right-wing press, he was condemned in advance: he was still and would always remain the one-time revolutionary who had mocked the colonial administration in Indochina, who had supported the Front Populaire, who had aided the 'Reds' in Spain. For the left-wing press, he had become the 'traitor' who had abandoned the progressive convictions of his youth by joining the camp of the 'usurper', de Gaulle. Between these two large reservoirs of ill-will were those who might be called the 'optimists' – such as André Parinaud and his colleagues of the weekly review, *Arts*. They had welcomed Malraux's appointment to the Ministry of Cultural Affairs, hoping that this superman would accomplish wonders, only to discover that he was letting a taste for the grandiose, the prestigious, the sensational take precedence over less 'showy' but indispensable initiatives.

Of all the 'wild ideas' hatched by Malraux during his ten years at the ministry, the wildest was surely his decision to lay 'bare' the foundations of the Louvre. At a time when an ever-increasing number of monuments were waiting to be restored, when the famous actor and stage director Jean Vilar was wringing his hands in despair and raising cries of alarm on behalf of his semi-bankrupt Théâtre National Populaire, Malraux suddenly felt the urgent need to pour large sums of money into enhancing the splendour of the 'greatest palace in the world' by digging a waterless moat around it, soon mocked by Paris wits as 'Monsieur Malraux's ditch'.

Some of his initiatives deserve high praise: for example, the organization in 1962 of a major 'retrospective' display of the canvases of Georges Braque: the first time in the history of the Louvre that such an honour had been shown to a living artist. The same can be said for other exhibitions Malraux sponsored – for Mondrian and Giacometti at the Orangerie, for Paul Klee at the Museum of Modern Art, for Archipenko at the Rodin Museum. But was it really necessary to 'recognize' (rather late in the day) the genius of Marc Chagall by asking him to repaint a new ceiling for the Paris Opéra? In a critical editorial published in the *Figaro* (November 8, 1963) the historian Pierre Gaxotte ridiculed the project: 'The Opéra is of value because it is, in all its parts, a perfect monument of the Napoleon III style. It is precious because of its unity, its exact concordance. This style is not ours? All right, let's put Chagall in a new theatre. At the Opéra, he will never be more than an intruder who destroys its harmony.'

The storm of protests, far from discouraging the impetuous minister, merely stimulated his combative ardour. Had Malraux not once confessed of himself: 'I have always felt more at home on the barricades than in a salon'? There was a smell of gunpowder in the air. So much the better. The petty bourgeois he had always detested, the philistines he had long despised had to be taught another lesson. And it was thus that another 'neglected' painter, André Masson, was invited to cover over the 'hideous' ceiling of the Odéon – that is, of Jean-Louis Barrault's pompously rebaptised Théâtre de France.

But this was merely the beginning, as the Boeotians of the world were soon to discover. In May 1962 André Malraux and Madeleine were invited to spend a few days in Washington by President John Kennedy and his wife Jacqueline, an ardent admirer of the author of *Man's Fate* and *The Voices of Silence*. On May 11th, during a luncheon offered to him by the Overseas

Writers Association, a *Washington Post* correspondent asked him in a bantering tone: 'Wouldn't it be a wonderful thing if the *Mona Lisa* could be seen at the National Gallery in Washington?' Although surprised, Malraux was not one to turn and flee. Picking up the gauntlet, he said:

'Yes, of course, why not?'

In Paris, there was an almost audible gnashing of teeth among certain curators of the Louvre, less than overjoyed by this new 'stunt' thought up by the former 'temple-robber of Cambodia'. But they were forced to comply. Specialists were dispatched to Washington to study its atmospheric conditions, security measures, and the possibilities of 'housing' Leonardo's masterpiece at the National Gallery. A special metal coffin was built for the secure transport of 'the world's most beautiful painting' and a first-class stateroom was reserved for its transatlantic crossing aboard the *France*.

Accompanied by Jacques Jaujard and Madeleine Hours, a veteran Louvre specialist, the *Gioconda* crossed the Atlantic and was met in New York on December 18, 1962 by a delegation of officials from the National Gallery, a small commando force of musclemen from the US Secret Service, and a swarm of journalists. Transported to Washington in a specially air-conditioned, armour-plated truck, the 'smiling one' was then relegated to the basement of the National Gallery, where for three humiliating weeks she waited on the good pleasure of the President of the United States and the gentlemen of the Congress, who had all gone home to celebrate Christmas and New Year's Eve with their families.

The actual unveiling did not take place until January 9th – a 'historic' evening which almost ended in catastrophe, caused by the presence in the hall of 2,000 persons: senators and representatives of Congress with their wives, State Department officials, Supreme Court justices, ambassadors and their spouses, and the inevitable swarm of journalists – all squashed and squeezed against each other, 'wishbones to backbones', as a survivor from this battlefield (John Skow) later wrote in a saucy article: 'The result was a triumph of geometry over aesthetics: nobody less than 6 feet 4 inches high had a chance to see the canvas. Nobody over 6 feet 5 inches could see much either, for the TV cameramen had aimed their floodlights in such a way that the reflections lit up the protective windscreen like a heliograph.' The noise at the back of the hall, where the congregated notables continued to prattle away, was such that, when his turn came to speak, Secretary of State Dean Rusk was forced to complain – without making himself properly heard. André Malraux, as was to be expected, delivered a stirring speech. ('The most powerful nation in the world today renders the most dazzling homage a masterpiece has ever received. May both of you' – this to President Jack and to his First Lady, Jackie – 'be praised, in the name of all the unnamed artists who thank you, perhaps from the depths of the funereal night.') But few persons in the overcrowded, overheated hall understood a word; nor, above all, that this 'historic' gesture on the part of an eternal France was intended to thank the American soldiers who, twice in twenty-five years, had come to 'save' this painting.

This experiment in cultural exhibitionism – later repeated with the far riskier dispatch to Tokyo of the Venus de Milo – simply added to the exasperation of his critics. As André Thierry wrote in *Arts* in September 1964:

> We needed a minister of Culture, we have an aesthete who amuses himself. We wanted a bold man, we have a publicist of grandeur. We wanted an organizer, we have a playboy who airs his whims.
>
> Did we really need a Malraux who did not commit his prestige to demanding a budget worthy of French culture, a Malraux who, instead of taking on the parliament and placing it in front of its responsibilities, finds that the essence of his task is to evoke Joan of Arc and the cathedrals before open-mouthed schoolchildren, a Malraux who, instead of acting, transformed himself into an official Versailles guide for passing highnesses? Give us back Cornu. He at least saved the château.

Harsh words, indeed – for André Malraux, as for Jacqueline Kennedy, here casually referred to as a 'passing highness' and who, if she had heard the name, would doubtless have replied, 'But who then is this Monsieur Cornu?'

Hurt by so much ingratitude for everything he was trying to accomplish, fed up with the plodding tedium of administrative work and the quarrels of his subordinates, worn out by the endless rounds of official dinners and receptions he could not ignore without offending some ministerial colleague or slighted ambassador, exasperated too by frequent disagreements with his wife Madeleine, whose musical gifts he did not sufficiently appreciate, André Malraux finally yielded to the advice of friends, who felt that what he needed above all was a good vacation.

Indeed, the tension on the domestic front, where meals were often consumed in grim silence, was becoming more unendurable with each day. For some time past, whenever André exploded on returning home because of some administrative contretemps at the office, Madeleine would say, 'leave this government and go back to writing' – advice which merely aggravated his ill humour, since it implied the unthinkable: that he should abandon the General. But a long sea voyage, undertaken to calm his nerves and with the approval of the Grand Charles, ready to entrust him with a diplomatic mission to China, was not in any sense an act of desertion.

And thus it was that in June 1965, accompanied by the faithful Albert Beuret, Malraux embarked on the *Cambodge*, repeating the voyage he had already made twice with Clara to Singapore and Hong Kong. From Canton he flew on to Peking, where he was received by the Minister of Foreign Affairs, Marshal Chen-yi, Prime Minister Chou En-lai, and finally by Mao

Tse-tung and the official president of the People's Republic of China, Liu Shao-shi.

From Peking Malraux took a plane to Delhi, where he stood in respectful silence in front of Gandhi's tomb, before revisiting the holy city of Benares. Here the Sanskrit University awarded him an honorary degree – the first foreigner to be thus honoured. He returned to Paris during the last days of August, a few days before the death of the architect Le Corbusier, in honour of whom, in the Cour Carrée of the Louvre and beneath a sky of scudding clouds, swept by a Vlaminckian wind, he delivered another funeral oration – in a voice so cracked and cavernous that it seemed to emerge from the realm of the dead.

While the trip to Asia had worked wonders in restoring his appetite for writing, it had failed to alter André's feelings towards Madeleine, who was brusquely informed that from now on he wanted to live alone at La Lanterne. Without protesting, she packed her bags and moved with her belongings to the new Paris flat, on the ninth floor of an apartment building on the Avenue Montaigne. Later, yielding to the entreaties of Manès Sperber, who, like Alain, was doing his best to patch things up, André Malraux agreed to resume his marital life with Madeleine. But this attempt soon ended in a new and particularly acrimonious exchange. He reproached her, in neo-Gaullist language, for 'not breathing at the altitude at which I breathe'.

Nettled, she replied: 'No one will have the courage to do so, but I must tell you: if you want to save yourself, you must stop drinking.'

'I was expecting that. Well, if I drink, it's because of you.'

'No,' she riposted. 'Because you were already drinking with Josette and she complained to me about it, saying that you finished *L'Espoir* on large doses of Pernod.'

A definitive separation was now unavoidable. André continued to inhabit La Lanterne with two Siamese cats, while Madeleine took over the apartment on the Avenue Montaigne.

Over the next few months Malraux was increasingly absorbed by the writing of a new book, partly inspired by his recent trip to the Orient. He still visited his Palais-Royal office, but was content to leave all routine problems of administration in the competent hands of Albert Beuret, the *eminence grise* of a ministry soon shaken by a new crisis.

In 1962 a commission had been created to determine what should be done for Music: an art so universally scorned at every level of the Ministry of Education that it was only grudgingly that the bureaucrats responsible would consider allowing even half an hour of musical instruction to be included in the weekly curriculum of France's primary schools and *lycées*. The members of this commission included two well known composers, Georges Auric and Henri Duthilleux, as well as the new director of the National Conservatory of Music, Raymond Gallois-Montbrun (son of the lawyer who had so ably defended Louis Chevasson during the Saigon trial of 1924). Malraux had prudently selected him for this post when he realized that his first choice, the rabidly 'modernist' composer, Pierre Boulez, would have used the opportunity to dismiss *all but one* of the Conservatory's 120 'reactionary' (too classically minded) teachers – a 'purge' which would inevitably have exposed Malraux to another storm of abuse.

After two years of desultory deliberations the Music Commission had still not produced a report when, in the autumn of 1964, Jacques Chailley, the president of the CNM (Comité National de la Musique, representing a number of musical guilds), began sounding the alarm bell. He had just returned from a trip to Budapest, where a young French violinist, Claire Bernard, had won the Georges Enesco Prize and had been enthusiastically acclaimed by the Hungarian press. In Paris not a single newspaper had bothered to report this musical triumph, whereas entire columns had been devoted to a banquet Georges Pompidou had organized at his residence for a famous French sports champion.

A couple of days later the *Figaro* published a biting editorial on the subject, bringing the matter into the open. Pompidou felt obliged to organize a second dinner at his residence – this time to honour the gifted young violinist, Claire Bernard. André Malraux was among those invited. He listened attentively as Chailley painted a sombre picture of France's musical 'wasteland', so neglected by its rulers that only four of its cities maintained full-time symphony orchestras, compared to eighty-eight in West Germany.

Working overtime during the next three months Chailley and his colleagues of the CNM prepared a concise report, suggesting a number of reforms. It was delivered to the Ministry of Cultural Affairs in early March of 1965.

On March 11th Malraux received Chailley, his designated successor, Darius Milhaud, and Raymond Lyon, the secretary-general of the CNM, in his ministerial office. The report was on his desk. 'All this seems to me very logical,' he explained to his three visitors. 'But, you understand, I can't undertake everything at once. I must therefore ask you to choose one point that you regard as absolutely overriding.'

In Malraux's new ministry, music had been casually placed under a general Directorate for Theatre, Music, and Cultural Action, where almost all of the available funds were channelled towards Paris's two opera houses, the two 'national' theatres (the Comédie-Française and Jean-Louis Barrault's Théâtre de France), and a number of Maisons de la Culture (cultural centres), which were supposed to arouse certain carefully chosen cities from their provincial torpor. Ignored, not to say banished from the banquet table, Music had been left to pick up the crumbs. Chailley, after consulting briefly with his two friends, accordingly declared: 'Music must be given its administrative autonomy and entrusted to a qualified person.'

'Fine,' said Malraux. 'Give me a name.'

This time Raymond Lyon spoke up: '*Monsieur le Ministre*, you already have a highly qualified person in your administration.'

'Who?'

'Marcel Landowski.'

A composer of distinctly classical tendencies, Landowski had recently been appointed Inspector of Musical Instruction at the ministry. He had helped the CNM prepare its report and was strenuously opposed to facile, short-cut solutions – such as a project, which had found favour with Pierre Boulez, of giving Paris two first-class symphony orchestras, which, acting like 'locomotives', would then pull the rest of the country out of its musical lethargy.

In noting Landowski's name, Malraux may have thought that the matter had been settled. Not so. For in the meantime Gaétan Picon and his deputy, Emile Biasini (head of the Directorate of Theatre, Music, and Cultural Action), had decided that there was only one man in France really worthy of directing an autonomous Music department in the Ministry of Cultural Affairs: Pierre Boulez. There ensued a long behind-the-scenes struggle, finally won by Albert Beuret. The former pianist, who had had to abandon his early keyboard exercises in order to help his mother run her hairdresser's salon, had not lost his love of music, and being someone who (to quote Landowski) 'chased and caught ideas as a squirrel does nuts', he soon grasped the imperative need to elaborate a long-term programme aimed at encouraging musical activities all over the country, and not simply – for reasons of prestige – in the pampered metropolis of Paris. This meant, among other things, the creation in a dozen French cities of musical conservatories worthy of the name.

In May 1966 Marcel Landowski was finally appointed head of an autonomous Service for Musical Affairs. The appointment was bitterly attacked in the weekly, *France-Observateur*, by Pierre Boulez who dismissed Landowski as a mediocre musician, a 'man of straw' totally lacking in imagination. This barrage of insults failed to impress Malraux, who had 'unfrozen' an allocation of 6 million francs for Landowski's new service. When he summoned Landowski, to find out what he intended to do with the money, he said, after hearing his report: 'Ah, I'm glad to see that you haven't been upset by the firework display of angry B flats.' After which, he added: 'Remember one thing: you can be insulted every day in two hundred newspapers; none of that has any importance if we are in agreement.'

Along with the preparation of the great Inventory for the preservation of historic monuments, sites, and urban districts against the perennial assaults of uncouth vandals and profit-seeking wreckers, this turned out to be Malraux's greatest victory during his ten-year term as minister. Four years later, in December 1970, a new Directorate for Music, Lyric Art (ie Opera), and Dance was established. André Malraux was no longer Minister of Cultural Affairs, but thanks to his initial support and to that of his successors, Edmond Michelet and Jacques Duhamel, Marcel Landowski's tiny service, which had started out with exactly three dedicated souls at no. 53, Rue Saint-Dominique, could now boast a staff of seventy. A new era was about to begin, one that was to see the creation of a Paris orchestra truly worthy of the name and the flowering of a 'golden age' such as the Opéra had not known since the long reign of Jacques Rouché. That was why Marcel Landowski could later write that 'Malraux is the first minister, since Louis XIV's time, who has done in depth something irreversible for music.'

The year 1967 was, for André Malraux, the year of his 'great return' to literature, a year of apotheosis. He was able to finish the book he had begun during his trip to Asia: an anti-autobiographical mosaic, a cubistic master-piece composed of fragmentary reminiscences put together with no heed to chronology, to which he gave the defiant title, *Antimémoires*. This was the gauntlet he was flinging down to his critics, to all those who for years had been deploring the 'disappearance' of the writer, the metamorphosis of the great novelist of yesterday into the pathetic *godillot* (footslogger) of General de Gaulle he had incomprehensibly become. 'I will show them that I am the greatest writer of the century,' he declared one day to his nephew Alain, with whom he often lunched (usually at Lasserre), whereas he never saw Alain's mother, who, freed at last, could resume her career as a gifted concert pianist.

Published in September, the *Antimémoires* were an instant best-seller. Two hundred thousand copies were sold in a few weeks, while contracts with fabulous advances were signed with foreign publishing companies. 'My Dédé is riding high,' wrote Louise de Vilmorin to her friend Diana Cooper. 'This consoles me a bit for my lost friend' – the writer Marcel Aymé, who had died a few days before, on October 16, 1967. 'I simply realize that ideas become important only when someone of importance expresses them. And my Dédé is someone of importance.'

Being herself an author whose poems and novelettes had been published by Gallimard, she had continued to catch glimpses of André Malraux – to whom she had dedicated her first book, *Sainte-Unefois* – despite the 1933 tiff provoked by her liaison with Friedrich Sieburg. Thirty years later, all that was forgotten. The tragic deaths of Gauthier and Vincent in 1961 had moved her to write André a letter of sympathy, and from 1964 on he had begun sending her brief notes. After his return from Asia, he had called on Louise at her lovely country house at Verrières-le-Buisson, which was only a few kilometres from Versailles. Realizing how emotionally disturbed he had become since the break-up of his marriage to his sister-in-law Made-leine, Louise had decided to enliven his solitude at La Lanterne, eventually spending much of each week there, but always returning on weekends to Verrières.

With the huge royalties earned by his *Antimémoires*, André bought an apartment overlooking the gardens of the Palais-Royal, a mere hundred yards from his ministerial office. The upper floor was for him, the lower floor for Louise, who was entrusted with the task of furnishing both. In this way they could have a place to stay in Paris on those evenings when they had a dinner to attend or a play to take in – a convenient arrangement which would eliminate the tedious, late evening return by chauffeured car to Verrières or Versailles.

Louise had also experienced an apotheosis, after the publication of a new novelette, *L'Heure maliciôse*, and particularly after a televised appearance ('Welcome to Louise de Vilmorin'), where she dazzled everyone by her charm and the spontaneity of her repartee. As she said of herself: 'I speak without reflecting. People who reflect never tell me anything of interest.' It was a daring thing to say at a moment when Malraux had again become part of her life, but the rapidity of his verbal delivery could give the impression that here was someone who did not need to reflect to say interesting things.

But, alas, this apotheosis was too lovely to last. 1967, the year of personal triumphs, was followed by 1968, the year of catastrophes. It began very badly for Malraux in the month of February when, irritated by the stubborn independent-mindedness of Henri Langlois, he decided to remove him from his post as director of the French Cinémathèque.

That the administration of the Cinémathèque, for which Malraux had found a new projection hall in a wing of the Palais de Chaillot, left a lot to be desired, even Henri Langlois' most fervent supporters could not seriously deny. But Langlois himself was too important a person to be shoved aside or treated badly. It was this sloppily clad bohemian, possessed of a single-minded passion and the faith of an apostle, who in 1936 had first had the idea of establishing a cinematographic 'library'. Since then he had spent his time tirelessly collecting all the old film reels he could lay his hands on. It was he who, with the help of friends, had managed during the terrible years of the German Occupation to hide an incalculable number of films which Gestapo agents would gladly have destroyed if they had been able to locate them – if only because their directors and certain of their actors were Jewish or because they represented the 'decadent' art that was condemned by Hitler, Goebbels, and their 'philosopher', Alfred Rosenberg. It was he who, long before Malraux's arrival at the Ministry of Cultural Affairs, had created the greatest 'reserve' or 'fund' of old films in the world, and which, without him, would not have existed. In short, this stubborn, headstrong fellow was a true creator, not a nondescript bureaucrat who could be dismissed with a stroke of the pen, to satisfy the fussy accountants and book-keepers of the Ministry of Finance. And above all not after the extraordinary ten-minute harangue which Malraux had delivered in early February to a number of Cinémathèque representatives, which was full of praise for Henri Langlois. Whence their stupefaction when, on February 9th, they learned that the French state, which had just acquired a majority of shares in the management of the Cinémathèque, was replacing Langlois by an egregious nonetity, Pierre Barbin.

In the conflict that pitted him against his 'friend' Langlois, it was an international community of outraged actors and film directors who rose, *en masse*, to defend him against Malraux and the Ministry of Cultural Affairs.

They were led by the pioneers of the *'nouvelle vague'* (New Wave) – François Truffaut, Jean-Luc Godard, Alain Resnais, Claude Chabrol – and thirty-six other French film directors. And that was merely a starter. By February 12th, no fewer than sixty film-makers had taken steps to forbid the projection of their films by the new state-run Cinémathèque. Telegrams of protest flooded in from everywhere – signed by Fritz Lang, Charles Chaplin, Orson Welles, Roberto Rossellini, Luis Buñuel, Carl Dreiser, Elia Kazan, and many more. It was no longer a French 'affair'; it had become an international scandal. French newspapers were filled with scathing comments. With cutting irony François Truffaut entitled an article, *'L'Anti-Mémoire courte'* ('A Short Anti-Memory'). In *Combat*, Philippe Tesson thundered: 'The Malraux Myth has lasted long enough!' From Switzerland the playwright Jean Anouilh added his voice to the chorus of protesters, ending his telegram with a typical flash of wit: 'Add in my name signatures of Sophocles and Shakespeare, often invoked by the Culture ministry.'

Far more damaging than the 'Appeal of the 121', which had precipitated a falling out with his daughter Florence, the 'Langlois affair' fatally tarnished Malraux's image as a 'liberal defender of the arts', giving him a completely different air – that of an intolerant despot.

This affair was the prelude to the revolt of French student youth, which broke out three months later against the 'pompous', 'old-fashioned', 'regal' regime of Charles de Gaulle. Once again Malraux found himself torn between his loyalty to the General and memories of his revolutionary youth. The crisis of May 1968 soon assumed a dramatic acuity when Daniel Cohn Bendit and his 'Apaches', not content to have placed 'imagination in power' in the lecture-halls of the Sorbonne, occupied the Odéon theatre – to the consternation of Jean-Louis Barrault, who nevertheless agreed to talk to the dishevelled debaters.

In 1966, when Barrault had scandalized the Gaullists (and many others) by staging Jean Genêt's *Les Paravents* – in which, among other 'values', the prestige of the French Army was dragged through layers of excremental mire – Malraux had courageously rebutted the criticisms formulated by Christian Bonnet (a conservative deputy from Brittany) by opposing all forms of censorship and citing as precedents the nineteenth-century uproars aroused by Charles Baudelaire's 'literature of rottenness' and the publication of *Madame Bovary*. But for Malraux this new 'Odéon affair' was far more serious. Not only had its director agreed to 'open a dialogue' (*dialoguer*) with the young enemies of the regime; not only had he gone as far as to declare, in a moment of servile self-abasement, that he was no longer 'the director of this theatre, but an actor like any other. Barrault is dead!'; he had also refused to hasten the evacuation of the theatre by the intellectual gypsies who had set up camp there by having the electric current and the telephone lines cut. If these were real grievances – and, according to Barrault, it was the Ministry of Cultural Affairs itself which, at the moment of the invasion, had urged: 'Open the doors and start a dialogue!' – what remained inexplicable was the strange silence observed by André Malraux and his stubborn refusal to receive Jean-Louis Barrault throughout the summer of 1968.

When, in early September, Barrault was finally sacked as director of the desecrated Théâtre de France (closed because of the damage done to its upholstery and interior decorations), the *Figaro*'s Jean-Jacques Gautier, who had been very severe in judging the première of *Les Paravents*, condemned the brusque manner in which he and Madeleine Renaud were informed of this dismissal. In *Le Monde*, Bertrand Poirot-Delpech was even harsher: 'The hypocritical praise of *La Nation*' – an organ of Gaullist propaganda – 'won't change anything. Installed at the Odéon like a prince, Barrault has been chased out of it like a lackey . . . After [a season of] fear has come, as was logical, *le temps du mépris*' ('the time of scorn'). Thus, held up before him as a mirror of reproach, the title of his weakest novel was used, thirty-three years later, to mock the mute, inscrutable Malraux of 1968.

Chapter 39

Last Years at Verrières

Late in the evening of Sunday 27 April, 1969, the French learned from radio and television broadcasts that Charles de Gaulle had lost his foolhardy bet. The referendum he had decided to hold in order to promote the 'regionalization' of France and the 'reform' (in fact, the emasculation) of the Senate had been rejected by a majority of more than 53% (who had voted 'No'), compared with less than 47% (who had voted 'Yes'). Shortly after midnight the General, in a laconic message transmitted by the Agence France-Presse, announced that he had ceased to exercise the functions of president of the Republic.

Like many other Gaullists, André Malraux was outraged by the 'foul blow' dealt by Valéry Giscard d'Estaing, to say nothing of the 'betrayal' perpetrated by Georges Pompidou, to whom Malraux, ten months before, had too hastily proposed a toast, promising him a 'national destiny'. On her return from Greece, from where she had sent him a postcard proposing a meeting for Monday 28 April, his former press attachée, Brigitte Friang, was greeted by a Malraux she had difficulty recognizing.

'What do you expect me to do for Greece' (the Greece of the Fascist colonels) he cried, 'when there is nothing I can do for France?' Malraux seemed in a state bordering on despair. 'His face even paler than usual, creased by twitches, he paced restlessly back and forth, describing the chaos into which France was going to tumble, now that it was deprived of General de Gaulle . . .

'Deploring, though I did, so much ingratitude . . .', Brigitte Friang later recalled, 'I was unable to believe the apocalyptic picture Malraux painted. We were entering an era of business, not of civil war.'

Seven weeks later, having resigned in his turn, André Malraux finally left his elegantly panelled office, on the Rue de Valois, handing over his ministry to his stout-hearted friend, Edmond Michelet. From 'La Lanterne', which he had decided to give up now that he was no longer minister of Cultural Affairs, he moved to Verrières with his books, his 'Greco-Buddhist' sculptures, his Caledonian masks, a Tibetan crown, the vase Mao Tse-tung had given him in Peking, as well as an extraordinary bull (fashioned from wire and strips of coloured paper), which he had one day picked up in a Mexican market-place. The Greco-Buddhist sculptures presented a problem which was not resolved until later, when they were placed in niches near to the main entrance, next to several Mexican cocks and the Chinese vase.

Louise offered André a small apartment on the second floor called 'The Boats' (because of the nineteenth-century sloops adorning the walls), where Orson Welles had once lodged on several occasions between 1954 and 1956. It included a bedroom, a study, and a bathroom. From the dormer windows on the eastern side, he could see the front gate and a small courtyard, from those on the western side, a generous expanse of green lawn, flanked by pines and birches and a magnificent Lebanese cedar, planted back in 1815. Here, beneath the eaves, he could make a new home for himself by hanging up a painting by Rouault, and above all a 'unique' Braque – a blue fishing-boat lying on the beige strand and as though crushed by a blackish sea and sky, whose darkness was enhanced by the black frame: a gift from the painter which Malraux placed so high that he claimed that it was with reference to this painting that all of Braque's other canvases should be judged. It was here, he thought, that he would camp until the duplex apartment of the Palais-Royal was properly fitted out and furnished by the spendthrift Louise, who was taking care of the internal decoration. ('Money ruins me,' Louise used to sigh with disarming insouciance, only too happy to be able to ruin herself so agreeably.)

In the meantime, André could content himself with Verrières' famous blue drawing-room, dominated by an equestrian painting of Louis XIV and where curtains, armchairs, and stools were all made of or covered by the same blue fabric with white flowers (a bit like the *fleur-de-lys* draperies of the Valois kings of France). It was here, with the full agreement of Louise's brothers, who occupied other parts of the house, that the former minister of Cultural Affairs established himself and where, except for several trips abroad, he was to spend the rest of his life.

Needless to say, many eyebrows were raised at this strange liaison between a former 'leftist', ever ready to adopt a revolutionary vocabulary – but an anti-Marxist, or rather a pre-Marxist one (in the stirring tradition of 1789) – and a *dame de lettres* from the topmost circle of French high society. It was the reverse of the friendship which in their old age had linked the beautiful bourgeoise from Lyon, Juliette Récamier, and the most noble Breton Viscount, René de Chateaubriand. A bold comparison Malraux would doubtless have dismissed as *farfelu* (fanciful), while being secretly flattered. To the accusation that he had betrayed his bourgeois origins by choosing a *vie de château* far more luxurious than the one he had known during the war, at Saint-Chamant and Fayrac, Malraux could always answer that Max Jacob had never betrayed his humble origins as the son of a Quimper tailor when he enlivened the evenings of certain salon hostesses in Paris. And what of Voltaire? His modest origins as the son of a Paris notary had not kept him from frequenting the salons of dukes and duchesses, the court of an English queen (Caroline), and from being lodged for fifteen years by a marquise. It is true that it had never occurred to the indulgent Madame du Châtelet to marry her illustrious guest, whereas certain 'friends' had, it seemed, thought of arranging a marriage between Louise and André – something that would certainly have helped to arrange matters with a tacitly disapproving *'Tante Yvonne'* (Madame de Gaulle). But when one day, during a television interview, a brash reporter had the temerity to ask Louise de Vilmorin why she didn't marry André Malraux, she shook her lovely head and with an infectious smile replied: 'But who today gets married? Priests are the only ones who do so.'

We know little of the intimate relations between Louise de Vilmorin and André Malraux, and it is better that it be so. But it was not always smooth sailing. There was, to begin with, the problem of the cats, for which Louise did not feel an overpowering passion. It was reluctantly and only after she had come to realize how inconsolable André was, when deprived of their company, that Louise agreed to take in several cats, for whom two tiny door openings were cut, so that they could come and go through the side door next to the fireplace in the drawing- room. But nothing vexed her more that to see *Fourrure* or *Lustrée* (a black cat with extraordinary green eyes) padding softly around – over the chairs and sofas and the tables of the *'salon bleu'*, gliding deftly among the glasses, the whisky decanter, and the Perrier bottle, before settling down, with the same casual nonchalance, in an armchair, from which she alone had the right to shoo away these creatures of divine ancestry. ·

Housed under the same roof, Louise and her illustrious guest belonged to two very different worlds. While André remained cloistered in his top-floor study, where at 5 o'clock in the afternoon he would see his secretary, to give her instructions (normally written out on bits of paper) as to the answers that were to be made to letters, bills, or incoming telephone calls – for he himself never telephoned nor replied to calls – Louise would receive the joyous band of her friends. Of a gregarious disposition and liking to shine in the midst of amusing dinner-table companions, she often risked eclipsing the sombre star seated opposite her. And if the hilarity she had a way of unleashing with some hasty quip or impertinent remark threatened to drag the level of discourse down into the shallow waters of frivolity, she would be called to order with a peremptory *'Définissez!'* or *'Approfondissez!'* More than once, when a carefree Louise ventured to criticize Stendhal, calling him something of a fraud, there was a moment of silence, broken by an imperious *'Dévelopez, Louise!'*

Years later the writer Jean d'Ormesson, who made several pilgrimages to Verrières, recalled that Malraux 'concerned himself solely with religion. He spoke of the Apocalypse, of Saint John, of the Gospels . . . He was Moses on Mount Nebo, crushing me beneath the tablets of the Law.

'Every now and then poor Louise would utter a few words. Malraux would interrupt and, pointing a finger, would say: "*Développez! Développez!*" in an authoritarian tone. Poor Louise was petrified. Yet she was very brilliant. But her puns and plays on words lost their effect next to Malraux's incandescent improvisations.'

This judgement may seem harsh – for others who saw him almost every day often saw Malraux melt and laugh at Louise's spontaneous repartee. But it probably captures the atmosphere that reigned at Verrières during the first months of Malraux's stay. While his departure from the Ministry of Cultural Affairs had brought him a certain relief from the irksome chores and obligations of administrative life, he had devoted too much time and nervous energy to the task not to be worried by the future of of a ministry he alone could have set up. And it was certainly not his intimate conviction that France, without De Gaulle, was headed downwards, if not plunging headlong into an abyss of mediocrity, which rendered him less trenchant, dogmatic, and sectarian: a mood aggravated, curiously enough, by the glasses of Scotch he emptied in the evening and which had the effect of exciting his caustic verve rather than of calming his tense nerves.

Toward the end of this unhappy summer of 1969 André Malraux slipped, fell, and broke a finger. The autumn was also painful for Louise de Vilmorin, who came down with a serious attack of 'flu. In December, after having been invited to lunch at Colombey-les-Deux-Eglises – it was the first time he had seen General de Gaulle since his abrupt resignation in April – André decided to offer Louise a change of climate. Leaving the wintry overcast of the Ile de France, they would go spend the New Year in the sun-blessed Moroccan oasis of Marrakesh. The idea delighted Louise, whose health remained frail.

Shortly before Christmas, several old friends came to dine at Verrières. Toward the end of the meal, Claude Bénédick, who had managed to get himself appointed secretary-general of the Comédie-Française while remaining the Agence France-Presse's accredited correspondent to the House of Molière, picked up a candlestick with which to light a cigarette. Louise promptly stopped him: 'Never do that. It brings bad luck.' She wanted to protect her friend Claude against misfortune, not suspecting that it was she herself·who was threatened.

The day after Christmas Louise, still plagued by 'flu, called the doctor, who prescribed an injection. It was close to 7 in the evening. André Malraux had returned upstairs after having come down, as he often did, to empty a glass of whisky with Louise who, this time, was propped up in her four-poster bed. A nurse prepared the syringe and gave her the prescribed injection. Louise then turned – and suddenly stiffened.

When, alerted by the unusual sound of running feet, André Malraux's secretary entered the bedroom a minute or two later, she found him gripping one of the bed-posts, his ashen face hideously contorted. The companion of his old age had just died of a heart attack.

The irresistible Louise, whose carefree gaiety and witty sallies had bewitched so many men and women – beginning with Antoine de Saint-Exupéry, Jean Cocteau, Gaston Gallimard, Pali Palffy, Duff Cooper and his wife Diana – would no longer be enlivening the blue drawing-room of Verrières. For the sixth time in his life – counting the disappearance of his two half-brothers Roland and Claude, the loss of his two sons and of their mother – the Angel of Death had struck André Malraux.

As a special favour (obtained from the local prefect) Louise de Vilmorin was buried in the park of Verrières, which she so loved. No upright slab, no marble tomb marks the spot, today completely overgrown by grass. Instead, there is a small stone bench on which were carved her personal emblem, a four-leaf clover, and her motto, *Au secours*, both as she liked to draw them. She had asked that a cherry tree be planted nearby, so that young people could come, sit on the little bench and eat cherries. This wish was faithfully respected by her three daughters, her four brothers, and André Malraux. Princess Marthe Bibesco added her own homage by having a magnolia planted not far away.

Inconsolable during the first few weeks, Malraux never set foot again in the duplex apartment overlooking the Palais-Royal, which he had bought for Louise and himself, but which she had not had time to furnish. With the full assent of her brothers, he became the first 'tenant' of the country-house at Verrières, where the ground floor and the *salon bleu* were kept virtually unaltered, as they had been when Louise was alive. The only change was the fitting out of a downstairs study where henceforth he could receive his friends or the journalists who wished to interview him.

After this terrible shock it is hardly surprising that 1970 should have been a year of gestation rather than of creation. It was marked by Gallimard's publication of *Le Triangle noir* – three variations on the theme of the demonic, in the form of essays devoted to Choderlos de Laclos and his *Liaisons dangereuses*, to Goya (previously published with illustrations under the title of *Saturne*), and to that uncompromising revolutionary, Saint-Just.

In June Malraux was shocked by the trip Charles de Gaulle undertook to Francisco Franco's Spain (to which he himself had never returned since 1939), but he was greatly moved by the extraordinary compliment the General paid to him by writing, in the first volume of his *Mémoires d'espoir* (published in October): 'To my right I have, and will always have, André Malraux, . . . a genius friend.'

The joy, however, was shortlived. For two or three weeks later, on November 10th, the news was ticker-taped by the Agence France-Presse and immediately flashed around the world: General de Gaulle had died the evening before, at Colombey-les-Deux-Eglises. The French government – which is to say, President Georges Pompidou and Prime Minister Jacques Chaban-Delmas – organized a grandiose funeral ceremony in Notre-Dame Cathedral, to be celebrated on 12 November in honour of the last remaining political giant of the Second World War. At the same time, in accordance with the wishes expressed in the General's will, his widow and the members of his family prepared a simple ceremony at Colombey-les-Deux-Eglises, which was to be held that same Tuesday, but in the afternoon.

Did Malraux first proceed to Notre-Dame, where at 11 in the morning so many heads of state and prime ministers (Richard Nixon, Indira Gandhi, King Baudoin of Belgium, Emperor Haile Selassie of Ethiopia, the Shah of Iran, etc.) gathered to pay their last respects? Be that as it may, in order to reach Champagne, he hired a helicopter at the Orly airport and had himself flown to Chalons-sur-Marne. At Colombey, the village church was already crammed with fervent Gaullists and the simple ceremony was about to begin when a Citroën DS braked to a screeching stop outside. From one door emerged André Malraux, from the other the novelist Romain Gary, already a rising star in the Gallimard firmament. To the astonishment of the mourners in the nave, Malraux now staggered forward (as his biographer Jean Lacouture described the scene three years later), 'his coat flung open, arms limp, a haggard phantom with an unsteady gait, a lock of mourning hair falling across the devastated brow . . . plunging ahead for a kind of charge. Groping his way up the central aisle like a blind prophet, he stumbled against the trestle that had been set up in front of the altar to receive the coffin, and seemed stunned before the plaster figure of Christ overhanging the choir.' Room was made for him in one of the front pews, and there he stood, strangely stooped and seeming absent, chewing his finger-nails as the church doors were opened to let in the corpse, borne by twelve young village lads.

From this second shock, which smote him eleven months after the death of Louise de Vilmorin, came a new book, or more exactly a chapter of a second autobiographical tome, which Malraux had not dared to write while the General was still alive. The title he gave to it, *Les chênes qu'on abat* (Felled Oaks), was drawn from the famous elegy Victor Hugo had composed after the death of Théophile Gautier:

> *O! quel farouche bruit font dans le crépuscule*
> *Les chênes qu'on abat pour le bûcher d'Hercule.*

If, quoting Hugo, Malraux employed the plural, it was because he considered himself to be one of the stout 'oaks' that those wretched 'traitors', Georges Pompidou and Valéry Giscard d'Êstaing, had managed to axe. The result, in any case, was a charming artistic reconstitution of the visit Malraux had made to Colombey-les-Deux-Eglises on 11 December, 1969. Into the dining-room table talk and the later conversation in the General's living-room, were freely interwoven phrases De Gaulle or Malraux had uttered on other occasions, along with – who knows? – remarks he would doubtless have liked to make during conversations with the General. But what does it matter? For the striking thing here – and it is astonishing that as shrewd a connoisseur of French literature as John Weightman (in *The Observer*) should not have appreciated this – is the relaxed, informal, anything but stilted nature of the portrait Malraux painted of the General, depicting him in his country-house, lunching with his wife, playing with his cat, Grigri,

408 · André Malraux

and speaking of everything – of death, women, Christianity, the illusion of happiness – in the peaceful setting of 'La Boisserie'.

It is these tiny descriptive touches, far more than the Chateaubriandesque heights to which the dialogue occasionally ascends, that give this little book a special flavour, making of Charles de Gaulle a genuinely human being rather than a remote, abstract, legendary figure. In 1954, after the publication of the first volume of General de Gaulle's *Mémoires de Guerre*, the Swiss journalist-historian Herbert Lüthy, in a brilliant critical review, pointed out that if one wished to know what had really happened in Bordeaux during the crucial day of 17 June, 1940, it was not to the first volume of De Gaulle's memoirs (*L'Appel*), where the events of this day were treated with Olympian aloofness, that one should go, but rather to *Assignment to Catastrophe* – the fascinating reminiscences of General Edward Spears, the principal architect of the historic flight to London which transformed a somewhat obscure two-star general into the legendary 'man of June 18th'. This, but with the added touch of genius, is what distinguishes, or rather separates, De Gaulle's *Mémoires d'Espoir* – where everything is solemn, cold, pretentious – from Malraux's *Les chênes qu'on abat*.

He had hardly finished *Les chênes qu'on abat* when, once again, he was possessed by the demon of action. In March 1971 a revolt broke out in eastern Pakistan, where an overwhelming majority of Bengalis had voted, along with their leader, Sheikh Mujibur Rahman, in favour of an autonomous Moslem regime, freed from the ponderous military tutelage of western Pakistan. Marshal Yahia Khan's reaction was to regard those elections as a form of mutinous behaviour, to have Sheikh Mujibur arrested and the revolt drowned in blood. Terrified by pitiless repression, millions of Bengalis fled their land and sought refuge in the neighbouring provinces of India. For the vast majority of Frenchmen, this was one more episode in the post-colonial history of Asia, in which Europeans would do well not to get involved. Not for Malraux. The fact that in 'his' Asia – comprising India, Pakistan, China, Thailand, Indochina, all of which he had visited – a subjugated people were rising up against a reactionary military regime seemed to him highly tragic and their dire lot intolerable. It was, transposed to the Orient, a new version of the 1934 revolt of the poor miners of Asturias against the conservative government of Gil Robles. It was time to act. But how? Well, by issuing a call for volunteers, as he had done in 1936 for the Republicans of Spain. The Spanish Republicans had lacked an effective bombing force; he had created one. The Bengalis of eastern Pakistan lacked officers (most of their officer corps came from western Pakistan); he would train and form them.

On September 17th Malraux made a radio broadcast announcing his intention of going to fight in Bengal. He appealed for volunteers – that is, for retired officers, like himself, through whose veins there still coursed a brave, courageous blood, a heart ready to throb for the cause of liberty.

Visibly, or rather inwardly, André Malraux had not changed. At the age of 27 he had wanted with several NRF authors to mount an expedition to free Leon Trotsky, whom Stalin had banished to distant Siberia. In 1971, just short of 70, he wanted to come to the rescue of the oppressed people of Bengal. But . . . there was the rub. Notwithstanding a ferocious will-power and a brain in a state of permanent fermentation, he was physically no longer the same man. When, toward the end of September, Brigitte Friang came to have tea with him at Verrières, she was struck by the change. 'His tallness sapped by the sagging curve of the spinal column, he now walked unsteadily. Where was the Malraux who used to gallop up and down the stairs of the Boulevards des Capucines?' She herself answered this question by writing (a couple of pages farther on in *Un autre Malraux*) that he was 'worn out by nerves that had been kept overly taut for years, by a mind ceaselessly solicited by too many interests, by too many nights torn from his daily labours in order to further his literary works, and with it all and for much too long, little pills to keep him from falling asleep in the evening, and little pills to wake him up in the morning, and all this without forcing himself to lay off alcohol.'

This did not keep Malraux from outlining his crazy project to his former press attachée, who had now become a roving reporter for *Le Monde diplomatique*. Already, he explained to her, he was being submerged by offers of enlistment from hardy volunteers, ready to follow him to a distant land which was soon to assume the name of Bengla-Desh. It was not enthusiasm that was lacking. And, by the way, he asked her – the tea by this time had probably given way to whisky – had she kept her hand in . . . how 'good a shot' was she? Though startled by the question, the undaunted *pistolera* hastened to reassure him: recently, in her village in the Vaucluse, she had challenged a gendarmerie captain to a match with an 11 mm Colt, 'a real jewel for ladies'.

The answer reassured Malraux. She had come to ask him for letters of recommendation to Indira Gandhi and to Yaprakash Narayan? So much the better. But she must forget the journalistic trip she was planning to make to the country of the Mahatma. He, Colonel Berger (1971 model) had something much more palpitating to propose to her: that she, who had had a taste or two of war and had won her parachutist wings, accompany him to India as his second-in-command.

One must read the succulent pages Brigitte Friang devotes to this extravagant adventure (in *Un autre Malraux*) to appreciate its wonderfully *farfelu* character. For the most flabbergasting thing of all is that this woman, who was frankly suspicious of Indira Gandhi's subtle machinations, was nevertheless ready to march; to pack her bags and her revolver and even to enlist the services of a tall, blue-eyed nephew whose English, picked up in South Africa, was so perfect that he could pass himself off any time as an officer recently graduated from Sandhurst.

And yet . . . this was no schoolboy prank, no casually envisaged exploit. Quite the contrary, it was with the utmost seriousness that Malraux-Berger talked to her of this Foreign Legion of officer-trainers he was planning to form. 'Once again,' as she later wrote, 'I was able to verify what I was already conscious of, to wit that while Malraux was gifted with a keen perception of the *drollerie* of situations, of the comic side of events, and above all of their incongruity, he was totally devoid of a sense of humour.' For what surprised her most in the course of their two-hour conversation was its tragic tone and, on the part of Malraux, the repeated evocation of death. ('If I die . . . If I am killed . . . If they kill me . . .') It was not simply the half-brother of Roland and Claude Malraux who was conjuring up this possibility; it was the romantic man of letters who could not forget that the great Lord Byron had died at Mussalonghi, where he had gone to help the Hellenes in their struggle for freedom.

In the end, nothing came of this extravagant project. Brigitte Friang was able to fly off to Montreal on a journalistic assignment in Canada. As for Indira Gandhi, she asked for a bit of patience from the almost septuagenarian friend of her father, Pandit Nehru, knowing full well (but without saying so) that she had no need of a resuscitated Colonel Lawrence to hasten the dismemberment of the two portions of a Greater Pakistan, which had been invented on the spur of the moment by the lawyer, Mohammed Jinnah. The Indian Army could take care of the job unaided.

But this was not the end of this incredible story. In December, exasperated by the attitude of the President of the United States (who had decided to send an aircraft-carrier and a war fleet into the Gulf of Bengal, in the hope that this might calm the bellicose ardour of India's prime minister), Malraux addressed an 'Open Letter to Mr Nixon', which was published on the front page of the Figaro on December 18th. It was both a plea on behalf of the oppressed peoples of Bengal and a severe critique of the foreign policy pursued by successive governments in Washington, which had effectively allied itself with an oppressive militarist regime. 'You are going to try to establish a dialogue with China which you have postponed for twenty years: the ancient dialogue of the richest country in the world with the poorest. Let us hope, with regard to a free Bengal, that you will not wait for twenty years before remembering that it ill behoves the country of the Declaration of Independence to crush [human] wretchedness fighting for its own independence.'

The distant successor of Thomas Jefferson might have taken umbrage. Not at all. During a stop-over in Paris, Indira Gandhi informed a crestfallen André Malraux that, for the time being, she could cope quite well on her own and without French volunteers. Richard Nixon, on the other hand, seized the ball on the rebound. As a stubborn *Realpolitiker* who was anxious to extricate his country from the Indo-Chinese morass, he invited André Malraux to visit him in Washington in order to offer him advice for the trip he was planning to make to Peking.

So here he was, in February 1972, once again making the trip to Washington he had undertaken nine years before for the unveiling of the *Gioconda*. But this time, it was at Uncle Sam's expense, in a TWA plane, and accompanied by his pretty secretary, Corinne Godfernaux. On their arrival at Dulles airport there was a comic mix-up when a zealous passport inspector from the Immigration Service refused to admit Malraux on the grounds that his diplomatic passport did not carry a proper visa. The misunderstanding was finally cleared up – but only after a telephone call had been put in to the White House, where, much embarrassed, an official confirmed that Yes, Monsieur André Malraux had been personally invited to the capital by the President of the United States.

Twice received during his brief stay by Richard Nixon – first in the Oval Office, then at a White House dinner thrown in his honour – Malraux talked at length of Mao (essentially 'an old man facing death') and of the terrible fear under which he had been labouring, when he had met him in 1965, that the Russians and the Americans were going to gang up on China by using a dozen atomic bombs to destroy his country's industrial centres. Above all, he insisted on the insular and continental character, far more than the expansionist aspect of Chinese foreign policy. He went as far as to declare that 'China's activity in Vietnam was simply an imposture. There was a period when the friendship between China and Russia was serene and cloudless, when the Chinese allowed Russian weapons to cross their territory to reach Vietnam. But China has never helped anybody. Neither Pakistan, nor Vietnam. Chinese policy is a brilliant lie. The Chinese don't believe it; they believe only in China. China alone. For Mao, China is a continent. It's a kind of Australia. China alone counts. If China must receive the Sultan of Zanzibar, it does so. Or the President of the United States. For the Chinese, it has no importance.' However, he congratulated Richard Nixon on the boldness he was showing in undertaking a trip to China, comparing him to those sixteenth-century explorers who set sail without knowing if they would ever reach the hoped-for lands.

On Saturday, 29 April, France's second television channel (*Antenne 2*) began broadcasting an extraordinary series entitled *La Légende du siècle*. Filmed at Verrières by Claude Santelli and Françoise Verny over a six-month period in 1971, this TV series revealed a Malraux who was totally unknown to most viewers, even to those who had read his novels.

After seeing the first episode, devoted to 'The People of the Night', Paul Guimard wrote enthusiastically in the weekly *L'Express*: 'This face whose disjointed features are filled with anguish, this glance which is either inward-gazing or projected far away, but rarely focused at the right distance for the viewer, this disarticulated voice such as the oracle at Delphi once had, these crumbled discourses of the Malraux of *La Légende du siècle*, how shall we ever forget them?' The praise was all the more remarkable, since Guimard had begun by predicting a 'less than plausible future' for *Les chênes qu'on abat*, had dismissed *Le Musée imaginaire* as 'a cocktail of abstruse postulates, of chaotic considerations, and whose finest pages owe too much to Elie Faure.' He had also quoted this interesting comment made by François Mitterrand: 'I wonder if Malraux doesn't belong to that lineage of writers whose genius is fully expressed in conversation and which is dissipated in writing.'

But let us continue quoting from this article, which graphically transcribes the impression made by this first broadcast – 'devoted to the Resistance it deals in fact with torture and freedom . . . . and is placed under the double patronage of Jean of Patmos and Victor Hugo. Saint John, because the Gospels are 'the apogee of the expression of Christ.' Hugo, because 'a great tragic poet is a prophet'. Which means that anecdotes merely figure here to help André Malraux's train of thought reach sometimes hazy heights, but there are illuminated by the magic of lyrical words. One must need have nothing but cinders in the place of a heart to remain insensitive to this driving, burning monologue, which revolves interminably around the agonizing condition of Man, even if the people for Malraux, are above all the formless mineral ore of History, which great men illustrate. . .

'Whether a sudden awakening or a product of remorse, this *Légende du siècle*, a masterpiece of televisual art, has made us hear accents we had long been deprived of.'

In November, just as the second series of *La Légende du siècle* (four successive Saturdays) was ending, Malraux was seized by nervous disorders of a troubling kind. His legs kept giving way beneath him, he kept falling down, he suffered, but without losing consciousness, dizzy spells and convulsive spasms which made him lose his balance. Doctors, and then specialists were urgently summoned to Verrières by Sophie de Vilmorin, a niece who had been adopted and partly brought up by Louise and who, now separated from her German husband, had come to Verrières to look after her aunt's posthumous works. Having become a faithful friend of André Malraux ever since 1966, when he had examined him for the first time, Dr Louis Bertagna, a first-rate psychiatrist with a robust sense of humour, had him hospitalized at the Salpêtrière Hospital, in southeastern Paris, where it was discovered that the cerebellum was threatened. Malraux spent one month here.

From this new ordeal came another book, as curious as those that had preceded it: a kind of commentary or journal (but without precise dates), where meditations about what he was experiencing or seeing round about him were linked to reminiscences in which past and present were constantly intermingled. Shamelessly plundering his past writings – notably the description of the gas attack in *Les Noyers de l'Altenburg* – he rewrote it in a slightly different form, like a player reshuffling a pack of cards before dealing them out. Variations on a theme, or rather on several themes, by André Malraux.

Later, Pierre Bockel said of *Lazare* that it was one of the most beautiful books ever written about Death. But, in reality, if the shadow of death hovers over all of this semi-oneiric book, in which the real and the unreal constantly merge and intermingle, it deals with everything: illness, the fear of death, courage, suicide, folly, suffering, forms of torture and among them, the agony of Christ.

Back at Verrières, where the gentle Sophie de Vilmorin continued to take care of him, it was a decidedly different André Malraux who greeted his daughter Florence and his increasingly rare friends. He no longer touched a drop of alcohol, not even wine, contenting himself with hot or iced tea, or fruit juice. He continued to frequent his favourite restaurant, Lasserre, where he went to have lunch two or three times a week with Sophie de Vilmorin, but without drinking any coffee at the end of the meal, nor – which was even more surprising – lighting up a cigarette. From one day to the next he had given up smoking. Completely and forever. This victory over a terrible temptation was one more triumph of the will, a manifestation of that *Selbstüberwinding* (self-overcoming), which was supposed to characterise the Nietzschean superman.

No less curiously, this total absence of intoxicants calmed him, made him less irritable, more tolerant. He no longer needed to embark on long ocean cruises, as he had done in the past with Sophie de Vilmorin and a painter and jewelry designer of Hungarian origin named Caroline ('Gogo') Karolyi, as far as Iceland and the Arctic Circle, or in the Mediterranean as far as Dubrovnik and the Dalmatian coast. He had settled down at last, had become a sedentary person. To be sure, since the death of the witty Louise, a great lover of fêtes and distractions, life at the château had greatly changed. One day Sophie de Vilmorin, who had originally come to Verrières to oversee the publication of three of her aunt's posthumous works before being asked to look after Malraux and his own writings, was asked by André: 'What are we going to do? Do you like to receive?' She hesitated, afraid to disappoint him, then decided to tell the truth. 'No,' she replied. 'Ouf!' said Malraux, with a gesture of relief.

With Sophie de Vilmorin, who was among other things an attentive 'listener', André Malraux had undoubtedly found a devoted companion who knew how to create a conjugal atmosphere (even though they were not married) of perfect serenity. Gone, vanished forever, were the frictions and rows that had marked his life with the tirelessly talkative Clara, an insanely jealous and embittered Josette, an often distraught Madeleine, lost in a world of music where, outclassed, he did not feel at home. Louise, of course, had been the glorious exception; for, as he explained to her niece Sophie, as a general rule he disliked women writers, often remarking after meeting one of them: 'That's a man'. After years and years of struggle, during which at every moment he had felt the need to assert himself, he could now at last relax, feeling himself surrounded and protected by a great tenderness, mingled with love and admiration. Hence the serenity one senses, even in the style of his last works. Hence also certain avowals which he would probably not have dared to make to others, such as saying, for example, that while admiring Buddhism, he could never dream of becoming a Buddhist, even preferring, if he had to choose, to become a Christian. But not, of course, just any sort of Christian. For one day, when Sophie startled him by asking if he would rather be a Pope than an anchorite, he pondered the question deeply before finally replying, 'Both.'

In April 1973 he left with her by plane for India, where he was graciously received by Indira Gandhi, no longer opposed to his visiting Bangladesh, now a fully independent country. He delivered several speeches at Dacca and Chittagong, and was awarded an honorary degree at the University of Rajshahi. After which, still accompanied by Sophie de Vilmorin, he continued his journey all the way up to Katmandu, where he was received by the King of Nepal.

This year, 1973, was almost a second apotheosis in the life of André Malraux – at any rate in the realm of art. It was at Saint Paul de Vence, on the Côte d'Azur, that the Maeght Foundation organized a special exhibition in his honour: 'André Malraux and the Imaginary Museum'.

In 1974 he published another fragment of the second volume of his reminiscences, for which he chose the decidedly Malrucian title of *Métamorphoses*. (The first volume, including the *Antimémoires*, had already been published; while both volumes were to carry the overall title of *Miroir des Limbes* – Mirror of Limbo). *La tête d'obsidienne*, which he dedicated to Gaston Palewski, 'who was the friend of Picasso and of whom Picasso was the friend', was, like everything Malraux wrote during these crepuscular years, a strange blend of reminiscences and meditation. In this case the 'plot' gravitated around two poles: modern art and Pablo Picasso, whom Malraux had frequented at the time when he was living and working on the Rue des Grands-Augustins, not far from the Seine. It was a very Malrucian Picasso who emerged from these pages, perhaps even more so than the transformed Charles de Gaulle of *Les chênes qu'on abat*.

With *Hôtes de passage*, published by Gallimard in 1975, it was another caravan of dialogues and descriptions that passed like a fairy-tale mirage before the marvelling reader's eye. Léopold Senghor, the great man of letters and President of Senegal; the museum of the Acropolis in 1922; Georges Salles (director of the Museums of France) and an astonishing Turko-Circassian soothsayer who claims to be a descendant of the last Ottoman Sultan, Abdul-Hamid, and who treats her dumbfounded guests to a dramatic reconstruction of some of the most dramatic moments in the life of Alexander the Great – an anthology item in the *farfelu* genre meriting a place alongside of the Clappique of the *Antimémoires*; Max Torres, secretary of State for Catalonia during the Spanish Civil war, coming to see Malraux in his ministerial office during the student riots of June 1968 – such are the principal figures in this astonishing mosaic. Which ends with these words, into which Malraux poured all of his pessimism: *Le temps des limbes* (The Time of Limbo).

Then, as though this firework display of the imagination needed to be corrected by a return to criticism, Malraux began a study of the evolution of modern literature. It was almost as though his career was closing in on itself to form a circle, or a horseshoe. The literary critic who had begun, half a century before, with an essay on cubist poetry, was thus ending his life with a metaphysical analysis of the evolution of the novel and of what awaits it in an epoch increasingly dominated by the tyranny of audiovisual sounds and images.

In November 1976, feeling greatly weakened by the treatment he had begun in August, André Malraux was transported to the Henri Mondor hospital centre at Créteil (southeast of Paris), where his daughter Florence and the faithful Sophie de Vilmorin came every day to sit beside his bed. This time it was no nervous disorder that was the trouble. The malady was incurable: an advanced state of cancer. At 9.30 a.m. on November 23rd he died, choked by a blood-clot in the lung.

Since his will made no stipulations regarding his burial, Florence and Sophie de Vilmorin opted for simplicity, knowing that in any case a grandiose ceremony would be held in his honour by his former comrades-in-arms of the Alsace-Lorraine Brigade. Having remained an agnostic, while fervently believing in the psychic value of every form of spiritual faith, André Malraux would certainly have refused a religious ceremony. He was therefore buried in the cemetery of the little town of Verrières-le-Buisson, not far from the country house where he had spent his final years of happiness.

The burial was conducted with extreme simplicity, in the presence of Pierre Bockel, who hurried over from Strasbourg, where he had risen to become archdeacon of the cathedral. As with De Gaulle, there was no funeral oration. The road leading to the graveyard was packed with mourners, many of them bearing flowers. Among the wreaths two in particular attracted considerable attention. The first expressed the deep sorrow of the restaurant Lasserre, of which which André Malraux had been such an assiduous client. The second was offered by the French Communist Party.

Acknowledgements

I would like, first of all, to thank Roger Straus, who most kindly introduced me to Antoine Gallimard. Words fail me when it comes to expressing all I owe to Jacqueline Blanchard, Albert Beuret's faithful assistant, and to Jean Grosjean, whose invaluable recollections of his experiences as a prisoner-of-war in 1940 filled an extraordinary lacuna in the reading public's knowledge of André Malraux's wartime experiences.

I would also like to express my great gratitude to Florence Malraux, who was unstinting in her support and encouragement, as well as to Madeleine Malraux, her son Alain, and Sophie de Vilmorin, who helped me in my research in many ways.

I also owe thanks to my friend, Claude Charpentier, who has done so much to preserve what can still be saved of the old 'commune libre' of Montmartre; Jean-Paul Dupont, of the Centre André-Malraux, and the historian, Jean Astruc, who was a mine of intelligent information on Bondy in the early years of this century; Jacqueline Paulhan, who kindly let me examine André Malraux's letters and postcards to Jean Paulhan; François Chapon, the urbane curator (since retired) of the Jacques Doucet library, and his two assistants, Nicole Prévot and the late, much regretted Jacqueline Zacchi; Albert Lebonheur and Francine Tissot, of the Guimet Museum, for their precious advice and information concerning Cambodia and the still mystery-shrouded art of Gandhâra; Vera Marigo and Michael Barry for useful background information on Afghanistan and ancient Bactria; Sir Ernst Gombrich for the interesting things he had to say about that distinctly odd duck, Josef Strzygowski; and Professor Walter Langlois, who with extraordinary generosity made available to me essays and articles he had written, which I would otherwise probably have missed.

I am also indebted to Jean-Claude Fasquelle and Martine Savary for allowing me to consult the press clippings of *La Tentation de l'Occident*, *Les Conquérants*, and *La Voie royale* preserved by the Bernard Grasset publishing company; to Ariane Fasquelle and André de Vilmorin for their help in obtaining a magnificent photo of Louise de Vilmorin playing the guitar; to Jean Bothorel, who most graciously let me see a few pages of his manuscript before his *Louise* had been published; to Ambassador Francis Lacoste and his daughter, Dominique Lacoste-Riggs, for so kindly lending me a copy of Gabriel Dardaud's scintillating recollections of his life as a journalist in Egypt; to General Lucien Robineau and Daniel Hary, of the SHAA (Service historique de l'Armée de l'Air) for information on Edouard Corniglion-Molinier; to Suzanne Chantal and José Augusto de Santos, who so graciously lent me photographs of Josette Clotis; and to Abidine Dino for his recollections of Roland Malraux in Moscow.

For the period of the Spanish Civil War I owe special thanks to Jean Lasserre, the enterprising editor of that unique aviation quarterly, *Icare*; to his friend and associate editor, Colonel Edmond Petit, who allowed me to consult a special Malraux file he had been compiling for years; to Colonel Victor Véniel and Jean Gisclon, both former fighter pilots in Malraux's international squadron; John Blake, who kindly put me in touch with General Jesús Salas Larrazábal; and, last but not least, to Paul Nothomb, the anything but doctrinaire 'political commissar' of *España* squadron.

I could not have written the seven chapters covering the Second World War without the generous aid offered to me by Monsignor Pierre Bockel, the former chaplain of the Alsace-Lorraine Brigade, its tireless 'Mercury', Dr Bernard Metz, and Antoine Diener-Ancel, the valiant commander of the Brigade's Strasbourg battalion. The same goes for the invaluable information I was offered by Jacques Poirier, author of the first detailed account of Colonel Berger's Resistance activities with the SOE in 1944. I also owe thanks to Raoul Verhagen (the 'Captain Arthur' of the 'Interallied Headquarters'); to Marc Gerschel, Gustave Houver, Henri Solbach, and to General Léon George, the son-in-law of Major (later General) Pierre Jacquot, who gave the Alsace-Lorraine Brigade the professional expertise it so badly needed. To this list I would like to add the names of Mireille Berl, Jean-Luc Jeener, Princess Tatiana Metternich, Herbert Lottmann, and Jean Lescure, the enterprising wartime smuggler and publisher of forbidden literature. To Madame Jenka Sperber I also owe special thanks, for the kindness she showed me in recalling certain moments in her and her husband's past.

For the post-war period I wish to thank Jacques Baumel for his helpful comments on the MLN Congress of January 1945, of which he was one of the principal organizers, and Brigitte Friang, who was most helpful in correcting certain errors I had made in the thirty-sixth chapter, devoted to Malraux's activities as the 'herald' of the Gaullist RPF.

In the field of Malraux's cultural activities, I must mention the help and advice offered to me by Claude Winter, Jean Meyer, Jean Piat, Jacques Sieyès, Claude Bénédick, and Madame Rasgonikov, the former librarian of the Comédie-Française; Pierre Moinot, Geneviève Gentil, and Martine Poulain for their comments on problems of book publishing; Maryvonne de Saint Pulgent for her expert advice on problems concerning opera; Marcel Landowski, Jacqueline Colin, Madeleine Rodlphe, Janine Merley, Bernard

Martinat, Jacques Masson-Forestier, Raymond Gallois-Montbrun, Jacques Chaillet, and Sandrine Grandgambe for their help in guiding me through the labyrithine world of Music in France; Renée Lichtig, Alain Marchand, and Glenn Myrent for their helpful cooperation in questions concerning Henri Langlois' Cinémathèque.

I would also like to thank for various services rendered, Jacques Maréchal, Paul Stebel, François Trécourt, Dominique Aury, Odette Poulain, Françine Rieu, Caroline ('Gogo') Karolyi, Vyonne Panitza, Rüdiger von Pachelbel, Bernard Morlino, M. and Mme Sosthènes de Vilmorin, who so warmly welcomed me at Verrières-le-Buisson, Dr Louis Bertagna, and Pierre Sudreau, the Frenchman chiefly responsible for the cleaning and 'face-lifting' of the grimy façades of Paris buildings.

I owe special thanks to Michelle Lapautre, and also to Françoise Verny, of the Flammarion publishing company, for the confidence they were willing to place in this biographical venture; as I do to Abel Gerschenfeld, who struggled valiantly with a manuscript which kept growing larger and larger.

I am also deeply indebted to Caroline Dawnay and Anthony Whittome for an equally and most heartening confidence in my biographical ability.

Finally, to close this already long list, I wish to suggest (being unable properly to express) all I owe to Robert von Hagemeister and to his widow, Annette, in whose lovely home some of the chapters in this book were written, with the more than helpful encouragement of their children, Viviane and Peter. More than grateful am I too to my step-son, Michael Aminoff and his wife Jan, without whose unwavering support I could never have sustained the effort needed to complete this book: one which my wife Elena, from the very start, wanted me to write.

Notes

These reference notes have been reduced to essentials. Readers interested in obtaining more precise page and line references can find them in the French edition of this book (title: *André Malraux*), published by Flammarion in 1994.

The following abbreviations have been used:

AG   André Gide.
AM   André Malraux.
Antim   *Antimémoires*.
BNms   Bibliothèque Nationale, Paris, manuscript department.
CdeG   Charles de Gaulle.
CH   *La Condition humaine*.
CM   Clara Malraux.
Corr   *Correspondance*.
CPD   'Cahiers de la Petite Dame' (vols. IV, V, VI of *Cahiers André Gide*).
Doucet   Bibliothèque littéraire Jacques Doucet (part of the Bibliothèque Sainte-Geneviève, Paris).
E&D   *Etre & Dire* (articles and essays collected by Martine de Courcel and published by Plon in 1976).
EFEO   Ecole Française d'Extrême-Orient.
MdeB   *Alain Malraux's Les Marronniers de Boulogne*.
NL   *Nouvelles littéraires*.
NRF   *Nouvelle Revue Française* (monthly).
Pl. I.   Malraux, *Oeuvres complètes*, Ed. de la Pléiade, I.
RLM   *Revue des Lettres modernes*.
TCL   *Twentieth Century Literature* (Autumn 1978).
VM   *Walter Langlois, Via Malraux*.
VR   *La Voie royale*.

1. FROM MONTMARTRE TO BONDY

Page

1 The details concerning Montmartre were obtained with the help of Claude Charpentier, founder and curator of the Musée du Vieux Montmartre.

Page
1–2 The information concerning Alphonse Malraux was obtained from the biographies of Robert Payne and Jean Lacouture; also from an AM interview granted to Jean Farran (*Paris-Match*, 19 June 1954).
1–3 For birth, marriage dates, etc. see *Chronologie*, Pl. I, LV–LVI.
4–6 When I visited Bondy (twice) in 1992, the house at no. 16, rue de la Gare was still standing, though threatened by plans to demolish it. Information about the Institution Dugand and other particulers about life in Bondy during the early years of this century were kindly provided by the historian, Jean Astruc.
 6 Chevasson quotation in Lacouture, *AM*, 18.
7–8 On AM and Henry Robert, Astruc, 'Le Fils de l'Epicière'.
 9 Unpublished fragment from *Les Conquérants*, in Pl. I, 1055–1056.
 10 'Long before I was sixteen', in Lacouture, *AM*, 22.
 11 Barrès, *Sous l'oeil des Barbares*, 59.

2. A MOST RESOURCEFUL REBEL

14–15 On Paris during the Great War of 1914–1918, see André Salmon, *Souvenirs sans fin*, II; J. Galtier-Boissière, *Mémoires d'un Parisien*, I; on Eugenia Errazuris, M. Cendrars, *Cendrars*, 302–305.
 15 On D. Galanis, AM Preface for an exhibition catalogue, reprinted in *Arts et métiers*, 1 April 1928.
15–16 René Doyon's reminiscences of AM can be found in his *Mémoire d'Homme*, 45–77.
16–17 On AM's first publishing suggestions, see André Vandegans, *La Jeunesse littéraire d'AM*, 21–26.
18–19 On Florent Fels, see his *Voilà*, 11–76; Walter Langlois, *VM*, 35–69; on Max Jacob, Roland Dorgelès, *Bouquet de Bohème*, 110–121, and G. Gabory, *Apollinaire*, 21–22.
19–20 On André Salmon, his *Souvenirs*, I, and Dorgelès, *Bouquet*, 279–282.
20–22 On Ducasse-Lautréamont, see Marcelin Pleynet, *Lautréamont par lui-même*; on the Dada uproar of 1920, Maurice Saillet, 'Les Inventeurs de Maldoror' (*Lettres nouvelles*, April–June 1954); M. Sanouillet, *Dada à Paris*, 144–154, 446–7.

3. AUTHOR, PUBLISHER AND TROUBADOUR

24–25 On Simon Kra, AM and the Editions du Sagittaire, see Langlois, *VM*, 13–15.
25–26 Gabory's reminiscences, *Apollinaire*, 13–27, 67–69.
26–27 *Lunes en papier*, see Pl. I, 3–31; Pierre Brunel's commentary (*ibid.*, 841–855); Vandegans, 96–140.
 28 On Kahnweiler and Max Jacob, R. Guiette, *La Vie de Max Jacob*, 118–125; Kahnweiler, *Entretiens*, 133–139.
29–30 On Pierre Durand, see Roger Grenier, *Pascal Pia*, 15–19.

4. CLARA

 31 On the 'anti-Boche' hysteria of 1915–1918, see Galtier-Boissière, *Mémoires*, I; J. Marnold, *Le Cas Wagner*.
 31 On Ivan Goll, see Claire Goll, *Oeuvres* I.
32ff. Most of this chapter is based on the first two volumes of Clara Malraux's autobiography – I. *Apprendre à vivre*, and II. *Nos vingt ans*. See also Isabelle de Courtivron, *Clara Malraux*.

5. NEW HORIZONS

42–43 AM's and Clara's trips to Prague, Vienna, Berlin, etc. are described in CM's *Nos vingt ans*.
 44 'But for you I would have remained a library rat' – CM, *Apprendre à vivre*, 274.
45–46 On Arland, see J. Duvignaud, *Marcel Arland*, and his own reminiscences, *Ce fut ainsi*.
 46 'Accordingly, since the world . . .' *Nos vingt ans*, 62–64.
 46 'bristling little bird of prey'—Mauriac, *Mémoires politiques*, 79.

6. A SHOT IN THE DARK

49 'We can only feel through comparison.' AM, 'La Peinture de Galanis', cited by Vandegans, *Jeunesse*, 90–91.

50 The draft-dodging trip to Strasbourg is described in all its drollery by CM (*Nos vingt ans*, 90–108).

53 On Paul Doumer and 'L'Inventaire officiel des temples khmers', see vol. I of EFEO's *Bulletin*, 5–78.

53–54 The first volume of Lunet de Lajonquiere's *Inventaire descriptif des monuments du Cambodge* was published in vol. IV of the EFEO's *Publications* (1902); the third and final volume in *Publications*, vol. XI (1911).

55 On preparations for the Cambodian foray, see W. Langlois, *The Indochina Adventure*.

7. FORTUNE FAVOURS THE BOLD

Most of the details in this chapter are taken from CM's detailed account of this 'archaeological expedition' in *Nos vingt ans*.

59 'Branches caked with mud . . .' *VR*, Pl I. 402–3.

8. THE TEMPLE-PLUNDERERS OF ANGKOR

64ff. In addition to CM's invaluable *Nos vingt ans*, this chapter owes a lot to W. Langlois' *Indochina Adventure* and, for details concerning the Phnom-Penh and Saigon trials, to Lacouture's *AM*.

71 *Le Matin*, 3 August 1924, front page.

75 'Clara is a good little wife . . .'—*Nos vingt ans*, 236–8.

76 'The undersigned, upset . . .' text in Pl I, LXVII.

9. CONVICTED, BUT NOT COWED

79ff. Most of this chapter is based on CM's *Nos vingt ans* and the third volume of her memoirs, *Les Combats et les jeux*.

81 Copies of the contracts were later published in *L'Indochine* (18, 22 July, 1925). See Langlois, *IA*, 54.

83ff. On conditions in Indochina at this time, see Virginia Thompson, *Indochina*; Léon Werth's *Cochinchine*; and Langlois, *IA*.

10. FISHING IN TROUBLED WATERS

86ff. Most of the details in this chapter are based on information provided in articles and editorials published in *L'Indochine*.

86 On Rouelle's victory, see *Courrier Saïgonais* (*CS*), May 2, 4, 11, 1925.

88 On Dr Lê-quang-Trinh, CM, *Combats*, 39; L. Werth (*Europe*, 15 Oct. 1925); Langlois, *IA*, 79–80.

89 On La Pommeraye, *ibid.*, 76–78; Lacouture, *AM*, 90–91; *CS*, 18 June 1925.

90 Monribot to Dê-Tu, quoted in *L'Indochine*, 25 June 1925.

94 'They were poor' – *L'Indochine*, 22 July 1925.

95 The dramatic scene with Hin is described by CM, *Combats*, 176–181.

11. THUNDER OUT OF CHINA

97–98 The idea that Abd-el-Krim was part of a world-wide 'Bolshevist' conspiracy had been 'confirmed' in the eyes of many Frenchmen by a trip made to Spanish Morocco by the French Communist rabble-rouser, Jacques Doriot. On the situation in China at this time, see Harold Isaacs, *The Tragedy of the Chinese Revolution*; on Sun Yat-sen and Lenin, Shao Chuan Leng and Norman Palmer, *Sun Yat-sen and Communism*.

102 Trip to Hong Kong etc., in CM's *Combats*, 211–215.

103 'Malraux never forgot'—see his Preface to Andrée Viollis' *Indochine S.O.S.*

105 AM: 'Now there's only one solution . . .' in CM, *CJ*, 228.

12. THE SIREN-CALLS OF THE ORIENT

107 4 Oct. 1925 letter to Louis Brun, publ. in special issue of *La Herne* (1982), p. 167.

107 On genesis of *La Tentation de l'Occident*, see Daniel Durosay's 'Notice' and 'Note sur le texte' in Pl. I, 887–904, 910–912.

108 On Tagore, Daniel Halévy article in *Revue de Genève*, 1921; cited by Henri Massis, *Défense de l'Occident*, 279–280.

109 Text of Massis article ('Mises au point'), in *Cahiers du mois* (winter 1924–1925), pp. 31–40.

110 W.M. Frohock, *AM and the Tragic Imagination*, 34.

13. THE 'BLACK DIAMOND' OF THE QUAI DE L'HORLOGE

112 AM and Paul Morand, meeting in Saigon, see Morand, *Papiers d'identité*, 170–172.

112–3 On AM's 'A la Sphère' publishing venture, see W. Langlois, 'Malraux, éditeur de livres d'art', lecture delivered at a Cerisy colloqium, organized by Christiane Moatti and David Bevan.

113 The Grasset publishing company's archives, which I was allowed to consult, contain 46 review articles devoted to *La Tentation de l'Occident*.

114–15 On D. Halévy and the 'Cahiers verts', see J. Bothorel's biography of *Bernard Grasset*, 141–149; and on André Chamson, his reminiscences, *Il faut vivre vieux*.

117 AM's financial troubles with Paul Valéry are the subject of a number of letters exchanged with Valéry's banker, Julien Monod (Doucet, VRY ms. 5832, 147–156).

117 On *La Quintessence satyrique du XXe siècle*, Pascal Pia, *Les Livres de l'Enfer*, II, 591–2; and on his other literary hoaxes, R. Grenier, *Pascal·Pia*, 29–40.

118 The illegal abortions 'clinic' is described by CM in fourth volume of her memoirs, *Voici que vient l'été*, 38–41.

119 Lucie Mazauric's description of D. Halévy's literary salon can be found in the first volume of her memoirs, *Avec André Chamson* ('Ah dieu! que la paix est jolie.'), 72–74.

14. A DARK, DANGEROUS HORSE

121 On Grasset's eventual willingness to finance AM's *Aux Aldes* rare-books venture, see Bothorel, *Grasset*, 167, but with wrong date indicated (December 1926, instead 1927).

122–4 On genesis and development of *Les Conquérants*, see Michel Autrand's 'Notice' in Pl. I, 976–998, and Christiane Moatti's essays in *Malraux et l'Histoire*, nos. 5, 6, 7.

122 Garine: 'He was generally thought to be ambitious'—Pl. I, 151.

123 'I prefer them, but only . . .' *ibid.*, 158.

124 On Pontigny, see *Paul Desjardins et les Décades de Pontigny* (1964) and RGM's 'Souvenirs' in *Oeuvres completes*, Pl. I, xc–xcii.

125 AM: 'In an argument one must always win'—recalled by Chamson, in *Il faut vivre vieux*, 42–45.

125 'the liveliest and the most successful (décade) of all I have attended'—*Corr.* AG—RMG, I, 686–7.

125 On the axe vs. the apple tree, Chamson, *op. cit.*, and Lucie Mazauric, 124–129.

126 The first Italian translation (*I Conquistatori*) was finally published by Mondadori in 1947.

126ff. Grasset's archives contain 89 press reviews of *Les Conquérants*, including some in Dutch, Danish, German, English, and even Russian.

126ff. P. Souday, *Le Temps*, 15 Oct.; *L'Humanité*, 22 Oct; A. Thibaudet, *Candide*, 11 Oct.; Rougemont, *Revue de Genève*, 1 Dec.; A. Thérive, *L'Opinion*, 24 Nov. 1928.

129 'Finally, on December 5th'—see *NL*, 8 December.

15. FAREWELL TO FANTASY

130 On Jean Paulhan, see *Jean Paulhan et la Nouvelle Revue Française* (NRF, 1969).

131 On Jean Prévost, see Adrienne Monnier, *Rue de l'Odéon*, and Prévost's portrait of AM in *Caractères*, 106.

131 On origin of the adjective *farfelu*, see CM, *Nos vingt ans*, 58; Vandegans, 118–9.

Page
131–2 On the historical and literary sources used for *Royaume-Farfelu*, see Michel Autrand's 'Notice', Pl i, 1088–1108, and the long chapter in Vandegans's *Jeunesse*.

132–3 'L'Expédition d'Isfahan', in *L'Indochine*, 6 August 1925. On Gide and the launching of the *NRF*, see P. Assouline, *Gallimard*, 19–45, 111–113; and, in contrast, Bothorel's *Grasset*, 165, 188; and on Grasset's dislike of AM's *style tremblé*, *ibid.*, 207.

133 AM's reply to Gallimard (about a 'Life of Edgar Allan Poe') has been preserved in the Jean Paulhan archives, which also contain a postcard, dated 20 January 1925, in which AM mentioned a 'Voyage to the Far East' he was thinking of writing.

134 In his biography, Jean Lacouture claims that AM's plans to 'rescue' Trotsky were actually committed to paper and hurriedly destroyed by members of the NRF-Gallimard staff shortly before the German occupation of Paris in June 1940.

135–6 On Benjamin Crémieux and Ramon Fernandez, see A.A. Eustis, *Trois Critiques de la NRF*, and Jérôme Garcin's preface to Fernandez's *Messages*; on Bernard Groethuysen, Paulhan's preface to BG's *Mythes et Portraits*; L. Mazauric, *op. cit.*, I, 42; CM, *Voici*, 59–60.

136 'Recreating in his own way . . .' Robert Aron, *Fragments d'une vie*, 70.

137 The story of Gide's liaison with Elisabeth Van Rysselberghe is related in considerable detail by Madame Théo in *CPD* IV, 149–179.

137 'A free spirit and a demolisher . . .' *ibid.*, 382–383.

137 For Gide's comments on *Les Conquérants*, *ibid.*, 383–4.

137–8 AM Preface to Madame Théo's Journal, *ibid.*, xxv.

16. THE ROYAL ROAD TO SUCCESS

139 On the move to Blvd. Berthier, CM, *Voici*, 68–69.

139–140 On Emmanuel Berl, *Chamson* I, 145–6; Morlino, *EB—Tribulations d'un pacifiste*; CM, *Voici*, 89–91.

139 On AM's 'extraordinary eloquence', *CPD* IV, 402, and Gide, *Journal* I, 912–913.

140 AM: 'For critics . . .' letter quoted by Vandegans, 284, from Eddy Du Perron's *Verzameld Werk* II, 163. On Du Perron, see Philippe Noble's Preface to EDP's *Pays d'origine*.

140 AM to Edmund Wilson, *The Shores of Light*, 573.

141–2 The trip to Persia is described by CM, *Voici*, 103–117.

142 For lunch with Martin-Chauffier, *ibid*, 81–83.

142–3 21 August, return to Paris: *CPD* V, 40–41.

143 AM to RMG (May 23), in RMG, *Corr.* 117 (no. 80), BNms. 'radiant Italian morning'—*Antimémoires*, 473.

144–5 For the different stages through which *VR* passed, see Pl. I, 1123–1209.

145 'Duco Perken', see Noble, Preface to DP's *Pays d'origine*.

145–6 On 'Baron' David de Mayrena and other adventurers, see W. Langlois's 'Notice', P. I, 1131–1133.

147ff. The trip to Afghanistan is described by CM, *Voici*, 117–136, but, writing it up more almost forty years later, she mistakenly placed it in 1931, instead of 1930. I am indebted to Michael Barry, author of *Le Royaume de l'Insolence*, for the historical details on the turmoil in Afghanistan in 1929.

151 'Meanwhile, the ten members of the Goncourt Prize jury,' *Candide*, 27 Nov. 1930.

151 'Within minutes AM's *VR*', *Le Matin*, 3 December.

151 'The outpaced ladies of the Femina . . .', *NL*, 6 December.

151–2 Bernard Lecache, in *La Gauche*, 3 December.

17. LITERARY IMPASSE

153 Fernand Malraux's suicide, CM, *Voici*, 161–163.

153–5 Copy of the pamphlet on the 'Gothico-Buddhist works from the Pamir' in Doucet, 570.18. Strygowski—thus misspelled by Clara, CM, *Voici*, 154.

155 I am indebted to Sir Ernst Gombrich for other, more accurate information regarding Josef Strzygowski.

155–6 For AM vs. Trotsky, Pl. I, 302–313.

156 'In early May of 1931 . . .'—journey related by Clara in such a disorderly fashion (*Voici*, 129–151) that it was difficult to figure out the exact itinerary.

156 On Jaipur, AM, *Antim*, 112; Benares, *ibid*, 262–264, 331; Darjeeling, CM, *Voici*, 128–9.

157 On Paul Monin's death, CM, *Combats*, 243–245.

158 AM's return to Paris (16 Nov. 1931), *CPD* V, 194–196.

Page
158–9 On the launching of *Marianne*, J. Bouissounouse, *La Nuit d'Autun*, 50–57; Morlino, *Emmanuel Berl*, 118–125.
159 On the move to the Rue du Bac, CM, *Voici*, 178.
161 'Such were the searching questions'—see *Antim*, 472: 'Eddy Du Perron used to tell me that *La Voie royale* was worthless.'

18. STORM CLOUDS OVER EUROPE

162 '*wie güt schmeckt mir Berlin*', AG-RMG, *Corr* I, 516–518.
162–3 On Berlin's cultural dynamism, see Manes Sperber, *Die vergebliche Warnung*, vol. II of his Memoirs: Fr. tr. *Le Pont inachevé*, 148–149; Gustav Regler, *The Owl of Minerva*, 128–129; Harry Graf Kessler, *Tagebücher*, 581.
163 On Gide's trips to Germany, AG, *Journal* I, 1143; *CPD* V, 247, 258, 267; breakfast with Kessler, *Tagebücher*, 693.
163 On Gide's pro-communist sentiments, *Journal* I, 1109–1110, 1116, 1117; RMG, 'Journal' (7 April 1932), quoted at end of AG-RMG, *Corr* I, 718; *CPD* V, 142–3, 220, 245–6, etc.
164 'For Stalin and his colleagues', see Babette Gross, *Münzenberg*, 228–9.
164 'It was simply a question of time—of three to six months', Sperber, *Pont*, 228–230.
164 AM: 'There is in Marxism . . .' *CH*, 116–7, or Pl. I, 611.
165 'Over the next few weeks . . .', on the exodus of German refugees, see Albrecht Betz, *Exil et Engagement* (1991).
165 On The International League against War and Fascism, Gross, *Münzenberg*, 235–238.
166 On Henri Barbusse, see Annette Vidal's *HB*, *Soldat de la Paix*; David Caute, *The Fellow Travellers* (*FT*), 55. On Vaillant-Couturier, Fernande Bussière's *PV-C*. On Romain Rolland, Bernard Duchatelet, *RR et la NRF*, 50–53.
166 On Gide's fear of becoming an *agité*, *CPD*, V, 228.
166 'In early March', *CPD* V, 282–*288*; and on Roland Malraux, 292–3.
167 Speeches made at the AEAR meeting were later published in a booklet entitled, *Ceux qui ont choisi*.
167 Gide, looking like an 'Ibsen preacher', and on AM's largely 'unintelligible' speech, Ehrenburg, *La Nuit tombe*, 11.
168 Fabre-Luce's art (in *Pamphlet*) was reprinted in *NL*, 8 April 1933.
169 On Gide and Einstein, *CPD* V, 299; AG, *Journal* I, 1162–6; 1166; AG-RMG, *Corr* I, 559–562.

19. A ROMANTIC INTERMEZZO

170 J. Bouissounouse, on *CH*, *Autun*, 55–56; Gide's opinion, *CPD* V, 286, 304–5; AG, *Journal* I, 1165.
171 Brasillach's critique of *CH* was later reprinted (along with AM's reply) in Pol Gaillard's *Les critiques de notre temps et AM*.
172 On birth of Florence Malraux, CM, *Voici*, 178–180.
172 'Will you never understand that for a Christian', *ibid*, 164.
172–3 AM being 'a bit lanky . . .' CM, *Nos vingt ans*, 101.
173 On the Pontigny 'rape', CM, *Voici*, 191–2.
173 On Louise de Vilmorin and AM, Bothorel, *Louise*, 76–80.
173 AM's long letter to 'Loulou', Doucet, ms. 30414.
173 'Tall, with lovely auburn hair', see André de V's portrait of his sister, *Louise de Vilmorin* (Seghers, 1962).
174 Cocteau: 'a tall, ravishing girl', *ibid.*, 47–48.
175 On the cruise ship, *Colombie*, AM letter to RMG, *Corr* 117, 89–90 (BNms).
175 'From the northern port of Hammerfest', undated letter, in Jean Paulhan archives.
175 'if it's to see penguins', letter to Josette Clotis, quoted in Suzanne Chantal's *Le Coeur battant*, 46.
175 On Trotsky's arrival in France, *L'Humanité*, 20, 21, 23 July; *Le Matin*, 24 July; Isaac Deutcher, *The Prophet Outcast*, 268–9.
176 On AM's trip to Saint-Palais, CM, *Voici*, 11–12, and his own account in *Marianne*, 25 April 1934.
178 'huge flight of seagulls . . .', Chantal, *Coeur*, 46–47. Except where otherwise indicated, other details on Josette Clotis' past, etc. come from this book, written by a friend.
179 On Janine Bouissounouse's negative opinion of Josette, see *Autun*, 54–55.
180 'For years a feeling of . . . frustration', CM, *Voici*, 50, 200.

Page
180 AM: 'It is better to be my wife . . .', *ibid.*, 34, 71.
180 '*Er hat sich eine kleine Jüdin* . . .', Aron, *Mémoires*, 77.
180 'Now, in late November', CM, *Voici*, 208–210.
180 On Friedrich Sieburg, see A. Betz, *Exil*, 46–47, 51–54, 74–78, 119–120; also art. in *Vu* (7 April 1933, p. 5), 'Dieu est-il nazi?'
180 On AM's discovery of Louise's liaison with Sieburg, Bothorel, *Louise*, 82–85.
181 'On November 7' and through to end of this chapter, Chantal, *Coeur*, 49–55.
181 On Roland Malraux, CM, *Voici*, 174–5; AG, *Journal* I, 1166; *CPD* V, 285, 289, 292, 301.
182 'In the taxi . . .'—CM, in the fifth vol. of her memoirs, *La Fin et le Commencement*, 127, later claimed that Josette had taken the initiative in kissing AM, but I have preferred to follow JC's own account of what happened, unaffected by any sense of bitterness.

20. THE ACTIVIST

183–4 On Otto Katz, Koestler, *IW*, 209–211; on Gustav Regler, his own memoirs, *Das Ohr des Malchus*, Eng. tr., *The Owl of Minerva*, and, for his Strasbourg 'coup', pp. 160–161.
184 The English title was *The Brown Book of the Hitler Terror*, prefaced by Lord Marley.
184 'On September 11th', *Le Populaire*, 12, 13 September.
184 On the 'counter-trial' in London, see J-M Palmier, *Weimar en exil* I, 462–465; Gross, *WM*, 265–6.
185 On Gide's and AM's trip to Berlin, see *CPD* V, 366–7; AG, *Littérature engagée* (Y. Davet), 42.
185–6 'He talks non-stop', J. Copeau, *Journal* II, 363–4.
186 On this turbulent period of French history, see Bertrand de Jouvenel's *Un voyageur dans le siècle*, 114–168; and André Thirion, *Révolutionnaires sans révolution*, 308–361.
186 AM and Clara, taking part in huge counter-demonstration, CM, *Voici*, 201–205.
186 On Paul Langevin, see his *La Pensée et l'Action*, 280–282; D. Caute, *FT*, 25, 155–6.
187 'Similar Vigilance Committees', Ehrenburg, *Nuit*, 39.

21. OVER THE DESERTS OF ARABIA

188 'In December,', Carlo Rim, *Grenier d'Arlequin*, 195.
188 'a German adventurer' (Jacobsthal), mentioned by AM in letter to Edmond Jaloux (12 Jan. 1934), Doucet, ms. 6098; CM, *Voici*, 129–130.
188 with 'elephants crowned', etc., *Antim*, 84.
189 'One of her feet, according to oriental legend', H. St. J Philby, *Sheba's Daughters*, 10–12.
189 'At the Société de Géographie', *Antim*, 88–89.
189 Information about Corniglion-Molinier obtained from SHAA and Colonel Edmond Petit; also Rim, *Arlequin*, 281–2.
190 'We have Clara's word for it', CM, *Voici*, 227.
190 'I find it perfectly ridiculous', *L'Intransigeant*, 5 May 1934
190 'The most violently opposed', CM, *Voici*, 225–231; also, Bouissounouse, *Autun*, 56, and *CPD* V, 357–8, 366.
190 'What you say of the adventurer', Doucet, ms. 6099.
190 'A little later M appeared', Rim, *Arlequin*, 204.
191 On preparations for flight and other valuable details, Edmond Petit, *Missions très spéciales*, 72–83.
191ff. AM in Cairo, details from Gabriel Dardaud's entertaining *Trente ans au bord du Nil*, 42–52.
194ff. The stop-over in Djibouti and the overflight of Yemen were all vividly described in the ten articles AM and Corniglion-M later wrote for *L'Intransigeant*, 3–13 May.
196 On hailstorm west of Tunis, *Antim*, 94–98.
197 Gide's unexpected presence at Lyon, CM, *Voici*, 233–236.
197 AM: 'Yes, I'm too impatient', *CPD* V, 366.
198 Petit and Jacqueline Pirenne, *Missions*, 83.

22. FOUR MONTHS IN THE USSR

199 'In early June', CM, *Voici*, 242; Ehrenburg, *Nuit*, 29–36.
199ff. On the Moscow Writers Congress, see special issues of *RLM* (nos. 304–309), 1972; Heller & Nekritch, *L'Utopie au pouvoir*, 221–227; Ehrenburg, *Nuit*, 36–40.
199 Boat trip to Leningrad, *ibid*, 39–40; CM, *Voici*, 241–2.

Page
199 On Leningrad, *Voici*, 244–5; *Antim*, 571.
200 'high-powered journalistic team', *RLM*, *op. cit.*, 135–6.
200 On Paul Nizan, see Annie Cohen-Solal's biography, 137–149, and Henriette Nizan's *Libres Mémoires*.
200 AM: 'But I am not a pacifist', *RLM*, 137.
200 'In Moscow', CM, *Voici*, 245–268.
200 On Joris Ivens, Regler, *Owl*, 201–203.
201 *Mezhrabpom* (*Mezhdunarodnaya Rabochaya Pomoshch*), the Soviet equivalent of the *IAH* (*Internationale Arbeiterhilfe* Münzenberg had founded in 1921 (Gross, 181–195).
201 The meetings with Meyerhold and Eisenstein are described by Clara, *Voici*, 251 *ff*. On Eisenstein's shattered plans, Bouissounouse, *Autun*, 47–49.
202 Text of Nizan's article, *RLM*, 131–134.
203 'a most unsexagenarian . . . Gorky', Regler, *Owl*, 203.
203 On Gorky's interminable speech, *ibid*, 225–229; and on Boleslavskaya and AM, II. Nizan, *LM*, 194–5.
203 Bukharin's Congress speech, in special issue of *Commune*, Oct.-Nov. 1934, pp. 54–59.
204 'moving, naive, and pathetic', Ehrenburg, *Nuit*, 47–49.
204 Shklovsky's attack on Dostoevsky, Heller, *Utopie*, 225.
206 'No less heretical', *RLM*, 137–142.
206ff. For banquet in Gorky's dacha, Regler, *Owl*, 208–214.
208 AM's toast to Trotsky, CM, *Combats*, 124–5.

23. THE REVOLUTIONARY MIRAGE

209 On trip to Novosibirsk etc., CM, *Voici*, 275–287.
209 AM abandoning his Baku petroleum workers novel, *CPD* V, 417; influence of Willi Bredel, CM, *Voici*, 268.
210 On Sperber's youth etc., see first vol. of his memoirs, *Die Wasserträger Gottes* (Fr. tr., *Les Porteurs d'eau*); and on his life in Berlin, 'L'Avertissement inutile' in vol. II
210 'Each being infinitely resembles', *ibid.*, 144.
210 'In this capitalistic world', *ibid*, 206.
211ff. Gide on *Temps du Mépris*, *CPD* V, 461; Thérive, *Le Temps*, 13 June; E. Mounier, *Esprit*, Sept. 1935.
212ff. Some of the speeches delivered at this International Writers Congress were later published in *Commune*, July 1935; see also AG, *Littérature engagée*, 82–99; Bouissounouse, *Autun*, 74; and, for Regler's stirring spech (also publ. in *Commune*), *Owl*, 230–232.
214 On the Victor Serge uproar, *CPD* V, 463–467; V. Serge, *Memoirs of a Revolutionary*, 317–319.
215 Henri-René Lenormand, on AM and the Writers Congress, *Confessions d'un auteur dramatique* II, 336–339.
216ff. On Pierre Laval, Bertrand de Jouvenel, *Un voyageur dans le siècle*, 344–350.
217 Hitler—that "sexual degenerate", cited by J. Toland, *Adolf Hitler* (Ballantine, 1976), 485–486.
219 Text of AM's Nov. 4th spech in *L'Herne* (special issue on AM, 1982), 170–173.
221 See Paul-Henri Spaak's curious apologia for Belgium's policy of neutrality, in *Combats inachevés* I, 40–42.
221 'words, words, words'—Raymond Aron, *Mémoires*, 137–8.

24. FROM MOSCOW TO MADRID

222 On Roland M, see CM, *Voici*, 103–4, 174–5; on Pierre Herbart in Moscow, *CPD* V, 495, 504, and his own reminiscences in *La Ligne de force*.
222 On rewriting of Soviet history, Heller, *Utopie*, 237–251.
223 Gide on 'pacific' nature of the nation-wide *kermesse*, AG-RMG, *Corr* II, 74.
223 CM and Madeleine Lagrange, *Fin*, 27–29.
224 ON AM's trip to Madrid, Lenormand, *op. cit.*, 375–377; Chantal, *Coeur*, 77–78.
225 On abortive Twentieth Century Encyclopedia project, see Ehrenburg, *Nuit*, 96–97; Sperber, *Avertissement*, 183.
225 AM speech on 'cultural heritage' in *L'Herne*, 294–299.
226 AM interrogated by J. Bouissounouse, *Autun*, 85–87.

25. THE LYRICAL ILLUSION

Page
228 Evening of Saturday 18 July, CM, *Fin*, 7–8.
228 Background information on Pierre Cot kindly furnished by Jean Lasserre; see also his *Procès de la République* I.
229 On the Potez 54, Patrick Laureau art. in *Le Fanatique*, Jan. 1981, with additional explanations from Col. Petit.
229 On AM's belief in airpower, *CPD* V, 426.
229–30 On flight to Madrid, *VM*, 157–8; CM, 10–13.
230 On Alvarez del Vayo, Gerald Brenan, *Spanish Labyrinth*, 308; Burnett Bolloten, *Spanish Revolution*, 132; Hugh Thomas, *The Spanish Civil War* (*SCW*), 200–201.
231 On Madrid, CM, *Fin*, 13–14; Thomas, *SCW*, 268–276; Regler, *Owl*, 273.
231ff. The Republicans' successes in neutralizing rebel artillery barracks are described in detail by participants in *Icare* (aviation quarterly), vol. 118 (1986), prepared by Patrick Laureau and Jean Lasserre. Other details are drawn from Hidalgo de Cisneros' *Virage sur l'aile* and J. Salas Barrazábal, *La Guerra de España desde el aire*.
232 The crisis overtaking the *Front Populaire* government is well described in Jean Lacouture's biography of *Léon Blum* and in Jules Moch's *Rencontres avec Léon Blum*.
233 On Baldwin: 'We hate fascism', Moch, *Rencontres*, 195.
234 AM and *Basler Rundschau* (30 July 1936), quoted in G. Schmigalle's *AM und der spanische Bürgerkrieg*, 90–91.
234 Adrienne Bolland later explained the reasons for her refusal to Jean Lasserre; Roger Beaucaire did the same when I interviewed him in the late 1960s.
235 Seizure by Spanish anarchists of MAP machine-guns—detail supplied to author by V. Véniel.
235 On fabulous salaries offered to volunteer pilots, Salas, *Guerra*, 84; J. Gisclon, *Avions*, 31–32; Angelo Emiliano, in *Icare* II (no. 130, 1989), 78–82.
235–6 Details on "mercenary" volunteers are taken from Gisclon's *Les Avions et les Hommes*, a fictionalized version of his experiences as a fighter pilot in AM's squadron. See also Jean Bernier's fine art. in *Icare* I, 144–5.
236 'It was probably on August 6th', CM, *Fin*, 18–19.
236 Unless otherwise specified, the details concerning the progress of Franco's forces are taken from Hugh Thomas' *SCW*.
237 On Colonel Hernandez Sarabia etc., see Mikhail Koltsov's fascinating *Diario de la guerra de España*, 40.
237–8 The exact dates of AM's squadron's sorties are given in P. Laureau's *La aviación republicana*, 45–47, and were verified for me by Victor Véniel.
239 'The bombers had hardly overflown', from AM's description of this bombing attack in *L'Espoir*, 91–95, in which the two raids (of August 16th and 20th) were merged into one.
240 Gisclon's fanciful account of the Sierra de Gredos incident was most kindly corrected for me by V. Véniel (letter of 23 Nov. 1992).
241 On bombing of War Ministry etc., Koltsov, *Diario*, 59–60.
241 'Three Nationalist warplanes were destroyed'—figure given by Salas, *Guerra*, 100: a far cry from the 16 claimed by AM in *L'Espoir*, 383–394, 401, in which, for purposes of fiction, this raid was moved in space from the region of Olmedo to Teruel, and in time from September to December.

26. THE ORDEAL

243 'I sleep three hours a night', Chantal, *Coeur*, 83–84.
243 On CM making herself 'useful' in Madrid, *Fin*, 54–55; on AM's brief glimpse of Gide, AG, *Journal* I, 1253.
244 Koltsov and Asensio Torrado, *Diario*, 80–81.
245 On CM's new trip to Madrid, *Fin*, 137–9.
245 'Here live the aviators . . .' Koltsov, *Diario*, 93.
246 Koltsov and Maria Osten, CM, *Fin*, 84–86.
247 'The first train load of foreign volunteers', J. Delperrie de Bayac, *Les Brigades internationales*, 78–80.
248 AM's return to Paris (Oct. 21), *CPD* V, 561, 562.
249 'On October 29th M . . .', *CPD* V, 565–9.
250 Hasty exodus of *los conejos*, Koltsov, *Diario*, 175.
250 On the increasingly dangerous missions from airbase at Alcalá, Bernier, in *Icare* I, 143.

Page
250 'There was no saluting . . .', Julien Segnaire's 'antimilitarisme du colonel', in *NRF*, July 1977, 31–32.
250 'On the evening of November 5th', Fischer, *Men*, 385.
251 On Hidalgo de Cisneros' unflattering judgement on AM essentially a 'dilettante', see his *Memorias* II, 324–5.
251 On Jean Darry, an exemplary 'mercenary' pilot, see Bernier, *Icare* I, 144–149.
251–2 On the two Potez 54 accidents of 27 December, see P. Laureau, 'La Mission de l'Espoir', *Icare*, II, 92–103.
252 The rescue of Florein and his wounded crewmen was later vividly described by AM in *L'Espoir*, 398–412.

27. SIERRA DE TERUEL

253 'Feast of the Three Kings', described by Robert Payne, in *This is War*, and quoted by Thornberry, *op. cit.*, 115.
253 The Resolution barring further shipments of volunteers to Spain was *unanimously* voted by the Chamber of Deputies (*Figaro*, 16 January 1937).
253ff. On Left Bank uproar over Gide's *Retour de l'URSS*, *CPD* V, 586; on January 16th lunch with Gide and Herbart, *CPD* V, 602–604, 623, 625–6; and Herbart's account of his woes in Spain, in *La ligne de force*, 125–139; Regler, *Owl*, 278–9.
254 Brasillach's attack on AM, in *Je suis partout*, 16 January; *CPD* V, 628–9.
255 On AM's trip to USA with Josette, Chantal, *Coeur*, 84–89; W. Langlois' account in *VM*, 212–232.
256 AM's row with Trotsky is well described by Thornberry, in *TCL* (vol. 24, no. 3), Autumn 1978, 324–334.
257 AM and Gide, 19 April and 5 May, in *CPD* VI, 13, 15. On Josette and Suzanne's *zenana*, Chantal, *Coeur*, 90–91.
257ff. On the International Writers Congress in Spain, Stephen Spender, *World within World*, 235–245; Ehrenburg, *Nuit*, 233–237.
259 AM's return to Perpignan, Chantal, *Coeur*, 92–93.
259 Frohock on *L'Espoir*'s cinematographic structure, *AM* 105 Suzanne Chantal art. in *Cinémonde*, Noël 1938.
260–1 AM's trip to Toulon to see Clara, CM, *Fin*, 173–176.
261ff. AM's return to Paris, *CPD* VI, 37; his trip to Toulouse followed by Josette, Chantal, *Coeur*, 94–95.
262 AM's crisis with Clara, Marcel Arland, *Ce fut ainsi*, 49–50; p. 71; H. Nizan, *Libres Mémoires*, 194–5.
262 'To keep Josette distracted', Chantal, *Coeur*, 98–99.
262–3 On *L'Espoir*, P. Nizan in *Ce Soir*, 13 January 1938; G. Friedmann, *L'Humanité*, 29 January; Louis Gillet, *NL*, 8 January; R. Brasillach, *Action Française*, 6 January, quoted by Thornberry, *op. cit.*, 189, fn. 43.
263–4 The information on Roland Malraux's return from Moscow with a message from Isaak Babel was kindly given to me by Abidine Dino.
264 On AM's 'smoke-filled den' at NRF, Denise Tual, *Le Temps dévoré*, 143.
265 Trip to Moulins during Easter, Chantal, *Coeur*, 100–101.
265 On Corniglion-M, Denise Tual, etc., ch. 13.
265 AM's sudden trip to Barcelona, Chantal, *Coeur*, 104–106.
265–6 On the filming of *Sierra de Teruel* (*S de T*), see Denis Marion's book on *AM*.
267 On Josette's stay in Barcelona, Chantal, *Coeur*, 107–119.
268 AM's return, beret on head, Tual, *Temps*, 150–153.
269 *Al fresco* lunches at the '*Pomme d'Api*', Chantal, 119.
269 On the musical finale, David Bevan's art. in *TCL*, 354–357, and D. Tual, *Temps*, 154–5.
269 Aragon, in *Ce Soir*, 11, 12 August 1939.

28. SITZKRIEG

270ff. Most of the details in this chapter are taken from Suzanne Chantal's *Le Coeur battant*, 123–183. The only references listed here come from other sources.
271 AM dinner with Aron, Aron's *Mémoires*, 158.
271 On Commissariat of Information, A. Maurois, *Mémoires*, 261–263.

Page
271 On incarceration of left-wing anti-fascists, see Koestler, *The Scum of the Earth*, and ch. 16 ('The undesirables') in Regler's *Owl*.
272–3 AM's 'plot' with André Beucler, in AB's *Plaisirs de Mémoire* II, 64–68.
274 On Jenka Sperber, Manès Sperber, *Au-delà de l'oubli*.
275 AM and Gen. Chardigny, Maurois, *Mémoires*, 263.
276 AM letter to RMG, in BNms. RMG, *Corr* 117 (94, 94 bis).
276 Information concerning Albert Beuret was kindly provided by Jean Grosjean and Jacqueline Blanchard.

29. THE DEBACLE

278ff. The events in this chapter concerning Josette Clotis are covered by Suzanne Chantal in *Coeur*, 185–229. The following notes refer to other sources.
279 'At Provins, on June 14th', AM's explanatory letter to Pascal Pia (Feb. 1941), Doucet, ms. 9570 (4–6).
279ff. 'Sleep and dysentery filled', Jean-Baptiste Jeener, *Paris-Soirs*, 13. Other details on the POW camp at Sens were kindly provided by Jean Grosjean, in several interviews.
282 'The camp life is tolerable', Chantal, *Coeur*, 213–4.
283 The *S de T* film is vaguely mentioned by Roland in letter to AM (23 Feb 1941), quoted by Alain M in *M de B*, 127.
284 Count Wolff Metternich, kindly identified by Princess Tatiana Metternich (letter dated 15 September 1991).
285 'In September M, Beuret . . .' from Grosjean's Preface to Pl. 1, XVI, and oral explanations.
285 On Gallimard and Paulhan near Carcassonne, Assouline, *Gallimard*, 270–271; Gide, *Journal* II, 44; *CPD* VI, 198.
286 Certain of the Graeco-Buddhist statues had been entrusted to Aunt Marie (Lamy). Information kindly offered by Florence Malraux.
286 On Dr Jean-Marie Sotty and Clara, CM, *Fin*, 204–207.
286 'The danger threatening M', from Jean Grosjean.
286 On Roland borrowing money for AM's escape, CM, *Fin*, 221.
286 On Phillippe de Gunsbourg, see M.R.D. Foot, *SOE in France*, 378, 398; Guy Penaud, *Histoire de la Résistance au Périgord*, 109–111, 171–173.
287 Alain Malraux's *M de B* (p. 123) contains a letter sent by Roland to Clara from Avignon (9 Nov. 1940) indicating that he had personally accompanied AM across the demarcation-line.
287 On AM in the cinema, see *Antim*, 598, and on friendly black cat, *Lazare*, 112.

30. THE STRUGGLE TO SURVIVE

288ff. Events in this chapter concerning Josette Clotis are covered by Suzanne Chantal, *Coeur*, 224–250. The reference notes here listed come from other sources.
289 On Dorothy Bussy, see her correspondence with Gide, *Cahiers AG*, vols 9 & 10; and many letters in RMG's *Corr générale*.
289 'On November 14th . . .' AM visit to Gide, *CPD* VI, 174–177.
290 On Emmanuel Berl in Vichy, Morlino, 320–336.
290–1 On Germans taking control of Havas News Service, see Pierre et Marthe Massenet, *Journal d'une longue nuit*, 91; and on threatened occupation of NRF premises, G. Heller, *Un Allemand à Paris*; Pierre Andreu & Frédéric Grover, *Drieu La Rochelle*.
291 'As it was, 153 NRF books', *CPD* VI, 198–200.
291 The 'La Souco' villa is described by S. Chantal in *Coeur*, 241, and by M. Sperber in *l'oubli*, 201.
292 On food crisis in southern France at this time, see Henri Michel, *Vichy Année 1940*, 95; Robert Murphy, *Diplomat among the Warriors*, 63–65; Robert Aron, *Histoire de Vichy*, 320–323; Henri Frenay, *La nuit finira*, 101–2. On the 'hungry' sea-gulls of Marseille, V. Serge, *Memoirs of a Revolutionary*, 363.
292–3 On the Emergency Rescue Committee, see Varian Fry's reminiscences in *Surrender on Demand* and Daniel Bénédit's equally fascinating *La filière marseillaise*.
293 On AM's correspondence with Robert Haas, see Langlois, *VM*, 258–267.
293–4 For AM's trip to Toulouse, CM, *Fin*, 222–226. The *échec vociférant* telegram was shown to me by Suzanne Chantal.

31. THE GALLEY SLAVE OF THE PEN

Page
295ff. Details in this chapter concerning Josette and AM have been taken from Suzanne Chantal's *Coeur*, 248–300.
295 On Pascal Pia in Lyon, H. Lottmann, *Camus*, 244–247.
295 On the DC-41's duffel-bags, etc. two letters written by Pascal Pia to Henri Calet (21 Feb. 1941), Doucet, ms. 9570/4–6.
296 Details on the 'Les Camélias' villa kindly supplied by José Augusto de Santos.
296 On AM's March 1941 visit to Marseille and his letter to De Gaulle, Bénédite, *filière*, 214–216; and on Roland's rescue of a copy of *S de T*, Alain M, *M de B*, 125–127.
297 'le forçat de la plume', Chantal, *Coeur*, 248–250.
297 AM letter to Robert Haas, in June 1939, in *VM*, 256.
299 'Let's not play at being boy scouts', Chantal, 255.
299 On Corniglion-M, information obtained from SHAA.
299 AM and Claude Bourdet, see CB's *Aventure incertaine*, 72. AM and Roger Stéphane, in RS's *Entretiens*, 96–97.
301 On Varian Fry's expulsion, *Surrender*, 214–239; Bénédite's *filière*; Langlois' account of how Fry smuggled film reels of *S de T* to Washington, *VM*, 233–252.
301 On Roland's departure for Toulouse, Alain M, 133–4.
301 'When . . . M reappeared in Nice', *CPD* VI, 283.
301 'The war, as M had been predicting', Simone de Beauvoir, *La Force de l'Age*, 509.
302 On Gide's departure for Tunis, *CPD* VI, 304–308.
302 Birth of Dan André Sperber, in *l'oubli*, 210, with details added (orally to author) by Jenka Sperber.
302 'It was not until weeks later', AM to RMG, BNms, RMG *Corr* 117 (nos. 106, 107).
303 On AM's trip to Corrèze, Mireille, *Avec le soleil pour témoin*, 131–2; Chantal, *Coeur*, 283.
303 'On November 16th', AM to RMG (BNms. RMG, *Corr* 117); AM to Pierre-Quint, 17 Nov. 1942 (BNms, NAF 18361, no. 329).
303–4 On Claude Malraux, CM, *Nos vingt ans*, 92–93; *Voici*, 114; Mouloudji, *La Fleur de l'âge*, 34–37; Alain M, *M de B*, 135–6.
304 On Philippe Liewer, Foot, *SOE*, 170, 173, 203–204, 262–264; Penaud, *Périgord*, 59–60, 81, 87–88.
304 AM's first meeting with Madeleine Lioux, Alain M, *M de B*, 144.
304 'Informed by telephone', Josette to RMG, 16 Dec. 1942, (BNms, RMG, *Corr* 117, no. 140).
305 On Roland's marriage to Madeleine and their 'strange new life', details from Mme Malraux (MM from here on).
305 AM to RMG, 2 Jan. 1943, RMG, *Corr* 177 (107, 108) BNms.
306 'I am completely intoxicated', *ibid.*, 111–113.
308 On desperate food situation in Nice, see RMG's letter (16 June 1943) to Jacques Copeau, and Copeau's reply, in JC-RMG, *Corr* II, 679–683.

32. THE RESISTER

309ff. Most of the details in this chapter are drawn from Jacques Poirier's autobiographical *La girafe a un long cou* and Léon Mercadet's *La Brigade Alsace-Lorraine*. The notes that follow cover information obtained from other sources.
309 'Henri Chevalier', the name indicated on Peulevé's (bogus) identity card and transmitted by the police commissioner of Brive to the Prefect at Limoges. (Photocopy offered to author by General Léon George.)
309 On Henry Peulevé, see Foot, *SOE*, 80, 199, 282.
311 On Violette Szabo, *ibid.*, 107, 262–264; other details from MM.
312 On Cyril Watney's radioed message to London, Foot, 107.
313 On AM's hurried trip to Paris, *CPD* VI, 314–316.
314 On Raymond Maréchal's death, Poirier, *girafe*, 93–95.
315 On AM recommending Camus' *L'Etranger* to Gallimard, H. Lottmann, *Camus*, 301, 320, 324.
316 Camus with Jean Lescure, as related by Lescure in Preface to Poirier's *girafe*.
318ff. Mme Théo recorded this AM visit to Paris (25–28 April) in (*CPD* VI, 316), but made no mention of Captain Jack's 'sequestration' in AG's apartment. On Josette's arrival in Paris, see Chantal, *Coeur*, 304–310; trip confirmed by details included in Lottmann's *Camus*, 322–3.

33. THE ALSACE-LORRAINE BRIGADE

Page
321ff. In this chapter too, most of the details come from Jacques Poirier's *La girafe a un long coup* and Léon Mercadet's *Brigade Alsace-Lorraine*. The following notes indicate other sources.
322ff. Diener-Ancel's first meeting with AM is described by Léon Mercadet (*Brigade*, 98–100) as having taken place at the Château de La Poujade. In fact, it took place in the 'fortress' of Castelnaud, as Antoine Diener discovered during a summer trip to Dordogne in 1993 (letter to author of 8 September).
324–5 AM's sudden trip to Toulouse, which still puzzles her, was related to me by MM (22 April 1992). See also Alain M's *M de B*, 349–352.
325 On the '*Das Reich*' SS Panzer Division, see Penaud, *Périgord*, 321–322.
326–7 Madeleine M's and Josette's tribulations at Domme were related to me by MM; see also her son's account in *M de B*, 352–357.
327 Details on his bicycle trip to Domme were kindly given to me in three letters from Raoul Verhagen (20 Feb., 11 and 23 March 1993).
327 'Never, more than at that moment'—Marc Gerschel to author in telephone conversation (26 Feb. 1993).
328 The details on Pierre Jacquot's personality, military background, and resistance activities were kindly furnished by his son-in-law, General Léon George.
329 On George Hiller's problems with the FTP, see Foot, *SOE*, 379–380.
330ff. AM's capture by the Germans etc. was later vividly described in *Antim*, 214–257.
334–5 On AM's visit to the Ritz Hotel, Carlos Baker, *Hemingway*, 497–8.
337 André Chamson's meeting with General de Lattre de Tassigny and what followed are described in his *La Reconquête*.

34. TRIUMPH AND TRAGEDY

340 AM: 'I salute, among you, your dead of yesterday . . .' etc., as told to author by Antoine Diener-Ancel (ADA), Dr Bernard Metz (BM), and Monsignor Pierre Bockel (PB) during an unforgettable visit to Strasbourg in December 1992.
341 On Pierre Jacquot being wounded while trying to reorganize a disorderly attack, I have followed Jean Baurès' sober account in the *Bulletin* de l'Amicale des Anciens de la Brigade indépendante Alsace-Lorraine (no. 222, II), July 1991, p. 18–22.
341 Description of car trip to Paris made to me by PB. On his first meetings with AM, see Pierre Bockel, *L'Enfant due rire*, 66–69; and AM's Preface, 19–20.
342–3 On Josette Clotis' tragic death, Chantal, *Coeur*, 312.
343 On AM stopping by to see Pascal Pia, Lottmann, *Camus*, 342–350, 365–366.
343 'On the evening of November 16th', *CPD* VI, 320.
344 'Perhaps on my dying day . . .' AM text, publ. in *L'Alsace française* (Nov. 1948).
346ff. On MLN Congress (23–28 January 1945), see Henri Frenay, *La nuit finira*, 475–478, 501–504; Janine Mossuz, *AM et le gaullisme*, 44–46.
347 Text of AM's speech was publ. in January 26th issue of *Combat*, which mentioned a second AM speech in its Jan. 27th number. On AM's suspicion of French Communists' machinations, see his remarks ('I'm not an innocent choirboy') to Roger Stéphane, in *Fin d'une jeunesse*, 43.
348–9 'On May 22, 1945 Antoine Diener's brother-in-law . . .' Gustave Houver's grim recollections, kindly transmitted to me by ADA; complemented by those of Henri Solbach, one of eleven French survivors from the *Cap Arcona*, who sent me a photocopy of an article by General Pierre Brunet in *Les Martyrs de Neuengamme* (pp. 54–78).

35. TWO MONTHS IN POWER

350 'On the 23rd of January', Arland, *Ce fut ainsi*, 55–57.
351 On AM's dislike of Sartre's works, see Gide to RMG, (18 Sept. 1941), AG-RMG, *Corr* II, 237.
351 'Yes, I've seen the trial number' (of *Les Temps Modernes*), AM to R. Stéphane, *Jeunesse*, 68.
351 On Avenue d'Orsay apartment, information from MM; on move to Boulogne, Alain M, *M de B*, 34–35.
352 AM tempted by cinema, Stéphane, *Jeunesse*, 57.
352 AM to Corniglion, on De G: 'What! That Fascist?' As quoted by Alain M, *M de B*, 157.
352 'General de Gaulle wishes to know', *Antim*, 123.
353ff. AM's description of this first meeting with De G, *ibid.*, 124–128.
355–6 On Claude Mauriac and De G, see his *Le Temps immobile* vol V, *Aimer de Gaulle*, 209–211.

Page
356ff. On AM as De G's minister of Information, see Raymond Aron, *Mémoires*, 205–8; on his inability to realize any of his grandiose projects, *Antim*, 119–120.
357 On AM's budget speech (29 Dec. 1945), see Janine Mossuz, *AM et le gaullisme*, 56–58.
358 On De G's sudden decision to resign, Lacouture, *DeG* II, 234–249; Georgette Elgey, *La République des Illusions*, 89–92.
358 'Economic activity is reviving . . .' De G, *Mémoires de Guerre* III, 286; Claude Mauriac, *Aimer de G*, 227–228, 258–9.

36. HERALD OF THE RPF

359 On Clara's experiences during the German occupation, see *Et pourtant j'étais libre*; on her return to Paris, 214.
359 AM's meeting with his daughter—as related to author by Florence Malraux.
359 'The prickly problem of the divorce, *ibid.*, 215–217.
360 AM continuing to see G. Palewski, Cl. Mauriac, *Aimer*, 232; Lacouture, *DeG* II, 260.
360 On embryonic Gaullist 'publicity and propaganda bureau', Brigitte Friang, *Un autre Malraux*, 7–10, 20–22.
360ff. 'In January 1947 . . .' Michel Debré, *Trois Républiques pour la France* II, 'La Fondation du RPF', 81–83.
361 De G, on 2 Feb. 1947, at Colombey, Lacouture, *DeG* II, 285.
361–2 Sulzberger on AM, in *A Row of Candles*, 315–317.
362 'The campaign was finally launched', B. Friang, 12–23; Lacouture, *DeG* II, 295–6, and on Strasbourg speech, 297–301.
362 'In the long interview', Sulzberger, *Candles*, 315–316; and later, with Soustelle, 327.
363 'It was even in M's villa', Cl. Mauriac, *Aimer*, 399–401. First number of *L'Etincelle*, 26 April 1947.
363 On May 15th Bordeaux speech, Cl. Mauriac, *Aimer*, 414.
364–5 On rising tension in France, Dominique Desanti, *L'année où le monde a tremblé: 1947*, 194–197, 311–315; Elgey, *Illusions*, 329.
364 Text of De G's July 27th speech in *L'Etincelle*, 2 August. Lacouture, *DeG* II, 310; Elgey, *Illusions*, 333–334.
365–6 'Many years later', J. Mossuz, *gaullisme*, 67, 72.
367 Bureau moving to Blvd. des Capucines, Friang, 46–49.
367–8 B. Friang's description of AM's oratory, *ibid.*, 138–9.
368 F. Mauriac on AM's oratory, *Mémoires politiques*, 258–260; Mossuz, 84–85.
368 'From the mighty voice of Michelet . . .' Text publ. in three successive issues of *Rassemblement*, 6, 13, 20 March 1948.

37. RETURN TO ART

369 MM's marriage to AM, 13 March 1948. Antoine Diener was AM's 'best man'. On *Tante Yvonne*'s sentiments, Alain M, *M de B*, 51.
370 AM's two main reasons for interrupting work on *Le Démon de l'Absolu* were explained to me by Jean Grosjean. The 'seven cardboard boxes' containing ms. fragments of *Démon* are presently stored in a special library reserve at the Sorbonne.
371 Claude-Edmonde Magny, *Esprit* (October 1948), p. 513.
371 '*conquérir, imposer, arracher*', R. Payne (Fr. ed.), 319. Frohock, *AM*, 160–161.
372 'Poussin drapes', *Musée imaginaire*, 61.
372 'The language of Phidias' forms', *ibid*, 99.
372 'There is in the David of Chartres', *ibid*, 136–7.
372 'Between the *Still Life with Clock*', 140–141.
372 'genius is inseparable . . .' *Création artistique*, 17.
372 'It is as vain to confuse . . .', *ibid.*, 17.
372 'Does the *Roncalli Pietà*' differ . . .', *ibid*, 105–106.
373 Gaucheron, in *Europe Magazine* (Nov. 1989), p. 33.
373 'Seamstresses like sunsets', quoted by Jeener, *Paris-Soirs*, 22. In *Création*, 33: 'Young girls like sunsets . . .'
374 'Wilbur Frohock was one of the first', *AM*, ch. 7.
375 'In 1950 . . . when the third volume'—information obtained from Madeleine and Alain Malraux.
375 AM: 'For a very small number', *Voix du Silence*, 617–619.

Page
375–6 Ernest Gombrich, 'AM and the Crisis of Expressionism', later reprinted in his *Meditations on a Hobby-Horse*, 79–85. In a later essay written for a volume edited by Martine de Courcel (*E&D*) and titled, 'Malraux's Philosophy of Art in Historical Perspective', Gombrich was less severe.
376 'From war, a major demon . . .' *Musée*, 129.
376–7 'encouraged by his former trainer . . . Albert Beuret', information obtained from his assistant Jacqueline Blanchard. AM, replying to *Daglig Nyhiter*, in *L'Herne* (1982), 435–439.

38. MINISTER OF CULTURE

378 'AM was visiting Venice', Gaston Palewski, 'M et De G', in *E&D*, 102–3; Alain M, *M de B*, 274–5.
378 AM and De G at Hôtel de la Pérouse, *Antim*, 146–149.
378 'A ministry of Algerian Affairs?', see Friang, 93; Cl. Mauriac, *Et comme l'espérance est violente*, 13, and where he repeats what AM had said to his father: 'There are only two men in France today, De Gaulle and myself.' See also François Giroud, *Leçons particulières*, 234.
379 'in the offices of the Avenue de Friedland', Friang, 34.
379 'strange feeling of *déjà vu*', Lacouture, *De G* II, 492.
379–80 On AM's press conference, *Le Monde*, 25 June 1958.
380–1 AM's account of his trip to Caribbean, *Antim*, 170–185.
381 AM's trip to New Delhi, *ibid*, 196–213; to Japan, 477.
382 On Jacques Jaujard and his work during the German occupation, see Rose Valland's *Le front de l'art* and Lucie Mazauric (Chamson), *Le Louvre en voyage*.
382 On Jacques Rouché, C. Dupêchez, *Histoire de l'Opéra*.
383 'By mid-March, rumours', see Robert Kemp art. in *Le Monde*, March 12, 13.
384 On AM's press conference, see Jean-Jacques Gautier's art. in *Figaro*, 10 April 1959; R. Kemp's in *Le Monde*.
384 'M is mad . . .', Jean Meyer, *Place au théâtre*, 222, and two chapters entitled 'Un sac de noeuds', 'La curée'.
385 'Everything up till then', in Claude de Boisanger's *Neuf mois à la Comédie-Française*, 9, 15–21.
386 On January 15th 'summit meeting', *ibid.*, 78–85.
387 On the grotesque staging of *Carmen*, Dupêchez, 271–2; on *Pelléas et Mélisande, ibid.*, 273, and René Dumesnil's art. in *Le Monde*, 18 April 1962.
388 On AM plans for theatre for Camus, P. Moinot, *Tous comptes faits*, 92–93.
388 On 'Manifesto of the 121', see *L'Express*, 6 Oct. 1960, 9–11; Guy Dumur, 'La Condition ministérielle' in *France Observateur*, 13 Oct. 1960.
388 AM: 'This time I've seen enough of her', Alain M, *M de B*, 197–200.
389ff. On Gauthier and Vincent Malraux, see Alain M, *M de B*.
390 'Pierre Bockel arrived . . .', as told to author (12 Dec. 1992).
390–1 On 'Malraux Law', André Holleaux art. 'Le Ministre', in *E&D*, 120–121.
391 'Early in 1962', Alain M, *M de B*, 221–225.
392 On AM's 'ditch', see Yvan Christ, 'Le cas du Louvre', in *Arts*, 16 Sept. 1964, p. 29.
392ff. 'On May 11th' (1962), according to John Skow, *Saturday Evening Post*, Feb. 16, 1963 ('Mona Lisa—Leonardo's famed masterpiece keeps a wacky date with America'). For a less critical description of this experiment in mobile exhibitionism, see Nicole Hervé Alphand's art. in *E&D*, 126–132.
393 'The result was a triumph of geometry', J. Skow, *op. cit.*
394 André Thierry, 'Les paris stupides d'AM', *Arts*, 16–22 Sept. 1964.
394 'Hurt by so much ingratitude', Alain M, *M de B*, 241–2, 252; and on scenes with Madeleine, 237, 275–279.
394–5 AM's description of his trip to China, *Antim*, 477–559.
395 'in a voice so cracked and cavernous', my ear-witness impression. New scenes with Madeleine, Alain M, *M de B*, 231–234.
395ff. The paragraphs devoted to the catastrophic situation in the realm of Music are based on conversations with Marcel Landowski, Raymond Gallois-Montbrun, and Jacques Chailley in particular.
397 Landowski on Beuret, *Batailles pour la musique*, 12–16.
397 Boulez's attack on Landowski, in *F-Observateur*, 25 May.
397 AM: 'Ah, I'm glad to see', Landowski, *Batailles*, 21.
398 'AM is the first minister, since Louis XIV', *ibid*, 12.

Page
398 'My Dédé is riding high', J. Bothorel, *Louise*, 305.
398 AM to Louise, after death of Gauthier, etc. Doucet, ms. 39413.
399 'I speak without reflecting', Bothorel, *Louise*, 302–3.
399ff. On the 'Langlois affair', ch 11 of Georges Langlois and Glenn Myrent's biography.
400 'In 1966, when Barrault', AM speech to National Assembly, (27 Oct. 1966; *Journal Officiel*, 27 Oct., pp. 3979–3980, and AM reply, p. 3989).
400 On Barrault's contention that it was the Ministry of Cultural Affairs that had urged him to open the doors of the Odéon Theatre and to 'dialogue' with the students, see his declaration to John Whitley, of *Sunday Times*, 23 July 1968.
401 Jean-Jacques Gautier, *Figaro*, 3 Sept. 1968; B. Poirot-Delpech, 'Le Temps du Mépris', *Le Monde*, 1 Sept. 1968.

39. LAST YEARS AT VERRIERES

402ff. Most of the details in this chapter were given to me orally by Sophie de Vilmorin, Florence Malraux, Dr Louis Bertagna, and AM's private secretary.
402 AM toast to Georges Pompidou, Lacouture, *DeG* III, 731.
402 'What do you expect me to do . . . ?', Friang, 149–152.
404 'Years later the writer . . .', Jean d'Ormesson, *Figaro* (literary supplement), 17 Feb. 1992, p. 3.
405 'Toward the end of the meal . . .' Claude Bénédick to author.
407 AM at De G's funeral, Lacouture, *CdeG* III, 796–7; John Weightman, *The Observer*, 27 February 1972.
408 In all, Lüthy published three articles in the monthly review, *Preuves*, on the three volumes of CdeG's *Mémoires de Guerre*. AM later told Manès Sperber that they were the best review articles he had read on the subject.
408ff. 'In March 1971'—on AM's pro-Bengal 'crusade', Friang, 106–127.
411 Richard Nixon, *Memoirs*.
411 Paul Guimard, *L'Express*, 27 May 1972.
412 'Later, Pierre Bockel said of *Lazare*', *Paris-Match*, 3 Dec. 1976.

Bibliography

WORKS BY ANDRÉ MALRAUX

Lunes en papier (with woodcuts by Fernand Léger), Éd. de la Galerie Simon, 1921.
La Tentation de l'Occident, Grasset, 1926.
Les Conquérants, Grasset, 1928.
Royaume-Farfelu, Gallimard, 1928.
La Voie royale, Grasset, 1930.
Vie de Napoléon par lui-même, Gallimard, 1930.
La Condition humaine, Gallimard, 1933.
Le Temps du Mépris, Gallimard, 1935.
L'Espoir, Gallimard, 1937.
La Lutte avec l'Ange, Éd. du Haut-Pays (Lausanne), 1943.
Les Noyers de l'Altenburg (new edition of *La Lutte avec l'Ange*), Albert Skira (Genève), 1945, puis
      Gallimard, 1948.
Esquisse d'une psychologie du cinéma et Scènes choisies, Gallimard, 1946.
La Psychologie de l'Art (vol. I), Le Musée imaginaire, Albert Skira (Genève), 1947.
La Psychologie de l'Art (vol. II), La Création artistique, Albert Skira (Genève), 1948.
Saturne (essay on Goya), Gallimard, 1950.
La Psychologie de l'Art (vol. III), La Monnaie de l'Absolu, Albert Skira (Paris), 1950.
Les Voix du Silence (condensed version of the three volumes of *La Psychologie de l'Art*), « Galeric de
      la Pléiade », Gallimard, 1951.
Tout l'art peint de Léonard de Vinci, « Galerie de la Pléiade », Gallimard, 1952.
Tout l'art peint de Vermeer de Delft, « Galerie de la Pléiade », Gallimard, 1952.
Le Musée imaginaire de la Sculpture mondiale:
    I. *La Statuaire*, « Galerie de la Pléiade », Gallimard, 1952.
    II. *Des bas-reliefs aux grottes sacrées*, « Galerie de la Pléiade », Gallimard, 1954.
    III. *Le Monde chrétien*, « Galerie de la Pléiade », Gallimard, 1955.
La Métamorphose des Dieux, « Galerie de la Pléiade », Gallimard, 1957.
Antimémoires, Gallimard, 1967.
Le Triangle noir (Laclos-Goya-Saint-Just), Gallimard, 1970.
Les Chênes qu'on abat, Gallimard, 1971.
Oraisons funèbres, Gallimard, 1971
L'Irréel (Métamorphose des Dieux, II), Gallimard, 1974.
Lazare, Gallimard, 1974.
La Tête d'obsidienne, Gallimard, 1974.
Hôtes de passage, Gallimard, 1975.
L'Intemporel (Métamorphose des Dieux, III), Gallimard, 1976.
L'Homme précaire et la littérature, Gallimard, 1977.
Œuvres complètes, Bibliothèque de la Plélade, Gallimard, 1969.

SPECIAL MAGAZINE
ISSUES DEVOTED
TO ANDRÉ MALRAUX
(in chronological order)

Esprit « André Malraux » (octobre 1948).
Revue des Lettres modernes (Minard) (éd. Walter Langlois, C. Moatti).
1. *André Malraux* – du « *farfelu aux* » *antimémoires* (1972).
2.   *visages du romancier* (1973).
3.   *influences et affinités* (1975).
4.   *Malraux et l'Art* (1978).
5   *Malraux et l'Histoire* (1982).
6.   « *Les Conquérants* » (éd. Moatti).
7.   « *Les Conquérants* », mythe, politique, histoire.
Fondation Maeght – *André Malraux* (catalogue, 1973).
Être & Dire – *André Malraux* (edited by Martine de Courcel, with « Néocritique » by André Malraux).
     London, Weidenfeld & Nicolson; Paris, Plon, 1976.
Nouvelle Revue Française (July 1977).
Twentieth Century Literature (1978/3).
L'Herne « André Malraux » (1982).
Magazine littéraire (October 1986).
Europe – « André Malraux » (November–December 1989).

ARLAND, Marcel, *Ce fut ainsi*, Gallimard, 1979.
ARON, Raymond, *Mémoires*, Julliard, 1983.
ARON, Robert, *Histoire de Vichy, 1940–1944*, Fayard, 1958.
– *Fragments d'une vie*. Plon, 1981.
ASSOULINE, Pierre, *Gaston Gallimard*, Balland, 1984.
ASTRUC, Jean, *Histoire des gens de Bondy*.
« Le Fils de l'épicière », *En Aulnaye jadis* (n°6), 1977.
AUB, Max, *Sierra de Teruel* (traducción y prólogo de Max Aub), Mexico, Ediciones Era, 1968.
BAKER, Carlos, *Ernest Hemingway. A Life Story*, London, Collins, 1969.
BARRÈS, Maurice, *Le Culte du Moi*.
     I. *Sous l'œil des Barbares*.
     II. *Un homme libre*.
     III. *Le Jardin de Bérénice*.
     Plon, 1922 (new edition, 1966).
BARRY, Michael, *Le Royaume de l'insolence*, Flammarion, 1984.
BEAUVOIR, Simone de, *La Force de l'âge*, Gallimard, 1960.
—— *La Force des choses*, Gallimard, 1963.
BENDA, Julien,
—— *La Trahison des clercs*, Grasset, 1927.
BÉNÉDITE, Daniel, *La Filière marseillaise. Un chemin vers la liberté pendant l'occupation*, Clamecy, Clancier-Guénaud, 1984.
BERL, Emmanuel, *Mort de la pensée bourgeoise*, Grasset, 1929.
—— *Mort de la morale bourgeoise*, Gallimard, 1930.
—— *Fin de la III République*, Gallimard, 1968.
BETZ, Albrecht, *Exil und Engagement – Deutsche Schriftsteller im Frankreich der dreissigen Jahre*, Munich, Text und Kritik, 1986. *Exil et engagement – les intellectuels allemands en France, 1930–1940*, Gallimard, 1991.
BEUCLER, André. *De Saint-Pétersbourg à Saint-Germain-des Prés*, Gallimard, 1980.
—— *Plaisirs de mémoire*, Gallimard, 1982.
BEVAN, David, *Via Malraux* (Écrits de Walter Langlois, réunis par David Bevan), Accadia University, Canada, et Minard (Paris), 1986.
BIDAULT, Georges, *D'une Résistance à l'autre*, Les Presses du Siècle, 1965.
BOCKEL, Pierre, *L'Enfant du rire* (preface by André Malraux), Grasset, 1973.
—— *Le Temps de naître*, Grasset, 1975.
—— *Alsace et Lorraine*, Strasbourg, Éditions des « Dernières Nouvelles », 1975.
BOISANGER, Claude Bréart de, *Neuf mois à la Comédie-Française*, Nouvelles Éditions Latines, 1964.
BOLLOTEN, Burnett, *The Spanish Revolution*, University of North Carolina Press, 1979.

BOTHOREL, Jean, *Bernard Grasset. Vie et passions d'un éditeur*. Grasset, 1989.
—— *Louise – ou la Vie de Louise de Vilmorin*, Grasset, 1993.
BOUISSOUNOUSE, Janine, *La Nuit d'Autun – Le Temps des Illusions*, Calmann-Lévy, 1977.
BOURDET, Claude, *De la Résistance à la restauration*, Stock, 1975.
BREDEL, Willi, *Die Prüfung – Roman aus einem Konzentrationslager*, Moskau-Leningrad, Verlagsgenossenschaft ausländischer Arbeiter in der UdSSR, 1935. Traduction française: *L'Épreuve*, Albin Michel, 1936.
BRENAN, Gerald, *The Spanish Labyrinth*, Cambridge University Press, 1950.
BRIGGS, Lawrence Palmer, *The Ancient Khmer Kingdom*, Philadelphia, 1951.
BURNHAM, James, *The Case for De Gaulle. Conversations with André Malraux*, New York, Random House, 1948.
BUSSIÈRES, Pernande, *Paul Vaillant-Couturier, ou l'histoire d'une amitié*, Rodez, Subervie, 1979.
BUSSY, Dorothy (née Strachey), Correspondence with André Gide, *Cahiers André Gide*, vol. 9 et 10.
CAUTE, David, *The Fellow Travellers*, London, Weidenfeld & Nicolson, Quartet Books, 1977.
CENDRARS, Miriam, *Cendrars*, Balland, 1984.
CHAMSON, André, *Roux le Bandit*, Grasset, 1925.
—— « L'Homme contre l'Histoire », dans *Écrits*, Grasset, 1927.
—— *Devenir ce qu'on est*, Paris, Namur, 1959.
—— *La Reconquête*, Plon, 1975.
—— *Il faut vivre mieux*, Grasset, 1984.
CHANTAL, Suzanne, *Le Cœur battant*, preface by André Malraux, Grasset, 1976.
CHASTENET, Jacques, *Quand le bœuf montait sur le toit*, Fayard, 1958.
—— *Histoire de la Troisième République: le Déclin de la Troisième – 1931–1938*, Hachette, 1962.
CHIAROMONTE, Nicola, *The Worm of Consciousness*, New York, Harcourt, Brace, Jovanovitch, 1953.
CLOTIS, Josette, *Le Temps vert*, preface by Henri Pourrat, Gallimard, 1932.
—— *Une mesure pour rien*, Gallimard, 1934.
COHEN-SOLAL, Annie, *Paul Nizan. Communiste impossible*, Grasset, 1980.
COPEAU, Jacques, *Journal*, vol. II, *1916–1948*, Seghers, 1991.
CORNIGLION-MOLINIER, Édouard Flaminius – under pseudonym of Dan Moligny, *Journal de F.L. Smith-Brown*, Fasquelle, 1946.
COT, Pierre, *Procès de la République* (2 vol.), New York, Éditions de la Maison Française, 1944.
COURTIVRON, Isabelle de, *Clara Malraux – Une femme dans le siècle*, Olivier Orban, 1992.
DARDAUD, Gabriel, *Trente ans au bord du Nil*, Lieu Commun, 1987.
DAVET, Yvonne, *André Gide – Littérature engagée*, Gallimard, 1950.
DEBRÉ, Michel, *Trois Républiques pour une France*, vol. II, Albin Michel, 1988.
DE GAULLE, Charles, *Le Fil de l'épée*, Berger- Levrault, 1944.
—— *Vers l'armée de métier*, Berger- Levrault, 1934 (2ᵉ éd. 1944).
—— *Discours et messages, 1940–1946*, Berger-Levrault, 1946.
—— *Mémoires de guerre:*
 I. *L'Appel, 1940–1942*, Plon, 1954.
 II. *L'Unité, 1942–1944*, Plon, 1956.
 III. *Le Salut, 1944–1946*, Plon, 1959.
—— *Mémoires d'espoir. Le Renouveau, 1958–1962*, Plon, 1970.
DELPERRIE DE BAYAC, Jacques, *Les Brigades internationales*, Fayard, 1968.
DESANTI, Dominique, *1947: L'Année où le monde a tremblé*, Albin Michel, 1976.
DESJARDINS, Paul, *Paul Desjardins et les Décades de Pontigny*. Études, témoignages et documents inédits présentés par Anne Heurgon-Desjardins. Préface d'André Maurois, PUF, 1964.
DEUTSCHER, Isaac, *The Prophet Outcast: Trotsky, 1929–1940*, Oxford University Press, 1963.
DORGELÈS, Roland, *Bouquet de bohème*, Albin Michel, 1989.
DOUHET, Giulio, *Il dominio dell'aire. Probabili aspetti delle guerra futura*, con prefazione d'Itali Balbo, Milano/Verona, Mondadori, 1932.
DOYON, René-Louis, *Mémoire d'homme*, La Connaissance, 1953.
—— *Livrets du Mandarin* (n° 8), La Connaissance (Sept. 1962).
DUCHATELET, Bernard, *Romain Rolland et la NRF*, Albin Michel, 1989.
DUPÉCHEZ, Charles, *Histoire de l'Opéra de Paris*, Perrin, 1984.
DU PERRON, *Charles Edgar. Verzammelt Werk* (vol. II): *Het Land van Herkomst*, Amsterdam, Oorschot, 1938 (2ᵉ éd. 1948); trad. fr. *Pays d'origine*, Préface par Philippe Noble, Gallimard, 1980.

DURRY, Marie-Jeanne, *Jules Laforgue*, Seghers, 1952.
DUTHUIT, Georges, *Le Musée inimaginable* (3 vol.), José Corti, 1956.
DUVIGNEAU, Jean, *Marcel Arland*, Gallimard, 1961.
EHRENBOURG, Ilya, *La nuit tombe. Souvenirs 1932–1940*, transl. from Russian by Vladimir Volkoff, Gallimard, 1966.
ELGEY, Georgette, *La République des illusions, 1945–1951*, Fayard, 1965.
ELLMANN, Richard, *James Joyce*, New York, Oxford University Press, 1959.
EUSTIS, Alvin Allen, *Trois Critiques de la NRF – Marcel Arland, Benjamin Crémieux, Ramon Fernandez*, Nouvelles Éditions Debresse, 1961.
FELS, Florent, *Voilà*, Fayard, 1957.
FERNANDEZ, Ramon, *Messages* (avec préface de Jérôme Garcin), Grasset, 1981.
FISCHER, Louis, *Men and Politics – an Autobiography*. New York, Duelle, Sloane & Pearce, 1941.
FOOT, M.R.D., *SOE in France*. London, His Majesty's Stationery Office, 1966.
FRANK, Joseph, *The Widening Gyre*, Rutgers University Press, 1963.
FRANK, Nino, *Mémoire brisée* (vol. I), Calmann-Lévy, 1967.
——— *Le Bruit parmi le vent* (vol. II), Calmann-Lévy, 1968.
FRENAY, Henri, *La nuit finira. Mémoires de Résistance, 1940–1945*, Robert Laffont, 1973.
FRIANG, Brigitte, *Un autre Malraux*, Plon, 1977.
FRONOCK, Wilbur Merrill, *André Malraux*, Stanford, 1951.
FRY, Varian, *Surrender on Demand*. New York, Random House, 1945.
GABORY, Georges, *Apollinaire, Max Jacob, Gide. Malraux et Cie*, Paris, 1982.
——— *Cœurs à prendre*, S. Kra, 1920.
GAILLARD, Pol, *Les Critiques de notre temps et Malraux*, Garnier, 1970.
GALANTE, Pierre, *Malraux*, Plon, 1971.
GALTIER-BOISSIÈRE, Jean, *Mémoires d'un Parisien* (3 vol.), Table Ronde, 1963.
GARAUDY, Roger, *Une littérature de fossoyeurs*, Éditions Sociales, 1947.
GARNIER, François, *Max Jacob – Correspondance* (vol. 1) et (vol. II, 1921–1924), Éditions de Paris, 1955.
GIDE, André, *Le Roi Candaule*, Aux Aldes, 1927.
——— *Pour Thaelmann* (Discours d'AG, André Malraux, Moro-Giafferi), Paris, 1935.
——— *Retour de l'URSS*, Gallimard, 1936.
——— *Retouches à mon « Retour de l'URSS »*, Gallimard, 1937.
——— *Journal (1889–1939)*, Gallimard (Bibliothèque de la Pléiade), 1939.
——— *Journal (1939–1942)*, Gallimard, 1946.
——— *Littérature engagée* (textes recueillis par Yvonne Davet), Gallimard, 1950.
——— *Correspondance André Gide-Roger Martin du Gard*, Tome I: *1913–1934*, Tome II: *1935–1951*, Gallimard, 1968.
——— *Cahiers André Gide* (n° 4), « Cahiers de la Petite Dame », *1918–1929*, Gallimard, 1973; *1929–1937* (n° 5), Gallimard, 1974; *1937–1945* (n° 6), Gallimard, 1975.
GIRAUDOUX, Jean, *Les Provinciales* (aquarelles de G. Gallibert), Aux Aldes, 1927.
GIROUD, Françoise, *Leçons particulières*, Fayard, 1990.
GISCLON, Jean, *Des Avions et des Hommes*, France-Empire, 1969. *La Désillusion*, France-Empire, 1986.
GLAIZE, Maurice, *Les Monuments du groupe d'Angkor*, Saigon, Albert Portail, 1948 (2ᵉ éd.).
GOLL, Yvan, *Œuvres* (2 tomes), préparées par Claire Goll, Emile-Paul, 1968.
GOMBRICH, Ernst, *The Story of Art*, London, Phaidon, 1950.
——— *Art and Illusion*, London, Phaidon, 1960.
——— *Meditations on a Hobby-Horse*, London, Phaidon, 1963.
GRASSET, Bernard, *La Chose littéraire*, Gallimard, 1932.
GREEN, Julien, *Œuvres complètes*: Tome I. *Journal, 1928–1939*. Plon, 1954.
GRENIER, Roger, *Pascal Pia*, Gallimard, 1989.
GROETHUYSEN, Bernard, *Introduction à la philosophie allemande depuis Nietzsche*, Gallimard, 1926.
——— *Origines de l'esprit bourgeois en France*, Gallimard, 1927.
——— *Mythes et Portraits*. Préface de Jean Paulhan, Gallimard, 1947.
GROSS, Babette, *Willi Münzenberg – Eine politische Biographie* (preface by Arthur Koestler), Stuttgart, Deutsche Verlags-Anstalt, 1967.
GROUEFF, Stephane, *Crown of Thorns*, Madison Books, 1987.
GROVER, Frédéric, *Six entretiens avec André Malraux*, Gallimard, 1971.
——— *Drieu La Rochelle* (avec Pierre Andreu), Table Ronde, 1989.
GUIETTE, Robert, *La Vie de Max Jacob*, Nizet, 1976.

GUILLOUX, Louis, *Carnets I: 1921–1944*, Gallimard, 1978.
—— *Carnets II: 1944–1974*, Gallimard, 1982.
HELLER, Gerhard, *Un Allemand à Paris*, Seuil, 1981.
HELLER, Michel (et Alexandre Nekritch), *L'Utopie au pouvoir*, Calmann-Lévy, 1982.
HERBART, Pierre, *La Ligne de force*, Gallimard, 1958.
HIDALGO DE CISNEROS, Ignacio, *Virage sur l'aile*, Éditeurs Français Réunis, 1965.
HOSTACHE, René, *Le Conseil National de la Résistance – Les Institutions de la clandestinité*, PUF, 1958.
HUGHES, H. Stuart, *Oswald Spengler – a Critical Estimate*, New York, Charles Scribner, 1952.
ISAACS, Harold R., *The Tragedy of the Chinese Revolution*, Stanford, 1951.
JACOB, Max, *Art poétique*, Emile-Paul, 1922.
—— *Le Cornet à dés*, Stock, 1923.
—— *Lettres aux Salacrou, 1923–1926*, Paris, 1957.
JEENER, Jean-Baptiste, *Paris-Soirs, Portraits-Souvenirs*, Éditions de Paris, 1958.
—— *La Barbe, ou un homme selon mon cœur*. Carnets Forces Vives, 1966.
JOUVENEL, Bertrand de, *Un voyageur dans le siècle, 1903–1945*. Robert Laffont, 1979.
JULIEN, Charles-André, *L'Afrique du Nord en marche*, Julliard, 1952.
KAHNWEILER, Daniel-Henry, *Entretiens avec Francis Crémieux*, Gallimard, 1961.
KESSLER, Harry Graf, *Tagebücher, 1918–1937*, Politik, Kunst, und Gesellschaft der zwanziger Jahre, Frankfurt, Insel-Verlag, 1961.
KEYSERLING, Hermann Graf, *Reisetagebücher eines Philosophen*, Darmstadt, 1920, trad. fr. *Journal d'un philosophe*, vol. I, Stock, 1928, vol. II, Stock, 1929.
KOESTLER, Arthur, *Scum of the Earth*, New York, Macmillan, 1948.
—— *The Invisible Writing* (Autobiography, 1931–1940), London, Hamish Hamilton, 1954.
KOLTSOV, Mikhaïl, *Diario de la guerra de España*, Paris, Ruedo ibérico, 1963.
KUPFERMAN, Fred, *Pierre Laval*, Masson, 1976.
LACOUTURE, Jean, *André Malraux: Une vie dans le siècle*, Seuil, 1973 (réimprimé 1976).
—— *Léon Blum*, Seuil, 1977.
—— *Charles de Gaulle:*
  II. *Le Politique (1944–1959)*, Seuil, 1985.
  III. *Le Souverain (1959–1970)*, Seuil, 1986.
LAFORGUE, Jules, *Dragées, Charles Baudelaire. Tristan Corbière*, Textes inédits, La Connaissance, 1920.
—— *Chroniques parisiennes. Ennuis non rimés*, La Connaissance, 1920.
—— *Exil, Poésie, Spleen*, La Connaissance, 1921.
LANDOWSKI, Marcel, *Batailles pour la musique*, Seuil, 1979.
LANGEVIN, Paul, *La Pensée et l'Action*, Éditeurs Réunis, 1950.
LANGLOIS, Georges (and Glenn Myrent), *Henri Langlois*, Denoël, 1986.
LANGLOIS, Walter, *André Malraux: The Indochina Adventure*. New York, Praeger, 1966.
—— *Malraux Criticism in English*, Lettres modernes, 1972.
LAUREAU, Patrick (avec Santiago Capillas et Enrique Pereira),
—— *La Aviación republicana, 1930–1939*, Toulouse, 1980.
—— *La Guerre d'Espagne: 1936–1939* (avec Jean Lasserre).
—— *Icare* (numéro spécial, 118), tome I (1986/3).
—— *Icare* (numéro spécial, 130), tome II (1989/3).
LENORMAND, Henri-René, *Les Confessions d'un auteur dramatique*, vol. II, Albin Michel, 1953.
LOTI, Pierre, *Un pèlerin d'Angkor*, Calmann-Lévy, 1912.
LOTTMAN, Herbert, *Albert Camus*, Seuil, 1985.
LUNET DE LAJONQUIÈRE, Edmond, *Inventaire descriptif des monuments du Cambodge*, Publications de l'École Française d'Extrême-Orient, n° 4 (1902), 8 (1909), 9 (1911).
MAITRE, Henri, *Les Régions moï du Sud Indo-Chinois, Le Plateau du Darlac*, Plon, 1909.
—— *Mission Henri Maître (1909–1911), Indochine Sud Centrale: les jungles moï*, Paris, 1912.
MALRAUX, Alain, *Les Marronniers de Boulogne*, (1) Plon, 1978. *Les Marronniers de Boulogne* (édition augmentée); (2) Ramsay/de Cortanze, 1989.
MALRAUX, Clara, *Portrait de Grisélidis*, Colbert, 1945.
—— *Le Bruit de nos pas* (Mémoires);
  1. *Apprendre à vivre*, Grasset, 1964.
  2. *Nos vingt ans*, Grasset, 1966.
  3. *Les Combats et les jeux*, Grasset, 1969.
  4. *Voici que vient l'été*, Grasset & Fasquelle, 1973.
  5. *La Fin et le commencement*, Grasset & Fasquelle, 1976.
  6. *Et pourtant j'étais libre*, Grasset & Fasquelle, 1979.

MARION, Denis, *André Malraux*, Seghers, 1970.

MARNOLD, Jean, *Le Cas Wagner: la Musique pendant la guerre*, Bossard, 1917.

MARQUET, Jean, *Un aventurier du XIXᵉ siècle: Marie I, roi des Sedang (1888–1890)*, Paris, 1927.

MARTIN DU GARD, Roger, *Œuvres complètes* (y compris, *Souvenirs*), Gallimard, Bibliothèque de la Pléiade (113), 1955.

—— *Correspondance générale*, tome V *(1930–1932)*, Gallimard, 1988; tome VI *(1933–1936)*, Gallimard, 1990.

MASSENET, Pierre et Marthe, *Journal d'une longue nuit*, Fayard, 1971.

MASSIS, Henri, *Défense de l'Occident*, Plon, 1927.

MAURIAC, Claude, *Malraux, ou le mal du héros*, Grasset, 1946.

—— *Un autre de Gaulle*, Hachette, 1970.

—— *Et comme l'espérance est violente* (tome 3 du *Temps immobile*), Grasset, 1976.

—— *Aimer de Gaulle*, Grasset, 1978.

MAURIAC, François, *Mémoires politiques*, Grasset, 1967.

MAUROIS, André, *Mémoires*, Flammarion, 1970.

MAZAURIC, Lucie, *Avec André Chamson*.

—— Tome 1. *Ah Dieu! que la paix est jolie*, Plon, 1972.

—— Tome 2. *Vive le Front populaire*, Plon, 1976.

—— Tome 3. *Le Louvre en voyage (1939–1945)*, Plon, 1978.

MERCADET, Léon, *La Brigade Alsace-Lorraine*, Grasset, 1984.

MICHEL, Henri, *Vichy – Année 40*.

MIREILLE (Berl), *Avec le soleil pour témoin*, Robert Laffont, 1981.

MOCH, Jules, *Mes rencontres avec Léon Blum*, Plon, 1970.

—— *Une si longue vie*, Robert Laffont, 1976.

MOINOT, Pierre, *Tous comptes faits*, Quai Voltaire, 1993.

MONNIER, Adrienne, *Rue de l'Odéon*, Albin Michel, 1960.

MONTHERLANT, Henry de, *Carnets – Années 1930 à 1944*, Gallimard, 1957.

MORAND, Paul, *Rien que la Terre*, À la Sphère, 1926.

—— *Papiers d'identité*, Grasset, 1931.

MORLINO, Bernard, *Emmanuel Berl – Les Tribulations d'un pacifiste*, La Manufacture, 1990.

MOSSUZ, Janine, *André Malraux et le gaullisme*, Armand Colin, 1970.

MOULOUDJI, Marcel, *La Fleur de l'âge*, Grasset & Fasquelle, 1991.

MURPHY, Robert, *Diplomat among the Warriors*, New York, Doubleday, 1964.

NENNI, Pietro, *La Guerre d'Espagne*, Maspero, 1959.

NIXON, Richard, *Mémoirs*, Montréal, New York, 1978.

NIZAN, Henriette, *Libres mémoires*, Robert Laffont, 1989.

NOIREAU, Robert (dit le « colonel Georges »), *Le Temps des partisans*, Flammarion, 1978.

OLIVIER, Fernande, *Picasso et ses amis*, Stock, Delamain, 1933.

OLLIVIER, Albert, *Saint-Just et la force des choses*. Préface d'André Malraux, Gallimard, 1955.

PALMER, Norman (avec Shao Chuang Leng), *Sun Yat-sen and Communism*, Stanford, 1954.

PALMIER, Jean-Michel, *Weimar en exil – Le destin de l'émigration intellectuelle allemande antinazie en Europe et aux États-Unls*, Payot, 1990.

PAULHAN, Jean, *Jean Paulhan et la Nouvelle Revue Française*, Gallimard, NRF, 1969.

PAYNE, Robert, *André Malraux*, Buchet/Chastel, 1970.

PENAUD, Guy, *Histoire de la Résistance en Périgord*, Périgueux, Pierre Fanlac, 1984.

PETIT, Colonel Edmond, *Missions très spéciales*, Pensée moderne, 1964.

PHILBY, Henry St. John Bridger, *Sheba's Daughters*, London, Methuen, 1939.

PIA, Pascal (Durand), *Les Livres de l'Enfer du XVIᵉ siècle à nos jours*, 2 vol., Coulet & Faure, 1977, 1978.

PICON, Gaëtan, *Malraux par lui-même* Seuil, 1959.

PLEYNET, Marcelin, *Lautréamont par lui-même* (« Écrivains de toujours »), Seuil, 1967.

POIRIER, Jacques, R.E., *La girafe a un long cou*, Périgueux, Fanlac, 1992.

PRÉVOST, Jean, *Les Caractères*, Albin Michel, 1948.

REGLER, Gustav, *Das Ohr des Malchus: eine Lebensgeschichte*, Cologne, Kiepenheuer & Witsch, 1958, Eng. tr.: *The Owl of Minerva*, London, Rupert Hart-Davis, 1959.

RIGHTER, William, *The Rhetorical Hero*, London, Routledge & Kegan Paul, 1964.

RIM, Carlo, *Le Grenier d'Arlequin – Journal, 1916–1940*, Denoël, 1981.

SAINT-CHÉRON, Philippe et François de, *Notre Malraux*, Albin, Michel, 1979.

SAINT-CLAIR, Maria (Mme Théo Van Rysselberghe), *Galerie privée*, Gallimard, 1947.

SAINT PULGENT, Maryvonne de, *Le Syndrome de l'Opéra*, Robert Laffont, 1991.

SALAS LARRAZABAL, Jesús, *La Guerra de España desde el aire*, Barcelona, 1972.
—— *Intervención extranjera en la guerra de España*, Madrid, Ed. Nacional, 1974.
SALMON, André, *Souvenirs sans fin*:
 Tome 1. *Première époque, 1903–1908*, Gallimard, 1955.
 Tome 2. *Deuxième époque, 1908–1920*, Gallimard, 1956.
 Tome 3. *Troisième époque, 1920–1940*, Gallimard, 1961.
SANOUILLET, Michel, *Dada à Paris*, Pauvert, 1965.
SAUVY, Alfred, *Histoire économique de la France entre les deux guerres*, Fayard, 1967.
SCHMIGALLE, Günther, *André Malraux und der Spansischer Bürgerkrieg*, Bonn, Bouvier, 1980.
SERGE, Victor, *Mémoires d'un révolutionnaire*, Seuil, 1951: *Memoris of a Revolutionary*, Oxford
 University Press (paperback), 1980.
SHIRER, William, *The Rise and Fall of the Third Reich*, Secker & Warburg.
SIEBURG, Friedrich, *Glücklich wie ein Gott in Frankreich?* Fr. tr. *Dieu est-il français?* Grasset, 1930.
—— *Es werde Deutschland. La Défense du nationalisme allemand*, Grasset, 1933.
SPAAK, Paul-Henri, *Combats inachevés* I, *De l'indépendance à l'alliance*, Arthème Fayard, 1969.
SPENDER, Stephen, *World within World*, London, Hamish Hamilton, 1951.
SPENGLER, Oswald, *Untergang des Abendlundes*, Fr. tr. *Le Déclin de l'Occident*, Gallimard, 1931,
 1948.
SPERBER, Manès, *Ce temps-là* (Mémoires):
 Vol. I. *Die Wasserträger Gottes*, trad. fr. *Les Porteurs d'eau*, Calmann-Lévy, 1976.
 Vol. 2. *Die vergebliche Warnung*, trad. fr. *Le Pont inachevé*, Calmann-Lévy, 1977.
 Vol. 3. *Alles vergangene*, trad. fr. *Au-delà de l'oubli*, Calmann-Lévy, 1979.
STÉPHANE, Roger, *Fin d'une jeunesse*, Table Ronde, 1954.
—— *André Malraux. Entretiens et précisions.* Gallimard, 1984.
—— *Portrait de l'aventurier.* Préface de Jean-Paul Sartre, Bernard Grasset, 1965.
SUDREAU, Pierre, *Au-delà de toutes les frontières*, Odile Jacob, 1991.
TANNERY, Claude, *Malraux, l'agnostique absolu, ou la Métamorphose comme loi du monde*, Gallimard,
 1985.
THIRION, André, *Révolutionnaires sans révolution*, Robert Laffont, 1972.
THOMAS, Hugh, *The Spanish Civil War*, Londres, Penguin Books and Hamish Hamilton, paper-
 back, 1977.
THOMPSON, Brian (and Carl A. Viggiani), *Witnessing André Malraux, Essays in honor of Wilbur
 Frohock*, Wesleyan University Press, 1984.
THOMPSON, Virginia, *French Indochina*, London, Allen & Unwin, 1937.
THORNBERRY, Robert, *André Malraux et la guerre civile espagnole, 1936–1937*, Paris, 1988.
TISSOT, Francine, *The Art of Gandhâra – Buddhist Monks' Art on the North West Frontier*, Librairie
 d'Amérique et d'Orient, 1986.
—— *Les Arts anciens du Pakistan et de l'Afghanistan*, Desclée de Brouwer, 1987.
TOLAND, John, *Adolf Hitler*, New York, Ballantine Books (paperback), 1977.
TUAL, Denise, *Le Temps dévoré*, Fayard, 1980.
VANDEGANS, André, *La Jeunesse littéraire d'André Malraux. Essai sur l'inspiration farfelue*, Pauvert,
 1964.
VANDROMME, Pol, *Malraux, du farfelu au mirobolant*, Alfred Eibel, 1976.
VIDAL, Annette, *Henri Barbusse, soldat de la paix*. Éditcurs Français Réunis, 1953.
VILLIERS DU TERRAGE, Mare, *Conquistadores et Roitelets*, Paris, 1906.
VILMORIN, André de, *Louise de Vilmorin*, Seghers, 1962.
VILMORIN, Louise de, *Sainte-Unefois*, Gallimard, 1934.
—— *L'Heure maliciôse*, Gallimard, 1967.
—— *Carnets*, Gallimard, 1970.
—— *Solitude, ô mon éléphant*, Gallimard, 1972.
—— *Le Lutin sauvage*, Gallimard, 1971.
VIOLLIS, Andrée, *Indochine SOS*, Préface d'André Malraux, Paris, 1935.
WERTH, Léon, *Cochinchine*, Rieder, 1926.
WILSON, Edmund, *The Shores of Light*, Farrar, Strauss & Young, 1952.
YAKI, Paul, *Le Montmartre de nos vingt ans*, Tallandier, 1935.

INDEX